──THE HEALTH OF──
ABORIGINAL AUSTRALIA

The cover painting illustrates a harmonious view of
Aboriginal health and well-being. The figures along the
bottom represent the community. The figures on the hill,
with energy from the sun, are rising above health problems,
and those in the circles on the left are the people who are a
catalyst for energy in the food chain. The snake, eggs and
fruit represent bush tucker.

Bronwyn Bancroft

THE HEALTH OF
ABORIGINAL AUSTRALIA

Edited by Janice Reid and Peggy Trompf

Centre for Cross-Cultural Studies
in Health and Medicine, University of Sydney.

Harcourt Brace Jovanovich, Publishers
Sydney London Orlando San Diego Toronto

Harcourt Brace Jovanovich Group (Australia) Pty Ltd
30–52 Smidmore Street, Marrickville, NSW 2204

Harcourt Brace Jovanovich Limited
24–28 Oval Road, London, NW1 7DX

Harcourt Brace Jovanovich, Inc.
Orlando, Florida 32887

Printed in Australia

National Library of Australia Cataloguing-in-Publication Data

---

The health of Aboriginal Australia

  Bibliography.
  Includes index.
  ISBN 0 7295 0385 2.

  [1]. Aborigines, Australian— Health and hygiene. [2]. Aborigines,
  Australian—Medical care. I. Reid, Janice, date– . II. Trompf, Peggy,
  date–

362.10899915

Cover illustration by Bronwyn Bancroft

Contents

Foreword   vii

Acknowledgments   viii

Contributors   ix

Introduction   xi
Janice Reid and Deborah Lupton

1. The history and politics of Aboriginal health   1
   Margaret-Ann Franklin and Isobel White

2. A review of Aboriginal health status   37
   Neil Thomson

3. The decline and rise of Aboriginal families   80
   Alan Gray, Peggy Trompf and Shane Houston

4. Food, nutrition and growth in Aboriginal communities   123
   Lindsey Harrison

5. Drug and alcohol use among Aboriginal people   173
   Maggie Brady

6. Aboriginal mental health: conflicting cultural perspectives   218
   Joseph Reser

7. In sickness and health: the sociocultural context of
   Aboriginal well-being, illness and healing   292
   Robyn Mobbs

8. Contemporary issues in Aboriginal public health   326
   Paul Torzillo and Charles Kerr

9. Policy and practice in Aboriginal health   381
   Sherry Saggers and Dennis Gray

Abbreviations   421

Index   423

*As we...bring our prayers for South Africa, we know that
we also are involved in racism and prejudice...Aboriginal people
still wait for justice in this land and we have not yet
created a community where people of different race, culture,
faith and social background can live together in peace
and equal opportunity.*

Prayers spoken by Bishop Heyward and Edmund Walker at the ecumenical
service for the people of South Africa on the occasion of the visit of
Nelson Mandela, Sydney, October 24, 1990

Foreword

During the fifties and sixties when I was a young person living on a cattle station community in the Northern Territory, waves of introduced diseases such as measles, mumps and chickenpox spread through our community. Often the whole community would be stricken and sometimes the struggle to survive would be lost. I can remember, as a 12-year-old, holding a baby who died in my arms of an illness I was later told was diphtheria, and comforting older people who were in pain or coughing up blood. In Aboriginal communities throughout Australia a similar story can be told of illnesses, striking down whole communities.

In earlier times, if we sought medical assistance we were often refused treatment, treated in the yard of the station homestead or in separate quarters in hospital, or would have to travel long distances in search of treatment or care. More often than not we would just have to cope. In some areas of Australia, feared diseases like leprosy led to Aboriginal people being removed to isolated institutions.

In the last 20 years, Aborigines have, in theory, had access to the same health services as non-Aborigines. However, across Australia there have been continuing difficulties in obtaining appropriate health care. One reason for this is the effect of living in poverty, dependent on others for services and lacking even basic living amenities. People may not have the confidence or knowledge to seek out adequate medical care or may be met by judgmental or racist attitudes when they do. Another issue that creates problems is the difference in the attitudes and values of health professionals and their Aboriginal clients. This can lead to negative experiences for Aboriginals and make seeking treatment so stressful that they delay going to a health centre, hospital or local professional.

However, this does not mean that progress has not been made. I would argue that we have come a long way in improving health care for our people through training Aboriginal health workers, doctors and nurses and setting up community-based medical services. But progress has been extremely slow and we are only now moving towards remedying the continuing inequalities that face us.

This book comes at a time when we are trying to ensure that health professionals have the range of skills needed to work effectively in a multicultural society, which includes first and foremost the indigenous people of Australia. It will help health professionals understand better the beliefs, concerns and social position of Aboriginal people within Australia and hence work more effectively with them. It will contribute to a better understanding of the historical, cultural, environmental and political aspects of health and health care. As a teacher of Aboriginal health workers and other health professionals, I believe it is a significant step forward for Aborigines and health services in Australia.

Veronica Arbon
Senior Lecturer, Aboriginal Education Unit,
Cumberland College of Health Sciences,
University of Sydney

Acknowledgments

This book is the product of a collective effort. It has involved Aboriginal and non-Aboriginal community workers, health professionals, tertiary teachers and researchers throughout Australia committed to the health and welfare of Aboriginal people.

This book, and its companion volume *The health of immigrant Australia*, were produced by the Centre for Cross-Cultural Studies in Health and Medicine, which was funded through the Department of Public Health of the University of Sydney by the federal Department of Education, Employment and Training under the Multicultural and Cross-Cultural Supplementation Program of the National Languages Policy. The centre is a joint project of the Department of Public Health and Cumberland College of Health Sciences, University of Sydney. We are grateful to the former Dean of Medicine, Richard Gye, and staff of the faculty office, and to Geoffrey Berry, Susan Quine, Tessa Guilfoyle, Sandra Cheng and other staff of the Department of Public Health for their support throughout the project. We also thank Jeffrey Miller and Graeme Watts for their encouragement and the staff of Cumberland College who contributed to the project.

The centre has received guidance from its advisory committee—Veronica Arbon, John Barrand, Lorna Channon-Little, Joy Higgs, Christine Inglis, Ilona Lee, Marie de Lepervanche, Jacqueline Lublin, Susan Quine and Toni Schofield. Lenore Manderson has provided valuable scholarly direction and editorial advice in her role as the centre's consultant, for which we extend our sincere thanks. Others whose assistance and knowledge have enhanced the content of the book include Leslie Houston, Anne Louis and Nancy Williams. We are grateful to staff of the centre and in particular to Glenn Richardson for his tenacity and enthusiasm in seeking out photographic material, and to Deborah Lupton for her research contributions. We also thank Tina Rae, whose organisational and secretarial abilities and good humour preserved order despite all.

Our thanks are also due to the editorial staff of Harcourt Brace Jovanovich who contributed to the production of the book: in particular, to Jeremy Fisher, managing editor of the College and Professional Division, for his encouragement, support and sound advice, and to senior editor Carol Natsis, whose editorial expertise greatly enhanced the final text. We would also like to thank Penny Taylor of the Australian Institute of Aboriginal and Torres Strait Islander Studies for her patience and assistance in providing photographs for various chapters. Finally we are grateful to Bronwyn Bancroft for her striking cover and to Glenda Browne for the preparation of a comprehensive index. Our friends and family, among them Amelia, Larissa and Colin, offered inspiration and support when most needed.

Note to instructors

As an aid to teaching, an instructor's manual is available upon written application to the publisher. It contains an annotated guide to audiovisual resources related to Aboriginal health issues, plus problem-solving case studies with suggested discussion topics and background notes.

Contributors

The numbers in parentheses indicate the pages on which the authors' contributions begin.

Maggie Brady (28, 139, 173, 200), Australian Institute of Aboriginal and Torres Strait Islander Studies, PO Box 553, Canberra, ACT 2601.

Gordon Briscoe (393), History Department, Faculty of Arts, Australian National University, GPO Box 4, Canberra, ACT 2601.

Patricia Fagan (400), Aboriginal Medical Service, 36 Turner Street, Redfern, NSW 2016.

Margaret-Ann Franklin, 8 Burgess Street, Armidale, NSW 2350.

Richard Glover (92), *Sydney Morning Herald*, GPO Box 506, Sydney, NSW 2001.

Michael Gracey (56), Aboriginal Health Unit, Health Department of Western Australia, 189 Royal Street, East Perth, WA 6004.

Alan Gray (80), National Centre for Epidemiology and Population Health, Australian National University, GPO Box 4, Canberra, ACT 2601.

Dennis Gray (381), Department of General Practice, University of Western Australia, Nedlands, WA 6009.

John Hargrave (62), Royal Darwin Hospital, PO Box 41326, Casuarina, NT 0810.

Lindsey Harrison (24, 123, 132, 160), Department of Public Health and Nutrition, University of Wollongong, PO Box 1144, Wollongong, NSW 2500.

Shane Houston (80), National Aboriginal and Islander Health Organisation, PO Box 414, Campbelltown NSW 2560.

Charles Kerr (326), Department of Public Health, University of Sydney, NSW 2006.

Amanda Lee (127, 369), Menzies School of Health Research, PO Box 41096, Casuarina, NT 0810.

Deborah Lupton (xi), Department of Public Health, University of Sydney, NSW 2006.

Margaret Miller (334), Australian Consumers Association, 57 Carrington Road, Marrickville, NSW 2204.

Robyn Mobbs (292), 18 Catherine Street, Ethelton, SA 5015.

Kingsley Palmer (139), Australian Institute of Aboriginal and Torres Strait Islander Studies, PO Box 553, Canberra, ACT 2601.

David Morrissey (372), Tranby College, PO Box 229, Glebe, NSW 2037.

Paul Pholeros (346), Nganampa Health Council (Consultant), Alice Springs, NT 0871.

Janice Reid (xi, 4), Centre for Cross-Cultural Studies in Health and Medicine, School of Community Health, Cumberland College of Health Sciences and Department of Public Health, University of Sydney, PO Box 170, Lidcombe NSW 2141.

Joseph Reser (218), Department of Psychology and Sociology, School of Behavioural Science, James Cook University of North Queensland, Townsville, QLD 4810.

Sherry Saggers (381), Edith Cowan University, Mt Lawley Campus, 2 Bradford Street, Mt Lawley, WA 6050.

Neil Thomson (37), Australian Institute of Health, PO Box 570, Canberra, ACT 2601.

Paul Torzillo (326), Suite 420, Royal Prince Alfred Hospital Medical Centre, 100 Carillon Avenue, Newtown, NSW 2042.

Peggy Trompf, Centre for Cross-Cultural Studies in Health and Medicine, Department of Public Health, University of Sydney, NSW 2006.

Bruce Walker (351), Centre for Appropriate Technology, Community College, PO Box 8044, Alice Springs, NT 0871.

Nancy Williams (4), Department of Anthropology and Sociology, University of Queensland, St Lucia, Qld 4067.

Joan Winch (402), Aboriginal Medical Service, 154 Edwards Street, East Perth, WA 6004.
Isobel White (1), Department of Anthropology, Research School of Pacific Studies, Australian National University, PO Box 4, Canberra, ACT 2601.

Introduction

Janice Reid

Centre for Cross-Cultural Studies in Health and Medicine, University of Sydney

Deborah Lupton

Department of Public Health, University of Sydney

Next to shooting indigenous peoples, the surest way to kill us is to separate us from our part of the Earth. Once separated, we will either perish in body or our minds and spirits will be altered so that we end up mimicking foreign ways, adopt foreign languages, accept foreign thoughts and build a foreign prison around our indigenous spirits, a prison which suffocates rather than nourishes as our traditional territories of the Earth do. Over time, we lose our identity and eventually die or are crippled as we are stuffed under the name of 'assimilation' into another society.

Senior official of the World Council of Indigenous Peoples (ICIHI 1987, p. 85)

Now I would like to tell you a story, about the time the first missionary came here. He used to preach and talk in those old days—that was the time of my mother's generation...The missionary...said that in the future the Whites would bring a great number of different things that are not too good for the Eskimos. We learned that there were going to be problems, problems of two cultures getting together, problems like drinking and war. The missionary talked of how things in each generation would get worse and worse...I believe that those things prophesied by the missionary are happening now.

Hugh Brody (Brody 1975, pp. 210–11

This is a story of an Anungu child
Who grew up in the bush so free and wild.
Who learnt about nature and things of this earth
And walked so proud in the land of his birth...

The white man came and took over the land
And did a lot of things he couldn't understand.
They raped mother earth and killed his people
To build their towns of spire and steeple.

No more would he hunt or search or track,
They took his land and gave nothing back.
He survived in the bush when things were down
But he couldn't make a living in a whiteman's town.

From 'The winds of change', a poem by Aboriginal writer Cyril Coaby (Coaby 1988)

This book is about the health of Aboriginal Australians, the diseases Aboriginal people suffer, the patterns of those diseases, their contexts and their causes—both historical and contemporary. It is intended for students and graduates in the health and welfare professions who have an interest in the social, economic and political factors that have shaped a legacy of ill-health in many Aboriginal communities.

The contributors to this volume write within a conceptual framework that is best represented by the 'new public health'. This perspective goes beyond the conventional paradigm of illness as the outcome of the assaults of pathogens, poor nutrition, addictions, unhygienic living conditions or genetic predisposition, to address the contribution of social justice, social action, power and access to resources to shaping people's health and life chances. The authors, Aboriginal and non-Aboriginal, come from a range of backgrounds and professions in the health field, including public health, anthropology, epidemiology, psychology, medicine, nutrition, sociology, demography and community health. Their contributions to the book include an overview of the invasion and colonisation of Aboriginal lands, the environmental and social conditions in which Aborigines live, government health policy and practice, the epidemiology of diseases that affect urban, rural and remote populations, nutrition and diet, the cultural context of illness and therapy, Aboriginal families and their health, the use of addictive drugs and substances, and current concerns in mental health.

A premise of this book, and a theme of most recent commentaries on Aboriginal health and sickness, is that much of the suffering of communities today can be traced to the alienation of Aboriginal lands. This alienation was wrought by the violence of guerilla warfare, massacres and rape, the deadly stealth of epidemic disease, malnutrition and poverty, and the good intentions of government agencies and missions which confined Aborigines to 'civilise' them, seized children of dual ancestry and stifled the religious and cultural expressions of Aboriginal people. As Gray et al. describe in this book, the appropriation of lands that sustained Aborigines and shaped their theology, social lives and economic activities had traumatising effects on families and local groups, effects that ramified through generations.

Aboriginal society today is known to most white Australians only through images in the media—reports of hangings in prison cells, of police raids on urban ghettos, of dilapidated shanty towns clinging to river banks or the edges of country towns, of intoxicated men and women, of sickly children, of Aboriginal protest, of dancers and artists, of rock bands and ceremonial performers. These paradoxical and, to an outsider, often perplexing portrayals convey a sense of a people apart, a people separated in time, place and culture from the 'mainstream' Australian society.

The supposed idiosyncrasies of Aborigines have been explained by some in terms of their collective predispositions (to drinking, fecklessness, 'going walkabout') or their culture (as inimical to education and enterprise; mystical and primitive). The Aborigines who run their own businesses, live in the suburbs, work in the public service or private sector, go to school and university, are internationally exhibited artists and successful authors, dancers and actors, rear well adjusted and healthy children, work for their communities or are prominent in public life rarely make headlines and so are invisible to most other Australians. Australian stereotypes about Aborigines, whether subtle or bald, are based on a belief that

Aborigines are different in their aspirations and values, unique in their position in Australia and therefore an intractable 'problem' for the society in which they live. In fact, Aborigines are not unique, either in their suffering or the challenges that suffering presents to the Australian state. Their experience is one that is shared by many communities in every continent of the world.

In order to understand the precursors of Aboriginal ill-health described in this book, it is important to recognise that any people subject to a similar broad set of historical conditions to that experienced by Aborigines will suffer a similar assault on their health and social integrity. Internationally, those communities that have histories of dispossession, dispersal and disease paralleled by that of Aborigines are known collectively as the 'fourth world'.

Dispossession and ill health: the fourth world experience

Fourth world communities are characterised by their experience of being colonised, or of being a minority in relation to the dominant, encompassing state. Many have been forced to assimilate, losing most of their land and their economic base, and therefore their autonomy. The United Nations uses the working definition of fourth world or indigenous populations as:

composed of the existing descendants of the peoples who inhabited the present territory of a country wholly or partially at the time when persons of a different culture or ethnic origin arrived there from other parts of the world, overcame them and, by conquest, settlement or other means, reduced them to a non-dominant or colonial situation; who today live more in conformity with their particular social, economic and cultural customs and traditions than with the institutions of the country of which they now form a part, under a state structure which incorporates mainly the national, social and cultural characteristics of other segments of the population which are dominant.

ICIHI 1987, p. 7

Fourth world communities exist within first world countries (for example, Aborigines, Basques, Bretons, Maoris and Native Americans), second world countries (such as the indigenous peoples of northern USSR) and third world countries (such as the indigenous peoples of Central and South America) (O'Neil 1986, pp. 119–20).

Indigenous populations are not, of course, homogeneous. Differences in social organisation, economic status, access to land, religious beliefs, history and health status exist among different tribes or geographical areas, as they do within states. For example, in the United States there are 507 federally recognised Native American communities, which differ widely in their cultural and genetic heritages, economic resources and ways of life (Rhoades et al. 1987b, p. 352). Similarly, Aborigines live in a spectrum of ecological zones, speak several hundred languages, and have differing religious and healing practices, diets, family traditions, political structures and economic strategies.

There are also historical differences between the ways the lands of indigenous peoples of different countries were invaded and exploited. These in part explain differences in their socioeconomic status and health status today (Fisher 1980).

Native Americans in British Columbia, for instance, forged a relatively autonomous relationship with Europeans by playing a crucial role in the fur-trade, but were subsequently relegated to a subordinate position, exploited, and became a marginal source of cheap labour. They offered little active resistance to the loss of much of their land. Subarctic Native Americans were initially also on an equal footing with Europeans as trappers and traders, but the latter's increasing control over the fur-trade, the depletion of game, low seasonal income, and the availability of extensive credit for consumer goods at trading posts and settlements all contributed to the creation of a 'welfare society' among northern Indians (Fisher 1980; Young 1988, p. 16). This loss of autonomy and subsequent pattern of dependency was mirrored amongst other Native American groups throughout the North American continent. Over three hundred treaties mediating the terms of the surrender of land were signed by Native Americans with the British, United States and Canadian governments. The vast majority of the treaties were later broken by these governments (ICIHI 1987, p. 16).

A similar pattern of economic colonisation and subsequent dependency upon welfare is evident in the history of the Maori peoples. After vigorously resisting the encroachment of the British, the Maoris signed the Treaty of Waitangi in 1840 and ceded sovereignty in exchange for exclusive land rights and 'all the rights and privileges of British subjects' (Fisher 1980, pp. 9–10; ICIHI 1987, p. 16). But by purchase or successive Acts of parliament most land was wrested from Maori hands, so that today they own only about 4 per cent of New Zealand territory.

In Australia, as British settlers annexed more and more land, Aborigines were forced to enter into some kind of relationship with them—to attempt negotiation or guerilla action. Attempts at organised resistance were hampered by the fact that they were outnumbered and did not have guns. The Europeans, many of whom considered Aborigines to be little more than vermin, killed local people or relocated them in reserves and settlements, as Franklin and White describe in chapter 1. Not even a nominal attempt was made to negotiate treaties similar to those in New Zealand and North America. Aborigines obtained jobs as pastoral workers and labourers as Australia's primary industry flourished, but this source of employment was eroded when industrialisation and mining interests became dominant, rural industries experienced recession and Aborigines were passed over for employment in favour of European immigrants, who were considered more 'dependable' (Stanner 1973–1974, pp. 256–7; Hewett 1990, p. 25). By the 1970s, Aborigines were increasingly being drawn into the economy of social welfare payments as a cushion against acute poverty and unemployment. These payments became especially important to women and children who had no other means of support. Such payments have undoubtedly contributed to the capacity to buy better food and other necessities, as well as luxury goods and alcohol, but despite the views of some that Aborigines would rather live on welfare payments than fend for themselves, few people enjoy or want to subsist on welfare, to be forced to depend on the legislated charity of others as a means of survival.

Many indigenous peoples now live on the margins of the dominant society, in the most underprivileged areas of cities and towns, and in remote settlements and reserves in which living conditions are far worse than those experienced by the people of the majority culture (Young 1988). Few of their number, especially in Australia and North America, complete high school, and even fewer go on to tertiary study and professional or high-paying jobs. They are concentrated in the ranks of the unemployed and the unskilled and poorly paid workers. All are in poorer health than the non-indigenous populations.

The ill-health of Aborigines and its precursors are discussed by Thomson in chapter 2 and by Torzillo and Kerr in chapter 8: the higher death rates at all ages, the impact of communicable and non-communicable diseases, and the environmental and lifestyle factors with which they are associated. Reser, writing on mental health issues in Aboriginal communities in chapter 6, draws attention to the rising death rate from suicide and violence among young men in particular, especially those who have been affected by alcohol. In chapter 5, Brady reviews the evidence for the effects of alcohol and substance use on individuals, families and communities, critically documenting the history and patterns of use. (See also NAHSWP 1989.)

The situation described by these authors for Australia is similar to that in North America . The age-specific death rate for Native Americans for injuries and violence is approximately double the national rate for the 15 to 45 year age group, and the mortality rate for infectious diseases is more than double that of all 'races'. Tuberculosis, diabetes and respiratory disease rates are much higher than those of the general population. Native Americans have the highest frequency of alcohol-associated health problems and deaths of any ethnic group in the United States. Abuse of inhalants is also common among Native American adolescents (Rhoades et al. 1987a). Native American children suffer the highest injury mortality rates of the major ethnic groups in at least one state (Olsen et al. 1990).

Similarly, compared to non-Maoris in New Zealand, Maori people suffer from much higher rates of coronary heart disease, cardiovascular disease, respiratory disease and hypertension. There are twice as many post-neonatal deaths among Maori children, and more Maori children have rheumatic fever, asthma, ear infections and hearing loss. Maori people have a much higher incidence of diabetes and higher death rates from cancer of the lung, stomach, breast, pancreas and cervix. Tuberculosis is still relatively common and Maoris die at a higher rate from digestive disorders, particularly from alcohol-associated cirrhosis of the liver. A disproportionate number of indigenous New Zealanders are in psychiatric institutions, and their rates for violent accidents are much higher. Life expectancy at birth is 7 years shorter for Maori males and 8.5 years shorter for Maori females, compared to the non-Maori population (Boddy 1988, pp. 31–2; Pomare and de Boer 1988, p. 27).

Infectious disease, degenerative disease, mental suffering, alcohol abuse and violence represent a common endpoint of the erosion of the resources, rights and autonomy of fourth world peoples. The processes by which dispossession is transformed into disease however are complex and interrelated.

Health, poverty and the environment

The fundamental changes that have occurred since the arrival of whites have resulted in a loss of control and autonomy of action by Aboriginal individuals and communities. Aborigines are subject at the local level to the attitudes, decisions, advice, actions and variable sympathies of whites. At the regional and national levels, the course of Aborigines' lives is significantly determined by politicians and administrators who are not of their culture. Access to community services is often blocked by poverty, remoteness, the cultural mismatch of many services, discrimination and a lack of knowledge of the structure and function of the services. Access to information is blocked by the language barrier, the withholding of information by some whites in service positions as a means of retaining control, poor communications, the lack of opportunities to share ideas and information with other Aboriginal groups or indigenous populations, and illiteracy in the language in which much necessary information is conveyed. The inaccessibility of many services and much information is magnified by the lack of access to assets and power. Very few Aborigines have had the opportunity to gain an understanding of the legal, financial and corporate structures of European society to enable them to take advantage of the economic system. Similarly, although increasing numbers of Aborigines are going to university, most do not have the educational qualifications that are required in Australian society for many positions of influence (Reid 1979, p. 9).

The visible manifestations of Aborigines' exclusion from the resources, wealth and knowledge of Australian society are the physical conditions in which many are forced to live, the food they eat, the hazards of an impoverished or exploited environment and the dwellings they inhabit. As Harrison shows in chapter 4, much Aboriginal ill-health can be related to poor diet and subsequent nutritional status. For many Aborigines in remote areas, for instance, who depend on a diet of refined carbohydrates such as sugar, flour, soft drinks and bread, together with fresh or tinned meat, it is simply not possible to obtain other foods. Often the local store has a limited range of foodstuffs, nutritious 'bush tucker' may be unavailable in the areas around a settlement, and households have neither places to store fresh food safely nor adequate cooking facilities. Many studies have shown that people of low socioeconomic status have a poorer diet than those who are more advantaged. Rural and urban Aborigines, as people who live in poverty, are subject to the same barriers to a good diet experienced by other disadvantaged Australians: a lack of money to buy nutritious food and of time or facilities to prepare it; the desire to eat those foods that are comforting, convenient and filling rather than nutritionally balanced; and the desire to conform to group norms in the choice of food.

For those Aborigines in rural, remote and city areas, as Torzillo and Kerr document in chapter 8, living conditions continue to fall far below the standard of those of other Australians. Sanitation, garbage disposal services, housing and water supplies are often of appalling standard, while stores, schools, telephones and recreational facilities are lacking (Commonwealth of Australia 1979). The housing of many Aboriginal communities in remote settlements, rural areas and towns, and in the poorer parts of large cities where Aborigines live, is substandard compared to the houses in which most non-Aborigines live. For instance, a Human Rights Commission inquiry which began in 1987 into conditions in Aboriginal communities on the New South Wales and Queensland border revealed that the houses (or more accurately, shacks) in these reserves had been constructed many years ago and had been patched up as they deteriorated with sheets of tin, 'creating heat-ravaged furnaces in summer and leaky ice-boxes in winter' (Totaro 1989, p. 3). People living in these reserves described how for decades they had endured a lack of sewerage systems and running water, and periods when food and supplies were cut off by floods. They were also subject to harassment by local whites. White children called the Aboriginal school bus 'the Vegemite bus', and armed white men would amuse themselves by shining hunting spotlights through the windows of the Aborigines' homes (Totaro 1989, p. 3).

Compounding the absolute poverty of the dwellings of many communities is the inappropriateness of many houses that have been designed on the basis of the values and cultural assumptions about the concept of a 'home' held by white bureaucrats, social planners and architectural firms. As Reser (1977) has pointed out, the values of those whose major life purchase is a house, who spend time and money improving it, and who assess people on the quality and appearance of their housing may be at odds with those of many Aborigines: 'A physical environment which departs from the European model is too readily seen as squalid, dirty, unhealthy' (Reser 1977, p. 52). Aborigines may reject or neglect conventional European houses offered to them, simply because these dwellings are not appropriate to their wants and needs. Many Aborigines do not value the isolation and privacy offered by the standard European house; they value human relationships, open living areas and space in which to be able to communicate freely with others and honour their obligations to offer accommodation to family and friends. Moreover, the burden of up to a dozen people using one dwelling may render plumbing inoperable, and without refrigeration, cupboards or the usual accoutrements of a conventional urban residence make it impossible to keep the house clean and tidy (by middle-class European standards) or in good repair.

When hardware is provided, it may be grossly inappropriate to the local environment. Flushed toilets, conventional washing machines, plastic piping that blocks easily, and electricity generators that run out of fuel all give an appearance of 'progress' but subvert householders' capacity to help plan facilities that are socially and environmentally appropriate and can be maintained locally. As Young (1988, p. 76) points out, writing of Canadian subarctic Native Americans, 'the construction of sanitation facilities does not alone guarantee their acceptance, proper use, and maintenance'. Reser (1977, p. 59) comments: 'If environments are perceived as meaningful and supportive, they are used and treated as such. If a person's home is not encompassed by our definition of a dwelling, however, heaven help the occupant'.

Priorities differ. At Yalata in South Australia, people have access to a store, houses, medical care and other amenities, and yet several families have moved to Oak Valley Outstation seven hours away by car, where they live in humpies, have no washing water, no green vegetables, no emergency medical services and no sanitary facilities; they subsist largely on damper and hunted meat. Their explanation is that they are 'looking after' their country (M. Brady, pers. comm.).

In sum, the built and physical environments both reflect and exacerbate the poverty and ill-health of Aboriginal communities. They promote a cycle of discrimination, neglect and sickness.

Ethnicity and social disadvantage

For many Aborigines, especially those who live in towns and cities, it is difficult to separate the disadvantage conferred by their ethnicity from the disadvantage conferred by their socioeconomic status. The Aborigines who live in the Sydney suburb of Redfern, for example, are subject to very different stressors from those who live in the remote areas of north and central Australia. One of the stressors in Redfern is being victimised by police. In 1989, the police shot dead an innocent Aboriginal man, David Gundy, in a dawn raid. This raid was later vehemently condemned by the Royal Commission into Aboriginal Deaths in Custody (H. Wootten) in a report tabled in parliament on 5 April 1991, which recommended that the possibility of laying criminal charges against the police be investigated. In 1990, another raid provoked prominent Aboriginal leaders to comment that the police were trying to drive the Aborigines out of Redfern (Cornwall 1990, p. 4). In the case of harassment such as this, ethnicity—that is, Aboriginality—is obviously the motivating factor.

Experiencing as they do the combined effects of racial prejudice and dispossession, it is little wonder that fourth world peoples are among those who suffer the greatest disadvantage from their low socioeconomic status. Langton (1981, p. 18) writes that 'few Aboriginal communities or groups in the modern Australian economy have lived out of poverty, and where they have, it has only been for short periods of time'. Aborigines are poorer, have higher rates of unemployment and have lower levels of education than non-Aboriginal Australians. The median annual income for Aborigines is 65 per cent of that for all Australians (see NAHSWP 1989). Again, other fourth world parallels are striking. Maoris have higher levels of unemployment, lower earning capacity, poorer education, lower rates of home-ownership and higher rates of incarceration in penal institutions than non-Maoris. Unemployment levels for Maoris are 2.5 times those of non-Maoris in New Zealand. Two-thirds of Maori people occupy the two lowest socioeconomic classes, a figure twice that of the non-Maori group. The income of the most common income group for Maori males in the full-time labour force in 1986 was half that of non-Maori males (Pomare and de Boer 1988, pp. 39–40). Similarly, the Native American population lags behind the general United States population (that is, all 'races') with respect to a range of income, education and employment measures. The median family income of Native Americans is 69 per cent that of the general United States population. Compared with the general population, there are more than twice as many Native Americans below the poverty line, and less than half as many Native Americans complete college. The unemployment rate for Native Americans is more than twice that of the general population (US Department of Health 1988, p. 16).

In the public health literature, the relationship between poverty, social isolation, material hardship, unemployment and ill-health is well documented (Lindheim and Syme 1983). Tesh (1988, p. 34) summarises it thus: 'People with the least education, people who live in the least desirable neighbourhoods, and people who work at the least prestigious jobs are all more likely to die earlier than people on the other end of these scales...virtually every disease strikes the lowest class most heavily'. For Aborigines, who, like Maoris and native Americans, bear the added burden of racism, the disadvantage conferred by living on the margins of Australia's economy and society is greatly magnified.

A fair share: health and social justice

Increasingly Aborigines are drawing their cause into the international arena, arguing in Australia and abroad for their rights to land, equal access to human services, economic justice, and social equality. For most Aborigines, equity in health and socioeconomic status and access to services are fine ideals, but rarely a reality. Hart's (1971, p. 405) 'inverse care law', which states that 'the availability of good medical care tends to vary inversely with the need for it in the population served' captures the dilemma Aborigines face. The 'inverse care law' is particularly apt for people who are both poor and black. During the last two decades, the development of the community-controlled Aboriginal medical services and the training of Aboriginal health workers, described in chapter 9 by Saggers and Gray, have served to bridge the gap between Aboriginal communities and the practitioners and institutions of Western medicine. These have been important programs, which have enhanced the access of Aborigines to health facilities and fostered community involvement and initiative. However, it is still the case that Aborigines seldom use mainstream services other than general practice, accident and emergency (outpatient) clinics, and certain inpatient services (such as obstetrics). Even when Aborigines do go into hospital, their experience can be intimidating or humiliating. For instance, the women of one New South Wales country town told a sympathetic female medical practitioner in 1987 that, when they were evacuated to the regional hospital to await the births of their babies, they were placed in an isolation ward away from other (white) expectant mothers, and given their meals in disposable containers. The hospital authorities justified their policy by explaining that they were treating all black women as presumptive hepatitis B carriers. Such stories of the neglect of cultural sensitivities or personal rights are common in the annals of Aboriginal interactions with mainstream health services.

As Robyn Mobbs explains in chapter 7, the cultural appropriateness of health service provision is an important dimension of access to appropriate care for Aborigines and other fourth world peoples. Many communities are alienated by the culturally inappropriate approaches of white personnel to their health problems. In New Zealand, Maori people have initiated moves to strengthen Maori cultures, values and contributions to health issues and to ensure that health workers recognise Maori ways of healing and treating illness (Boddy 1988; Duric 1985, p. 484). Maoris have expressed the wish to

define health for themselves, to identify their own specific health concerns and devise solutions to meet their own needs. They see health as a part of who they are, where they have come from and where they are going, and they wish to take responsibility for their own health at the level of the whanau (extended family), hapu (subtribe) or iwi (tribe) rather than as individuals.

Boddy 1988, p. 36

Tesh (1988, p. 81) suggests that there is a real need for individuals to feel as if they can do something to improve the conditions of their lives, a need for actions individuals can rely on while awaiting longer-term structural change based on progressive public policies; for it 'would verge on the suicidal to advocate only prevention policies that require someone else to take action'. Community participation that starts at the local and regional level has the potential to expand into state and national arenas. Success at the local level gives impetus to the erosion of obstacles and the establishment of truly local initiatives. It gives a chance to the individual to do something, to become empowered with the support of like-minded others. It is in this spirit that the Aboriginal medical services were conceived and for this reason that they increased rapidly, until they number over 60 today. The Aboriginal medical services are based on the philosophy of community control, a strategy that 'promotes responsibility, understanding and allows communities to be active participants' rather than passive recipients (NAHSWP 1989, p. xvi) and espouses a view of health similar to that captured by the Ottawa Charter on Health Promotion.

The new public health, as espoused by the Ottawa Charter, revolves around reducing inequalities in health, building social policies conducive to health, improving access to health resources, developing an environment conducive to health, strengthening social supports and community action, promoting positive health behaviour, appropriate coping strategies and knowledge, and reorienting health services towards prevention and health promotion (WHO 1986). Lindheim and Syme (1983, p. 354) maintain that in general there is ample evidence that for good health, both physical and mental, people need to 'connect'—not only with others, and with their biological and cultural heritage, but also with the future: 'They need the opportunity to shape situations, places, and activities that affect their lives'. The Victorian Aboriginal Health Service Co-operative (VAHSC 1989, pp. 4–5) outlines a similar set of requirements for an individual's mental health: the assurance of his or her identity; a belief in something external to himself or herself; the availability of options for future personal decision making; and the possession of a language common to the individual's group or community (particularly in an alien and threatening society).

Earth and body

Aborigines today hold that the restoration of sovereignty over land or restitution for losses are basic to the attainment of Aboriginal health and identity (VAHSC 1989, p. 1). For some people living in remote areas of Australia, particularly in northern South Australia and the Northern Territory, title to land has now been vested under white Australian law in clans and tribes that still live there. This recognition of their ownership of the land has been of profound spiritual and economic importance to such communities, placing them in a position to negotiate its use with outsiders and giving them the security of tenure that underpins community identity and self-determination. This is not to say that the depredations of history or their effects on health and social life have been removed—rather that a foundation for the future has been secured.

As Hayden Burgess of the World Council of Indigenous Peoples has expressed it: 'The earth is the seat of our spirituality, the fountain from which our cultures and languages flourish. The earth is our historian, the keeper of events and of the bones of our forefathers' (ICIHS 1987, p. 10). Land rights to people in Perth or Port Pirie, Canberra or Cherbourg, Broome or Bourke represent not only a securing of natural assets but a spiritual anchor, an island of autonomy in a sea of dependence, a tangible recognition by non-Aborigines of dispossession and the need for social justice, and a focus for action to remedy the sequelae of chronic social and economic disadvantage (see also Rowley 1981, pp. 81–2).

It is important for those who wish to understand 'the Aboriginal experience' as a fourth world nation to see contemporary patterns of ill-health as shadows on the wall of the cave cast by events on a broader horizon. Morbidity and mortality statistics reflect an inheritance of loss and social upheaval that remains a central feature of Aboriginal consciousness today. The rhetoric of the struggle for land rights is a language for expressing and engaging broader concerns, and the activities and activism of the Aboriginal medical services encompass more than 'illness' or 'health' as they are commonly understood. Thus, health professionals who want to be effective need to 'hear' what Aborigines have to say, not just about their immediate health concerns but about the broader impediments to their well-being and about their own ways of tackling their concerns. This book is written as one starting point in this endeavour.

References

Boddy, J. M. (1988), 'Maori health—is the future determined by the past?' *Recent Advances in Nursing* **20**, pp. 27–38.

Brody, H. (1975), *The people's land: Eskimos and whites in the eastern Arctic*, Penguin, Harmondsworth, Middlesex.

Coaby, C. (1988), 'The winds of change', *Aboriginal Health Worker* **12** (2), p. 33.

Commonwealth of Australia (1979), *Aboriginal Health. Report of the House of Representatives Standing Committee on Aboriginal Affairs*, AGPS, Canberra.

Cornwall, D. (1990), 'Drive to get us out, say blacks', *Sydney Morning Herald*, February 19, p. 4.

Durie, M. H. (1985), 'A Maori perspective of [sic] health', *Social Science and Medicine* **20** (5), pp. 483–6.

Fisher, R. (1980), 'The impact of European settlement on the indigenous peoples of Australia, New Zealand and British Columbia: some comparative dimensions', *Canadian Ethnic Studies* **12** (1), pp. 1–13.

Hart, J. T. (1971), 'The inverse care law', *Lancet* **27**, February, pp. 405–12.

Hewett, T. (1990), 'On the black side of Plonk Valley', *Sydney Morning Herald*, March 24, p. 25.

ICIHI (Independent Commission on International Humanitarian Issues) (1987), *Indigenous peoples: a global quest for justice*, Zed Books, London.

Langton, M. (1981), 'Urbanising Aborigines: the social scientists' great deception', *Social Alternatives* **2** (2), pp. 16–22.

Lindheim, R., and Syme, S. L. (1983), 'Environments, people and health', *Annual Review of Public Health* **4**, pp. 335–59.

NAHSWP (National Aboriginal Health Strategy Working Party) (1989), *A National Aboriginal Health Strategy*.

Olsen, L. M., Becket, T. M., Wiggins, C. L., Key, C. R., and Samet, J. M. (1990), 'Injury mortality in American Indian, Hispanic, and non-Hispanic white children in New Mexico 1958–1982', *Social Science and Medicine* **30** (4), pp. 479–86.

O'Neil, J. (1986), 'The politics of health in the Fourth World; a Northern Canadian example', *Human Organisation* **45** (2), pp. 119–28.

Pomare, E. W., and de Boer, G. M. (1988), *Hauora: Maori standards of health*, Special Report Series 78, New Zealand Department of Health, Auckland.

Reid, J. (1979), *Aboriginal Health in the 1970s and 1980s*, Cumberland College Reports 16, Cumberland College of Health Sciences, Sydney.

Reser, J. (1977), 'What is a "decent" house?' *Aboriginal Health Worker* **1** (2), pp. 50–60.

Rhoades, E. R., Hammond, J., Welty, T. K., Handler, A. O., and Amler, R. W. (1987*a*), 'The Indian burden of illness and future health intervention', *Public Health Reports* **102** (4), pp. 361–8.

Rhoades, E. R., Reyes, L. L., and Buzzard, G. D. (1987*b*), 'The organisation of health services for Indian people', *Public Health Reports* **102** (4), pp. 352–6.

Rowley, C. D. (1981), *A matter of justice*, ANU Press, Canberra.

Stanner, W. E. H. (1973–1974), 'Aborigines in the affluent society: the widening gap', *Anthropological Forum* **3**, pp. 249–63.

Tesh, S. (1988), *Hidden arguments: political ideology and disease prevention policy*, Rutgers University Press, New Brunswick.

Totaro, P. (1989), 'Toomelah—two years after the public tears', *Sydney Morning Herald*, September 11, p. 3.

US Department of Health (US Department of Health and Human Services) (1988), *Indian Health Service, Chart Series Book*, US Department of Health.

VAHSC (Victorian Aboriginal Health Service Co-operative Limited) (1989), 'Land rights, sovereignty, and health', *Contact* **112**, pp. 1–5.

WHO (World Health Organization) (1986), *Ottawa Charter for Health Promotion: an international conference on health promotion*, November 17–21, Ottawa.

Young, T. Kue (1988), *Health care and cultural change: the Indian experience in the central Arctic*, University of Toronto Press, Toronto.

CHAPTER 1

The history and politics of Aboriginal health

Margaret-Ann Franklin

Sociology Department, University of New England, Armidale, New South Wales

Isobel White

Research School of Pacific Studies, Australian National University, Canberra

The 1986 Australian census data include information concerning 227 645 Aborigines and Torres Strait Islanders living in widely varying environments throughout the continent. Surveys conducted during the 1970s and 1980s reveal that their health status is essentially the same as that of people of developing countries. Yet when Captain James Cook's *Endeavour* anchored in Botany Bay in 1770, the health of Australian Aborigines and Torres Strait Islanders was almost certainly better than that of the crew. It is now generally accepted that the average Aborigine, in fact, enjoyed better health than the average Englishman. Nothing much had changed when Captain Arthur Phillip arrived with his soldiers and the first convicts in 1788. The two centuries that have elapsed since then have seen a remarkable improvement in the health of the white population both in Australia and in Britain but a catastrophic decline in the health of Aborigines, with improvements only in very recent times.

The World Health Organization has defined health as a 'complete state of physical, mental and social well-being and not merely the absence of disease or infirmity'. Even in terms of a much narrower definition, such as 'absence of disease', the Aboriginal people in Australia could not generally be characterised as healthy. International aid agencies such as Community Aid Abroad, Freedom From Hunger and War on Want are funding projects to improve Aboriginal health.

Before the invasion

It is not possible to understand the present status of Aboriginal health without setting it in historical perspective. It is still a matter of debate how long Aborigines had been living in Australia before Europeans invaded the continent, and various theories of Aboriginal origin have been proposed. At Lake Mungo, in New South

Wales, 30 000-year-old pellets of ochre have been found with the remains of a burial, together with indications that the body had been covered with ochre before burial (Flood 1983, pp. 42–46). The burial of a woman at Lake Mungo dated 26 000 years ago indicates that Aborigines may have performed the earliest cremation in the world; other pellets of ochre 32 000 years old found at Lake Mungo suggest that Aborigines may have been the first artists (Bowler et al. 1970, pp. 39–60; Flood 1983, p. 46).

It is likely that Aborigines had been living in Australia for at least 50 000 years before its colonisation by the British. Sixty years ago, Radcliffe-Brown estimated that in 1788 the Aboriginal population of the whole continent was about 300 000, a figure subsequently generally adopted by historians, anthropologists and demographers (Radcliffe-Brown 1930, pp. 687–96). In 1983, Noel Butlin, an economic historian, challenged this estimate, suggesting that in south-eastern Australia in 1788 there were probably five times the number proposed by Radcliffe-Brown for that area. He calculated that there could have been 250 000 Aborigines in Victoria and New South Wales alone (Butlin 1983, p. 175).

We can never know exactly whether the total population of the continent in 1788 was about 300 000 or more than one million, but White and Mulvaney (1987, p. 117) consider that 'an estimate of about 750 000 is a reasonable one'. It had fallen to less than 70 000 in the 1930s, after 150 years of exposure to white 'civilisation' (Borrie et al. 1975, p. 478). There are arguments as to whether the chief cause of the decline was massacre or disease. Barwick (1971, pp. 288–315), Reynolds (1982, pp. 200–2), and the authors of the National Population Enquiry (Borrie et al. 1975, p. 175) all stress that in Australia the history of colonisation has shown a marked tendency to play down 'the role of outright slaughter'. Upon re-examination of the Victorian historical data, Barwick (unpub.) found no unequivocal evidence of a

Figure 1.1 *The health and welfare of Aborigines suffered a catastrophic decline as a result of the three-pronged attack launched by the white invasion of their land. (Larry Pickering,* The Bulletin, *24 November 1987)*

smallpox epidemic sweeping inland ahead of the English settlers . She suggested that it might have been convenient for squatters to claim that the Aboriginal population had been virtually eliminated before they arrived.

At the time of the arrival of the First Fleet, the Aborigines had developed an economy based on gathering and hunting, and a technology and way of life finely tuned to their environment. An important aspect of all Aboriginal religions deals with how spirit beings (totemic ancestors) shaped the physical world, named plants and animals and allocated them to the land-owning groups. These ancestors still exist today in recognisable transformations, each associated with particular animals, plants, or other natural phenomena. All Aboriginal people have special relationships with their land and its resources, and these relationships are expressed and mediated by totems. Aboriginal men and women in many areas continue to perform ceremonies to ensure that the local plants and animals survive and flourish.

Records written by European settlers and explorers often state that upon first encounter the Aborigines appeared to be in good health and free from disease. These records certainly give no indication that Aborigines were disease-ridden or were handicapped by ill-health. Abbie (1970, p. 95), who studied the health of traditionally oriented Aborigines, proposed the following hypothesis about the situation at the time the British arrived. The estimated life span was 40 years; the probable order of frequency of causes of death was injury (including warfare and murder), disease, sorcery and old age. Thirteen per cent of all children died within their first year of life and a total of 25 per cent had died by the end of their fifth year. Most of these children died from natural causes, but infants with obvious severe disabilities were not assisted to survive. Aborigines suffered from relatively few endemic diseases; two of the most prevalent seem to have been trachoma and yaws. They rarely suffered from high blood pressure, and diabetes was unusual, as were cancer and arthritis (Cowlishaw 1978, pp. 37–55).

Aborigines ate well except in times of drought in the more arid areas and of prolonged cold and wet in areas with substantial rainfall. In general, their environment provided the resources for a nutritious diet, the available food comprising both protein and vegetable foods with adequate vitamins and minerals. Furthermore, their diet was low in salt, sugar, and fat, and they carefully regulated the use of the few narcotics then available. Since their lifestyle dictated frequent exercise, they were not overweight. The small group size discouraged the spread of infectious diseases. Infanticide of the newborn may at times have been practised when a baby was born before its next older sibling could be weaned, although in general births were well-spaced (Cowlishaw 1978, pp. 262–83; 1981, pp. 37–55). Cowlishaw argues that spacing and a small completed family size were achieved by post-partum taboos on intercourse, by the hormonal effect of breast-feeding and by periods of low kilojoule intake. (However, in chapter 3 of this volume, Gray et al. argue that small family size can be explained in terms of infant and young child survival.) We therefore gain a picture of the pre-colonial Aborigines as a healthy vigorous people, with each family raising few, but robust, children. It is reasonable to assume that the population, in total and in each area, could have had periodic increases and decreases. Current research suggests that about 6000 years ago there was a continent-wide increase in population accompanied by changes in technology (White and Lampert 1987, p. 21).

Armed conflict in north-eastern Arnhem Land

Even in remote areas of Australia, Aboriginal people did not entirely escape being attacked and shot by men on horseback, although the scale of the massacres was relatively small compared to that in the southern part of the continent.

In a brief account of the police presence in the Roper River area, police historian Peter Young (1985, p. 3) writes that in 1910, following a report that 'a party of white prospectors had been murdered by Aboriginals [sic]', a police party including a mounted constable and six Aboriginal 'trackers' searched for the Aborigines 'for two months in unmapped country...The irony of this arduous patrol lay in the fact that the prospectors were not dead'.

Accounts of a mounted expedition recorded by Yolngu people who were quite old in 1970 probably refer to this patrol, but their version is very different. Birrikitji, who was born in about 1898, referred to several incidents in which a number of his close relatives were killed. Translated in 1985 by Maypilama Gurruwiwi, the following are excerpts from Birrikitji's account. This information would have been given to him by survivors, one of whom was his mother's brother.

'People were camped by the billabong at Burarr. After breakfast, the men on horseback went off through the camp and started collecting the spears and breaking every one. They kept on breaking them, on and on, until one man said, "Hey, why are you breaking our spears? What are you up to? What are you going to do to us?" So one man turned round and picked up the rifle [probably the white man who was handling the gun] and he hit him with the rifle butt on the forehead. The man who was hit by the gun was my [Birrikitji's] *gathu* [nephew], Pangaypangay. He dropped to the ground. His children were shocked to see their father fall down. They cried out, "Our father's down!" So everyone turned round and ran for their spears. Before they could reach

them, the other men tried to shoot them with guns so they didn't have a chance to get them.

'The second one down was Gudaltji, whom I call *mari* [grandfather]. Then my other *mari*, called Birrkuda, was the third down. Wangarrwiryuna was the fourth down (he was *mari*, too). Then they turned and shot my *ngapipi* [mother's brother], Mirringini. After Mirringini, they shot Djewiny, then Wuliwuli, my *mukul* [aunt], who was a Gumatj woman. They threw them all in the water. They killed almost everyone in the camp. The women and children were frightened, and some of them ran and hid in the big thick jungle of Rupawiliya. One man escaped: he dived into the water and stayed under. When he came up for air, they'd shoot, and he'd go down again. He finally came up in a cave at the side of the creek where he was safe. The men on the horses were there for only the day: they arrived the afternoon of the day before, and this surprise attack occurred after breakfast. They were trying to wipe out everyone in the camp. And then they were off. Nobody wanted to go back there...

'Djulama was taken away...They got one other lady from Burarr, where they shot everyone, and took her too, and her name was Bunuthul, my *mukul*. And they took another woman, too, from the Djambarrpuyngu clan, and [the white man] took her, too; she's a sister of my *galay* [cousin], Barpar. He got three women and took them away...'

A Yolngu man, who was also listening to the account, asked, 'Did he [the white man] travel through many places killing people?' Birrikitji said, 'Yes. He started from Roper, through all those [named] places to Biranybirany and other places, and shot all these Yolngu and from Biranybirany back to Bal, and then he came back to Banggawupa, shooting people, not visiting. At Banggawupa, that's where he wiped out everybody. They didn't come as far as Garrthalala...

Nancy M. Williams, Department of Anthropology and Sociology, University of Queensland, St Lucia
Janice Reid, Centre for Cross-Cultural Studies in Health and Medicine, University of Sydney

A three-pronged attack

In addition to killing 'twenty thousand blacks before federation' (Reynolds 1982, p. 200) (and many more in the twentieth century as the frontier moved north and west in the Northern Territory and Western Australia), the conquerors launched a three-pronged attack on the health and welfare of Aborigines:

1. by introducing new diseases, some immediately fatal, others fatal in the long term;
2. by taking away ancestral land, thus causing psychological illness and spiritual despair;
3. by herding Aborigines into small reserves and settlements, destroying their healthy lifestyle and substituting conditions and diet poorer than those of the poorest of the newcomers.

Introduced diseases

Some figures for the population decline in Victoria have been carefully compiled from archival records and other contemporary sources by Barwick (1971, p. 288): 'Early estimates of the original native population of Victoria range from 5000 to 15 000...Fewer than 2000 remained by 1863'. This was only 28 years after the first European settlement of Victoria, and Barwick (1971, p. 288) regarded the main cause of this decline to have been 'the introduction of alien diseases'. Certainly the disease pattern began to change fundamentally after European settlement.

Butlin based his estimate of rapid depopulation in south-east Australia on the existence of a smallpox epidemic (see also Gray et al., chapter 3 in this volume), and suggests that the introduction of the disease could have resulted from letting loose, either accidentally or on purpose, what was called 'variolous matter' (that is, scabs from smallpox victims, used during the eighteenth century for inoculation) (Butlin 1983, pp. 19–24; Butlin 1985).

Another epidemic occurred in 1829–30, shortly after the arrival in Port Jackson of a ship that had had cases of smallpox on board. Butlin (1983, pp. 24–37) regards the most likely cause of this outbreak to have been the distribution of the ship's infected blankets to Aborigines (again this could have been by accident or by design). Contrary to Butlin's interpretation, some historians argue that both the 1789 and the 1829–30 smallpox epidemics originated on the north coast of the continent, and were introduced by smallpox-infected trepang fishermen from the islands that now form part of Indonesia (Campbell 1985, pp. 336–58; Macknight 1986, pp. 136–37). Historian Macknight (1986, p. 136) implies, however, that by emphasising the significance of a smallpox epidemic the 'demographic effect of direct violence' is played down.

Smallpox was only one of many introduced diseases. Influenza, pneumonia, typhoid fever, measles, chickenpox, whooping cough, mumps, scarlet fever, diphtheria, tuberculosis, gonorrhoea, granuloma venereum (another form of venereal disease) and syphilis were mainly introduced by European colonists, although tuberculosis and venereal disease were probably also introduced by Indonesians, Melanesians, Chinese and Japanese (Abbie 1970, pp. 92–3). Leprosy is believed to have been introduced by Chinese labourers in the 1880s (Hargrave 1968). By the early 1840s venereal disease was widespread, as noted by Reece (1974, pp. 54–5):

According to Foster Fyans, Commissioner for Portland Bay, it had been introduced from Van Diemen's Land and, while 'hardly a shepherd was without disease', two-thirds of the Aborigines of the Port Phillip district had been destroyed by the infection. Bingham at Tumut and settlers in the Albury district also testified to its prevalence. Sometimes referred to as 'native pox' or 'black pox', the disease was believed by the whites to have originated from the Aborigines and it undoubtedly caused a good deal of bitterness between the races. At Glenormiston, in the Western District, Neil Black was told 'it is no uncommon thing for these rascals to sleep all night with a Lubra—and if she poxes him or in any way offends him perhaps shoot her before 12 next day'.

Throughout the nineteenth century, tuberculosis caused many deaths. Of Victoria, Barwick (1971, p. 309) writes:

In 1879 [the Aborigines Welfare Board] asked the government to authorise an investigation of mortality at the stations, explaining that the Aborigines who came young or were born there mostly died under the age of twenty-five and the usual cause was 'a disease of the lungs peculiar to the natives which ends fatally in every case'.

Barwick goes on to note that William Thomson, a Melbourne surgeon, thought the cause of the disease might be contagion and

deplored the Board's failure to provide isolated quarters for the sick, suggesting that their infectious spittle impregnated the cottages...Another physician corroborated Thomson's opinion that the Aborigines were specially susceptible to an extraordinary rapid and fatal 'tubercular consumption'.

In nineteenth-century Europe, the childhood infectious diseases were major causes of death for children. For example, between 1841 and 1910 whooping cough killed up to 13 000 annually in England and Wales, with higher death rates in some other parts of Europe. Between 1838 and 1911 measles caused up to 19 133 deaths a year in Great Britain, decimating each generation of children and leaving many with permanent eye and ear defects (Smith 1979, pp. 104–11, 142–8). (The harsh therapeutic measures advocated by the medical profession may have contributed considerably to the death rate, which fell with the better nursing practices of the twentieth century.) When these diseases were first brought to Australia, they had disastrous consequences for the Aboriginal population.

All epidemics, whether of smallpox, influenza or childhood diseases, proved especially disastrous for Aborigines because all members of a community were equally susceptible. All tended to fall ill at the same time—grandparents, parents, and children. This meant that no immediate family member was available to nurse the sick, to bring food, or even water, which was so essential for survival of those with high fevers. Barwick (1971, p. 308) gives an example of the high death rate from measles in Victoria in 1875 'when the last major epidemic of measles occurred, 31 of approximately 150 Coranderrk residents died of measles or subsequent pleuro-pneumonia'. There is evidence, too, about what happened as the colonial frontier moved into the desert areas in this century. Measles swept through the Western Desert in 1948 and again in 1957, killing adults as well as children (Hilliard 1968, pp. 131–41).

The last 40 years have seen the development of vaccines against the most serious of the childhood diseases, and immunisation is available to Aboriginal children as it is to all other Australian children. However, in this century, influenza has wiped out whole families and groups of Aborigines. Bobbie Hardy writes of 'the influenza epidemic that raged in the wake of the returning troops' in 1919. 'Aborigines were tragically susceptible, and some say that its effect on the Barkindji was practically exterminating' (Hardy 1976, p. 194). Clancy McKenna told Kingsley Palmer that in the 1930s influenza struck Aborigines gathered for a ceremony in the north-west of Western Australia:

The Ngala people were very few in number and that summer their strength was reduced even further. Men, women and children lay in the camp with the terrible cold sickness—the coughs and cries of the sick and bereaved hung on the still air with a frightening immediacy. There were no doctors, no help, no medicine. The station people stayed away from the camp for fear of catching the disease. Peter and Clancy did all they could, but many died. They dug a big hole and handed the bodies down, eight or nine in all and buried them in the same grave...there are no Ngala people left today.

Palmer and McKenna 1978, p. 69

In 1970 at Yalata two brothers, then middle-aged, said that as little boys they were the sole survivors of an influenza epidemic that killed their parents and all other members of their family group then living near Yalata (I. White, field notes).

The loss of ancestral land

The British who colonised Australia did not officially acknowledge the rights of the indigenous people to the land they occupied, yet Governor Phillip was instructed to 'live in amity and kindness' with the Aborigines and to punish any person who 'shall wantonly destroy them or give them any unnecessary interruption in the exercise of their several occupations...' (*Historical Records of New South Wales,* vol. 1, part 2, 1787, p. 52).

The early colonists believed that the Aborigines were nomads who roamed at random. This was a false picture, for although they might have moved camp often, each group hunted and gathered within a set area, usually returning to a particular place at the same season each year. Moreover, as Stanner (1979, p. 230) has pointed out:

No English words are good enough to give a sense of the links between an Aboriginal group and its homeland. Our 'home', warm and suggestive though it be, does not match the Aboriginal word that may mean 'camp', 'hearth', 'country', 'everlasting home', 'totem place', 'life source', 'spirit centre' and much else all in one. Our word 'land' is too sparse and meagre. We can now scarcely use it except with economic overtones unless we happen to be poets. The Aboriginal would speak of 'earth' and use the word in a richly symbolic way to mean his 'shoulder' or his 'side'. I have seen an Aboriginal embrace the earth he walked on. To put our words 'home' and 'land' together in 'homeland' is a little better but not much. A different tradition leaves us tongueless and earless toward this other world of meaning and significance.

Once it was found that sheep and cattle flourished in Australia, conflict between the two peoples was exacerbated and hard to contain. Colonists regarded the land as an economic asset to be developed for economic gain, but to Aborigines it was sacred, a part of themselves. As Aborigines did not till the soil or live in settled villages, the intruders felt justified in moving them from one area to another. Yet most Aborigines attempted to remain in their own country and many engaged in guerrilla warfare. The length and ferocity of the resistance depended on the density of the Aboriginal population, the number of white settlers, and the type of terrain. Certain areas became notorious for prolonged guerrilla activities led by great warriors such as Yagan and Midgigoroo of Western Australia or Durmugam of the Northern Territory (Durack 1964; Stanner 1960, pp.63–100).

Such extraordinary terrorism

Aboriginal fear both stimulated European assertiveness and entrenched black submission. The frontier was a finishing school for white arrogance and brutality. For their part the Aborigines had 'learnt in their terror to submit to anything the conquering race' chose to do. In 1891 a South Australian police constable provided the Government Resident of the Northern Territory with a detailed inventory of brutalities suffered by outback Aborigines. 'No matter what it is these poor creatures have to submit to,' he explained, 'it is simply through fear...it is the one word fear all through.' At the turn of the century Archibald Meston conducted a survey of the Aborigines in south-west Queensland, an area first settled 50 years before...Never before, he recalled, 'had I seen aboriginal [sic] men living under such extraordinary terrorism, many of them fine athletic fellows who could in case of a row have settled with their terrorisers in a very summary fashion. But many of them had long been treated as the dogs are treated and were scared into a belief that their employers wielded the power of life and death'.

Large-scale killing of Aborigines came to an end when they moved onto pastoral stations and into fringe camps. Yet life remained hazardous. There was little protection from the law, from public opinion, established custom or even from settler self-interest. An unknown number of Aborigines died from injuries received while being 'disciplined' with whip and fist and boot. Such cases were occasionally reported in the papers and infrequently taken before the courts. Every now and then the violence of the frontier washed back into the pioneer towns. In Queensland the Native Police occasionally arrested 'town blacks', marched them a mile or two down the road and shot them...In April 1861 Sub-Lieutenant Bligh led his troopers into Maryborough to disperse the town blacks. A couple were shot in the street, others were picked off while swimming in the river. By then a crowd had gathered to witness the spectacle...Townspeople undertook their own vigilante action to capture presumed offenders or to drive the local blacks out of town. In 1863 a Rockhampton Aborigine escaped from the police and plunged into the nearby Fitzroy river. He was 'actively pursued by the European mob in boats, who struck his head with their oars every time it appeared above the water'...But despite sporadic violence, the towns were safer for blacks than the bush. Even small settlements had residents opposed to the use of indiscriminate violence and who afforded protection to local Aborigines. In the large towns newspapers and police forces restrained the more brutal members of the community. In the bush many squatters developed a tradition of stern paternalism which stopped short of murder. Yet in the absence of restraint it is likely that Aborigines were often killed, their fate passing unnoticed outside the immediate district. One such incident was reported in passing in Curr's book *The Australian race* published in 1886–87. One of Curr's informants, while describing the funeral customs of clans living along the Belyando River, instanced the case 'of a girl of 15 years of age, who with several others were *dispersed* for unwittingly allowing the grass to take fire on the bank of a river on which they were fishing. This was on the territory of the tribe. She was brought here, and died the day after she received the shot.'

Keeping them in their place

Government policy from the 1790s, and conditions on the Australian frontier, had conspired to arm the settlers and encouraged them to engage in innumerable petty, private wars with the Aborigines. When the guns were put aside settlers continued to act on their own initiative, turning instead to whips and fists and boots. Defeat and dispossession of the blacks was not enough; white supremacy had to be constantly asserted district by district, even person by person...'Every man seems to consider himself,' a writer in the *Queenslander* observed in 1884, 'as quite justified in carrying out the utmost vigour of the law towards an Aboriginal, often for some very trivial and insignificant crime.' A correspondent in the *Moreton Bay Courier* twenty years earlier argued that it was time that the police were authorised to do 'what every private individual takes the liberty of doing when the occasion demands—administer a sound thrashing for offences against the decency or peace of the neighbourhood'...

Aborigines were expected—and usually compelled—to conform to a role created for them in advance of their entry into European society. The name changed over time and from place to place—nigger, coon, boong, abo, Jacky—but the role remained much the same. It was compounded of racial ideas shipped in from Europe, the experience of frontier conflict, the economic interests and psychological needs of the settlers. It was a demanding, constricting role to play. And it had to be played all the time, at least whenever Europeans were watching or listening. There was no room for initiative or independence or self-assertion. Speaking out of turn, looking a white man straight in the eye, assuming a facial expression considered inappropriate for a 'nigger'—each one could merit a fist in the face, a boot in the balls or a stockwhip around the shoulders. Above all else Europeans where united in their determination to keep the blacks in their place...'Keep them under', 'keep them down', 'keep them in their place'. These and similar expressions ran like a litany through the history of colonial Australia and can still be heard in some parts of the country. People who have grown up in metropolitan Australia since the Second World War often fail to appreciate how recently such ideas held sway unchallenged. The novelist Jean Devanny toured the Gulf country in the late 1940s. One of her hostesses told her seriously, 'You got to keep them down...otherwise they become as cheeky as they are stupid'. She found that the belief that blacks were ruined if whites actually talked to them was 'subscribed to by almost the entire white population of the Gulf'. She was told, 'Apart from giving them orders we don't acknowledge their existence. If you talk to them they will walk over you in no time. Cheeky b—s'...

When the settlers wanted the land they used guns; when they needed cheap labour they put them down and picked up their whips, brandishing them just as freely and with as little interference from the law...Outback settlers 'did not look upon the flogging of a black girl or the ill treatment of a black boy as anything wrong', a West Australian politician explained in 1905. 'These things to them are only discipline, only means of improving the race.'...A West Australian squatter reminded a meeting of colleagues in 1893 that 'a native had a hide, and not an ordinary skin like a human being'...A New South Wales clergyman, with a long history of involvement with the Aborigines, recalled in 1889 that there used to be common maxim among bushmen: ' "It is no use to hit a blackfellow with your fist, he won't feel it", and the corollary was that a heavy boot or a stout stick, or an iron bolt or a stock whip, were legitimate and suitable instruments for hortatory or punitive purposes.'

Extracted from Reynolds 1987, pp. 66–71.

Reserves and missions

Despite heroic attempts, the Aborigines were unable to check the advancing frontier, a frontier that has been described as 'a finishing school for white arrogance and brutality' (see Reynolds, 'Such extraordinary terrorism', in this chapter). Alarmed by reports of massacres and the gross maltreatment of Aborigines, the British government brought pressure to bear on colonial administrators to protect the indigenous people. The answer of the colonial administrators was to set aside reserves, mostly quite small. These reserves were not given to Aborigines but administered by government departments or religious missions and staffed by resident full-time white officials. The first victims were the hapless Tasmanians for whom the policy proved near fatal. On the mainland, many Aboriginal settlements were founded and free movement of Aborigines became more and more restricted. In Victoria, to quote Long (1970, p. 14):

The policy of dealing with the problem of the Aborigines by settling them in one spot and improving 'their moral and social conditions' was followed from the start of officially recognised settlement in the Port Phillip area.

Similar policies were introduced in the other Australian colonies. These reserves became 'total institutions' (Goffman 1961), which separated Aborigines from contact with the outside world. Long (1970, p. 4) estimated that as late as 1961 'nearly one-third of all Australians recorded as being of Aboriginal descent lived in settlements'.

Part of Eliza Kennedy's story, recorded by the linguist Tamsin Donaldson (Kennedy and Donaldson 1982, pp. 16–18), is about the consequences of one of the compulsory uprootings in New South Wales. Donaldson states that in September 1933 the Aborigines Protection Board moved all the Ngiyampaa people (but not all their possessions) from Corowa to Menindee. They were taken by truck and then by train out of their own country and sent

into the country of the Paakantji [or Barkindji]...to live in a white-run institution with Paakantji people whose own recent experiences had scarcely been more reassuring. The Ngiyampaa people were not consulted, nor even given a chance to contact absent relatives: 'I don't know what their ideas was, to get them onto a permanent water I suppose, mainly'. The period which followed was one of fear, disease and death: 'They averaged one a month, the deaths. Nine of our people died in the first nine months they were there... [The huts] all had cement floors which wasn't right because most of them lied on the floor, and I think that's why a lot of them died. Cold and pneumonias, I suppose, because the ground would warm up quicker than the concrete...When people fell sick they were taken off to hospital in Broken Hill, which only increased their relatives' fears. My poor old uncle reckoned, 'They must be doping them in Broken Hill, they don't seem to come back from there'.
Kennedy and Donaldson 1982, pp. 16–18

Another similar forced removal was suffered by the family of Lorna Dixon. She recalls that all the Aborigines living at Tibooburra, including Lorna's large extended family, were forcibly removed to the government settlement at Brewarrina. They had had a house of their own at Tibooburra, but on arrival at Brewarrina:

All the women were told to sleep on the schoolhouse floor and the men on the verandah...Granny died very soon after we got there, and a bit later our step-great-grandfather died, as well as lots of other old people...We were given some rations, but they never lasted the full week.

Mathews 1985, pp. 98–101

Soon after the move, Lorna's sister had a baby in Brewarrina Hospital. 'Her baby girl had arrived safely, but my sister died....She was young and healthy, and we just couldn't believe it...We were not allowed to get in touch with the doctor or hospital and never knew what caused her death.' (Mathews 1985, p. 100)

Throughout the nineteenth century, and for most of the first half of the twentieth, 'looking after' Aborigines was regarded as a suitable occupation for people who had some pretensions to respectability and honesty, but who were unsuited for any other employment. To gain a responsible position on a mission station, a further requirement was adherence to a particular branch of Christianity; missionary zeal was often more important than sympathy for Aborigines. Whether the post was on a government or mission settlement, no training, aptitude or experience was required, with the consequence that there was wide variation in the treatment of Aboriginal people who lived in such settlements. Whether they were kind and loving paternalists, or rigid, cruel disciplinarians, none of the whites employed in settlements believed that Aborigines deserved equal treatment, none consulted their charges about their present or their future, none regarded Aboriginal men and women as fully adult and therefore capable of caring for their children in a proper manner, none saw anything inhuman in removing children from their parents, or in uprooting families to suit the convenience of Europeans (see Gray et al., chapter 3 in this volume).

With the change to settlement life, major alterations in food habits were introduced. One reason for herding Aborigines onto settlements and reserves was to prevent hunting and gathering on land that had been taken over for stock-raising and agriculture. This meant the abandonment of the traditional healthy mixed diet and the substitution of rations, which needed to be cheap, portable and non-perishable. The rations consisted mainly of white flour, sugar, tea, rice, tinned meat and salt beef (Taylor 1977, p. 154). In the 1950s when stores were opened on the settlements and Aborigines began to use money, they found the ration-type foods cheap and available. Some settlement dwellers were able to supplement their diet by hunting or fishing, but there was a serious shortage of fruit and vegetables. Even when available, fruit and vegetables were expensive. Moreover, Aborigines were also spending money on alcohol and tobacco, which had become available by that time.

In central, north-western and northern Australia, European penetration began in the late nineteenth century, and was both slow and sparse. At first Aborigines resisted and were massacred (see Williams and Reid, 'Armed conflict in north-eastern Arnhem Land' in this chapter), but they were finally forced to adapt to the colonists' presence. Between 1908 and 1954, large reserves were set aside comprising land that was of little use for grazing or agriculture. The title to these lands was never returned to their original owners but remained in the possession of the Crown. In the mining boom of the 1960s and 1970s, until new legislation was passed, portions of reserves were excised to establish mining towns and mining leases were granted without reference to traditional Aboriginal ownership of the land.

On many reserves, mission and government settlements were set up to 'look after' Aborigines, who were attracted to them because they supplied food and water, to which otherwise Aborigines no longer had access, and those other goods, such as tobacco, that Aborigines soon learned to want. In 1928 the Aborigines' Friends Association and other similar organisations pressed for further areas of central Australia to be added to the reserves, but historian Peter Biskup (1973, p. 90) writes that, in his opinion, those organisations 'envisaged the reserves as preserves for the missionaries rather than real reserves for aborigines [sic]'. This view is shared by anthropologist Robert Tonkinson (1974, p. 120). Moreover, from the nineteenth century until recent times, little or no instruction in Aboriginal culture and Australian colonial history was required for those who staffed mission or government settlements in remote areas. In addition, health care was either neglected or misunderstood.

Smaller reserves were declared on the outskirts of remote new towns, where local Aborigines who had been turned off their own land, with uncertain employment and little money, lived in wretched poverty in makeshift housing. Few services were provided for them: fresh water and sanitation were minimal or entirely lacking, their children were not admitted to the local school, and there was no provision for their health needs.

Aborigines living on reserves were allotted rations by the responsible government. These were not generous but set the standard for Aborigines employed on the large cattle and sheep stations outside the reserves. During the Depression, state governments, who were responsible for administering the 'dole', drew a distinction between the rations necessary to sustain whites and those necessary for Aborigines,

Figure 1.2 *Clothes and blankets are distributed at Nymboida Mission, New South Wales, c. 1920, one of many missions set up to 'look after' Aborigines. (Courtesy Howard Creamer)*

although in both cases the scale of rations varied with the size of the family. In 1931, Sir James Mitchell, then premier of Western Australia, was able to assure Western Australians that their unemployed were the best off in Australia. The standard sustenance allowance was 7 shillings a week for a single man, 14 shillings for a married couple and 7 shillings for each child under 14 years of age up to a maximum of five children. Two-thirds of this dole was in the form of cash—a greater proportion than in any other Australian state—and the rest came in the form of orders for food, meals or accommodation for single men (Bolton 1972, p. 98). Money, the premier pointed out, went further in Western Australia. Milk could be bought at 2 pence a pint (500 mL approx.) compared with 4 pence elsewhere, while bread cost 3½ pence a loaf compared with 5 pence in other states. Furthermore, the unemployed received free firewood and hospital treatment (Bolton 1972, p. 170). These figures were fixed in a postwar boom in 1919 when no-one anticipated a long period of unemployment. At the worst point of the depression in 1932, Western Australia had 7000 white men on sustenance, but no attempt was ever made to reduce these rates (Bolton 1972, pp. 186, 99). Aborigines were not so fortunate; their rations were considerably reduced (see table 1.1). Legally, before the Depression, some employed Aborigines earning award rates were entitled to the 'white dole', but administrators usually forgot this (Biskup 1973, p. 163).

It is interesting to compare the 'black dole' of 1930 with the ration allotted to black indigents in Western Australia in 1865 (table 1.1). These figures suggest that in 1930 it was assumed that a Western Australian Aboriginal man needed 8 pounds (3.6 kilograms) less flour and could do completely without meat except in approved cases, but that he needed 2½ more ounces (approximately 70 grams) of tea (Biskup 1973, pp. 41, 163).

Table 1.1 Comparison of the 1865 black rations with the 1930 black 'dole' in 1930, Western Australia

	1865 dole	1930 dole
Flour	16 lb	8 lb
Meat	5¼ lb	
Sugar	1½ lb	1½ lb
Tea	1½ oz	4 oz
Tobacco	1 stick	1 stick

1 oz (ounce) = 28 grams approximately
1 lb (pound) = 454 grams approximately
Source: Biskup 1973, pp. 41, 163

Health on the reserves

Within the central and northern reserves, the mission and government settlements proved disastrous for the health of the Aboriginal inhabitants. Living habits suitable for a handful of people who moved camp regularly were totally unsuitable for several hundred settled permanently in one area. Authorities were slow to provide facilities such as piped water and sanitation. Houses built at some settlements were rudimentary and not acceptable to the Aboriginal occupants. Moreover, it was difficult to provide shelter and water for a camp that was moved whenever one of its people died. At some of the settlements, most of the Aboriginal inhabitants lived within sight of the administrative headquarters, and moved the camp perhaps half a kilometre after a death. At others, for example at Yalata in South Australia, the main camp was up to 30 kilometres from the headquarters and might move 40 kilometres after a death. In Arnhem Land, settlement houses were accepted more readily and re-occupied after a short period of abandonment following a death (I. White field notes).

Most of the settlements had poor facilities for dealing with the health problems that arose. In addition, few of the staff were properly trained to deal with people of a culture very different from their own. Attempts to solve the problems were misguided to say the least. For example, in 1957 in the Northern Territory the Commonwealth government replaced rations with the provision of meals, and wages were paid partly in the form of meal tickets for all family members (see Harrison, 'Communal feeding: a Northern Territory example of assimilation', in chapter 4 of this volume). Communal feeding had a number of very negative effects. Aborigines who had spent much of their time gathering food now found that most of the responsibility for feeding themselves had been taken away from them. Settlement life offered them little to do. Communal feeding also disrupted family life, because men, women and children were seated separately, in order to avoid the danger of contact with those in proscribed relationships. Although authorities claimed that the system educated Aborigines to prepare well-balanced meals from foodstuffs available on the settlements, only those few employed on the kitchen staff had any chance to learn. Colin Tatz has suggested that 'the only educational value of the system was that it seemed to familiarise the Aborigines with eating in cafeteria conditions and with the taste of mass produced, European style meals' (Cited in Middleton and Francis 1976, pp. 86–7).

The worst effect of communal dining was cross-infection. Much of this had been attributed to overcrowding in humpies, but a survey of infant mortality rates in the southern region of the Northern Territory between 1964 and 1971 showed that overcrowding represented a minimal source of infection compared with the communal dining room (Wagner 1981). This survey showed that communal dining rooms were a health hazard. It was there that children, whose ages ranged from 8 weeks to 3½ years, were exposed to infection when solid foods were introduced to them. Hygiene arrangements in the dining rooms and kitchens were very unsatisfactory. Wagner (1981, pp. 9–10) quotes from a health inspector's report on the communal dining room facilities at Yuendumu in 1966:

a.   *The hot water system had been defective for six days. This was caused by a shortage of kerosene, which is used in this hot water system.*

b.   *Plates and other utensils remained dirty and greasy after being washed.*

c.   *Shelves in the kitchen were littered with food scraps and dirty utensils.*

d.   *Window ledges in the dining room contained food scraps.*

e. *The area surrounding the kitchen was littered with tins, bones and other refuse.*

f. *All grease traps were dirty and appeared to have not been closed for several days.*

g. *Garbage drums were not being washed after being emptied.*

h. *The area under the garbage stand was dirty and covered with food particles. The area was very damp and could provide an attractive breeding area for flies.*

i. *Food for the children's meals was placed on the table approximately twenty minutes before commencement of the meal.*

j. *The food supplied for infant feeding was supplied on the plates fifteen minutes before the meal. Flies swarmed over the food.*

In 1969, communal feeding was discontinued on most settlements. Instead, Aborigines were given their full wages in cash (however, not generally award wages), so that they could purchase their own provisions. No spectacular improvement in diet resulted, because, with little money and little choice of foodstuffs, they had no option but to make do with a poor diet consisting mainly of white flour, sugar, tea and meat.

Hospital facilities on many Aboriginal settlements and missions were poor. In the period 1964–1971, hospitals did little to reduce the high death rate of Aboriginal infants, and may even have contributed to it. Wagner (1981, p. 9) found that there were chronic staff shortages, and that while many staff were well-qualified and conscientious others had little or no medical training. A report made of a visit to Yuendumu in 1966 revealed, for example, that milk for infants was prepared in the hospital's dressing room where open buckets containing soiled disposable napkins and used dressings from purulent wounds were also kept (Wagner 1981, p. 9).

In an address to a 1972 conference on Aboriginal health, anthropologist Stanner (1974, pp. 6–7) (one of the three members of the Council for Aboriginal Affairs established by the Commonwealth Government in 1967) made the following remarks about outback settlements:

Consider a situation which now gives us a lot of anxiety...In recent years we have set up several settlements in the dry-arid zone of central Australia. We have encouraged the growth of quite large concentrations of Aborigines in them...But the people themselves, sometimes of several dialects and contrastive cultures, had no traditional experience of living cheek-by-jowl with large numbers of their own kind—indeed, of any kind, for long periods, let alone permanently...Under their own ecological wisdom, which we as yet barely understand, they had found it advisable to live in quite small numbers because of the gossamer web of life on which flora, fauna, and humankind could associate over time in these life-spaces...The settlements themselves have been well described as 'total institutions'. Every Aborigine in them lives in a virtually complete dependency on authority for practically everything. I am at a loss to grasp on what model of human or social reality we built such institutions. I have often wondered why we supposed that they would work out humanely and formatively. They would not do so for us...I have sometimes felt that I was looking at something between a plantation and a corrective institution—a plantation without a marketable crop...and a house of correction in which inconvenient old habits could be, in time, eliminated and convenient new habits—convenient, mainly, to us—could be engendered. I am not sure who is teaching whom, and what, in this lesson.

Aborigines on cattle stations

On each of the large cattle stations of the north, a short distance from the homestead was the 'blacks' camp', where lived the remnants of the traditional owners of the land on which they were now poor hangers-on. The adult able-bodied were employed (but not necessarily paid), the men and some of the women as labourers and stockriders, while other women worked as domestic servants in the homestead and were often expected to provide sexual services as well.

Most pastoralists showed little concern for the health of their Aboriginal workers. In the 1930s, Charles Duguid (1963, p. 24), an Adelaide medical practitioner, wrote after a journey in central and northern Australia:

My visits to the cattle station made me depressed and ashamed beyond measure. As I approached one homestead on a cold, cheerless, rainy day, old men, women, and children came running down a hillside. They were all painfully thin and hungry, their clothes were mere rags. Later, over a cup of tea in the homestead, I asked why the Aborigines we had seen did not get more food. 'They get Government rations', was the reply. At that time official instructions were as follows: the rations or weekly allowance to each person receiving relief must not exceed: flour, 5 lb [2.3 kilograms], sugar 1 lb [454 grams], tea ¼ lb [113 grams].

Duguid had assumed certain Christian missions in the inland would be involved in ministering to Aborigines, but he soon found that he was mistaken. Instead, representatives of the missions told him that if they cared for Aborigines 'their work on behalf of white people on cattle stations would soon come to an end' (Duguid, p. 24).

In 1945, anthropologists Catherine and Ronald Berndt found no improvement and reported that Aborigines working for Vesteys were poorly fed. (Vesteys was the popular name for the Australian Investment Agency, the leaseholder of many properties in the Northern Territory. Lord Vestey was the founder and head of this agency.) The Berndts recorded that at Wave Hill 'each working man and woman was given three times daily a slice of dry bread, one piece of usually cooked meat (sometimes in the form of a bone), and a dipper of tea' (Berndt and Berndt 1987, p. 72). Officially each station set aside a day each week on which rations were distributed to the aged and infirm and to the dependants of employees. The Berndts discovered, however, that the weekly ration consisted of:

two to three pounds [900–1460 grams] of flour, sometimes with rising (to those requesting it); one half to one pound [226–454 grams] of sugar (often less), to which was added a small handful of tea (under one ounce [28 grams]); and one stick of tobacco (to those requesting it). At the time of our visit a slightly larger amount of flour was sometimes issued because it contained weevils. A number of Aborigines refused to use it, complaining that it caused pain and discomfort after eating.

Berndt and Berndt 1987, pp. 72–3

From time to time a beast was killed, but Aboriginal dependants 'received only bones and offal' (Berndt and Berndt 1987, pp. 72–3).

The plight of pregnant Aboriginal women particularly concerned the Berndts (1987, pp. 76–7). They found that neither pregnant women nor nursing mothers received any extra food to supplement their diet of bread and cooked beef. They reported that during their visit to Wave Hill, three births took place. In the first case, the mother was a young woman usually employed in the homestead, who had four surviving children. Her last-born child had died in infancy. The new arrival was stillborn, and the mother was very ill, but nothing was known of this at the homestead until the Berndts supplied the information. The second birth was normal, but in the third case both the mother and child (first born) died within a few hours of each other. Shortly after the Berndts left Wave Hill, another birth took place. The mother was a young woman who was usually employed at the homestead. Her infant also died, and although the doctor was summoned from Katherine, she died too (Berndt and Berndt 1987, pp. 76–7). Thus, in a two-month period only one out of four births was normal. The Berndts drew Vesteys' attention to this fact and suggested that lack of sufficiently nourishing diet had an important bearing on this question. They also pointed out that discontent, disillusionment and distrust of the future were all factors helping to keep the birth rate low. At Limbunya, for instance, at the time of the Berndts' visit, there were only three young children too young to be employed, comprising only approximately 6 per cent of the total population. Both men and women asserted that they could see no sense in rearing children to grow up under the conditions that Aboriginal workers were then experiencing. They asked 'Why should we breed more people for kadia [or kardiya—Europeans], to use the way they use us?' (Berndt and Berndt 1987, p. 91).

The Berndts (1987, p. 255) assumed that the pastoral company would see that it was in its own interest to maintain its Aboriginal employees and their dependants in reasonable contentment and good health. They knew that Vesteys was in a position to make the necessary financial arrangements for improving its native labour position. They took it for granted that the company would do this, not as a matter of charity but of personal interest and expediency. They reasoned that if such a policy were carried over the extensive areas controlled by the company, other stations would be obliged, in self-protection, to adopt similar measures. The company, however, was not interested. It wanted the Berndts to use their anthropological skills to recruit 'bush' and 'outside' natives to labour on its properties (Berndt and Berndt 1987, p. 221–255).

Another study of the living conditions of Aborigines on the cattle stations of the Northern Territory was carried out by Frank Stevens in 1965, 1966 and 1968. On the basis of his account published in 1974, it appears that little change in conditions had occurred since the reports of Duguid and the Berndts. For example:

The contrast between peacocks in full plume and the crude provision made for the accommodation of the native work force seemed generally typical of the small importance attached to the physical circumstances of the employees primarily responsible for the industry. Indeed, the social and economic gap existing between

*management and labour on properties in the Northern Territory must have very few
parallels throughout the world. For while the masters at some stations sat down to dine
in virtual baronial splendour, being waited on by up to as many as six highly trained
domestics, occasionally decked out in monogrammed aprons and caps, the husbands
and children of the maids sat in the dust picking at the offal from their disgusting
pottage and eventually crawling into 'dog-kennel-like' structures to sleep.*

Stevens 1974, p. 108

Stevens also described in negative terms the health of the Aborigines:

*Our inquiries concerning native health brought many references to sore throats,
chest complaints, pussy ears, dysentery, malnutrition, eye complaints, scabies,
ringworm and diarrhoea. From a general survey the Aboriginal work force did not
look well.*

Stevens 1974, p. 101

He found that adequate medical care was lacking.

It is not surprising that in 1946 hundreds of Aboriginal employees and their
families walked off pastoral stations in the Pilbara district of Western Australia, nor
is it surprising that nearly 20 years later the occupants of the 'blacks' camp' deserted
Wave Hill Station in the Northern Territory and moved to Wattie Creek, to which
they demanded rights of ownership.

Demands for reform: the 1930s

With improved communications in the 1930s, there was better contact with the outback and more interest in it among non-Aboriginal city dwellers, who learned from
the press about the injustices suffered by Aborigines both in the remote areas and
nearer to the cities. Non-Aborigines began to clamour for reform. Equally important
were the organised protests by Aborigines in the large cities and the rural areas of
the south-east and south-west of the continent. In 1926 in Western Australia, a union
of Aborigines led by William Harris demanded equal protection for all Aborigines
under the law and a lessening of restrictions for the more assimilated (Biskup 1973,
pp. 85, 158–60). In the 1930s, William Cooper in Victoria and William Ferguson in
New South Wales formed Aborigines' associations, which exposed the ill-treatment
Aborigines were suffering, and demanded justice and reform (Miller 1985, pp. 150–
7; Horner 1974; Markus 1988).

In 1937, a meeting of all state and federal ministers responsible for Aborigines
was held in Canberra. With the exception of the ministers from Tasmania and Victoria (who claimed they had no problem), the meeting agreed that white Australia's
Aboriginal 'problem' was best divided into two: that of the 'full bloods' and that of
the 'half-castes'. It was felt that the first 'problem' was partly soluble: as the 'uncivilised full bloods' were dying out, all that was needed was to establish a few in-
violable reserves. As for the 'semi-civilised full bloods', their fate was more complicated. It was decided that the best thing to do with them would be to keep them
'under benevolent supervision' on 'small local reserves selected for tribal suitability'.
It was felt that they would be better off if they lived 'as nearly as possible a normal

Figure 1.3 *The appalling conditions of Aborigines living in camps on cattle stations contrasted starkly with the 'baronial' lifestyle of the station owners, whose Aboriginal domestic staff were often clothed in elaborate uniforms. 'Biddy', pictured in Walgett, New South Wales, in 1887, was nursemaid to John Kenneth Gordon. (Bicentennial Collection, Mitchell Library, State Library of New South Wales, Sydney)*

tribal life' and, as a measure of white society's benevolence, it was agreed that these Aborigines would be allowed to retain 'unobjectionable' tribal ceremonies. Delegates were troubled about the children of detribalised natives who lived near centres of white population. Eventually it was agreed that these youngsters should be given a white education and employed in occupations that would not bring them into economic and social conflict with the white community.

Having dealt with those of full descent, the conference set out to solve the mixed descent 'problem'. Since the days of the gold rushes, white Australians had treated those of part-European, part-Aboriginal descent as being black rather than white. This, the conference decided, was a mistake, for it was obvious that their destiny lay 'in their ultimate absorption by the people of the Commonwealth' (Reynolds 1972, pp. 172–3).

While all state Aboriginal administrators were anxious to 'breed out' the 'part-Aborigines', some doubted whether absorption into the white population was possible. A representative of the University of Adelaide suggested that the university

AUSTRALIAN ABORIGINES CONFERENCE

Sesqui-Centenary

DAY OF MOURNING & PROTEST

to be held in

THE AUSTRALIAN HALL, SYDNEY
(No. 148 Elizabeth Street)

on

WEDNESDAY, 26th JANUARY, 1938

(Australia Day)

from

10 a.m. to 5 p.m.

THE FOLLOWING RESOLUTION WILL BE MOVED:

"WE, representing THE ABORIGINES OF AUSTRALIA, assembled in Conference at the Australian Hall, Sydney, on the 26th day of January, 1938, this being the 150th Anniversary of the whitemen's seizure of our country, HEREBY MAKE PROTEST against the callous treatment of our people by the whitemen during the past 150 years, AND WE APPEAL to the Australian Nation of today to make new laws for the education and care of Aborigines, and we ask for a new policy which will raise our people to FULL CITIZEN STATUS and EQUALITY WITHIN THE COMMUNITY."

Aborigines and Persons of Aboriginal Blood only are invited to attend. Please come if you can!

Signed for and on behalf of

THE ABORIGINES PROGRESSIVE ASSOCIATION

J. T. Patten, President.
W. Ferguson, Organising Secretary

Address: c/o Box 1924 KK
General Post Office, Sydney

Figure 1.4 *In the 1930s, Aboriginal associations were formed to demand justice and reform. In this notice published by the Aborigines Progressive Association, Aborigines were called to attend a protest on Australia Day 1938. (From Horner 1974, p. 199)*

Figure 1.5 *Aboriginal girls at the Cootamundra Girls Training School, New South Wales, in the 1940s. (Archives Authority of New South Wales)*

should study the problem. The research was undertaken by a Harvard–Adelaide Universities Anthropological Expedition in 1938–9 and its results were published by one of the research workers, Norman Tindale, ethnologist for the South Australian Museum. The results of the survey must have been pleasing to those who favoured elimination of the Aboriginal 'problem' by absorption into the white community, for Tindale (1941, p. 67) told them that:

Complete mergence of the half-castes in the general community is possible without detriment to the white race. Their Aboriginal blood is remotely the same as that of the majority of the white inhabitants of Australia, for the Australian Aboriginal [sic] is recognised as being a forerunner of the Caucasian race. In addition, the half-castes are increasingly of our own blood, in places the majority of them already are more than half white. Two successive accessions of white blood will lead to the mergence of the Aboriginal [sic] in the white community. There are no biological reasons for the rejection of people with a dilute strain of Australian Aboriginal blood. A low percentage of Australian Aboriginal blood will not introduce any aberrant characteristics and there will be no fear of reversions to the dark Aboriginal type.

Those who feared the so-called 'throw-back' must have felt relieved to learn from Tindale that their fears were groundless.

Implementation of the assimilation policy included the practice of state welfare officers taking light-skinned children from their dark tribal mothers. This happened to Charles Perkins, who later became Secretary of the Department of Aboriginal Affairs. He writes:

The troopers would ride up and say, 'All right, get all the half-caste kids!' Like rounding up the lambs from the rest of the sheep, they would separate them, put them in a truck and off they would go. These kids were brought up in institutions across the Territory. That is why a lot of us have hangups. How else could it be? You miss the love of a mother and all the other things that go with it, the family circle. As a young kid, four or five years old, dumped with a lot of strangers, you can be emotionally scarred for life. We were not, as children, allowed to meet any of the tribal people. I only met my grandmother once in my life, and that was through the fence of the reserve. I was then told I could not talk to her. That was the only time I ever saw her, for a few minutes. Then she died, and that was the end of my hope of knowing her. It was a really peculiar set-up; all through the Northern Territory. The programme was handled by people who really did not have any idea of what they were doing. They were all motivated by the wrong ideas as far as I was concerned. I do not think they had much humanity really.

Perkins 1975, pp. 14–15

Towards change and improvement: the 1940s and after

In northern and central Australia, the Second World War began to change the material conditions of the Aboriginal population. Aborigines were employed by the army in various capacities, paid the same wages and given the same conditions as whites. 'For the first time since colonisation began the Aborigines received decent food and the same medical care as whites...' (Middleton 1977, p. 83). In 1941, Aboriginal women who were not nomadic or dependent on the Commonwealth or state became entitled to receive child endowment payments, and in 1942 amending legislation provided that children in institutions maintained by state governments could also receive the same payments. Rowley (1971, p. 38) has suggested that 'these measures, and especially perhaps the 1942 amendment, appear to have marked a turning point in Aboriginal welfare, especially for Aboriginal families'.

When Paul Hasluck became Minister for Territories in 1951, he promised that there would be a new deal for Aborigines, but he soon discovered that it was one thing to attempt to change a policy and quite another to change the practice (Franklin 1976, pp. 141–56). In the area of health, the government began compiling information about the growth and development of Aboriginal infants in the Northern Territory in 1958. Before that date, Ellen Kettle, a nursing sister, had noted that her records revealed that one out of every five Aboriginal babies born between 1954 and 1957 did not live to adulthood (Kettle 1967, p. 217).

Improvements in public health measures for Aborigines met with considerable opposition from white Australians. For example, the 1957 Annual Report of the Alice Springs Hospital recorded that the ward used for Aboriginal patients was so dilapidated and overcrowded that there could be no adequate isolation of infectious cases. The report stated that during the forthcoming year a new ward would be built for Aboriginal patients. In the following year the ward was built, 'but agitation by local citizens that it was "unfair" for Aborigines to get new facilities while they suffered inadequate ones, resulted in the new ward being allocated to white patients' (Tatz 1972, p. 7).

A similar situation existed in New South Wales. On at least two occasions in the 1960s a New South Wales minister for health found it necessary to threaten that hospitals practising racial discrimination would lose the government subsidy. At Moree 'the Chairman of the Moree hospital board replied [to the minister's threat] that any order by the government would be ignored, that any attempt to alter the current situation would "lead to trouble" '. In 1965, the minister repeated his threat and drew attention to the effect of segregation on international opinion (Rowley 1971, pp. 263–4).

In other states, government action to ameliorate the condition of Aborigines was slower still. Douglas Gordon dated any significant change in Queensland to the late 1960s. He wrote:

I worked for many years in the state with the largest Aboriginal population. I can honestly say I never once thought about their health, in particular their infant mortality, as a concern any different from these matters in the population as a whole. It was a subject which we did not advert to, let alone discuss as a specific problem. When various social groups in the last decade or so began to query the welfare of Aborigines this made little impact on either doctors or the average citizen. However all of this changed when a series of papers appeared from 1968 onwards associated with the names of F. W. Clements, P. M. Moodie and D. J. Jose. These set out, in no uncertain fashion, the appalling infant mortality rate among our Aboriginal populations. Since then of course most sane, thinking people have completely changed their attitudes.

Gordon 1976, p. 652

The change in attitudes of white doctors about race coincided with a shift in government policy from segregation to assimilation. In 1952, the *Medical Journal of Australia* stated in a leading article:

It would be easier, of course, to let the aborigines [sic] die out but fortunately conscience and a sense of human responsibility still remain. The aborigines must be helped to adjust themselves to, and perhaps be assimilated into, our community and way of life so that they may be in it and of it.

Medical Journal of Australia 1952, p. 633

Recognising the problem: from the 1960s

Research continued, influenced by the idea of assimilation. During the 1960s, the medical profession apparently realised for the first time the enormity of the Aboriginal health problem. Aboriginal morbidity and mortality rates were found to be far higher than those of white Australians.

In the 1950s and 1960s, the health of Aborigines in the rural areas as well as in small towns and cities was no better than in the remote areas and showed little or no improvement over that of the last century. For example, in 1957 after failing to

Medical attitudes and health care

An examination of articles in the *Medical Journal of Australia (MJA)* from its inception in 1914 to 1950 shows that medical views, and medical activity, were influenced strongly by the belief that Aborigines were doomed to extinction in the inevitable race struggle, because they were lower on the evolutionary scale, primitive remnants of the Stone Age.

In this period, scientific evidence for assumptions about racial differences was largely derived from the investigation of perceived physical characteristics, from which moral and intellectual defects were inferred. The strength of contemporary racial stereotypes and the eminence of the men who demonstrated racial inferiority by apparently scientific means fed the prewar consensus.

As it was believed that extinction was inevitable, medical services for Aborigines were neglected. Where Aborigines were provided with hospital accommodation it was, as Rowley (1971, pp. 263–4) has suggested, because certain diseases such as leprosy and trachoma were regarded as threats to the white population.

It should not be forgotten that assumptions of Aboriginal racial inferiority were firmly rooted in scientific belief. That the 'proofs' no longer stand up to critical examination does not alter the impact they made at the time. In 1928, for example, the *MJA* published the Joseph Bancroft Memorial Lecture 'Functional anatomy and medical practice', given by William Colin Mackenzie, Professor of Comparative Anatomy at the University of Melbourne and Director of the Australian Institute of Anatomy. In it he stated:

Remember that primitive man, with abducted lower limbs and sagging knees, had a fight to maintain the erect posture. The aboriginal [sic] with his [sic] thin legs and long arms is nearer to these people than we and his so-called laziness has a physiological basis. The aboriginal boy sitting at school on seats without backs directs only part of his attention to lessons; the rest is devoted to keeping himself erect. (Mackenzie 1928, p. 429)

Aborigines were considered to be extremely suitable for various kinds of research. In a 1937 study of the causes of high blood pressure and the effects of civilisation, L. Jarvis Nye, a Brisbane physician, explained that he had used Aboriginal subjects because 'they stand at the bottom of the evolutionary ladder of anthropological relationships and they are considered to be the prototype of man as he appeared in the Stone Age in Europe' (Nye 1937, p. 1000).

It was also alleged that Aborigines did not suffer like white people. A 1918 report on hookworm eradication in Queensland stated:

Like Negro races in other parts of the world the Australian aborigines [sic] seem to possess a relative immunity towards the ill effects of hookworm infection. They are, however, nonetheless dangerous from a public health viewpoint as distributors of disease among the white communities. (Waite 1918, p. 505)

The material published in the *MJA* shows a remarkable consensus among doctors about Aborigines throughout this period, but in the 1940s there was a change in one respect. The activities of army doctors in the north of Australia during the war revealed a more detailed picture of Aboriginal ill-health than was previously known. The first article to be innocent of derogatory stereotyping of Aborigines appeared in the *MJA* in 1945. It was a review of diseases seen in Aboriginal patients by an army doctor, Lieutenant Colonel Binns (Binns 1945).

It may well be that the entry into the field of Aboriginal research of younger men, such as these army doctors, trained in specialties with a more clinical bias, was a critical factor in the broadening of interest beyond physical anthropology and in the eventual inclusion of Aborigines within the medical profession's general sphere of interest.

Lindsey Harrison, Department of Public Health and Nutrition, University of Wollongong, New South Wales save the life of an Aboriginal baby, the local medical practitioner Archie Kalokerinos visited the Aboriginal cemetery at Collarenebri, a prosperous north-western New South Wales township:

I found that more than half of the graves belonged to infants. A few short miles away was the European cemetery. An accurate count there was impossible, for the graves of some were not clearly marked; but one thing was clear: only a small percentage belonged to infants. I visited the police station and examined the records of births and deaths. The Aboriginal infant mortality rate for Collarenebri was over a hundred per thousand; that is, out of every 1000 babies born, over a hundred die in infancy, compared with the European death rate in the area of about 20 per 1000. A little research gave me figures from overseas. The result of these few simple hours of work convinced me that we had, amongst the Aboriginal infants in Collarenebri, a problem that was bad even compared with the worst one overseas. It was difficult to believe.

Kalokerinos 1974, pp. 23–4

Max Kamien, physician and psychiatrist, studied Aboriginal health and social conditions in the New South Wales town of Bourke in the early 1970s. Living conditions were very poor, particularly on the reserve outside the town. Infant mortality was 88 per 1000 live births. He questioned 343 mothers about their children's health: 17 per cent of children were said by their mothers to be generally unwell. He found that 63 per cent had intestinal parasites, 50 per cent had trachoma, 27 per cent had recurrent coughs, sore throats and bronchitis, and 38 per cent of children between 5 and 14 years old had active dental caries. Thirty-one per cent of the 282 adults interviewed by Kamien complained of persistent ill-health.

In adults the most common diseases found were dental caries and gum infections, a variety of eye disorders, fungal infections of the skin, chronic bronchitis, urinary tract infections, intestinal parasites, high blood pressure and anaemia...Between 1967 and 1971, twenty-four per cent of the adult Aboriginal population of Bourke were admitted to hospital on at least one occasion with chronic bronchitis, emphysema or pneumonia.

Kamien 1978, pp. 84–107.

The situation at Bourke would be representative of many such towns in south-eastern Australia.

One of the little-recognised dimensions of ill-health in some country areas was that of occupational diseases. Such was the case of Aboriginal asbestos miners at Baryulgil in New South Wales, for instance. Similarly, Labrador keratopathy is an eye disease suffered by Aboriginal stockmen working in dry, hot, dusty areas, who developed crippling or fatal lung disease (see Hills 1989).

By the middle of the twentieth century many thousands of Aborigines were living in Australia's capital cities. They lived in overcrowded conditions in the poorest housing. They filled the lowest paid jobs and were often unemployed, with consequent malnutrition and ill-health on a massive scale. Their vital statistics, hospital admissions, and ailments echo those of rural areas. Nevertheless, Gale's

(1972, p. 203) study of Adelaide Aborigines in the mid-1960s concludes that 'the degree of ill-health is greater in rural areas than in the city'. Rowley (1971, pp. 362–79) also suggests that although conditions in the cities were bad, they were better than in the rural areas. It was to take advantage of these better conditions that so many Aborigines had migrated to the cities.

New policies and definitions

Meanwhile, at the level of the official formulation of policy, federal and state ministers for Aboriginal affairs defined Australia's assimilation policy in 1961 as meaning:

that all Aborigines and part-Aborigines are expected eventually to attain the same manner of living as other Australians and to live as members of a single Australian community, enjoying the same rights and privileges, accepting the same responsibilities, observing the same customs and influenced by the same beliefs as other Australians.

Reynolds 1972, p. 175

This definition aroused considerable controversy among white Australians who were familiar with Aboriginal culture. Linguist T. G. H. Strehlow tried to explain how Aborigines felt about the matter. He was probably one of the few non-Aboriginal Australians who could have done this: he had grown up with Aboriginal people at Hermannsburg in central Australia, and could speak the Arrernte language. Strehlow explained that:

the majority of the Aboriginal and part-Aboriginal population are not very enthusiastic in their collaboration in plans designated by their white conquerors for their physical and cultural extinction, no matter how much they desire to be regarded as fellow citizens in their own right in what has been their country for thousands of years. Moreover, the dark Australian generally does not have a very high regard for the white man's morals, ethics, religion, or social behaviour. The white man is still admired mainly for his material possessions or his money...

'The stupid whiteman' is still a common description applied to us in many parts of central Australia, where the greatest measure of contempt for the intelligence of a native who has lived 'too much' among white men is conveyed in the phrase that he is a person 'as ignorant as a white man'.

Strehlow 1964, pp. 6, 16

Although few white Australians could understand how Aborigines felt about being assimilated into Australian society, there was a move to alter the wording, if not the goal, of government policy. As a result, in 1965 the official goal of the assimilation policy was 'that all persons of Aboriginal descent *will choose* to attain a similar manner of living to that of other Australians and live as members of a single Australian community' (Reynolds 1972, p. 175, italics added). The implication was meant to be that Aborigines should not be forced to become culturally the same as white Australians.

A referendum in 1967 gave the Commonwealth government power to legislate for Aborigines. In the following year, the Commonwealth government established the Office of Aboriginal Affairs, and in 1969 the states, which had tended to ignore the special health needs of Aborigines, agreed to establish special units funded by the Commonwealth. Although this has led to some improvement in Aboriginal health, white administrators and medical personnel have largely excluded Aborigines from both the decision-making processes and the delivery of health care. Australia has trained indigenous medical doctors in Papua New Guinea but has produced in Australia only 14 Aboriginal doctors, and these only comparatively recently. The 1986 census revealed that there were only 437 registered and 329 enrolled Aboriginal nurses and 55 Aboriginal dental nurses (NAHSWP 1989, p. 27), small numbers compared with the non-Aboriginal population in these occupations. Until Aboriginal-controlled health services were funded, 'the majority of health care networks provided for Aboriginal communities [were] directed by centralised white bureaucrats who [were] usually both physically and culturally separated from their clients' (House of Representatives Standing Committee on Aboriginal Affairs 1979, p. 113). Even today, with over 60 such services established, the major hospitals, public health programs, community health services and specialist services are dominated by white practitioners and administrators and are underused by Aborigines.

In 1973, the Labor government recognised Aborigines as a distinctive cultural and ethnic group with a right to determine their own future, and the Department of Aboriginal Affairs became fully fledged. The Aboriginal Land Rights Commission was also established, with Mr Justice Woodward as Commissioner, to examine the land issue in the Northern Territory. In 1975, a Land Rights Bill for the Northern Territory was introduced into parliament, and in 1976 the *Aboriginal Land Rights (Northern Territory) Act* became law. Every state except Tasmania has now legislated in some form for land rights. Today, Aborigines hold some kind of title to quite small areas of New South Wales, Queensland and Victoria, and to larger areas in the Northern Territory, South Australia and Western Australia. Except in South Australia and the Northern Territory, however, most of these do not provide secure, long-term tenure. It should be remembered that the largest areas are mostly arid desert unsuited to pastoral activities and there is serious and mounting opposition to Aboriginal rights by powerful mining interests because some of these desert lands have been shown to be rich in minerals of various kinds. An expensive and well-orchestrated campaign by the mining lobby has had considerable success in turning public opinion against Aboriginal land rights. As a result the federal government has modified the *Aboriginal Land Rights (Northern Territory) Act 1976* and the Western Australian government has trimmed its Aboriginal land policy in the direction of more power to the mining interests. Changes in both places deny the Aboriginal owners a strong right of veto over mining and exploration.

Aboriginal action

Since the mid-1960s, the most important gains in Aboriginal political, social and economic status—with consequent improvement in health—have been the results of the actions of Aboriginal people themselves (Lippmann 1981, pp. 71–99, 176–211). The demand for land rights began to be heard throughout the country in 1966 when the Gurindji people walked off Wave Hill Station in the Northern Territory with a demand they be given rights to the land surrounding their new village at

Dispersal, alienation and re-possession: the southern Pitjantjatjara

Many Aboriginal groups throughout Australia have been dispossessed or dispersed from their lands under unhappy circumstances. The story of the people associated with Maralinga in South Australia is just one example of government expedience taking precedence over Aboriginal rights.

Even before the arrival of Europeans in the Great Victoria Desert region (crossing the borders of the Northern Territory, South and Western Australia), considerable Aboriginal population movement had been occurring, as the Pitjantjatjara and others moved east, and other dialect groups moved south. Ooldea Soak, a natural permanent source of water on the eastern edge of the Nullarbor, was visited by hundreds of desert dwellers, as well as being known to coastal people. The soak was not only drought-resistant; it was also a centre where both trade and ceremony took place. With European expansion, it became the focus of activity associated with the building of the Trans-Australian Railway (1912–17). The European activity along the line, and in the vicinity of Ooldea, attracted the attention of Aboriginal people. Mrs Daisy Bates and, later, missionaries of the United Aborigines Mission (UAM) became established there, and a semi-permanent Aboriginal camp developed, increasingly dependent on hand-outs.

The first loss to the Aboriginal people occurred probably unbeknown to them. The Commonwealth Railways took possession of the land upon which the line was built, and acquired Ooldea Soak itself from the state government in 1916. The waters of Ooldea Soak were bored and thousands of litres a week were pumped out to supply the railway, a practice that continued until 1926 when pumping was abandoned because of overuse and increasing salinity. The construction of the railway, which employed over 1000 men just on the eastern side, was responsible for the devastation of local Aboriginal groups. Diseases such as measles and chickenpox, the introduction of alcohol and prostitution, and the destruction of the environment all accompanied the construction of the line. Mrs Bates, who watched in despair wrote:

Each group through whose territory the line was passing saw its waters absorbed, its game driven away, its food and water trees cut down, the whole country turned to strange uses, and its own people intruders on their own ground. (Australasian *1 May 1920, p. 886*)

By 1920 the area was devoid of the animals usually hunted for meat by Aborigines; the railways had even leased some of the Ooldea land to the butcher who supplied meat to the railway, so that he could graze 400 sheep there.

While the construction of the line was indirectly responsible for the destitution of the Aboriginal people who frequented the region, the authorities disapproved of Aborigines appearing in tattered clothes and begging from passengers. They also attempted to discourage Aboriginal people from travelling free of charge on the cattle trucks. Ooldea people had begun to use the railway as transportation to attend ceremonies in Western Australia in conjunction with Kalgoorlie and Cundeelee groups—their kin and ceremonial associates. Remembering this time, Aborigines now living at Yalata talk of 'stealing the train' to Kalgoorlie—getting a free ride.

With growing disapproval and alarm on the part of the railway and government authorities about the numbers of 'derelict natives' in and around Ooldea, the first of many attempts was made to remove the 'nuisance'. Suggestions were made for new locations for the Aborigines, well away from the railway. But in 1938 several thousand square kilometres at Ooldea were declared an Aboriginal reserve. The UAM then established a school with dormitories for boys and girls, and attempted unsuccessfully to discourage the performance of traditional ceremonial practices and the observance of customary beliefs and obligations on the part of its charges. By the late 1940s, several hundred desert or 'spinifex' people camped for extended periods at Ooldea, making occasional trips back into the desert to contact relatives still there, to visit sacred sites and to hunt for meat.

In 1947 a rocket-testing range was established at Woomera, to the east, and there were suspicions in some quarters, officially denied, that ultimately atomic warheads would be tested in the region. The range over which the rockets were fired incorporated parts of the Central Reserves (the country from which many of the Ooldea people came) and there was a public outcry about the potential impact on Aborigines of roads, surveying parties and control of movement. By the early 1950s, Australia was secretly agreeing with the British government to make land available for the testing of atomic weapons; the official announcement came in February 1952. Two areas north of the Trans-Australian Railway were selected: first Emu and later a site which came to be named 'Maralinga' (not, incidentally, a local Aboriginal term), just 53 kilometres north-west of Ooldea Soak. Maralinga was located directly on the north–south walking route used by the spinifex people to and from Ooldea.

Meanwhile, life at the Ooldea mission had become physically untenable, and the mission had suffered an internal split of its own, which meant that the Ooldea establishment had to be closed down. In June 1952, without warning, the missionaries packed up, and their Aboriginal charges were given rations for the last time and told to disperse. While the exact location of the future atomic testing site was unknown at this juncture, the Aborigines were actively prevented from travelling north by the Woomera-based native patrol officer. A large contingent had set off to join relatives in the north, at Ernabella. Instead, the remnants of the Ooldea people were taken, against their wishes by all accounts, to a property in the south purchased by the South Australian government, called Yalata. There, on alien territory, away from the spinifex and the red sand of the Great Victoria Desert, they remained until comparatively recently.

The Ooldea Aboriginal Reserve, proclaimed in 1936, encroached on the area earmarked for the atomic tests, and so in 1954 this proclamation was revoked. The native patrol officer took men from the new settlement at Yalata back to Ooldea so that they could retrieve ritual paraphernalia they had left hidden in bush. He was then able to report that 'all active tribal interest' in the area was at an end. Once the construction and use of Maralinga (serviced by the railway) was under way, the ex-Ooldea people were discouraged from walking north from Yalata to the railway, and their movements east and west on the railway were strictly monitored. A large portion of the lands containing their sites and water sources, which they had previously traversed, became a prohibited area. This meant that young men were not taken to visit significant sites on the land, and the memories of the elderly became more vague. Above all, people were homesick for the desert landscape, the trees and animals peculiar to it.

The British undertook seven major atomic blasts at Maralinga, and hundreds of minor trials which dispersed highly radioactive contamination over wide areas. A royal commission was convened in 1984, with Mr Justice J. R. McClelland as its president, to investigate the conduct of the tests and the adequacy of safety measures, among other matters (McClelland et al. 1985). In the same year, freehold title was granted to the Aboriginal owners of the Maralinga lands, from which a portion containing the test sites was excised. This successful land claim meant that an embryonic camp, established in the spinifex in 1982, could be officially supported as an outstation community. While there are fears among many Aboriginal members of the community about the damage done to the land, its waters and its animals by the 'poison' (radioactive contamination), the outstation has had a thriving population for much of the time since 1984. At least one of the rockholes that supplied water to desert people as they walked into Ooldea Soak from the north and the west has been found to be contaminated; in addition the Aboriginal people sometimes fear that the hot summer sun brings the 'poison' out of the ground. The Aboriginal owners of the land want nothing less than a total clean-up of the contaminated debris.

Maggie Brady, Australian Institute of Aboriginal and Torres Strait Islander Studies, Canberra

Wattie Creek. In 1968, the Yirrkala people of Arnhem Land began a case against a bauxite mining company and the Commonwealth with the aim of gaining recognition of their title to land under Australian law. In January 1972, an Aboriginal tent embassy was set up on the lawns of Parliament House, Canberra, and this was backed throughout Australia by marches and demonstrations demanding land rights. Not only did these actions raise the consciousness of many white Australians but they also attracted worldwide media attention. Internal and external pressures on the Australian government have continued to be fully exploited by Aboriginal activists. For example, when sacred sites were destroyed and others threatened on Noonkanbah Station in Western Australia, the organised resistance by local Aborigines gained nationwide and worldwide television coverage, and an Aboriginal delegation was sent to Geneva to plead their case before the United Nations Subcommission on the Prevention of Discrimination and the Protection of Minorities.

The mining lobby is proving effective in pursuing mining company interests, both in Canberra and in state capitals, with a number of consequences. One important consequence is that Aborigines' power to veto mining and exploration on the land granted or leased to them has been extensively eroded (Jennett 1986, pp. 11–14). Aboriginal groups, however, have protested strongly, and a delegation of Aborigines took the matter to Geneva to put it before the United Nations subcommission.

When the Commonwealth government adopted its national Plan for Aboriginal Health in 1973, it was then envisaged that within 10 years the health of the Aboriginal people would be improved to a level equal to that of the rest of the Australian population (see Saggers and Gray, chapter 9 in this volume). This called for the development of comprehensive morbidity and mortality statistics so that progress towards this goal could be monitored. Most state bureaucracies refused to cooperate, however, despite requests for Aboriginal health statistics from such prestigious bodies as the National Health and Medical Research Council, the Senate Select Committee on Aboriginal Affairs and Torres Strait Islanders, the House of Representatives Standing Committee on Aboriginal Affairs, the Commission of Inquiry into Poverty, the National Population Inquiry, Aboriginal Medical Services, the National Aboriginal Consultative Committee and the National Aboriginal Conference Executive. This stalling has occurred partly because many state bureaucrats hold assimilationist views, but it has also been caused by bureaucratic inertia (Borrie et al. 1975, p. 462). In Australia many bureaucracies are involved in the provision of Aboriginal health care and there has been little cooperation or coordination. This problem has been addressed by the federal Task Force on Aboriginal Health Statistics, which was set up in 1984 to establish a national system of Aboriginal health statistics (see 'The availability of Aboriginal health statistics', in Thomson, chapter 2 in this volume). All states and territories, apart from Queensland, cooperated. But the National Aboriginal Health Strategy Working Party (NAHSWP) reported in 1989 that the goal of a national statistical collection had still not been fully realised. In some jurisdictions, identification of Aboriginality has been implemented only since 1985, and it is widely known that underenumeration of Aborigines is common. The working definition of an Aborigine is a person who identifies as an Aborigine and is accepted as one by the Aboriginal community where he or she lives; but staff often fail to inquire whether patients identify as Aborigines and this means that many Aboriginal people are classified as non-Aboriginal. This has probably led to an underestimation of the prevalence of ill-health in the Aboriginal community (NAHSWP 1989, p. 10).

Actions by Aborigines have been instrumental not only in changing government policy but also in raising their own self-esteem. Moreover, their actions have not been limited to the field of politics. In July 1971, several Aborigines who were concerned about the failure of conventional health care delivery systems to meet the needs of their people established the Aboriginal Medical Service in Redfern, an inner city suburb of Sydney (see 'Self-determination in action', in chapter 9). This group was assisted by a number of white doctors who were concerned about the low health levels of Aborigines. Financial assistance was sought and obtained from the Office of Aboriginal Affairs. The experiment proved to be extremely successful and other Aboriginal communities established their own medical services. By 1990 68 community-controlled Aboriginal medical services (AMSs) were being funded.

Community-controlled Aboriginal health services are an important innovation. Since their introduction more Aboriginal people than ever before are receiving health care in a sympathetic and accessible form, and Aboriginal communities are generally more aware of health issues. The AMSs provide a range of services including primary health care and health education in areas such as nutrition, hygiene and strategies for preventing illness. Some employ medical practitioners and dentists. All employ nurses and health workers, and all provide a referral service for Aboriginal people needing mainstream or specialist medical attention or consultations with allied health professionals (see Franklin 1982). While it is clear that community-controlled medical services have improved the health of Aboriginal people in the areas they serve, the issue of control itself is not simple. Some of the problems involved in understanding what control can mean to local Aboriginal people and the white health care providers who wish to facilitate Aboriginal initiatives are revealed in Fred Myers' discussion of the medical service at Papunya in the Northern Territory during the early 1980s (see case study: Myers, 'A community-controlled health service: different agendas'. Myers' commentary illustrates one way in which non-Aboriginal interpretations of the best interests of Aboriginal communities can inadvertently be at odds with Aborigines' own wishes or concerns. The pressures on communities to manage resources and programs and to take direct responsibility for local services are, paradoxically, sometimes much greater than those placed on non-Aboriginal communities by government agencies, be they in rural or metropolitan centres. The most viable and successful community-controlled services have been those initiated by Aborigines themselves and shaped by the local needs and perceptions. This is not to say that the white staff referred to in this case study lacked commitment and dedication—on the contrary. The lesson that Myers draws from this case is that power and control are complex realities which are difficult to ensure without broader changes in the political position and influence of Aborigines and a keen understanding of the economic and cultural imperatives of local communities.

In December 1987, a meeting of Commonwealth, state and territory ministers for Aboriginal affairs and health agreed upon the development of a coordinated

A community-controlled health service: different agendas

In 1980–81, Papunya's independent medical service was officially controlled and administered by the Village Council. Operating costs were provided in grants from the Department of Aboriginal Affairs, to whom the council was accountable, but the selection of employees was a local matter. The medical service consisted of a doctor, two nursing sisters, and a number of Aboriginal 'health workers'. These last workers were the only employees drawn from the local community and the only medical personnel able to speak Aboriginal languages. While some of the health aides worked at a clinic housed in Papunya, others provided emergency care and administered a stock of medical supplies for people at the distant outstations. These remote settlements were visited by the doctor or nursing sisters on a regularly scheduled basis.

The white Australian doctor was extremely capable and dedicated to the political ideal of Aborigines administering their own medical services. This was his understanding of 'self-determination' when he arrived at Papunya in early 1981. He hoped to educate the community to the health dangers they faced, so that they could take responsibility for corrective and preventive action. The percolation of medical knowledge to more accessible and culturally sensitive local workers would place health care more strongly under Aboriginal control. While recognising that medical specialists would be needed to treat acute conditions, the doctor hoped that an 'Aboriginalization' of the health service could achieve the self-reliance that would free them from dependence on white outsiders. To accomplish this goal would require not only that Aboriginal health workers be able to diagnose and treat a variety of recurrent ailments, but also that they be willing to undertake the responsibility for such care. Yet this sort of self-determination proved to conflict with local values.

Most of the Aboriginal health workers were women, and usually young women. This situation reflected the facts of education, the primary Aboriginal identification of medical activity with children's sicknesses ('women's business'), and the fact that the nursing sisters were usually women, whose aides would naturally be of the same sex. According to the doctor, many of the health workers showed considerable skill in diagnosis. To improve their abilities to relate diagnosis to treatment, the teacher in charge of bilingual education was asked to prepare a visual chart and a set of mnemonics to serve for instruction. The workers' intelligence, combined with this training and their familiarity with the common sicknesses in the area, it was hoped, would lead them to take over responsibility for a significant portion of health care. Unusual cases could be handled by conferences over the medical service radio channel or by flying visits or evacuation. If the major obstacle to Aboriginalization were a combination of white domination and Aboriginal lack of confidence, these steps would lead to 'Aboriginal control'. In other words, the local people would take over running the health service, along the lines of the Chinese village medical program.

During the first several months of 1981, I was able to observe this system in Papunya and at the outstations...Rather than going to the health workers for care, local people continued to seek out the nursing sisters even for such simple remedies as pain tablets...For the most part, the health workers were viewed as 'translators' or 'interpreters' rather than as health experts... Knowing that they were hired and fired by the Village Council constituted the health workers' understanding of Aboriginal control...

With the exception of ritual duties, the sacrifice of an individual's interests and personal obligations for the continuing performance of a task supposed to contribute generally to 'community welfare' has little precedence or significance in traditional Pintupi life...The specialization embodied in the health workers' role was quite unusual...

In Papunya, absenteeism among health workers was common, often to the distress of the white staff when emergencies arose. Sometimes the health workers simply found their medical responsibilities to be in conflict with other obligations—especially obvious when ceremonies were under way. Viewed as 'flexibility', this is precisely the quality said to be valued or desirable by Aboriginal people (Nathan and Japanangka 1983, p. 165).

The chief issue in the case of the health workers, then, was whether they took responsibility for the medical service's operation and continuation as a whole. At Papunya the expectation was that it would continue whether or not an individual took part. While there was an Aboriginal obligation for the Pintupi workers to 'help' people, this was not represented as an obligation to sustain the particular institution in which this 'help' could be transacted—especially when one's energies were required elsewhere.

Similar perspectives on the medical service underlay the Papunya Village Council's position... The council did not think of itself as having to sustain the medical service...This agency was sustained from outside, although local people could control its action as it affected them. They viewed the service as separate in some sense, as a 'different business' rather than as an institution for the general welfare of an autonomous community...

The Australian doctor interpreted this unwillingness to take on 'responsibility' as a product of living in the 'total institutions' of government settlements (citing Goffman 1961, in fact). This condition would take time to dispel, he thought, because Aborigines were used to having whites deliver services for them. Reasoning further that those with authority in the community had not been sufficiently involved in the medical service, he asked an older man, whom he believed to have 'traditional authority', to head the medical service. While this man was able to give the doctor good political advice, he had neither a basis for authority over the health workers nor the desire to command them. The doctor's goal of 'Aboriginalization' meant making the medical service 'represent' the community. However, the concepts of 'representation' and of 'community' were themselves elements of a different cultural tradition...

We can see how this arrangement satisfies the condition 'Aboriginal control' but it may endanger the very autonomy that the Aboriginal people seemingly seek to preserve... To some extent, control of this sort is an illusion, since the Aborigines do not control the means of its reproduction. The money for health services is produced by others and by political activity in an arena beyond the settlement. Obviously, Aborigines' ability to control the policy of, for example, the Northern Territory government is limited. These problems may eventually drive Aboriginal people to seek political control at a higher level of organization.

Extracted from Myers 1986, pp. 276–82

national strategy to improve Aboriginal health services. Its report (available only on application to the Department of Aboriginal Affairs) was published in March 1988, and its findings and recommendations were considered at a further joint meeting of Commonwealth, state and territory ministers. The ministers agreed to work together on ways of implementing a national Aboriginal health strategy. They also decided to set up a development group to assess the working party's report and to develop areas for early action.

What is the present legacy of this interplay between history and politics? It is clear that the Australian Aboriginal situation today has very much in common with the nineteenth-century picture in which many of the Western world's battles for adequate housing, drainage, sanitation, refrigeration and facilities for personal hygiene had still to be won. Many Aborigines living in an otherwise affluent Australia are still trapped in a vicious cycle of poverty and powerlessness from which they feel they can never hope to escape. This demoralising hopelessness is itself one of the major health problems. Related to this is the cultural gap between Aborigines and other Australians, who cannot understand what it is like to be an Aborigine, or do not care. The one constant pattern is that whether whites are hostile or well-intentioned, whether they know themselves to be ignorant or believe themselves to be well informed, the 'Aboriginal problem' is the problem of how white people should decide to deal with Aborigines. Only very recently are there signs that some whites in the community and government may be learning from Aborigines what Aborigines want and need, and acknowledging that local autonomy is crucial to the process of self-determination and self-management.

References

Abbie, A. A. (1970), *The original Australians*, A. H. and A. W. Reed, Sydney.

MJA (1952), 'The Australian Aboriginal and ourselves', *Medical Journal of Australia* **2**, pp. 663–4.

Barwick, D. (1971), 'Changes in the Aboriginal population of Victoria, 1863–1966', in D. J. Mulvaney and J. Golson (eds), *Aboriginal man and environment in Australia*, Australian National University Press, Canberra, pp. 288–315.

Berndt, R. M., and Berndt, C. H. (1987), *End of an era: Aboriginal labour in the Northern Territory*, AIAS, Canberra.

Binns, R. T. (1945), 'A study of diseases of Australian natives in the Northern Territory', *Medical Journal of Australia* **1**, pp. 421–6.

Biskup, P. (1973), *Not slaves, not citizens*, University of Queensland Press, St Lucia.

Bolton, G. C. (1972), *A fine country to starve in*, University of Western Australia, Nedlands, WA.

Borrie, W. D., Smith, L. R., and Di Julio, O. B. (1975), *National Population Inquiry: population and Australia, a demographic analysis and projection, first report*, vol. 2, AGPS, Canberra.

Bowler, J. M., Jones, R., Allen, H., and Thorne, A. G. (1970), 'Pleistocene human remains from Australia: a living site and human cremation from Lake Mungo, Western New South Wales', *World Archaeology* **2**, pp. 39–60.

Butlin, N. G. (1983), *Our original aggression*, Allen and Unwin, Sydney.

Butlin, N. G. (1985), 'Macassans and Aboriginal smallpox: the "1789" and "1829" epidemics', *Historical Studies* **21** (84), pp. 315–35.

Campbell, J. (1985), 'Smallpox in Aboriginal Australia, the early 1830s', *Historical Studies* **21**, pp. 336–58.

Cowlishaw, G. (1978), 'Infanticide in Aboriginal Australia', *Oceania* **48**, June, pp. 262–83.

Cowlishaw, G. (1981), 'The determination of fertility among Australian Aborigines', *Mankind* **13**, pp. 37–55.

Curr, E. (1886–87), *The Australian race: its origin, languages, customs*, 4 vols, Melbourne.

Duguid, C. (1963), *No dying race*, Rigby, Adelaide.

Durack, M. (1964), *Yagan of the Bibbulmun*, Nelson, Melbourne.

Flood, J. (1983), *Archaeology of the Dreamtime*, Collins, Sydney.

Franklin, M.-A. (1976), *Black and white Australians*, Heinemann Education, Melbourne.

Franklin, M.-A. (1982), 'Delivering health care to Aborigines', *Australian Journal of Social Issues* **17** (4), pp. 276–87.

Gale, F. (1972), *Urban Aborigines*, Australian National University Press, Canberra.

Goffman, E. (1961), *Asylums*, New York, Doubleday.

Gordon, D. (1976), *Health, sickness and society*, University of Queensland Press, St. Lucia.

Hardy, B. (1976), *Lament for the Barkindji: the vanished tribes of the Darling River region*, Rigby, Australia.

Hargrave, J. C. (1968), *Leprosy in Northern Territory Aborigines*, Government Printer, Darwin.

Hilliard, W. (1968), *The people in between: the Pitjantjatjara people of Ernabella*, Hodder and Stoughton, London.

Hills, B. (1989), 'A handful of dust', Sydney Morning Herald ('Spectrum'), 30 September, p. 68.

Historical Records of New South Wales (1787), vol. 1, part 2, p. 52.

Horner, J. (1974), *Vote Ferguson for Aboriginal freedom*, ANZ Book Co., Sydney.

HRSCAA (House of Representatives Standing Committee on Aboriginal Affairs) (1979), *Aboriginal health*, AGPS, Canberra.

Jennett, C. (1986), 'The great Australian backlash: growing opposition to land rights', *National Outlook*, December 1985 – January 1986, pp. 11–14.

Kalokerinos, A. (1974), *Every second child*, Nelson, Melbourne.

Kamien, M. (1978), *The dark people of Bourke*, AIAS, Canberra.

Kennedy, E., and Donaldson, T. (1982), 'Coming up out of the nhaalya: reminiscences of the life of Eliza Kennedy', *Aboriginal History* **6**, pp. 5–27.

Kettle, E. (1967), *Gone bush*, Leonard, Sydney.

Lippmann, L. (1981), *Generations of resistance: the Aboriginal struggle for justice*, Longman Cheshire, Sydney (see especially pp. 71–99, 176–211).

Long, J. P. M. (1970), *Aboriginal settlements: a survey of institutional communities in eastern Australia*, Australian National University Press, Canberra.

McClelland, J. R., Fitch, J., and Jonas, W. J. A. (1985), *The report of the Royal Commission into British Nuclear Tests in Australia*, AGPS, Canberra.

Mackenzie, W. C. (1928), 'Functional anatomy and medical practice', *Medical Journal of Australia* **2**, p. 422–30.

Macknight, C. C. (1986), 'Review of *Our original aggression* by N. G Butlin', *Historical Studies* **22** (86), pp. 136–7.

Markus, A. (1988), *Blood from a stone: William Cooper and the Australian Aborigines' League*, Allen and Unwin, Sydney.

Mathews, J. (1985), 'Lorna Dixon', in I. White, D. Barwick and B. Meehan (eds), *Fighters and singers: the lives of some Aboriginal women*, Allen and Unwin, Sydney, pp. 90–105.

Middleton, H. (1977), *But now we want the land back*, New Age Publishers, Sydney.

Middleton, M. R., and Francis, S. J. (1976), *Yuendumu and its children*, AGPS, Canberra.

Miller, J. (1985), *Koori, a will to win: the heroic resistance, survival and triumph of Black Australia*, Angus and Robertson, Sydney.

Myers, F. R (1986), *Pintupi country, Pintupi self: sentiment, place and politics among Western Desert Aborigines*, AIAS, Canberra.

Nathan, P., and Japanangka, D. L. (1983), *Health business*, Heinemann Education, Richmond, Vic.

NAHSWP (National Aboriginal Health Strategy Working Party) (1989), *A national Aboriginal health strategy*, Department of Aboriginal Affairs, Canberra (limited circulation).

Nye, L. J. J. (1937), 'Blood pressure in the Australian Aboriginal, with a consideration of hyperpiesia and its relation to civilisation', *Medical Journal of Australia* **2**, p. 1000.

Palmer, K., and McKenna, C. (1978), *Somewhere between black and white*, Macmillan, Melbourne/Sydney.

Perkins, C. (1975), *A bastard like me*, Ure Smith, Sydney.

Radcliffe-Brown, A. R. (1930), 'Former numbers and distribution of the Australian Aborigines', in *Official Yearbook of the Commonwealth of Australia* **23**, pp. 687–96.

Reece, R. H. W. (1974), *Aborigines and settlers*, Sydney University Press, Sydney.

Reynolds, H. (1972), *Aborigines and settlers*, Cassell Australia, Sydney.

Reynolds, H. (1982), *The other side of the frontier*, Penguin Australia, Ringwood, Vic.

Reynolds, H. (1987), *Frontier: Aborigines, settlers and land*, Allen and Unwin, Sydney.

Rowley, C. D. (1971), *Outcasts in white Australia: Aboriginal policy and practice*, vol. 2, Australian National University Press, Canberra.

Smith, F. B. (1979), *The people's health 1830–1910*, Australian National University Press, Canberra.

Stanner, W. E. H. (1960), 'Durmugam, a Nangiomeri', in J. B. Casagrande (ed.), *The company of man: twenty portraits by anthropologists*, Harper and Row, New York, pp. 63–100.

Stanner, W. E. H. (1974), 'Some aspects of Aboriginal health', in B. S. Hetzel, M. Dobbin, L. Lippman and E. Eggleston (eds), *Better health for Aborigines: report of a national seminar at Monash University*, University of Queensland Press, St Lucia, pp. 3–13.

Stanner, W. E. H. (1979), 'After the Dreaming', reprinted in *White man got no Dreaming*, (1978), ANU Press, Canberra, pp. 198–248 (first published 1968).

Stevens, F. (1974), *Aborigines in the Northern Territory cattle industry*, Australian National University Press, Canberra.

Strehlow, T. G. H. (1964), *The Aboriginal viewpoint*, Aboriginal Advancement League of South Australia, Adelaide.

Tatz, C. M. (1972), 'The politics of Aboriginal health', *Supplement to Politics* **7** (2), November.

Taylor, J. C. (1977), 'Diet, health and economy: some consequences of planned social change in an Aboriginal community', in R. M. Berndt (ed.), *Aborigines and change: Australia in the 70s*, AIAS, Canberra, pp. 147–58.

Tindale, N. B. (1941), 'Survey of the half-caste problem in South Australia', *Proceedings of the Royal Geographic Society of Australasia (South Australian Branch)* **42**, pp. 66–161.

Tonkinson, R. (1974), *The Jigalong mob: Aboriginal victors of the desert crusade*, Cummings, Menlo Park, California.

Wagner, H. (1981), 'Aboriginal infant mortality', *The Lamp*, September, pp. 5–16.

Waite, J. H. (1918), 'The Queensland hookworm campaign: first progress report', *Medical Journal of Australia* **2**, pp. 505–10.

White, J. P., and Lampert, R. (1987), 'Creation and discovery', in D. J. Mulvaney and J. P. White (eds), *Australians to 1788*, Fairfax, Syme and Weldon, Sydney, pp. 3–23.

White, J. P., and Mulvaney, D. J. (1987), 'How many people?', in D. J. Mulvaney and J. P. White (eds), *Australians to 1788*, Fairfax, Syme and Weldon, Sydney, pp. 115–17.

Young, P. (1985), *Roper River Centenary 5, 6, and 7 July*, newsletter no. 1.

Unpublished material

Barwick, D. (unpub.), Smallpox in Victoria? Some questions about the evidence, seminar paper, Australian National University, 1986, available from AIATSIS library.

CHAPTER 2

A review of Aboriginal health status

Neil Thomson

Aboriginal Health Unit, Australian Institute of Health, Canberra

Aborigines and Torres Strait Islanders comprise the least healthy identifiable sub-population in Australia. Although there have been some improvements since the 1970s, the conclusion of the House of Representatives Standing Committee on Aboriginal Affairs (HRSCAA) in 1979—that the standard of health Aborigines experience would not be tolerated if it existed in the population as a whole (HRSCAA 1979)—remains true today.

In this chapter, the term 'Aborigines' generally will be used to refer to both Australian Aborigines and Torres Strait Islanders. Aboriginal identification is in accordance with the accepted 'working definition': 'an Aboriginal or Torres Strait Islander is a person of Aboriginal or Torres Strait Islander descent who identifies as an Aboriginal or Torres Strait Islander and is accepted as such by the community in which he (she) lives' (DAA 1981).

The health problems of Aborigines vary across Australia, reflecting the different circumstances of communities. Although communities in more remote areas have not seen the improvements in their physical environment experienced by other Australians, many have managed to maintain some social and cultural integrity in their lives. Their health problems, however, largely reflect their very poor physical environment. At the other extreme, the health problems of the many Aborigines living in urban and less remote areas resemble those of other socioeconomically disadvantaged Australians, with an extra component reflecting their adverse social environment.

Although their health problems differ, the overall standard of health of Aborigines is low throughout the country. For almost all disease categories, rates for Aborigines are worse than for other Australians; death rates are up to four times higher, and life expectancy is up to 21 years less. The causes of their lower health status are complex, but the social and economic inequality of Aborigines is clearly of central importance.

In the absence of reliable comprehensive data about individual diseases (see 'The availability of Aboriginal health statistics'), this chapter will focus on the information available through the general administrative collections on births and pregnancy outcomes, deaths and hospitalisation.

The availability of Aboriginal health statistics

The adequacy of Aboriginal health statistics depends first on the identification of Aborigines in the population and on health-related statistics. However, a number of key collections do not provide for Aboriginal identification, and the level of accuracy of identification, when provided, is less than satisfactory in many of the collections. The need for national Aboriginal health statistics has been recognised for many years (see Smith 1978, 1982), but until recently very little progress has been achieved.

In 1984, the Federal Task Force on Aboriginal Health Statistics reached agreements with all states and territories except Queensland (which it did not visit) to identify Aborigines in a number of 'priority' health statistics collections (Task Force on Aboriginal Health Statistics 1985). Priority collections were identified as the birth and death registration systems, and the hospital morbidity and maternal/perinatal collections.

A number of states and territories already had the capacity to identify Aborigines in some of their collections, but there was clearly a need to extend the coverage to all states and territories (see Thomson 1986a for a more detailed summary of the issues involved). In general, progress in the implementation of the changes necessary to permit the identification of Aborigines in the various statistical collections has been much slower than expected. The following information summarises the present situation in each state or territory.

New South Wales. Before the task force, provision for Aboriginal identification already existed on death notification forms, on medical certificates of cause of perinatal death, and in the hospital morbidity and maternal/perinatal collections. Birth notification forms were modified in 1990 to provide for Aboriginal identification, but no progress has been made in modifying medical certificates of cause of death. Cancer and communicable disease notifications do not identify Aborigines.

Victoria. At the time of the task force, the hospital morbidity and maternal/perinatal collections provided for Aboriginal identification. Since November 1986, the forms of notification of birth and death have provided for Aboriginal identification, as have cancer notifications since January 1988. Communicable disease notifications still do not do so.

Queensland. Although Queensland was not visited by the task force, changes have been made to provide for Aboriginal identification in the maternal/perinatal and hospital morbidity collections, and moves are under way for the modification of the birth and death notification forms to include a question on Aboriginality. Some communicable disease notifications provide for Aboriginal identification, but none of the other systems do so.

Western Australia. In 1984, medical certificates of cause of death, and the hospital and maternal/perinatal collections provided for Aboriginal identification. Since the state's maternal/perinatal collection provides quality data on Aboriginal births, Western Australia decided against changing the form of notification of birth. Provision for Aboriginal identification on death notification forms was implemented in 1985. Cancer registrations have identified Aborigines since 1980, but communicable disease notifications still do not do so.

South Australia. Prior to the task force, provision for Aboriginal identification already existed on medical certificates of perinatal death, and in the hospital and maternal/perinatal collections. The necessary changes to the birth and death notification forms were made in 1985, but South Australia decided against changing the medical certificate of cause of death. Cancer notifications provide for Aboriginal identification, but communicable disease notifications do not.

Tasmania. At the time of the task force, the maternal/perinatal collection and medical certificate of cause of perinatal death included provision for Aboriginal identification, and in 1989 changes were made to birth and death notification forms. No provision is made for Aboriginal identification in cancer registrations or communicable disease notifications, but a new centralised hospital morbidity collection will provide for Aboriginal identification.

Australian Capital Territory. In 1984, provision for Aboriginal identification existed on medical certificates of cause of death and cause of perinatal deaths, and in the hospital morbidity and maternal/perinatal collections. The changes to the birth and death notification forms were introduced in 1985. Neither cancer registrations nor communicable disease notifications provide for Aboriginal identification.

Northern Territory. Before the task force, provision for Aboriginal identification existed in the hospital morbidity and maternal/perinatal collections. Changes to the birth and death notification forms were made in 1988, and the Northern Territory now provides for the identification of Aborigines in all main health-related collections.

In major national health-related surveys, developments have been just as slow. The first two national health surveys undertaken by the Australian Bureau of Statistics (ABS), in 1978 and 1983, did not provide for the identification of Aborigines. The third survey, in 1989–90 did make provision for Aboriginal identification, but no special sampling procedures were employed to ensure that an adequate sample of Aborigines was included.

Two recent national surveys of disabilities, undertaken by the ABS in 1981 and 1988, did not include provision for Aboriginal identification, nor did any of the three National Heart Foundation of Australia's surveys of the prevalence of cardiovascular risk factors.

Of course, providing for the identification of Aborigines does not guarantee that they will be so identified. This problem is recognised as most significant in the larger urban centres in the south of the continent. To ensure that adequate levels of Aboriginal identification are achieved in the health-related collections, intensive validation studies, and often remedial procedures, are required. It is therefore likely to be some time before reliable statistics are routinely produced as a result of the major changes that have occurred in recent years.

Neil Thomson

The Aboriginal population

According to the 1986 Australian Census of Population and Housing, the Aboriginal population was 227 645, breaking down into 206 104 Australian Aborigines and 21 541 Torres Strait Islanders (table 2.1).

The Aboriginal population is relatively young compared with the total Australian population. About 40 per cent of Aborigines are less than 15 years of age, compared with 23 per cent of the total population. Only 4 per cent of Aborigines are aged 60 years or over, compared with almost 15 per cent of the total population. Two-thirds of Aborigines live in urban areas (centres with a total population of 1000 or more), compared with 86 per cent of non-Aborigines. The remaining one-third

Table 2.1   Australian Aboriginal and Torres Strait Islander population, by states and territories, 1986

State / territory	Total	Aust. Aborigines	Torres Strait Islanders	Proportion of total population %
Qld	61 268	48 098	13 170	2.4
NSW	59 011	55 672	3 339	1.1
WA	37 789	37 110	679	2.7
NT	34 739	34 197	542	22.4
SA	14 291	13 298	993	1.1
Vic.	12 611	10 740	1 871	0.3
Tas.	6 716	5 829	887	1.5
ACT	1 220	1 160	60	0.5
Total Aust.	227 645	206 104	21 541	1.4

Source: ABS 1987*a*

live in rural communities (15 per cent) and other rural areas (18.5 per cent). In all about 25 per cent of Aborigines live in remote areas of Australia: probably about 5 per cent in small groups in their ancestral homelands, and the rest in Aboriginal towns and settlements on Aboriginal lands and reserves.

Fertility and pregnancy outcomes

The fertility of Aboriginal women remains much higher than that of non-Aboriginal women, despite the fact that Aboriginal fertility has declined substantially since the late 1960s, largely in parallel with the decline in fertility in the total population (Gray unpub. *a*; Gray 1983). ('Fertility' is used in the technical sense, denoting actual, rather than potential, reproductive performance.)

The higher present-day fertility of Aboriginal women is largely due to the great excess of births occurring at young ages, particularly in the teenage years. Table 2.2 shows the very high fertility rates among Aboriginal teenagers living in Western Australia, the Northern Territory and the Queensland Aboriginal communities. The rates shown in the table for Aboriginal women aged 20 to 24 years are also well above those for all Australian women.

Beyond the 20–24 year age group, the pattern varies slightly. The fertility rates of Aboriginal women living in the Queensland communities and in Western Australia closely resemble the overall Australian rates, while Aboriginal women in the Northern Territory experience higher rates.

Although it appears that the South Australian Maternal/Perinatal Collection identified only about 70–75 per cent of births to Aboriginal mothers in that state in 1981–86, a similar pattern of higher fertility at younger ages has been reported (South Australian Health Commission 1988).

The great differences in maternal age mean that about 30 per cent of Aboriginal women having babies were 19 years of age or younger, compared with 5.8 per cent of all Australian women. This difference is even more marked at younger ages, with 9.3 per cent of Aboriginal women having babies in Western Australia in 1985 being 16 years of age or younger, compared with only 0.5 per cent of non-Aboriginal women (Hill 1987). Of the 228 births to mothers aged 16 years or younger, 115 (50.4 per cent) occurred to Aborigines. While at these young ages non-Aboriginal fertility has declined in Western Australia since 1979, it appears that Aboriginal fertility may have increased slightly (Stanley and Mauger 1986).

Probably the best summary index for fertility is the total fertility rate, which is the sum of the age-specific fertility rates for females of each age. It represents 'the number of children that would be born (ignoring mortality) to a hypothetical group of 1000 women who, as they pass through the reproductive years, experience the particular age-specific birth rates on which the index is based' (Pollard et al. 1981, p. 91). Compared with the total fertility rate of 1873 per 1000 women for all Australian women in 1986, the rates for Aboriginal women were each in excess of 3000 per 1000: 3170 for women living in the Queensland communities in 1987, 3273 for those living in Western Australia in 1986, and 3451 for those living in the Northern Territory in 1986.

Figure 2.1 *Two-thirds of Aborigines live in urban areas. Here, some of Sydney's Aboriginal residents participate in a street march in 1981. (E. Pelot Kitchener)*

Table 2.2   Births and age-specific fertility rates: Aborigines and total Australia

| | Aborigines | | | | | | Total Australia 1986 | |
| | Qld 1987[a] | | WA 1986 | | NT 1986 | | | |
Age group	No.	Rate	No.	Rate	No.	Rate	No.	Rate
15–19[b]	113	164.7	338	161.5	385	173.8	14 236	21.7
20–24	130	224.9	463	226.2	385	200.6	59 045	89.6
25–29	65	137.1	239	147.8	241	148.2	94 561	142.5
30–34	22	63.0	108	85.8	126	103.1	56 187	88.9
35–39	10	35.1	26	26.8	44	45.1	17 021	27.3
40–44	3	9.2	5	6.4	13	17.6	2 233	4.3
45+	0	0.0	0	0.0	1	1.6	35	0.2
All ages[c]	343	122.9	1229	126.7	1195	128.3	243 408	66.3

Sources
Australian Institute of Health, unpublished, from data supplied by the Queensland Department of Health, the Health Department of Western Australia and the Northern Territory Department of Health and Community Services; Australian Bureau of Statistics 1987*b*

Notes
[a] The Queensland figures are for the Aboriginal reserve communities.
[b] Included in the 15–19 age group are births occurring to females aged 14 years or less.
[c] The rate shown for 'All ages' is the general fertility rate: the number of births per 1000 females aged 15 to 49 years.

Birth weight

Babies born to Aboriginal women are 150–350 grams lighter than those born to non-Aboriginal women, in terms of both mean and median birth weight (see table 2.3).

Of particular significance is the proportion of babies of low birth weight (LBW), that is, less than 2500 grams. Compared with the combined non-Aboriginal proportion (for Western Australia in 1983–86, South Australia in 1983–86 and the Northern Territory in 1986–87 of 5.7 per cent, 13.5 per cent of babies born to Aboriginal women were of low birth weight (see table 2.4). Among Aborigines, the proportion varied: 17.0 per cent for the Queensland communities; 15.2 per cent for the Northern Territory; 12.9 per cent for Western Australia; and 11.7 per cent for South Australia.

Table 2.3   Mean and median birth weights (grams): babies born to Aboriginal and non-Aboriginal women

	Aboriginal				Non-Aboriginal 1983–87
	Qld[a] 1987	WA 1983–86	SA 1983–86	NT 1986–87	
Mean weight	3011	3138	3168	3041	3362
Median weight	3029	3192	3233	3082	3383

Sources
Australian Institute of Health, unpublished, from data supplied by the Queensland Department of Health, the Health Department of Western Australia, the South Australian Health Commission and the Northern Territory Department of Health and Community Services

Notes
[a] The Queensland figures are for the Aboriginal reserve communities.
[b] The non-Aboriginal data are for WA, 1983–86, SA, 1983–86 and the NT, 1986–87.

Table 2.4   Birth weight distribution: babies born to Aboriginal and non-Aboriginal women

Weight (grams)	Aboriginal								Non-Aboriginal	
	Qld 1987[a]		WA 1983-86		NT 1986-87		SA 1983-86			
	no.	%	no.	%	no.	%	no.	%	no.	%
<2500	58	17.0	624	12.9	360	15.2	144	11.7	7577	5.7
2500–2999	107	31.2	1109	22.9	683	29.0	273	22.0	20140	15.4
3000–3499	112	32.7	1781	36.8	828	35.1	434	35.0	49340	37.7
3500–3999	51	14.9	1001	20.7	363	15.4	303	24.5	39920	30.5
>=4000	15	4.4	321	6.6	122	5.2	85	6.5	13980	10.7
All weights	343	100.0	4836	100.0	2356	100.0	1239	100.0	130957	100.0

Sources
Australian Institute of Health, unpublished, from data supplied by the Queensland Department of Health, the Health Department of Western Australia, the South Australian Health Commission and the Northern Territory Department of Health and Community Services; Australian Bureau of Statistics 1987 *b*

Notes
[a] The Queensland figures are for the Aboriginal reserve communities.
[b] The non-Aboriginal data are for WA, 1983–86, SA, 1983–86 and the NT, 1986–87.

Although it appears that the proportion of LBW babies in the Northern Territory may have declined, the proportion in other places has shown little change. Compared with the current overall level in the Northern Territory of 15.2 per cent, 23.2 per cent of 3617 babies born to Aboriginal women at the Royal Darwin Hospital in the period 1968–83 were of low birth weight (Gogna et al. 1986), as were 26 per cent of the 216 babies born at Galiwin'ku (Arnhem Land) in the period 1979–82 (Watson 1984).

In Western Australia, the LBW proportion among babies born to Aboriginal women has not changed significantly since the mid-1970s. Compared with more than 4000 babies born to Aboriginal women in the period 1975–78, of whom 13 per cent weighed 2500 grams or less (using an earlier definition of LBW) (Seward and Stanley 1981), 12.9 per cent of babies born to Aboriginal women in the period 1983–86 were of low birth weight.

Although based on a small number of births, the higher proportion of LBW babies in the Queensland communities, 17.0 per cent, is consistent with figures reported earlier (Streatfield unpub.).

Mortality

The level of mortality experienced by Aborigines has long been recognised as much worse than that of other Australians (Moodie 1973). Although the overall situation has probably improved over the past 20 years, the current level is still much higher than that of non-Aborigines, and there is some evidence that the death rates of young and middle-aged Aboriginal adults may have worsened in that time, at least in some parts of the country.

Standardised mortality ratios

With the substantial difference between the age structures of the Aboriginal and non-Aboriginal populations, it is necessary to standardise death rates. Indirect standardisation has been used to provide an estimate of the number of deaths expected by the various Aboriginal subpopulations if they were to experience the same age-specific death rates as the non-Aboriginal population. The ratio of the number of deaths observed to the number expected is known as the standardised mortality ratio (SMR). However, as a result of incomplete reporting of Aboriginal deaths, precise details of non-Aboriginal death rates are not known. Consequently, the age-specific death rates for the total Australian population have been used, thus slightly overestimating the expected number of deaths, and slightly underestimating the SMRs.

After standardisation, Aboriginal death rates are generally between two and four times those of the total Australian population. Table 2.5 shows the number of observed and expected deaths for Aborigines in various regions, as well as the standardised mortality ratios.

Expectation of life at birth

The other figure summarising mortality is expectation of life at birth. For males, the calculated life expectancies at birth range from 53 years for Aborigines living in the Northern Territory in 1985 to 61 years for those living in the Kimberley region of

Table 2.5   Aboriginal observed and expected number of deaths, and standardised mortality ratios[a]

	Males			Females		
	Observed no.	Expected no.	SMR	Observed no.	Expected no.	SMR
Queensland communities, 1985–1986	113	41.2	2.7	95	22.5	4.2
Western Australia, 1985–1986	404	163.0	2.5	285	96.9	2.9
Northern Territory, 1985	209	56.1	3.7	151	40.3	3.7
Western New South Wales,1984–1987	205	59.0	3.5	110	37.0	3.0
Kimberley, WA,1983–1984	108	68.0	1.6	81	34.1	2.4

Sources
Holman and Quadros 1986; Gray and Hogg 1989; Australian Institute of Health, unpublished, from data supplied by the Queensland Department of Health, the Health Department of Western Australia and the Northern Territory Department of Health and Community Services

Notes
[a] See text for details of standardisation and SMRs.

Western Australia in 1983–84 (see table 2.6). For females, the range is from 58 years for Aborigines living in the Queensland communities in 1985–86 to 65 years for those living in the western areas of New South Wales in 1984–87. Even the highest expectations of life at birth are well below those of the total Australian population in 1986: 73 years for males and 79 years for females.

In the absence of details of Aboriginal deaths in other parts of Australia, an intercensus survival analysis has been applied to population figures from the 1981 and 1986 Australian censuses (see table 2.7) (Gray unpub. *b*). This analysis reveals a striking similarity of Aboriginal mortality throughout Australia.

The best levels of expectation of life at birth for Aborigines, 12 to 15 years less than those experienced by other Australians, are comparable with those documented for Colombia, Mongolia, the Philippines and Thailand (United Nations Children's Fund 1988). The worst levels, about 20 years less than overall Australian figures, are comparable with levels recorded in India, Haiti, Ghana and Papua New Guinea.

Age-specific mortality

The lower expectations of life at birth for Aborigines largely reflect the much higher mortality experienced by young adults. The age pattern of Aboriginal mortality is strikingly different from that of other Australians, with the ratio of Aboriginal to total Australian age-specific death rates being highest for young and middle-aged adults. The combined age-specific death rates for 1985 for Aborigines in the Queensland communities, Western Australia and the Northern Territory are shown in table 2.8, as well as the rates for the total Australian population and the Aboriginal/total Australian population age-specific death rate ratios.

The limited data available suggest that the death rates for young and middle-aged Aboriginal adults have increased over the past 20 to 30 years. For Aborigines in the Northern Territory, estimates of recent age-specific death rates for all age groups beyond 30–39 years are higher than those estimated for 1958 to 1960 (Moodie 1973). For country areas of New South Wales, the deterioration appears even greater: death rates for all age groups from 20–29 years are almost one and a half times those estimated for 1955 to 1964 (Moodie 1973; Thomson and Smith 1985).

Table 2.6   Expectation of life at birth of Aborigines for selected regions, by sex

	Male	Female
Queensland[a] communities, 1985–1986	56.2	57.8
Western Australia, 1985–1986	55.2	61.9
Northern Territory, 1985	53.0	63.0
Western New South Wales, 1984–1987	53.5	64.8
Kimberley, WA 1983–1984	60.8	64.2

Sources
Holman and Quadros 1986; Gray and Hogg 1989; Australian Institute of Health, unpublished, from data supplied by the Queensland Department of Health, the Health Department of Western Australia and the Northern Territory Department of Health and Community Services

Notes
[a]The Queensland figures are for the Aboriginal reserve communities.

Table 2.7   Expectation of life at birth of Aborigines for states/territories, based on intercensal survival estimates (years)

	Male	Female
New South Wales/Australian Capital Territory	57.3	65.4
Victoria/Tasmania	58.1	67.6
Queensland	55.8	64.0
Western Australia	55.0	63.5
South Australia	56.2	65.3
Northern Territory	54.7	62.2

Source: Gray unpub. b

Table 2.8   Aboriginal[a] and total Australian age-specific death rates and rate ratios,[b] 1985

Age group (years)	Males			Females		
	Aborigines	Total Australia	Rate ratio	Aborigines	Total Australia	Rate ratio
0–4	9.5	2.7	3.5	9.2	2.2	4.3
5–9	0.6	0.3	1.9	0.2	0.2	1.0
10–14	2.2	0.3	7.7	0.4	0.2	2.5
15–24	3.2	1.4	2.4	2.7	0.5	5.7
25–34	10.1	1.3	7.7	3.3	0.6	5.9
35–44	18.7	1.8	10.5	6.9	1.0	6.8
45–54	26.8	5.1	5.2	22.5	3.0	7.4
55–64	58.3	15.0	3.9	38.3	7.6	5.0
65+	94.8	61.0	1.6	75.9	45.6	1.7

Source
Australian Institute of Health, unpublished, from data supplied by the Queensland Department of Health, the Health Department of Western Australia and the Northern Territory Department of Health and Community Services

Notes
[a] The Aboriginal figures represent the combined data from the Queensland communities, Western Australia and the Northern Territory.
[b]Any discrepancy in the tabulated figures is due to rounding for presentation.

Causes of Aboriginal deaths

In 1985, for both Aboriginal males and females, the leading cause of death was disease of the circulatory system (International Classification of Diseases [ICD] 390–459) (see tables 2.9 and 2.10). Deaths from diseases in this ICD category, which includes heart diseases, were 2.2 times more frequent than expected for males, and 2.6 times for females.

The second leading cause of death for Aboriginal males, and third for females, was the ICD category 'External causes of injury and poisoning' (ICD E800–E999). Deaths in this category were 3.6 times more frequent than expected for Aboriginal males, and 4.3 times for females.

Diseases of the respiratory system (ICD 460–519), formerly the leading specific cause of death for Aborigines (Moodie 1973), now rank second for Aboriginal females, and third for males. However, whereas in the past the vast majority of Aboriginal deaths from diseases of the respiratory system were due to pneumonia and influenza (ICD 480–487), these diseases now contribute less than half the deaths certified in this category, with chronic respiratory conditions generally being at least as important (Hicks unpub.; Plant unpub.; Smith et al. 1983). Overall, for Aboriginal males, deaths from diseases of the respiratory system were 5.6 times more frequent than expected. For Aboriginal females, they were 7.7 times more frequent than expected.

Of increasing importance as causes of Aboriginal deaths are neoplasms (ICD 140–239), which now rank fourth for both males and females. Although contributing a much lower proportion of deaths among Aborigines than among other Australians, the actual number of Aboriginal deaths from neoplasms is slightly higher than the number expected from the age-specific rates of the total Australian population.

Table 2.9   Causes of male Aboriginal deaths: observed and expected death rates, and rate ratios

Cause of death	Observed rate	Expected rate	Rate[a] ratio
Circulatory system (ICD 390–459)	3.2	1.4	2.2
Injury and poisoning (ICD E800–E999)	2.2	0.6	3.6
Respiratory system (ICD 460–519)	1.7	0.3	5.6
Neoplasms (ICD 140–239)	1.0	0.8	1.3
Infectious and parasitic (ICD 001–139)	0.6	0.0	27.9
Conditions originating in perinatal period (ICD 760–799)	0.6	0.1	4.6
Mental disorders (ICD 290–319)	0.4	0.1	8.0
Digestive system (ICD 520–579)	0.4	0.1	3.4
Symptoms, signs and ill-defined conditions (ICD 780–779)	0.4	0.1	4.7
Other	1.6	0.4	4.5
All causes	12.2	3.9	3.2

Source
Australian Institute of Health, unpublished, from data supplied by the Queensland Department of Health, the Health Department of Western Australia and the Northern Territory Department of Health and Community Services

Notes
[a]Any discrepancy in the tabulated figures is due to rounding for presentation.

Table 2.10   Causes of female Aboriginal deaths: observed and expected death rates, and rate ratios

Cause of death	Observed rate	Expected rate	Rate[a] ratio
Circulatory system (ICD 390–459)	2.4	0.9	2.6
Respiratory system (ICD 460–519)	1.1	0.1	7.7
Injury and poisoning (ICD E800–E999)	0.9	0.2	4.3
Neoplasms (ICD 140–239)	0.9	0.5	1.7
Digestive system (ICD 520–579)	0.5	0.1	7.3
Endocrine, nutritional etc. disorders (ICD 240–279)	0.5	0.1	9.5
Infectious and parasitic (ICD 001–139)	0.4	0.0	19.4
Conditions originating in perinatal period (ICD 760–799)	0.4	0.1	3.8
Genito-urinary system (ICD 580–629)	0.3	0.0	8.7
Other	1.1	0.4	3.6
All causes	8.5	2.4	3.5

Source
Australian Institute of Health, unpublished, from data supplied by the Queensland Department of Health, the Health Department of Western Australia and the Northern Territory Department of Health and Community Services

Notes
[a] Any discrepancy in the tabulated figures is due to rounding for presentation.

The other causes of death warranting specific mention are the infectious and parasitic diseases (ICD 001–139). The impact of diseases in this composite category, including intestinal infectious diseases and tuberculosis, as well as a range of other bacterial, viral, rickettsial, fungal and parasitic diseases, has declined substantially over the last quarter of a century. In the past, these infectious causes of death, particularly some of the intestinal infectious diseases (commonly referred to as gastroenteritis and dysentery), were among the leading causes of death for Aborigines (Moodie 1973). Now ranking fifth for Aboriginal males, and seventh for females, these diseases are still much more frequent among Aborigines than among the general Australian population, for whom deaths from these diseases have become uncommon. The number of deaths documented for Aboriginal males was 28 times the number expected from the age-specific rates of the total population. For Aboriginal females, the number documented was 19 times the number expected.

Fetal and infant mortality

The infant mortality rate (deaths in the first year of life per 1000 live births) has been the focus of considerable attention since the documentation of rates of almost 150 infant deaths per 1000 live births for Aborigines in the Northern Territory in the 1960s. During the 1970s there was a steady and statistically significant decline in the Aboriginal infant mortality rate (Thomson 1983). As shown in table 2.11, since 1972–74 the infant mortality rates have declined substantially for Aborigines living in the Northern Territory and in the Queensland communities, from levels around 80 infant deaths per 1000 live births. The best estimate for Aborigines in Western Australia at about this time, produced by a special survey in 1971, was 76 infant deaths per 1000 live births. For each state/territory, the major decline occurred during the 1970s, and further improvements in the 1980s have been less impressive.

Figure 2.2 *Infant mortality is some three times higher for Aborigines than for other Australians, but it is still relatively low by world standards. Joanne Hooper and her baby pictured here live in West Bre (Dodge City) in the country town of Brewarrina in north-west New South Wales. (From P. Taylor, ed.,* After 200 years, *Aboriginal Studies Press, Canberra, 1988, p. 72; photo by S. Edwards)*

The infant mortality rate ratios have declined substantially from the initial levels, but, except for the Queensland communities, the ratios have remained fairly static since the late 1970s. For the most recent triennium, 1984–86, the rates are still between 2.3 times (Queensland communities) and 3.5 times (Northern Territory) the overall Australian rates for the period.

The key indicator of fetal outcome is the perinatal mortality rate, including late fetal deaths and deaths of live-born infants within the first 28 days of life. (Some caution needs to be used in comparing the figures quoted here with international figures, some of which relate only to late fetal deaths and deaths of live-born infants within the first seven days of life.)

Table 2.11   Infant mortality rates:[a, b] Aboriginal and total population, by triennium

	Aborigines			Total Australia
Triennium	Queensland[c] communities	Western Australia	Northern Territory	
1972–1974	78.4 (4.8)	n/a	74.3 (4.5)	16.5
1975–1977	58.3 (4.8)	n/a	59.0 (4.9)	12.1
1978–1980	33.9 (3.0)	27.6 (2.4)	43.0 (3.8)	11.4
1981–1983	29.4 (2.9)	23.1 (2.3)	35.4 (3.5)	10.0
1984–1986	21.3 (2.3)	25.0 (2.7)	32.5 (3.5)	9.3

Source
Australian Institute of Health, unpublished, from data supplied by the Queensland Department of Health, the Health Department of Western Australia and the Northern Territory Department of Health and Community Services

Notes
[a] Rates are infant deaths per 1000 live births.
[b] Numbers in parentheses are the Aboriginal/total population rate ratios.
[c] The Queensland data apply to the Aboriginal reserve communities.

Table 2.12 Perinatal mortality rates:[a, b] Aboriginal and total population, by triennium

| | Aborigines | | | |
| | | | | |
Triennium	Queensland[c] communities	Western Australia	Northern Territory	Total Australia
1972–1974	63.3 (2.7)	n/a	60.3 (2.6)	23.3
1975–1977	49.8 (2.6)	n/a	58.7 (3.0)	19.4
1978–1980	36.1 (2.4)	26.9 (1.8)	48.9 (3.2)	15.1
1981–1983	26.1 (2.0)	28.0 (2.2)	43.1 (3.3)	12.9
1984–1986	29.4 (2.5)	23.6 (2.0)	41.7 (3.6)	11.7

Source
Australian Institute of Health, unpublished, from data supplied by the Queensland Department of Health, the Health Department of Western Australia and the Northern Territory Department of Health and Community Services

Notes
[a] Rates are stillbirths plus neonatal deaths per 1000 total births (live births plus stillbirths).
[b] Numbers in parentheses are the Aboriginal/total population rate ratios.
[c] The Queensland data apply to the Aboriginal reserve communities

Aboriginal perinatal mortality rates have declined substantially since the early 1970s, but the recorded rates reveal that they have declined only at the same rate as that of the total population (see table 2.12).

While Aboriginal infant mortality remains about three times higher than that of other Australians, it is relatively low by world standards, being comparable with levels in the Soviet Union, Portugal, Yugoslavia and Korea (United Nations Children's Fund 1988). In contrast to overall mortality, the Aboriginal infant mortality rate is highest in the more remote areas of Australia, such as the Kimberley region of Western Australia and the Northern Territory, where it is around 30 infant deaths per 1000 live births.

Maternal mortality

For the 1982–84 triennium, the last period for which full data for Australia are available (NHMRC 1988), 8 Aboriginal deaths were identified among the total of 94 maternal deaths occurring in Australia. Of the 8 Aboriginal deaths, 5 (63 per cent) were attributed to direct causes, compared with 37 (43 per cent) of non-Aboriginal deaths (see NHMRC 1988 for definitions of direct and total maternal deaths).

Table 2.13 shows the number of direct and total maternal deaths for Aborigines and non-Aborigines for the 1982–84 triennium, along with data for the previous triennia. In 1982–84, the proportion of Aboriginal deaths (8.5 per cent) was much lower than in 1979–81 (15.3 per cent), but similar to the levels in earlier triennia: 1970–72, 7.4 per cent; 1973–75, 4.4 per cent; 1976–78, 8.5 per cent.

Although data are not available for the states or the Australian Capital Territory for the 1985–87 triennium, it is known that 6 Aboriginal maternal deaths occurred in the Northern Territory in this triennium (reported in the annual reports of the Northern Territory Department of Health and Community Services).

Complete data on all Aboriginal pregnancies, the appropriate denominator for the calculation of death rates, are not available. However, it is possible to make a rough estimate of the total number of Aboriginal confinements, based on the assumption that known Aboriginal birth rates apply to the total Aboriginal population. Table 2.14 shows the rates and rate ratios calculated from these estimates. Although rough estimates, they provide an indication of the differences between Aboriginal and non-Aboriginal people, revealing that Aboriginal death rates were three to five times those of non-Aboriginal people.

Of the Aboriginal maternal deaths occurring in 1982–84, one woman died from eclampsia, two from classical postpartum haemorrhage, two from ruptured uterus, and one from supine hypotension associated with a snake bite (NHMRC 1988). The causes of the other two Aboriginal deaths were not provided.

Table 2.13   Maternal deaths: Aboriginal and non-Aboriginal, by triennium

Triennium	Aboriginal deaths		Non-Aboriginal deaths	
	Direct	Total	Direct	Total
1970–1972	13	18	137	226
1973–1975	5	6	55	131
1976–1978	5	9	47	97
1979–1981	6	15	48	83
1982–1984	5	8	37	86

Source: NH&MRC 1988

Table 2.14   Maternal death rates[a] and rate ratios, Aboriginal and non-Aboriginal deaths, 1982–84

	Aboriginal	Non-Aboriginal	Rate ratio
Direct[b]	24.3	5.3	4.6
Total[b]	38.9	12.3	3.2

Source: NH&MRC 1988

Notes
[a] The maternal death rates have been estimated according to the current NHMRC method: maternal deaths per 100 000 confinements.
[b] See source for definition of direct and total deaths.

Hospitalisation

While not necessarily accurately reflecting the extent or pattern of treatable illness in the community, hospital statistics, generally reflecting more serious types of morbidity, confirm the relatively poor health status of Aborigines, both in terms of the rate of hospitalisation and the length of stay in hospital.

Overall, Aborigines are admitted to hospital two-and-a-half to three times more frequently than non-Aborigines, and, once admitted, tend to stay slightly longer. They are admitted more frequently for virtually every cause, and for every age-group, than are non-Aborigines. However, hospital separation practices (discharges, transfers and deaths) are influenced by many factors, including state/territory variations in admission policies and differential geographic accessibility of hospitals, so separation data must be interpreted with caution.

Separation rates

The combined separation data (data on hospital admissions and discharges) for Aborigines and non-Aborigines living in Western Australia, South Australia and the Northern Territory, directly standardised using the World Standard Population as the reference population, reveal that the Aboriginal male separation rate of 431 per 1000 was 2.5 times that of non-Aboriginal males, which was 169 per 1000 (see table 2.15). The rate for Aboriginal females, 563 per 1000, was 2.8 times the non-Aboriginal rate, which was 200 per 1000.

The combined data, however, conceal significant regional differences in both Aboriginal and non-Aboriginal separation rates (see table 2.15). After allowing for the overall differences in separation rates between Western Australia and South Australia, Aboriginal separations were around three times more frequent than non-Aboriginal separations in those states. For the Northern Territory, the Aboriginal/non-Aboriginal separation rate ratio was 1.6 for both males and females. While non-Aboriginal separation rates for the Northern Territory were intermediate between those for the two states, the Aboriginal rates were substantially lower. Judging from other measures of health status, it would appear that these lower rates are most probably due to the relative geographic inaccessibility for many Aborigines of the five public acute hospitals in the Northern Territory.

Age-specific separation rates

Whereas the highest separation rates for non-Aborigines occurred for older people, for Aborigines the highest rates were for infants and young children in the 0–4 year age group (both males and females) (see table 2.16). The next highest rate ratios for Aborigines were found among young and middle-aged adults (age group 35–44 years for males, and 45–54 years for females). Aboriginal separations were higher than those of non-Aborigines for all age groups.

Table 2.15   Standardised hospital separation rates[a]: Aboriginal and non-Aboriginal population, by sex and state/territory[b]

	Males			Females		
	Aboriginal	*Non-Aboriginal*	*Rate ratio*	*Aboriginal*	*Non-Aboriginal*	*Rate ratio*
Western Australia	541	191	2.8	744	234	3.2
South Australia	465	147	3.2	514	164	3.1
Northern Territory	286	179	1.6	345	219	1.6
Total	431	169	2.5	563	200	2.8

Source
Australian Institute of Health, unpublished, from data supplied by the Health Department of Western Australia, the South Australian Health Commission and the Northern Territory Department of Health and Community Services

Notes
[a] The rates, directly standardised using the World Standard Population as the reference population, are expressed as separations per 1000 population.
[b] Reliable comprehensive separation data for Aborigines are not available from the other states and the Australian Capital Territory.

Table 2.16 Age-specific hospital separation rates[a] and rate ratios[b]: Aboriginal and non-Aboriginal population, by sex

Age group (years)	Males			Females		
	Aboriginal	Non-Aboriginal	Rate ratio	Aboriginal	Non-Aboriginal	Rate ratio
0–4	929	241	3.9	826	173	4.8
5–14	168	95	1.8	160	76	2.1
15–24	195	108	1.8	589	219	2.7
25–34	337	110	3.1	684	306	2.2
35–44	445	120	3.7	494	185	2.7
45–54	489	174	2.8	735	191	3.9
55–64	635	261	2.4	592	224	2.6
65+	686	487	1.4	741	359	2.1

Source
Australian Institute of Health, unpublished, from data supplied by the Health Department of Western Australia, the South Australian Health Commission and the Northern Territory Department of Health and Community Services

Notes
[a] The rates are expressed as separations per 1000 population.
[b] Any discrepancy in the tabulated figures is due to rounding for presentation.

Causes of hospitalisation

From the combined data for Western Australia (1986), South Australia (1986) and the Northern Territory (1984), the leading causes of hospitalisation for Aboriginal males were conditions classified within the ICD group 'external causes of injury and poisoning' (ICD E800–E999), with a standardised separation rate of 79.4 per 1000 population, 2.7 times the non-Aboriginal rate of 29.6 per 1000 (see table 2.17). The second highest rate was for diseases of the respiratory system, with a standardised separation rate of 69.8 per 1000 population, 3.7 times the non-Aboriginal rate of 18.9 per 1000. After the miscellaneous ICD group, 'symptoms and ill-defined conditions', the group 'infectious and parasitic diseases' (including gastroenteritis) was the next most frequent cause of hospitalisation, with 34.8 separations per 1000, 9.1 times the non-Aboriginal rate of 3.8 per 1000.

For Aboriginal females, the leading cause of hospitalisation was the ICD supplementary classification, which includes a number of conditions associated with reproductive function, such as normal pregnancy, contraceptive management, procreative screening, antenatal screening, and healthy live births (see table 2.18). The separation rate for this category was 94.1 per 1000 population, 4.0 times the non-Aboriginal rate of 23.4 per 1000. The next leading cause was the ICD group 'complications of pregnancy, childbirth, and the puerperium' with a separation rate of 75.0 per 1000, 2.0 times the non-Aboriginal rate of 38.1 per 1000. The ICD category 'external causes of injury and poisoning' was the third most frequent reason for hospitalisation, being responsible for 64.7 separations per 1000, 3.7 times the non-Aboriginal rate of 17.6 per 1000. Diseases of the respiratory system were responsible for 62.1 separations per 1000, 4.4 times the non-Aboriginal rate of 14.3 per 1000.

Table 2.17 Causes of male hospital separations[a]: Aboriginal and non-Aboriginal standardised separation rates[b] and rate ratios[c]

Cause	Aboriginal	Non-Aboriginal	Rate ratio
Injury and poisoning (ICD E800–E999)	79.4	29.6	2.7
Respiratory system (ICD 460–519)	69.8	18.9	3.7
Symptoms, signs and ill-defined conditions (ICD 780–779)	42.7	13.6	3.1
Infectious and parasitic (ICD 001–139)	34.8	3.8	9.1
Nervous system and sense organs (ICD 320–389)	28.7	9.2	3.1
Skin and subcutaneous tissues (ICD 680–709)	27.6	4.0	6.8
Digestive system (ICD 520–579)	26.7	18.2	1.5
Other causes	89.7	56.5	1.6
All causes	430.5	169.0	2.5

Source
Australian Institute of Health, unpublished, from data supplied by the Health Department of Western Australia, the South Australian Health Commission and the Northern Territory Department of Health and Community Services

Notes
[a] Figures for both Aborigines and non-Aborigines represent the combined data for Western Australia 1986, South Australia 1986 and the Northern Territory 1984.
[b] The rates, directly standardised using the World Standard Population as the reference population, are expressed as separations per 1000 population.
[c] Any discrepancy in the tabulated figures is due to rounding for presentation.

Table 2.18 Causes of female hospital separations[a]: Aboriginal and non-Aboriginal standardised separation rates[b] and rate ratios[c]

Cause	Aboriginal	Non-Aboriginal	Rate ratio
Supplementary classification (ICD V01–V82)	94.1	23.4	4.0
Complications of pregnancy etc. (ICD 630–676)	75.0	38.1	2.0
Injury and poisoning (ICD E800–E999)	64.7	17.6	3.7
Respiratory system (ICD 460–519)	62.1	14.3	4.4
Symptoms, signs and ill-defined conditions (ICD 780–779)	47.3	14.0	3.4
Genito-urinary system (ICD 580–629)	42.2	20.6	2.0
Infectious and parasitic (ICD 001–139)	33.9	4.1	8.3
Skin and subcutaneous tissues (ICD 680–709)	22.8	3.4	6.7
Nervous system and sense organs (ICD 320–389)	22.9	8.8	2.6
Other causes	93.3	56.8	1.6
All causes	562.6	199.9	2.8

Source
Australian Institute of Health, unpublished, from data supplied by the Health Department of Western Australia, the South Australian Health Commission and the Northern Territory Department of Health and Community Services

Notes
[a] Figures for both Aborigines and non-Aborigines represent the combined data for Western Australia 1986, South Australia 1986 and the Northern Territory 1984.
[b] The rates, directly standardised using the World Standard Population as the reference population, are expressed as separations per 1000 population.
[c] Any discrepancy in the tabulated figures is due to rounding for presentation.

Duration of hospitalisation

The duration of hospital stay has generally been reported as longer for Aborigines than for non-Aborigines. The most recent estimate, for Western Australia for 1986, reported that Aboriginal patients spent an average of 6.5 days in hospital for each separation, compared with an average of 5.9 days for non-Aborigines (HDWA 1987*b*). Separate figures for each sex were not provided. Based on more complete information, for Western Australia for 1983, the average stay for Aboriginal males was 7.2 days, compared with 6.2 days for non-Aboriginal males. For females, the average stay for Aborigines was 6.9 days, compared with 6.5 days for non-Aborigines. After allowing for the different age structures of the populations, the average duration of hospitalisation for Aboriginal males was 1.5 times longer than expected (Thomson 1986*c*). For Aboriginal females, the average duration was 1.4 times longer than expected.

Aborigines living in rural areas of South Australia in 1982 had an average duration of hospital stay of 6.7 days; in urban areas the average stay was 5.4 days (Hart n. d.). For the fourth quarter of 1980, Aborigines in the Northern Territory had an average stay of 9.6 days, compared with 5.2 days for non-Aborigines (Northern Territory Department of Health 1980). In contrast to the other areas, in country regions of New South Wales in 1977 the average duration of hospital stay for Aborigines was 7.8 days, compared with 9.7 days for non-Aborigines (Armstrong 1979).

A recent Australia-wide study of hospital utilisation has provided some indirect estimates of duration of stay for 1985–86 (Mathers and Harvey 1988). For Western Australia, the average duration of stay for Aborigines was estimated at 6.0 days, compared with 6.1 days for non-Aborigines; for South Australia, the average duration of stay for Aborigines was estimated at 5.8 days, compared with 6.5 days for non-Aborigines; and, for the Northern Territory, the average Aboriginal duration of stay was estimated at 9.2 days, compared with 5.1 days for non-Aborigines.

Sickness and disease

Growth and nutrition

Throughout their lives, many Aborigines suffer from major disorders of nutrition and growth (see Harrison, chapter 4 in this volume). In fetal life, infancy, childhood and the first years of adulthood these disorders present characteristically as poor growth, in terms of both height and weight (Thomson unpub.).

As shown in table 2.4, babies born to Aboriginal women are substantially lighter than those born to non-Aboriginal women. Most significantly, the proportion of babies of low birth weight born to Aboriginal women is more than twice that of babies born to non-Aboriginal women. The available data suggest that there have been, at most, only slight improvements over recent years (see 'Birth weight'). The lower birth weights of babies born to Aboriginal women, most likely reflecting the relatively poor health and nutritional status of Aboriginal mothers, and their greater exposure to a number of risk factors (Gracey et al. 1984), have clear implications for postnatal growth.

From birth, the growth of most Aboriginal infants is satisfactory until breast milk becomes insufficient by itself, at which time they become more directly exposed to the substandard environment in which many Aborigines live. At this time in life, they become vulnerable to a wide range of infections, related to unhygienic living conditions and high levels of environmental contamination (Gracey 1987), in many cases entering the vicious synergistic cycle of infection–malnutrition. Many Aborigines carry this legacy of impaired growth into early adulthood, where it has its major impact on the health of mothers and of the next generation (Gracey et al. 1984) (see also 'Kylie's first two years').

From the early adult years, many Aborigines start to gain weight excessively, eventually becoming overweight or obese (Thomson unpub.). The weight gain is generally related to relative physical inactivity and a high intake of highly refined carbohydrates and, not infrequently, alcohol (Gracey et al. 1984). Associated with the high levels of obesity in adulthood, there now are alarming levels of the lifestyle diseases, particularly diabetes mellitus, hypertension, and coronary heart disease, previously virtually non-existent among Aborigines.

Diabetes mellitus

An important consequence of the present high levels of obesity among many Aboriginal groups is the emergence of a new health problem—diabetes mellitus—a disease unlikely to have been present to any great extent among Aborigines living a hunter-gatherer lifestyle. It is likely that the prevalence of diabetes among Aborigines lies between about 7.5 per cent and 16 per cent. These levels compare with a prevalence of diabetes of 3.4 per cent for non-Aborigines in Busselton, Western Australia, in 1980 (Glatthaar et al. 1985).

The complications of diabetes, particularly retinopathy and peripheral neuropathy, are at least as common among Aborigines as among non-Aborigines Stanton et al. 1985). (See also Harrison, chapter 4 in this volume.)

Circulatory system disorders

Diseases of the circulatory system have become the leading causes of death for Aborigines, as they are for non-Aborigines (see tables 2.9 and 2.10). However, the situation is much worse for Aborigines. Not only are overall death rates for Aborigines substantially higher than non-Aboriginal rates, they are between 10 and 20 times higher for young and middle-aged adults (Thomson unpub).

While the relativity of the specific causes of circulatory system disorders differs significantly between areas, overall deaths are caused predominantly by degenerative changes to the circulatory system, such as ischaemic heart disease, heart failure and cerebrovascular disease. In the more remote areas of Australia, rheumatic heart disease is still responsible for a significant number of deaths among Aborigines.

In contrast to early surveys, which reported relatively low blood pressures among Aborigines (see Moodie 1981 for a detailed review of a number of surveys from 1926), recent surveys generally have found blood pressure levels higher than among non-Aborigines. However, these levels are not uniformly higher, and the largest recent survey, of 1705 Aborigines throughout South Australia, concluded

Kylie's first two years

Kylie* was born in the obstetric ward of the Derby Regional Hospital, Western Australia, on 5 November 1987. Her mother had been transferred there three weeks previously from the nursing post in Lizard Flat, which serves her community of 300 people at Emu Creek, on the edge of the Great Sandy Desert. She had driven 60 kilometres into Lizard Flat in the community's four-wheel drive vehicle and waited there for two days for the 290-kilometre journey into Derby on the flying doctor plane. Kylie's mother had already given birth to three children in the Derby hospital, one of whom had died at 10 days of age of an overwhelming respiratory infection. When Kylie was born, her mother was 24 years old, 160 centimetres tall and weighed 48 kilograms.

*Not her real name.

Kylie weighed 2.95 kilograms at birth and was transferred home when she was one week old. She was a chubby, happy baby, who was breast-fed and grew well until she was 5 months old, when she developed a cold and loose, frequent stools and began feeding poorly. She was feverish, fretful and unhappy. Some of the other children in the Lizard Flat camp had similar illnesses. The community chairman thought the illnesses were due to the hot weather, recent thunderstorms and the blocked toilets, which were overflowing; the community had been waiting three weeks for the toilets to be fixed. He also blamed the high levels of illness in the community's children on the large numbers of diseased and mangy dogs that roamed around

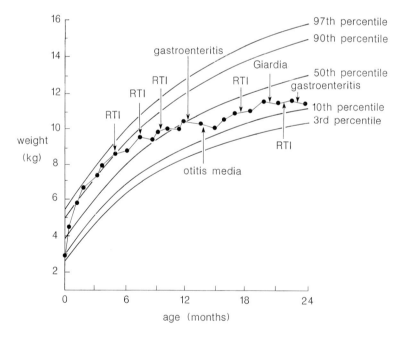

Figure 2.3 *Kylie's growth chart from birth to 2 years old, showing her main illnesses: respiratory tract infection (RTI), gastroenteritis, otitis media and giardiasis. Kylie shows the common Aboriginal growth pattern: adequate growth in the first 6 to 8 months, followed by faltering growth associated with repeated episodes of infections and, eventually, 'failure to thrive' and undernutrition. The 97th, 90th, 50th, 10th and 3rd percentile weight-for-age curves are shown (WHO reference values); the 50th percentile is the median value.*

the camp. Many of the dogs belonged to the old people, who were very reluctant to get rid of them.

The Aboriginal health worker arranged for Kylie to be admitted to the nursing post at Lizard Flat. When she and two other sick children and their mothers and other relatives arrived in an old Toyota, the doctor was away on flying clinics for the rest of the day. The senior nurse at the nursing post arranged for the sick children and their mothers to be taken the 290 kilometres to the regional hospital at Derby by ambulance: it was late at night by the time they arrived. Kylie spent two weeks in the children's ward before she was discharged and sent home. That was the first of five hospital admissions, mostly for respiratory tract infections, before she was two years of age; in all, she spent 9 weeks in hospital during that time.

It took months for Kylie to recover from these bouts of sickness. In fact, she never regained the chubby, happy appearance that she had before her first hospital admission. She looked scrawny and unhappy, her nose was always running, she often had sore ears and was given repeated courses of antibiotics for respiratory infections. When she was admitted to hospital, it was usually because the treatments available at the nursing post 'didn't seem to work'. The fact that her sibling had died of a respiratory infection put more pressure on nursing staff to admit Kylie to hospital.

Although Kylie was on a full diet and shared meals with the rest of her family, and was still sucking at the breast, her weight gain seemed to be unsatisfactory. The Aboriginal health worker showed Kylie's mother how her daughter's growth pattern had 'fallen off' the pattern expected for her age (see figure 2.3). From about 6 to 8 months of age, many other children in the Lizard Flat camp had also begun to show a similar, unsatisfactory growth pattern, which persisted at least through the first two years of life.

A new community nurse had recently arrived from Melbourne. She said that Kylie had 'failure to thrive' and the locum doctor arranged for Kylie to see the paediatrician the next time she came with the flying doctor plane from Derby on her two-monthly round of clinic consultations. The paediatrician had seen Kylie before when she had been in hospital in Derby. She arranged for some investigations to be carried out, including a blood film, x-rays and sputum culture. Kylie's blood showed that she was moderately anaemic and had eosinophilia. The appearance of the red blood cells suggested that the anaemia was due to iron deficiency; the iron deficiency was probably the result of a combination of inadequate diet, her mother's use of an unfortified powdered cow's milk preparation to feed Kylie after her first hospital admission plus the extra demands put on her by repeated infections. The eosinophilia was probably due to intestinal parasites. In her first two years, Kylie had two courses of Flagyl for the parasite *Giardia lamblia*, which is endemic in some Aboriginal communities and is thought to be a major cause of diarrhoea and failure to thrive. Although Kylie was given some iron-containing mixtures to treat her anaemia, her haemoglobin remained below 11 g/dL. Her sputum cultures grew various micro-organisms including *Escherichia coli*, *Staphylococcus aureus*, streptococci and *Haemophilus influenzae*.

Kylie's growth curve (see figure 2.3) showed that she never achieved satisfactory 'catch up' growth in her first two years after the deficits which had occurred starting with her respiratory tract infection at 5 months of age. Her mother decided not to have any more babies; she said she'd had too much trouble already, especially as her man was 'always in trouble in town' and 'didn't give [her] enough money to look after the kids properly'.

Michael Gracey, Aboriginal Health Policy Unit, Health Department of Western Australia, Perth

that high blood pressure was 'no more a problem among Aboriginals than among the general Australian population' (AHOSA n. d., p. 68).

Circulatory system disease highlights the complexities of Aboriginal health inequalities, with Aborigines experiencing those diseases more often associated with developing countries, such as rheumatic heart disease, as well as those more often associated with developed countries, such as ischaemic heart disease.

Respiratory disorders

Respiratory system disease has probably claimed more Aboriginal lives over the past 200 years than any other cause, and even today remains one of the leading causes of death (see tables 2.9 and 2.10). Morbidity from respiratory disease is an important cause of significant illness in the Aboriginal community (see tables 2.17 and 2.18).

The most marked differences between Aborigines and non-Aborigines occur with the infective respiratory diseases, but, in terms of both mortality and hospital separation rates, the level of chronic respiratory disease is also substantially higher for Aborigines than for non-Aborigines.

The pathogenesis of respiratory disease among Aborigines is multifactorial, with biological, environmental and lifestyle factors all playing significant roles. The poor nutritional status of many Aborigines, particularly children, is likely to be of central importance, but substandard housing and the high prevalence of smoking also make substantial contributions. The actual contribution of the relative inaccessibility, for many Aborigines, of medical and health services is less clear.

As with other aspects of Aboriginal ill-health, it is most unlikely that the elimination of the respiratory disease differentials between Aborigines and other Australians will occur until the differentials in nutrition, housing and lifestyle factors are largely eliminated.

Ear disease

The high level of chronic ear disease among Aborigines, particularly children, does not appear to have decreased over the last 15 to 20 years, despite the great attention paid to the problem (Bear 1985). The prevalence of perforations of the eardrum (generally between 10 per cent and 30 per cent) and of hearing loss (generally between 10 per cent and 40 per cent) among Aborigines is particularly high, and almost certainly much higher than for non-Aborigines, among whom the extent of these disorders is unknown (Thomson unpub).

However, whereas there does not appear to have been much progress either in understanding the aetiology of the disorder or in reducing its prevalence, greater and more encouraging attention has been paid to its well-recognised major complication—hearing loss significant enough to interfere with education, particularly in the delayed acquisition of language skills (Lewis 1976; Stuart et al. 1972).

Eye disorders

The prevalence of preventable eye disorders among Aborigines is unacceptably high, and an increased commitment is needed if the 'overburden of avoidable blindness' (Royal Australian College of Ophthalmologists 1980, p. 100) is to be substantially reduced.

Between 1976 and 1979, the National Trachoma and Eye Health Program surveyed almost 62 000 Aborigines and more than 38 000 non-Aborigines, largely in rural and remote areas Australia. The program found that the proportion of blindness for the Aborigines examined was 15 per 1000, compared with 2 per 1000 for non-Aborigines (blindness was defined as a visual acuity of no better than 6/60 in either eye, the level of vision entitling a person to a blindness invalid pension). Of the people examined aged 60 years or more, 1 in every 5 Aborigines was blind, compared with about 1 in every 20 non-Aborigines, and the latter figure was noted as possibly higher than in the general Australian population. A large proportion of the avoidable blindness among Aborigines was secondary to trachoma, a form of conjunctivitis caused by the bacterium, *Chlamydia trachomatis.*

Overall, 38 per cent of the Aborigines examined showed signs of trachoma, either follicular or cicatricial or both, compared with only 1.7 per cent of the non-Aborigines examined. The extent of the severe forms, particularly of cicatricial trachoma, is clearly implicated in the high level of avoidable blindness described above. A review undertaken in 1985 found that the overall prevalence and severity of both follicular and cicatricial trachoma among Aborigines had declined by between 20 and 40 per cent since 1976–79, but that the reduction in follicular trachoma, in particular, was not uniform, with the prevalence actually increasing in a number of communities.

The present level of the disease among Aborigines is still unacceptably high, and efforts to eradicate it need to be intensified. The program confirmed the totally substandard conditions in which many Aborigines in rural Australia live. To effect the needed massive reductions in the prevalence and severity of trachoma, substantial improvements in these conditions are necessary. The cornerstone of appropriate strategies was seen as community-based action, including the provision of health-related hardware to permit improvements in personal hygiene (Hollows 1985; Taylor 1987). Accompanying this community-based action, the treatment and surveillance campaigns need to be maintained, and probably expanded, for some time, if this potentially sight-threatening disease is to be eliminated.

If further reductions in the level and severity of trachoma can be achieved, it is probable that diabetic retinopathy will become the most frequent threat to the vision of many Aborigines. To date, little work has been undertaken into this condition. Clearly, this aspect needs to be addressed urgently, in order to assess accurately the potential impact, and to develop prevention and treatment strategies.

Specific communicable diseases

Despite the emergence of ischaemic heart disease as the leading cause of Aboriginal mortality, a number of communicable diseases continue to have a much greater impact among Aborigines than among other Australians.

Invasive childhood diseases

The most dramatic of the other communicable diseases are the invasive diseases of childhood, which, although uncommon, illustrate well the health disadvantages experienced by Aborigines. For example, an exceptionally high incidence of invasive disease caused by *Haemophilus influenzae* has been documented for young Aboriginal children in Central Australia (J. Hanna, pers. comm.; Hansman et al. 1986). For Aboriginal children aged up to 5 years in 1985–86, the average annual incidence of invasive *H. influenzae* disease was estimated at 990 cases per 100 000 (Hanna unpub..), much higher than for non-Aboriginal children in central Australia (350 per 100 000). These levels contrast with the very much lower incidence documented for children of the same age group admitted to the Adelaide Children's Hospital, which was 30 per 100 000 (Hansman et al. 1986). The incidence among these Aboriginal children is exceptionally high, even by world standards, being more than twice as high as that documented for the dispossessed Eskimos of southern Alaska and the Navajo Native Americans of New Mexico (Hansman et al. 1986).

Meningitis accounted for 37 per cent of all diagnoses of invasive *H. influenzae* disease, with bacteremia and pneumonia being the other diagnoses (Hanna unpub.; Hansman et al. 1986). Interestingly, there were no cases of epiglottitis, the other severe form of invasive disease found in non-Aboriginal children. The case-fatality rate for invasive *H. influenzae* disease was 3.7 per cent. The other striking aspect of the epidemiology of the disease was that, as found in developing countries, a significant proportion (15 per cent) of the cases were caused by strains other than type B, the strain responsible for virtually all of the disease occurring among non-Aborigines in Australia.

Over 70 per cent of the cases occurred in infants (less than 12 months of age), and there was a slight female preponderance (Hanna unpub.). Environmental crowding and other adverse socioeconomic factors were seen as likely to be of importance in the pathogenesis of the disease (Hanna unpub.; Hansman et al. 1986).

For all causes of juvenile meningitis admitted to the Alice Springs Hospital in the period 1981–86, the average annual incidence for Aborigines was 568 per 100 000, 'as high as any previously reported worldwide', and very much higher than the non-Aboriginal incidence of 56 per 100 000 (McIntyre and Erlich unpub.).

Of the cases in which a causative agent was identified, 38 (59 per cent) were caused by *Haemophilus influenzae*, 14 (22 per cent) by *Streptococcus pneumoniae*, three by *Neisseria meningitidis*, one by *Pseudomonas aeruginosa* and one by *Cryptococcus neoformans* (McIntyre and Erlich unpub). Unfortunately, this breakdown did not differentiate between Aborigines and non-Aborigines.

More recently, central Australia (including the southern areas of the Northern Territory and neighbouring parts of Western and South Australia) experienced an epidemic of disease caused by *Neisseria meningitidis*, a pattern of this disease most typically seen in developing countries (Cook 1988; Hanna et al. 1988; Hansman 1983). This contrasts with the endemic form of the disease more generally found in western industrialised countries like Australia, and usually caused by organisms of the B or C serogroups (Cook 1988; Hansman 1983).

Between the middle of 1987 and the middle of 1988, 23 cases, all Aboriginal, were identified at the Alice Springs, Kalgoorlie and Tennant Creek hospitals (Hanna et al. 1988). In line with the epidemic pattern (Cook 1988), a large proportion of the cases (78 per cent) occurred among people aged 5 years or more, with serogroup A being the most frequently isolated serotype (Hanna et al. 1988). It is understood (Hanna et al. 1988) that the epidemic commenced in the Pilbara region of Western Australia (for which no details have been published), and then moved to central Australia.

Tuberculosis

In contrast to these acute diseases of childhood, a number of the 'old' communicable diseases such as tuberculosis (probably the leading cause of death in

Figure 2.4 *Invasive childhood diseases have a higher incidence among Aboriginal than among non-Aboriginal children. (M. Brady)*

the late nineteenth century for Aborigines in many parts of the country) still occur much more frequently among Aborigines than non-Aborigines. In 1984, the last year for which there are national data, the average incidence among Aborigines was between 15 and 20 times that of other Australians (Penny and Thomson 1987). The higher incidence of tuberculosis among Aborigines is probably related to poor housing, malnutrition, other chronic chest diseases and alcohol abuse.

Leprosy

Ever since its introduction into Australia in the late nineteenth century (Hargrave 1980), leprosy has always been primarily a disease affecting Aborigines (although some non-Aborigines are also affected), and the bulk of the cases have occurred in the Northern Territory, the northern half of Western Australia, and, to a lesser extent, northern Queensland.

Despite the fact that the annual number of notifications among Aborigines has declined significantly over the past decade, for the period 1984–86 Aborigines still accounted for more than a quarter of all new cases reported in Australia. There were 26 new cases among Aborigines. Of the 66 new cases reported for non-Aborigines, about half were reported for recent arrivals to Australia, particularly refugees from South-East Asia. The persistence of leprosy among Aborigines highlights the great differences in health status between Aborigines and other Australians.

Leprosy in the Northern Territory

No-one who travels along the north coast of Australia can fail to be impressed with its isolation. There are a few small settlements and missions, but throughout the entire length Darwin, with a population of about 75 000 people, and Nhulunbuy, with about 3000, are the only major towns in existence to this day. The rest of the coast is flanked by low hills, rough scrub and kilometre upon kilometre of uninhabited low-lying swampy mangrove country. Inland there is a gradual transition from scrub to broken rocky outcrops, wide semi-arid plains and finally desert. During the north-west monsoon season, however, travel by land is almost impossible away from the sealed highways.

There are now about 33 000 Aborigines in the Northern Territory belonging to more than 80 different groups. The area they occupy is approximately 1.3 million square kilometres. Before white settlement, only small groups of people occupied any given area and contact between groups was rare apart from ceremonies and other significant occasions, such as a birth or death. Moreover, these small groups were in turn split into smaller family groups and subgroups.

About the middle of the last century, change came with settlement of Europeans and Asians on the north coast. These people introduced leprosy to the Northern Territory. A similar situation existed in Western Australia and Queensland, but in Queensland early cases were found in Pacific Islanders. Today leprosy is endemic throughout the northern half of the Northern Territory, particularly in Arnhem Land, and the Kimberley region of Western Australia. A few cases still appear in Queensland. Most cases are now inactive following treatment, but in recent years there has been a very slow peripheral spread to involve some of the desert groups as well.

When the first cases of leprosy were recognised, steps were taken to isolate patients. Aborigines soon became adept in diagnosis themselves. Their remedy was different from that of the Europeans: they carefully hid their infected relatives in the bush and cared for them in remote parts of the country. For the infected, the results were just about the same: isolated by Europeans, they died or were never seen again; if they were hidden by their own people, they died or became deformed. The important thing to the Aborigines,

then and now, was that they died in their own ancestral territory.

Leprosy is caused by *Mycobacterium leprae*, which closely resembles the tubercle bacillus. However, the leprosy bacillus attacks the skin, the mucous membrane of the nose and above all, the peripheral nerves. Its destruction of the peripheral nerves leads to sensory loss and paralysis of muscles in the eyes, hands and feet. Sensory loss and paralysis lead to the serious deformity commonly associated with leprosy.

Most Aborigines are still quite unaware of the cause of the disease. Some stockmen believe that the claw-hand of leprosy is caused by pulling too hard on the reins of a hard-mouthed horse; foot drop is attributed to injury; others believe that ulcers are caused by walking in rough bush country, as indeed they are in people who have no feeling in their feet; deformities occurring in early life are generally thought to be congenital; some blame eating of fish; others believe their enemies have caused their illness through magic or sorcery; yaws, ringworm, birthmarks and dermatitis are jumbled together with other signs and symptoms; some believe that it is a punishment for an error they have made in disposing of the dead; others do not philosophise at all. The concept of passing infection from one person to another is often not understood or believed, but there is a recognition that leprosy is an entity. Most are aware that certain well-known presenting signs previously presaged either isolation or deformity. Some call it 'the big sickness'. The rest of the world has taken centuries to classify patients into infectious and non-infectious groups; indecision and argument have preceded every change in policy, even in recent years. It is small wonder, then, that Aborigines have been hesitant in accepting new and changing ideas about the disease. If they know they have leprosy, they often conceal it but, unlike the rest of the world, seldom attach any stigma to it.

It was not until the end of the Second World War that ideas about leprosy began to change, when sulphones were first used in its treatment. Although they had been discovered years before, they were not used because of their toxicity in large doses. A comparatively small dose was found to be effective and, as soon as a satisfactory dosage regimen had been worked out, the benefits became so obvious that sulphones were heralded as 'miracle drugs'. Patients who had shown no clinical improvement for years began to recover and tentative moves made to treat people in the bush met with a gratifying response. Whereas the prospect of enforced isolation in hospital far from home resulted in concealment, patients now began to present for treatment. In turn this led to further liberalisation of the once strict policy: infectious patients were not necessarily isolated at all, or at most for only a short time, and were able to receive visits from their relatives.

It was gradually realised that the sulphones did little to change or prevent the deformities traditionally associated with leprosy. Patients who also realised this tended to look on these drugs as useless and in some cases the sulphones fell into an undeserved disrepute. More recently, other valuable drugs have been discovered that prevent complications and quickly render patients non-infectious.Basic scientific research in India established the fact that deformity is directly related to peripheral nerve lesions. As already mentioned, destruction of these nerves is now known to be responsible for paralysis and loss of sensation in the limbs and the eyes. Whilst sensation is rarely restored by treatment, it has been possible to teach patients to protect their insensitive hands, feet and eyes from injury. In the case of paralysis, reconstructive operations are used to replace paralysed muscles and tendons with active ones, so that useful function is restored.

In summary, the discovery of the sulphones and other drugs, a liberal policy and surgical reconstruction of deformity have all helped to produce an atmosphere of cooperation from which rational measures may be taken to control leprosy in northern Australia. Gradually the public has become aware that not all leprosy is infectious and that it need not be attended by gross mutilation and social ostracism. Aborigines do not ostracise patients. On the contrary, they go out of their way to help them and to care for them when they can no longer care for themselves. It is therefore important that the general Australian population should not stigmatise Aborigines with leprosy and that medical services aimed at treating leprosy should be integrated with other health services. Nurses in rural areas should be prepared to treat leprosy and all other ills in the same clinics, in the same wards and under similar circumstances. In this way, they can provide a sound basis for the education of patients and for cooperation, without which success is impossible. Education is one of the most important duties of Aboriginal health workers, who are now taking over the care and control of leprosy among Aborigines. They are the people who see the disease where others do not, and they are the people who will ultimately determine the success of the whole leprosy program.

John Hargrave, Royal Darwin Hospital, Darwin

Sexually transmitted diseases

A number of sexually transmitted diseases, particularly syphilis and gonorrhoea, have emerged as major health problems for Aborigines in many parts of Australia. Unfortunately, as with information about many other health problems, most data relate to Aborigines living in remote and rural areas of the country. Little has been documented about the prevalence of these diseases for the majority of Aborigines, who live in less remote areas of Australia. The current notification rate for Aborigines in the Northern Territory is some 60 times that for non-Aborigines, and the disease is also known to be much more frequent among Aborigines living in the Kimberley region of Western Australia, and in at least some of Queensland Aboriginal communities (Thomson, unpub.).

Information about gonorrhoea is less comprehensive, but notifications for Aborigines in the Northern Territory have shown a substantial increase over the past decade, with notification rates for Aborigines now being about four times those of non-Aborigines (Devanesen et al. 1986; NTDHCS 1987*a*). In 1985 and 1986, the rate of notifications among Aborigines was much higher in central Australia than in the

Darwin or Katherine regions, and the rate for the east Arnhem Land region was lower than the overall rate for non-Aborigines.

Even less is known about other sexually transmitted diseases, but granuloma inguinale still occurs sporadically among Aborigines. Genital infection with *Chlamydia trachomatis* appears less frequent among Aboriginal women than among non-Aboriginal women (Thomson unpub.). However, its occurrence is enough to justify an active anti-chlamydial program in Queensland (Queensland Health and Medical Services 1986). Genital herpes appears to be less prevalent among Aborigines than among non-Aborigines in the Northern Territory (NTDHCS 1987*a*).

Sexual intercourse is an important means of transmission in two other communicable diseases: hepatitis B virus (HBV) and human immunodeficiency virus (HIV), which is responsible for the acquired immune deficiency syndrome (AIDS). There is widespread evidence of the exposure of Aborigines to hepatitis B virus, with the prevalence of serological markers of HBV ranging from 23 to 90 per cent (Thomson unpub.). More important, the prevalence of chronic carriers, evidenced by the presence of hepatitis B surface antigen (HBsAg), ranges from around 3 to 26 per cent. For virtually all regions for which data are known, the prevalence of HBsAg was above, or around the borderline of, the high risk level of 8 per cent, as defined by the World Health Organization (Deinhardt and Zuckerman 1985). These levels are well above the prevalence of 0.07 per cent documented for blood donors in Sydney (Britton et al. 1985).

In view of the greater susceptibility of chronic carriers of HBV to the long-term sequelae of the infection, including cirrhosis and primary liver cancer, particularly hepatocellular carcinoma, these diseases could be expected to be more common among Aborigines than among other Australians. Available data suggest that deaths from cirrhosis are 2.5 times more frequent for Aboriginal males than for non-Aboriginal males, and 5.4 times more frequent for Aboriginal females than for non-Aboriginal females (Plant unpub.). Detailed studies in Western Australia found the incidence of primary liver cancer to be between 5 and 8 times higher for Aborigines than for the general Australian population (Armstrong and Joske 1979; Frazer et al. unpub). More recently, data from the Western Australian Cancer Registry revealed that the incidence of hepatocellular carcinoma for Aboriginal males was 12.6 per 100 000 person years, compared with 1.7 for non-Aboriginal males (Hatton and Clarke-Hundley 1986; Health Department of WA 1987*c*). For females, the incidence for Aborigines was 6.4 compared with 0.4 for non-Aborigines. Although cirrhosis and primary liver cancer occur more frequently among Aborigines than among the general Australian population, the actual contribution of HBV is not known. Dietary factors and alcohol are also likely to play a significant role, certainly for cirrhosis.

While little can be done to prevent current carriers proceeding to their possible long-term sequelae, the availability in Australia since 1982 of an effective vaccine provides the means for interrupting transmission and reducing the reservoir of carriers (Burrell 1984). Most Aboriginal babies are now offered hepatitis B vaccination under a program funded largely by the Commonwealth government.

Ever since the deadly impact of the acquired immune deficiency syndrome (AIDS) was first recognised, concern has been expressed about the likely impact if the causative organism, the human immunodeficiency virus (HIV), were introduced

Figure 2.5 *A pamphlet published by the Aboriginal Health Unit of the New South Wales Department of Health aims to inform the Aboriginal population about hepatitis B and explains how to prevent infection. (NSW Department of Health, Sydney)*

into the Aboriginal population. Over the last year or two, there have been a number of unpublished reports of Aborigines with serological evidence of exposure to the virus, and of deaths from AIDS. Great attention has been paid to the education of Aborigines about the dangers of the virus. The only published report on screening for HIV comes from an analysis of serum specimens from 1150 Western Australian Aborigines originally tested in 1986 for hepatitis B (Bucens et al. 1988). No evidence of HIV antibodies was found, but the report adds that the authorities in Western Australia were aware of two cases of HIV infection in urban Aborigines in that state. A newspaper article (*Sydney Morning Herald,* August 6 1990, p. 5) reported that seven Aborigines living on Palm Island in Queensland had returned HIV-positive blood tests, an infection rate 11 times the Queensland average. There has been one confirmed death of an Aborigine from AIDS, that of a young child in western New South Wales who acquired the HIV infection from a blood transfusion following a kidney transplant (Gray and Hogg 1989).

Even in the relative absence of hard data, the concerns expressed by Aborigines and health authorities about the threat of HIV infection, and of AIDS, are justified. This is particularly so in view of the high transmission among Aborigines of hepatitis B virus, which utilises some of the same routes of transmission as HIV, namely through sexual intercourse and exchange of blood products. Some Aborigines living in urban areas would appear to be at greatest initial risk, mainly through the sharing of needles for the administration of illicit intravenous drugs. In addition, the ceremonial practices of circumcision and scarification among some Aborigines, mainly those living in the more remote areas, provide other opportunities for transmission of the deadly virus.

Intestinal infections and infestations

Intestinal infections and infestations remain a major cause of Aboriginal ill-health and of hospitalisation. Acute diarrhoeal disease, generally non-specific gastroenteritis, was second only to respiratory disease as a cause of hospitalisation for Aboriginal children less than 10 years of age in Western Australia in 1986 (M. Gracey pers. comm.; HDWA 1987*b*). Diarrhoeal diseases were responsible for more than 10 per cent of the deaths of Aboriginal children aged less than 5 years in the Northern Territory in the period 1979 to 1983 (Plant unpub.). In Western Australia in the period 1981 to 1986, hospital separations for Aboriginal infants remained 16 to 20 times more frequent than for non-Aboriginal infants, and 11 to 15 times more frequent for young Aboriginal children.

Skin infections and infestations

The limited available data show that skin infections and infestations are much more common for Aborigines than for non-Aborigines (see Thomson unpub). For both Western Australia and the Northern Territory, skin diseases, based on principal diagnosis, were within the seven leading causes of hospitalisation for Aborigines (Devanesen et al. 1986; HDWA 1987*b*), with separation rates up to twice those of non-Aborigines. However, these figures underestimate the prevalence of skin conditions among Aborigines, and probably among non-Aborigines. A recent study of paediatric admissions to the Royal Darwin Hospital found that many patients admitted for other reasons had identifiable skin infections (M. J. Ferson pers. comm.). These skin conditions included both bacterial infections, not uncommonly secondary to scabies, and various fungal infections. The greater impact of skin conditions

Figure 2.6 *Dogs drinking from a dripping tap on a mobile water tank at an outstation in the Great Victoria Desert, South Australia. Unhygienic living conditions such as these may lead to intestinal infections and infestations which are a major cause of Aboriginal ill-health. (M. Brady)*

was also documented by the National Trachoma and Eye Health Program in its Australia-wide survey in 1976–79.

Apart from the social morbidity associated with the various skin conditions, there is the ever-present risk of glomerulonephritis resulting from streptococcal skin infections, commonly secondary to scabies. Communities in the north of the country not infrequently experience epidemics of acute poststreptococcal glomerulonephritis, fortunately generally quite mild (Gogna et al. 1983; Devanesen et al. 1988).

The skin conditions experienced by Aborigines have attracted much less professional attention than they deserve. The much higher rates of skin infections and infestations are clearly further examples of avoidable morbidity.

Mental health

Population-level data for Aborigines in the area of mental health are even more deficient than data on most areas of physical ill-health. Additionally, two other aspects complicate an overall assessment of Aboriginal mental health. First, great difficulties are encountered in cross-cultural interpretation, particularly for many Aborigines living in the more remote parts of Australia. Second, the diversity of social environments confronting different Aboriginal groups and communities is probably more influential in the area of mental health than in physical health (see Reser, chapter 6 in this volume).

Despite the fundamental and great difficulties in assessing mental health disorders, a National Health and Medical Research Council working party concluded that the available evidence suggested that the overall level of psychotic disorders among Aborigines was much the same as among non-Aborigines, with the extent of non-psychotic disorders being more variable (Urquhardt 1981). It is noteworthy that the evidence on which this conclusion was based had been accumulated in the 1950s, 1960s and 1970s, mainly from studies in remote parts of the country. In contrast to many of the physical disorders, there have been few recent studies from which population-level information can be deduced.

Since the establishment in 1987 of the Royal Commission into Aboriginal Deaths in Custody, increasing attention has been focused on suicides, and suicide attempts, by Aborigines, including an examination of the generally accepted belief that suicide was not originally part of Aboriginal culture. The evidence from more remote parts of Australia suggests that suicide was very uncommon among traditionally oriented Aborigines (Eastwell 1982, 1988; Jones and Horne 1973), but, based on overall mortality data (Plant unpub.), it is probably not so uncommon today among the total Aboriginal population of the Northern Territory, nor for Aborigines in Queensland (Reser unpub.).

The indirect evidence of the increasing incidence of suicide and attempts among Aborigines has been confirmed in worrying detail by a thorough study of Aboriginal deaths occurring in the Kimberley region of Western Australia since 1957 (Hunter 1988a, 1988b, 1989). This study suggests that in the Kimberley region suicide is a very recent, and localised, phenomenon. The two main factors identified as being associated with the male suicides were alcohol abuse and a recent or threatened disruption of an important interpersonal attachment. The latter association was also identified in one of the two female suicides.

Of the 103 Aboriginal deaths documented by the Royal Commission into Aboriginal Deaths in Custody (1988) to have occurred in custody, 30 have been by hanging. Only 8 of the deaths by hanging occurred in the period 1980–85, with 22 in the period 1986–88. Of course, not all hangings are necessarily suicides.

Thus, while suicide was probably once of a very low incidence among Aboriginal communities living in traditional ways, it appears that since the 1970s this, and other self-inflicted injury, has become more frequent for many Aboriginal communities. If anything, the incidence of suicide appears to have increased markedly in the 1980s, and 'suicide and suicide attempts are [now] endemic in many communities throughout much of Australia' (Reser unpub., p. 2).

The rise in the incidence of suicide appears to 'accompany a decline in the traditional values, an unfortunate side-effect of...modernisation' (Eastwell 1988, p. 340), but the cause is likely to be much more than that. As the differences in different shires in the Kimberley region suggest, it appears that the rise in suicide is an example of a differential worsening of the social environment for some Aboriginal communities. Hunter (1988a, p. 270) suggests that, despite the apparent economic and political gains since the early 1970s, a detailed socio-historical analysis of Aboriginal suicides 'must confront the subtle and covert psychological consequences of cultural exclusion, in which the dominant society's aims and ideals are offered, but the means of attainment...are unavailable'.

The increasing occurrence of suicides among some Aboriginal communities provides a tragic illustration of the enormous social and psychological pressures to which many Aborigines are exposed. It is also probable that the completed suicides are just the tip of a large iceberg of increasing mental distress and disorders experienced by many Aborigines.

Alcohol and substance abuse

Alcohol

Alcohol abuse has long been recognised as a major problem for many Aborigines and Aboriginal communities (House of Representatives Standing Committee on Aboriginal Affairs 1977), but, again, hard data are scarce. While very few deaths are directly attributed to alcohol abuse, there is little doubt that alcohol plays a major role in the present high levels of Aboriginal mortality. Unfortunately, the role of alcohol is rarely acknowledged in the information provided on the medical certificate of cause of death, whether for Aborigines or for non-Aborigines.

Using supplementary information provided by Aboriginal health workers, a study of Aboriginal deaths occurring in country areas of New South Wales in 1980–81 found that alcohol abuse was a significant medical problem in 27 per cent of all deaths (34 per cent of male deaths, and 15 per cent of female deaths) (Smith et al. 1983; Thomson and Smith 1985). The impact of alcohol was particularly important in the 35–44 year age group, the age group for which the ratios of overall Aboriginal death rates to those of the total New South Wales population were also highest.

Alcohol abuse was also found to play a significant role in Aboriginal deaths occurring in Western Australia in 1983 (Hicks unpub.), particularly in relation to deaths caused by diseases of the respiratory system (usually pneumonia). In addition, attention was drawn to the association of alcohol abuse with deaths from epilepsy.

A 1986–87 survey of alcohol consumption among 1764 adult (aged 15 years and over) Aboriginal residents of the Northern Territory, excluding those resident in urban households, found that almost three-fifths of the Aboriginal adults questioned did not consume any alcohol (Watson et al. 1988). Almost two-thirds of males, and a fifth of females did consume alcohol. Of those Aborigines who did consume alcohol, most started drinking during their teenage years. A greater proportion of Aborigines living in the Katherine and central Australian regions consumed alcohol than did those living in the Top End. People living in town camps consumed substantially more than those living in other types of communities.

Two-fifths of drinkers consumed alcohol on at least four days every fortnight, and more than a quarter consumed it on at least four days per week. People living in town camps consumed alcohol much more frequently than other Aborigines, with the next most frequent consumers being people living in major communities. Somewhat surprisingly, almost three-tenths of people living on outstations consumed alcohol on at least four days every fortnight, and more than a sixth consumed it on at least four days per week.

About two-thirds of drinkers, both males and females, consumed alcohol in harmful amounts, according to the current National Health and Medical Research Council's guidelines (NH&MRC 1987): more than 60 grams per day for males, and more than 40 grams per day for females.

A 1985 survey in Bourke (New South Wales) found that the proportion of Aboriginal males consuming hazardous amounts of alcohol had declined from more than 50 per cent in 1971–72 to 28 per cent (Harris et al. 1987). The proportion of Aboriginal females consuming hazardous amounts had increased slightly from 3 to 5 per cent. The study also found that the proportion of Aboriginal hospital admissions that were directly or indirectly alcohol-related had declined from 39.5 per cent in 1971–72 to 25.4 per cent in 1985 (Harris et al. 1987). Of non-Aboriginal admissions, only 4.8 per cent were directly or indirectly related to alcohol. Two-fifths of admissions of Aboriginal males were alcohol-related, as were an eighth of Aboriginal female admissions. In 28 per cent of the Aboriginal admissions (both sexes), trauma was the primary diagnosis. The second most frequent primary diagnosis was a seizure (31 cases, 20 per cent).

Numerous other studies (see, for example, Brady, chapter 5, this volume; Brady 1988; Brady and Palmer 1984; Collman 1979; Healy et al. 1985; Lake 1989; Larsen 1979; Larsen 1980; O'Connor 1984; Sansom 1980) confirm the widespread use of alcohol, often excessively, by Aborigines, but most focus largely on the social aspects, and do not provide detailed consumption data.

The available evidence confirms that the consumption of alcohol by many Aborigines is higher than that of Australians generally, in terms of both the proportions consuming alcohol, and the average quantities consumed.

While the factors underlying Aboriginal use of alcohol are undoubtedly complex, and multifactorial, it is probable that, for many Aborigines, a sense of powerlessness, and an awareness of that powerlessness, are of key importance.

Petrol inhalation

Petrol inhalation (or sniffing) has become a major problem for children and young adults in many Aboriginal communities, particularly in Arnhem Land, central

Australia (including the southern areas of the Northern Territory, the north-west regions of South Australia, and the Warburton Ranges area of Western Australia) and the eastern goldfields region of Western Australia (SSCVSF 1985).

Mainly because of the cyclical nature of the practice, but also because of its secretive nature in some groups/communities, it is virtually impossible to estimate the actual prevalence, even within a particular community. However, a survey of the Pitjantjatjara communities of Amata, Pukatja and Aparawatatja, undertaken in 1984 by staff of the Nganampa Health Service, revealed that 112 (34 per cent) of 330 children and young adults aged 10 to 24 years sniffed (Freeman 1987). Of the 112 sniffers, 66 (59 per cent) were chronic users.

A recent report from the Department of Community Services in Western Australia examined the fate of 73 known petrol sniffers from the 1958–66 birth cohort (Smith and McCulloch 1986). Of these, 24 had died (19 had been chronic sniffers), 11 were still chronic sniffers, 3 were still sniffing regularly but were not chronic, 14 were sniffing occasionally, and 21 had given up. While no details were provided about the deaths that had occurred, the overall mortality documented is exceptionally high, even compared with other Aboriginal data.

In the Pitjantjatjara areas served by the Nganampa Health Council, there have been three deaths attributable to petrol inhalation (time period unstated) (Freeman 1987), while the Yalata community in south-western South Australia has had two confirmed deaths, in 1984 and in 1986 (Brady 1988; see also Brady, chapter 5, in this volume).

Dental health

The assessment of Aboriginal dental health is complicated not only by the very limited availability of data on the dental health status of Aborigines, but also by the changing patterns of dental disease. The two major causes of dental disease, for both Aborigines and the general population, are dental caries and periodontal disease, the frequency of both of which has undergone substantial changes over recent years.

Dental caries

The extent of dental caries in Aboriginal communities is quite variable, probably as a result of varying levels of protection offered by natural fluoride. Adequate levels of natural fluoride probably counteract, to some degree, the other acknowledged risk factors for caries: food products containing large quantities of sugar, generally poor health in childhood, salivary abnormalities, and an uncommon hereditary predisposition of dental tissue to caries (Leus 1983). After a period of apparent increase in the prevalence of caries among some Aboriginal communities, there is some evidence of recent decreases in the prevalence and severity (Cooper et al. 1987; AHOSA 1986; NTDHCS 1987a).

In 1979, a sample of Aboriginal children in the Top End of the Northern Territory had on average less caries in their deciduous dentition than a large sample of the total population had achieved by 1985 (NTDHCS 1987). In contrast, the level of caries in a smaller sample in western New South Wales was somewhat higher than that of the total population (Cooper et al. 1987). The caries prevalence of the

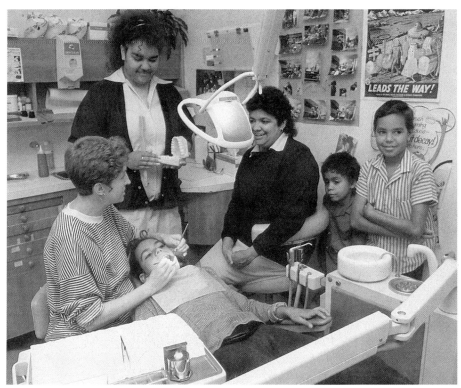

Figure 2.7 *Dental care for Aborigines is provided by the Aboriginal Medical Service in the inner Sydney suburb of Redfern. (From* Australian Society, *February 1990; photo by M. Olah)*

permanent dentition was similar: Aboriginal children in the Northern Territory had slightly lower mean levels, while those in western New South Wales had slightly higher levels.

The New South Wales study documented a substantial improvement in the dental health status of Aboriginal children since 1978, with the level of caries of children aged 6–8 years declining by 50 per cent, and that of children aged 10–11 years by 33 per cent (Cooper et al. 1987). The reduction in the severity of the carious lesions was even more marked: 73 per cent for the younger age group, and 34 per cent for the older group.

In a number of small surveys between 1982 and 1985, the mean caries levels of Aborigines living in remote communities in South Australia were found to be similar to those of the general South Australian community (AHOSA 1986), but it was noted that much of the dental decay had not been treated.

Periodontal disease

The other major dental health problem encountered by Aborigines is periodontal disease, the development of which depends on the accumulation of food debris or plaque (Schamschula 1982), permitting the growth of a range of anaerobic micro-organisms in the grooves between the gums and teeth. In its simplest form, periodontal disease is seen as inflammation of the gums, gingivitis. Chronic inflammation typically involves the deeper supra-alveolar connective tissues, leading to progressive recession of the supporting structures of the teeth, with resultant tooth mobility and possible loss.

Research in the 1970s suggested that the level of periodontal disease among Aborigines had increased over the previous 20 to 30 years to levels worse than those documented for the general Australian population (Homan 1977; Schamschula 1982). Unfortunately, there is little detailed information available about recent trends in periodontal disease. The South Australian survey found that 79 per cent of the people examined had periodontal disease, with 23 per cent having advanced disease (AHOSA 1986).

Overall, the high levels of periodontal disease among Aborigines reflect relatively poor oral hygiene. For many Aborigines, the lack of adequate dental care, including restorative work, means that they will continue to be exposed to the risk of becoming edentulous.

Cancer

As discussed previously, the overall mortality of Aborigines from malignant neoplasms (cancers) is slightly higher than that of non-Aborigines. However, the overall figures conceal significant differences, in which deaths from some cancers are much more common among Aborigines than among non-Aborigines, and deaths from others much less so.

For Aboriginal males in the Northern Territory in 1979–83, the most significant differential in mortality was for cancer of the liver and intrahepatic bile ducts (ICD 155) (see section on hepatitis B virus, under 'Sexually transmitted diseases'). Interestingly, while cancer of the trachea, bronchus and lung (lung cancer, ICD 162) was the leading cause of cancer deaths for Aboriginal males, the death rate was only three-quarters that of non-Aboriginal males.

For Aboriginal females in the Northern Territory, the most common causes of cancer deaths were cancer of the trachea, bronchus and lung (lung cancer, ICD 162) and cancer of the cervix uteri (ICD 185), in each case with rates substantially higher than those for non-Aborigines.

Interestingly, in contrast to cancer mortality the available data suggest that the overall incidence of cancers among Aborigines is lower than, or at most equal to, that among non-Aborigines (Hatton and Clarke-Hundley 1987; Honari and Saint-Yves 1987). This probably reflects, to some degree, the differential access of Aborigines and non-Aborigines to health services.

Urinary tract disorders

Although urinary tract disorders have long been suspected of being major contributors to Aboriginal morbidity (Moodie 1973), their actual importance has only recently been fully recognised.

A 1982–84 survey of more than 3000 Aborigines living in remote, rural and urban areas of South Australia found a prevalence of presumed serious renal disease at least 10 times that of the general population (AHOSA n. d.). Females had a higher prevalence of any urinary abnormality than did males. The prevalence of such abnormalities was also noted to be high among obese and/or diabetic subjects.

The high level of serious renal disease among Aborigines is also reflected in the numbers requiring artificial kidney treatment. Over recent years, the number commencing treatment at Queen Elizabeth Hospital in Adelaide suggests that such abnormalities are between six and eight times more common for Aborigines than for non-Aborigines, with at least part of the difference being due to the higher prevalence of diabetes mellitus found among Aborigines (see section on diabetes mellitus in this chapter) (Pugsley unpub.).

It is also likely that a higher frequency of urinary tract infections among Aborigines plays a significant role in the pathogenesis of serious renal disease, as does a past history of acute glomerulonephritis. As previously mentioned, periodic epidemics of acute poststreptococcal glomerulonephritis are still known to occur among Aborigines in the Northern Territory (Devanesen et al. 1988; Gogna et al. 1983).

Injuries

In terms of both mortality and morbidity, injuries have a much greater impact for Aborigines than for non-Aborigines (Wood and Thomson unpub.) The term 'injury' is used generally in reference to those conditions classified within the ICD group 'external causes of injury and poisoning' (E888-E999).

Aboriginal mortality from injuries is at least three times that of the general Australian population. For both males and females, motor vehicle accidents (ICD E810-E819) and injury purposely inflicted by others (ICD E960-E969) are the main causes of Aboriginal deaths.

As discussed under 'Hospitalisation', injuries were the leading cause of hospitalisation for Aboriginal males, and the third leading cause for Aboriginal females, and the leading cause of admissions not related to pregnancy. Clearly, injuries contribute disproportionately to the health disadvantages experienced by Aborigines. In view of their position among the leading causes of mortality and hospitalisation, it is surprising that so little attention has been directed to the prevention of injuries among Aborigines.

Aboriginal health status: summary

By virtually every health status measure, the health of Aborigines is much worse than that of other Australians.

With Aboriginal mortality roughly two to four times that of the total Australian population, Aborigines can expect to live many years less than other Australians: for males, between 12 and 20 years less, and, for females, between 4 and 21 years less. Throughout the country, the major cause of Aboriginal deaths is disease of the circulatory system, including heart disease.

The mortality of Aboriginal infants, despite substantial improvements since the early 1970s, remains about three times higher than that of non-Aboriginal Australians. Aboriginal maternal mortality is still three to five times that of other Australians.

Overall, the hospitalisation of Aborigines is two to three times higher than that of non-Aborigines, and up to five times higher for children less than five years of age.

Malnutrition appears to be a persistent problem for many Aborigines, characterised by high rates of mild to moderate undernutrition in infants and young children, and of obesity in adulthood.

The communicable diseases, though less important now in terms of mortality, remain significant causes of morbidity among Aborigines. Of major importance are respiratory tract and middle ear infections. For many Aboriginal infants and children, diarrhoeal disease still poses a major threat, and in most parts of remote Australia trachoma remains common. Other common communicable diseases among Aborigines are skin infections and infestations, the sexually transmitted diseases and hepatitis B, which is being increasingly recognised. A number of other diseases, such as meningitis, affect Aborigines disproportionately. Although there are a relatively low number of new cases each year, tuberculosis and leprosy still cause problems for some Aborigines. Grave concern has been expressed about the potentially devastating impact of AIDS if the human immunodeficiency virus becomes established in the Aboriginal population.

Despite the continued significance of communicable diseases, the so-called 'lifestyle diseases' have probably emerged as the major causes of Aboriginal morbidity. Hypertension among Aborigines, virtually non-existent in the past, is probably more than twice as frequent as among non-Aborigines. It is also likely that this problem is compounded by less successful hypertension control.

Diabetes mellitus, almost exclusively type 2 (non-insulin dependent), is between two and five times more prevalent among Aborigines. Again, it is probable that in many cases the management of Aboriginal diabetes is less than optimal.

While the prevalence of psychotic mental disorders among Aborigines is similar to that of the general population, a number of other mental health problems are possibly more common, and suicide appears to be emerging as a major problem for many Aboriginal communities.

In many instances, Aboriginal use of alcohol is hazardous, contributing substantially to both morbidity and mortality. Among Aboriginal children and adolescents, petrol inhalation has reached crisis proportions in some parts of Australia.

The impact of injuries among Aborigines is much greater than among other Australians.

The health inequalities experienced by Aborigines are so great, and so extensive, that only broad-ranging strategies have any chance of eliminating them. The strategies must aim at redressing the social inequalities, including the discrimination experienced by many Aborigines, and be complemented by appropriate supportive strategies within the health sector. However, the elimination of the substantial social and health inequalities experienced by Aborigines will require much more commitment than has been shown to date by any Australian government, or by the Australian people. Unless governments, and the Australian people, are prepared to commit themselves fully to achieving social and health justice for Aborigines, the standard of Aboriginal health will remain at levels that 'would not be tolerated if it existed in the population as a whole' (HRSCAA 1979, p. i).

References

ABS (Australian Bureau of Statistics) (1987*a*), *Aboriginals and Torres Strait Islanders: Australia, states and territories*, catalogue no. 2499.0, ABS, Canberra.

ABS (1987*b*), *Births Australia 1988*, catalogue no. 3301.0, ABS, Canberra.

AHOSA (Aboriginal Health Organisation of South Australia) (n.d. [1986]), *Renal survey report*, AHOSA, Adelaide.

AHOSA (1986), *A report of the dental survey and treatment of Australian Aborigines in the north-west communities of South Australia, Port Augusta (and surrounds), Ceduna, Yalata (and surrounds)*, AHOSA, Adelaide.

Armitage, P., and Berry, G., (1987), *Statistical methods in medical research*, Blackwell Scientific Publications, Oxford.

Armstrong, B., and Joske, R. A. (1979), 'Incidence and etiology of primary liver cancer in the Pacific basin', National Cancer Institute Monograph **53**, pp. 127–32.

Armstrong, M. (1979), *Aboriginal hospital morbidity in NSW, 1977*, Working Paper no. 1, Health Commission of New South Wales, Sydney.

Bear, V. (1985), 'Chairman's welcome', in Australian Deafness Council, *Ear disease in Aboriginal children: proceedings of a seminar held in Perth, 8 September 1985*, pp. 6–7.

Brady, M. (1988), *Where the beer truck stopped: drinking in a northern Australian town*, Australian National University North Australia Research Unit, Darwin.

Brady, M., and Palmer, K. (1984), 'A study of drinking in an Aboriginal community', in M. Brady and K. Palmer, *Alcohol in the outback: two studies in drinking*, Australian National University North Australia Research Unit, Darwin.

Britton, W. J., Cossart, Y., Parsons, C., Burnett, L., and Gallagher, N. D. (1985), 'Risk factors associated with hepatitis B infection in antenatal patients', *Australian and New Zealand Journal of Medicine* **15**, pp. 641–4.

Bucens, M. R., Reid, P. M., Holman, C. D. J., and Quadros, C. F. (1988), 'Survey of HIV infection in Aborigines' (letter), *Australian and New Zealand Journal of Medicine* **18**, p. 179.

Burrell, C. J. (1984), 'Nipping hepatitis B in the bud', *Medical Journal of Australia* **141**, pp. 204–5.

Collman, J. (1979), 'Social order and the exchange of liquor: a theory of drinking among Australian Aborigines', *Journal of Anthropological Research* **35**, pp. 208–24.

Cook, I. (1988), 'Meningococcal disease and immunisation', in N. Thomson (ed.), *Immunisation in Australia: proceedings of the first national conference, July 1987, Canberra*, Public Health Association of Australia and New Zealand, Canberra.

Cooper, M. H., Schamschula, R. G., and Craig, G. G. (1987), 'Caries experience of Aboriginal children in the Orana Region of New South Wales', *Australian Dental Journal* **32** (4), pp. 292–4.

DAA (Department of Aboriginal Affairs) (1981), *Report on a review of the administration of the working definition of Aboriginals and Torres Strait Islanders*, Department of Aboriginal Affairs (Constitutional Section), Canberra.

Deinhardt, F., and Zuckerman, A. J. (1985), 'Immunisation against hepatitis B: report on a WHO meeting on viral hepatitis in Europe', *Journal of Medical Virology* **17**, pp. 209–17.

Devanesen, D., Furber, M., Hampton, D., Honari, M., Kinmonth, N., and Peach, H. G. (1986), *Health indicators in the Northern Territory*, Northern Territory Department of Health, Darwin.

Devanesen, D., Bernard, E., Stokes, M.-L., Daby, J., Withnall, K., Falls, G., and Peach, H. (1988), 'Lessons from an outbreak of glomerulonephritis in an Aboriginal community', in Menzies School of Health Research, *Annual report, 1987–88*, Menzies School of Health Research, Darwin.

Eastwell, H. D. (1982), 'Psychological disorders among the Australian Aborigines', in C. Friedman and R. Faguet (eds), *Extraordinary disorders of human behaviour*, Plenum Publishing Corporation, New York.

Eastwell, H. D. (1988), 'The low risk of suicide among the Yolngu of the Northern Territory: the traditional Aboriginal pattern', *Medical Journal of Australia* **148**, pp. 338–40.

Freeman, P. (1987), 'Petrol sniffing in Amata, South Australia', in Nganampa Health Council, *Anangu winki nyaa:ku pikatjararinganyi nya a-nguru (Why are we becoming sick and what is it from?)*, Nganampa Health Council, Alice Springs, p. 88–97.

Glatthaar, C., Welborn, T. A., Stenhouse, N. S., and Garcia-Webb, P. (1985), 'Diabetes and impaired glucose tolerance: a prevalence estimate based on the Busselton 1981 survey', *Medical Journal of Australia* **143**, pp. 436–40.

Gogna, N. K., Nossar, V., and Walker, A. C. (1983), 'Epidemic of acute poststreptococcal glomerulonephritis in Aboriginal communities', *Medical Journal of Australia* **1**, pp. 64–6.

Gogna, N. K., Smiley, M., Walker, A. C., Fullerton, P. (1986), 'Low Birth weight and mortality in Australian Aboriginal babies at the Royal Darwin Hospital: a 15 year study', *Australian Paediatric Journal* **22**, pp. 281–4.

Gracey, M. (1987), 'Malnutrition and infections: interactions and wider implications', *in Proceedings of the Menzies Symposium, Nutrition and Health in the Tropics, held in Townsville, 26–27 August 1987*.

Gracey, M., Spargo, R. M., Bottrell, C., Hammond, K., Mulholland, K., and Valentine, J. (1984), 'Maternal and child nutrition among Aborigines of the Kimberley region', *Medical Journal of Australia* **141**, pp. 506–8.

Gray, A. (1983), 'Aboriginal fertility in decline: current research', *Aboriginal Health Project Information Bulletin* **3**, pp. 16–22.

Gray, A., and Hogg, R. [1989], *Mortality of Aboriginal Australians in western New South Wales, 1984–87*, New South Wales Department of Health, Sydney.

Hanna, J., Thomas, D., and Thurley, J. (1988), 'Meningococcal meningitis in central Australia, 1984–88', *Communicable Disease Intelligence* **16**, pp. 11–13.

Hansman, D. (1983), 'Meningococcal disease', *Medical Journal of Australia* **1**, pp. 77–8.

Hansman, D., Hanna, J., and Morey, F. (1986), 'High prevalence of invasive *Haemophilus influenzae* disease in central Australia, 1986', *Lancet* **2**, p. 927.

Hargrave, J. C. (1980), *Leprosy in the Northern Territory of Australia*, Government Printer of the Northern Territory, Darwin.

Harris, M., Sutherland, D., Cutter, G., and Ballangarry, L. (1987), 'Alcohol related hospital admissions in a country town', *Australian Drug and Alcohol Review* **6**, pp. 195–8.

Hart, G. (n. d.), *Hospitalisation of Aborigines in South Australia, 1979–1982*, Technical Monograph Series no. 4, South Australian Health Commission, Adelaide.

Hatton, W. M., and Clarke-Hundley, M. D. (1986), *Cancer in Western Australia, 1984*, HDWA, Perth.

Hatton, W. M., and Clarke-Hundley, M. D. (1987), *Cancer in Western Australia, 1985: an analysis of age and sex specific rates*, Statistical Series 6, HDWA, Perth.

HDWA (Health Department of Western Australia) (1987*a*), *Annual report, 1986–87*, Government Printer, Perth.

HDWA (Health Department of Western Australia) (1987*b*), *Hospital morbidity statistics: short-stay hospitals, 1986*, HDWA, Perth.

HDWA (Health Department of Western Australia) (1987*c*), *Occurrence and distribution of hepatitis B infection in the Aboriginal population of Western Australia*, Occasional Paper 11, HDWA, Perth.

Healy, B., Turpin, T., and Hamilton, M. (1985), 'Aboriginal drinking: a case study in inequality and disadvantage', *Australian Journal of Social Issues* **20** (3), pp. 191–208.

Hill, C. (1987), *The 1985 Western Australian birth cohort: perinatal and infant mortality identified by maternal race*, Statistical Series 9, HDWA, Perth.

Hollows, F. C. (1985), 'Community-based action for the control of trachoma', *Reviews of Infectious Diseases* **7** (6), pp. 777–82.

Holman, C. D. J., and Quadros, C. F. (1986), *Health and disease in the Aboriginal population of the Kimberley region of Western Australia, 1980–1985*, Occasional Paper 3, HDWA, Perth.

Homan, B. T. (1977), 'Changing periodontal status in a changing environment', *Journal of Dental Research*, Special Issue C, pp. C46–C54.

Honari, M., and Saint-Yves, I. F. M. (1987), *The Northern Territory cancer report, 1981–1985: an analysis of ethnic, age and sex specific rates*, Northern Territory Department of Health, Darwin.

HRSCAA (House of Representatives Standing Committee on Aboriginal Affairs) (1977), *Alcohol problems in Aboriginals: interim report on Northern Territory aspects*, Acting Commonwealth Government Printer, Canberra.

HRSCAA (House of Representatives Standing Committee on Aboriginal Affairs) (1979), *Aboriginal health*, AGPS, Canberra.

Hunter, E. M. (1988*a*), 'On Gordian knots and nooses: Aboriginal suicide in the Kimberley', *Australian and New Zealand Journal of Psychology* **22**, pp. 264–71.

Hunter, E. M. (1988*b*), 'Aboriginal suicides in custody: a view from the Kimberley', *Australian and New Zealand Journal of Psychology* **22**, pp. 273–82.

Hunter, E. M. (1989), 'Changing patterns of Aboriginal mortality in the Kimberley region of Western Australia, 1957–1986: the impact of deaths from external causes', *Aboriginal Health Information Bulletin* **11**, pp. 27–32.

Jones, I. H., and Horne, D. J. de L. (1973), 'Psychiatric disorders among Aborigines of the Australian Western Desert: further data and discussion', *Social Science and Medicine* 7, pp. 219–28.

Lake, P. (1989), 'Alcohol and cigarette use by urban Aboriginal people', *Aboriginal Health Information Bulletin* **11**, pp. 20–22.

Larsen, K. S. (1979), 'Social crisis and Aboriginal alcohol abuse', *Australian Journal of Social Issues* **14** (2), pp. 143–60.

Larsen, K. S. (1980), 'Aboriginal group identification and problem drinking', *Australian Psychologist* **15** (3), pp. 385–92.

Leus, P. A. (1983), 'Dental caries', *World Health*, pp. 11–13.

Lewis, A. N. (1976), 'Otitis media and linguistic incompetence', *Archives of Otolaryngology* **102**, pp. 387–90.

Mathers, C., and Harvey, R. (1988), *Hospitalisation and costs study, vol. 2. Survey of public hospitals and related data*, AGPS, Canberra.

Moodie, P. M. (1973), *Aboriginal health*, Australian National University Press, Canberra.

Moodie, P. M. (1981), 'Australian Aborigines', in H. C. Trowell and D. P. Burkitt (eds), *Western diseases: their emergence and prevention*, Edward Arnold, London, pp. 154–67.

NH&MRC (National Health and Medical Research Council) (1987), *Is there a safe level of daily consumption of alcohol for men and women? Recommendations regarding responsible drinking behaviour*, AGPS, Canberra.

NH&MRC (National Health and Medical Research Council) (1988), *Report on maternal deaths in Australia 1976–78*, AGPS, Canberra.

Northern Territory Department of Health (1980), *Bulletin 29*, pp. 36–40.

NTDHCS (Northern Territory Department of Health and Community Services) (1987*a*), *Annual report for the financial year, 1986–87*, Government Printer, Darwin.

NTDHCS (Northern Territory Department of Health and Community Services) (1987*b*), *Annual report: Mental Health Act, 1987*, NTDHCS, Darwin.

O'Connor, R. (1984), 'Alcohol and contingent drunkenness in central Australia', *Australian Journal of Social Issues* **19** (3), pp. 173–83.

Penny, M., and Thomson, N. (1987), 'Preliminary analysis of tuberculosis in Aborigines, 1984', *Aboriginal Health Information Bulletin* **8**, pp. 15–18.

Pollard, A. H., Yusuf, F., and Pollard. G. N. (1981), *Demographic techniques*, Pergamon Press, Sydney.

Queensland Health and Medical Services (1986), *1985–1986 annual report*, Government Printer, Brisbane.

Royal Australian College of Ophthalmologists (1980), *National Trachoma and Eye Health Program*, Royal Australian College of Ophthalmologists, Sydney.

Royal Commission into Aboriginal Deaths in Custody (1988), *Interim report: Commonwealth, New South Wales, Victoria, Queensland, Western Australia, South Australia, Tasmania, and Northern Territory*, AGPS, Canberra.

Sansom, B. (1980), *The camp at Wallaby Cross: Aboriginal fringe dwellers in Darwin*, Australian Institute of Aboriginal Studies, Canberra.

Schamschula, R. G. (1982), 'Social causes of dental disease', *Aboriginal Health Project Information Bulletin* **2**, pp. 21–4.

Seward, J. F., and Stanley, F. J. (1981), 'Comparison of births to Aboriginal and Caucasian mothers in Western Australia', *Medical Journal of Australia* **2**, pp. 80–4.

Smith, A., and McCulloch, L. (1986), *Petrol sniffing: report on a visit to Alice Springs to see the work of the NT petrol sniffing prevention team*, Department of Community Services, Perth.

Smith, L. R. (1978), *Aboriginal health statistics in Australia: a survey and a plan*, Health Research Project, Australian National University, Canberra.

Smith, L. (1982), 'Aboriginal health and Aboriginal health statistics', *Aboriginal Health Project Bulletin* **1**, pp. 14–24.

Smith, L., Thomson, N., and Gray, A. (1983), *Aboriginal mortality in New South Wales country regions, 1980–1981*, State Health Publication (IDS) 83-169, New South Wales Department of Health, Sydney.

South Australian Health Commission (1988), *Aboriginal births in South Australia, 1981–1986: an analysis of perinatal outcomes*, South Australian Health Commission (Epidemiology Branch), Adelaide.

SSCVSF (Senate Select Committee on Volatile Substance Fumes) (1985), *Volatile substance abuse in Australia*, AGPS, Canberra.

Stanley, F. J., and Mauger, S. (1986), 'Birth-weight patterns in Aboriginal and non-Aboriginal singleton adolescent births in Western Australia, 1979–83, *Australian and New Zealand Journal of Obstetrics and Gynaecology* **24**, pp. 49–54.

Stanton, K. G., McCann, V., Knuiman, M., Constable, I. J., and Welborn, T. (1985), 'Diabetes in part-Aborigines of Western Australia', *Diabetologia* **28**, pp. 16–21.

Stuart, J. E., Quayle, C. J., Lewis, A. N., and Harper, J. (1972), 'Health, hearing and ear disease in Aboriginal school children', *Medical Journal of Australia* **1**, pp. 855–9.

Task Force on Aboriginal Health Statistics (1985), *Towards a national system of Aboriginal health statistics*, Commonwealth Department of Health, Canberra.

Taylor, H. R. (1987), 'Strategies for the control of trachoma', *Australian and New Zealand Journal of Ophthalmology* **15**, pp. 139–43.

Thomson, N. (1983), 'Aboriginal infant mortality, 1976–1981', *Australian Aboriginal Studies* **1**, pp. 10–15.

Thomson, N. (ed.) (1986*a*), *Aboriginal health statistics: proceedings of a workshop, Darwin, April 1986*, Australian Institute of Health, Canberra.

Thomson, N. (1986*b*), 'Recent developments in Aboriginal health statistics', in N. Thomson (ed.), *Aboriginal health statistics: proceedings of a workshop, Darwin, April 1986*, Australian Institute of Health, Canberra, pp. 14–19.

Thomson, N. (1986*c*), 'Recent Aboriginal hospitalisation data', in N. Thomson (ed.), *Aboriginal health statistics: proceedings of a workshop, Darwin, April 1986*, Australian Institute of Health, Canberra, p. 44–52.

Thomson, N., and Smith, L. (1985), 'An analysis of Aboriginal mortality in NSW country regions, 1980–1981', *Medical Journal of Australia*, Special Supplement 143, pp. S49–S54.

United Nations Children's Fund (1988), *The state of the world's children, 1988*, Oxford University Press, Oxford.

Urquhardt, G. (1981), 'Address to a conference, Aboriginals and mental health', in *Aboriginals and mental health*, Australian National Association for Mental Health, Sydney, pp. 49–53.

Watson, C., Fleming, J., and Alexander, K. (1988), *A survey of drug use patterns in Northern Territory Aboriginal communities: 1986–1987*, NTDHCS, Darwin.

Watson, D. S. (1984), 'Obstetrics at Galiwin'ku', *British Journal of Obstetrics and Gynaecology* **91** (8), pp. 791–6.

WHO (World Health Organization) (1977), *International classification of diseases, 1975 revision*, WHO, Geneva.

Unpublished material

Frazer, A., Hocking, S., and Hansen, B. (unpub.), Primary liver cancer and Aborigines. Fifth year social and preventive medicine project, Department of Medicine, University of Western Australia, Perth.

Gray, A. (unpub. *a*), Australian Aboriginal fertility in decline, PhD thesis, Australian National University, Canberra, 1983.

Gray, A. (unpub. *b*), Reference estimates of Aboriginal mortality, 1981–1986, paper presented at the Annual Conference, Australian Population Association, Brisbane, September 1988.

Hanna, J. (unpub.), The epidemiology of invasive Haemophilus influenzae infections in children under five years of age in the Northern Territory and central Australia, Master of Public Health thesis, University of Adelaide, 1988.

Hicks, D. G. (unpub.), Aboriginal mortality rates in Western Australia, 1983, Master of Public Health thesis, University of Sydney, Sydney, 1985.

McIntyre, P., and Erlich, J. (unpub.), Epidemiology of childhood meningitis in central Australia, 1981–1986, paper presented at the Annual Scientific Meeting, Australian Society for Infectious Diseases, Sydney, May 1988.

Plant, A. J. (unpub.), Aboriginal mortality in the Northern Territory, 1979–1983, Master of Public Health thesis, University of Sydney, Sydney, 1988.

Pugsley, D. (unpub.), Renal disease in the Aboriginal population, unpublished paper.

Reser, J. (unpub.), Aboriginal deaths in custody and social construction: a response to the view that there is no such thing as Aboriginal suicide, unpublished paper for the Royal Commission into Aboriginal Deaths in Custody.

Streatfield, R. W. (unpub.), Primary health care approach to maternal and child health services for Aboriginal and Islander communities, Queensland, Master of Public Health thesis, University of Sydney, Sydney, 1983.

Thomson, N. (unpub.), Inequalities in Aboriginal health, Master of Public Health thesis, University of Sydney, 1989.

Wood, B., and Thomson, N. (unpub.), The impact of injury among Aborigines: a priority for surveillance and prevention, paper presented at the National Injury Surveillance and Prevention Project: National Review and Future Directions Conference, Adelaide, 1987.

CHAPTER 3

The decline and rise of Aboriginal families

Alan Gray

National Centre for Epidemiology and Population Health, Australian National University, Canberra

Peggy Trompf

Centre for Cross-Cultural Studies in Health and Medicine, University of Sydney

Shane Houston

Tharawal Aboriginal Medical Service, Airds, New South Wales

As it was

The concept of family is an essential component of the analysis of the determinants of health. People come to exist through their families and they live in families. If we agree on this much, it is very likely that we will fail to agree on much more about what a family actually is.

Greer (1984, p. 263) notes that:

almost all discussions of the family founder because of the difficulty in deciding what the family is, as distinct from what it was or will be, because families are always building up and breaking down, acquiring new members by marriage and procreation and losing them by estrangement and death.

She goes on to argue convincingly that the family has always been perceived by Church, State and social planners in Europe and Asia as a threat to their authority, despite their attempts to neutralise the threat by regulation and idealisation. The family is a threat to authority because its functions, at some level in most societies at most points in time, have usually included precisely those functions that the State and Church claim for themselves: religious, judicial, protective, economic, socialising and cultural functions (Mitterauer and Sieder 1982, pp. 71–84). In a society without Church and State all these roles, and more, are necessarily found within the family, or within a group of families functioning as a community. Such was Australian Aboriginal society until the end of the eighteenth century and in some parts of Australia until the third quarter of the twentieth century. A discussion of what an Aboriginal family was, and has now become, should be based in the first instance on how related people carry out social functions for each other. In this way, we cannot be led to wrong conclusions by an imposed concept of what a family is or should be.

It is, of course, true that, just as in other societies, families in Aboriginal societies contain procreating couples and children at their core. In a discussion of the multi-faceted Aboriginal kinship system, Berndt and Berndt (1988) record that the elementary or nuclear family is the basic kinship as well as social unit in Aboriginal societies. There is a large body of information about the economic function of (nuclear) family units in Aboriginal societies and the division of labour between men and women. Malinowski (1913, p. 281) summarised the evidence available at that time in a way that is only contradicted in interpretation by subsequent studies. Hunting, the making of weapons and the protection of his wife and children were the responsibility of the husband; the wife provided vegetable food, did camp work, carried heavy burdens, manufactured nets and usually caught the fish. Malinowski remarked (1913, pp. 282, 283) that 'it is easy to see that the amount of work allotted to women is considerably greater and that their labour is much harder than the men's work' and 'the woman's share in labour was of much more vital importance to the maintenance of the household than the man's work'. This applied especially to the supply of food (see also Hiatt 1978).

Figure 3.1 *Alice Mark and Laura Scott of Napranum, a community in Cape York Peninsula, collecting arrowroot at Bung Point on the Embley River. (From P. Taylor, ed.,* After 200 years, *Aboriginal Studies Press, Canberra, 1988; photo by C. Lewens)*

The primary sources on which Malinowski drew pointed out that all or most of the wife's productive activity was directed to the needs of her husband, herself and her children, but that the game obtained by the husband's hunting was not solely or even mainly for the members of the nuclear family. Other related people stood to gain from the husband's productive activity, particularly, but not exclusively, his wife's parents and brothers (see also Berndt and Berndt 1988, p. 81). Malinowski's interpretation of this was that it showed that the women were economically subservient to their husbands. However, Kaberry (1939, pp. 1–36) refuted this judgment, pointing out that it was the economic roles of women that enforced good treatment and justice from their husbands. Kaberry also pointed out that in sexual and social aspects of their lives, apart from their economic responsibilities, Aboriginal women had privileges and duties that set them apart from, but did not necessarily make them subservient to, their husbands.

Kinship systems

It is in the obligation of Aboriginal men and women to supply food outside the nuclear family unit that the term 'family' acquires a wider meaning in Aboriginal societies than would be allowed by a direct application of the functions of Western nuclear families to an Aboriginal social context. When aspects of kinship systems are examined, it becomes increasingly clear that this wider sense of family is pervasive in Aboriginal societies. The most outstanding aspect of Aboriginal kinship systems was, and in many places still is, the existence of whole classes of people identified by an Aboriginal person as his or her 'brothers', 'fathers', 'sisters', 'mothers', 'husbands', 'wives' or the various other classes of affines. These classificatory relationships governed almost all social interactions, including marriage (see Berndt and Berndt 1988, pp. 85–90 for a summary of these relationships). The classification of an individual was signalled by membership of named subsections within sections or moieties and clans, and usually could be identified across contiguous linguistic or tribal boundaries. In these kinship systems, marriages were permitted only between partners who stood in the classificatory position of prospective husband and wife to each other, although in some systems there were other relationships that were not particularly 'wrong' in this sense. In the past, really 'wrong' liaisons (for example between classificatory brothers and sisters) attracted the severest sanctions that the society could impose, including death.

Marriage in many Aboriginal societies permitted polygyny (multiple wives) and encouraged the levirate (remarriage of a widow to her husband's natural brother, not just classificatory brother). Polygyny resulted in a characteristic pattern of large age differences between wives and their first husbands in some areas. In response to a lack of marriage opportunities for young men, there were often 'counter-cultures' with their own rules for extramarital or informal sexual relationships (Shapiro 1979, pp. 81–8). Women in polygynous marriages were often closely related—some may have been sisters—and thus provided support for one another in child rearing, hunting and foraging, and other aspects of daily life. The advantages of a large household, however, could be offset by strain and hostility between co-wives.

These wider kinship roles carried economic obligations as well. The reason that a man was expected to present gifts such as meat to his wife's father, mother and brothers was to compensate them for the loss of his wife's economic value (Berndt and Berndt 1988, p. 81). The Berndts also note that the exchange of brothers and sisters in marriage created a tight network of economic cooperation between families. Besides economic roles, kin relationships carried a whole series of social regulatory functions which correspond to the religious, judicial, socialising and cultural functions with which the term 'family' is associated. While there were common threads in different parts of Australia, the range of these functions was extensive.

Child-rearing

One aspect of family life that is important in the context of health outcomes is the rearing of children. A number of studies have investigated the circumstances of Aboriginal child-rearing practices in the past. Malinowski (1913, pp. 234–73) provided a very useful survey of nineteenth-century sources. On the basis of these, he hypothesised a pattern of very long periods of breast-feeding (at least three years and frequently much longer), infanticide immediately after birth in instances where an older child was still being breast-fed or of an older unweaned infant if the mother died, and a resulting total of no more than two surviving children under the age of puberty at any time. Cowlishaw (1982) has more recently argued that physiological factors, such as the contraceptive effect of prolonged breast-feeding, could help explain the low fertility of Aboriginal women in the past, but Gray (1983) has pointed out that a small completed family size could be explained purely in terms of the survival rates of infants and young children.

Malinowski's sources also remarked on the great love and affection of parents for their children, and on what seemed to observers of Victorian times and to Malinowski himself (1913, p. 252) to be extremely lenient treatment and lack of

Figure 3.2 *Della Shillingsworth with her children Cecil and Marjorie at Dodge City, Brewarrina, a community in north-western New South Wales (From P. Taylor, ed.,* After 200 years, *Aboriginal Studies Press, Canberra, 1988; photo by S. Edwards)*

chastisement of children's errant behaviour. More recent sources (Kaberry 1939; Meggitt 1962; Reay 1963) suggest that it was the role of the mother or an older sister to scold or discipline a child, although Hamilton (1981, p. 99) notes that punishment by mothers was a rather rare occurrence among the Anbarra women of north-central Arnhem Land in the recent past.

Malinowski noted that decisions affecting children were not always made by the father or mother. Decisions by other relatives could extend to matters such as infanticide or marriage of a daughter. (There are, however, some semantic difficulties with the concept of decision-making, as reported by Middleton and Francis (1976, p. 63). Investigating the roles of parents at Yuendumu, central Australia, in 1970 by asking Aboriginal children about events at home, they discovered that questions about 'decisions' had to be framed very carefully, because the only Warlpiri word equivalent to 'decision' was not known by young people at all and was used only by older people for ceremonial purposes.) Both parents played a major role in their children's practical and social education until the age of puberty, but at that time daughters left their parents to be married and sons joined the fraternity of uninitiated youths to be educated in tribal traditions and beliefs and become men.

The detailed survey by Hamilton (1981) of child-rearing practices among the Anbarra people provides the most complete picture available about the everyday practice of child-rearing in a traditionally oriented Aboriginal community, a practice that was apparently little affected by changes in roles at that time. While the role described for mothers seems very clearly close to its precedents, comments about the role of fathers should be interpreted carefully. In their analysis of family roles at Yuendumu, central Australia, in 1970, Middleton and Francis (1976) detail many instances of apparent changes in relative responsibilities of mothers and fathers since the previous description of the same Warlpiri (Walbiri) people by Meggitt (1962). It is obvious that if men's roles in Aboriginal societies operated more at the group level than did women's roles, which were more family-centred, then it was these societal roles of men that were probably most affected by the way authority operated in a concentrated settlement such as Maningrida (Arnhem Land) or Yuendumu.

Survival of infants

In all human societies up until about 200 years ago, the first few years of life were the most hazardous. Estimates of Aboriginal infant and early childhood mortality levels in the period before colonial times are not precise. While many observers have pointed to low survival rates of infants in Aboriginal communities before the introduction of extensive health services began in the 1960s, these rates would have been partly the result of introduced infections and of diarrhoeal and respiratory diseases associated with concentrated settlement and not characteristic of earlier Aboriginal communities.

Nevertheless, such evidence as we do have—for example, for a group of women in the period before they came to the Maningrida settlement in Arnhem Land in 1958, (Hamilton 1981, p. 126)— shows that the first months and years of life were indeed hazardous, with accidental deaths contributing substantially to mortality in the post-neonatal period. The Maningrida data, even though based on very small numbers, suggest a mortality rate for children under the age of 5 of about 40 per cent, a level close to the lower levels of mortality in most human populations 200 years ago. Evidence from a large burial site on the south Queensland coast (Haglund 1976) also suggests a mortality rate for children under the age of 5 of around 40 per cent. Similarly, unpublished data from a baptismal register in the Daly River area of the Northern Territory shows that, in the 1880s and 1890s when the mission was operating, the mortality rate for children under 5 was at least 33 per cent. (While a baptismal register might seem an unlikely source for reliable pre-colonial demographic data, it has been argued that the conditions of the Jesuit mission on the Daly River were such that Aboriginal lifestyle was little affected: see Gray 1983.) Such figures may seem high, but they are actually quite favourable compared with the historical record of human populations. Aboriginal children may have had some advantages because of the absence of some disease agents that operate in concentrated settlements. On the other hand, a relatively high level of accidental death may have offset these advantages.

The reports of an American–Australian expedition to Arnhem Land in the late 1940s (Billington 1960) contained considerable information about the pattern of child-bearing and infant survival of Aboriginal populations whose contacts with non-Aboriginal society were at that time not substantial enough to have caused great disturbance to traditional practices. Whether the health outcomes of infants and children also remained unaffected is a more difficult issue. The reports record that the number of children born to a woman did not appear excessive, that breast-feeding was almost continuous (except during pregnancies) and lasted for up to three years if there was no intervention by further pregnancy, and that miscarriages were not uncommon. A total of 202 mothers at Angurugu, Yirrkala and Oenpelli had, between them, had 653 live births, 24 still births (a still-birth rate of 35 per 1000 births, somewhat higher than is found in Aboriginal populations now), 63 miscarriages and abortions, 83 infant deaths (an infant mortality rate of 127 per thousand live births), and one case of purported infanticide. The rather high incidence of recorded fetal deaths suggests that poor maternal health might have reduced the survival chances of babies *in utero*. Note also that the one purported case of infanticide suggests a very low incidence, and places emphasis on infanticide in earlier sources into a proper context.

Health and disease

Many observers have commented on the pattern of health, morbidity and mortality that would have characterised Australian Aboriginal societies in the past. Aboriginal people lived in a continent too sparsely populated to support some types of disease, especially viral human-borne diseases with a high morbidity and short illness and infection stages, which require large population concentrations in order to become endemic. For example, measles requires a population base of at least 500 000. The introduction of such a disease might cause an epidemic but, without a sufficiently large population, the disease would inevitably die out after the initial epidemic, because the number of people without antibodies would be insufficient to maintain the disease and allow it to spread during the infectious stages. Some other types of disease, particularly illnesses associated with contaminated water supplies or pest carriers, would also have been absent from mobile hunting and gathering populations. It has been argued that diseases such as smallpox and measles could have evolved perhaps only 10 000 years ago with the development of agriculture in Eurasia (Kunitz in press).

The characteristic diseases of a hunter-gatherer population are those with low morbidity and long illness and infection stages, such as the treponemal and chlamydial diseases, or with causes in the natural environment, for example insect-borne diseases such as malaria (but it is not clear whether any form of malaria ever became established before the colonial period, even in northern Australia: see Black 1972). It is also probable that parasitic infestations such as lice and intestinal worms also afflicted original Australian populations.

It has been pointed out by Aboriginal people that their languages had no words corresponding to the English word 'health', and that it would have been difficult for Aboriginal people to conceptualise 'health' as an aspect of their lives separate from other aspects (NAHSWP 1989, p. ix; see also Mobbs, chapter 7 in this volume). Approached from the perspective of health as an integral aspect of everyday family life, the history of Aboriginal population change and health in the last two centuries can be seen as the history of dislocation, desecration and destruction of Aboriginal society's basic unit, the family.

Dislocation, desecration, destruction

In the late nineteenth century Curr (1886, p. 110) commented that he had 'never heard of a female over the age of sixteen years who, prior to the breakdown of Aboriginal customs after the coming of the Whites, had not a husband'. The reference to the breakdown of Aboriginal customs is the interesting part of this statement, for Curr and other writers of his time regarded the breakdown of customs, and therefore of family, as something so obvious that it was not necessary to comment further. Today, the reasons for the breakdown of customs related to family life are of extreme interest and importance to historical analysis of the processes of depopulation accompanying the European invasion of the continent. Yet we have surprisingly little information about what actually happened to Aboriginal families during the early colonial period, and we need to reconstruct hypothetical scenarios largely by a process of deduction.

Early epidemics and introduced diseases

Disease can disrupt a society if it affects enough people to disrupt basic social functions. We have already identified the nuclear family group as the basic economic unit in Aboriginal societies at the time of the first European settlement, and for most of the period since then. For a disease to have an impact on the survival of the society, as distinct from the survival of individuals, it must affect the economic functions within the basic family unit of man, woman and children in the first instance. A case has been made that some of the earliest introduced diseases could have had precisely this effect. Butlin (1983) refers to the evidence of devastating epidemics of smallpox in the Aboriginal populations of south-eastern Australia in 1789 and again around 1829, and of the capacity of this disease to destroy economic viability within the family group for a long enough period to affect the survival of all the family's members.

In assessing the evidence, the nature and extent of the early epidemics needs to be considered (see also Franklin and White, chapter 1). The epidemic of 1789 is presumed by Butlin to have originated from the Sydney Cove settlement, but the settlers themselves did not have cases, except for one American Negro who died in the epidemic, and had not had cases since leaving Cape Town 17 months before, a period much longer than the latent and infectious stages of the disease. Estimates made in official reports were that perhaps half the Aboriginal people living between the Hawkesbury River to the north of the settlement and Botany Bay to the south died in this epidemic, so it was undoubtedly severe. Reports about later epidemics in northern Australia (Mulvaney 1989) suggest that locally high mortality rates of this order might not be as unreasonable as they at first appear.

Butlin made three assumptions about these epidemics: that the first epidemic hit a population that had not been exposed to smallpox previously; that both epidemics affected almost all the peoples of south-eastern Australia; and that mortality at the time followed the pattern of age-specific rates in unvaccinated patients in a later epidemic in India (but it was much higher in level). All three assumptions are open to dispute. If we agree that a smallpox epidemic began in Port Jackson in 1789 and spread widely, as Butlin maintained, then it is reasonable to ask why possible epidemics from earlier Indonesian landings in northern Australia would not also have spread widely across the continent and so introduced some immunity. Earlier writers (Cumpston 1914) argued that a north–south movement was consistent with the evidence available about the 1829 epidemic, and so with Indonesian introduction on that occasion. There is a great deal of evidence from northern Australia pointing to the introduction of smallpox epidemics from Indonesia at several times in the nineteenth century, and the journals of the earliest European explorers included reports of pockmarking from previous epidemics observed in the remotest parts of the continent. As for the second assumption, that almost all tribes in south-eastern Australia were hit uniformly and with very high fatality rates, there is little evidence for or against except that the history of pandemics shows that they have usually had very uneven impact. The third assumption, assigning an age-specific mortality pattern based on mortality among patients in an Indian epidemic, ignores any actual age-specific pattern of infection; in addition, Butlin made arbitrary upward adjustments to these rates and arrived, for example, at massive uniform mortality rates for children aged less than 5 years.

Whether the impact on individuals was severe or mild, we can be left in no doubt that the characteristics of smallpox would have affected family economic activity. Every person who contracts the disease is not only debilitated but afflicted with pustules and, in areas of thick skin such as hands and feet, severe cracking and splitting, which seriously curtail any hunting or gathering activity. The reports that are available, of the dead and dying simply left where they lay by other group members, do indicate serious societal disruption in smallpox epidemics in Australia.

It might be supposed that, as with smallpox, other epidemic disease introductions would also have had a very serious effect. Surprisingly, there is little evidence of this, mainly because most other epidemic diseases made no appearance in the European settlements in Australia until much later. The first was influenza in 1820, then whooping cough in 1828, scarlet fever in 1833, measles in 1850 and diphtheria in 1858 (Young 1969). While scattered reports can be found of the serious impact of some of these diseases, particularly measles in the middle of the century, by the time they were introduced the pressures on the Aboriginal population were generally of quite a different order.

Among these other pressures were introduced chronic diseases, at least some of which can be presumed to have spread beyond the frontiers of European settlement. Venereal diseases were certainly present in the European settlements right from the start, and the earliest reports from settlers also mentioned the presence of 'venereal' among Aboriginal peoples of the inland. What the Aboriginal diseases were is not clear. Yaws, a treponemal disease that confers cross-immunity against the closely related treponematosis syphilis, was present in Aboriginal populations as an endemic childhood disease. Because of the presence of yaws, syphilis was rarely found in Aborigines of the Northern Territory, for example, until the 1970s when yaws was fast disappearing and a generation was reaching adulthood without having acquired yaws in childhood. The sexually transmitted chlamydial disease, lymphogranuloma venereum, has been found to be widespread in Aboriginal populations and may be indigenous. There was another disease, possibly much less contagious, called granuloma inguinale. Gonorrhoea can definitely be assumed to have been introduced to Aboriginal people through direct contact quite early.

Sexually transmitted chlamydia and gonorrhoea are diseases that can have a serious social impact because they affect the capacity of women to bear children. The mechanism is one of primary infection, leading in some cases to pelvic inflammatory disease and associated blockage of the Fallopian tubes (salpingitis), sometimes followed by permanent scarring damage of the tubes. A woman with active pelvic inflammatory disease is infertile. In addition, before antibiotics were available, an estimated 60 per cent of cases of pelvic inflammatory disease led to permanent incapacity to bear children (Westrom and Mardh 1975; Taylor-Robinson 1977). However, the proportion of women with untreated cervical gonorrhoea who actually develop pelvic inflammatory disease is quite low (8 to 20 per cent by various estimates), and the proportion appears to be similar or lower in the case of cervical chlamydial infections (Eschenbach et al. 1977; Westrom and Mardh 1978). While chlamydial infections appear to have an effect on the capacity to bear children similar to that of gonorrhoea, it is also important to note that active chlamydia is frequently imparted to infants during birth and results in a characteristic pneumonia which is often fatal, thus increasing infant loss. Transmission of gonorrhoea from male to female occurs in about one-third of instances of sexual intercourse where the male has the active disease. Taking all the factors together, an infected male will cause permanent damage to the Fallopian tubes of a fertile woman (without treatment) in something under 5 per cent of instances of sexual intercourse.

There can be no doubt that even at these low rates of permanent damage, gonorrhoea and its insidious effects would have spread slowly into Aboriginal populations, first as a result of sexual abuse of black women by white men, then possibly beyond the frontier of white settlement. The impact of sterility on Aboriginal families would have depended on whether a woman had already borne children or not, for without children she would not be considered to have fully become a woman (Berndt and Berndt 1988, pp. 196, 207). Cases of secondary sterility would have the effect of lowering the reproductive capacity of the society but would not be as socially disruptive as primary sterility, which would prevent the completion of family formation. Syphilis, if and where it did spread into Aboriginal populations, would possibly not have had such a serious social impact, even if it did eventually cause deaths in those affected. This is because although syphilis can cause an increased incidence of fetal wastage, and result in children being born with the disease and with congenital defects, it does not cause infertility as such.

Direct physical effects of European settlement

Most of the effects of disease were not immediate consequences of the 1788 settlement at Sydney Cove, but were the result of recurrent invasions during the course of the nineteenth century as the characteristic diseases of Eurasia entered Australia. These diseases represented additional pressure on Aboriginal societies at a time when the physical effects of advancing European settlement were being felt. It was the actual presence of European settlers that threatened the basis of Aboriginal society, not disease at a distance (Gray 1988). Even the most extravagant reconstructions of the effects of introduced diseases cannot refute the contention that the rate of depopulation was proportionately much greater within the frontier of European settlement than beyond it. The presence of European settlers directly attacked the economic basis of Aboriginal society.

In most parts of Australia, Aboriginal people were forewarned of the approach of Europeans, because they knew about the expeditions and settlers in other areas, they had encountered feral animals and they were already familiar with many introduced implements, and with the use of iron and glass. What they did not expect, and everywhere resisted, was forced dispossession of their homelands, and the introduction of grazing animals that fouled water resources, destroyed the habitats of native animals and changed the vegetation so much that traditional gathered foods could no longer be found. Aborigines resisted, and often there was open warfare. It has been estimated that at least 20 000 Aborigines died as a result of conflict, about 10 times the number of Europeans that died (Reynolds 1981). Massacres of Aborigines continued right through to the 1920s and 1930s, and ended only when the entire country was effectively under white domination.

Within the expanding frontier of European settlement, pastoralists and Aborigines reached uneasy agreement, especially as the size of squatters' holdings grew quickly larger. Curr (1886, p. 101) perceptively noted that the earliest squatters' runs were only 'twenty thousand to one hundred thousand acres', and at first employed a great many more men than the much larger runs subsumed later. The large stations offered greater opportunity for sustained conflict, but once conflict was settled they also could afford means of sustenance for both Aborigines and settlers, and some employment for those Aborigines willing to accept it. The stations also served as distribution points for rations issued by the colonial governments. This initial period of accommodation was already coming to an end by the middle of the nineteenth century in Victoria and later in the same century in New South Wales, as the squatters' runs were broken up into selections by a new wave of settlers (Read 1980). In the Northern Territory, western Queensland and the north-west of Australia, however, the initial period of accommodation lasted almost to the present day. Berndt and Berndt (1987) record the characteristics of the Aboriginal populations of stations in the Northern Territory in the mid-1940s, including interesting compilations of vital statistics that demonstrate that recently arrived 'bush' Aborigines had higher birth rates and lower incidence of childlessness than the 'station' populations. The Berndts' figures were retrospective and tended to disguise the likelihood that Aboriginal population decline in the Northern Territory had ended by that time, but they demonstrated forcefully that it was those Aborigines who had reached accommodation with the settlers who had suffered the worst demographic outcomes. These comments refer to the most recent manifestations of the first period of accommodation between Aborigines and settlers. It was a disrupted society dependent on the agents of disruption.

It is not surprising that social disruption was reflected in the demographic characteristics of Aboriginal populations. The first official counts in different parts of Australia in the second half of the nineteenth century revealed two gross anomalies. The first was a large surplus of adult men over adult women, and the second was that there were too few children to sustain future population numbers. The surplus of men over women is something that the discussion so far has given no reason to expect. There are many likely explanations: it is possible, for instance, that mortality of women was heavier than mortality of men in pre-colonial times; it is also possible that the populations recorded in early enumerations contained excess numbers of men because they included men who had entered the settled areas for employment or other purposes, leaving their womenfolk and children behind; and it is possible that the depredations of conflict and abuse took a greater toll of women. Before dismissing the last of these, it would be well to remember Hill's (1951) recollection of the retribution riders' genocidal aim in the Northern Territory of shooting 'the breeders', and the many recorded instances of kidnapping and abuse of Aboriginal women for sexual purposes by stockmen (see instances cited by Reynolds 1972, pp. 27–34).

Small numbers of children relative to numbers of women of reproductive age were also found in all the earliest population counts from settled areas. We can be absolutely certain that this was not a feature of Aboriginal populations before white settlement, because it would have resulted in the complete disappearance of the Aboriginal population in only a few generations. There appear to have been two causes, namely a high incidence of childlessness and low numbers of children for those women who did have children. Even if we accept that in pre-colonial times some sterility might have existed in Aboriginal populations as a result of indigenous disease agents, the information cited by the Berndts (Berndt and Berndt 1987) suggests that in the Northern Territory in the mid-1940s there was less childlessness among 'bush' Aborigines. The Berndts raise four questions about the apparent depopulation in station populations and other settled populations (Berndt and Berndt 1987, p. 186):

1. *Diet—how did station diet compare with 'bush' diet; how did it compare with a reasonably balanced diet; and what was the minimum basis for such a diet?*
2. *Were women (and men) unhappy and insecure in the contact situation to such an extent that they refused to have children?*

3. *The abortion rate required consideration.*
4. *Disease, infections, illness (especially venereal disease), or other physically based factors could be responsible for long-term or short-term sterility in both men and women.*

While by the mid-1940s these questions had been repeatedly addressed in successive parts of Australia for almost 100 years, the summary is succinct enough to cover the main competing explanations and to suggest that all of these issues played some role, if we read 'abortion' in its old sense of 'miscarriage'.

The second period of accommodation was even more catastrophic than the first. As the squatters' estates were broken up, first in Victoria and later in other parts of Australia, there was literally nowhere for the remaining Aboriginal populations to go. In Victoria, it was their own efforts at obtaining farming land to work that led to the establishment of government-controlled stations in 1860. These became the model for concentrating Aboriginal populations in similar institutions in all the mainland states and the Northern Territory, although it was only in Victoria that they could be seen as due to Aboriginal initiative. At first, the stations or missions were mostly established only when land partly occupied by Aborigines was required for more intensive European use, although in the north Church mission stations were often established in remoter areas with a missionary purpose. Later, even the populations of areas not affected by the pastoral frontier, in central Australia, Arnhem Land and Cape York, were also concentrated on such stations because governments found it convenient. Stanner (1974, pp. 6–7) called the establishment of these settlements a 'bureaucratic scientology of human affairs':

The settlements themselves have been well described as 'total institutions'. Every Aborigine in them lives in a virtually complete dependency on authority for virtually everything. I am at a loss to grasp on what model of human or social reality we built such institutions. I have often wondered why we supposed they would work out humanely and formatively. They would not do so for us. Why for Aborigines? Did we have in mind the medieval village? The monastery? The plantation? The corrective institution?

We have already noted that the essence of the conflict between Church and State and family is that, given a free hand, the family seeks to administer precisely those functions that Church and State claim for themselves. The concentrated settlements for Aboriginal people can be seen as an orderly attempt to assert claims of authority in religion, the administration of justice, protection, economic order, socialisation and culture. (Even after death, possession of a body could pass out of the control of Aboriginal people — see Glover, 'The bones of our ancestors' in this chapter.) In fact, elements of all these can be found in the administrative practice of the mission and settlement authorities as they developed. At first, the stated emphasis was on protection, and state-appointed officials were actually known as protectors. The imposition of the state justice system was implicit in all arrangements for concentration and control, and local protectors were in many cases the police. The economy of each settlement was totally controlled, even to the extent of control of personal finances. Socialisation was attempted through disrupting families: children were placed in dormitories and there were mass eating arrangements.

The bones of our ancestors

Few of us worry about the bones of our ancestors. We know they will have been laid to rest with proper ceremony. But for many black Australians such confidence is not possible. The bones of their ancestors were spread throughout the world as part of an extensive trade in Aboriginal skulls and skeletons, which has left the remains of as many as 3000 Aborigines in Britain alone. The bones, which Aboriginal people are now demanding back, were collected in the name of a totally discredited branch of anthropology whose aim was to demonstrate white supremacy.

In the latter half of the nineteenth century, Australia might have been regarded by most as an insignificant British colony—but to the world's evolutionary scientists it was the place which would furnish the proof of Darwin's theory that humanity descended from the apes. This, after all, was the point on which Darwin's theory had been most criticised: how, asked the critics, could creatures as noble as human beings bear any relation to the animal kingdom? The answer, said Darwin in his *Descent of man*, was to consider the female Australian savage, 'who uses very few abstract words, and cannot count above four, exert her self-consciousness, or reflect on the nature of her own existence'.

Darwin's supporters were quick to follow his lead. Over the following decades, the bodies of both living and dead Aborigines were measured and remeasured in increasingly frantic attempts to prove that their bodies lay somewhere between those of the animal kingdom and modern whites.

It was hardly accidental that Australia's Aborigines were selected to fill this lowest rung on the evolutionists' ladder. This was the period in which whites and blacks were still fighting a frontier war in Australia. For many decades the work of these scientists provided society with a tailor-made justification for Aboriginal genocide. In their work, the Aborigine was seen not only as the missing link that proved Darwin's theory, but also as a living fossil that showed how humanity had lived thousands of years before.

Evolution, the scientists believed, followed a single road: the European male represented the vanguard; the Aborigine was an arrested stage in that progress. To watch him dance or hunt was to learn about the infancy of mankind. 'Ape-like' was no longer a metaphor of racist abuse, but a scientific statement to be backed by exact measurements and complex formulae. The Aborigine, with his 'fossil' body and brain, could not help but die out in the face of a more advanced race, the scientists told an eager public.

It was an ultimate example of blaming the victim: Aboriginal dispossession was proof of inferiority—an unchangeable inferiority of bones and blood. But that 'inferiority' was also the unchallengeable assumption from which the scientists' proceeded.

Looking back through the hundreds of studies piled in our state libraries, one comes again and again across fudged results and ignored evidence. The common technique was to show that selected features of the Aboriginal body were similar to those found in some lower form of life. The exercise encountered few problems, since the animal chosen for comparison could be varied at will.

From an infinite number of possible bodily measurements, scientists also searched for what they called 'meaningful characters'—measurements which would yield the desired result: ape, Aborigine, European. Such results were studied by later workers and a standard list emerged of 'good things to measure'. By the end of the century, it was a motley assortment of bones that provided the proof of Aboriginal inferiority: the short big toe, the narrow thorax and pelvis, longer upper members, large teeth and the low angle of torsion in the humerus.

These scientists were not conscious cheats: they were merely working from the known 'fact' of European supremacy, and disregarding unhelpful data. Modern scientists agree their conclusions were faulty, but some still insist the collections should be kept—particularly bones older than 10 000 or 15 000 years. All Australia's major museums have now agreed not to display any recent skeletal material, and wherever possible to return it to descendants, although British institutions are resisting any handback.

Yet tough questions remain. Should older bones be kept? If so what should be the cut-off point? And does science today still serve its society's interests to the same extent as nineteenth-century anthropology?

Richard Glover

The dominant culture was imposed through the education system (see Rowley 1970). It is difficult to avoid the conclusion that the underlying purpose of the 'concentration' camps was to destroy Aboriginal families by denying them all functions. Government and Church settlements were places where all the diseases of concentrated human habitation could wreak their havoc. Besides the diarrhoeal and parasitic diseases that sprang from contaminated water supplies and unsatisfactory disposal of waste, tuberculosis and other respiratory diseases that flourish where people are in constant close contact were also rife. Long (1970) records early data on the vital statistics of many institutional settlements in eastern Australia, and these data establish that it was normal for deaths to outnumber births, sometimes for an extended period.

Policy effects and responses

Protectionism

Aboriginal settlement patterns were defined by the colonial experience, as government policy was instrumental in the dispersal of the indigenous population . An instance here was the establishment of the Aborigines Protection Board in 1883 by the New South Wales government and the passing of the *Aborigines Protection Act 1909*, which enabled children to be removed from their parents if a magistrate deemed them to be 'neglected'. The policy of protectionism resulted in the removal of people from ancestral lands and the settlement of unrelated people in permanent areas such as missions and reserves, which led to familial, social and cultural disruption. The history of the establishment of the Yalata settlement in South Australia (Brady and Morice 1982) provides a synopsis of the way in which this disruption occurred (see also Brady, 'Dispersal, alienation and re-possession: the southern Pitjantjatjara', in Franklin and White, chapter 1 in this volume).

In the alien circumstances of reserves and missions, Aborigines were successful in establishing viable enterprises, including wool-washing plants and farms, and built cottages, schools and meeting rooms (Gilbert 1973). However, in 1886, the Victorian *Aborigines Act* was passed, which stated that only 'full bloods' or 'half castes' over the age of 34 could live on reserves. This policy was another attempt to breed out Aborigines, since it was the government's intention to merge part-Aborigines into the white population. Variations on this policy were adopted in all the states and finally as national policy in the 1930s (Rowley 1970). Its eventual effect was to break up the successful communities as residents were forced to leave. White settlers were quick to seize opportunities. For example, by 1893 half of the Coranderrk settlement (Victoria) had been leased to whites. By 1923 the remaining Aboriginal population had been moved to a reserve of poor quality land, and the rest of Coranderrk was sold (Parbury 1986).

Assimilation and the 'stolen generations'

Protectionism gave way to assimilation in the 1930s. 'It was a dual policy involving the acculturation of the mixed race fringe and urban dwellers, and the segregation of traditionally oriented Aborigines' (Healy et al. 1985, p. 292). Reynolds (1972) notes that in 1937 the Conference of Commonwealth and State Authorities on Aborigines concluded that a twofold problem existed. In the first place, it was felt that 'uncivilised full bloods' were in imminent decline, and the strategy would be to make their passing as painless as possible. Those 'full bloods' who were 'semi-civilised' should be supervised on small reserves. But what was to be done with those Aborigines of mixed descent? The answer lay in a policy of assimilation, which led to the notorious strategy later to be dubbed the 'stolen generations' (see Swann, 'Two hundred years of unfinished business' in this chapter). The general policy aim of the conference was 'that the destiny of the natives of Aboriginal origin, but not of the full blood, lies in their ultimate absorption by the people of the Commonwealth and it therefore recommends that all efforts be directed to that end' (Rowley 1971, p. 28). Light-skinned children were forcibly removed from their darker parents and later this 'special treatment' was extended to include the removal of children from rural town reserves as well. Among others, Aborigines have described this policy as 'a systematic attempt at cultural genocide [which]...has been the background for many years of horrific memories, distress and mental health problems that continue to this day' (Swann 1989, p. 9). The *Aborigines Protection Act 1909* (NSW) defined a neglected child as one who had no visible means of support or who had no fixed place of abode. This definition provided ample scope for magistrates to order the removal of children in circumstances where Aborigines were forced to leave stations or where children lived in fringe areas. The Act was made more draconian with an amendment in 1915, which stated that if the board considered that a child's moral or physical welfare was endangered, the child could be removed from the family immediately on the orders of the police or the reserve manager.

The racial intention was obvious enough for all prepared to see, and some managers cut a long story short when they came to that part of the committal notice 'Reason for Board taking control of the child'. They simply wrote 'for being Aboriginal'.

Read n.d., p. 6

The conceptual category of 'half-caste' has not only served to regulate relations between the non-Aboriginal population and people of Aboriginal descent, but has also reinforced the dominance and control of Anglo-Celtic social, racial and cultural ideals. Government and mission attempts to take Aborigines from their 'uncivilised' backgrounds and thus 'give them a chance' had focused on children (Towers 1982, p. 48), who, having had minimum socialisation with their own families, would most benefit from the positive influence of white 'civilisation'. Towers (1982, p. 49) continues:

Similarly, the white ancestry of the 'half caste' gave them a potential for absorption into the white community. As only 'part' Aborigines they could be considered, firstly, as not fully developed Aborigines. Secondly, as 'part' Europeans, they held a possible potential capability to function as Europeans within white society, after adequate training. Thirdly, with some contention, many believed that Aboriginal racial characteristics were not dominant: by continued interbreeding with whites over a number of generations they would become indistinguishable from the general population.

Figure 3.3 *Some of the Aboriginal children who were separated from their parents and sent to Kinchela School in New South Wales in the 1920s. (Archives Authority of New South Wales)*

Thus, the most successful subject for this policy was the lighter skinned child.

For a variety of reasons, the numbers of children removed from their families between 1883 and 1969 can only be estimated. Read (n.d., p. 9) estimated the number to be 5625 in New South Wales. In 1930, the Queensland Aborigines Chief Protector stated that 'Quadroon or octoroon children destined for absorption with the white communities should be rescued from the Aboriginal atmosphere as soon as possible' (cited in Towers 1982, p. 51). As late as 1960, a contributor to the *Medical Journal of Australia* could say:

Take a full blood native baby, bring it up from early infancy, with white children and away from squalid surroundings, and the resulting adult should fit into the general community as reasonably as most people do, save for the important matter of colour, which may give rise to an inferiority complex.

Cleland 1960, p. 28

The effects of the policy are evident at the present time, despite the fact that the practice of removing children from parents ceased in 1969 in New South Wales. Read (n.d.) points out that these relatively recent events are not widely known among the white community and that, where they are known, there is little understanding of the effects this had on Aboriginal communities. One effect is detailed by an Aboriginal health worker, who explains that, for some young adults who as children had been removed from their parents in this way, the result is frequently

Two hundred years of unfinished business

A mother was at her home on a New South Wales mission with her five children, John (9), Sally (7), June (6), Normie (3), and Ruth (6 months). Her husband was away working. She had just put her children to bed. There was a crash at the door, followed by the sound of heavy footsteps. Two policemen and another stranger announced they were there to collect the children. Of course, mother and children fought and objected.

The children were loaded into a truck and taken to the local railway station where they were handed over to welfare workers who threatened and bribed them to stop them crying. They were told they were going on holidays and that they could go to the pictures if they kept quiet. After arriving at Sydney's Central Station, the oldest boy was taken on a train to Kinchela Aboriginal Boys' Home and the youngest to Bomaderry Children's Home. The girls were taken to the Aboriginal Girls' Home at Cootamundra. On arrival they were deloused and their heads shaved. The two older girls, June and Sally, were separated and placed in separate dormitories, each with 50 other girls.

The youngest child, Ruth, was placed with a staff member. The following week, June was sent to the school classroom, but Sally and nine other girls were told to stay behind. After school, June was told that her two sisters and the other fairer skinned girls had gone to live with 'nice families'. Sally was fostered with a . Dutch family. She learned to speak Dutch fluently. She said that she first noticed her 'difference' at her new school while playing games. Other children refused to join hands with her, and they called her names.

Her foster parents said she was well behaved until she was about 13 years old, when she started smoking, getting around with the wrong crowd, and running away from home. At 16, she ran away definitely, and little else is known about her except that at the age of 22 she was battered to death in Sydney.

An Aboriginal organisation was notified of her death. Her natural mother was contacted for the first time since her removal, and her body was taken back to the mission for burial.

June was in Cootamundra for 10 years. She describes life in the home as one of sadistic regimentation, where cleanliness, 'godliness', and domestic duties were substituted for love and affection. There she received clear negative messages about her Aboriginality, Aboriginal culture, and her 'no-good black family'. At 14, she was placed as a domestic servant on a farm where, for over 12 months, she was physically and sexually assaulted by the station owner. She tells of occasions when she was in bed and the station owner would walk into her room and masturbate on her face and body. She became pregnant and was sent back to Cootamundra.

She was then sent to an unmarried mothers home in Sydney. Her son was taken from her at birth and put up for adoption. From there she was given accommodation at the Parramatta Girls' Home and had several 'placements' with Corrective Services.

Today June has problems coping with her two children, who have been placed in care by Youth and Community Services. She has been told that, if she wants her children back, she must 'get her act together' or her children will be made state wards.

Ruth was fostered to a white family, who changed her name. At the age of eight, she was placed with another family for one year while her foster mother received psychiatric care. At the age of 12, her foster family returned her and her belongings, packed in plastic bags, to the local office of Youth and Community Services. Her stepfamily said they felt Ruth had always been 'weird' and that her behaviour was now quite strange (she talked and made noises into a tape recorder while crouched in a closed wardrobe). She was then fostered by another white family and, again her surname changed. This young woman, today in her early 30s, is attempting to work through an assortment of problems.

After seven years in Kinchela Boys' Home, John was sent to work at a dairy farm where he stayed until he was 18. Little else is known about him. He died at the age of 27 of liver disease caused by excessive alcohol consumption.

Normie was in Bomaderry until he was nine years old, when he was transferred to Kinchela. Normie will not talk about the time he spent in these institutions. He has been diagnosed as an alcoholic. With the help of Alcoholics Anonymous he remains sober, but suffers episodes of depression and often becomes emotional and withdrawn...

The three survivors in this family are Aboriginal Australians of this generation...when their records were examined, the reason for their removal was recorded. It read...Aboriginal.

Pat Swann, Aboriginal Medical Service, Redfern, Sydney; reprinted from Contact **112***, December 1989, pp. 10–12* seen in 'chronic cycles of alcoholism, gaol and further family disintegration' (Askham 1985, p. 31). The files of the South Australian Aboriginal Child Care Agency (ACCA) indicate that:

of 55 children and natural parents who contacted ACCA in regard to adoption into non-Aboriginal families, 52 were experiencing, or had experienced, severe emotional stress and disturbance. This stress was in relation to identity crisis, and inability to locate natural family members due to Government regulations on adoption. Twenty of the cases had severe drug or alcohol problems relating to their family, and identity issues. Anxiety, overeating, and inability to care for their own children, were other associated problems which came to our notice. Departmental files on adoption of Aboriginal children are not accessible to ACCA.

Askham 1985, p. 32

Figure 3.4 *Margaret Kay, an Aboriginal girl in domestic service around 1920. Under the assimilation policy, lighter-skinned children were deemed potentially able to function as Europeans if they were given adequate training. (Archives Authority of New South Wales)*

The problem of poor parenting on the part of the 'stolen' children themselves and, in some cases, the carry-over of this to *their* children, has only recently been discussed by some Aboriginal health and welfare workers (Anne Louis, pers. comm.). Finally it should be remembered 'that the view that children need a stable and permanent home, appropriate for children in an individualistic society, has less force in an Aboriginal context, where a child is part of an extensive and interlinking kin network' (Askham 1985). Formal adoption in an Aboriginal context means care by close relatives, and most states now have policies that recognise that care for Aboriginal children is best handled within the Aboriginal community.

Aboriginal settlements today

As a result of the dislocation mentioned earlier in this chapter, Aboriginal populations now live in several types of settlements that are usually categorised as remote or traditional settlements, town camps, rural communities and urban communities. Since the social and environmental conditions and health status of remote Aborigines is extensively dealt with in this text (see Thomson, chapter 2, and Torzillo and Kerr, chapter 8), the discussion in this chapter will concentrate on rural and urban communities.

Briefly, however, remote or traditionally oriented Aboriginal people number from 15 000 to 20 000, living in 150 to 200 communities. Here, initiation rites are performed, and traditional forms of law, behaviour and communication are observed. About 100 tribal languages are in use. Included in these figures are people who have returned to their ancestral homelands.

Recent years have seen the growth of the outstation movement: Aborigines have been leaving the large settlements that were created by European pastoralists and white policy makers and that, as mentioned before, brought together disparate tribal groups. Where possible, they have returned to their traditional country and are instigating land claims. In 1981, 540 remote Aboriginal communities or outstations were identified by the Department of Aboriginal Affairs. Many of these had air strips, bores, durable housing and were developing 'village style communities'. Communities such as these are found in Western Australia, South Australia, Arnhem Land and Queensland. No such communities exist in New South Wales, Victoria, Tasmania or the ACT (Healy et al. 1985).

Urban communities

If urban areas are defined as containing populations of 1000 or more people, then about 66 per cent of Aborigines can be classed as urban dwellers (AIH 1988). According to McConnochie et al. (1989, p. 21):

Urban cultures must...be studied in part from an historical perspective. The history of culture contact and 'chain migration' of Aborigines to the cities and towns has meant that Aborigines have responded to many different European situations, and brought their changing cultures and identities with them, forming diverse, unique urban communities with one thing in common, their Aboriginality.

Figure 3.5 *At Strelley, an Aboriginal-owned cattle farm in the Pilbara, Western Australia, an Aboriginal teacher conducts a class in the Nyangumarta language. Strelley is the administrative and resource base for an education system controlled by Aborigines and designed to preserve their culture and identity. (Mike Brown/Australian Overseas Information Service, Department of Foreign Affairs and Trade, Canberra)*

Many Aborigines who have been born and bred in the city still identify with the former settlement areas of their kin (Young 1981; Barwick 1974; Beasley 1975). The term 'part-Aborigine' that is often used to describe these urban people gives rise to certain conceptual problems. Langton (1981) argues that white social scientists analyse 'part-Aborigines' from an assimilationist and ethnocentric standpoint, which does not recognise the ways in which Aborigines adjust to city life. Furthermore, specific cultural practices and behaviours exist, albeit in the context of industrial life (see also Keen 1988). Gray (1989) points out that many 'urban' Aborigines are in fact recent migrants from the country and many return to the country, especially as their family commitments increase.

Special features of urban Aboriginal life identified by Langton include methods of conflict resolution, funerary rites and matrifocality as an accepted and even desired family form. Matrifocality may be attributed to the following:

Aboriginal men are unable to reside permanently with wives and children because of itinerant labour patterns, unemployment, imprisonment, regulations pertaining to social security benefits for supporting mothers and so on. Aboriginal social and cultural values may also contribute to the incidence of the woman focused family, in that mother, grandmother, aunts and other female relations provide a cultural core, remembering and passing on to their children the knowledge that provides them with an identity in a crowded, impersonal urban environment.

Langton 1981, p. 18

Further kinship allegiances through these networks enhance the viability of the group, and the family can offer emotional and economic support, and act as a buffer against prejudice, hostility and the ethnocentrism of the wider society. Group membership generates a sense of belonging, of comradeship and security: 'Belonging is a pleasure and often a matter of defiant pride. Consequently the policy of assimilation [when interpreted as dispersal and disappearance of Aboriginal groups] has little appeal' (Langton 1981, p. 155). A large proportion of Aboriginal households in Sydney, Adelaide and Brisbane are composed of extensive and extended family groups, which are fairly fluid in their composition. Barwick found that Melbourne households tended to be rather mobile, with people attaching more importance to locality rather than to actual place of residence: 'For Aborigines the basic subcultural ties are those of locality and family. They identify or place one another not by asking "what work do you do?" but rather "what place do you come from?" "which family is yours?" ' (Barwick 1974, p. 27). Thus, regional allegiance plays a strong part in maintaining kin ties, obligations and responsibilities. Aborigines are sustained by a subculture that demonstrates their pride in distinctiveness, coming from a certain place and belonging to a community, 'bonded by shared experience, common memories and inherited legends of oppression as a depressed indigenous minority' (Barwick 1974, p. 27) In Adelaide, Gale (unpub.) found that older Aboriginal women maintained close links with their country origins, and were instrumental in transmitting information between rural and urban groups. Kin and friendship ties were maintained through mutual visitation. In a study of Aboriginal households in Adelaide, 41 per cent of respondents reported 'strong and meaningful' ties to outside Aboriginal communities, 20 per cent reported 'real but not so strong' ties, and the remainder mentioned weak or totally non-existent ties (Radford et al. 1990).

Beasley (1975) found that the search for employment appears to be the most important reason Aborigines have for migrating to cities, although Young (1981) found employment to be much less important in migration in central Australia. Other reasons cited by Young were the need to gain access to health services and to provide better opportunities for children. The range of housing available to these 'migrants' corresponded to that available to other low-income groups and most Aboriginal households were occupied by kin related by blood or marriage.

Urban Aborigines are subject to the same economic deprivations as very poor whites, that is, those whose income depends solely on social security. However, the difference is that most Aborigines are dependent on such payments. In 1984, the median family income for Aborigines and Torres Strait Islanders was slightly more than half (54.5 per cent) that of all Australians (DAA 1984, p. 48). Urban-dwelling Aborigines suffer from diseases related to nutrition deficiency, from poor health care and stress-related conditions. They are exposed to social problems related to drug and alcohol use, and they are victims of racism. Aboriginal unemployment is very high and Aborigines are over-represented in imprisonment rates. In fact, Aborigines living in major urban areas appear to suffer the worst effects of poverty (HTIC 1988, p. 88; see also McDonald 1990; Wilson 1982).

Women and families

In Brisbane we visited a three-bedroom house that is home for sixteen family members. The house is rented by a woman and her husband. Their six surviving children (three are deceased), four grandchildren and daughter-in-law are also living with them along with the woman's youngest brother and her husband's parents. The children's ages range from 8 to 22. A daughter is pregnant with her second child.

Four generations live in the house. The 'lounge room' is used as a bedroom. A single bed is in one corner and two mattresses are stored underneath it during the day. On fine evenings, members of the family sleep outside. Occasional visits from other extended family members, who may stay for a number of months, add to the congestion.

None of the family members was refused accommodation. The three eldest children have had their names on housing lists for up to four years. They and their families have nowhere else to go. The father is the only one who has been able to find a job.

Six children are attending school. Three of them are in high school. There is no room for a book shelf with books, little room for clothes, and no room for studying, so no homework is done.

The house is full to overflowing and essentials such as shower, toilet, refrigerator and stove are rarely working properly. Windows are broken and patched up with whatever is available. Doors do not close, much less lock. The occupants do not notify the State housing authorities of much needed maintenance because they fear eviction. There is nowhere else to go!

Despite these living conditions the atmosphere was warm and welcoming. When we visited, children were arriving home from school and were everywhere. There was bread and jam appearing and disappearing, laughter, tears, nappies and noise. Although companionship was evident, immense strain and tiredness were clear on the woman's face. She looked much older than her 41 years. Nevertheless she was strong and determined and full of hope that everything would work out and get better. Her angry demands were for a better understanding by governments and authorities of the needs of large Aboriginal families. She could only stand by and watch as her husband and three eldest children drank more alcohol than they should. She could only stand by and watch the violence that erupted on many occasions after heavy drinking bouts. Often she would be the victim of this violence. She had no idea what to do about the complaints that kept coming from the school about the children. The idea of visiting the school was for her too traumatic—she did not have the confidence to talk to the teachers. She was not well but did not want to see a doctor for fear of what she would be told and because she did not feel comfortable with doctors.

When families break down and members move away from the community the pattern of obligation which underpinned the family is fragmented and consequently obligations are not met. This causes particular problems for the care of aged people. When people spoke of services for old people in their communities they were referring to more than health services. We met a number of elderly people who were not sick but who were not able to look after themselves. They were dependent upon people other than family members to care for them. This departure from traditional practice of the extended family caring for and supporting its members arises from factors such as family breakdown, shortage of accommodation and low income.

Overcrowding was cited as one of the reasons for family breakdown by a woman in Charleville. Certainly several older women expressed concern about living with their children because it was 'too crowded and too noisy'. This woman expressed a desire for a small place of her own.

From Daylight and Johnstone (1986)

Radford et al. (1990) found that levels of stress associated with 'economic, medical and other social conditions' have resulted in the one or more attempted suicides or consideration of suicide reported by a predominantly female sample. Certain factors were identified as being more often associated with suicide attempts than attributable to chance. These were:

employment instability of partner or care giver, lack of knowledge of at least one parent and foster home (but not institutional) experience by age 12, being in receipt of a pension or benefit, in receipt of past emergency aid, living in rented housing which was deemed unsatisfactory, personal mobility, lack of access to a private vehicle, frequent changes in employment, unemployment, a present major health problem in self or partner, drug abuse not including alcohol, number of police calls to the house, being bashed or sexually assaulted, a personal perception of non-acceptance by the rest of society, that 'minor violations of the law' bring major distress, frequent feelings of anger and that one did not have 'reasonable control' of one's life.

Radford et al. 1990 p. 2

The same or similar social conditions have been reported by Aboriginal women in other urban areas in New South Wales. Aboriginal women from the Newcastle Awabakal Cooperative described their distress associated with low income, welfare dependency, alcohol abuse and domestic violence (WHPRC 1985), and in its national consultations with Aboriginal women, the Aboriginal Women's Task Force (Daylight and Johnstone 1986) identified violence as an area of concern to Aboriginal women.

The current Royal Commission into Aboriginal Deaths in Custody (RCADC) has highlighted many of the problems that Aboriginal people in both urban and rural areas face in dealing with the justice system:

Aboriginals [sic] are arrested and imprisoned at many times the rate of non-Aboriginals [and] the numbers in custody and...dying in custody are very high in proportion to the Aboriginal population in the community at large.

RCADC 1989, p. 4

The National Police Custody Survey for August 1988 showed that 'Aboriginal people were apprehended and placed in police cells at a rate over twenty times that of non-Aboriginal people' (McDonald 1990, p. 5). The Northern Territory and Western Australia had the highest proportions of Aboriginal custodies (76 per cent and 54 per cent, respectively): these states also have the proportionately largest Aboriginal populations in Australia (see table 3.1).

The 1988 National Police Custody Survey found that, in every jurisdiction, repeat detentions were more common for Aborigines, who were generally incarcerated for longer periods of time than non-Aborigines. Although Aboriginal women represent less than 1.5 per cent of the national female population, they comprised nearly 50 per cent of all female custodies, with Queensland and Western Australia showing the highest female custody rates (McDonald 1990). Offences for which Aborigines were incarcerated and for which they were over-represented were disorderliness, assault and drunkenness. In contrast to non-Aborigines,

Table 3.1 Police custody rates per 100 000 population (1986 Census), August 1988

State	Aboriginal per 100 000 pop.	Non-Aboriginal per 100 000 pop.	Total custody per 100 000 pop.	Level of over-representation[a]
NSW	1312	87	103	15
Vic.	1570	117	123	13
Qld	2840	170	237	17
WA	7730	180	385	43
SA	4877	187	239	26
Tas.	640	123	135	5
NT	4776	429	1415	11
ACT	1967	185	197	11
Aust.	3539	131	183	27

[a] Rate ratios, i.e. ratios of Aboriginal custody rates to non-Aboriginal rates.

Source: McDonald 1990

they were under-represented for homicide, robbery, theft, fraud, sexual offences, drink driving and other driving-related matters, and drug offences (McDonald 1990).

In the inner Sydney suburb of Redfern there have been complaints about police activities from Aboriginal residents for some 20 years. The first Aboriginal Legal Service (ALS) was established in Redfern in 1970 as a result of these complaints. During the 1980s the area was the target of many police raids (Cuneen 1990), resulting in 1989 in the death by police shooting of an innocent Aboriginal man, and

Figure 3.6 *Helen Corbett laying wreaths at Long Bay Gaol, Sydney, during a protest on 27 January 1988. (S. Edwards)*

Figure 3.7 *A cartoon that appeared in the* Sydney Morning Herald *after a police raid on several Aboriginal homes in Redfern, Sydney, in February 1990 (A. Noir/*John Fairfax Group)

the intimidations of scores of other Aboriginal residents. Commenting on a raid that involved 128 police, the executive superintendent of police said, 'Our normal surveillance activities can't operate in a place like the black community. You stand out like you know what. Where do you survey the activity of people when they are all of the one breed?' (*Sydney Morning Herald*, 10 February 1990)

It is in this context that a discussion paper of the Royal Commission into Aboriginal Deaths in Custody examines the question of racism as perceived and experienced by Aboriginal people.

Although many non-Aboriginal people contend that there is little racism in Australia, many Aboriginals experience Australian society as highly racist, whether they be children at school, people seeking employment or accommodation, or people in contact with police or other public officials. Non-Aboriginal people who lack knowledge of Aboriginal history and society are often heard to ask why individual Aborigines do not in greater numbers pursue and achieve material success like many immigrants, some of whom come from disadvantaged backgrounds...self esteem, self respect and equality of opportunity will not readily develop in an atmosphere of hostility, prejudice and ignorance on the part of the non-Aboriginal community.

RCADC 1989, p. 9

Town camps

So-called fringe-dwelling Aborigines were defined by the House of Representatives Standing Committee on Aboriginal Affairs (HRSCAA) as:

Aboriginal persons who live on the fringes of both the Aboriginal and non-Aboriginal cultures but belong fully to neither; in particular, it refers to Aboriginals [sic] who live on the outskirts of, or within, a non-Aboriginal community who have acquired some of the traits or values common to it, but who are neither typical of nor accorded the same status as other members of that community.

HRSCAA 1982, p. 3

Whether there exists any person who meets this definition is open to debate.

Such a definition assumes the 'intactness' of Aboriginal society, and ignores the sociostructural position of Aborigines. It also overlooks the fact that Aboriginal culture has been dominated by that of the Anglo-Celtic colonisers. In this sense, all Aborigines are fringe dwellers. Submissions to the HRSCAA were critical of this definition, pointing out that it was a non-Aboriginal one of opprobrium, which had little currency for Aborigines and overlooked the fact that sociocultural structures, outside and different from those of non-Aborigines, existed in these settings. Accordingly, the term 'town camper' was adopted, meaning:

groups of Aborigines living at identified camp sites near or within towns or cities which form part of the socio-cultural structure of the towns and cities, but which have a life style that does not conform to that of the majority of non-Aboriginal residents and are not provided with essential services and housing on a basis comparable to the rest of the community.

HRSCAA 1982, p. 6

Altogether, about 20 000 people live in communities such as this.

Torzillo and Kerr (chapter 8, this volume) detail the conditions and the lack of adequate health care and other necessities referred to in this definition. Here, we describe some of the functions of these settlements and the effects that living in such locales has on families. We have already discussed some of the mechanisms that attracted or forced Aborigines to move to the edges of towns and cities and adopt a more settled lifestyle. Town camps provide an enclave for Aborigines who either do not wish to, or are not encouraged to, participate fully and equally in the (white) town community. Rented housing is often seen as an economic burden. For many Aborigines, town camps provide a satisfying environment, enabling Aboriginal values and beliefs to be transmitted. Apart from outstations, town camps also avoid the direct control of Anglo-Australian authority. The Aboriginal Development Commission (ADC) identified some positive features of town camps for Aborigines (HRSCAA 1982, p. 9):

- they allow some control over the environment;
- they give a degree of stability;
- there are less personal restrictions;
- they allow families to regroup;
- they alleviate racial tension;
- they provide cheaper living costs and readier access to services in the town;
- they may be situated on areas that have traditional significance.

Aboriginal people in transit use town camps as stopover points for a variety of reasons: to use town services, sell artefacts, attend meetings, funerals or conferences, and to visit friends and relations. Families also come to town to visit relatives in prison. During the wet season, pastoral workers visit the towns and people come in for special events, either traditional or non-traditional. The existence of a 'home-less drifter' group appears to be brought about by alcoholism and poverty, which in turn has led to the breakup of families, kinship systems, community structures and cultural heritage. The Kalano Community Association in Katherine reported that:

the authority of older Aboriginal people is on the decline and this decline is directly attributable to social pressures caused by drinking. Also, families have broken up, resulting in communities whose age structures provide them with unbalanced so-cial systems. Under these conditions, and coupled with lost traditional land ties, some Aboriginals [sic] have become apathetic and assumed the lifestyle of homeless drifters.

HRSCAA 1982, p. 11

For town campers, economic problems encompass housing, land tenure, employment, community facilities and transport. Visitors place strains on financial resources and on hospitality. Overcrowding causes tension, and the presence of several tribal groups living in the same camp can increase this tension and lead to open conflict. Aborigines give housing high priority, in that poor housing is seen as contributing to ill-health which then affects educational chances, thus reducing employment and train-ing opportunities. The former general manager of the ADC commented:

If we can provide housing, children will have somewhere to sleep, they will not get sick, they will have somewhere to study, they will be able to keep warm and employ-ment will be given at the time to people to construct the housing.

HRSCAA 1982, p. 21

By 1982, little authoritative data had been amassed on town campers' health status. The HRSCAA (1982) was told that environmental conditions were the cause of numerous health problems. For children, these included head lice, ringworm and scabies, conditions that also resulted in absence from school. Other problems men-tioned included poor nutrition, gastroenteritis, poor mental health and suicides. Aboriginal medical services are available to about 80 of the 206 town camps iden-tified by the HRSCAA. Because they are community controlled, these services are particularly responsive and accessible to Aboriginal patients.

Aboriginal communities are subject to discrimination by Anglo-Australian in-stitutions and individuals, as evidenced by the lack of improvement of camps. The federal Department of Health commented:

The level of action by officials on these matters is frequently determined by local political demands which are mainly expressed by local government councillors. It would appear that racial intolerance may be a strong factor in determining whether action of this type is taken.

HRSCAA 1982, p. 36

The social pressures placed on these populations cause Aborigines to worry about the disintegration of traditional authority structures, the breakdown of family units and the lessening of respect for elders.

Housing on the reserve

The first recognised, permanent settlement of Aboriginal people at La Perouse was in about 1880. It was illegal, but allowed to stay, because of the policy of keeping the blacks segregated from the whites. It is believed most of the people came from the south coast and that they came for the fish. Aboriginal people have always moved between La Perouse and the south coast. At the end of the 1870s and the beginning of 1880s twenty-six Aborigines camped permanently at La Perouse. Ten of these were reported to be full bloods. Missionaries worked at the camp since its beginning. Before managers were introduced the camp was looked after by resident missionaries and a policeman.

The camp was then established as a reserve under the Aborigines Protection Board in 1883. Tin houses were erected. They were on the shore of Botany Bay where the original camp was. It was an area of seven acres. The land was set aside for use by Aborigines but was not officially gazetted until 1895. At this time it was called Aborigines Camp. The Board's policy was to make reserves economically self supporting and independent by establishing farms on them, but this wasn't possible at La Perouse because the soil was too sandy. Instead they had to be self supporting fishermen at Frenchmans Bay beach adjoining the reserve. The Board provided boats and nets. Males over eleven years old were to participate. This plan wasn't successful because the fishing was seasonal. The Aborigines continued to visit the south coast for seasonal picking.

In 1929–1930 because the tin houses were sinking in the sand, the settlement was moved back to where we are today. New homes were built. These homes had two bedrooms, a kitchen and a fuel stove. There was a communal laundry with two sets of cement tubs, two coppers and everyone had to share days to do the washing. At one end of the laundry there was showers for the men, and at the other end there were showers for the women. This was depression time. Two unauthorised unemployment camps were settled north of the reserve, known as Hill 60 and Happy Valley. Blacks and whites lived alongside each other. Another unauthorised camp was set up called Frogs Hollow, on the southern boundary of the reserve, and it was predominantly Aboriginal.

After the Second World War Aborigines, whites and new Australians built their own shacks at Frogs Hollow. There were a lot of Russians living there. Randwick Council had a meeting with the people and told them that they couldn't stay, so the white people moved away from the area. This was the early 1950s. Aboriginal people were housed on the reserve or moved to Tasman Street. Some moved out of the area. The Board built ten new homes amongst the older ones on the reserve. The largest of these consisted of three bedrooms, five light switches and again a fuel stove. We used coal for fuel and we had an ice chest with a large block of ice that would last for two or three days. They had no bathrooms but a pump in the shower with a piece of hose put into a bucket and we would pull the handle back and forwards, but we later made changes ourselves. Ones that had regular employment, bought their own electric stoves, hot water systems and washing machines.

We were constantly protected by a manager who lived on the reserve. The manager would just walk into anyone's house without knocking to inspect it. If the Board thought you weren't looking after your children, they would just have them taken away. Those children never saw their people again. When they were old enough to work they were put out as house servants. We paid seventeen shillings a week rent. Housing had always been a major problem. There is no excuse for the government. We could have been looked after better than we have. Monies that were given to the Aborigines Protection Board by the government for repairs to the houses were put back into revenue, rather than making our living standard better.

By 1972 the Board was abolished and a new government body was formed to represent us. It was called the Directorate for Aboriginal Welfare. Because the houses were dilapidated there was a new housing project at La Perouse. The scheme for Aboriginal housing involved replacing the old houses with newly constructed ones, so the old and very old houses were demolished and twenty-eight houses and four aged units now exist on a seven acre site. These houses have three, four or five bedrooms and were built up to Housing Commission standard. In these houses we have thirteen or more light switches, an electric stove, a power point in every room and separate toilet and bathroom. We paid rents to the Housing Commission which then handed them over to the Aboriginal Lands Trust set up in 1973. It was abolished in March 1983 when new legislation came in and set up Local Land Councils so now we are responsible to ourselves only. We pay rent and are much happier and freer, free to have our white friends in our home. The children are not taken away.

Iris Williams (reprinted from Williams 1988, pp. 7–9)

Town campers are economically reliant on social welfare payments and seasonal pastoral employment. De facto marriages are common, as is the female-headed household. Women are widely regarded as being the most important members of the household, as it is the mother who provides economic stability through welfare income, provides care and nurturance and is often a leader in community initiatives (Daylight and Johnstone 1986). However, economic deprivation and the disruption of the traditional marriage responsibilities of men have left women in a vulnerable position. There is less obligation for husbands to stay with the family and women may not have appropriate 'care-taking' relatives to whom they can turn, for instance in the case of male violence.

Specific health and welfare issues

Infants, children and adolescents

In the mid-1960s, the appearance of information about Aboriginal infant mortality levels provoked much comment in Australia. Striking as it did at the very core of responsiveness of an Australian population then preoccupied with marriage and motherhood, the revelations about large numbers of little black Australian babies dying provoked a groundswell of community demand for action. Community concern was attested in newspaper headlines as every new piece of information emerged in the late 1960s and early 1970s.

The result of this attention was the expansion of Commonwealth-funded health services for Aborigines. The new programs concentrated their initial attention almost entirely on maternal and child health, operating mostly through state governments at that time. There were impressive results, as discussed by Thomson in chapter 2 of this volume. From infant mortality rates above 100 per 1000 live births in the late 1960s and early 1970s, in some parts of Australia, the rates fell to below 40 per 1000 live births by the early 1980s in all parts of Australia for which data were available (Smith 1980*a*; Thomson 1983). Since then, there has been much more gradual change, although in most parts of Australia Aboriginal infant mortality rates may now be less than 30 per 1000 live births.

It is helpful to consider these figures in perspective. First, in the past Aboriginal infant mortality rates were very much higher than non-Aboriginal rates, and they remain very much higher today. Since the mid-1960s, infant mortality rates for the total Australian population have declined by more than 50 per cent to about 9 per 1000 live births. It can be seen that the Aboriginal rates remain about three times as high as those of the total Australian population, compared with rates that were possibly five to six times as high two or three decades ago. However, during most of the period of decline the two series were moving mostly in step, and during the 1980s the rate for the total population possibly declined even faster than the Aboriginal rate. If the aim of health programs has been to remove disparities between Aboriginal health and the health of the Australian population in general, then these results establish that the target has kept shifting even as improvements have been made.

Yet, from an absolute perspective, the declines in infant mortality have resulted in levels that are lower than in any less-developed country and are very low compared with the levels that have prevailed throughout the history of human mortality experience. Until within the last 200 years, all human populations had very high levels of infant and early childhood mortality, levels that respected neither social class, the economic strength of nations, the type of economy nor type of social organisation. There were undoubtedly differences between populations both in scale and nature of mortality in infancy and early childhood, but there were no populations in which risk of early mortality was almost negligible, as it is today in high-income countries. Muhsam (1979) notes that the absence of the conditions for many

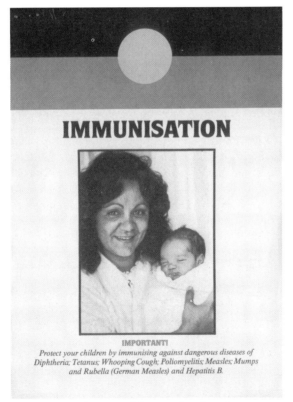

IMPORTANT!
Protect your children by immunising against dangerous diseases of Diphtheria; Tetanus; Whooping Cough; Poliomyelitis; Measles; Mumps and Rubella (German Measles) and Hepatitis B.

Figure 3.8 *The Aboriginal Health Unit of the New South Wales Department of Health publishes health information pamphlets such as this one on immunisation to encourage Aboriginal communities to protect their children against disease (Aboriginal Health Unit, NSW Department of Health, Sydney)*

diseases in hunter-gatherer societies implies that a transition from hunting and gathering to agriculture must have been accompanied by a demographic transition to higher mortality and fertility than prevailed beforehand. On the other hand, the same change would have decreased maternal mortality, and conditions that are more favourable for the survival of the mother are also more favourable for the successful gestation and neonatal survival of the child. The higher mortality to which Muhsam refers would have been the result of post-neonatal mortality from infectious diseases and pest vectors encouraged by more concentrated settlement. However, as we have already noted, accidents were apparently very common causes of death for children in hunting and gathering Aboriginal populations.

In the case of Aboriginal populations in Australia, it has been pointed out that lower-bound estimates of Aboriginal mortality before 1788 would mean that the English invaders would have encountered people with death rates lower than their own and birth rates very much lower, and that observations by nineteenth-century writers (for example, Curr 1886, pp. 70, 208) possibly support that view (Gray 1985).

The history of mortality of Aboriginal infants and young children during the last 200 years was probably as follows: little change at first, then increases in mortality levels as a result of introduced diseases, particularly in concentrated settlements; then gradual improvement until by the 1960s levels were similar to those experienced by the total Australian population in the early part of the twentieth century and to those which were and still are prevalent in many less-developed countries; then very rapid improvement in a short space of time, but to a new low level still well above the Australian population standard.

The determinants of relative ill-health in infancy and early childhood start to work their effects at birth and before birth. Various studies report a high incidence of low birth weight babies linked with poor survival in the perinatal period: that is, a higher incidence of late fetal death or early neonatal death (for example, Seward and Stanley 1981; Kliewer and Stanley unpub.; Julienne 1983). Growth patterns of Aboriginal infants deviate below international standards (Gracey et al. 1983), but not if living conditions are similar to those of other Australians (Cockington 1980).

The nature of illness in childhood is substantially different for Aboriginal and non-Aboriginal Australians. Aboriginal infant mortality includes a very high proportion of deaths from respiratory and infectious diseases, which are much less prominent in non-Aboriginal morbidity and mortality data (Devanesen et al. 1986). These illness patterns are a reflection of the unhygienic living conditions of many Aborigines, which also contribute to the characteristic illnesses suffered by Aboriginal children and their resulting developmental disadvantages, such as those associated with ear disease.

Adults

Contemporary patterns of ill-health of Aboriginal adults would hardly be explicable outside the historical context that has been outlined in earlier sections of this chapter. This premise is one that should be kept in mind, but it is unfortunately also true that there is so little evidence about the development of these contemporary patterns of ill-health that it is necessary to start from a rather more prosaic description and infer aspects of development with reference to the historical context.

The main sources of quantitative information about the health of people in Australia are in the first instance descriptions of their ill-health, especially mortality, but also included here are the collections of data on hospital patients, known as hospital morbidity collections. Only in recent years have whole-population surveys of aspects of health itself been attempted. Until the last few years, there has never been any attempt to provide separate information about Aboriginal morbidity, mortality and health in these collections of data (see the case study by Thomson, 'The availability of Aboriginal health statistics', in chapter 2) . In this way, the patterns of Aboriginal adult health remained hidden from official perception and action, except where specific classes of problem were noted. Only recently has any information about Aboriginal health started to emerge from the standard collections of information about the general population.

Surprising as it may seem, one of the best sets of information that we have about the health of a population, as distinct from its ill-health, is a by-product of data on mortality. A life table derived from mortality data usually contains information on 'expectation of life' at exact ages. Expectation of life at birth (the average number of years that a baby would live if it experienced the death rates of the table) is usually considered to be a measure of the level of mortality in a population. It is no such thing. Every population has exactly the same level of mortality, eventually; that is, everyone dies. The expectation of life is certainly a measure of the age distribution of mortality. By implication, what it actually measures is the level of intensity of survival in the population. This is certainly a measure of health, one of the best we could possibly have, except that it takes no account of those aspects of health that determine the quality rather than quantity of survival.

Information about the survival prospects of Aboriginal people, measured in this way, was scanty until the 1980s. There were previous estimates for some parts of Australia, sometimes based on model life tables and sometimes on actual distributions of deaths (Jones 1963; Moodie 1973; Boundy unpub.; NSWHC 1979; Smith 1980b). It was not until the early 1980s when some life tables for the Aboriginal population of New South Wales were produced that it was definitely recognised that the pattern of Aboriginal mortality resembled no model life table pattern (Smith et al. 1983). It was only the accumulation of direct evidence from different parts of Australia that prompted this realisation.

What was found was a pattern of very high rates of mortality in middle adulthood. This is illustrated ·in figure 3.9, using various series of data from different points of time. Some of the data are from unpublished sources; other data are from Australian Institute of Health (1988) and Gray and Hogg (1989). The diagram for males establishes that adult mortality rates are extremely similar in all the sets of data, but the 1960s data from the Northern Territory show much higher mortality rates for infants, children and teenagers. A slightly different picture is conveyed by the equivalent data for females; in this case, the higher rates for the Northern Territory in the 1960s extend through the ages of childbearing to women in their early forties.

Few would have expected that the pattern and level of Aboriginal male adult mortality in New South Wales in the mid-1980s would be almost identical to those of the Northern Territory 20 years earlier. Neither was it to be expected that mortality patterns for Aboriginal women in the 1980s, at all ages, would be similar in the

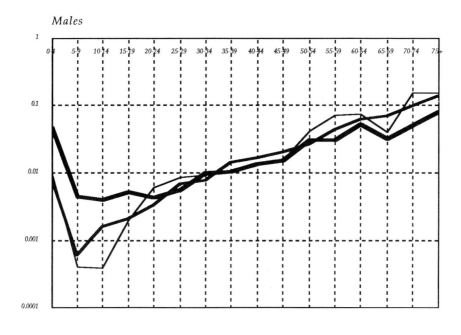

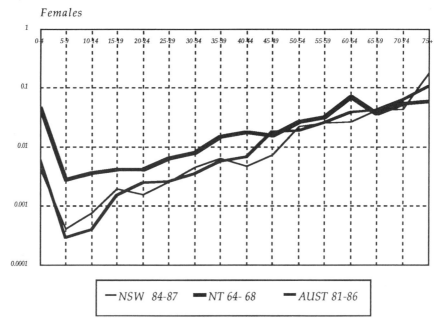

Figure 3.9 *Aboriginal mortality estimates for the Northern Territory in the 1960s, Australia as a whole in the early 1980s, and western New South Wales in the mid-1980s show close similarity at adult ages. This is especially marked for males. The rates are expressed on a logarithmic scale, for five-year age groups. (Based on data from Australian Institute of Health 1988, Gray and Hogg 1989, and unpublished sources)*

western parts of the country to those in the eastern parts. There are vast differences in environmental conditions in different parts of Australia. Even more striking than these similarities is the fact that we could overlay mortality rates for Canadian Indians and obtain a reasonably close correspondence.

When life tables are constructed from these sets of data, it is found that the survival prospects of young adults are extremely low by any standards. Expectation of life at age 20 is less than 40 years for men in all but one of the four sets of data in figure 3.9, and it is about 45 for women in the data from the 1980s. From other parts of the world, national life tables with such low levels of expectation of adult life are rare. In a recent set of life tables (United Nations 1986), the only tables for males at age 20 with a life expectation lower than the highest value derived from the Aboriginal male series (there were none lower than the lowest value) were Liberia in 1971, Malawi in 1977, Rwanda in 1978, Swaziland in 1976, Bangladesh in 1974 (but not 1981), Sabah in 1980 and Sarawak in 1980. For females the results were similar, with the addition of Cape Verde in 1979–1981, Iran in 1976, the Maldives in 1982 and Nepal in 1981. Most of these countries are among the least-developed countries of Africa and Asia.

It must be emphasised in this context that it is Aboriginal *adult* survival that is extremely low by world standards. There are very many countries with expectation of life at birth lower than the Aboriginal population in the 1980s, because there are still very many countries with extremely poor levels of infant and child survival. There are only a handful of countries, however, that have such poor survival prospects for adults. Even though the measure of health that is being used here is a measure of quantity of survival and not its quality, it is clear that low quantity must also imply low quality of survival. Why are Aboriginal adults so unhealthy?

A conventional answer to this question is to enumerate the causes of death that contribute to high death rates, or to fill pages with tables of statistics of treatment of illness in hospitals. This approach leads to the conclusion that Aboriginal death rates are higher than the death rates of other Australians in virtually every major class of cause of death. It is therefore not very helpful except to identify some categories of illness that seem to contribute disproportionately to mortality. The most outstanding category of illness in this sense is circulatory system disease (see also Thomson, chapter 2 in this volume).

Circulatory system diseases

Gray and Hogg (1989) found that in western New South Wales in 1984–87, diseases of the circulatory system made up approximately 40 per cent of the excess risk of mortality of Aboriginal people compared with the total population of the state. They also found that the relative risk of ischaemic heart disease for Aboriginal men and women was a risk approximately 13 times higher than for the total New South Wales population. Data from other parts of Australia (see Plant 1990 and Khalidi 1990 for the Northern Territory; Hicks 1990, p. 73, for Western Australia; Australian Institute of Health 1988 for various parts of Australia) show a similar pattern of causes of mortality but usually with a somewhat lower contribution from ischaemic heart disease.

There are two major issues concerning the classification of Aboriginal deaths due to ischaemic heart disease: the first is that apparent low occurrence in the past in remote parts of Australia was partly mediated by a conventional view among medical practitioners that Aborigines did not suffer from ischaemic heart disease at all; the second is that, in cases of sudden death, ascription of the cause to an ischaemic-disease-related infarction (heart attack) may be a matter of pure convenience in the absence of an autopsy. The second of these issues was of some concern in the study in western New South Wales (Gray and Hogg 1989), but it was found that causes of death involving ischaemic heart disease usually referred to pre-existing conditions known to the practitioner certifying the death and so were genuine cases. As for the contention made repeatedly by medical practitioners in remote areas of Australia that circulatory system disease is a relatively recent phenomenon that has become apparent only in the 1980s, Khalidi (1990) found that on the contrary there had been little change in age-specific incidence in the decade from the mid-1970s through to the mid-1980s. The idea that Aborigines did not suffer heart disease may have been purely perceptual and conventional.

There are many extant questions about the causation of high levels of heart disease among Aborigines. It is also linked with other prevalent disease syndromes such as diabetes mellitus and with dietary changes that accompanied the historical processes of concentration of the Aboriginal population.

Effects of high mortality

Let us adopt a different perspective on Aboriginal adult mortality, and look not at its antecedents but at its effects. The death of a parent in early adulthood directly affects the economic conditions of a family and the family environment of children who are frequently still young. Not only are such people the fathers or mothers of young children, but they are also the main supports of elderly parents and family rent-payers. Table 3.2 shows the extent of parental loss among some Aboriginal people on the far north coast of New South Wales in 1986.

Table 3.2   Survival of parents of Aboriginal people, Aboriginal Family Demography Study, 1986

| Age group | Numbers of Aborigines | | | | |
	Both parents living	Mother living	Father living	Neither parent living	Total
0–4	65	1	2	–	68
5–9	57	3	–	–	60
10–14	63	4	5	2	74
15–19	53	13	9	1	76
20–24	52	6	5	6	69
25–29	28	6	1	12	47
30–34	10	8	3	7	28
35–39	4	7	4	11	26
40–44	5	10	3	17	35
45–49	–	4	4	12	20
50+	–	6	–	24	30

Source: Gray 1987

From table 3.2, it can be calculated that at least one parent had been lost through death by: 8 per cent of children aged less than 15 years, 28 per cent of 15–24-year-olds, 49 per cent of 25–34-year-olds and 92 per cent of people aged 35 or more. Not one out of 50 people aged 45 or more had both parents living, and not one of 30 people aged 50 or more had a living father. This progression demonstrates that the major impact of adult mortality begins in the teenage years. It is a part of growing up as an Aborigine; its effects are felt either directly or through the traumatic experiences of cousins and close friends; and it occurs right in the crucial period of a young person's education and transition into adulthood.

It is reasonable to expect that a society whose families experience this kind of mortality impact will be geared to attempt to cope with it. In fact, of 40 children and young people under the age of 20 who had lost at least one parent, most were not in single-parent households: 9 were in households with a surviving parent and a step-parent, 12 were in households with the surviving parent, 11 were in households in which they had no parents but they did have grandparents, and the remaining 8 were with brothers, sisters, uncles, aunts and cousins. There is obviously a very considerable role for grandparents and other relations in assuming responsibility for children whose parents have died.

In a social environment in which death occurs frequently, it is also natural to expect that there will be a degree of expectation of mortality. In the area of the study mentioned above (Gray 1987), there are many adherents of fundamentalist Aboriginal church groups. There are also portents of death, including a 'death bird', whose call proclaims the death of the hearer or close relations. Other birds are also considered to be bearers of important news. Such beliefs are held strongly by Aboriginal people in the study area, and variants can be found in most parts of Australia.

Mortality patterns

How did these patterns of mortality develop? How do they compare with mortality in the past? While there is little data available for points progressively further back in time, information on orphanhood of Aboriginal children under 16 years of age in 1933 from the Australian census of that year sheds some light on the direction of change since that time. Of the total 13 000 Aboriginal children born between 1917 and 1933, 11 422 or 85.3 per cent still had both parents living, a further 872 or 6.5 per cent had living mothers, a further 791 or 5.9 per cent had living fathers, and 303 or 2.3 per cent had neither parent living. (Interestingly, the proportions for those people classified at the time as 'full blood' and those classified as 'half blood' are very similar, indicating very similar adult mortality for the two groups.)

When these results are compared with the recent data in table 3.2, the proportions of those with deceased parents seemed to be much higher in the past. However, this is to be expected because child bearing in more recent times has tended to occur at much younger ages, particularly of the fathers, than in the past. When allowance is made for these differences, it still appears that adult Aboriginal female mortality approximately 60 years ago was higher than it has been recently, although adult male mortality may have been lower then than now. Higher female mortality in the past is consistent with the large excesses of adult males that were observed in the earliest population counts. It is difficult to be conclusive because there are no obvious ways to push the mortality analysis back any further in time. Yet the effects of white settlement, such as disruption of families, were clearly even more severe 60 years ago than they have been in recent times. We can infer that the coping structures of Aboriginal societies were either stronger in the past than now or stretched to the point of intolerance. It was this period that saw the reversal of the decline of the Aboriginal population that had occurred since the beginning of white settlement and a movement towards positive population growth (Smith 1980*b*).

The renewal of the family

This chapter has outlined the practical implications for Aboriginal families of the attempted control of Aboriginal societies by the regulation of families. It has also been suggested here that it is not possible to look at the health of communities outside the context of the history of relations between Aborigines and non-Aborigines. Significantly, this history is not dissimilar to the history of many other conflicts between coloniser and colonised elsewhere in the world, and the health issues are very similar for many indigenous populations today. This alone tells us something about cause and effect, about what it is that Aboriginal people have tried to protect and nurture and what, as a consequence, the colonisers had to overcome in order to subdue and disenfranchise them. Aboriginal families were placed both as defenders and targets in the confrontation. They were a source of strength and therefore a prime target for the colonial authorities. Aboriginal people would argue that there was a systematic campaign of violence and 'pacification' against their communities in an attempt to provide stability for the newly founded Australian colonies. There can be no doubt that there was a campaign, but it is open to debate whether in most cases it was systematic or simply a set of pragmatic actions. The land was the objective of the campaign and Aboriginal peoples were the barrier to its successful acquisition. As violent confrontation passed into uneasy accommodation and unequal sharing of land, colonial policy makers focused their attention on the family as the core unit of Aboriginal communities.

The stolen generations are the most recent manifestation of these policies and the policy effects are still felt. Children were taken 'for being Aboriginal'. The justification given was often put in terms of moral or physical threat to the children by their own families. Many young women were taken, if not 'for being Aboriginal', for being said to be in moral danger so long as they remained with their people. However many were then trained to be domestic servants, later went into service in white households and sometimes became the sexual property of the men who headed those households.

Today Aboriginal families are in a constant state of flux as the result of these depravations and their appallingly high mortality rates relative to the rest of the Australian population. The impact of reduced life expectancy in Aboriginal communities was eloquently summarised by the question 'Where are all the grandfathers?' posed by one Aboriginal commentator (pers. comm. by Aboriginal elder to S. Houston). Yet by any standards, and certainly from an Aboriginal perspective, the Aboriginal family has endured and retained a commonality across all regions of Australia. This may seem all the more remarkable given the evidence presented in this chapter of the concerted attacks on Aboriginal family life. Why has this commonality survived? What is it about Aboriginal families that compels us to accept the essential Aboriginality of families even after 200 years of systematic attempts at destruction? Surely there must be some greater influence than acknowledged common genetic inheritance, which informs most dictionary definitions of the term 'family'.

Anthropologists have described the complexity of Aboriginal kinship, and we have noted that in Aboriginal ways of life members of the so-called extended family assume functions, duties and rights which in non-Aboriginal communities would be assumed either by the biological parents or by the State or the Church. These rights can extend from discipline to education, birthing and decisions about marriage and settlement of disputes.

In the birthing process, for instance, grandmothers and aunts play a significant midwifery role, as they combine both a practical service and a religious function in terms of the ceremonies carried out before, during and after birth. In the urban context, these traditional assistants may or may not be present. The Aboriginal Medical Service in Tharawal, New South Wales, which serves a large urban community 80 kilometres from Sydney, has an antenatal program that focuses on providing information to aunts and grandmothers. Teenage mothers are frequently not well grounded in parenting skills, and find that child-rearing places restrictions on normal teenage activities. The older and more experienced women therefore play an important role as they step in to care for the child during the early years and, at the same time, educate and advise the young mother on parenting skills. In this way,

Figure 3.10 *Arthur Hooper, Priscila Boney and family live at Dodge City, Brewarrina, in north-western New South Wales. Through the vehicle of the family, Aborigines can guarantee an Aboriginal future for their children. (S. Edwards)*

traditional child-care practices are carried on, and the child may return to the biological mother or stay with relatives. Either way, the crucial point is that the child remains in touch with his or her Aboriginality and family. Thus the relationship between the biological parent and child is in no way diminished, while an appreciation of the valuable contribution made by members of the wider family to the nuclear group is gradually established.

Traditionally, the education of children was a family affair until puberty, when responsibility passed to significant elders. In the urban context, children face the conflicts engendered by being Aboriginal in a sea of non-Aborigines. One way to gain strength and confidence to face this challenge is to understand who they are and where they are from. Most Aboriginal children know where their parents' ancestral land is located , and where they were born. Even in the urban context, there is a preoccupation with education about identity, home and country, and it is invariably older people who fulfil this function. As parents reach their late twenties and thirties they begin to take on the elders' roles and 'settle down'. One of the reasons for this haste to maturity is found in the deaths that surround Aboriginal people. As one Aborigine said, 'You see so many deaths, and when you start to see your contemporaries die, it makes people sit down and take stock. Can I regain what I've lost?' (pers. comm.) When deaths occur, it is important to affirm family genealogy, because a consolidation of kinship at this time is necessary.

Elders have always been the key people to inform others about marriage rules, about who can marry whom. While traditional marriage laws are largely absent in the urban context, there is a re-emergence of prohibitions on marriage between certain close relatives. In the situation arising from the policy of taking children from their natural parents, it is very important that there are some people who are 'kinship custodians'. In this way, the unique Aboriginal family, with its repository of kinship knowledge, is able to ensure, to a great degree, that marriage between siblings does not occur. Many communities have 'cultural gatekeepers' who are consulted on marriage eligibility and on matters of history. As Aboriginal people say, 'Culture is not people's song and dance and speech, it is an attitude and way of doing things. You can't kill Aboriginal culture until you kill Aboriginal people' (pers. comm.).

Given all the objective facts relating to Aboriginal morbidity and mortality, it may seem that we should be speaking solely of the decline of the Aboriginal family, rather than the decline and rise. However, Aboriginal people at the community level say that Aboriginal communities are strong and getting stronger. It is at this 'grass roots' level that fundamental changes are being noticed and it is here that a reassertion of the Aboriginal concept of the family is occurring. There is an impetus to Aboriginalise ways of doing things, to introduce Aboriginal values and aspirations into everyday living, which results in the emergence of a culture strengthened by adaptation and readaptation. Some sectors of the Aboriginal community are pressing for parallel development, that is to remain a distinct, yet viable and equal society within the Australian nation. This distinctness would entail control of those processes that make Aborigines unique. By the 'rise' of the Aboriginal family we mean this demand for community control and for the processes of establishment of identity and development that have given Aborigines the strength to carry on. Families are becoming the vehicle through which Aborigines guarantee an Aboriginal future for their children.

References

AIH (Australian Institute of Health) (1988), 'Aboriginal Health—a case study', in *Australia's health*, the first biennial report of the Australian Institute of Health, AGPS, Canberra.

Askham, H. (1985), 'Aboriginal health issues—our children and the bureaucracy', in *Women's health in a changing society* (conference proceedings), vol. 2.

Barwick, D. (1974), 'The Aboriginal family in south-eastern Australia', in J. Krupinski and A. Stoller (eds), *The family in Australia*, Pergamon Press, Sydney, pp. 153–67..

Beasley, P. (1975), 'The Aboriginal household in Sydney', in R. Taft, J. Dawson, P. Beasley, *Attitudes and social conditions*, ANU Press, Canberra, pp. 137–87.

Berndt, R. M., and Berndt, C. H. (1987), *End of an era: Aboriginal labour in the Northern Territory*, AIAS, Canberra.

Berndt, R. M., and Berndt, C. H. (1988) *The world of the first Australians: Aboriginal traditional life past and present*, Aboriginal Studies Press, Canberra.

Billington, R. P., (1960), 'Report of the nutrition unit—chapter 3: the health and nutritional status of the Aborigines', in C. P. Mountford (ed.), *Records of the American-Australian expedition to Arnhem Land*, vol. 2: 'Anthropology and nutrition', Melbourne University Press, Melbourne.

Black, R. H. (1972), *Malaria in Australia*, AGPS, Canberra.

Brady, M., and Morice, R. (1982), 'Defiance or despair? Petrol-sniffing in an Aboriginal community', in J. Reid (ed.), *Body land and spirit: health and healing in Aboriginal society*, University of Queensland Press, St Lucia, pp. 72–88.

Butlin, N. (1983), *Our original aggression: Aboriginal populations of southeastern Australia 1788-1850*, George Allen and Unwin, Sydney.

CARPA (Central Australian Rural Practitioners Association) (1990), *Newsletter* **11**, February, PO Box 8143, Alice Springs, NT.

Cleland, J. B. (1960), 'The future of the Australian Aboriginal', *Medical Journal of Australia*, 2 January.

Cockington, R. A. (1980), 'Growth of Australian Aboriginal children related to social circumstances', *Australian and New Zealand Journal of Medicine* **10**, pp. 199–208

Cowlishaw, G. (1982), 'Family planning: a post-contact problem', in J. Reid (ed.), *Body, land and spirit: health and healing in Aboriginal society*, University of Queensland Press, St Lucia, pp. 31–48.

Cumpston, H. H. L. (1914), *The history of smallpox in Australia*, Government Printer, Melbourne.

Cuneen, C. (1990), *Aboriginal police relations in Redfern: with special reference to the 'police raid' of 8 February 1990*, report commissioned by the National Inquiry into Racist Violence, Human Rights and Equal Opportunity Commission, May.

Curr, E. M. (1886), *The Australian race: its origin, languages, customs, place of landing in Australia and the routes by which it spread itself over that continent*, 4 vols, Government Printer, Melbourne.

DAA (Department of Aboriginal Affairs) (1984), *Aboriginal social indicators*, AGPS, Canberra.

Daylight, P., and Johnstone, M. (1986), *Women's business: report of the Aboriginal Women's Task Force*, AGPS, Canberra.

Devanesen, D., Furber, M., Hampton, D., Honari, M., Kinmonth, N., and Peach, H. G. (1986), *Health indicators in the Northern Territory*, Northern Territory Department of Health, Darwin.

Eschenbach, D. A., Harnisch, J. P., and Holmes, K. K. (1977), 'Pathogenesis of acute pelvic inflammatory disease: role of contraception and other risk factors', *American Journal of Obstetrics and Gynaecology* **128** (8), pp. 838–50.

Gilbert, K. (1973), *Because a white man'll never do it*, Angus and Robertson, Sydney.

Gracey, M., Murray, H., Hitchcock, N. E., Owles, E. N., and Murphy, B. P. (1983), 'The nutrition of Australian Aboriginal infants and young children', *Nutrition Research* **3**, pp. 133–47.

Gray, A., (1983). 'Aboriginal fertility at the time of European contact: the Daly River Mission baptismal register', *Aboriginal History* **7**, pp. 80–9.

Gray, A. (1985), 'Limits for demographic parameters of Aboriginal populations in the past', *Australian Aboriginal Studies* **1**, pp. 22–7.

Gray, A. (1988), 'Aboriginal society: demographic and social history', in J. Jupp (ed.), *The Australian people: an encyclopedia of the nation, its people and their origins*, Angus and Robertson, Sydney, pp. 135–40.

Gray, A. (1989), 'Aboriginal migration to the cities', *Journal of the Australian Population Association* **6**, p. 2.

Gray, A., and Hogg, R. (1989), *Mortality of Aboriginal Australians in western New South Wales 1984–1987*, New South Wales Department of Health, Sydney.

Greer, G. (1984), *Sex and destiny*, Harper and Row, New York.

Haglund, L. (1976), *An archaeological analysis of the Broadbeach Aboriginal Burial Ground*, University of Queensland Press, St Lucia.

Hamilton, A. (1981), *Nature and nurture: Aboriginal child-rearing in north-central Arnhem Land*, AIAS, Canberra.

Healy, J., Hassan, R., and McKenna, R. B. (1985), 'Aboriginal families', in D. Storer (ed.), *Ethnic family values in Australia*, Prentice Hall, Sydney, pp. 291–332.

Hiatt, B. (1978), 'Woman the gatherer', in F. Gale (ed.), *Woman's role in Aboriginal society*, AIAS, Canberra, pp. 4–15.

Hicks, D. G. (1990), 'Aboriginal mortality rates in Western Australia', in A. Gray (ed.), *A matter of life and death: contemporary Aboriginal mortality*, Aboriginal Studies Press, Canberra, pp. 71–6.

Hill, E. (1951), *The Territory*, Angus and Robertson, Sydney.

HRSCAA (House of Representative Standing Committee on Aboriginal Affairs) (1982), *Strategies to help overcome the problems of Aboriginal town campers*, October.

HTIC (Health Targets Implementation Committee) (1988), *Health for all Australians: report to Australian Health Ministers' Advisory Council*, AGPS, Canberra.

Jones, F. L. (1963), *A demographic survey of the Aboriginal population of the Northern Territory, with special reference to Bathurst Island Mission*, AIAS, Canberra.

Julienne, A. (1983), *A comparative study of perinatal outcome among Aboriginal and non-Aboriginal hospital confinements in rural New South Wales*, Working Paper 3, New South Wales Department of Health, Sydney.

Kaberry, P. (1939), *Aboriginal woman: sacred and profane*, Routledge, London.

Keen, J. (ed.) (1988), *Being black: Aboriginal culture in 'settled' Australia*, Aboriginal Studies Press, Canberra.

Khalidi, N. A. (1990), 'Levels and trends of Aboriginal mortality in central Australia', in A. Gray (ed.), *A matter of life and death: contemporary Aboriginal mortality*, Aboriginal Studies Press, Canberra, pp. 85–94.

Kunitz, S. (in press), 'Disease and the destruction of indigenous populations', in T. Ingold (ed.), *Humanity, culture and social life: an encyclopaedia of anthropology*, Routledge and Kegan Paul, London.

Langton, M. (1981), 'Urbanizing Aborigines: the social scientists great deception', *Social Alternatives* **2** (2), pp. 16–22.

Long, J. P. M. (1970), *Aboriginal settlements: a survey of institutional settlements in eastern Australia*, ANU Press, Canberra.

McConnochie, K., Hollensworth, D., and Pettman, J. (1989), *Race and racism in Australia*, Social Science Press, NSW.

McDonald, D. (1990), *National Police Custody Survey August 1988: national report*, Royal Commission into Deaths in Custody, Research Paper 13, March.

Malinowski, B. (1913), *The family among the Australian Aborigines: a sociological study*, University of London Press, London (reprinted 1963, New York, Schocken Book).

Meggitt, M. J. (1962) *Desert people: a study of the Walbiri Aborigines of central Australia*, Angus and Robertson, Sydney.

Middleton, M. R., and Francis, S. H. (1976), *Yuendumu and its children: life and health on an Aboriginal settlement*, AGPS, Canberra.

Mitterauer, M., and Sieder, R. (1982), *The European family: patriarchy to partnership from the middle ages to the present*, Basil Blackwell, Oxford.

Moodie, P. M. (1973), *Aboriginal health*, ANU Press, Canberra.

Muhsam, H. V. (1979), 'The demographic transition: from wastage to conservation of human life', in *Population science in the service of mankind*, International Union for the Scientific Study of Population, Liège, pp. 143–63.

Mulvaney, D. J. (1989), *Encounters in place: outsiders and Aboriginal Australians 1606–1985*, University of Queensland Press, St Lucia.

NAHSWP (National Aboriginal Health Strategy Working Party) (1989), *A National Aboriginal health strategy*, Department of Aboriginal Affairs, Canberra (limited circulation).

NSWHC (New South Wales Health Commission, Aboriginal Policy Committee) (1979), *Aboriginal mortality in country areas of New South Wales, 1978, 1979*, Working Paper 2, New South Wales Health Commission, Sydney.

Parbury, N. (1986), *Survival: a history of Aboriginal life in New South Wales*, Ministry of Aboriginal Affairs, Sydney.

Plant, A. J. (1990), 'What do we know about premature adult mortality', in A. Gray (ed.), *A matter of life and death: contemporary Aboriginal mortality*, Aboriginal Studies Press, Canberra, pp. 77–84.

Radford, A. J., Harris, R. D., Brice, G. A., Van der Byl, M., Monten, H., Matters, D., Neeson, M., Bryan, L., and Hassan, R. J. (1990), *Taking control: a joint study of Aboriginal social health in Adelaide with particular reference to stress and destructive behaviours, 1988–89*, Monograph 7, Department of Primary Health Care, Flinders University of South Australia, Adelaide.

RCADC (Royal Commission into Aboriginal Deaths in Custody) (1989), *Underlying issues*.

Read P. (n.d.), *The stolen generations: the removal of Aboriginal children in New South Wales, 1883–1969*, Occasional Paper 1, Ministry of Aboriginal Affairs, Sydney.

Read, P. (1980), 'Fathers and sons: a study of five men of 1900', *Aboriginal History* **4** (1–2), pp. 97–116.

Reay, M. (1963), 'Aboriginal and white Australian family structure: an enquiry into assimilation trends', *Sociological Review* **11**, pp. 19–47.

Reynolds, H. (1972), *Aborigines and settlers: the Australian experience, 1788–1939*, Cassell, Melbourne.

Reynolds, H. (1981), *The other side of the frontier: an interpretation of the Aboriginal response to the invasion and settlement of Australia*, James Cook University, Townsville.

Reser, J. (1989), 'Aboriginal deaths in custody and social construction: a response to the view that there is no such thing as Aboriginal suicide', *Australian Aboriginal Studies* **2**.

Rowley, C. D. (1970), *The destruction of Aboriginal society*, ANU Press, Canberra.

Rowley, C. D. (1971), *Outcasts in white Australia*, ANU Press, Canberra.

Seward, J. F., and Stanley, F. J. (1981), 'Comparison of births to Aboriginal and Caucasian mothers in Western Australia', *Medical Journal of Australia* **2**, pp. 80–4.

Shapiro, W. (1979), *Social organization in Aboriginal Australia*, ANU Press, Canberra.

Smith, L. R. (1980*a*), *Aboriginal vital statistics: an analysis of trends*, Commonwealth Department of Health Aboriginal Health Bulletin 1, AGPS, Canberra.

Smith, L. R. (1980*b*), *The Aboriginal population of Australia*, ANU Press, Canberra.

Smith, L. R., Thomson, N., and Gray, A. (1983), *Aboriginal mortality in country areas of New South Wales, 1980–1981*, New South Wales Department of Health, Sydney.

Stanner, W. E. H. (1974), 'Some aspects of Aboriginal health', in B. S. Hetzel, M. Dobbin, L. Lippmann, and E. Eggleston (eds), *Better health for Aborigines?* University of Queensland Press, St Lucia.

Swann, P. (1989), '200 years of unfinished business', in *Contact* **112**, December, pp. 10–12.

Taylor-Robinson, D. (1977), 'Infections and infertility in man and animals', in C. R. Coid (ed.), *Infections and pregnancy*, Academic Press, London.

Thomson, N., (1983), 'Aboriginal infant mortality, 1976–1981', *Australian Aboriginal Studies* **1**, pp. 10–15.

United Nations (Department of International Economic and Social Affairs) (1986), *Demographic yearbook 1985*, United Nations, New York.

Westrom, L., and Mardh, P.-A. (1975), 'Acute salpingitis: aspects on aetiology, diagnosis and prognosis', in D. Danielson, L. Juhlin and P.-A. Mardh (eds), *Proceedings of the Symposium on Genital Infections and their Complications, Stockholm, October 9–11 1974*, Almqvist and Wiksell, Stockholm.

Westrom, L., and Mardh, P.-A. (1978), *Pelvic inflammatory disease. 1: Epidemiology, diagnosis, clinical manifestations and sequelae*, World Health Organization, Geneva.

WHPRC (Women's Health Policy Review Committee) (1985), *Women's health services in NSW*, final report to the Hon. R. J. Mulock, September.

Williams, I. (1988), *La Perouse: the place, the people and the sea*, Aboriginal Studies Press, Canberra, 1988.

Wilson, P. (1982), *Black death, white hands*, Allen and Unwin, Sydney.

Young, E. (1981), *Tribal communities in rural areas*, Development Studies Centre, ANU, Canberra.

Unpublished material

Boundy, C. A. P. (unpub.), Aboriginal population of the Kimberley: a projection, unpublished report commissioned by the Office of the North West.

Gale, F. (unpub.), No relation poor fella—the city Aborigine's dilemma, lecture, Northern Territory University, Darwin, 1981.

Kliewer, E. V., and Stanley, F. J. (unpub.), Aboriginal and Caucasian births in Western Australia, 1980–1986. II: perinatal and infant mortality by birthweight and gestational age, manuscript.

Towers, L. (unpub.), The 'half caste' Aborigine in Australia: racial classification and social ambiguity, BA Hons thesis, Department of Anthropology, University of Sydney, 1982.

Young, C. M. (unpub.), Population growth and mortality of cohorts in Australia, PhD thesis, Australian National University, Canberra, 1969.

CHAPTER 4

Food, nutrition and growth in Aboriginal communities

Lindsey Harrison

Department of Public Health and Nutrition, University of Wollongong, New South Wales

Although the last 30 years have seen substantial improvements, most indicators continue to reflect the unfavourable health and nutritional status of Aboriginal children. The Aboriginal infant mortality rate (IMR), for example, still remains three times higher than that of the non-Aboriginal Australian population, and Aboriginal infants are still more likely to be of low birth weight (less than 2.5 kilograms) than their non-Aboriginal peers (Thomson 1985; Thomson and Honari 1988; Thomson, chapter 2 in this volume). Reports of growth retardation in childhood continue to be found in the literature, together with accounts of high rates of infection and intestinal parasites (e.g. Gracey et al. 1983; Cameron and Debelle 1986; Gracey and Sullivan 1987; Roberts et al. 1988; Cheek et al. 1989). Most of these studies have a biomedical focus and there is now a significant body of such research. However, biomedical researchers have not usually been willing or able to investigate the political, economic and sociocultural aspects of nutrition. Nutrition is not just a biomedical issue. As we shall see in this chapter, the nutrition-related problems that many Aboriginal children continue to experience are closely linked to social and economic disadvantage and to an unequal access to resources. The nutrition of Aboriginal adults has received comparatively little attention, although it is now known that they suffer disproportionately from the so-called lifestyle diseases such as obesity, hypertension, diabetes and cardiovascular disease and that, as a consequence, their life expectancy is considerably shorter than that of other Australians (see Thomson, chapter 2 in this volume). Epidemiological evidence from the United Kingdom and elsewhere now suggests that there may be a link between adverse circumstances in childhood and later risks of hypertension and cardiovascular disease (*Lancet* 1988; Barker and Osmond 1986; Barker et al. 1989; Gennser et al. 1988; Whincup et al. 1988). These findings require further research, but could obviously be of great importance to the Aboriginal community.

Despite the apparent importance of nutrition as a determinant of Aboriginal health, many aspects remain unclear. For example, there is in general a paucity of data about dietary intake, so that conclusions about its role must be tentative at best. Problems of method are largely to blame here. It is extremely difficult to study with any degree of accuracy the diet of any free-living population going about its day to day affairs (Marr 1971; Bingham 1987).

The dietary information that *is* available for Aborigines comes mainly from remote rather than urban or rural Australia. This is despite the fact that, according to the 1986 census, 24.4 per cent of Aborigines and Torres Strait Islanders live in major urban centres (population of 100 000 and over). The geographic distribution of the Aboriginal population varies by state; in Victoria, for example, the majority are urban dwellers, while in the Northern Territory most live in rural localities. Because Aboriginal communities live in different locations, and in different social and economic circumstances, it can be quite inappropriate to extrapolate dietary data gathered from one group in one area to another group in another area.

This overview of Aboriginal food and nutrition commences with a discussion of the present-day sources of food supply and the contemporary diet. The chapter continues with a discussion of the nutritional status of Aboriginal children and the nutrition-related health problems of Aboriginal adults, and concludes by considering nutrition interventions.

Figure 4.1 *Aborigines gathering food at Port Macquarie, New South Wales, in 1905 (D. Thomas/Bicentennial Collection, Mitchell Library, State Library of New South Wales, Sydney)*

Food supply and the contemporary diet

It is often assumed that the diet of Aboriginal people is uniformly bad and that this alone is responsible for many health problems. In the popular imagination, this is certainly the belief. 'Black diet blamed for child sickness' states a *Sydney Morning Herald* headline (Margo 1988), referring to an article in the *Medical Journal of Australia*. In fact, the article in question does not discuss diet at all, but is concerned with growth and with the high incidence of infection and intestinal parasites in Aboriginal children in a remote area of the Kimberleys (Roberts et al. 1988). A more accurate headline might have been 'High incidence of infection and intestinal parasites influence child growth'.

Preconceived notions about Aborigines and their lifeways frequently lead to conclusions about diet that the available evidence cannot sustain with any certainty. There have been very few quantitative studies and most of these have a very small sample size, which limits their reliability and the extent to which they may be generalised to the population as a whole.

There are a number of techniques commonly used to estimate usual dietary intake. The accuracy of these techniques varies enormously from the most accurate, such as the duplicate analysis method (where all food and drinks are weighed and measured, and duplicate weighed samples are taken at the same time for chemical analysis), to the least satisfactory, in quantitative terms, when the subject is asked to recall habitual intakes.

The weighed methods are time consuming, expensive and likely to cause great intrusion into the lives of the subjects, possibly altering usual dietary patterns. Only one such study has been attempted with Aborigines and that had a sample size of two families (Kamien et al. 1975*a*). More commonly used are the diary method (in which the subject or researcher keeps a detailed diary of food consumed, usually in household measures) and the recall method (in which subjects are asked about their actual food intake during — usually — the previous 24 hours).

Three quantitative studies using the 24-hour recall method are available for Aborigines (Hitchcock and Gracey 1975; Heywood and Zed 1977; Sibthorpe unpub.). These involved 14 preschool children in a rural town in Western Australia, 29 school children (and 43 white school children) in Walgett, New South Wales, and 38 adults in Kempsey, New South Wales, respectively. Another study used 24-hour recalls to gather qualitative data about the types of food available to 21 children under three years of age at Milikapiti, a Tiwi community in the Northern Territory (Harrison unpub.).

All methods are to some extent intrusive and all assume that the time period of the survey represents the 'normal' diet, though in fact food intakes may vary markedly, especially over different seasons, but even on different days. The 24-hour recall method is also subject to problems of honesty and memory.

The use of tables of food composition, which most methods require, can also present difficulties. The nutrient content of food is not constant, but varies according to factors such as geographic location, climate, season and length of storage. The ingredients, and hence the nutrient content, of composite dishes can also vary from cook to cook ('recipe error'). As local foodstuffs and diets differ, each country has its own food tables and it is important to use the most recent edition (for Australian tables, see DCSH 1989).

The literature dealing with dietary survey methods and their problems is vast and has been reviewed by Marr (1971) and more recently by Bingham (1987). In view of the many problems it is important that the level of accuracy of the method chosen fits the objective of the survey. Without clinical, anthropometric or biochemical evidence of nutritional status, the significance of dietary data can be difficult to determine.

Much of the information we have about Aboriginal diet comes not from intake studies of the type already discussed, but from community studies. These deal only with communities in remote Australia and often have an economic rather than a nutritional focus. Amounts of food entering the community are ascertained either from store turnover figures or from records of individual purchases made over a specified period of time (for example, Young 1984; Harrison unpub.). This type of study is only possible because these communities possess a single food outlet.

The food purchased, or apparently purchased, is converted to nutrients using food composition tables and compared to a community profile of theoretical nutrient requirements calculated from recommended daily allowances (RDAs). As with food tables, each country publishes its own RDAs, which may differ from one another. These are updated periodically as more information becomes available. Because the study of human nutrient requirements is extremely difficult and complex, each update can vary significantly from the earlier edition and can be the subject of scientific controversy (Pellett 1988). Diets thought to be deficient in certain nutrients may in fact be adequate in the light of new (though not necessarily definitive) knowledge. In addition, the RDA for most nutrients is always increased to a 'safe' level to ensure that most of the population is covered, whatever their circumstances, though this then overestimates the requirements of many (Truswell et al. 1983; Dreosti 1989; Warwick 1989).

What is being assessed in community studies is not the adequacy of the diet, but the possible adequacy of nutrients apparently available for consumption. However, in large Aboriginal communities, the contribution of bush foods may not be taken into account (Taylor 1977). As this source is likely to be significant, depending on the time of year, community studies often underestimate food supplies. The weighing of bush foods available for consumption is generally only feasible in small outstations (Altman 1982, 1984a and b; Meehan 1977, 1982a). The term 'bush food' here refers to any naturally occurring food harvested by Aborigines, including sea foods. It should also be remembered that, even where nutrient availability appears satisfactory, food distribution patterns may mean that not all individuals satisfy their requirements. The case study 'A dietary survey in a remote community' is an example of this type of study.

Some of the available dietary studies are now rather old, the earliest dating from 1948 (McArthur 1960). The majority, however, were carried out in the 1960s and early 1970s, before the period of profound social and economic change that occurred with the adoption by the federal government, in 1972, of the policy of Aboriginal self-determination. Funding for medical and other community services was increased at this time and Aborigines were more fully incorporated into the cash economy, with the granting of award wages and the extension of the unemployment benefit to those eligible. Such changes are likely to have affected diet, just as the earlier government policy of assimilation had done. During the

A dietary survey in a remote community

There is a small coastal community of approximately 360 people on a large island north-west of Oenpelli in the Northern Territory. The community receives most supplies from Darwin via a fortnightly barge which now has refrigeration. Perishable items, such as fruit and vegetables, are occasionally flown in on the daily air service. Air freight charges are in excess of 2 dollars per kilogram. Storage and refrigeration facilities at the community store are minimal and most stocks are depleted before the barge's arrival.

A recent health survey of 95 per cent of the adults living in the community found that 36 per cent were overweight, with a body mass index greater than 25 (BMI >25). The crude prevalence of diabetes was 16 per cent. Twelve per cent were underweight (BMI <18), 12 per cent were anaemic (haemoglobin 11 g/L) and 85 per cent had low red blood cell folate (115 µg/L).

Data were meticulously collected from the store over a period of 12 weeks. All food items delivered to the store were listed, total quantities supplied were tabulated and the average daily supply was calculated. Owing to limited availability of refrigeration and storage in the community store, the fact that many lines were depleted prior to the arrival of the barge and the very regular ordering patterns, daily supply was assumed to approximate average daily store turnover (purchases).

The average population of the community was determined by population census repeated at fortnightly intervals. Adjustments were made for the number of European and other community members who purchased food from sources other than the community store. Apparent consumption of food and nutrients was determined by dividing average daily store turnover by the average number of people using the store. Appropriate dietary allowances were determined from current Australian dietary allowances for each age and sex category (including pregnant and breast-feeding women) and proportioned for the community using age and sex distribution figures obtained from each census. Data were analysed using computer software incorporating Australian food composition data. Calculations were also entered into the data base to adjust for the observed high proportion of fat weighed in meat cuts available in the store.

This dietary study indicated that:

1. Of all the foods stocked in the store, only 18 contributed significantly (that is, over 2 per cent) to the total energy intake. Of these, four foods (sugar, flour, bread and meat) provided over 55 per cent of the total energy intake.

2. Sixty per cent of the high total sugar intake (258 grams per person per day) was derived from white sugar per se, which is equivalent to 143 grams or 38 teaspoons per person per day. Forty-five per cent of the high fat intake was derived from the fatty meat available. Take-away foods and snack foods like potato chips contributed nearly 20 per cent of the total fat intake.

3. Community-adjusted intakes of energy, sugars and fat were excessive, while the apparent intake of dietary fibre, some minerals (calcium and zinc) and some vitamins (retinol equivalents, riboflavin, vitamin E, vitamin B6 and folic acid) were inadequate.

The major advantages of this dietary methodology are that it is relatively non-invasive, inexpensive and can be collected retrospectively. It does not rely on the subjective assessment of diet and avoids language, literacy, numeracy and cultural factors, which may make direct measurement or dietary recall in Aboriginal communities problematic.

The limitations of the store method include the need to consider problems such as wastage, bulk storage and slow movement of stock, seasonality and foods from other sources (including bush foods, foods purchased from stores outside the community, alcohol and kava), and the application of appropriate nutrient composition values for foods available in community stores.

It should be remembered that this method does not measure dietary intake, but the nutrients apparently available for consumption. Food distribution patterns within the community are not taken into account. Nonetheless, surveys such as these can provide valuable information where nutritional status is known to be poor, as in the case of the community described here, and may assist in improving the food supply by demonstrating its role in community health.

Amanda Lee, Menzies School of Health Research, Casuarina, Northern Territory assimilation era (1951–72), the attempted incorporation of Aborigines into the dominant society caused a transformation of diet for most Aboriginal communities. Bureaucratic control extended to the food supply and systems of communal feeding and food rationing were widespread. Close attention should therefore be paid to the date of dietary studies and to the circumstances under which they were carried out, as they may now have historical value only.

Aboriginal communities in settled Australia

There is very little dietary information for Aboriginal groups in settled Australia, whether urban or rural dwellers. This is partly because it is extremely difficult to study a community that may be physically dispersed and has access to many food outlets. Aboriginal groups are also concerned to protect their privacy and may not welcome the attention of non-Aboriginal researchers, however benign their motives. Until recently, Aborigines were subject to discriminatory and restrictive legislation. Many still remember their houses being 'inspected' without their consent by non-Aboriginal people in various official capacities (Sibthorpe unpub.). Control extended to the food supply and various ration schemes operated at different times. A ration scheme for unemployed Aborigines in New South Wales is described in the case study 'Eight—two—and a quarter'.

Four quantitative studies were carried out during the early 1970s. In a study in Walgett, New South Wales, foods consumed by 17 members of two families were weighed for six days and aliquots were analysed for vitamin content (Kamien et al. 1975*a*). Energy intakes were low and it is possible that this was because of the method used, which disturbed normal eating habits. Protein intakes were generally above recommended dietary allowances. Meat and bread consumption was high, but fruit, vegetables and dairy products were less frequently consumed. Blood analysis revealed various vitamin deficiencies, but these may also have been the result of the infections present in six of the subjects. The authors concluded that bread fortification would address the vitamin deficiencies and this was subsequently carried out for a short period of time (Kamien et al. 1975*a*; Kamien 1978). Hitchcock and Gracey (1975) quantified nutrients apparently available for consumption from the food purchases of eight households in a country town in south-west Australia. Again available energy appeared to be low, although apparent protein intakes were either very close to, or well above, recommended dietary allowances. Vitamin availability was generally satisfactory, except for the three households with the lowest energy intakes. This could have been a problem of reporting, or overall food intakes may have been low. There are many possible explanations.

In the same study, Hitchcock and Gracey obtained 24-hour recalls from the mothers of 14 children aged between 3 and 4 years. In spite of this small sample, and the fact that only one 24-hour recall was made per child, the study claimed to document poor dietary practices in this group, but the figures that were generated by the study presume an accuracy that the method used cannot sustain.

The third study (Wise et al. 1970) involved a survey of 210 people for hyperglycaemia in an urban community in Port Augusta, South Australia. Diet histories were obtained from 98 of the participants, from which was estimated the daily

Eight—two—and a quarter

Whenever elderly Aboriginal people from New South Wales reminisce, the expression 'eight—two—and a quarter' will undoubtedly be used. This expression refers to the Government food ration of eight pounds [3.6 kilograms] of flour, two pounds [900 grams] of sugar, and a quarter of a pound [113 grams] of tea, which was issued to eligible Aboriginal adults. Each dependent child was entitled to half of this amount. Other rations such as meat and jam were intermittently supplied, but it was the 'eight—two—and a quarter' that were the ingredients of their mainstay diet of damper or johnny cakes and sweet black tea. The cost of the rations was recovered whenever people joined the workforce.

In some areas, the police issued coupons which were negotiable at selected local stores for the rations. Where an established government reserve or authorised mission existed, the ration issue would be made directly from the ration store that would normally be situated on such establishments.

When the system of issuing rations was discontinued, these store-houses were either dismantled or modified for other uses...It was thus a pleasant surprise for me to hear my uncle, Reg Murray of Walgett [New South Wales], identify one such building on Dungalear Station, a property where he had worked and lived for many years, but had not revisited since 1939...

Dungalear Station is situated about 40 kilometres north of Walgett...Dungalear was reputedly the only private land holding, not being a mission, that was authorised to issue government rations to the Aboriginal people.

The ration shed was erected in the early part of the century at about the same time as the other station buildings...I found that the store was probably in as good condition as it was in its busiest times, with perfectly preserved shelving and with its original serving counter still intact. And there in a prominent place in front, were the three large wooden bins which, Reg Murray informed me, were used to store the flour, sugar and tea. The store itself measured about 12 metres by 4.5 metres, with shelving covering the walls from the floor almost to the ceiling, while the other storage racks ran down the centre of the room...

The estimate of the numbers of Dungalear's Aboriginal population varied, but there were certainly several hundred at times, and this was one of the factors leading to the requirement for such a large storage area. Another factor...was the irregularity in the delivery of supplies. Prior to the establishment of the railhead at Walgett in 1908, supplies had to be transported by bullock wagon from Narrabri, a distance of about 250 kilometres...Whenever there was rain, these tracks (and they were little more than that) became impassable. This remained a factor for some years even after the arrival of the railway, for there was still some 40 kilometres of this terrain to be traversed.

As well as issuing Government rations, the store supplied every other requirement of the people, such as food, soap, clothing, and patent medicines. These were normally obtained on credit; the company later deducted the amount directly from the employee's salary. A Dungalear wage book entry, selected at random, shows an employee indebted to the store for 68 per cent of his total wages. One is reminded of the once-popular ballad which had the line 'I owe my soul to the company store'.

*From Paul Behrendt, 'A remnant from the past', Australian Aboriginal Studies **2**, 1986, pp. 58–9*

carbohydrate, protein and total energy intake. The diet history method does not, however, lend itself to this type of quantification.

In the fourth quantitative study, Heywood and Zed (1977) assessed the nutrient intakes of 29 Aboriginal and 43 white children in Walgett by 24-hour recalls. The differences in energy and iron intakes for the two groups was not significant and the risk of protein deficiency in either group was very low. The intakes of thiamine, riboflavin and ascorbic acid were significantly lower in the Aboriginal group, although this does not imply deficiency. However, the authors concluded that the Aborigines were at greater risk of vitamin deficiency than the white group and more likely to have intakes below the recommended levels for more than one nutrient.

In a more recent study in settled Australia, in Kempsey in New South Wales, Sibthorpe (unpub.) called into question the 'damper, syrup and tea' diet of anecdote. The study was based on 126 24-hour recalls from 38 adults in 31 households. Sibthorpe concluded that the relative proportions of energy derived from carbohydrate, protein and fat were similar to those of the rest of the Australian population. Energy intakes appeared to be under-reported, especially given the number who were overweight in the sample (83 per cent of males and 69 per cent of females). If the under-reporting was uniform, then the diets of most Aborigines in the sample were composed of foods adequate to meet the requirements of most of the vitamin and minerals studied.

For this Aboriginal community, the contribution of bush foods to the diet is small and irregular. The people are even reluctant to talk to non-Aboriginal people about bush food because, during the era of assimilation (1951–72 in most of Australia, apart from Queensland), the denigration and suppression of Aboriginal foods and cooking ('dirty blackfella food') was part of the attempted incorporation of Aborigines into the dominant society. As in remote Australia, diet was profoundly altered during this period. Fishing remains a popular leisure activity at Kempsey for both Aboriginal and non-Aboriginal residents, which is why it probably escaped sanction (Sibthorpe unpub.).

Aboriginal towns in remote Australia

The community store now provides most of the food supply to the larger Aboriginal communities in remote Australia. The availability of bush food fluctuates according to the season, and transport and other cash outlays may be required to exploit it, but stores are a constant source. Hunting and gathering are more usually weekend and leisure-time activities, but they are nonetheless important for social and cultural reasons, although their contribution to the diet may be variable and sometimes infrequent (Harrison unpub.). Fisk (1985) suggests that, on average, only 5 per cent of the food supplies of Aborigines who live in Aboriginal towns on Aboriginal lands comes from hunting and gathering.

At Milikapiti, a small town of over 300 Tiwi on Melville Island in the Northern Territory, hunting and gathering still occupy an important place in Tiwi life, even though the Tiwi, like other residents of Aboriginal towns, are part-time hunters and gatherers. Most hunting takes place during the dry season after burning off, usually at the weekends. During the wet season, hunting becomes more sporadic, and oriented more towards the sea and sea shore than the land, as the rains and new growth make land travel difficult and obscure the game.

It is extremely difficult to estimate the contribution to the Tiwi diet of bush foods as it varies throughout the year, but, during the dry season of 1983, the principal item of approximately one quarter of meals was a bush food, either meat or fish. Children under 3 years of age consumed 16 different types of bush food, which represent the full range available on and around the island, but exclude plant foods, which the Tiwi now rarely collect. Turtle was the most common item in the children's diet, followed by fish (Harrison unpub.).

At Wujalwujal (then Bloomfield River Mission) a community of 263 Kuku-Yalanyji in Queensland, Anderson (1982) reports that out of 148 midday and evening meals surveyed, a total of 46 (31 per cent) contained one or more food items obtained from the bush. These were usually fish, pig or marine turtle meat, shellfish or yams. The figures refer to 1977–78. However, the European administration (the Lutheran Church) considered subsistence production to be a waste of time and inimical to the Queensland government's policy of assimilation. The dietary and other inputs of bush trips were not recognised, nor was the significant role of women and unemployed men in this sphere. The mission staff and other whites even denied that the Kuku-Yalanyji used of the bush to any extent, which, in Anderson's view, fitted in with white ideas of Aborigines being lazy and dependent on hand-outs.

As far as European foods are concerned, food choice has been only a recent possibility for most Aboriginal communities in remote areas. Until the early 1970s, Aborigines resident at government settlements and missions were restricted by systems of communal feeding and food rations (see case study 'Communal feeding: a Northern Territory example of assimilation').

The creation of settlements had other important effects on the food supply. The bush could not support a large, static population and areas surrounding the settlements became depleted of game and vegetable food (McArthur 1960; Peterson 1978). The success of hunting and gathering expeditions then depended on the availability of motor transport, but the purchase of vehicles by Aborigines remained an impossibility until the late 1960s, when they began to receive social security benefits and cash wages.

By the early 1950s, the contribution of bush foods to the diet in the Northern Territory was described by Wilson (1953) as not significant, but this may have been an inaccurate generalisation, especially as she supplied a list of foods still exploited. At Milingimbi (Northern Territory), it has been estimated that, during the 1950s, at least half the population depended mainly on hunting and gathering for their food supply (Turnbull 1980). In Queensland, where a similar development of settlements took place, it was reported that, in 1967, hunting and fishing still provided a significant proportion of total food (Jose and Welch 1970).

Rations

Initially, Aborigines who resided at settlements were issued with dry rations, such as flour, rice, tea, sugar, jam and some canned goods. The American-Australian Expedition to Arnhem Land in 1948 found that Aborigines who depended on rations ate a monotonous diet low in fat and, though no clinical signs of deficiency were observed, the diet was probably deficient in ascorbic acid and vitamin A for many months of the year. At one mission, the meal pattern for most of the year was as follows (McArthur 1960, p. 15):

Breakfast: Ground wheat porridge with golden syrup or honey; damper, tea and sugar.
Dinner: Wheat porridge or rice; fresh vegetables or golden syrup or honey; damper, tea and sugar.
Supper: Damper and fish (if fish not available, then more wheat porridge or sweet potatoes or cassava); tea and sugar.

Communal feeding: a Northern Territory example of assimilation

In the mid-1950s, the Northern Territory Administration (NTA) admitted that there existed a high infant mortality in the Aboriginal community and that one of the causes, direct or indirect, was malnutrition (NTA 1957–58, p. 33). The administrative solution to this problem was to introduce a system of communal feeding. From 1955, all government settlements and missions in the Northern Territory commenced building programs for communal feeding. The aim was to provide three meals a day, seven days a week and to phase out the issue of food rations. Non-Aboriginal staff were hired to supervise the proceedings. However, the efficient provision of an adequate diet was not the only goal:

Promoting changes in the Aborigines' diet and eating habits is a very important factor in achieving their assimilation. A variation in diet is expected to bring about major improvements in health, and the adoption of European eating habits should have the effect of making Aboriginal people more acceptable in the community generally…[C]ommunal feeding is being introduced to ensure that all residents in the settlements will be adequately fed, as a means of inculcating European tastes in food (and) as a means of training people in regard to regular eating habits involving the use of European eating utensils. (NTA 1958–59, p. 10)

In this scheme, the social setting was equally if not more important than the adequacy of the food itself. Communal feeding was seen as part of the socialisation process towards a European lifestyle, which Aborigines must inevitably undergo.

The system monopolised the time of women by requiring them to walk to and from the feeding centre with their infants and small children three times a day. Even when cash became available at the end of the 1960s and adults preferred to purchase food from the community store, mothers were still required to present their infants for feeding at the times laid down. If attendance dropped, women would be 'reminded' that they should attend. This example is from Yuendumu:

When there was a general falling off in the numbers using the dining room, the superintendent or one of his European or Aboriginal assistants drove around the village, telling the women to take their children to the meals and sometimes driving them there.

This usually produced a temporary increase in attendances, particularly when carried out by Europeans, after which women might even be seen approaching the dining room at a jog trot. (Middleton and Francis 1976, p. 78)

By 1961, food rationing had all but disappeared in northern settlements. The NTA reported that food services continued to improve and cookery courses were held in Darwin for selected Aborigines (or 'wards' as Aborigines were called). Despite this official enthusiasm, the communal feeding system was never popular with Aborigines:

Despite a wide range of well-cooked and nutritious meals provided by the Kitchen Supervisor and staff, a large proportion of the Bagot population [a settlement on the outskirts of Darwin] refused to eat in the communal dining room. They were able to do this because of the greater wage earning potential in the Darwin area, and the easy access to shopping facilities. (NTA 1961–62, p. 58)

Although Aborigines in remote areas did not have this choice, failure to attend meals was one of the few means of protest available to them. In 1960, most Aborigines at Papunya attended the dining room only once a day. On paper, meals served from the communal kitchen provided a higher percentage of essential nutrients than the rations had provided, but there was no guarantee that this food was adequately distributed to the population (Corden 1973).

Kettle (1966) noted that supervised communal feeding had not brought about a significant change in the mean weight curves of the infants on the three missions that she visited in Arnhem Land.

This should not be construed as a reflection on the work of the missions. The services for Aborigines, including the supervised child feeding, are considered by the author to be as good as, if not better than, in many other places. Much more information is required… about the attitudes of the individual Aboriginal mother to interference with the feeding and management of her babies. At no time could it be considered that all Aboriginal mothers have been fully cooperative in communal feeding; there are, undoubtedly, reasons for this which have not been fully explored. (Kettle 1966, p. 977)

During the 1970s, as cash became available to Aborigines through award wages and the social security system, attendances at meals at the settlements declined to the extent that communal feeding was gradually phased out, although schemes for preschool children were the last to disappear. Regrets were expressed in government reports over opposition by some Aborigines to closure of the feeding centres. In fact, at Papunya, efforts were made to counteract an 'expectation' held by some parents that it was the government's responsibility to care for Aboriginal children. At Areyonga, infant meals were still provided because 'regrettably' the women now expected this service (NTA 1971–72, p. 13). Ten years earlier, the NTA would have been delighted at this sign of acceptance of the system it had imposed. That this acceptance was belatedly occurring was probably because the younger parents had known no other way.

Lindsey Harrison

It is possible that damper and wheat porridge would have proved too bulky for a small child to achieve an adequate energy intake, though the addition of golden syrup and jam would have helped. Evidence collected by the expedition suggests that the children were actually energy deficient at the time of the survey.

A broader survey of the ration system in the Northern Territory was carried out by Wilson (1953) in the early 1950s. It included government settlements of different sizes, missions of different denominations and cattle stations. The assessment was based on food issued (not food consumed). Food distribution patterns and seasonal variations were not taken into account and no allowance was made for nutrient losses in cooking. Nonetheless, it was concluded that Aborigines were seldom over-fed and sometimes short of food.

On missions and government settlements the diet was inferior to that of stockmen, but better than that of station workers who provided labour around the homestead, although Stevens (1974) suggests that station workers considered themselves better off than Aborigines at settlements or missions, because they had almost unlimited access to meat, which they prized. Consumption of butter and fats was low. Garden produce and eggs from settlement hens were usually just enough for non-Aboriginal staff. With the exception of meat, no foodstuffs were produced locally in sufficient amounts to provide regular supplies for all Aborigines. On most missions and settlements, water had to be carried some distance.

Community stores

When cash became available at the end of the 1960s, community stores became the main providers of food. Many were not able to stock a variety of foodstuffs, because of the lack of refrigeration and the long distance from wholesalers. These problems were originally solved by stocking only those foods likely to keep for some time without refrigeration, such as flour, sugar, tea and tinned goods. Conditions have much improved in most cases, with community generators supplying power for refrigeration, but the quality of the food available still varies widely between communities; small stores, in particular, may be able to stock only basic items.

Community stores are often run by progress associations or social clubs, which frequently employ non-Aboriginal managers. Unfortunately, there are many tales of these managers absconding with store takings, although managerial inefficiency is probably an even greater cause of financial crises in stores (Young 1984) and may have a drastic effect on the food available (Nathan and Japanangka 1983).

The larger stores generally have a greater capacity than smaller ones for making profits, because they are able to save on costs such as staffing, capital investment, accountancy and insurance, and have better facilities for bulk buying and storage. Smaller stores often manage only to break even because the generation of profits would entail an unacceptable increase in retail mark-ups (Young 1981, 1982, 1984).

Nonetheless, food costs for remote Aboriginal communities are far higher than for other centres. In 1978 at Wujalwujal (Queensland), the prices were 34 per cent higher than Brisbane prices (Anderson 1982). At Milikapiti (Northern Territory) in 1983, prices were approximately 30 per cent higher than Darwin prices (Harrison unpub.). In some communities in the Kimberleys (Western Australia), basic food items cost over 66 per cent more than they did in the Perth metropolitan area (Sullivan et al. 1987).

Aboriginal per capita incomes, on the other hand, have always been lower than those of other Australians (Altman and Nieuwenhuysen 1979). The median family income of Aborigines and Torres Strait Islanders is now slightly more than half (54.4 per cent) that of all Australians (DAA 1984, p. 48). Incomes vary according to location; however, they are highest in the cities and lowest on outstations (Fisk 1985).

Where evidence is available, it suggests that in remote communities, store food needs can be met by these low levels of income, leaving a surplus for other items. The Tiwi at Milikapiti (Northern Territory), for example, spend approximately 30 per cent of their income on food. This is much higher than the Australian average (19.7 per cent: ABS 1985) and indicative of the lower Tiwi incomes and higher prices at the community store. Nonetheless, it demonstrates that the Tiwi feel able to utilise most of their income for other purposes (Harrison unpub.). Similar findings have been reported by other workers (such as Peterson 1977; Taylor 1977; Anderson 1982).

The adequacy of the store diet is difficult to assess from the available studies. Those dating from the 1970s tend to show a monotonous diet, reflecting foods available in the stores at that time, but give no information about nutritional status. Taylor (1977) quantified the diet purchased from the store at Edward River in north Queensland and found that it was low in some vitamins and minerals when compared with RDAs, but he did not include nutrients from bush food.

Detailed data on the turnover from four community stores, Fregon (South Australia) and Yuendumu (Northern Territory) in the central desert region, Galiwin'ku (Northern Territory) in the northern region and Oombulgurri (Western Australia) in the Kimberleys, showed that foods purchased were sufficient to meet the recommended dietary allowances for energy, protein, calcium, vitamin C and thiamin. They did not cover the recommended allowances for iron, retinol (vitamin A), riboflavin or niacin. Available protein was 267 per cent of RDA. These figures do not take into account consumption variations due to seasonal factors or to fluctuations in the availability of money. Also, during the trading periods in question, the number of people actually consuming the food could have been significantly above or below the figure calculated (Young 1984).

The store diet in 1983 was much more varied at Milikapiti (Northern Territory) than at the communities described earlier by Anderson (1982) and Taylor (1977).

Based on records of individual purchases over a fortnightly pay cycle, the store was apparently providing 85 per cent of theoretical energy requirements (Harrison unpub.).

The largest contributor to available energy at Milikapiti was sugar (24.9 per cent), a category that includes honey, jam, syrup and soft drinks. The average Australian diet obtains approximately 15 per cent of its energy from sugar (Commonwealth Department of Health 1984). Alcohol contributed another 17.8 per cent, compared to 5 per cent in the average Australian diet. In contrast to the larger contribution made to total energy by sugar and alcohol, the Milikapiti store diet contained a lower percentage of energy from fat than the average Australian diet (27.2 per cent compared to nearly 40 per cent). This was mainly from meat, rather than from fats or oils. The Tiwi typically boil or grill their food and moisten bread or damper by dipping it in tea. Protein sources provide 14.3 per cent of available energy and this is higher than the Australian average of 12.3 per cent (Henderson 1975). These figures do not include bush food.

These studies tend to show that meat is much prized in the Aboriginal diet and it can be available in large amounts. Protein lack is unlikely, at least at the community level. The source of the meat (store or bush) also affects fat consumption, as bush animals are usually leaner than domesticated species. However, Aborigines place a great deal of emphasis on the fat depots of hunted animals. Fat is synonymous with 'good' in the context of bush food (Altman 1982). High intakes of sugar have been recorded and, as a concentrated source of energy, sugar has a role to play in the development of obesity in adulthood, as does the regular consumption of significant amounts of alcohol (see Brady, chapter 5 in this volume). Consumption of dairy products and store-bought fruit and vegetables appears low and this is reflected in the low values for some vitamins and minerals when compared to RDAs. The difficulties of transporting and storing perishable items in remote areas are factors that limit their availability.

Outstation groups in remote Australia

The outstation or homeland movement, in which small, related groups of people move away from the large communities to live on their ancestral lands, was made possible by the policy of self-determination adopted in 1972. By 1978, there were 113 decentralised communities in the Northern Territory alone with a population of 3300 (DAA 1979). Outstations are also common in the northern parts of Queensland, South Australia and Western Australia. This process of decentralisation was easier to accomplish for groups who, despite resettlement during the assimilation era, had remained physically close to their ancestral lands. It was not possible for groups whose lands had been alienated and more difficult for those whose lands were situated a long way from the established centralised communities. In general, the outstation movement has been most significant for Arnhem Land communities and more difficult to sustain in the harsher environment of central Australia (Young 1981).

Outstation communities have two sources of food supply; the bush and the local store. The extent to which each contributes to the diet depends on locality and time of year. Outstations in the tropical north can satisfy many of their nutrient needs from bush foods (Altman 1982, 1984*a* and *b*; Jones 1980; Meehan 1977, 1982*a*). The edible resources available to outstation groups such as the Yolngu in northeastern Arnhem Land are 'diverse and plentiful' and they are supplemented with supplies including rice, flour, powdered milk, breakfast cereals, tea, sugar, jam and syrup from the main community at Yirrkala (Reid 1986).

Altman (1984*a* and *b*) and Meehan (1977, 1982*a*) have quantified the nutrients apparently available for consumption at two Arnhem Land outstations, one coastal and one inland. Altman estimated that, at the Momega outstation from 1979 to 1980, 47 per cent of the energy and 81 per cent of the protein available for consumption came from bush foods. These were mainly fauna, which contributed over 90 per cent of the bush foods diet each month. In all, Altman observed 90 species of fauna and 80 species of flora consumed by the 30 Gunwinggu people during his year-long residence at the outstation. The European food from Maningrida tended to replace the labour intensive gathering of bush carbohydrates such as yams.

From 1972–73, Meehan studied the diet of the 30-strong Anbarra community located on the Blythe River. The Anbarra bought flour, rice, sugar and porridge from Maningrida with money derived from wages, social security benefits and the sale of arts and crafts. All of their flesh food was hunted. This was mainly fish and shellfish, but included fresh and saltwater turtles, birds, wallabies, snakes and goannas.

Figure 4.2 *People of Oak Valley Outstation, Great Victoria Desert, South Australia, buying stores. (K. Palmer)*

Foods such as yams, water chestnuts and wild fruits still formed an important part of their diet, and eggs and wild honey were collected when available. Bush foods contributed from 42.2 per cent to 64.8 per cent of the available energy and from 76.7 per cent to 80.3 per cent of available protein depending on the time of year. In general, the diet provided more than the recommended allowances for energy and protein. Altman made a similar finding.

Cane (1986) has reported intensified use of traditional resources on Aboriginal outstations in central Australia. He surveyed 53 outstations near Kintore, Papunya, Yuendumu, Docker River and Ernabella and estimated that bush foods provided up to 50 per cent of the diet in some Pintupi camps (6 per cent of total outstations), between 20 and 30 per cent of the diet of most Warlpiri and Luritja camps (44 per cent of outstations) and between 10 and 15 per cent of the diets of most of the camps around Docker River and Ernabella. However, no quantitative data were collected and it is not possible to estimate the nutrient composition of the diet.

Vegetable foods are less important than animal foods in this region and seeds are no longer processed because it is time consuming and difficult. Traditionally, about 40 to 50 different types of seeds, *Eucalyptus*, *Acacia* and grass seeds were eaten. Most fruits are still gathered including bush tomatoes, konkle berries, wild figs, bush plums and quandongs. Bush tomatoes are the most important of these. It is possible to gather 5 kilograms per hour giving a return of 9000 kcal (37 656 kilojoules).

By far the most important of the bush foods used by these outstations is animal meat, especially kangaroo. A similarly heavy reliance on kangaroo meat, estimated to be 900 grams per capita per day, has been found by Palmer and Brady at Oak Valley, an outstation near Maralinga in South Australia (see case study, Palmer and Brady, 'The food quest at Oak Valley Outstation, South Australia').

There are few data about the nutritional status of outstation groups. O'Dea et al. (1988*a*), however, have reported no biochemical evidence of malnutrition at one outstation in north-eastern Arnhem Land. Eighteen adults and six children under the age of 15 were tested out of a total population of 31. Only one person was anaemic, while plasma protein and albumin levels were in the normal range. This is despite the fact that, by standard criteria, all were underweight (see 'Nutrition in adulthood' section).

It has been suggested that child growth patterns in northern outstation groups indicate an overall diet of adequate quantity and quality (Rae et al. 1982). It may well be, however, that the lack of infectious diseases at the outstations compared to the larger townships is an important reason for this rather than diet alone, though evidence is scarce either way. Infections increase the body's food requirements, but may at the same time decrease appetite and/or cause malabsorption, resulting in weight loss and growth retardation.

Meehan (1982*a*) has reported that elderly women who are unable to accompany hunting and gathering groups tend not to fare so well in the outstation system, because most food is immediately cooked and eaten before returning to the outstation. It is important, therefore, to look at food distribution patterns and not just at food available for consumption by the community as a whole. Some individuals may eat more than they require and others less.

Figure 4.3 *Birds are among the flesh foods hunted in many remote Aboriginal communities. (From P. Taylor, ed.,* After 200 years, *Aboriginal Studies Press, Canberra, 1988, p. 45; photo by J. Rhodes)*

Figure 4.4 *Breakfast at a hearth on an outstation in the Great Victoria Desert, South Australia, photographed in 1987, consisted of frankfurters, tea, cereal and a piece of red kangaroo meat. (M. Brady)*

The food quest at Oak Valley Outstation, South Australia

The Royal Commission into British Nuclear Tests in Australia, which made public its findings in 1985, proposed that a series of major scientific studies be undertaken at Maralinga, South Australia, to examine the feasibility of rehabilitating areas contaminated by radioactive debris. A technical assessment group set up after the royal commission, in conjunction with the land council (Maralinga Tjarutja) representing the Aborigines, arranged for us to undertake an anthropological study of the diet and lifestyle of the Aborigines living at Oak Valley Outstation, some 160 kilometres north-west of Maralinga village.

An important aspect of the research was to collect detailed information on Aboriginal diet, including both bush foods and European stores, and to note the storage of food and its preparation. We both knew the outstation residents well, as a result of sustained contact over several years, so the intrusion of asking people what they had eaten, noting their purchases and weighing their kangaroos was somewhat minimised.

The camp residents at Oak Valley are great meat eaters. There are usually vehicles available, young men who can acquire rifles and ammunition, and several open plain locations favoured by red kangaroo. Minimal supplies of fresh meat were available from other sources. Hunting is therefore energetically pursued, and vehicles return with red kangaroo, bush turkeys and goannas. Another source of fresh meat consists of rabbits purchased by Oak Valley people from railway workers on the Trans-Australia line 200 kilometres to the south. The purchased rabbits are usually already skinned and gutted, so they are stewed along with a few onions, or a packet of soup. Unskinned rabbits are cooked belly down, whole, in the ashes.

There is 61.3 per cent edible tissue in a red kangaroo, and virtually all parts of the animal are consumed, although the lungs may be given to the dogs. The bones are broken up and the marrow sucked out. Marrow is said to be 'like egg' and is given to children as a special treat. Joeys are cooked whole, and are often consumed by the hunters at a temporary camp during the day's hunting. The highest number of kangaroos was hunted in our winter sample (August 1987), totalling 766 kilograms in two weeks, in a population of 73 at the beginning, and 107 at the end of the period.

The edible tissue of a rabbit is 49 per cent of the whole body weight, and we noted minimal wastage. As with kangaroo, the heart, kidney and liver are eaten, but the stomach contents are discarded. Oak Valley people not only consume hunted meat and fresh rabbit, but also tinned meat products (steak and kidney pies, braised steak and onions). We estimate, therefore, that the per capita daily intake of meat to be up to 900 grams. The Australian daily average meat intake for men and women is 192 grams (Commonwealth Department of Health 1986) However, other researchers have reported high levels of meat consumption among Aboriginal and other hunter-gatherer societies (O'Dea et al. 1988a).

Kingsley Palmer and Maggie Brady, Australian Institute of Aboriginal and Torres Strait Islander Studies, Canberra

Bush foods

Recently, there has been an awakening of interest in bush foods by some sections of the wider Australian community and lavishly illustrated books on the topic are now available (such as Isaacs 1987; Low 1989). The ABC television series 'Bush Tucker Man' was also extremely popular and subsequently released on video. The Aboriginal contribution to these enterprises is often implicit rather than explicitly acknowledged, but the best do relate their subject matter to its cultural context. These books and videos also enable non-Aboriginal Australians to appreciate the depth of knowledge required for the successful exploitation of bush foods.

Aborigines have well-defined ideas about what constitutes a balanced diet in the bush. The foods consumed are diverse and fresh and the methods of cooking, usually grilling or roasting, maximise the retention of trace elements and vitamins (Meehan 1982b).

Totemic significance

Most of the species used for food have totemic significance and many have an important part to play in ritual. In Aboriginal society, relationships with the land, and the plants and animals on it, date from the Dreaming, when the ancestor beings or totemic spirits created the earth and human institutions. These creative powers are depicted to have animal or plant characteristics as well as human qualities. Because of this, human ties to the land are also bound up with ties to other forms of life (Maddock 1982).

People become associated with particular species and particular tracts of land through their membership of a group, usually referred to as a clan in English. Membership is acquired at birth, either from the mother or the father, depending on the particular form of local organisation. This varies in different parts of the country. People may also be linked with a site or species that is associated with their conception.

In some parts of the country, people do not eat their totemic species, although they do in others. Even though these restrictions, where they exist, are permanent, they are unlikely to have, or have had, any nutritional significance, since they apply to only a small part of the food supply.

Some species may also be prohibited or taboo to certain groups of people for other reasons. This again varies in different parts of the country. Food restrictions may apply, for example, to the close relatives of a person recently deceased. Altman (1982) has distinguished four main categories of food taboo among the Gunwinggu of north-central Arnhem Land. These taboos are based on:

1. kin relations;
2. the seasonal cycle;
3. ceremonial experience;
4. women's sexual cycles.

Kin-based taboos are universal among the Gunwinggu, the main one being that a sister cannot eat meat shot by her brother. Some foods cannot be eaten at certain times of the year. Altman gives the example of large river sawfish and river sharks. Only the elders may eat these fish during the wet season, otherwise all the children will fall ill.

Consumption taboos affect youths of 14 to 16 years of age when they are initiated into the Gunabibi cult. All foodstuffs associated with the Gunabibi song cycles are forbidden until the youths are familiar with the cult four or five celebrations later. The same rules hold for the other major ceremonies. Taboos also restrict a youth's access to the game he hunts.

When a woman is menstruating or pregnant, most reptiles and a large range of ceremonially significant flora and fauna are forbidden. A range of food taboos also applies if she is breast-feeding a young infant.

In the past, food restrictions during pregnancy and early lactation were common in Aboriginal society and may still be important for some groups. The restrictions demonstrate the vulnerability of a woman and her unborn child or infant and retrospectively explain any abnormalities. The extent to which they had any nutritional significance in the past is difficult to determine, since it would have depended on the overall food supply and the types of food that were restricted. Both would have varied across the country. Today, European foods are also available and they tend not to be the subject of taboos. Another point is that young Aboriginal women have usually had different life experiences from their mothers and certainly from their grandmothers, so they may not subscribe to the belief system underlying the taboos. However, they may still observe some or all as a matter of respect for the wishes of older people. This is the case with young Tiwi women. Some, though not all, abstain from certain types of fish during pregnancy, but not all who abstain accept the reasons given by older people. Many other varieties of fish are available, so that giving up one or two (usually) is no hardship and does not have nutritional consequences (Harrison unpub.).

Nutrient content

An important factor in increasing our understanding of bush foods has been the systematic analysis of their nutrient content over the last decade. This is useful because it makes possible the more accurate examination of the contemporary Aboriginal diet where bush foods still play a significant part.

On the whole it appears that most bush foods are similar in composition to cultivated varieties in the same food category. For example, the composition of the waterlily stalk is similar to celery (Brand et al. 1982*a*; Brand et al. 1983). An

Figure 4.5 *The stalks and corms of waterlilies are among the plant foods harvested in central Arnhem Land. The corms are collected and washed on paperbark and then roasted in ashes. (J. Reid)*

exception is the green plum (*Terminalia ferdinandiana*) which is claimed to have the world's highest vitamin C content. In three samples, which were obtained from different locations in different seasons, the vitamin C content was found to be 3150, 2850, and 2300 milligrams per 100 gram edible portion; citrus fruits have around 50 milligrams per 100 grams (Brand et al. 1982*b*; Brand et al. 1983).

Other foods rather high in vitamin C include the Indian gooseberry (*Phyllanthus emblica*, 316 milligrams per 100 grams) and the cheeky yam (*Dioscorea bulbifera*, 233 milligrams per 100 grams). Some fruits and vegetables have been found to be relatively higher in protein compared with most Western varieties. These include the bush banana (*Leichhardtia australis* and *L. leptophylla*), containing 8.1 and 9.8 grams per 100 grams, and the waterlily root (*Nymphaea macrosperm*), containing 9.6 grams per 100 grams. For comprehensive lists, see James (1983), Brand et al. (1982*a*), Brand et al. (1983), and Brand and Cherikoff (1985).

Nuts and seeds have also been analysed. The results indicate that many are rich sources of protein and fat, and of trace elements such as iron and zinc. Seeds of several of the *Acacia* species, for example, are higher in energy, protein and fat than crops such as wheat and rice. In the arid and semi-arid areas of Australia, some 50 of the 800 species of *Acacia* were used by Aborigines for food (Brand et al. 1984; Brand and Cherikoff 1985; Cane 1987). Caution must be used in interpreting such data as all foods vary widely in their composition. The nutrient content of plant food varies according to species, soil conditions, rainfall and season. Animal foods vary with age, species, breed, sex and season. Both plant and animal foods are altered by methods of storage, processing and cooking. These are some of the problems inherent in the use of any food composition tables. At the present time, much of the bush food data derives from the analysis of a single sample of food, often small in quantity and possibly unrepresentative. However, they are useful as a guide and probably provide a better estimate than extrapolating from Western foods (Brand and Cherikoff 1985).

There have been fewer analyses of animal foods compared to plant foods, but it has been shown that these foods tend to be low in fat, with a high proportion of polyunsaturated fatty acids (greater than 20 per cent). It has been hypothesised that this may have protected Aborigines against cardiovascular disease, obesity and diabetes, even when the diet contained a high proportion of these foods (Naughton et al. 1986).

There is some evidence, too, that there are differences in the type and quality of the carbohydrate in traditional Aboriginal diets compared to that in Western diets (Fitz-Henry and Brand 1982; Thorburn and Brand 1987; Thorburn et al. 1987). The rate of starch digestion has been studied *in vitro* in 37 foods (20 Aboriginal foods, 10 Pacific Island foods and seven Western foods) and the rate of absorption of nine foods (eight bush foods and one Western food) has been studied in seven volunteers. It was found that 23 of the 30 traditional foods were digested more slowly than the seven Western foods. In the human subjects, there was a good correlation between starch digestibility and plasma glucose response; six of the eight traditional foods produced a significantly smaller rise in plasma glucose than potatoes. Again, it is hypothesised that because carbohydrate in traditional diets is slowly digested and absorbed, thereby requiring a small insulin response, it may once have been protective against diabetes (see 'Nutrition in adulthood' section).

Nutrition in infancy and childhood

The nutrition of Aboriginal infants and children has received much publicity over the last two decades and can still command sensational headlines in the press. This response is understandable, given that the relative affluence of Australia should ensure that all citizens are well nourished, but the evidence can become entangled in the emotion generated by the topic.

Measurement of growth

Evaluating the evidence is not an easy task. Nutritional status in children is most often measured by growth, but the problem lies in establishing 'normal' growth and the point at which deviation from the norm increases the risk of disability and even death. These issues need to be addressed before we turn to the Aboriginal data.

To be analysed, growth data are related to the measurements of a reference population and there are several ways of doing this. A measurement can be expressed by any of the following:

1. as a percentage of the reference;
2. as falling in a particular percentile of the reference population;
3. as deviating from the reference mean by so many standard deviations.

Reference populations are usually derived from North America or the United Kingdom. One of the most widely used have been the American Harvard Standards, but the World Health Organization currently recommends the growth data collected by the United States National Center for Health Statistics (NCHS) in the 1960s and 1970s (Hamill et al. 1979). There are some differences of opinion as to whether these and other reference standards more accurately reflect the growth of formula-fed infants than that of breast-fed infants (Dewey et al. 1989; Roche et al. 1989*a* and *b*).

Some researchers have objected to the use of British or North American standards for other populations (for example, Goldstein and Tanner 1980). However, others argue that the use of an international reference population is appropriate, though it should not be regarded as a standard in the sense of a target or ideal (Waterlow 1980; Graitcer and Gentry 1981). Indeed, evidence suggests that growth potential in the early years of life is less likely to be affected by ethnic differences than by socioeconomic factors (Habicht et al. 1974; Graitcer and Gentry 1981). This finding is also applicable to Aboriginal children (Maxwell and Elliott 1969; Jose and Welch 1970; Cockington 1980; Muller et al. 1984). However, although children of all ethnic groups may have the genetic potential to approach the European or American norm, there is no evidence that this represents the optimum or that it is advantageous for children to be so heavy or so tall, even when the environment is favourable (Waterlow 1980).

It should be emphasised that we are discussing here the assessment and analysis of group growth data. When assessing the development of the individual child, the clinician will take into account other factors, including gestational age, birth weight and length, and parental size.

Weight-for-age (weight of child as a percentage of the weight of a standard child of the same age) is the most widely used index of nutritional status, although it does not distinguish between present poor nutrition or past poor nutrition (Waterlow 1972; Waterlow and Rutishauser 1974). Present poor nutrition or wasting is better assessed by weight-for-height (weight of child as a percentage of the weight of a standard child of the same height). Past poor nutrition or stunting is better assessed by height-for-age (height of child as a percentage of the height of standard child of the same age). The choice of which to use will vary with the purpose of the measurement process (Habicht 1980).

Cut-off points rank children into various categories of nutritional status, defining who is normal and who is mildly, moderately or severely malnourished. Conventionally, researchers have used 80 per cent for weight and 90 per cent for height as cut-off points, because these points roughly correspond to two standard deviations below the mean or the third percentile of the Harvard Standard (Waterlow 1980). Others prefer to use the tenth percentile (Harvard or NCHS), below which growth is considered to be unsatisfactory or to require further investigation or treatment (Hamill et al. 1979). These decisions will alter the numbers considered to be undernourished. In practice, the choice of cutoff point depends on the purpose of the study or the survey.

Ideally, cut-off points should be related to the increased risks of morbidity, disability or death associated with particular weight or height deficits, but such information is rarely available. To derive quantitative estimates of risk requires large numbers of subjects and the study must be done without medical or nutritional intervention. Two examples are the study by Kielmann and McCord (1978) in the Punjab which related mortality rates to weight-for-age, and that by Sommer and Loewenstein (1975) in Bengal, which looked at arm circumference and height. Chen et al. (1980), also in Bengal, looked at a range of anthropometric measurements and showed that the risk of mortality was similar for normal, mild and moderately malnourished children, but climbed sharply for the severely malnourished. It is not clear how far the risks identified in these studies would apply to different populations in different circumstances, but they do show that the relationship of risk with degrees of malnutrition is not a linear one (Wheeler 1980).

Mortality is obviously a crude index of risk. Payne (1985, p. 3) has defined 'real' malnutrition as physiological states carrying penalties in terms of loss of function. People have the capacity to adapt to a fairly wide range of dietary situations and only when that adaptive capacity is stretched beyond its limits does the body fail to maintain its functional capacity and malnutrition ensue. This means that malnutrition, as distinct from 'otherwise benign deviations of growth or body size' is much less frequent than has previously been believed.

Are Aboriginal children malnourished, according to Payne's definition of functional capacity, or do they suffer from 'benign deviations of growth or body size'? It is inescapable that many Aboriginal children are shorter and lighter than their non-Aboriginal peers (Brown and Townsend 1982; Hitchcock et al. 1987), but this is unlikely to have any functional significance, either physically or intellectually (Dobbing 1985). However, these children are the survivors of cohorts with much higher levels of infant mortality and morbidity than the rest of the Australian population and this should be a cause of great concern. Aboriginal Australians have experienced, and continue to experience, social discrimination and economic dis-advantage. It should come as no surprise that this is reflected in their health status.

Growth studies

It was during the 1950s and 1960s that reports began to appear in the medical litera-ture, notably in the *Medical Journal of Australia*, of the unsatisfactory growth per-formance of Aboriginal children when compared to their non-Aboriginal peers. High rates of infection and intestinal parasite loads were also recorded. It was studies like these (for example, Crotty 1958; Jose and Welch 1970; Kirke 1969; Max-well and Elliott 1969) that helped to alert the wider Australian community to the rela-tive deprivation of Aboriginal Australians.

Similar studies continue to appear in the literature. Some improvements are evi-dent in more recent papers, notably in the numbers of those whose nutritional status is judged to be unsatisfactory, but the types of problems that are described remain essentially unchanged. It is not always possible to compare these studies because they use different reference populations, different cut-off points (that is, different definitions of 'undernourishment') and different ways of displaying the data.

Kettle (1966) was one of the first to describe the 'typical' growth curve. Kettle's study was an attempt to prepare standard weight and height curves for Aboriginal infants and children, based on longitudinal weight and height records of 400 Aboriginal children born between 1958 and 1965 at three Arnhem Land missions. This is a good illustration of why using an international reference population is preferable to constructing local standards. Not only is the sample size very small and drawn from a restricted area, but also few of the children studied by Kettle 'had a normal infancy, as the individual medical records of many show a history of intes-tinal and chest infections, hookworm infestation and gross anaemia, all factors which may have influenced growth' (Kettle 1966, p. 972).

Kettle showed that Aboriginal infants at the missions (Goulburn Island, Milin-gimbi and Elcho Island) grew very rapidly during the first half of the first year, al-most doubling their birth weight at three months of age. The increase continued to about five months of age but from then on the increments were smaller than for other Australians. Other studies since then have reported similar findings, such as: Jose and Welch (1970) in six Queensland communities; Cox (1979) in north Queensland; Kirke (1969) in central Australia; Coles-Rutishauser (1979), Gracey and Hitchcock 1983, Gracey et al. (1983) and Gracey et al. (1984) in Western Australia. In Western Australia, where Aboriginal communities in different locations have been compared, the falloff appears to be most pronounced in remote areas (Gracey et al. 1983). At 18 months, there can be a maximum difference of 3.5 kilograms be-tween Aboriginal and non-Aboriginal children which continues during the remain-ing preschool years (Kirk 1981). Figure 4.6 shows a 'typical' growth curve. Mean weights of Tiwi children are plotted against the conventional cut-off points on the Harvard Standard. Despite the small sample size, the rapid increase in weight in the first six months of life followed by a slowing down is evident.

Most of the growth studies discussed so far have been cross-sectional, which means that, while providing a description of the state of affairs at the time of the study, they are not able to determine the role of the various factors involved in

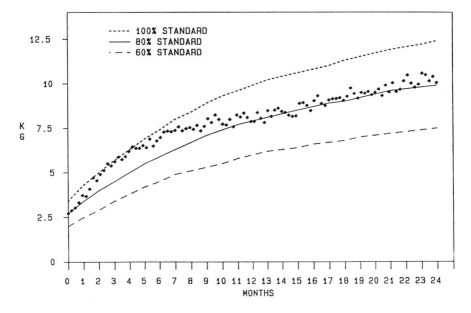

Figure 4.6 *Mean weights of Tiwi children in the first two years of life, compared to the Harvard standard*

growth faltering. One prospective longitudinal study is that of Gracey and Sullivan (1987), who are following a cohort of infants born in several remote communities in the Kimberleys. The sample size, however, is small (*n* = 48). So far the infants have shown the typical growth pattern. They grew well in the first three months, but their rate of growth then slowed between three and six months. This faltering became more severe after six months. They also have had recurrent and chronic infections, mainly gastroenteritis and chest infections, and intestinal parasites (see Gracey, 'Kylie's first two years', in Thomson, chapter 2 in this volume).

Although the typical growth curve flattens and dips in the second six months of life, growth velocity may decline much earlier. Waterlow et al. (1980) compared monthly increments of weight in the first six months of life from longitudinal studies made in several less developed countries (but including Kettle's Arnhem Land data) with the United Kingdom mean. They point out that although it is not known whether the United Kingdom mean is optimal, it is associated with lower morbidity and mortality than prevail in many other countries. The exercise showed that the rate of growth falls off substantially, compared with the United Kingdom mean, between three and four months of age and in many cases earlier. The relative contributions of inadequate diet and infection are not known. Few data are available for Australia, but the pattern seems to be similar (Cox 1979; Harrison unpub.; Gracey and Sullivan 1987).

There are far fewer studies for older Aboriginal children, particularly adolescents, so it is not clear how far or how long growth retardation persists. Beck (1985) has found that, in the town camps of Alice Springs (Northern Territory), where 202 children under 14 were measured, growth retardation is most pronounced in infancy and early childhood, peaks in the third year of life and subsequently gradually improves. In a study of 1887 Aboriginal children aged 4 to 16 in the Kimberleys (Western Australia), Hitchcock et al. (1987) found that the median weights (fiftieth percentile) of both boys and girls approximated the tenth percentile weights of their non-Aboriginal Perth counterparts.

In a longitudinal study of adolescent growth at Yuendumu ($n = 62$), Brown and Townsend (1982) found few differences between Aborigines and British children in the ages at take-off (TO) and peak height velocity (PHV), in adolescent gain or in percentage of adult height achieved at TO and PHV. Aboriginal boys were however shorter than British boys at TO, PHV and adulthood. As PHV was higher in Aborigines than the British children and as there were known levels of infant mortality and morbidity at Yuendumu between 1953 and 1979, the authors postulate that the high PHVs are indicative of catch-up growth after early childhood retardation.

Low birth weight

Low birth weight (LBW) is a common feature of many Aboriginal growth studies. During the late 1960s, Maxwell and Elliott (1969) reported a rate of 12.5 per cent in central Australia, twice the national average at that time and, almost 20 years later, Cameron and Debelle (1986) reported a rate of 12 per cent in the Murray Valley, again twice that for the local non-Aboriginal population. An analysis of Western Australian figures for 1975 to 1978 by Seward and Stanley (1981) showed that 13 per cent of Aboriginal births in the state were of low birth weight compared with 5.5 per cent of non-Aboriginal births. The most reliable recent data for Aborigines from Australian departments of health (Western Australia 1983-1985 and the Northern Territory 1986) show that 13 to 15 per cent of Aboriginal babies were of low birth weight, compared to about 6 per cent for non-Aboriginal Australians (Thomson and Honari 1988; Thomson, chapter 2 in this volume).

The high proportion of LBW babies is an important factor influencing the number of Aboriginal infant deaths. Thomson (1983) has noted that the decline in the infant mortality rate for the years 1976 to 1981 was due to fewer post-neonatal deaths, while the improvements in stillbirths and neonatal mortality have been less marked. Neonatal mortality, which is the number of deaths during the first month of life, reflects events during the antenatal and birth period. It is more closely related to birth weight than is post-neonatal mortality, which is also influenced by environmental factors such as infectious diseases and by socioeconomic disadvantage (McCormick 1985).

Low birth weight (less than 2500 grams) may be the result of prematurity or due to factors which adversely affect growth *in utero*, or both. A distinction is made clinically between infants with the appropriate weight for their gestational age and infants who are small for their gestational age, because each group gives rise to different health problems and to different mortality rates. Infants of low birth weight who are small for their gestational age are more likely to survive than are premature infants of the same birth weight (McCormick 1985). Lancaster (1989) has noted that the findings in the Kimberleys of rapid weight gains in early infancy followed by a slowing of the growth rate are typical of infants who are small for their gestational age.

Kliewer and Stanley (1989), however, have suggested that Aboriginal infants are more likely to be born earlier than white infants as well as to have a definite shift towards pathological growth retardation at term. Further, they suggest that Aboriginal infants normally may be smaller than white infants, which implies that genetic factors may be more important than environmental factors in determining size at birth.

Lancaster (1989) argues that the results of such studies must be open to question unless the method of calculating gestational age is validated. Lancaster also questions the high proportion of Aboriginal births for which gestational age was able to be calculated (91.9 per cent), when a previous study (Seward and Stanley 1981) found that the date of the last menstrual period was unknown in 40 per cent of Aboriginal pregnancies.

Many factors, including nutrition, are implicated in the aetiology of intrauterine growth retardation. Indeed, an analysis of 895 studies published between 1970 and 1984, has identified 15 factors that directly affect intrauterine growth (Kramer 1987). These include the infant's sex, racial/ethnic origin, maternal height and pre-pregnancy weight, paternal height and weight, maternal birth weight, parity, history of prior low birth weight infants, gestational weight gain and energy intake, general morbidity and episodic illness, malaria, cigarette smoking, alcohol consumption and tobacco chewing. Factors whose impact is expressed indirectly through one or more of the direct factors include maternal age and socioeconomic status. Substantial overlap obviously exists between several of the factors and their prevalence will vary from setting to setting, but the multiplicity of factors is the point to keep in mind.

It has been suggested in the Australian context that later growth may be predicted by low birth weight. A longitudinal study in the east Kimberleys Western Australia has found that Aboriginal children who were underweight at 5 years of age were also significantly lighter at birth than those who were not underweight at five (Roberts et al. 1988). However, as the authors point out, there are many possible explanations for the association of low birth weight in Aboriginal infants with undernutrition in later childhood. Low birth weight may just be a proxy for other factors that also affect nutritional status at that time, such as substandard, unhygienic living conditions and high rates of infection and parasitic diseases.

Infection and the environment

Reports of high rates of infection in Aboriginal communities persist in the literature and the situation appears not to have altered substantially over the last 30 years. This indicates that many Aboriginal communities are still forced to live in poor and contaminated environments, particularly in remote areas. Growth faltering is likely to reflect the disease pattern as much as the dietary pattern.

Infections or illnesses increase nutrient requirements, but often cause a reduction in food intake because of lack of appetite. In some illnesses, particularly diarrhoea, food may be withheld by care-givers and/or malabsorption occurs. Energy deficiency results in the depletion of body fat stores and in the breakdown of tissue protein. Body weight is lost and growth rate is retarded. A child with nutritional deficiencies may also have a decreased ability to resist infections

Figure 4.7 *After the first three months of life, Aboriginal infants often show evidence of growth faltering, which may be partly attributed to intestinal, chest and other infections. (P. Lucich/AIATSIS, Canberra)*

through impairment of the immunological system (Rosenberg et al. 1976; Scrimshaw et al. 1968; Suskind 1977).

Aboriginal children are known to suffer disproportionately from gastroenteritis and from other diseases, notably upper respiratory tract infections, trachoma and ear and skin infections (see Thomson, chapter 2 in this volume). Evidence suggests that the quantity of water available is a crucial factor in preventing many diarrhoeas and other diseases such as impetigo and scabies, although quality of water may be relatively more important for the under 3-year-olds (Hebert 1985; Iseley 1983). Many Aboriginal communities still lack essential services such as a reticulated water supply and safe sewage disposal (see Torzillo and Kerr, chapter 8 in this volume)

The adverse effects of diarrhoeal disease on growth in developing countries are well documented (Black et al. 1984). Rowland et al. (1977) studied the role of infection in determining nutritional status in Gambian village children. They demonstrated a strong negative relationship between growth and gastroenteritis, which also prevented normal and 'catch-up' growth in the second and third year of life. Lutter et al. (1989) have put the cumulative effects of diarrhoea at between 2.5 and 10 centimetres at the age of 36 months, representing the range of deficits that could be expected given variations among populations in the incidence of diarrhoea and in weaning patterns.

An association of poorer growth with poor environment has been reported by a number of studies in Australia. It has been found, for example, that Aboriginal children living in settled Kimberley towns (Western Australia) are taller and heavier than those who live in more remote localities; they are also heavier at birth and throughout their preschool years. It is suggested that this difference in size is the result of the better environmental conditions of the towns (Hitchcock et al. 1987).

Cockington (1980) studied growth in three Aboriginal communities of differing socioeconomic circumstances; rural town dwellers, rural town fringe dwellers and 'nomadic' reserve dwellers. The main differences between the communities were in standards of housing and provision of essential services. Cockington reports that marked growth retardation was most evident in the reserve population with the worst socioeconomic environment. Moderate retardation was observed in the fringe-dwelling group, while 'normal' growth, that is, similar to that of non-Aboriginal children, was shown by children living in the rural town, with housing and facilities of the same standard enjoyed by the local non-Aboriginal Australians.

Similar results were found in communities in the Murray Valley of north-west Victoria and south-west New South Wales (Cameron and Debelle 1986). Seven per cent of 297 children ranging from newborn to 11 years old were stunted or less than 90 per cent standard-height-for-age (SHFA), four per cent were wasted or less than 80 per cent of standard-weight-for-height (SWFH) and 17 per cent were less than 80 per cent standard-weight-for-age (SWFA). These are similar figures to those found by Gracey and Sullivan (1987) in the Kimberleys (Western Australia). There, higher figures (26 per cent were less than 80 per cent SWFA) were found in the community housed in camps on the outskirts of town, where dilapidated housing lacked all amenities, compared to 11 per cent with less than 80 per cent SWFA found in Aboriginal communities accommodated in the town in standard three-bedroom European-style housing.

Not all researchers have linked improved growth with environmental conditions, however. In Queensland, Muller et al. (1984) have reported that at Cherbourg, a community 270 kilometres west of Brisbane, infant growth rates are now similar to those of non-Aboriginal children. The proportion of children below 90 per cent SWFA (NCHS) appears to be the same as for non-Aboriginal children. The data upon which the analysis was based were drawn from health records dating from 1952 to 1981. The authors attribute the improvement in growth to the more active participation of the people in their own health care and to the preventive efforts of a team from the Aboriginal Health Program at work in the community since 1972, rather than to changes to the environment.

Roberts and Rutishauser (1978), on the other hand, argue that stress, anorexia and malabsorption associated with repeated infections have a much greater influence on Aboriginal nutrition than does food availability. Significant improvement in nutritional status can be expected only in conjunction with improvements in the overall environment. A similar point is made by Payne (1985) in a discussion of the nature of malnutrition. He points out that malnutrition in children is so intimately related to infectious disease that it makes no practical sense to pursue programs aimed at improving food consumption without also ensuring improvements in water, sanitation and housing.

Breast-feeding and supplementation

We have seen that growth faltering in Aboriginal infants occurs during the second half of the first year of life and that infections play a significant role. These events are occurring as milk alone is becoming inadequate for growth and supplementation is necessary. How and when is this achieved and to what extent are Aboriginal babies breast- or formula-fed? This is an important question because breast milk contains antibodies that can help protect the infant from infections to some extent, and it may be difficult to prepare bottle feeds safely when facilities are inadequate.

Australia followed other industrialised countries with a rapid decline in breast-feeding between the 1930s and the 1960s. The low point (only 50 to 60 per cent of mothers breast-feeding on leaving hospital) was in the late 1960s and early 1970s. The shift from breast-feeding to bottle-feeding in the postwar years was the result of many factors, including improved material conditions, promotion by health personnel and changes in hospital routine to favour bottle feeding (Baghurst 1988). Aboriginal women in many communities, particularly in settled Australia, came under the same pressure from health personnel to adopt bottle-feeding. In more remote areas, however, prolonged breast-feeding has remained the norm (Gracey et al. 1983).

There now appears to be a return to breast-feeding in Australia and this is being led by educated women from the higher socioeconomic groups. A joint survey of infant-feeding practices in Western Australia and Tasmania in 1984–85 showed that 86 per cent and 81 per cent of mothers, respectively, were breast-feeding their babies on hospital discharge. Forty-five per cent were still breast-feeding at 6 months (Hitchcock and Coy 1988). An earlier study had shown that 79 per cent of non-Aboriginal mothers in Perth were breast-feeding at 6 weeks and this had declined to 11 per cent at 12 months (Hitchcock et al. 1983).

A study of urban Aborigines, also in Perth (Phillips and Dibley 1983), showed a pattern of breast-feeding similar to that of non-Aboriginal mothers. Eighty-two per cent of the Aboriginal mothers (n = 127) initiated breast-feeding but many failed to maintain lactation and, by 12 weeks, only half were still breast-feeding. This had declined to 19 per cent at 12 months. Coyne and Dowling (1978) earlier surveyed infant-feeding practices among Aborigines in rural New South Wales. Fifty-two per cent of infants (n = 146) were breast-fed at birth; by 3 months this had declined to 25 per cent and by 6 months to 16 per cent.

The reasons given by the Perth Aboriginal mothers for ceasing breast-feeding were similar to those often given by non-Aboriginal mothers. These include anxiety over an inadequate milk supply and sore nipples. Many of these problems could be overcome with sympathetic support (Phillips and Dibley 1983).

The question of when breast-feeding alone becomes inadequate is a difficult one because it depends on the requirements of the individual baby and the lactational performance of the individual mother. The timing is especially important for babies in unhygienic circumstances who may be at risk from contaminated food (Waterlow 1981). Researchers have tackled this problem by attempting to calculate infants' theoretical nutrient requirements, by analysing breast milk and studying the growth of different populations in different social and economic circumstances (for example, Rowland 1985; Whitehead 1985). It remains a controversial area, however (see Waterlow 1979; Waterlow and Thomson 1979; Jelliffe and Jelliffe 1979; Waterlow et al. 1980).

The timing of the introduction of supplementary foods varies in Australia. In the Perth study of non-Aboriginal mothers, almost all infants were eating a variety of foods by six months of age (Hitchcock et al. 1983). In the Western Australia and Tasmania study, solid and non-milk foods were introduced earlier to infants who were fed 'artificially'. Nearly all infants were being fed these foods by the age of six months (Hitchcock and Coy 1988). The Aboriginal group in Perth introduced solids early. By 16 weeks of age, 65 per cent were receiving solid food (Phillips and Dibley 1983). In rural New South Wales, solid foods were introduced before the age of 2 months to 20 per cent of the infants (Coyne and Dowling 1978).

Prolonged lactation and early supplementation with additional fluids and semi-solids have been traditionally practiced in many societies (Raphael 1984). The duration of breast-feeding, however, tends to change with increasing urbanisation and the availability of processed milks (King and Ashworth 1987). Paradoxically, prolonged breast-feeding may be associated with poor nutritional status (Victora et al. 1984; Brakohiapa et al. 1988). This has also been observed in remote Aboriginal communities where prolonged breast-feeding is common. Gracey et al. (1983) found that the fall-off in growth in the second half of infancy was more pronounced in remote areas, where breast-feeding is almost universal up to two years of age. They speculate that breast-feeding is beneficial in this group and that health patterns would be worse if the infants were 'artificially' fed. However, milk alone is inadequate for most babies by the second half of infancy (Whitehead 1985) and the growth pattern described may either be the result of infections and/or a failure of supplementation. It is possible, for example, that suckling blunts appetite to the extent that infants do not appear hungry or demand other food. On the other hand, it is possible that suitable supplementary foods are not regularly available.

Too little is known about supplementary feeding practices in remote Aboriginal communities to answer these questions with any certainty. However, children are required to make their food needs known to their caretakers from an early age and are presumed to know what they need. If they request food and it is available they are given it. Demanding infants and children do well under this system. They are not encouraged to eat if they appear reluctant to do so, which might be the case if they are experiencing frequent infections and/or have just suckled (Middleton and Francis 1976; Hamilton 1981, 1982; Harrison unpub.).

Nutrition in adulthood

Comparatively little attention has been paid to nutrition in adulthood, although it is known that Aboriginal adults have a shorter life expectancy than the rest of the Australian population and that some so-called lifestyle diseases such as hypertension and diabetes are relatively more common in the Aboriginal population. Most work to date has focused on diabetes and, to a lesser extent, body fat distribution and its relationship to increased health risk.

Body mass index and body fat distribution

Disorders such as diabetes are frequently associated with obesity and it appears, from the few studies that are available, that many Aboriginal adults, particularly women, tend to gain weight rapidly in early adulthood (Rutishauser and McKay 1986). What happens to the diet then, or what other factors there might be, is not known.

In adults, weight status is usually defined by the body mass index (BMI), the formula for which is W/H^2, where W is weight in kilograms and H is height in metres. The National Health and Medical Research Council (NH&MRC) has reviewed evidence relating BMI to mortality and morbidity and recommended that acceptable weights-for-height in Australia should be based on a BMI range of 20 to 25 (NH&MRC 1984). However, individuals with the same BMI can differ in their body fat content, depending on their body build and composition.

Rutishauser and McKay (1986) suggest that the use of anthropometric data such as the BMI to assess nutritional status in populations other than the Anglo-Australian population requires caution and more research. The authors carried out a detailed cross-sectional anthropometric survey of 114 women aged 15 and over at five Aboriginal communities in the Kimberleys (Western Australia), partly in response to an earlier survey by Gracey et al. (1984), who had reported widespread poor nutrition among Aboriginal girls and women of childbearing age. As already discussed, maternal nutrition influences birth weight. Maternal nutrition has been a neglected area in Aboriginal health, in spite of the high percentage of LBW babies. Gracey and his colleagues examined 388 females aged from 15 years to 34 years in seven communities in the Kimberleys. In the 15 to 19 age group, 36 per cent were judged to be 'undernourished' (BMI less than 17.6 kg/m^2); the figure for the 20 to 24 age group was 24 per cent. In all, only 51 to 63 per cent of the women had a BMI within 'acceptable' limits (defined as 17.6–27.5 kg/m^2). Gracey et al. (1984, p. 507) concluded that the women's nutritional status was substandard, although 'there is no simple anthropometric measurement which will clearly define malnutrition in adult life in individuals or in groups'.

Rutishauser and McKay (1986) calculated body fat content from the sum of four skin folds using the age- and sex-specific prediction equation of Durnin and Womersley (1974), although this was derived from a different ethnic group and may itself not be appropriate. The authors found that even in Aboriginal women with a BMI below 20, the estimated percentage of body fat (24 per cent) was well within the normal range for young women. The lowest BMI of the youngest women, usually associated with undernutrition, is clearly not associated with a lack of subcutaneous fat.

In this study, Rutishauser and McKay (1986) also found a rapid increase in body weight in women between the ages of 25 and 35 years. The women showed a central pattern of fat distribution which became more pronounced with increasing BMI.

The type of fat distribution in obesity is now thought to have a substantial impact on health risk. (Obesity is defined as a BMI greater than 30.) An android or central distribution of body fat is associated with stroke, hypertension, ischaemic heart disease and non-insulin-dependent diabetes mellitus (Seidell et al. 1987). This distribution is most common in men when they become obese, while a gynoid or peripheral fat deposition pattern is more common in women when they become obese. Women who have a central fat distribution are more at risk from the metabolic complications of obesity than are women who have a peripheral fat distribution.

O'Dea (1987) has reported similar findings to Rutishauser and McKay for Aboriginal women. O'Dea found that body fat distribution was of the android pattern (waist to hips ratio greater than 0.9) in both men and women. The numbers in these studies are small, but the findings may help to explain why Aboriginal women, in contrast to non-Aboriginal women, appear to have similar risks for the disorders associated with obesity (such as diabetes) to those of men at the equivalent level of obesity.

Dugdale (1988) has suggested that early malnutrition can produce this high-risk distribution of body fat. When data from a survey of 495 Aboriginal children and 3971 non-Aboriginal children from all parts of Queensland were analysed, it was noted that although they weighed less, the Aboriginal children had more fat in the subscapular region and less in the triceps region than the non-Aboriginal children (Dugdale et al. 1980; Dugdale and Lovell 1981). A further 145 children aged 5 to 10 years from the Aboriginal community at Cherbourg (Queensland) were investigated. It was found that a tendency to a higher subscapular/triceps skinfold (SSF/TSF) ratio was associated with a lower birth weight or weight gain in the first two years of life. In children who had been well nourished in infancy, the subscapular/triceps skinfold ratio was similar to that of the non-Aboriginal children. However, more research is required to determine if there is a relationship between poor nutrition in infancy and a tendency to central obesity in adulthood.

Diabetes

Non-insulin-dependent diabetes mellitus (NIDDM, type 2 diabetes) has become a significant health problem in many Aboriginal communities. Studies have put the likely prevalence of NIDDM among Aborigines from between 7.4 per cent to 17 per cent depending on the area surveyed and, it is assumed, the length of exposure of the population to the risk factors for development of the disease. The lower figure comes from a study of three small, isolated communities in the desert region of north-west Australia (O'Dea et al. 1988b) and the higher figure from a survey of coastal Aborigines from the west Kimberleys (Bastian 1979). Intermediate prevalence figures have been reported from four communities in different parts of South Australia (Wise et al. 1976) and from rural towns of south-west and central Western Australia (Stanton et al. 1985). A recent study has estimated that the prevalence of NIDDM in the non-Aboriginal population of Australia, aged 25 years and over, is 3.4 per cent (Glatthaar et al. 1985; Larkins 1985).

NIDDM has severe long term consequences, although initially symptoms may be mild and easily ignored. However, it can cause microvascular complications in the eyes, kidneys and the peripheral nervous system and is associated with hypertension and coronary artery disease (Stern 1988).

In a study of American Indian Health Service data, Gohdes (1986) found that 76 per cent of all those with lower limb amputations were diabetics, while 33 per cent of those hospitalised with chronic renal failure and 29 per cent of those hospitalised with ischaemic heart disease were diabetics. The rate of diabetic complications for Aboriginal Australians is less well known, but Stanton et al. (1985) found that some complications were more prevalent. For example, retinopathy (haemorrhages into the retina leading to permanent loss of vision) within 10 years of onset of diabetes was more common in Aborigines than in the non-Aboriginal groups they studied.

NIDDM is characterised by both a deficiency in insulin secretion and by tissue resistance to insulin-stimulated glucose uptake, although the exact aetiology is not yet understood. Insulin is a hormone secreted by the beta cells of the pancreas. When blood glucose rises after a meal, insulin secretion is stimulated and the combination of hyperinsulinemia and hyperglycaemia promotes glucose uptake by the liver and peripheral muscles. Glucose is used for fuel or converted to glycogen for storage. Insulin also inhibits hepatic glucose production and the breakdown of stored fats for fuel (DeFronzo 1988).

The primary lesion appears to be insulin resistance, which may be genetic or acquired (Eriksson et al. 1989; Stern 1988). Obesity causes insulin resistance, although it cannot by itself explain the difference in prevalence rates in different populations (DeFronzo 1988). Insulin resistance is also present in approximately 25 per cent of non-obese individuals with normal oral glucose tolerance. One explanation seems to be that some people who have inherited or, by becoming obese, acquired insulin resistance can overcome it by secreting more insulin and maintaining a state of chronic hyperinsulinemia. In others, the pancreatic beta cells become exhausted and insulin secretion declines. Impaired glucose tolerance and, subsequently, NIDDM develop (Reaven 1988). Once insulin secretion declines and fasting hyperglycaemia develops, further metabolic complications ensue. Sustained chronic hyperglycaemia may be a pathogenic factor in its own right, leading to defects in both insulin secretion and insulin action (DeFronzo 1988).

Some populations, including Aborigines, appear to be genetically predisposed to develop NIDDM when they undergo rapid lifestyle changes (variously described as 'urbanising' or 'modernising' in the literature). It has been hypothesised that these populations possess a 'thrifty' gene which would have enabled them to survive in a harsh and unstable environment. In times of food abundance, efficient hepatic glucose production, which is not sensitive to suppression by insulin, would have promoted the conversion of large intakes of dietary protein to glucose. Active hepatic lipogenesis would have facilitated the conversion of this excess energy to triglyceride for storage in adipose tissue. Fat stores provide a protein-sparing effect by limiting the need for dietary or body protein to be used for energy in times of food scarcity. However, changes in lifestyle, in particular in food consumption patterns and physical activity, have led instead to obesity and insulin resistance (O'Dea 1982, 1983).

Other populations that have undergone lifestyle changes similar to those experienced by Aborigines are also suffering increasing rates of NIDDM. These include Melanesians of the Torres Strait, Mexican-Americans and Native Americans (Duffy et al. 1981; Ritenbaugh and Goodby 1989; Urdaneta and Krehbiel 1989). In Native Americans, the prevalence varies from tribe to tribe, but values of 20 to 30 per cent are common and they are higher in older adults

(Weiss et al. 1989). The highest known diabetes prevalence in the world, 50 per cent among those aged 35 years and over, occurs among the Pima Indians of Arizona (Bennett et al. 1971).

Not all of the available studies are comparable as sample sizes vary, and are often small, and not all use the same diagnostic criteria. Most recent studies use the World Health Organization (WHO) criteria, which define diabetes as a plasma glucose concentration of greater than 7.8 mmol/L in the fasting state, or greater than 11.1 mmol/L two hours after the administration of a standardised oral glucose load. Impaired glucose tolerance (IGT) is defined as a plasma glucose concentration between 7.8 mmol/L and 11.1 mmol/L two hours after a standardised oral glucose load. Some studies use the United States National Diabetes Data Group (NDDG) criteria. These are similar but require that an intermediate glucose level also exceed 11.1 mmol/L if the fasting criterion is not met (Stern 1988).

O'Dea et al. (1982) have identified a number of metabolic characteristics that appear to be associated with susceptibility to NIDDM in Aborigines. These include impaired glucose tolerance, hyperinsulinemia and hypertriglyceridemia in young, relatively lean subjects (BMI of approximately 21 kg/m^2). These Aborigines have been 'Westernised' for 50 years. In order to understand the biomedical consequences of lifestyle change, O'Dea et al. (1988a) compared the carbohydrate and lipid profile of these Aborigines with a small group living on an outstation in north-eastern Arnhem Land and eating a diet containing a large proportion of traditional foods. It was found that although the outstation people had a much lower BMI (14–19 kg/m^2) than the urban group, their insulin levels were similar. In addition, their insulin levels were higher than those of a group of non-Aboriginal Australians with a BMI of 21 kg/m^2. The outstation group also exhibited mild elevation in triglyceride levels consistent with inappropriately high fasting insulin levels and insulin resistance. These factors put them potentially at risk of diabetes should further lifestyle changes and obesity occur.

Temporary reversion to a traditional lifestyle has been shown to reduce hyperinsulinemia in non-diabetic urban Aborigines (O'Dea and Spargo 1982, O'Dea et al. 1980). Improvement has also been shown in diabetic Aborigines if they revert to a 'traditional' diet and lifestyle for as little as seven weeks (O'Dea 1984). Reasons for the improvements include weight loss, increased physical exercise and the low fat content of the bush diet. Reduction in stress may also play a part, as stress has been implicated in the aetiology of NIDDM (Surwit and Feinglos 1988).

These studies have helped to elucidate the aetiology of NIDDM in Aborigines, but they do not tackle the problems of prevention or management. Although it has been shown that dietary change is possible in the short term, it is obviously not a practical proposition for most Aborigines periodically to 'go bush' or to return to a more traditional way of life. Dietary control, which means changing food habits for life, is difficult for all diabetics (Campbell et al. 1989).

Further research could with benefit be directed to understanding the meaning for Aboriginal groups of chronic diseases like NIDDM. Lang (1989), for example, has demonstrated the complexities of the Dakota (Sioux) interpretation of NIDDM. The Dakota are a Native American people whose experience of this disease is similar to that of Aborigines. Lang makes the point that the Dakota interpretation differs substantially from the medical model in which health-care workers are trained. This type of research, by increasing the understanding of health-care workers, could facilitate cooperative efforts to design culturally appropriate diabetes education and treatment programs. People who participate in setting goals for treatment are more likely to follow therapeutic regimes than those who are told what to do (Weiss et al. 1989).

Nutrition programs

Overwhelmingly, nutrition programs that have been targeted to the Aboriginal population have been concerned with diet. Yet, as we have seen, the role of diet in the aetiology of nutrition problems is not a clear one. In particular, as far as children are concerned, the quality of the environment is equally, if not more, important. This aspect has not been addressed because nutrition tends to be seen as a medical problem, and hence the province of departments of health, while the responsibility for housing, water supply and sewage lies elsewhere in the bureaucracy.

Even if it were proved that diet is to blame for Aboriginal health problems, further questions would need to be asked. Is the problem a lack of food, either at the community or household level? If so, is the problem one of supply or cost? If not, do distribution patterns within the community or the household disadvantage some groups or individuals? Or is the problem a lack of knowledge of food values, so that poor food choices are made? The questions are potentially endless and the available evidence hardly begins to answer them. What we can say is that these problems, and the extent to which they are implicated in nutrition problems, are not likely to be uniform across the country. It is worth repeating that Aboriginal communities are found in different locations and in different socioeconomic circumstances. It is only with extreme caution that the findings from a study undertaken in one community can be applied to another.

Are more studies therefore needed? This is not an easy question to answer, but the issues raised by it are important. More information on the one hand may mean that the situation may be better understood and remedied. On the other hand, studies can be costly and, particularly if not geared to intervention, may raise the expectations of the community involved but fail to satisfy them. It is no wonder that some communities become sceptical about the research enterprise and question its benefits for them. Indeed, more studies about the deplorable state of some Aboriginal communities and their appalling lack of resources are hardly needed. The problem is well known but remains unsolved.

But who decides what interventions are required? Rarely is it the community concerned and this is one of the reasons why programs have had little demonstrable effect. Aborigines do not share the value systems of non-Aboriginal Australians and it cannot be assumed that they perceive problems in the same way, or with the same order of priority, as government departments or well-meaning non-Aboriginal individuals or groups. Without an appreciation of this point, programs and policies imposed from outside, however well intentioned, tend to increase Aboriginal dependency and sense of powerlessness, as the history of the co-existence of the two cultures amply demonstrates.

Since Aboriginal medical services have been established, some Aboriginal groups have set up their own nutrition programs (see Winch, 'An Aboriginal nutrition program', in Saggers and Gray, chapter 9 in this volume), but these usually depend on government financial support which is rarely long term. Sykes (1977) has discussed some of these problems.

Most nutrition programs or interventions fall into three categories—food fortification, food supplementation and nutrition education—and all three have been used at some time in different parts of the country. (Nutrition rehabilitation is also a type of intervention, but is not considered here.) Some programs are government initiatives, but many are local, non-government responses. Since it is impossible to detail them all here, this text concentrates on the types of program, the assumptions they make and the problems with each approach.

Food fortification

There is only one example of food fortification in the literature as far as I am aware and it demonstrates the problems of this approach.

Some of the dietary studies discussed earlier showed that Aboriginal diets may be deficient in certain vitamins and minerals and that consumption of fruits and vegetables appears to be low. In response to this, at the beginning of the 1970s a group of non-Aboriginal workers in Bourke, New South Wales, fortified the local white bread supply with iron, vitamins B1 and B2 and niacin (Kamien et al. 1974; Kamien et al. 1975*b*; Kamien 1978). Bread was chosen because it was considered to be the staple in the Bourke diet, contributing nearly 30 per cent of the intake of kilojoules and protein. Bread fortification is common in North America, the United Kingdom, Scandinavia and parts of Europe, but not in Australia. However, the substances and amounts added to the bread at Bourke were permissible under the New South Wales Pure Food Regulations. Blood sampling of Bourke Aborigines showed that half of those who were deficient in these substances when tested in 1971 were no longer deficient in 1974 after bread fortification. The fortification program was short-lived, however, because it was denounced in the press as a secret experiment, potentially harmful to certain individuals with rare genetic diseases. These claims were exaggerated, although there were certainly problems with this approach.

The fortification of foodstuffs with a particular nutrient or nutrients can be the answer when the diet of the target population is known to be deficient in that nutrient, but is otherwise satisfactory, and when the nutrient is unlikely to be supplied by any other means. A well-known and successful example is the addition of iodine to salt or bread to prevent endemic goitre and cretinism in areas where the soil is iodine deficient (in Australia this occurs in Gippsland and Tasmania). The amount required is small and iodine is well tolerated, absorbed and utilised by this route.

The addition of other nutrients to foodstuffs is more open to question. Dosage can be a problem. How much people eat and how this may relate to their need for the nutrient cannot be assessed or controlled. The fortified food may come to be regarded as especially healthy or 'good', increasing usual consumption to the detriment of other foods and, possibly, other nutrients. The absorption of the added nutrient may be enhanced or prevented by other constituents in the food or in foods consumed with it. Iron absorption, for example, is affected by the phytates found in bread.

If the reliance in Bourke on bread as a staple was, for some reason, deplored (which it seems to have been), why reinforce or promote its use? Indeed, the researchers in Bourke appear to have believed that the food supply was restricted, but the evidence for this is rather suspect, based as it was on a survey of two families. Bread, incidentally, is a good source of carbohydrate, protein, fibre and a significant source of some micronutrients; these are present in greater amounts in wholemeal bread.

A more relevant approach would have been to encourage the consumption of a wider variety of food. What factors were involved here? There are some hints in the accounts. The local butcher is described as expensive so the Aboriginal population did not patronise him. However, they bought and killed their own sheep instead, so meat appears not to have been a problem, though storing it was. Eggs were purchased and some families fished regularly. Cheap citrus fruit was available in local orchards, but the Aboriginal population felt 'uncomfortable' going to them, possibly because of prejudice. Yet they readily purchased fruit and vegetables once a week from the visiting greengrocer, so these items were known and enjoyed. Food storage facilities, however, were obviously inadequate so that perishables had to be quickly consumed after purchase. Cooking facilities were described as primitive. The picture which emerges is a complex one with many contributing variables including low incomes. It is not surprising then that the quick, short term solution of bread fortification was attractive.

Food supplementation

Supplementary feeding programs apparently provide a concrete and practical way of alleviating nutritional problems. They are not, however, as widespread as they used to be during the 1970s, although local examples may still be found (see, for example, the case study 'Good intentions: a community nutrition program'). Feeding programs can be costly and difficult to evaluate, so they are not favoured by governments. Also the distribution of food is now more likely to be regarded as a patronising welfare hand-out than a positive benefit, but it has recently been suggested that food vouchers might be used instead to combat poor nutrition in women and children in the Kimberley region (Sullivan et al. 1987).

Government supplementary feeding programs have been most extensive in the Northern Territory, where they grew out of the communal feeding system; programs for mothers and babies were the last to disappear. They were replaced during the 1970s by nutrition assistance programs targeted to those 'at risk' and based on health centres (Commonwealth Department of Health 1976/77). Some feeding programs around the country have been school based (see, for example, Coyne et al. 1980 for a nutritional evaluation of a preschool feeding program in New South Wales).

Food supplementation, usually of preschool children and pregnant women, remains one of the most common nutritional interventions in third world countries and is often tied to food aid programs. Nutritional advice and/or medical care may

Good intentions: a community nutrition program

In 1983, the doctor employed by the local council of a remote Aboriginal community in the Northern Territory initiated a nutrition program to combat infant growth faltering. He felt a major cause was the inability of young mothers to cope with large families. These mothers received free supplies of a multimix (a combination of mashed potatoes, pumpkin and egg) to feed to their children. They were also encouraged to join a small group of women who, at the doctor's suggestion, were manufacturing the multimix in large quantities and freezing it. Meanwhile, the doctor financed the program by raffling meat trays at the social club.

The nurse who worked under the doctor's direction at a neighbouring community resisted the introduction of the multimix there, partly because she was not convinced that it would address the nutrition problems in her community, where large families were not the norm, and partly because, anticipating apathy from both Aboriginal health workers and mothers, she feared that the cooking would be left to her.

However, the nurse felt obliged, under pressure from the doctor, to undertake some kind of special program. Accordingly, health and nutrition films were screened for all women once a fortnight at the health centre. An afternoon tea of sandwiches was served. The idea was that a more informal environment than the clinic itself would encourage discussions about child-rearing and feeding to take place.

As a social occasion, it was a great success. Attendance varied from 20 to 40 women, plus many children and babies, and the women enjoyed both the films and the tea. However, the program lasted only a few weeks. Frequently the films did not arrive on time and the health workers, who had to prepare the tea, did not hold the meetings when the nurse was making her regular visit to another community. They had agreed to the program when the nurse had put the idea to them, but only for her sake. They were not committed to it.

Apart from the occasion when the dietitian was fortuitously present and delivered a short talk, no nutrition discussion took place. This part of the program was never attempted. The whole scheme had no clear aim beyond presenting information through film. This was done on a rather haphazard basis, because it depended on which films were available. It was also hard to choose suitable and relevant films from a catalogue, without first viewing them.

Films (or videos) are probably a good way to present health information to this community, because watching videos is a popular local pastime, but the program did not last long enough to assess their potential.

Shortly after this, the doctor left the community and the multimix disappeared too.

Lindsey Harrison

also be available as part of the program. Supplementation assumes that nutritional problems are caused by a physical lack of food, either at the community or household level. A number of problems have been identified with this approach, some of which are applicable to the Australian situation. For a number of reasons, the food may not reach those most in need, who indeed may not be identified. Distance and the responsibilities of caretakers (other children, work or both) may preclude attendance at the supplementation centre. Traditional distribution patterns may not favour children (particularly female children) or women, so that the extra food, if it is taken home, may be eaten by other members of the family. The foodstuff itself may not be known by, or be acceptable to, the recipient population, so it is rejected. Paradoxically, the supplementary food may depress still further the amount of food available in the community. This occurs when the food is eaten instead of the usual diet rather than in addition to the usual diet. Overall demand for food is therefore reduced. Naturally, nutritional status is not improved, because

Figure 4.8 *This nutrition poster, designed for Pitjantjatjara children in 1987, shows both bush and store foods available to the communities. (Leonie Lane/Redback Graphix for Nganampa Health Council, Alice Springs, Northern Territory)*

food consumption does not increase. Since program evaluation is difficult and costly to carry out, it may not be attempted. Without evaluation, however, it is not possible to gauge the effectiveness of these programs, but it has been suggested that they are rarely cost-effective (Beaton and Ghassemi 1982; Kennedy and Knudsen 1985).

Nutrition education

Today, nutrition education is the main aim of government departments of health. Attempts are made to produce educational materials that are relevant to the Aboriginal population and not just altered white messages. In some areas, such as the Northern Territory, materials are produced in Aboriginal languages where these have been written down and are now taught in schools.

Nutrition education assumes that the 'problem' is one of lack of knowledge and that, with the right information, people will be able to choose a nutritious diet. It is often assumed that Aborigines choose unwisely from European foods because they lack knowledge of food values and perceive all European foods to be 'good' (Taylor 1977), but this point has not been systematically studied. It is likely that this type of knowledge depends on exposure to the Australian education system and the media. Young Tiwi women, for example, appear to have a knowledge of nutrition and food values similar to that of their non-Aboriginal counterparts with similar education (Harrison unpub.).

Nutritional knowledge does not necessarily have an effect on behaviour. Indeed, the range of possible influences on dietary behaviour is extremely large and not all are amenable to change by the individual or the group. The most important influence on food choice is obviously the physical availability of food and its cost. The individual also makes decisions about food. These are likely to be influenced by such factors as: the physical properties of the food; its taste, appearance and texture; personal preferences; the influence of parents, peers and the mass media; and beliefs about the food itself.

Food plays a central role in all human societies. It not only appeases hunger and provides nutrients for body maintenance, growth and reproduction, it also has a wide range of other functions as well. Food is used to create and express relationships between people, for example. What we eat and who we eat with reflects our position in society and our relationship with others. Certain foods can have special significance and be reserved for particular people or occasions. Food can also express relationships not only between people, but also between people and the natural or supernatural worlds (de Garine 1972). These factors mean that people can be extremely resistant to change in their dietary habits.

Figure 4.9 *The New South Wales Department of Health distributes health and nutrition promotion material such as this to Aboriginal families. (Aboriginal Health Unit, NSW Department of Health, Sydney)*

The importance of these issues is shown by the experience of Stacey (1977, 1978, 1979), who was involved with nutrition education programs for Aboriginal women in central Australia. Although the women would readily repeat what Stacey taught them about European food values and the appropriate diet for small children, she found that for them the most important use of food was to express relationships with other adults. Adults gave children what food they requested if they were there when food was available, but children did not have adult obligations. Further, the women did not link diet with physical health. Although Stacey ignores completely the economics of the food supply, her articles are useful reminders of the social role of food. Above all, she stresses the importance of listening to and respecting the client group and not assuming that the health professional knows best.

All the approaches to Aboriginal nutrition described here have been concerned with diet and all make assumptions about the causes of the particular problems they are meant to address. Almost inevitably, the assumptions are a simplification of the situation. This is because there are rarely prime or single causes for the sorts of nutritional problems we have discussed and, hence, rarely single or easy solutions. As far as many Aborigines are concerned, the problems they experience stem from their structural position in Australian society, their economic disadvantage and the social discrimination that they regularly face. No dietary approach *per se* will rectify this, but undoubtedly the method of implementing programs will either exacerbate the situation or, through consultation and involvement, help people make the most of the choices they have, even though those choices are often more limited than those available to other sections of the Australian population. No purely dietary approach increases education and employment opportunities or provides adequate housing and essential services to those communities that still lack them. All these factors have an impact on nutrition.

Appropriate interventions

Food and nutrition are sensitive issues and, to avoid repeating the mistakes of the past, it is vital to evaluate critically the evidence and be aware of its limitations. This process should prevent the drawing of dubious conclusions. The concentration on diet as the major cause of Aboriginal ill-health and on mainly dietary interventions, rather than tackling structural and environmental factors, is an example of this. The growth patterns of Aboriginal children resemble those of non-Aboriginal children when their living conditions are similarly favourable, but they more often experience high rates of infection and growth faltering, due in large part to poor and contaminated environments. Until these areas are addressed, little further improvement can be expected in the various indicators used to measure Aboriginal health status. However, the sorts of interventions required would involve a greater transfer of resources to the Aboriginal population than is currently the case and is unlikely to be politically feasible.

Inappropriate interventions not only fail to remedy structural and environmental factors, they often increase the dependency of Aboriginal communities on non-Aboriginal decision makers and resource holders. Involvement in the decisions that vitally effect them is likely to have health dividends for Aboriginal people, although this is not always understood by economic rationalists.

Lack of education and employment opportunities for Aborigines, and the daily experience of discrimination, which few non-Aboriginal people can appreciate, are issues which must be tackled by the Australian population as a whole. Nutrition problems are not medical problems and will not be eliminated by medical solutions. They are the product of an unequal access to resources and require social and political action.

References

ABS (1985), *1984 household expenditure survey, Australia*, AGPS, Canberra.

Altman, J. C. (1982), 'Hunting buffalo in north-central Arnhem Land: a case of rapid adaptation among Aborigines', *Oceania* **52** (4), pp. 274–85.

Altman, J. C. (1984*a*), 'The dietary utilisation of flora and fauna by contemporary hunter-gatherers at Momega Outstation, north-central Arnhem Land', *Australian Aboriginal Studies* **1**, pp. 35–46.

Altman, J. C. (1984*b*), 'Hunter-gatherer subsistence production in Arnhem Land: the original affluence hypothesis re-examined', *Mankind* **14** (3), pp. 179–90.

Altman, J. C., and Nieuwenhuysen, J. P. (1979), *The economic status of Australian Aborigines*, Cambridge University Press, Cambridge.

Anderson, C. (1982), 'The Bloomfield community, north Queensland', in E. A. Young and E. K. Fisk (eds), *The Aboriginal component in the Australian economy. Vol. 3: Small rural communities*. Development Studies Centre, ANU, Canberra.

Baghurst, K. I. (1988), 'Infant feeding: public health perspectives', *Medical Journal of Australia* **148**, pp. 112–113.

Barker, D. J. P., and Osmond, C. (1986), 'Infant mortality, childhood nutrition and ischaemic heart disease in England and Wales', Lancet **1**, pp. 1077–81.

Barker, D. J. P., Osmond, C., Golding, J., Kuh, D., and Wadsworth, M. E. J. (1989), 'Growth in utero, blood pressure in childhood and adult life, and mortality from cardiovascular disease', *British Medical Journal* **298**, pp. 564–7.

Bastian, P. (1979), 'Coronary heart disease in tribal Aborigines: the west Kimberley survey', *Australian and New Zealand Journal of Medicine* **9**, pp. 284–92.

Beaton, G. H., and Ghassemi, H. (1982), 'Supplementary feeding programmes for young children in developing countries', *American Journal of Clinical Nutrition* **35**, pp. 864–916.

Beck, E. J. (1985), *The enigma of Aboriginal health*, AIAS, Canberra.

Bennett, P. H., Burch, T. A., and Miller, M. (1971), 'Diabetes mellitus in American (Pima) Indians', *Lancet* **2**, pp. 125–8.

Bingham, S. A. (1987), 'The dietary assessment of individuals; methods, accuracy, new techniques and recommendations', *Nutrition Abstracts and Reviews* (Series A) **57** (10), pp. 705–42.

Black, R. E., Brown, K. H., and Becker, S. (1984), 'Malnutrition is a determining factor in diarrhoeal duration, but not incidence, among young children in a longitudinal study in Bangladesh', *American Journal of Clinical Nutrition* **37**, pp. 87–94.

Brakohiapa, L. A., Yartey, J., Bille, A., Harrison, E., Quansah, E., Armar, M. A., Kishi, K., and Yamamoto, S. (1988), 'Does prolonged breast feeding adversely affect a child's nutritional status?' *Lancet* **2**, pp. 416–18.

Brand, J. C., and Cherikoff, V. (1985), 'Australian Aboriginal bushfoods: the nutritional composition of plants from arid and semi-arid areas', *Australian Aboriginal Studies* **2**, pp. 38–46.

Brand, J. C., Cherikoff, A., Lee, A., and McDonnell, J. (1982*a*), 'Nutrients in important bush foods', *Proceedings of the Nutrition Society of Australia* **7**, pp. 50–4.

Brand, J. C., Cherikoff. V., Lee, A., and Truswell, A. S. (1982*b*), 'An outstanding food source of vitamin C', *Lancet* **2**, p. 873.

Brand, J. C., Rae, C., McDonnell, J., Lee, A., Cherikoff, V., and Truswell, A. S. (1983), 'The nutritional composition of Australian Aboriginal bushfoods: 1', *Food Technology in Australia* **35** (6), pp. 293–8.

Brand, J. C., Cherikoff, V., and Truswell, A. S. (1984), 'The nutritional composition of seeds and nuts eaten by Australian Aborigines', *Proceedings of the Nutrition Society of Australia* **9**, p. 174.

Brown, T., and Townsend, G. C. (1982), 'Adolescent growth in height of Australian Aborigines analyzed by the Preece-Baines function: a longitudinal study', *Annals of Human Biology* **9** (6), pp. 495–505.

Cameron, F. J., and Debelle, G. D. (1986), 'Nutrition of Aboriginal infants and children in the Murray Valley', *Medical Journal of Australia* **144**, pp. S5–S8.

Campbell, L. V., Barth, R., and Gosper, J. (1989), 'Unsatisfactory nutritional parameters in non-insulin-dependent diabetes mellitus', *Medical Journal of Australia* **151**, pp. 146–150.

Cane, S. (1986), 'Bush tucker: intensified use of traditional resources on Aboriginal outstations', in B. Foran and B. Walker (eds), *Science and technology for Aboriginal development*, CSIRO and Centre for Appropriate Technology, Melbourne.

Cane, S. (1987), 'Australian Aboriginal subsistence in the Western Desert', *Human Ecology* **15** (4), pp. 391–434.

Cheek, D. B., McIntosh, G. H., O'Brien, V., Ness, D., and Green, R. C. (1989), 'Malnutrition in Aboriginal children at Yalata, South Australia', *European Journal of Clinical Nutrition* **43**, pp. 161–8.

Chen, L. C., Chowdhury, A. K. M., and Huffman, S. L. (1980), 'Anthropometric assessment of energy-protein malnutrition and subsequent risk of mortality among preschool aged children', *American Journal of Clinical Nutrition* **33**, pp. 1836–45.

Cockington, R. A. (1980), 'Growth of Australian Aboriginal children related to social circumstances', *Australian and New Zealand Journal of Medicine* **10**, pp. 199–208.

Coles-Rutishauser, I. H. E. (1979), 'Growing up in Western Australia: if you are Aboriginal', *Proceedings of the Nutrition Society of Australia* **4**, pp. 27–33.

Commonwealth Department of Health (1976–77), *Northern Division annual report*, Commonwealth Department of Health, Darwin.

Commonwealth Department of Health (1984), *Dietary guidelines for Australians*, AGPS, Canberra.

Commonwealth Department of Health (1986), *National dietary survey of adults: 1983. No. 1: Foods consumed*, AGPS, Canberra.

Corden, M. W. (1973), 'The dietary situation at Yuendumu and Papunya', in *Some observations on the diets and nutrition of Aboriginal people in central Australia*, Commonwealth Department of Health, Canberra.

Cox, J. W. (1979), 'A longitudinal study of the changing pattern in Aboriginal infants' growth, 1966–76', *Journal of Biosocial Science* **11**, pp. 269–79.

Coyne, T., and Dowling, M. (1978), 'Infant feeding practices among Aboriginals in rural New South Wales', *Proceedings of the Nutrition Society of Australia* **3**, p. 91.

Coyne, T., Dowling, M., and Condon-Paoloni, D. (1980), 'Evaluation of preschool meals on the nutritional health of Aboriginal children', *Medical Journal of Australia* **2**, pp. 369–75.

Crotty, J. M. (1958), 'Anaemia and nutritional disease in Northern Territory native children', *Medical Journal of Australia* **2**, pp. 322–25.

DAA (Department of Aboriginal Affairs) (1979), *Statistics Section Newsletter* **1** (8), AGPS, Canberra.

DAA (Department of Aboriginal Affairs) (1984), *Aboriginal social indicators, 1984*, AGPS, Canberra.

DCSH (Department of Community Services and Health) (1989), *Composition of foods: Australia*, AGPS, Canberra.

DeFronzo, R. A. (1988), 'The triumvirate: beta-cell, muscle, liver: a collusion responsible for NIDDM', *Diabetes* **37**, pp. 667–87.

de Garine, I. (1972), 'The socio-cultural aspects of nutrition', *Ecology of Food and Nutrition* **1**, pp. 143–63.

Dewey, K. G., Heinig, M. J., Nommsen, L. A., and Lonnerdal, B. (1989), 'Infant growth and breast feeding', *American Journal of Clinical Nutrition* **50**, p. 1116.

Dobbing, J. (1985), 'Infant nutrition and later achievement', *American Journal of Clinical Nutrition* **41**, pp. 477–84.

Dreosti, I. E. (1989), 'Recommended dietary intake for protein in Australia', *Australian Journal of Nutrition and Dietetics* **46** (4), pp. 82–92.

Duffy, P., Morris, H., and Nielson, G. (1981). 'Diabetes mellitus in the Torres Strait region', *Medical Journal of Australia*, special supplement 1, pp. 8–11.

Dugdale, A. E. (1988), 'Infant nutrition and adult health', *Lancet* **1**, p. 948.

Dugdale, A. E., and Lovell, S. (1981), 'The effect of early growth on distribution of subcutaneous fat in Aboriginal children', *Ecology of Food and Nutrition* **11**, pp. 53–5.

Dugdale, A. E., May, G. M. S., and O'Hara, V. M. (1980), 'Ethnic differences in the distribution of subcutaneous fat', *Ecology of Food and Nutrition* **10**, pp. 19–23.

Durnin, J. V. G. A., and Womersley, J. (1974), 'Body fat assessed from total body density and its estimation from skinfold thickness: measurements on 481 men and women aged from 16 to 72 years', *British Journal of Nutrition* **32**, pp. 77–97.

Eriksson, J., Franssila-Kallunki, A., Ekstrand, A., Saloranta,C., Widen, E., Schalin, C., and Groop, L. (1989), 'Early metabolic defects in persons at increased risk for non-insulin-dependent diabetes mellitus', *New England Journal of Medicine* **321** (6), pp. 337–43.

Fisk, E. K. (1985), *The Aboriginal economy in town and country*, George Allen and Unwin/AIAS, Canberra.

Fitz-Henry, A. W., and Brand, J. C. (1982), 'Rate of digestion and absorption of Australian Aboriginal starchy bushfoods', *Proceedings of the Nutrition Society of Australia* **7**, p. 214.

Gennser, G., Rymark, P., and Isberg, P. E. (1988), 'Low birth weight and the risk of high blood pressure in adulthood', *British Medical Journal* **296**, pp. 1498–500.

Glatthaar, C., Welborn, T. A., Stenhouse, N. S., and Garcia-Webb, P. (1985), 'Diabetes and impaired glucose tolerance: a prevalence estimate based on the Busselton 1981 survey', *Medical Journal of Australia* **143**, pp. 436–40.

Gohdes, D. M. (1986), 'Diabetes in American Indians: a growing problem', *Diabetes Care* **9** (6), pp. 609–13.

Goldstein, H., and Tanner, J. M. (1980), 'Ecological considerations in the creation and the use of child growth standards', *Lancet* **1**, pp. 582–5.

Gracey, M., and Hitchcock, N. E. (1983), 'Nutritional state of Aboriginal infants and young children in Western Australia', *Aboriginal Health Project: Information Bulletin* **4** (August), pp. 22–7.

Gracey, M., and Sullivan, H. (1987), 'Growing up in the Kimberley: a study of nutrition, growth and health in Aboriginal infants in the far north of Western Australia', *Australian Aboriginal Studies* **1**, pp. 57–61.

Gracey, M., Murray, H., Hitchcock, N. E., Owles, E. N., and Murphy, B. P. (1983), 'The nutrition of Australian Aboriginal infants and young children', *Nutrition Research* **3**, pp. 133–47.

Gracey, M., Spargo, R. M., Bottrell, C., Hammond, K., Mulholland, K., and Valentine, J. (1984), 'Maternal and childhood nutrition among Aborigines of the Kimberley region', *Medical Journal of Australia* **141**, pp. 506–8.

Graitcer, P. L., and Gentry, E. M. (1981), 'Measuring children: one reference for all', *Lancet* **2**, pp. 297–9.

Habicht, J.-P. (1980), 'Some characteristics of indicators of nutritional status for use in screening and surveillance', *American Journal of Clinical Nutrition* **33**, pp. 531–5.

Habicht, J.-P., Martorell, R., Yarbrough, C., Malina, R. M., and Klein, R. E. (1974), 'Height and weight standards for preschool children: how relevant are ethnic differences in growth potential?' *Lancet* **1**, pp. 611–15.

Hamill, P. V. V., Drizd, M. P. H., Johson, C. L., Reed, R. B., Roche, A. F., and Moore, W. M. (1979), 'Physical growth: National Center for Health Statistics percentiles', *American Journal of Clinical Nutrition* **32**, pp. 607–29.

Hamilton, A. (1981), *Nature and nurture*, AIAS, Canberra.

Hamilton, A. (1982), 'Child health and child care in a desert community 1970–1971', in J. Reid (ed), *Body, land and spirit: health and healing in Aboriginal society*, Queensland University Press, St Lucia, pp. 49–71.

Hebert, J. R. (1985), 'Effects of water quality and water quality on nutritional status: findings from a south Indian community', *Bulletin of the World Health Organization* **63** (1), pp. 143–55.

Henderson, R. F. (1975), *Australian Government Commission of Inquiry into Poverty: food consumption patterns*, AGPS, Canberra.

Heywood, P. F., and Zed, C. A. (1977), 'Dietary and anthropometric assessment of the nutritional status of Aboriginal and white children in Walgett, NSW', *Proceedings of the Nutrition Society of Australia* **2**, pp. 21–7.

Hitchcock N. E., and Coy, J. F. (1988), 'Infant-feeding practices in Western Australia and Tasmania: a joint survey, 1984–1985', *Medical Journal of Australia* **148**, pp. 114–17.

Hitchcock, N. E., and Gracey, M. (1975), 'Dietary patterns in a rural Aboriginal community in south-west Australia', *Medical Journal of Australia*, special supplement 2, pp. 12–16.

Hitchcock, N. E., Owles, E. N., Gracey, M., and Gilmour, A. (1983), 'Development of eating and drinking patterns in the first two years of life', *Journal of Food and Nutrition* **40** (4), pp. 161–4.

Hitchcock, N. E., Gracey, M., Maller, R. A., and Spargo, R. M. (1987), 'Physical size of 1887 Aboriginal schoolchildren in the Kimberley region', *Medical Journal of Australia* **146**, pp. 415–19.

Isaacs, J. (1987), *Bush food: Aboriginal food and herbal medicine*, Weldon, Sydney.

Iseley, R. B. (1983), 'Relating improvements in water supply and sanitation to nutritional status: the issue of using anthropometry as an evaluation measure', *Food and Nutrition Bulletin* **5** (4), pp. 42–51.

James, K. W. (1983), 'Analysis of indigenous Australian foods', *Food Technology in Australia* **35** (7), pp. 342–3.

Jelliffe, D. B., and Jelliffe, E. F. P. (1979), 'Adequacy of breastfeeding', *Lancet* **2**, pp. 691–2.

Jones, R. (1980), 'Hunters in the Australian coastal savanna', in Harris, D. R. (ed.), *Human ecology in savanna environments*, Academic Press, London.

Jose, D. G., and Welch, J. S. (1970), 'Growth retardation, anaemia and infection, with malabsorption and infestation of the bowel: the syndrome of protein-calorie malnutrition in Australian Aboriginal children', *Medical Journal of Australia* **1**, pp. 349–56.

Kamien, M. (1978), *The dark people of Bourke*, AIAS, Canberra.

Kamien, M., Nobile, S., Cameron, P., and Rosevear, P. (1974), 'Vitamin and nutritional status of a part Aboriginal community', *Australian and New Zealand Journal of Medicine* **4**, pp. 126–37.

Kamien, M., Woodhill, J. M., Nobile, S., Rosevear, P., Cameron, P., and Winston, J. M. (1975a), 'Nutrition in the Australian Aborigine: dietary survey of two Aboriginal families', *Food Technology in Australia* **27** (3), pp. 93–103.

Kamien, M., Woodhill, J. M., Nobile, S., Cameron, P., and Rosevear, P. (1975b), 'Nutrition in the Australian Aborigines: effects of the fortification of white flour', *Australian and New Zealand Journal of Medicine* **5**, pp. 123–33.

Kennedy, E., and Knudsen, O. (1985), 'A review of supplementary feeding programmes and recommendations on their design', in M. Biswas and P. Pinstrup-Andersen (eds), *Nutrition and development*, United Nations University, Oxford University Press, Oxford.

Kettle, E. S. (1966), 'Weight and height curves for Australian Aboriginal infants and children', *Medical Journal of Australia* **2**, pp. 972–7.

Kielmann, A. A., and McCord, C. (1978), 'Weight-for-age as an index of risk of death in children', *Lancet* **1**, pp. 1247–50.

King, J., and Ashworth, A. (1987), 'Historical review of the changing pattern of infant feeding in developing countries: the case of Malaysia, the Caribbean, Nigeria and Zaire', *Social Science and Medicine* **25** (12), pp. 1307–20.

Kirk, R. L. (1981), *Aboriginal man adapting*, Oxford University Press, Melbourne.

Kirke, D. K. (1969), 'Growth rates of Aboriginal children in central Australia', *Medical Journal of Australia* **2**, pp. 1005–9.

Kliewer, E. V., and Stanley, F. J. (1989), 'Aboriginal and white births in Western Australia, 1980–1986. Part 1: birthweight and gestational age', *Medical Journal of Australia* **151**, pp. 493–502.

Kramer, M. S. (1987), 'Intrauterine growth and gestational duration determinants', *Pediatrics* **80** (4), pp. 502–11.

Lancaster, P. A. L. (1989), 'Birthweight percentiles for Aborigines?' *Medical Journal of Australia* **151**, pp. 489–90.

Lancet (1988), 'Infant nutrition and cardiovascular disease', *Lancet* **1**, pp. 568–9.

Lang, G. C. (1989), ' "Making sense" about diabetes: Dakota narratives of illness', *Medical Anthropology* **11** (3), pp. 305–27.

Larkins, R. G. (1985), 'To screen or not to screen: the diabetic dilemma', *Medical Journal of Australia* **143**, p. 537.

Low, T. (1989), *Australia's wild food harvest*, Angus and Robertson, Sydney.

Lutter, C. K., Mora, J. O., Habicht, J.-P., Rasmussen, K. M., Robson, D. S., Sellers, S. G., Super, C. M., and Herrera, M. G. (1989), 'Nutritional supplementation: effects on child stunting because of diarrhoea', *American Journal of Clinical Nutrition* **50**, pp. 1–8.

McArthur, M. (1960), 'Report of the nutrition unit', in C. M. Mountford (ed.), *Records of the American-Australian Scientific Expedition to Arnhem Land. Vol. 2, Anthropology and nutrition*, Melbourne University Press, Melbourne.

McCormick, M. C. (1985), 'The contribution of low birth weight to infant mortality and childhood morbidity', *New England Journal of Medicine*, Jan. 10, pp. 82–90.

Maddock, K. (1982), *The Australian Aborigines: a portrait of their society*, 2nd edn, Penguin Books Australia, Ringwood, Vic.

Margo, J. (1988), 'Black diet blamed for child sickness', *Sydney Morning Herald*, 18 January.

Marr, J. W. (1971), 'Individual dietary surveys: purposes and methods', *World Review of Nutrition and Dietetics* **13**, pp. 105–64.

Maxwell, G. M., and Elliott, R. B. (1969), 'Nutritional status of Australian Aboriginal children', *American Journal of Clinical Nutrition* **22**, pp. 716–24.

Meehan, B. (1977), 'Hunters by the seashore', *Journal of Human Evolution* **6**, pp. 363–70.

Meehan, B. (1982a), *Shell bed to shell midden*, AIAS, Canberra.

Meehan, B. (1982b), 'Ten fish for one man: some Anbarra attitudes towards food and health', in J. Reid (ed.), *Body, land and spirit: health and healing in Aboriginal society*, University of Queensland Press, St Lucia, pp. 96–120.

Middleton, R. M., and Francis, S. H. (1976), *Yuendumu and its children: life and health on an Aboriginal community*, AGPS, Canberra.

Muller, M., Eaton-Evans, J., and Dugdale, A. E. (1984), 'Growth of Aboriginal infants', *Medical Journal of Australia* **141**, pp. 228–30.

Nathan, P., and Japanangka, D. L. (1983), *Health business*, Heinemann Educational Australia, Melbourne.

NH&MRC (National Health and Medical Research Council) (1984), 'Tables of acceptable weight for height for Australians: nutrition statement adopted by the NH&MRC', *Journal of Food and Nutrition* **41**, p. 191.

Naughton, J. M., O'Dea, K., and Sinclair, A. J. (1986), 'Animal foods in traditional Australian Aboriginal diets: polyunsaturated and low in fat', *Lipids* **21** (11), pp. 684–90.

NTA (Northern Territory Administration) (1957–58), *Annual report*, Northern Territory Administration, Darwin.

NTA (1958–59), *Annual report*, Welfare Branch of the Northern Territory Administration, Darwin.

NTA (1961–62), *Annual report*, Welfare Branch of the Northern Territory Administration, Darwin.

NTA (1971–72), *Annual Report*, Welfare Division of the Northern Territory Administration, Darwin.

O'Dea, K. (1982), 'The relationship between urbanisation and diabetes in Australian Aborigines', *Proceedings of the Nutrition Society of Australia* **7**, pp. 30–6.

O'Dea, K. (1983), 'Lifestyle change and diabetes in Australian Aborigines', *Aboriginal Health Project Information Bulletin* **4**, pp. 17–21.

O'Dea, K. (1984), 'Marked improvement in carbohydrate and lipid metabolism in diabetic Australian Aborigines after temporary reversion to traditional lifestyle', *Diabetes* **33**, pp. 596–603.

O'Dea, K. (1987), 'Body fat distribution and health outcome in Australian Aborigines', *Proceedings of the Nutrition Society of Australia* **12**, pp. 56–65.

O'Dea, K., and Spargo, R. M. (1982), 'Metabolic adaptation to a low carbohydrate-high protein ("traditional") diet in Australian Aborigines', *Diabetologia* **23**, pp. 494–8.

O'Dea, K., Spargo, R. M., and Akerman, K. (1980), 'The effects of transition from traditional to urban lifestyle on the insulin secretory response in Australian Aborigines', *Diabetes Care* **3** (10), pp. 31–7.

O'Dea, K., Spargo, R. M., and Nestel, P. J. (1982), 'Impact of westernisation on carbohydrate and lipid metabolism in Australian Aborigines', *Diabetologia* **22**, pp. 148–53.

O'Dea, K., White, N. G., and Sinclair, A. J. (1988a), 'An investigation of nutrition-related risk factors in an isolated Aboriginal community in Northern Australia: advantages of a traditionally-orientated life-style', *Medical Journal of Australia* **148**, pp. 177–80.

O'Dea, K., Traianedes, K., Hopper, J. L., and Larkins, R. G. (1988b), 'Impaired glucose tolerance, hyperinsulinemia, and hypertriglyceridemia in Australian Aborigines from the desert', *Diabetes Care* **11** (1), pp. 23–9.

Payne, P. R. (1985), 'The nature of malnutrition', in M. Biswas and P. Pinstrup-Andersen (eds), *Nutrition and development*, United Nations University/Oxford University Press, Oxford, pp. 1–19.

Pellett, P. L. (1988), 'Commentary: the RDA controversy revisited', *Ecology of Food and Nutrition* **21**, pp. 315–20.

Peterson, N. (1977), 'Aboriginal involvement with the Australian economy in the Central Reserve during the winter of 1970', in R. M. Berndt (ed.), *Aborigines and change: Australia in the 70s*, Social Anthropology Series no. 11, AIAS, Canberra/Humanities Press, New Jersey, pp. 136–46.

Peterson, N. (1978), 'The traditional pattern of subsistence to 1975', in B. S. Hetzel and H. J. Frith (eds.), *The nutrition of Aborigines in relation to the ecosystem of central Australia*, CSIRO, Melbourne, Vic., pp. 25–35.

Phillips, F. E., and Dibley, M. J. (1983), 'A longitudinal study of feeding patterns of Aboriginal infants living in Perth, 1980–82', *Proceedings of the Nutrition Society of Australia* **8**, pp. 130–3.

Rae, C. J., Lamprell, V. J., Lion, R. J., and Rae, A. M. (1982), 'The role of bush foods in contemporary Aboriginal diets', *Proceedings of the Nutrition Society of Australia* **7**, pp. 45–8.

Raphael, D. (1984), 'Weaning is always: the anthropology of breastfeeding behaviour', *Ecology of Food and Nutrition* **15**, pp. 203–13.

Reaven, G. M. (1988), 'Role of insulin resistance in human disease', *Diabetes* **37**, pp. 1595–607.

Reid, J. (1986), ' "Land of milk and honey": the changing meaning of food to an Australian Aboriginal community', in L. Manderson (ed.), *Shared wealth and symbol: food, culture and society in Oceania and southeast Asia*, Cambridge University Press, Cambridge, pp. 49–66.

Ritenbaugh, C., and Goodby, C.-S. (1989), 'Beyond the thrifty gene: metabolic implications of prehistoric migration into the New World', *Medical Anthropology* **11** (3), pp. 227–36.

Roberts, D., Gracey, M., and Spargo, R. M. (1988), 'Growth and morbidity in children in a remote Aboriginal community in north-west Australia', *Medical Journal of Australia* **148**, pp. 68–71.

Roberts, R. W., and Rutishauser, I. H. E. (1978), 'Are Aborigines underfed?' *Australian Paediatric Journal* **14**, p. 218.

Roche, A. F., Guo, S. and Moore, W. M. (1989*a*), 'Weight and recumbent length from 1 to 12 mo of age: reference data for 1-mo increments', *American Journal of Clinical Nutrition* **49**, pp. 599–607.

Roche, A. F., Guo, S., and Moore, W. M. (1989*b*), 'Reply to K. G. Dewey et al.: infant growth and breast feeding', *American Journal of Clinical Nutrition* **50**, pp. 1117–18.

Rosenberg, I. H., Solomons, N. W., and Levin, D. M. (1976), 'Interaction of infection and nutrition: some practical concerns', *Ecology of Food and Nutrition* **4**, pp. 203–6.

Rowland, M. G. M. (1985), 'The "why" and "when" of introducing food to infants: growth in young breast-fed infants and some nutritional implications', *American Journal of Clinical Nutrition* **41**, pp. 459–63.

Rowland, M. G. M., Cole, T. J., and Whitehead, R. G. (1977), 'A quantitative study into the role of infection in determining nutritional status in Gambian village children', *British Journal of Nutrition* **37**, pp. 441–50.

Rutishauser, I. H. E., and McKay, H. (1986), 'Anthropometric status and body composition in Aboriginal women in the Kimberley region', *Medical Journal of Australia* **144**, pp. S8–S10.

Scrimshaw, N. S., Taylor, C. E., and Gordon, J. E. (1968) *Interaction of nutrition and infection*, World Health Organization, Geneva.

Seidell, J. C., Deurenberg, P., and Hautvast, J. G. A. J. (1987), 'Obesity and fat distribution in relation to health: current insights and recommendations', *World Review of Nutrition and Dietetics* **50**, pp. 57–91.

Seward, J. F., and Stanley, F. J. (1981), 'Comparison of births to Aboriginal and Caucasian mothers in Western Australia', *Medical Journal of Australia* **2**, pp. 80–4.

Sommer, A., and Loewenstein, M. S. (1975), 'Nutritional status and mortality: a prospective validation of the QUAC stick', *American Journal of Clinical Nutrition* **28**, pp. 287–92.

Stacey, S. (1977), 'Nutrition education: a point of view', *Proceedings of the Nutrition Society of Australia* **2**, pp. 17–20.

Stacey, S. (1978), 'Who should learn what: health education amongst traditionally oriented Aborigines', *New Doctor* **8**, pp. 42–4.

Stacey, S. (1979), 'Showing the way to good health poses questions', *Aboriginal News* **3** (7), pp. 18–19.

Stanton, K. G., McCann, V., Knuiman, M., Constable, I. J., and Welborn, T. (1985), 'Diabetes in part-Aborigines of Western Australia', *Diabetologia* **28**, pp. 16–21.

Stern, M. P. (1988), 'Type 2 diabetes mellitus: interface between clinical and epidemiological investigation', *Diabetes Care* **11** (20), pp. 119–26.

Stevens, F. (1974), *Aborigines in the Northern Territory cattle industry*, ANU Press, Canberra.

Sullivan, H., Gracey, M., and Hevron, V. (1987), Food costs and nutrition of Aborigines in remote areas of northern Australia, *Medical Journal of Australia* **147**, pp. 334–7.

Surwit, R. S., and Feinglos, M. N. (1988), 'Stress and autonomic nervous system in Type 2 diabetes: an hypothesis', *Diabetes Care* **11** (1), pp. 83–5.

Suskind, R. M. (ed.) (1977), *Malnutrition and the immune response*, Raven Press, New York.

Sykes, B. (1977), 'An analysis of some of the difficulties confronting Aboriginal community-controlled nutrition programs', *Proceedings of the Nutrition Society of Australia* **2**, pp. 32–6.

Taylor, J. C. (1977), 'Diet, health and economy: some consequences of planned social change in an Aboriginal community', in R. M. Berndt (ed.), *Aborigines and change: Australia in the 70s*, Social Anthropology Series no. 11, AIAS, Canberra/Humanities Press, New Jersey, pp. 147–58.

Thomson, N. (1983), 'Aboriginal mortality, 1976–1981', *Australian Aboriginal Studies* **1**, pp. 10–15.

Thomson, N. (1985), 'Recent trends in Aboriginal birth weights', *Aboriginal Health Project Information Bulletin* **7**, pp. 14–18.

Thomson, N., and Honari, M. (1988), 'Aboriginal health: a case study', in *Australia's health: the first biennial report by the Australian Institute of Health*, AGPS, Canberra.

Thorburn, A. W., and Brand, J. C. (1987), 'Digestion and absorption of carbohydrate in Australian Aboriginal, Pacific Island and Western foods', *Australian Aboriginal Studies* **1**, pp. 61–4.

Thorburn, A. W., Brand, J. C., and Truswell, A. S. (1987), 'Slowly digested and absorbed carbohydrate in traditional bush foods: a protective factor against diabetes?' *American Journal of Clinical Nutrition* **45**, pp. 98–106.

Truswell, A. S., Irwin, T., Beaton, G. H., Suzue, R., Haenel, H., Hedja, S., Hou, X.-C., Leveille, G., Morava, E., Pederson, J. and Stephen, J. M. L. (1983), 'Recommended dietary intakes around the world', *Nutrition Abstracts and Reviews* **53** (11), pp. 939–1015.

Turnbull, S. (1980), *Economic development of Aboriginal communities in the Northern Territory*, AGPS, Canberra.

Urdaneta, M. L., and Krehbiel, R. (1989), 'Cultural heterogeneity of Mexican-Americans and its implications for the treatment of diabetes mellitus type 2', *Medical Anthropology* **11** (3), pp. 269–82.

Victora, C. G., Vaughan, J. P., Martines, J. C. and Barcelos, L. B. (1984), 'Is prolonged breast feeding associated with malnutrition?' *American Journal of Clinical Nutrition* **39**, pp. 307–14.

Warwick, P. M. (1989), 'Predicting food energy requirements from estimates of energy expenditure', *Australian Journal of Nutrition and Dietetics* **46**, supplement, pp. S3–S28.

Waterlow, J. C. (1972), 'Classification of protein-calorie malnutrition', *British Medical Journal* **3**, pp. 566–9.

Waterlow, J. C. (1979). Adequacy of breast-feeding. Lancet ii, 897-898.

Waterlow, J. C. (1980), 'Child growth standards', *Lancet* **1**, p. 717.

Waterlow, J. C. (1981), 'Observations on the suckling's dilemma: a personal view', *Journal of Human Nutrition* **35** (2), pp. 85–98.

Waterlow, J. C., and Rutishauser, I. H. E. (1974), 'Malnutrition in man', in J. Cravioto, L. Hambroeus, and B. Vahlquist (eds), *Early malnutrition in mental development*, Symposia of the Swedish Nutrition Foundation XII, Almqvist and Wiksell, Stockholm, pp. 13–26.

Waterlow, J. C., and Thomson, A. M. (1979), 'Observations on the adequacy of breast feeding', *Lancet* **2**, pp. 238–42.

Waterlow, J. C., Ashworth, A., and Griffiths, M. (1980), 'Faltering in growth in less-developed countries', *Lancet* **2**, pp. 1176–7.

Weiss, K. M., Ulbrecht, J. S., Cavanagh, P. R., and Buchanan, A. V. (1989), 'Diabetes mellitus in American Indians: characteristics, origins and preventive health care implications', *Medical Anthropology* **11** (3), pp. 283–304.

Wheeler, E. F. (1980), 'Nutritional status of savanna peoples', in D. R. Harris (ed.), *Human ecology in savanna environments*, Academic Press, London, pp. 439–55.

Whincup, P. H., Cook, D. G., Shaper, A. G., MacFarlane, D. J., and Walker, M. (1988), 'Blood pressure in British children: associations with adult blood pressure and cardiovascular mortality', *Lancet* **2**, pp. 890–3.

Whitehead, R. G. (1985), 'Infant physiology, nutritional requirements, and lactational adequacy', *American Journal of Clinical Nutrition* **41**, pp. 447–58.

Wilson, W. (1953), 'A dietary survey of Aborigines in the Northern Territory', *Medical Journal of Australia* **2**, pp. 599–605.

Wise, P. H., Edwards, F. M., Craig, R. J., Evans, B., Murchland, J. B., Sutherland, B. and Thomas, D. W. (1976), 'Diabetes and associated variables in the South Australian Aboriginal', *Australian and New Zealand Journal of Medicine* **6**, pp. 191–6.

Wise, P. H., Edwards, F. M., Thomas, D. W., Elliot, R. B., Hatcher, L., and Craig, R. (1970), 'Hyperglycaemia in the urbanised Aboriginal: the Davenport survey', *Medical Journal of Australia* **2**, pp. 1001–6.

Young, E. (1981), *Tribal communities in rural areas: the Aboriginal component in the Australian economy*, Development Studies Centre, Australian National University, Canberra.

Young, E. (1982), 'Aboriginal community stores', in P. Loveday (ed.), *Service delivery to remote communities*, North Australia Research Unit Monograph, ANU, Darwin.

Young, E. (1984), *Outback stores: retail services in north Australian Aboriginal communities*, North Australian Research Unit Monograph, ANU, Darwin.

Unpublished material

Harrison, L. J. (unpub.), Diet and nutrition in a Tiwi community: a study of factors affecting the health status of under threes at Milikapiti, North Australia, PhD thesis, Australian National University, Canberra, 1986.

Sibthorpe, B. (unpub.), All our people are dyin': diet and stress in an urban Aboriginal community, PhD thesis, Australian National University, Canberra, 1988.

CHAPTER 5

Drug and alcohol use among Aboriginal people

Maggie Brady

Australian Institute of Aboriginal and Torres Strait Islander Studies, Canberra

The use of drug and alcohol substances to achieve alteration in mood is an issue fraught with misunderstanding in popular opinion, and is made more complex by conflicts of opinion on both theory and treatment among health professionals.

When the use of substances is engaged in by a minority group or an indigenous population, in this case Aboriginal Australians, the conventional opinions become more entrenched, and the theoretical issues deepen in complexity. This chapter addresses some of the conventional wisdoms and myths that surround the use of drugs and alcohol by Aboriginal people, and traces the development of a professional and academic position on their use of these substances. Along with the views of what might be termed the dominant society on this issue, Aboriginal opinions have become increasingly influential. These Aboriginal perceptions are, however, no less controversial than the dominant views, and are in the process of change.

The history of the use of psycho-active, or mood-altering, substances by Aborigines is an important starting point, for two reasons: first, because conventional wisdom asserts, incorrectly, that few, if any, such substances were used by Aborigines before contact with Europeans; and second, because the history of the use of such substances by Aborigines is one in which crude legislative controls have had an unprecedented influence on present attitudes and patterns of use. What follows in the first part of this chapter is a brief examination of the range of indigenous and imported mood-altering substances and the subsequent legislative attempts to control their use by Aboriginal people. Having established this historical framework, it is possible to explore the development in both the social and medical sciences of a body of research into Aboriginal use of mood-altering substances. This research has arisen out of the concerns of the 1960s and early 1970s, expressed largely by welfare and church-based observers.

Psycho-active substances

Before European settlement

One of the most common myths about Aboriginal uses of intoxicating or otherwise mood-altering drugs and alcohol is that these substances were introduced by Europeans after the landing of the First Fleet in 1788; and that until then, Australia was the world's only 'dry' continent (Dingle 1980, p. 228). From the 1950s to the present, some commentators have asserted that Aborigines were one of the few peoples (if not the only people) of the world to have had no traditional alcoholic beverages (Cleland 1957, p. 159; Millar and Leung 1974, p. 92; Larsen 1980; Spencer 1988, pp. 15, 17), and to have had minimal use of other drugs (Eastwell 1988, p. 1). It was (and is) not unusual for writers to draw the conclusion that this apparent absence of indigenous alcohol and drug substances (and by implication the absence of indigenous controls) has been the cause of later widespread abuse of intoxicating beverages (Spencer 1988). On the contrary, there is evidence that Aborigines in a variety of Australian regions knew how to collect and prepare natural substances which, when ingested, produced changes of mood. In addition, there is some evidence that the processes of preparation and distribution in themselves served as a means of social control of use.

As Dwight Heath observes in an informative overview of anthropological studies of alcohol use, a remarkable fact about alcohol is how simple it is to make; the process of fermentation occurs naturally, even without human intervention (Heath 1987*a*, p. 20). Although some of the historical evidence is fragmentary, and we are reliant upon the reports of untrained observers, references to drug and alcohol use are diverse. Aborigines prepared intoxicating beverages from the sap of *Eucalyptus gunnii* in Tasmania (Plomley 1966, p. 534), and from bauhinia blossom and wild honey in the Diamantina region of western Queensland (Duncan-Kemp 1934, p. 76). In south-western Australia, Aborigines made a drink called *mangaitj* with the soaked cones of *Xanthorrhoea*, a grass tree: the thick mixture was allowed to ferment for a few days (McCarthy 1957, p. 71; Carr and Carr 1981, p. 17). Basedow describes a 'mild pandanus-cider' made by Roper River (Northern Territory) Aborigines from the pounded and soaked cones of the palm-like *Pandanus* plant, or screw-pine (Basedow 1929, p. 154).

Although these beverages may have been only mildly intoxicating, observers note that, having drunk them, people became 'excited and voluble' (McCarthy 1957, p. 71), and Robinson was told that eucalyptus sap beverage 'frequently makes them drunk' (Plomley 1966, p. 534). Basedow notes that on festive occasions the people 'imbibe more than ordinarily, and thereby bring themselves into a condition of indubitable merriment'. He continues by observing: 'This is the only instance I am aware of where Australian natives, intentionally or unintentionally, make an intoxicating drink' (Basedow 1929, p. 154).

The most notable drug substance available from the natural flora was the psycho-active drug, pituri, made from the dried, cured leaves and growing tips of *Duboisia hopwoodii*, a desert plant from the central areas of Australia. Like the indigenous tobaccos of the *Nicotiana* species, pituri was mixed with the ash derived from the burned leaves of particular species of tree, and was chewed, not smoked.

Figure 5.1 *The desert plant,* Nicotiana ingulba, *found in the central areas of Australia, from which indigenous tobacco was made. (P. Latz/AIATSIS, Canberra)*

The addition of ash produces an alkaline action, which facilitates the liberation of nicotine. P. Watson's 1983 monograph provides the most detailed and accurate appraisal of the use of pituri, although the drug has aroused interest for many years (Liversidge 1880). Pituri has been described as 'a powerful stimulant' and a 'habit-forming drug' (Thomson 1939, p. 82); in 1861 a member of the Burke and Wills expedition likened its effects to 'two pretty stiff nobblers of brandy' (Watson, P., 1983, p. 8).

There were also strong indigenous tobaccos, which were chewed; and northern coastal people smoked tobacco using pipes of Papuan or Malay origin (Thomson 1939, pp. 82–7). Thomson, in a richly detailed article on smoking pipes, describes a method of smoking and inhaling from a pipe used on Cape York which had a 'powerful narcotic effect...I have seen a native so affected by a single inhalation, as to be rendered nearly senseless' (Thomson 1939, p. 85). Ngaanyatjarra women in Western Australia report that 'bush tobacco' was so strong that it made people sick until they became used to it (Brady 1989*a*).

Apart from these alcohols and nicotine-based substances, early writers also documented the use of other drugs. In his Tasmanian journals Robinson notes that wattle tree blossoms would be suspended in Aboriginal huts 'as an opiate to cause sleep' (Plomley 1966, p. 302); Aborigines in New South Wales made a stupefying beverage by adding liquid to the trunks of cork trees (*Duboisia myoporoides*) and drinking the decoction the next day (Carr and Carr 1981, p. 25); the Murray River 'Tattayarra [sic]' tribe are reported by Angas to have used an 'intoxicating root' growing in the scrub, which had 'much the same effect as opium' (Angas 1847, p. 73); and in Victoria, the Lake Boga people made a 'stupefying' drink from the root and bark of the bitter quandong, or ming (*Santalum murrayanum*) (Stone 1911, p. 445; Clarke 1988, p. 71).

Procuring and processing these substances required skill, knowledge and labour; the absence of any tradition in the use of metals or clay meant that containers made of plant products or shells were used for the collection and fermentation of beverages. Such difficulties, as well as ecological factors, probably served to control the production of these drugs. In addition, as P. Watson (1987) points out, there were social controls in operation (at least in the case of pituri), which affected production, distribution and consumption of the drug. For example, knowledge of the whereabouts of suitable plants was restricted, as was familiarity with preparation techniques; consumption was controlled by age and sex statuses. Basedow notes that the collecting grounds with clearly marked boundaries were owned by particular men (Basedow 1929, p. 155). Most importantly, Aboriginal people themselves monitored production and distribution of the drugs, something that is not possible today (Watson, P., 1987).

The evidence given here indicates that Aboriginal people in a wide variety of regions used psycho-active substances before the first European settlement on their land. The effects brought about by such substances were valued enough for people to engage in the labours associated with their collection, preparation and trade. A variety of factors, however, served to control the quantity, distribution and ingestion of these drugs.

Imported substances

The English were not the first to make landfall in Australia. It is sometimes forgotten that Macassan (Indonesian) fishermen visited Australia's northern coasts annually from perhaps the sixteenth century to collect trepang (bêche-de-mer). The Macassans brought dug-out canoes, cloth, knives, tobacco, pipes and alcohol, and entered into exchanges with Aborigines for these items (Thomson 1939; Macknight 1976). The alcohols they brought included arrack (palm wine), brandy and gin (Macknight 1976, p. 31). Warner, who worked in north-east Arnhem Land between 1926 and 1929, notes that 'the gin traded to the natives caused occasional great drunken orgies...However, the alcohol seems to have had no effect upon the general well-being of the people' (Warner 1969, p. 449).

The First English Fleet in 1788 brought with it rum and wine, and keen efforts were made within the first few years of settlement to grow hops and vines, and to start distilleries. Illicit stills developed which produced 'noxious and unwholesome spirits' (*HRA* 1796, p. 555), and rough liquor was imported from India, the Cape of Good Hope and South America. All inhabitants of the colony soon gained access to spirits, as Dingle (1980) and Powell (1988) point out. In 1830, less than a year after the establishment of the Swan River settlement in Western Australia, the colonial secretary issued licences for three hotels and six ale houses; six years later, Perth offered one licensed house for every 75 people (Welborn 1987, p. 17). Welborn documents the new wealth that was to be made from brewing and the monopoly that was established (in Western Australia at least) by 'powerful ruling families' in the industry (Welborn 1987, p. 48). Meanwhile Aborigines were provided with alcohol for the amusement of Europeans and in exchange for women. Backhouse (1843) and Evans et al. (1975) note that Aborigines were provided with the mixed dregs of bottles and glasses, and with adulterated liquor. Fifty years after the English invasion, the first Australian legislation was passed in New South Wales that prohibited the sale or supply of liquor to Aborigines (McCorquodale 1987, p. A129).

Tobacco was, of course, another imported drug that found a ready clientele among Aborigines, some of whom already used indigenous tobacco and pituri. Thomson (1961) suggests that Aborigines were already addicted to their indigenous tobacco. On Cape York, where Aborigines did not grow tobacco, Thomson provides evidence of intermittent trade with Torres Strait Islanders, whose material culture had been heavily influenced by Papua New Guinea. 'It is probable', he writes, 'that tobacco was one of the important articles of exchange brought down during these voyages' (Thomson 1939, p. 82). Tobacco quickly became an important item once the English colony was established, and squatters and missionaries alike used it to win over and pacify the Aborigines (Walker 1980; Stanner 1979). Several ethnographers have documented that the craving for tobacco by Aborigines induced them to undertake long journeys, endure hardship, and even to abandon their homelands, moving into centres of white settlement (Thomson 1939; Read and Japaljarri 1978; Stanner 1979). Tobacco became part of regular government rations issued to Aborigines in later years, a matter that became cause for controversy in the 1940s when the Church Missionary Society in northern Australia refused to distribute tobacco to its Aboriginal charges. The society believed that tobacco was addictive and 'detrimental to the Christian principle of healthy living' (Cole 1980, p. 67).

Opium was also imported, being used by Europeans, Chinese workers and Aborigines. The blame for the distribution and use of opium was frequently laid on the Chinese, but in the 1880s Queensland station managers supplied opium to Aborigines in exchange for their labour, and Aborigines also obtained the opium dross—the charcoal ash remaining after the opium had been smoked—which was mixed with water and eaten. This concoction caused the death of numbers of Aborigines (Evans et al. 1975, p. 94). There was sensational coverage in the newspapers of the era, in which the Chinese were held responsible for the degradation of Aboriginal opium-users. This has been interpreted by Evans et al. (1975, p. 96) as a means of diverting attention from the very high Aboriginal death rate caused by introduced disease and the effects of venereal disease and liquor. In 1897, the first law was passed to prohibit the sale of opium to Aborigines (Manderson 1987, p. 5).

Kava, a beverage made from the crushed root of the pepper plant *Piper methysticum*, was used in 1911 by Saibai Islanders in the Torres Strait, according to a first-hand report by a resident teacher (Chief Protector of Aborigines 1911, p. 22). Kava has anaesthetic and sedative effects and has been used by Pacific Islanders for centuries. The 1911 report documents the method of preparation of the root by chewing and mixing it with saliva, and the consumption rituals (drinking from a half coconut, clapping of hands), which were presumably also imported, learned behaviours.

Strictly speaking, then, neither alcohol nor other mood-altering drugs were 'white man's poison' introduced to populations unused to psycho-active substances. In at least some regions of the continent, Aboriginal people already had sufficient skills and knowledge of their flora to pursue actively the sensations achieved by the ingestion of these substances. Apart from the indigenous alcohols, nicotine and other drugs, at least some Aborigines and Islanders had engaged in trade with outsiders who were not Europeans, so that the range of items was expanded to include kava, gin, palm wine, and processed tobacco. They were unprepared, however, for the sheer volume of substances (particularly beverage alcohol) that became available after 1788 (and, indeed, that were thrust upon them in some instances), over which they had no control in terms of production or distribution. Once the problems of heat and humidity were overcome, locally produced beer, wine and spirits flourished in the new colony; shareholders in the new companies received high dividends; breweries bought or leased hotels, which became tied houses (selling draught beer from only that brewery); alcohol production and distribution in Australia became big business (Welborn 1987, p. 51).

Legislative controls

Limitation and prohibition have long been the mechanisms whereby the state has attempted to restrain the otherwise apparently unrestrained ingestion of psycho-active substances by its people, particularly by its 'minors', the Aboriginal people. In the early days of settlement, attempts were made to control the supply of liquor to colonists by means of limited licences, and by limiting the volume of imported spirits (Dingle 1980, p. 229). However, local breweries were developed from 1804 onwards in an attempt to 'act as a substitute for the sea of rum in which the young colony appeared to be floating' (Dingle 1980, p. 235). The local wine industry gained momentum from about 1830, after a slow start.

Although the quality of both beer and wine was dubious, alcohol was freely available to town dwellers. In rural and outback regions, however, colonists did not have access to alcohol, which meant that bush workers interspersed periods of work with short bouts of intensive drinking in the towns (Evans et al. 1975, p. 93). Dingle comments that this 'work and bust' tradition, which emphasises drinking as much as possible in a short period of time, has had a lasting influence on Australian drinking habits, and was reinforced by legislation such as 'six o'clock closing', instituted in 1916 (Dingle 1980, p. 237). Until this time, Australian drinkers flourished under liberal drinking laws, with pubs open from the early hours of the morning until midnight. Not until the growth of the temperance movement before the First World War were white Australians in any danger of having their 'personal liberty' to drink freely curtailed (Phillips 1980; Powell 1988).

Aboriginal people, on the other hand, had been subject to prohibitive laws long before the white population. Legislation that prohibited the supply or sale of liquor to Aborigines was passed in New South Wales in 1838; Western Australia in 1843; Victoria in 1864; South Australia in 1869; Queensland in 1885; Tasmania in 1908 and the Australian Capital Territory in 1929 (see McCorquodale 1987 for details of this legislation). These laws also encompassed Aborigines of mixed descent (referred to at the time as 'half-castes'), as well as Queensland's Pacific Islanders and Polynesians. The justification for the early prohibitions of Aboriginal alcohol use lay in the belief that alcohol inflicted 'serious evil' on the natives. The concerns of the times were undoubtedly mixed; while missionaries and temperance workers considered the sight of intoxicated Aborigines a degradation of their proud 'natural' state, settlers and squatters moving onto Aboriginal land perceived drunken Aborigines to be dangerous (Millar and Leung 1974, p. 91).

Other laws were passed to prohibit Aborigines from being supplied with opium: in Queensland in 1891 and 1897; South Australia, 1895; the Northern Territory, 1918, and Western Australia, 1940. The Queensland legislation of 1891 is interesting, as it makes it an offence to supply opium to an Aborigine except for medicinal purposes. Manderson (1987) documents how Australian policies designed to control opiate use changed between 1900 and the 1930s: from a tolerant acceptance of widespread self-medication with patent medicines (whose ingredients included narcotics) to restrictive laws controlling use. He associates these changes with the growing power of doctors, and changing attitudes to illness:

Throughout the world, the status which doctors were beginning to enjoy not only confined the acceptable use of opium to limits and contexts defined by them, but subjected those who used opium outside these parameters to a critical medical and scientific analysis; the 'bad habit' of earlier generations became a disease— 'addiction'—and, with the development of psychiatry, physical addiction became mental weakness and thence moral vice.

Manderson 1987, p. 7

A Northern Territory Act banned the supply of methylated spirits to Aborigines in 1936, although Sansom documents that between 1939 and 1962 there were 108 charges or convictions against Aborigines for drinking methylated spirits (Sansom 1980, p. 46).

Drinking rights and citizenship

In his study of Aboriginal fringe-dwellers in Darwin, Basil Sansom posits that the meaning of alcohol and of drinking for Aborigines is 'rooted in a history that...is a development from legally imposed and racially unequal restrictions to an era of greater liberty' (Sansom 1980, p. 44). Legal restrictions on Aboriginal access to alcohol have persisted until comparatively recently, and their influence on Aboriginal uses of, and attitudes towards, drinking should not be underestimated. While the earlier total prohibitions have passed into history, the many discriminatory and racist permutations of these laws remain part of what Sansom calls the 'remembered past' for all Aboriginal people.

The aspects of prohibition that rankle most are those that exempted certain Aborigines from the restrictions. Several states developed legislation that allowed alcohol to be purchased and consumed by Aborigines of mixed descent and others who could establish that they complied with the required standards of hygiene, intellect and good (that is, non-Aboriginal) company. Aboriginal people thus ceased to be 'Aborigines' for the purposes of this legislation (Eggleston 1976, pp. 198–202).

For example, in the Northern Territory, the Welfare Ordinance of 1953 declared that all Aborigines were wards of the government unless they could claim exemption by way of their 'standard of personal habit and behaviour'. The welfare authorities kept a register of wards, known by Aboriginal people at the time and since as the 'stud book'. Exempted Aborigines were entitled to obtain alcohol (Brady 1990).

In Western Australia, Aborigines could apply for 'citizenship' if they had 'dissolved tribal and native associations', adopted the 'manner and habits of civilised life', or served in the armed forces (*The Natives [Citizenship Rights] Act 1944*). The certificate of 'citizenship' was referred to by Aborigines, derisively, as the 'dog tag'. The case study, 'Somewhere between black and white', from the biography of Clancy McKenna, a Western Australian Aborigine of mixed descent, reveals something of an Aborigine's ambivalence about 'citizenship', as well as Clancy's ongoing relationship with alcohol.

Citizenship bestowed the right to drink, but could be withdrawn following two convictions for an offence, including habitual drunkenness (McCorquodale 1987, p. A702). In this way, legislation passed in 1944 in one state set the scene for the association between the notion of 'citizenship' and the right to consume alcohol. When Aboriginal people were granted the right (but not the obligation) to vote in federal elections in 1962, Aborigines all over Australia interpreted this as also giving them 'citizenship', and the right to drink alcohol legally. In fact, each state and territory repealed laws restricting the sale of alcohol to Aboriginal people over a period of several years. In South Australia, Aborigines could drink legally in 1962 unless they lived in 'primitive' conditions, and all restrictions came to an end in 1967. In Victoria, prohibition was repealed in 1957; in Queensland, in 1961; in New South Wales, in 1963; in the Northern Territory, in 1964; and in Western Australia all restrictions were finally repealed in 1972. Notwithstanding these variations, Aborigines interpreted the right to vote as giving them the right to drink, and Sansom noted that in the Northern Territory, during the interim period between voting rights in 1962 and the end of prohibition in 1964, Aborigines began to drink openly (Sansom 1980, p. 75).

Other ethnographers have documented Aboriginal people referring to drinking rights and citizenship as inseparable concepts (Myers 1986; Nathan and Japanangka 1983). Bain even suggests that Aboriginal people interpreted the new equality as requiring expression in the act of drinking (Bain 1974, p. 45). Elkin, in a pamphlet on citizenship published in 1958, observed that 'citizenship for the Aborigine includes, if it does not mean, the right to go where white citizens go, particularly into the hotel. Thus, alcohol has come to bear a symbolic value' (Elkin 1958, p. 16). Collmann (1988) and Brady and Palmer (1984) document that Aboriginal drinkers think drinking in itself confers symbolic equality with whites; that they become less shy and more forward with whites when they have been drinking; and that they speak English in such encounters. Marshall, in a rich ethnography of alcohol use in Micronesia, makes similar observations (Marshall 1979).

Drinking alcohol has thus become inextricably associated with equality and status among Aboriginal people, as it has for many other minorities and indigenous groups (Heath 1987*a*, p. 31). The fact that discriminatory laws existed for so long and in such a complex variety of forms has meant that the right to drink has a high premium among Aboriginal people; in some instances this has thwarted local community-based attempts by Aborigines themselves to ban alcohol once again from their environs.

Somewhere between black and white

It was about this time that they both began to drink. Neither had citizenship rights, but it was easy enough to get alcohol from old Malays, or from a friend who had obtained his rights. It was hard to refuse a friend. Drinking generally took place down at the beach, away from the town proper, or over behind the limestone ridge. Either way they were more or less safe from the raiding parties of the police, who delighted in filling up the paddy waggon with drunks and carting them off to the gaol. Apart from a few encounters with the law, Clancy managed to keep out of trouble, but he was careful, and having neither his rights nor a vehicle he was not eligible for the more serious offences of supplying or drunken driving.

Away from the town...there was time to reflect on the world again, and to try for the citizenship rights that had become such an objective for Clancy. With his rights, he felt, he would be the equal of any other man, but there was some confusion in his mind as to why he had to have the rights, whereas white men appeared to have them automatically. The government man told him to apply for the exemption first of all, and in time, if he proved himself reliable, he would be granted full rights. They were not able to answer his questions as to why he didn't have rights in the first place...

Most nights they would have a drink or two. Clancy would visit the pub on his way home from work. He received his rights six months after Topsy, because of his six-month prison sentence. Some mornings Clancy would wake up as dry as a bone, feeling like death. He'd have a drink of water and be drunk again. He felt his veins filling up with the warm sweet alcohol, and that helped to make the world recede...The work at the mine went well and Clancy seldom drank much when he was living out there. But the attractions of town proved too much, and after a while he came in and started drinking again. A group sat together behind the post office, but their raucous laughter and cries of complaint were too loud and the policeman was upon them before they knew what had happened.

In court the next morning most of them were fined one pound. But Clancy was in for greater things. Not only had he been before the bench countless times before, but he was the only person to be accused who had citizenship rights. Thus, theoretically at least he was the only one who could have bought the alcohol in the first place. He had therefore supplied the others. He was given six months for being drunk in town, and six months for supplying. The sentences were to run concurrently. So it was off to Broome once more. Sometimes Clancy thought that it would have been better if he had not got the rights after all. But what was he supposed to do? It seemed that whatever he did things would come out wrong, sooner or later...'You going to keep off the supplying now, eh? Now look, Clancy, you want to get away from this mob. You're a clever bloke, there's no denying that. You'd be better off. You could do well'.

Clancy looked at the policeman...and thought for a moment. Then he said, 'Don't you tell me that, I know. I was leader of them, I was born amongst them, and I always been a part of them. But I tell you something. You cut my head off, and I reckon I might forget about them then'. Clancy laughed...

'The grog came up pretty recently really. Lot of fellows been drinking, they can't seem to stop somehow. You see they never had much of anything, and when they given a little they want to have more than anyone else. I suppose he's afraid whitefella might come and take it away again, so he got to get as much as he can while it's there. I hit it very hard when I got up to '48 Christmas, on the whisky. Old Rob Lucas was pretty good to his workers, and he gave me a bottle of whisky for a Christmas box. Well two of us drunk that. But in the long run the grog got me wary. I used to be pretty noisy, then I used to get into trouble. Then I got arrested. Now I drink without moving about and go to sleep. That's the only chance they got to pick me up now, when I fall asleep. It's in me, just like with the smoking. See if I had a good blow-out, it do me for five or six weeks, or three months. But after all the grog's gone from my system, I gets very dopey and tired, and I got to go in and have a skinful, and then go back again. It's in the habit I think, but I think it got hold of my system. I tell you the truth, if a doctor like to have a look, I think he'll prove that. I'll never stop. So every now and again, I say to Peter, "Look, my skin's drying out. I got to go in and have a skinful, and I'll be all right again". He know I gotta go. I always come back again...

'See, I got two names mudamuda and half-caste. See I wanted nowhere. See whitefella call me half-caste, well I don't want it there, Aborigine he call me mudamuda, I'm not there. I'm in the middle, and I'm strong on both sides, I'm half way in between. I tell the other blokes that I'm half a white bloke and half an Aborigine. But I reckon I'd have been better off an Aborigine, 'cause I was more with them and got the feeling for them here.' He pointed to his stomach.

From Palmer and McKenna 1978, pp. 110–19, 123–4

The 1967 Referendum, passed overwhelmingly in all states, gave the federal government the responsibility to legislate for Aborigines, and enabled Aborigines to be officially counted in population censuses. It did not, contrary to popular belief, give drinking rights to Aborigines, for as we have seen in the preceding discussion, this was a matter for the individual state governments. Nevertheless, some commentators assume that the referendum allowed Aborigines to consume alcohol legally, and more than 20 years later they still suggest that this was an act of 'misguided benevolence' because Aborigines are in danger of becoming 'extinct' as a result of alcohol use (Spencer 1988, p. 19). The years of prohibition and semi-prohibition had never prevented Aboriginal people from having access to alcohol (or other drugs), as Clancy McKenna's story (see 'Somewhere between black and white') and others confirm, but the repeal of these liquor laws meant that Aborigines could drink openly and in public, and were subject to arrest on charges of drunkenness, disorderly conduct and so on. In a discussion of the discriminatory legislation, Eggleston notes that in several police divisions there was indeed an increase in Aboriginal convictions following the repeal of liquor restrictions (Eggleston 1976, 219–22). She mentions that Aborigines with no previous liquor convictions were appearing in court charged with being drunk. Eggleston suggests that the reasons for this were associated with depressed conditions and high Aboriginal visibility; later, and perhaps in contradiction, she posits that:

Aborigines, whose status had been considerably reduced by legislation, show themselves no more than human by rushing to take advantage of rights and privileges which the rest of the community takes for granted, once legal barriers are removed.
Eggleston 1976, p. 222

As a result of discrimination in licensed premises as well as from choice, Aborigines often drink in public in the open air, thus coming more easily to the attention of the police. Aboriginal people have thus become disproportionately represented in alcohol-related charges coming before the courts. 'Alcohol', writes Eggleston, 'is of crucial importance in the involvement of Aborigines with the criminal law' (1976, p. 213).

Conflicting models

Before turning to some of the early attempts to study and understand the meaning and outcomes of Aboriginal uses of alcohol, it is important to bear in mind that there are several contentious aspects in the current understanding of drug and alcohol

Figure 5.2 *By choice and because of discrimination in licensed premises, Aborigines often drink in the open air. This notice at Port Augusta, South Australia, puts the foreshore area out of bounds for drinkers. (From P. Taylor, ed.,* After 200 years, *Aboriginal Studies Press, Canberra, 1988, p. 131; photo P. Sumner)*

use. The first of these relates to the concept of addiction and the disease model; another concerns the causes of dysfunctional drug and alcohol use in the general population, and among Aborigines in particular.

The disease model

The notion of addiction, heavily influenced by psychiatric diagnostic criteria, has fallen from favour in recent years. As one author explains:

Because the treatment of alcoholism and other drug dependence is a relatively young field, there is much controversy as to what addiction is on the most fundamental levels. Traditional psychiatry had taught that addiction is a symptom of an underlying psychopathology, while other treatment professionals who rely on the so-called disease concept of addiction describe addiction as a primary disorder rather than a pathology that is secondary to another problem that is psychiatric in nature. Consequently, there has been confusion as to what constitutes appropriate diagnostic criteria for alcoholism and other drug dependencies.

Landry 1987, p. 379

The confusion deepened because two influential models developed, one in the United States, and the other in the United Kingdom. While the American Psychiatric Association's *Diagnostic and statistical manual of mental disorders* (*DSM*) (American Psychiatric Association 1987) relied on the US model, the International Classification of Diseases (ICD) of the World Health Organization used the British model (WHO 1977). Landry (1987) provides a useful outline of recent revisions of DSM which attempt to merge the two models (see also WHO 1981). The disease model, first advanced in the United States towards the end of the eighteenth century, asserted that those who 'lost control' of their drinking suffered from the 'disease of inebriety'; it meant that consumers were characterised as hapless victims. Over the years the model was refined until it became the dominant metaphor, taken up by Alcoholics Anonymous and other self-help groups. However, epidemiological research began to document that a wide range of drinking problems are distributed throughout the general population, and that people move in and out of problem drinking over time. As a result, the orthodox disease model began to disintegrate. Now it is felt that 'the disease concept...is in a state of "crisis" because of wide fissures in the fundamental propositions at its core' (Walsh and Hingson 1987, p. 283; Heath 1987b, p. 114). The disease concept of alcoholism is also a decidedly ethnocentric construct, as Room points out:

A disease concept centering on loss of self-control, in this view, is not just differentially distributed among cultures, nor just manifested differently in different cultures; instead, it is at its heart a culture-bound syndrome, a concept which has meaning only in a culture in which individual self-control is the normative mode of social control.

Room 1984, p. 176

One of the few Australian anthropologists to confront directly the theories of alcohol dependence and hold them up against the realities observed in town camps is O'Connor (1984). His conclusion is that the people he observed simply do not fit into the categories associated with the alcohol dependence syndrome.

In Australia, key publications and health professionals have taken a broad view, which tends to de-emphasise the notion of addiction. For example, a popular review of drug use in Australia states:

The World Health Organization (1982) defines drug dependence as a state in which self-administered drugs cause damage to self or society. Terms such as 'alcoholic' and 'addict' have been commonly used in the past, often with strong moral overtones. It is preferable to refer to a person being (physically or psychologically) dependent on a drug.

Brown et al. 1986, p. 62

Notwithstanding this current direction of thinking about drug and alcohol use and abuse, the literature on Aboriginal uses of drug substances still abounds with loosely defined concepts of disease, addiction and alcoholism. For example, in 1988 Spencer wrote in a government publication that 'Alcoholism of a severe socially and physically damaging type is presently endemic amongst Australian Aboriginal peoples' (Spencer 1988, p. 15). Alcoholics Anonymous, co-dependency counselling and other therapeutic regimes are based thoroughly on the 'disease' concept, and many Aboriginal people (some of whom have been influenced by these organisations) espouse the view today that alcoholism is a disease (Bryant 1987; Hunt 1981; Mills 1985, pp. 105–6). Kunitz and Levy (1974) provide an interesting discussion of the influence of 'anglo definitions' upon the changing ideas of alcohol use among Navaho Indians. The National Aboriginal Health Strategy Working Party report (NAHSWP 1989), in its discussion of alcohol and other substance abuse, reveals some of the confusion among Aboriginal people and others over the terms and definitions associated with alcohol use. For example, the report states unequivocally, 'Non-Aboriginal Australia must realise that alcoholism is an introduced illness caused primarily by political, social, economic and cultural deprivation' (NAHSWP 1989, p. 192). Later in the same document, the alcohol problem is said to be a symptom of dispossession, leading to loss of self-esteem, rather than a disease.

A guide to *Terms and definitions for use in drug-related research in Australia* recommends the discontinuation of the use of the term 'addiction' with respect to alcohol use and suggests:

Alcohol Dependence Syndrome (i) Cluster of symptoms including a narrowing of drinking repertoire, salience of drinking behaviour, increased tolerance to alcohol, repeated alcohol withdrawal symptoms, relief or avoidance of symptoms by further drinking, subjective awareness of compulsion to drink and reinstatement of syndrome after abstinence.

Richards et al. 1989, p. 1

Similarly, the Australian Drug Offensive prefers categories such as unsanctioned use, hazardous use, problem-related use and dependent use, and states:

Although terms such as 'alcoholic' and 'addict' may be useful to some people, generally they are used too loosely...When assessing drug using behaviour, we need to consider:

> *drug (its type and effects)*
> *context (i.e. social or cultural setting)*
> *person or persons using it*
> *how it is used*
> *why it is used*
> *consequences of that use.*

CEIDA 1986, pp. 39–40

These criteria are similar to those proposed by Norman Zinberg as being aids to the social understanding of drug use. He suggests that three determinants must be addressed in the consideration of what impels individuals to use drug substances, and how the drug use affects the user. These are the drug (its pharmacological actions); the set (the attitude of the person at the time of use), and the setting (the influence of the social and physical setting within which use occurs) (Zinberg 1984, p. 5). Of the three, the setting has been most neglected in studies of drug use, which may explain why so many current viewpoints are oriented to individual psychopathology.

Antecedents

This leads into another of the issues on which there are conflicting views in the overall understanding of drug and alcohol use: the presumed antecedent causes of problematic or dysfunctional use of such substances by people in general, and by Aborigines in particular.

For many years it was assumed that an individual became involved in drug use or abuse as a result of ignorance or misconception of the effects and dangers of drug use. However, as Miller and Ware point out, little evidence was found to support such assumptions upon empirical investigation (Miller and Ware 1989, p. 23). In recent years, however, intrapersonal factors (such as low self-esteem, lack of social values) and interpersonal factors (influence of family and peers) have been suggested as major contributors to the initiation of drug use and abuse in the general population. In a review of studies of antecedents, initiation into the use of all drugs including alcohol was most strongly related to interpersonal factors (Miller and Ware 1989, p. 25). Other influential factors were said to be psychological depression, delinquency, non-conformity, and stressful family circumstances. Significantly (for this discussion) sociodemographic factors (class, occupation) 'in both absolute terms and relative to other variables, add very little to the explained variance of initiation into drug use' (Miller and Ware 1989, p. 25).

In contradistinction to these views of the factors that may precipitate drug abuse in the general population, the explanations for Aboriginal drug and alcohol use and abuse are posited to be entirely historical, social and political in nature. They relate to dispossession, colonisation, low socioeconomic status and rapid social change. These are all thoroughly social factors. For example, lawyer Elizabeth Eggleston asserts that Aboriginal heavy drinkers are not suffering from mental illness, but:

The origins of their chronic alcoholism lie less in personal inadequacy than in community defects. It is not simply a question of the disorganization of the Aboriginal community; more important is the pathology of the white community which rejects the Aborigines in so many ways.

Eggleston 1974, p. 60

The list of supposed 'causes' of certain drug uses among Aborigines is long and varied. In a Senate Select Committee enquiry into the inhalation of volatile solvents, including the inhalation of petrol fumes among Aborigines, Aboriginal witnesses proposed that petrol sniffing and substance abuse were symptoms of the 'appalling socio-economic environment forced upon us'. A Victorian spokesperson said in evidence:

Communities have identified a number of causes of petrol sniffing and substance abuse and these include the destruction of Aboriginal culture; the denial of Aboriginal rights; enforced isolation; inadequate housing, community facilities and appropriate educational opportunities; the destruction of the traditional economy; the enforcement of inappropriate laws, values and social systems...It follows in our minds that the unacceptable practice of petrol sniffing and substance abuse is a symptom of that environment and thereby directly attributable to the planned destruction of our society.

Australia, Senate Select Committee, 18 March 1985, pp. 807–8

While this view is widespread among some sections of the Aboriginal population, there are some dissenting voices (Gibson unpub.; Langton 1989). The case study, 'A contemporary Aboriginal viewpoint' is an excerpt from a paper presented by Merv Gibson, an Aboriginal man from Hopevale, Queensland, at the 1987 ANZAAS conference. His remarks were also reported in the press at the time (*Northern Territory News*, 26 August, 1987).

A contemporary Aboriginal viewpoint

This paper is the product of my own personal consideration of anthropology and Aboriginal society. Having studied anthropology and archaeology at the University of Queensland, I took a year off my studies to return to the Aboriginal community at Hopevale. In my work as projects officer in the community, I had the opportunity to observe my own society, equipped with the ideas that my years of study had given me. My practical experience there, considering the community's social problems and talking to community members, has led me to believe that there seems to be a vast disparity between the science of anthropology and its ideas about Aboriginal society, especially with regard to their social problems, and Aboriginal society itself. In this paper I have chosen to dwell on the problem of alcohol among Aboriginal people.

Anthropologists and other white people who have set themselves up as 'experts' on Aboriginal society, such as missionaries and government officials, have contributed to the creation and perpetuation of the myths that now *shackle* Aboriginal society. This paper argues that Aboriginal society has *internalised* these myths, and that these myths are necessary to justify social exploitation by sections of the Aboriginal community.

Alcohol has become such a *particular problem* for Aboriginal people because, under the Myth, it has become an expression of *identity* and *culture* for them. For black people, to drink alcohol is to *be* an Aboriginal. Social relationships and community [are] expressed through the consumption of alcohol. This paper is concerned with the question of whether the social phenomenon of alcohol among Aboriginals is the expression of *true culture and identity*, or whether it is a *distortion* and an *exploitation* of that culture and identity.

For example: Jack collects his pay cheque or social security cheque and spends most of it providing alcohol for himself and his cousins. His wife is unable to purchase enough food for their children until the next cheque, and therefore the children are hungry and his wife has to borrow food from a neighbour to feed them. Because Jack regularly appropriates the family income in this way, it is highly unlikely that his wife will ever repay what she was given. What was once a relationship of equal cadging between her family and the neighbours becomes unequal. What was once dependency by Jack's wife and children based on *necessity* becomes dependency by Jack based on *social exploitation* and *parasitism*.

Why is such exploitation and parasitism allowed to continue? It is allowed to continue because the Myth has convinced the members of the society, that it is part and parcel of Aboriginal culture and tradition...Jack justifies his appropriation of the family income for the purposes of buying alcohol for his cousins, as a true expression of cultural identity and as a fulfilment of cultural and kinship obligations. Consuming alcohol for Jack in the way that he does is all about reinforcing kinship and cultural ties. During the course of consuming the alcohol Jack can be heard explaining his kinship ties to his fellows...It is a gross denial and distortion of true Aboriginal tradition...

The consequences of the operation of such myths is that alcoholism and social responsibility is associated with Aboriginal identity. Health, hygiene and care about nutrition and economic welfare are associated with a white identity. There is this assumption amongst Aboriginals that achievement and social responsibility is the preserve of white people...

The ideas that form the Myth are those that have been internalised from the white interpretation of black people. Anthropologists, through their advice to policy-makers and in their contribution to the public perception of Aboriginals, have contributed to the construction of the Myth, which has been used to explain some of the most ridiculous things. It is time to stop portraying gambling in Aboriginal society as some kind of traditional re-distribution of wealth. It is time to stop interpreting alcoholism as some kind of helpless result of culture clash. Rather we should be seeing it for what it is. That is: the deliberate distortion of tradition for the sake of fulfilling an individual physical desire for alcohol. It is time to *stop* portraying the contemporary Hopevale alcoholic as a passive victim of colonisation. Rather we must consider how he has actively created his own problems. My generation at Hopevale cannot honestly point to colonisation and dispossession as the immediate cause of their social problems... Rather, our social problems stem from our inability to recognise how members of our community, and indeed we ourselves, are using 'tradition' and 'culture' and 'kinship' to exploit our own society. If anthropology is to serve any purpose for Aboriginal people, surely it must be to help recognise these problems.

From Gibson unpub.

Merv Gibson's paper raises some thought-provoking issues, particularly about the role of researchers and their interpretations of Aboriginal alcohol use; this point will be pursued later. The idea that problematic drug or alcohol use results from 'culture clash' has been influential in Australia, as it was in North America. The acculturation hypothesis suggests that minority or indigenous groups are subject to stresses resulting from value conflicts, identity crises and the loss of traditional institutions, and that those individuals most stressed by these factors engage in 'maladaptive' behaviours, including drug and alcohol use (Bonnheim and Korman 1985; Barnes 1985; May 1982). According to this view there is a supposedly natural progression from people who are still entrenched in their traditional culture (and therefore less likely to produce high levels of 'deviant' behaviour), to those who are undergoing rapid social change and are subject to modernisation (who exhibit high levels of 'deviance'). The acculturation argument permeates much work on Aboriginal alcohol and drug use (Nurcombe et al. 1970; Hunt 1981). The problem with acculturation as an explanation for Aboriginal (and other minority) drinking is that the argument assumes that 'traditional' cultures were unchanging and unstressed, and also that cultural change is necessarily stressful. MacAndrew and Edgerton (1969), Beauvais and La Boeff (1985), and Peele (1985) make some pertinent comments on the variability of drinking styles and subsequent pathology between and within groups, which also tend to undermine the acculturation or culture clash argument.

With respect to problem drinking, some researchers de-emphasise the supposed differences between indigenous populations (such as Australian Aborigines or American Indians) and others in similar socioeconomic circumstances. For example, while stressing particular deprivations suffered by American Indians, Dozier states:

It is clear, then, that the causes of Indian drinking must be sought in historical, social and cultural circumstances. Among all those who drink to excess, whether Indian or non-Indian, there is a background of emotional troubles, frustrations and disappointments. Alcohol under these circumstances temporarily gives a sense of superiority and confidence, while dulling the senses so that the unpleasantness of life may be forgotten.

Dozier 1966, pp. 74–5

Similarly, in an attempt to characterise intratribal differences in drinking levels of American Indians Wiesner et al. found that:

Drinking levels and style may be unique in some respects among Indians and influenced by cultural heritage but the overall differences in drinking levels and the life-time drinking patterns parallel the general drinking patterns in our society as a whole.

Wiesner et al. 1984, p. 244

Heath notes research that concluded that much Navaho drunkenness could be accounted for without recourse to the fact that the subjects were Navahos; drunkenness, unemployment and involvement with police were said to be not so much features of Indian culture as factors common to all those who find themselves in a disadvantaged, economically deprived class (Heath 1989, p. 219).

Mention also needs to be made of a controversial topic: the apparent ethnic variation in sensitivity to the short-term physiological effects of ethanol. While many of the studies are marred by methodological shortcomings and others found no significant differences, as Heath observes in his discussion of this issue, some investigators have reported significant differences between or among populations ('Whites', 'Orientals', 'Indians' etc.) with respect to the rapidity with which alcohol is metabolised within the body (Heath 1987*a*, pp. 28–9). Marinovitch et al. (1976) found no significant differences in the metabolism of ethanol between Aborigines and non-Aborigines.

In summary, then, it can be said that contradictory explanations are offered for the prevalence of drug and alcohol abuse in one section of the population (Aborigines), and in Australian society as a whole. There are also uncertainties and differences of opinion about definitions of drug and alcohol-related problems, including the disease of addiction, dependence, abuse and dysfunction. The possibility that there are inherent differences in the metabolism of alcohol by different peoples remains an on-going controversy. In many respects, all these issues constitute an underlying dialogue in the research literature on Aboriginal use of psycho-active substances.

Three decades of studies

Much of the early published work on Aboriginal alcohol use was not founded on research at all, but arose from the expressed concerns and experience of church and welfare workers in the field. Not until comparatively recently did the focus move from opinion to research, and from a concentration on alcohol use to other drug uses. Pastor P. G. E. Albrecht was one of the first church workers to write at length on Aboriginal alcohol use (Symonds et al. 1963; Albrecht 1974). Having grown up among the Arrente people in central Australia, he displays an unprecedented degree of understanding, but his work is marred by the preoccupations of the 1960s (assimilation policies) and anachronistic views of land rights (in the 1970s). His most widely read assessment of the causes of 'the alcohol problem among Aborigines' was published in 1974. While it reiterates the myth that 'since Aborigines had no indigenous beverage alcohol, they evolved no rules governing its use in their communities' (Albrecht 1974, p. 36), the article highlights some key issues. Albrecht documents the abuse of Aboriginal kinship expectations by drinkers who rely on others for sustenance, the fact that citizenship was associated with drinking and with equality, and that alcohol allows the release of tensions and frustrations that are otherwise kept under control. He sees the solution to lie within the Aboriginal communities themselves, in the creation of a community consensus.

As Heath (1987*a*) observes, much anthropological work on alcohol use was previously a serendipitous byproduct of fieldwork that had other emphases; few people went into the field with the intention of focusing on alcohol use. It is only recently that ethnographic studies have specifically dealt with the use of alcohol and other drugs. Australia is no exception in this respect; for example, Calley's study of race relations on the north coast of New South Wales (Calley 1957) refers to the social impact of alcohol prohibition, to drinking as a predominantly male activity, and compares criminal charges against Aborigines and with those against whites. Jeremy Beckett also published work from New South Wales, undertaken in 1957, and his 1965 article was the first anthropological paper specifically on alcohol use. It was an important publication, and remains one of the few studies of alcohol use among rural (rather than remote, 'traditionally oriented') Aborigines. Beckett documents the social distance between the races, as well as Aboriginal perceptions of drinking, alcohol choices and drinking styles celebrated in popular 'folk' songs. Above all, his ethnography shows why alcohol use and drunkenness was valued among the people he studied. For them it was a means of achieving a state of well-being and letting off steam. It also indicated adult male status, and consuming large amounts of alcohol showed great physical prowess. The emphasis in Beckett's work is a welcome change from the entirely problem-oriented approach of many earlier writers.

Another anthropologist whose work touched upon alcohol use in the course of her central Australian field study is Bain, who in 1974 published an article containing insights that have been reiterated in the work of others since then. In this article she emphasises the group nature of drinking, the adoption of a drinking identity among regular users, and the pressures on heavy indulgence:

Once a start is made, it becomes impossible to refuse. The process may be rapid, intermittent, or develop over weeks or months, but no one remaining in camp was able, or was permitted, to exercise moderation, though many have wished to do so...Refusal, however, is possible if a whole group of kin abstains or an individual is teetotal altogether or for a limited period. Ignorance of liquor is also an acceptable reason. If a person can say, 'No, I have no knowledge of it', then he is not, ideally, pressed to drink.

Bain 1974, p. 47

She thus raises two crucial points: the collective nature of the drinking act, which in itself precludes moderation, and the acceptable ways of refusing alcohol.

Later social scientists have taken up the idea of the drinking group and the drinking way of life, notably Sansom (1980), who studied fringe-dwelling Darwin Aborigines, and O'Connor (1984), who worked with town campers in Alice Springs. O'Connor stresses that heavy drinking among town campers has become a way of life, and that the drinking style constitutes a 'group dependence':

To belong to the group and to live in the fringe camp is to drink with the group. If one does not drink with the group one may have a physical presence there, but one does not belong. The choice is simple: drink and belong, or abstain and remain outside.

O'Connor 1984, p. 181

Similarly, in Sansom's ethnography the pathology of the drinking sprees (and their physical aftermath) is defused because the reader is presented with intricate details of lives that revolve around drinking:

[O]ne is presented with people who neither shame-facedly admit nor reluctantly confess to the grogging proclivities of their camp's membership. Rather one comes to a community whose members roundly announce that grogging is an activity that, on the one hand, gives each person style, and, on the other, endows the collectivity with a style of life...In the grogging community...the moral onus is reversed and it is the abstainer who must make apologies. Because they are deviant, temperate men in grogging communities are put on the defensive.

Sansom 1980, pp. 48–9

Collmann is another anthropologist who considered alcohol use as part of his overall work. His 1980 doctoral dissertation (published in 1988), provides more data on alcohol as a component of social identity and relatedness among Alice Springs Aborigines. He also provides data on drinkers' ranking of and tastes for different beverages, from spirits (rum or ouzo), beer, port and sweet sherry to methylated spirits. He assesses the meaning of being drunk for these town campers as an experience of personal power. Like Sansom, he concludes that drinking makes action possible (Collmann 1979, 1988). The studies of Beckett (1965), Bain (1974), Sansom (1980), O'Connor (1984) and Collmann (1988) provide major insights into Aboriginal attitudes to drinking, how drinking is valued, and into the style and strongly collective nature of the drinking act. The contribution of psychiatrist Max Kamien deserves mention here too. In addition to dealing with the physical and psychological pathology associated with Aboriginal alcohol use in Bourke, New South Wales, Kamien (1978) also provides interesting case studies of individuals. He quotes a 51-year-old man who had, he said, been drunk every day for the previous 11 years:

If you want to give up drink you have to go where you don't have mates. It is important to me to go with my mates, that's all I've got. If I refused a mate the next time I pick up with him he won't want anything to do with me. He would lend me anything. Now he won't lend me nothing. I'd be sort of insulting him.

Kamien 1978, p. 153

In the last decade, anthropologists have begun to focus specific studies on alcohol use, including Sackett (1977, 1988), Stead (unpub.), Brady and Palmer (1984), and Brady (1988). The authors of all these studies have lived in and with the drinking communities, which were remote and relatively isolated enclaves of Aborigines with strong traditional practices. Sackett (1977) and Brady and Palmer (1984) document the existence of informal, locally accepted 'rules' associated with drinking, but note that these did not succeed in preventing an erosion of the Law (Aboriginal religious law), or high rates of morbidity and mortality. Brady and Palmer's study of a South Australian community attempts to present a holistic view of alcohol use by using both qualitative and quantitative data. They show that alcohol is used by Aborigines to achieve personal power and give them the courage to confront whites, but also that the violence that often follows drinking sprees exacts a heavy toll. This is documented using presentations for alcohol-related incidents at the community clinic over a six-month period.

While anthropologists and other social scientists have focused on the value placed upon alcohol use (in the creation of conviviality, social exchanges, and action), the psychological approach (as with earlier welfare-oriented work) has dwelt more on the pathology surrounding alcohol and its effects. Kamien says that Aboriginal men in Bourke, New South Wales, drank alcohol to relieve their inner tensions, while the women in the same town used analgesic powders to achieve the same effect (Kamien 1978, p. 145). However, he stresses that drinking 'was more due to group psychosocial pressures rather than to individual psychological need' (1978, p. 160). Larsen (1980), in a rather tortuously argued paper, suggests that alcohol abuse was associated with un-assimilated Aborigines who preferred the company of their own groups, rather than multiracial company. The tone of his paper intimates that assimilation is unquestionably desirable, and that black identity has a negative connotation. Apart from Kamien (1978), and more recently Hunter (1989) who quantified intake and collected case studies, there is a tendency for the psychiatric researchers to present little actual data but much generalisation (Eastwell 1988; Spencer 1988). Spencer asserts that 'Aborigines' (presumably as a whole) have a severe form of alcoholism which is difficult to treat be-cause theirs is a 'non-scientific culture' and they think 'in a historically earlier mode' (Spencer 1988, p. 19).

As Aboriginal organisations have grown since the mid-1970s, particularly in central Australia, Aboriginal attitudes towards research into drug and alcohol issues affecting Aborigines have undergone considerable change. Initially, local organisations con-cerned (primarily) with alcohol use were confined to organising pick-up services (so that inebriated Aborigines were taken home rather than being picked up by the police), and running 'rehabilitation' centres. More recently, the lobbying power of research has been recognised by these organisations. Tangentyere Council (which administers the affairs of Aboriginal town campers in Alice Springs) has a liquor committee which has commissioned several studies (Lyon 1990), as has the Central Australian Aboriginal Congress (a health organisation) (Simmons 1988). As well as these organisations, Aboriginal land councils have hired their own researchers to collect detailed data on alcohol-related morbidity in order to object to the increasing numbers of liquor licences issued in the vicinity of Aboriginal communities. In this way, research is increasingly being viewed, not as an exploitative tool of white academics, but as a necessary con-tribution to assist Aboriginal people who are organising themselves to mount local awareness campaigns, lobby governments and oppose the burgeoning liquor industry. Alcohol use among Aboriginal people is not an easy issue to explore, and communities are understandably sensitive to investigators who dwell on social pathology. Undertak-ing such work in close cooperation with, and under contract to, Aboriginal organis-ations means that the studies are facilitated, and some degree of control is exerted over methodology and publication.

Avoiding alcohol related pathology?

Associated with the issue of control, and the sensitivities aroused by researching so-cial problems, a particular criticism has been levelled at anthropological studies which suggests that anthropologists have minimised the seriousness of drinking problems in the societies they have studied. Robin Room, a prominent United States alcohol researcher published an article on this issue—what he terms 'problem deflation'—in a major anthropological journal in 1984 (Room 1984). Room suggests that ethnographic methods may be better tuned to measuring the pleasures rather than the problems of drinking, and that this 'deflation' of problems is not just an oversight, but tends to be inherent in the functionalist perspective (Room 1984, p. 171). In other words, because anthropologists are preoccupied with understanding the meanings and values attached to alcohol use (its use in social and economic exchanges, for example), they have avoided facing up to the damage it causes. Notwithstanding the protestations to the contrary by some of Room's commentators, including Jeremy Beckett and Lee Sackett (Room 1984, pp. 178–91), the anthropological avoidance of the pathological consequences of alcohol use has been raised before. Graves (1967) suggests that there is an 'unspoken taboo' on the part of ethnographers against exposing dysfunctional behavioural patterns. Certainly some Australian anthropologists have examined the social exchanges among Aborigines, and the creation of credit among drinkers, to the exclusion (one cannot help thinking) of any meaningful consideration of the violence and despair that can also be part of the drinking groups and their milieu such as that described by Reser in chapter 6 of this volume. The work of Sansom (1980) and Collmann (1988), for example, could be critically examined with this perspective in mind. As Room notes, the tendency to focus on collective behaviour 'directs the fieldworker towards the pleasures of the drinking group, usually male, and away from the private agonies the men's drinking may involve for women and children' (Room 1984, p. 172).

The countervailing argument is that anthropological studies have defused the problems associated with alcohol as a corrective to the excessively negative, sometimes moralistic, and certainly ethnocentric treatment given to alcohol use among indigenous groups by researchers (usually) from other disciplines. The case study, 'On problem deflation' presents part of Jeremy Beckett's reply to Room's article.

Notwithstanding the debate highlighted by Room's accusation that anthropologists have downplayed the negative aspects of alcohol use, it is possible to say that the contribution of the social sciences to alcohol studies (and potentially to policy making) is growing. Characteristics of a variety of Aboriginal uses of alcohol have emerged from the social sciences, including the predominant pattern of opportunistic and binge drinking; the strong collective nature of the drinking act and way of life; the division within the population between heavy drinkers on the one hand and abstainers on the other; the role of women as abstainers; the absence of impact (so far) of low-alcohol beverages and of price on Aboriginal purchases; and the relatively low exposure of remote Aborigines to mass-media anti-drinking campaigns.

Patterns of drug and alcohol use

To date, very little work has been undertaken that attempts to characterise the patterns of drug and alcohol abuse among Aborigines, including intra- and inter-community patterns, or regional differences. Certainly there has been no research undertaken in Australia approximating the thoroughness of some overseas work, which has brought together diverse research studies of particular societies and their

On problem deflation

A member of the 'wet generation', I wanted to counter the accepted view that people only drank to the point of intoxication out of misery. Instead I proposed a view, expressed by a local songwriter, to the effect that 'if we didn't drink there'd be no fun around here'. I also wrote in indignation that the law should deny alcohol to Aborigines while allowing it to Europeans. In place of psychological reductionism, I presented Aboriginal drinking in its historical, social and cultural contexts. I argued that the Aborigines had adopted the hard drinking of the frontier to reconstitute their shattered society and that in defying official prohibition they were conducting a pre-political resistance. I did recognise that the positive functions were achieved at a high price in terms of domestic upheaval, police harassment, imprisonment and fines. However I ignored arguments from addiction, dismissed the few acute alcoholics as aberrant, and took no account of the long-term physical consequences of heavy drinking. An attack of delirium tremens, known as 'the horrors', was remarkable principally as the subject of an entertaining song. This nonchalant approach, however, was a consequence less of my functionalism than of an anthropology designed to handle social rather than biological facts. The people did not take these matters seriously, so neither did I.

Subsequent work has varied a good deal in its approach. Psychologists have continued to take such notions as stress and 'feelings of dis-ease' as their starting point, while giving some recognition to sociocultural factors (Cawte 1974, p. 201; Kamien 1978). Sackett (1977), an anthropologist, has described the disruptive effects of alcohol in a traditionally oriented community and the inability to control them. Collmann (1979), on the other hand, has described the use of alcohol in fostering sociability.

I meanwhile have maintained contact with the community I first visited in 1957, and my attitude to their drinking is no longer so nonchalant. The legal restrictions on drinking were lifted in 1963, but my prediction that this removed a major factor for drunkenness could not be checked because other things had not remained equal. Simultaneously there was a sharp downturn in employment, which meant that men no longer spent extended periods 'in the bush' and away from alcohol. Drinking became continuous, involving males at an earlier age and including some women as well. 'News' from the community consists of a dismal chronicle of alcohol-related deaths, often of men in their twenties and early thirties.

This case may indicate a variable that Room appears to have missed. My own easy-going attitude to drinking was part of a general shift in public opinion which made it easier for Aborigines to increase their consumption. Most of those I got to know in 1957 were in the early stages of their drinking careers and did not yet show the ill effects that would one day emerge as the consequence of alcoholic liberalism.

The Aborigines are slowly forming their own critique of drinking, seeing it as a product of joblessness and the boredom of small-town life. But the relation between biological and social facts is never simple, and habitual heavy drinking remains an integral part of daily life. Understanding its centrality in social and cultural terms still seems to me to be the contribution that the anthropologists should be making, even if it is only a part of a total understanding.

From Jeremy Beckett, 'Comments on Robin Room's "Alcohol and ethnography: a case of problem deflation?"', Current Anthropology 25 (2), 1984, pp. 169–91

uses of alcohol and other substances. Marshall's edited volume on beer and modernisation in Papua New Guinea is such an example (Marshall 1982). The volume also includes studies of kava and betelnut as well as beer, and traces historical developments, liquor laws and the role of old and new religious movements as they articulate with alcohol use. Lindstrom (1987) edited a volume on drug use in Western Pacific societies which, because of its regional focus, allows patterns to emerge and comparisons to be made. Marshall devoted a book to an ethnography of alcohol use on Truk, Micronesia (Marshall 1979). Kunitz et al. (1971) contributed to the debate on acculturation in their work on the epidemiology of alcohol-related morbidity among two neighbouring American Indian groups. Their comparative work on cirrhosis rates suggests that there are many important cultural differences between different groups that influence styles of drinking, social behaviour, and subsequently the degree of morbidity.

In New Zealand, the University of Auckland has coordinated a major study on the place of alcohol in the lives of New Zealand women, from which a series of publications has emerged exploring alcohol use in different sections of New Zealand society including Maori and Islander people (National Council of Maori Nurses 1988; Neich and Park 1988). North American research has produced informative review articles on drug and alcohol use among its ethnic groups and indigenous peoples, which cover the wide range of available literature. Notable reviews include Everett et al.(1976), Heath (1975, 1987*a*, 1987*b*) and May (1977).

While the Australian studies from the social and psychological sciences already mentioned provide documentation of drinking patterns, these are generally studies of discrete groups and environments, with little regional comparison. The first survey to attempt such a task was undertaken by the Northern Territory Drug and Alcohol Bureau in 1986 and 1987 (Watson, C., et al. 1988). The survey design divided the Northern Territory into three regions (the 'Top End', Katherine and central Australia), and the Aboriginal populations questioned were selected from major communities, town camps, cattle stations and outstations. Ten per cent of the target population was sampled, using both an individual questionnaire and a group survey. People were asked about their use of alcohol, tobacco, analgesics and kava, as well as combinations of these. The use of petrol as an inhalant (widespread in two of the regions of the survey) was not included, for reasons that are unexplained in the report of the survey. The report presents quantitative data on the age and sex of users, frequency of use, estimates of quantities (in the case of alcohol, grams of alcohol per day), as well as qualitative data on perceptions and subjective reasons for use. The Northern Territory survey is one of the few published studies to document estimated intake (of alcohol and other drugs) and to make comparisons between intake in different environments and regions of the country. Other studies that have attempted to quantify intake include Kamien (1975, 1978) and Harris et al. (1987), working in Bourke; some data from Sydney (HRSCAA, 1977, p. 7); and Lake (1989) with a small sample from Adelaide. Skowron and Smith (1986) and Smith et al. (n.d.) collected data on alcohol intake in two Western Australian Aboriginal communities, but these reports remain in limited circulation. Similarly, Gray et al. (1981) quantified alcohol intake among Aboriginal people in Collie, a rural town in Western Australia. The findings of the Northern Territory survey, including the preponderance of male drinkers of kava and alcohol, female analgesic users, male tobacco smokers and female tobacco chewers, as well as regional variations, help to undermine the oversimplistic nature of many 'grand theories' about drug and alcohol use among indigenous people, typified by the acculturation model.

Some studies have compared the patterns of white Australian and Aboriginal drinking in rural towns. Harris et al. (1987) provide comparative data on intake and morbidity in New South Wales. Healy et al. (1985) and Hamilton (1985) have published research on alcohol consumption in both populations in Mount Isa, Queensland, and Brady (1988) studied alcohol use in Tennant Creek, Northern Territory.

Aboriginal versus white drinking in the Northern Territory

Perhaps the most obvious differentiation between groups in Tennant Creek as far as drinking is concerned is that between Aboriginal people and Europeans. Apart from purchasing takeaway alcohol, there is only one venue where numbers of Aboriginal people in the town drink—the front bar of the Swan. Until early 1983 Aboriginal people also drank at the Goldfields, in a section of the front bar which was divided off from the main area...this section of the bar was subsequently closed down. Aborigines in Tennant have, then, two choices: to drink 'at home' (or outside the 2 kilometre limit) or to drink in one bar...Some 'town' Aborigines (many of mixed descent, with government jobs, or adopted by European families) belong to the town's clubs but these people are unusual and are treated by Europeans as being exceptional Aborigines (or, as one explained it, 'Aborigines who are really like white fellers').

As a rule, then, Aborigines and whites do not drink at bars alongside one another...Europeans have, by virtue of their status and compliance with dress requirements, a comparatively wide choice of drinking venues—two restaurants, two taverns, two hotels and five clubs...this variety of establishments enables the Europeans to sort themselves into chosen social class groupings, so that they may avoid encounters with certain others (e.g. management and workers, police and public). Aboriginal people do not have the same range of environments at their disposal. This means that grievances, annoyances and disputes may not be dissipated by a distribution between premises (i.e. controlled, bounded environments

rather than the open air) as they are with Europeans. Rather, those Aboriginal people who wish to drink in a bar are all forced to use one small room for this purpose...In a tight area, containing determined drinkers who are inevitably of a variety of language groups, visitors and residents, the slightest push or wrong word is potentially volatile. The door of the front bar opened directly onto the main street, with no entrance hall or doorway—drinkers and arguers spill out onto the main street...where they are in full view of vigilant citizens or cruising police...

To some extent, a double standard exists whereby social life in town is resolutely centred around alcohol, whilst members of the community direct attention to 'others' among whom, it is said, the 'real' problem lies. Frequently Aboriginal drinking is denounced in this way. It is clear that the rules by which to drink, which are established by each racial group, provide clues to the understanding of the intolerance of one group towards the other. Greater visibility, audibility, and the lack of formalised venues for intra-group differentiation whilst drinking mark Aboriginal drinking sessions. Europeans, on the other hand, exist within a culture of outback isolation which proclaims and rationalises the rightness of their style of drinking and drunkenness. Clubs, organisations and a variety of premises provide choices for Europeans in Tennant Creek within which their friendship, work and class groupings can be reinforced. Aboriginal drinkers have limited formal venues and must construct their social groupings elsewhere, at a decreasing number of 'safe' drinking places out of sight of police and public.

From Brady 1988, pp. 28–32, 43–4

Both sets of research commented on the high number of social events that revolved around alcohol use in each town, and the social imperative to consume large amounts of alcohol. In both towns, the social drinking of Aborigines was restricted to a single hotel and public places. In the Northern Territory, however, Aboriginal drinking has been further constrained by the imposition of what has come to be known as the 2 kilometre law. The legislation was set in place in 1983 and prohibits the consumption of liquor in public within 2 kilometres of any licensed premises (Brady 1988, pp. 58–62). Since it was primarily Aborigines who drank in public parks, waste ground and so on, and official barbecue areas (used by whites for public drinking) are exempt, the law has effectively made public drinking illegal for Aboriginal people. The case study, 'Aboriginal versus white drinking in the Northern Territory' illustrates some of the ecological factors in a small country town that serve to mould the drinking patterns of its Aboriginal and non-Aboriginal residents.

Volatile substance use

Apart from the use of alcohol, tobacco and analgesics, the most notable use of a mood-altering substance by Aborigines is petrol sniffing—the deliberate inhalation of petrol fumes. While the earliest sporadic reports of petrol sniffing among Aborigines date from the 1940s and 1950s, the practice has escalated over the last 20 years. Petrol sniffing is engaged in, both habitually and occasionally, by children and young adults of both sexes in a variety of communities, primarily in the Top End of the Northern Territory, in central Australia, and in the Eastern Goldfields region of Western Australia. There are also large areas in these 'outback' regions where sniffing is either rare or unknown. Petrol, glue and other inhalant use has been reported among Aboriginal youth in urban and rural parts of 'settled' Australia, for example in Brisbane and New South Wales country areas (SSCVSF 1985; NSWAECG 1986). The extent of the use of glue and other inhalants among urban and rural Aboriginal youth is virtually impossible to establish: the methodology employed by the NSW Aboriginal Education Consultative Group (NSWAECG) survey meant that individuals were asked to comment not on their own use, but on the numbers of known others who used a variety of drugs, which provided only a vague estimation of prevalence. Some usage of volatile substances is practised among Aboriginal prison inmates, a fact which has emerged from the Royal Commission into Aboriginal Deaths in Custody.

The inhalation of volatile substances is an appealing form of drug use for young Aborigines, particularly those living in remote or outback communities, because of the cheapness and availability of these substances, and the lack of access to other substances. While some communities have curbed the use of petrol among their young people, there has been a steady rise in the number of locations reporting sniffing, particularly in the decade 1970—80. In the 1960s, approximately seven communities (in South Australia, Western Australia and the Northern Territory) reported sniffing, but between 1970 and 1980 the number of new locations noting the practice was 14 (Brady 1989a, p. 147). The increased prevalence of petrol sniffing has accompanied the greater availability of petrol itself, for up until the late 1960s many communities had limited on-site supplies and few privately owned vehicles. Petrol is obtained from derelict and other vehicles, or by stealing it from bowsers; despite the prevalence of diesel vehicles, every community requires petrol for light machinery or (in coastal communities) for outboard motors. The increased private ownership of vehicles has also intensified inter-community travel and in many instances residents apportion blame for the outbreak of petrol sniffing in their community to the arrival of visiting sniffers from elsewhere. The practice has also grown in popularity alongside the development of larger peer groups of adolescents; several researchers have documented the high population growth and decline in infant mortality between the 1950s and 1970s (although fertility also declined in some areas) (Gray 1985; Young 1981; McKnight 1986). The youth population aged 19 years and under is often approximately 50 per cent of the total in both Arnhem Land and central Australian communities (Brady 1989*a*). Petrol is inhaled from soft drink cans or cardboard drink containers, often shaped to fit over the nose of the user; euphoria and hallucinations are experienced, and users demonstrate their altered state by excited shouting and laughter, playing loud rock music and engaging in acts of disobedience aimed at the status quo. Wilful damage of school buildings is common among petrol sniffers (Folds 1987).

The first published research study of sniffing was by a team of psychiatrists (Nurcombe et al. 1970) who visited Arnhem Land in 1968, 1969 and 1970. The team compared sniffers and non-sniffers, but found no significant differences in the types of home and family prestige of the two groups; they did, however, note that more sniffers were members of two particular clan groups. Their findings are reported in several subsequent and similar publications (Nurcombe et al. 1973; Nurcombe 1974; Hetzel 1975). Several years later, another psychiatrist (Eastwell) began research into petrol sniffing. As well as approaching the issue from a psychiatric point of view (emphasising sniffing as a symptom of stress, malaise and the absence of outstations among particular subgroups in the population), he undertook studies of lead toxicity in bone and blood (Eastwell 1978, 1979*a*, 1979*b*, 1984, 1985; Eastwell et al. 1983). As with alcohol use, church and welfare workers have also studied and

Figure 5.3 A poster designed for a campaign against petrol sniffing in Aboriginal communities (Health Promotion Unit, NT Department of Health and Community Services, Darwin)

published their findings on petrol sniffing (Clark 1984; Downing 1985; Nichols 1985; Sargent 1977; Tomlinson 1975), as have educationalists (Folds 1987; McClay and Christie 1980; Rogers 1980). Others have reported on juvenile crime associated with petrol sniffing (Hope 1987; Worrall 1982; Brady 1985*a*). Interventions in specific communities are described by Brady (1989*a*), Dalton-Morgan (1978), Franks (1989) and Morice et al. (1981). The only study to attempt a social epidemiology of the practice, examining the notable regional distribution of petrol use, is Brady (1989*a*).

The treatment of this drug use by Australian researchers and commentators has been almost entirely problem-oriented in perspective, with the early published work being dominated by psychiatrists. In recent years physicians and epidemiologists have started to document the physical sequelae of the chronic use of petrol (Freeman 1985; Hayward and Kickett 1988; Rischbieth et al. 1987). Morice et al. (1981) produced a resource manual for health professionals in the field, which provides an overview of published literature on physical and psychological effects of sniffing, treatment protocols (with chelating agents) and community interventions. Similarly, a Commonwealth information booklet reviews the medical and psychiatric literature (Department of Health 1985). A senate select committee, having received numerous submissions and toured several communities engaging in petrol sniffing, reported its findings in 1985 (SSCVSF 1985). While the report fails to distinguish between knowledgeable observation and generalising opinion, the Hansard records (Australia, Senate Select Committee, various dates) make interesting reading, and enable researchers to draw their own conclusions.

Few social scientists have dealt with the use of petrol, although Folds (1987) provides a provocative account of the practice, suggesting that it constitutes an active resistance on the part of young male Aborigines. In several publications, (Brady 1985*b*, 1988, 1989*a*, 1989*c*) I have provided an anthropological perspective, suggesting that Aboriginal perceptions of the substance and its effects on users are crucial in any understanding of its dynamics. In many communities there is a high level of tolerance and a lack of decisive intervention on the part of adults, which is related to existing non-authoritarian socialisation practices and a belief that petrol sniffers are unamenable to rational instruction. I have argued that the existence of petrol sniffing, and the difficulties experienced by many Aboriginal communities in eliminating it, are not related to the supposed deterioration of 'culture' or to family breakdown. The persistence of the practice can be related to factors that are also relevant to alcohol use: the pleasures of the drug itself, and of shared group meanings; and the expressions of autonomy and daring that the altered state makes possible (Brady 1989*a*). The case study, 'Number One for Action: an ex-sniffer's account' is an account of petrol sniffing given to me by a young woman of 20 living in an east Arnhem Land community; she is now no longer a user of petrol, and attributes her ability to abandon the drug use to her conversion to Christianity. This was in the form of participation in a Aboriginal-organised revival movement which used synchronised dance movements to gospel rock music, known as 'Action' (Brady 1989*c*). The music, learned movements and group focus of the activity attracted large numbers of young people, and Action spread rapidly through Arnhem Land during 1988 (as have many earlier revival movements). Numbers of petrol sniffers publicly vowed to eschew their drug use as a result.

Number One for Action: an ex-sniffer's account

My brothers and cousin-brothers was learning me to sniff. How to get the tin, scrape tin on cement to get the top off. They taught me. It was killing my brain and the petrol been go all over my body and I been sick. After that I been sniffing again and then I went to A... with boys and girls to steal car and drink beer. Went to steal truck, skid around. We got petrol from workshop where cars staying, from old car. After that I was stealing too much, sniffing 24 hour. After that I went to court...they tried to give me a fine...but sent me to B... gaol in 1985, four months...good life in gaol, play volleyball inside, pool, colouring, play game. I like B... sometime, but not too much. Single room, but after that not lonely, happy all the time, one side for woman one side for boys. We got everything, good tucker. Sometimes I was homesick, sometimes not.

I always go to Church, Fellowship. I'm Number One for Action. Came out of gaol November 1987. I was doing Action this year...when I was home back from hospital I didn't do any silly things because I was doing well at Fellowship. Doing very good with my friends, they like me.

They like to sniff 24 hour. I don't know why. Parents tell them and try to help them, they try to tell them to worship to God. They don't take any notice. They walk around, shout away, too much

petrol all over the body, they kill your brain, eh? It's true. When I was sniffing first, I had horrors. Snake, ghost or devil, dog, animals, try to bite you, chase. They do it to make feel strong. My favourite horror only snake. Start from morning, maybe afternoon or night, then you get a picture of snake, animals. It make you feel, make you funny way...they shout...Because I been used to it, make daylight, till six o'clock in the morning and went back home. Sometime it makes you hungry, my side it not. If I want to eat something else, fruit, [if] I been feel eating, dinner time I been eat. Not much, I was really skinny. Twenty-four hour. I been have maybe one bottle, two bottle petrol in my room, and cordial bottle. Not this time, I been Christian. I been baptised and confirmed in river. I'm good life, health, getting strong and too much tucker. I got good life and getting fat and strong. I been forget about it, sniffing. I got a good Action. Everyday I always go worship God at church...When I was sniff, and my parents told me not, [I said] 'I got my own life. If I want to die, I die. You don't have to tell me what to do. I don't take notice from anyone!' They said maybe you got little brain. 'That's right!' I said. I been want to die, I don't like this place. They [the others] want to die. Christians got a good power inside.

From an account given to M. Brady in east Arnhem Land

Accounts of individuals such as that of the woman in 'Number one for Action: an ex-sniffer's account' stress the fearful enjoyment of hallucinations (the 'horrors'), the unwillingness to take notice of parental remonstrances, and the lack of concern about ill-effects, even death. In some regions, petrol sniffers wear determinedly outrageous clothing, daub graffiti on community buildings, listen to 'heavy metal' rock music and belong to named gangs; in this way they signify during the adolescent and young adult years their difference from, and aloofness to the norms of their own society (Brady 1989a). Marriage and family responsibilities for both sexes usually bring with them an abandonment of petrol sniffing. As with studies of alcohol use, such accounts of drug use are crucial in order to correct an oversimplified and deterministic view that substance use and abuse by Aboriginal people necessarily demonstrates the demise of the structures and belief systems of that society.

Kava use among Aborigines

Notwithstanding the report from 1911 that Torres Strait Islanders consumed kava (Chief Protector of Aborigines 1911), kava made a reappearance in Australia from approximately 1982, when the use of this beverage from the crushed root of the pepper plant was introduced in Arnhem Land, Northern Territory. Legally imported to Australia as a 'food beverage', not a drug, kava acts as a local anaesthetic, a muscle relaxant, and has sedative and soporific qualities (Alexander et al. 1987, p. 6). Shulgin describes the chemistry and pharmacology of *Piper methysticum* (Shulgin 1973). Alexander et al. (1987) and Alexander (1985) provide a clear account of the introduction and use of kava in northern coastal Aboriginal communities, and document the spread of kava drinking to other communities.

While kava has been used for centuries in Melanesia and Polynesia (Cawte 1985; Bott 1987; Prescott and McCall 1988; Alama and Whitney 1990), its arrival and spread among Aborigines caused concern among Aboriginal people and some observers (Gordon et al. 1987; Cawte 1988). Psychiatrist John Cawte interpreted the new interest in the beverage as a 'macabre cult' (Cawte 1988, p. 545). He is taken to task for this value judgment by P. Watson (1988, p. 342) who points out that the social incorporation of novel drugs occurs quite commonly in many societies. Aboriginal people themselves were instrumental in the introduction of kava. Although initially its use was confined to Fijian and Samoan community workers in communities, some Yirrkala men visited Fiji, where they were impressed with the tension-reducing effects of kava there and arranged for supplies to be sent to their own community. In part, it was hoped that kava would take the place of alcohol and thus minimise alcohol-related violence (Downing 1985; Alexander et al. 1987). Gerrard describes its use as an adjunct to alcohol (Gerrard 1988). Two studies of kava use in Arnhem Land report that in kava-using communities male drinkers predominate (between 70 and 80 per cent of men, compared with 20 per cent of women), with ages ranging from about 15 years to 60 and over (Mathews et al. 1988; Alexander et al. 1987). Consumption, notoriously difficult to estimate, was suggested to be approximately 1.6 litres of kava per person at each sitting (Alexander et al. 1987, p. 20); over 440 grams per week was categorised by Mathews et al. (1988) as 'very heavy' consumption. An anonymous author writing in the *Aboriginal Health Worker* suggested that Arnhem Land people may drink 'up to a hundred times the amount normally drunk in the Pacific Islands' ('Kava: a challenge to alcohol' 1986, p. 12). The effects upon health of 'heavy' usage were pursued by Mathews et al. (1988) in a pilot study in one Arnhem Land community where they found that heavy users complained of bad health, were more likely to have scaly skin and were 20 per cent underweight. They suggested 'circumstantial' evidence for a toxic effect on the liver, but their results are queried by Douglas (1988, p. 341), who points out that examinations of liver and spleen were not recorded. High-ranking individuals in Hawaii (who drank kava regularly and over long periods) showed the physical symptoms of kava overuse, according to historical records noted by Alama and Whitney (1990). These included redness of the eyes and scaliness of the skin. Even before the publication of the research results by Mathews and his colleagues from the Menzies School of Health Research in Darwin, some Aborigines were calling for kava to be prohibited, and in 1988 Western Australia limited its availability by placing kava under the *Poisons Act*, so that its use is legal only with a permit.

It is hard to identify the exact nature of the concerns expressed by Aboriginal people and others; used in moderation, together with normal dietary intake, kava is a harmless, even beneficial, substance. Negative comments include its cost, the length of time devoted to consuming kava, reported mixing of kava with alcohols, fatigue at school and work (from late nights drinking kava), the fact that it has become a 'fad', and the uncertainty regarding the health effects of heavy use. As Alexander et al. point out, none of these factors is associated with kava in itself, but with the uses made of it by adherents (1987, pp. 31–4). In an overview of drugs in Oceania, Marshall (1987) observes that while abstention after habitual use does not produce withdrawal symptoms, 'a definite craving for the social experience of kava drinking...if not also a mild addiction to the drug...is well attested' (Marshall 1987, p. 26). In response to public pressure, the Northern Territory Department of Health and Community Services has produced a 'casualty reduction' style pamphlet, which discourages the use of kava by those breast-feeding, those suffering from liver, heart or lung disease, and children. Users are encouraged to wash their hands before preparing the beverage and to eat before consuming kava.

Other drug use

There is only limited available research on analgesic use by Aborigines, the most detailed being Kamien's work in Bourke (Kamien 1978). He found that analgesic use by Aborigines was more common among women than men and that 68 out of 92 households revealed 142 separate containers of analgesics. In their survey of Northern Territory Aboriginal communities, C. Watson et al. (1988) found that 76 per cent of Aborigines surveyed took analgesics and benzodiazepines, and again found that more women than men took tablets of this kind. Many anthropologists with field experience in Australia are aware of the prevalence of 'pain tablet' use among Aboriginal people, usually paracetamol and aspirin.

Tobacco use was also surveyed by the Northern Territory Drug and Alcohol Bureau team, who found that over half of those interviewed smoked tobacco and one quarter chewed tobacco. Pipes are commonly used by both men and women in some areas, and Arnhem Land people still use pipes of the Macassan type or made out of crab claw (Brady 1985*b*; Thomson 1939). Lake (1989) surveyed tobacco (as well as alcohol) use among 102 patients of the Aboriginal Medical Service in Adelaide, finding that 78 per cent of the men and 64 per cent of the women surveyed smoked tobacco. Men smoked an average of 22 cigarettes a day, while women averaged 20 cigarettes (Lake 1989, p. 20). Given that circulatory and respiratory diseases are among the leading causes of death of Aborigines (Watson, C., et al. 1988; Devanesen et al. 1986), and that 66 per cent of Aboriginal smokers in the Northern Territory are aged between 15 and 20, it is clear that tobacco use is a major preventable health problem.

From time to time there are reports of Aboriginal people ingesting unusual substances as drugs, for example, the consumption of duplicating fluid (Mitchell 1984), or soap powder (Watson 1983). The ethical problems associated with reporting such rare instances (and attendant problems of imitative behaviour) are not often addressed by the medical profession. D. Watson's communication (two cases), although published in a British journal, was reported one week later by the Northern Territory press (*Northern Territory News*, 12 March 1983).

The discussion has focused so far on use of licit drugs: alcohol, inhalants, kava, tobacco and analgesics. The use of illicit drugs by Aborigines is difficult to quantify, and there have been only anecdotal accounts of their use, reported for the most part in the press. The NSW Aboriginal Education Consultative Group survey of Aboriginal school students (NSWAECG 1986) included questions on the use of marijuana, tranquillisers, cocaine and heroin. Despite the vagueness of the 'other-directed' questions ('do you know any young Aboriginal people in your town or suburb who use any of these?'), 51 (19 per cent) replied that they knew someone using cocaine, and 53 (19 per cent) knew of someone using heroin. The National Aboriginal Health Strategy Working Party report (NAHSWP 1989, p. 201) asserts that heroin use became 'a significant problem in the Aboriginal communities in Sydney as early as 1982', that young Aborigines can obtain heroin easily and that the number of users is growing steadily. Aborigines who are part of prison populations, particularly in urban areas, have access to illicit drugs, as the reports from the Royal Commission into Aboriginal Deaths in Custody (RCADC) reveal (Muirhead 1989). Intravenous drug use in all sections of Australian society is obviously of major concern because of the risks of HIV infection. In this respect any growth in injection drug use among Aborigines deserves urgent attention.

Morbidity and mortality

Comparatively little is known about overall patterns of mortality and morbidity among Aboriginal people as a result of drug and alcohol use; the extent to which Aborigines are identified in hospital and mortality statistics varies from state to state as Thomson observes in chapter 2 in this volume. Nevertheless, a limited number of useful publications exist that document the sequelae of chronic drug and alcohol use.

Alcohol use

Devanesen et al. have compiled statistics on health indicators in the Northern Territory. These provide data on morbidity and mortality from a variety of causes that can be both directly and indirectly associated with drug and alcohol use. For example, deaths from injury and poisoning are often related to alcohol or drug use, as are diseases of the circulatory system. The authors devote a section to alcoholism, documenting mortality and hospital separation data (discharge rates), and note that Aborigines appear to have a higher than expected mortality from all alcohol-related diseases except suicide and self-inflicted injury (Devanesen et al. 1986, p. 244). This is surprising in view of many of the findings of the Royal Commission into Aboriginal Deaths in Custody, in which alcohol was implicated in a high proportion of accidental deaths and suicides (see also Reser 1989; Graham 1989). (The issue of Aboriginal suicides is discussed by Reser, chapter 6 in this volume.) Paul Wilson's popular account of the case of Alwyn Peter, a Queensland man who stabbed his girlfriend to death, notes that heavy alcohol use was associated with both homicides and self-inflicted injuries among Aborigines (Wilson, P., 1982). David Bradbury's film *State of shock*, also based on Peter's life, provides a graphic depiction of how alcohol affects the Weipa community (Langton 1989). Justice Muirhead, in his *Interim Report on the Royal Commission into Aboriginal Deaths in Custody*, observes:

The evidence before the commission...suggests that both in Australia and overseas alcohol is the single factor most consistently linked with deaths in police custody. Intoxication at the time of arrest or detention plays a predominant role in ensuing tragedies. The vulnerability of an intoxicated person...cannot be overemphasised. There is much medical evidence and material which shows that a person who is intoxicated or suffering from withdrawal may be under a great deal of stress, both physiological and psychological, and thereby at risk if unsupervised.

Muirhead 1988, p. 26

Epilepsy, heart disease, diabetes, hypoglycaemia and past and recent head injuries are just some of the overt causes of death noted by the RCADC; some of these were masked by intoxication; others were associated with years of heavy drinking. The RCADC has highlighted, among other things, the inadequate training of the police in the recognition of alcohol-related health problems.

Hospital separation rates for homicide and injury deliberately inflicted by others were found to be higher among Aborigines than among non-Aborigines in the Northern Territory (Devanesen 1986, p. 222). Harris et al. (1987) studied alcohol-related admissions to Bourke (NSW) hospital, comparing the rate of admission for Aboriginal and non-Aboriginal patients. They found that 25.4 per cent of all Aboriginal admissions were directly or indirectly alcohol-related, compared with 4.8 per cent of non-Aboriginal admissions. Trauma was the most common reason for Aboriginal alcohol-related admissions, followed by seizures and gastritis (Harris et al. 1987, p. 197). Between 1979 and 1986, 32 per cent of premature deaths (under 60 years of age) were due to trauma or seizures, according to findings by Thomson and Smith (1985) that showed that an unusually high proportion of such deaths were due to trauma. A study showing the differences in morbidity and mortality between adult Aborigines and adult non-Aborigines in New South Wales notes that the most frequent other significant health problem recorded in Aboriginal deaths was alcohol abuse, reported for 27 per cent of all deaths. Aboriginal relative mortality risks were greatest between the ages of 35 and 44, also the peak years for the reporting of alcohol use as a significant medical problem (Julienne et al. 1983, p. 6).

Brady and Palmer (1984) examined presentations at a community clinic for alcohol-related causes, and found that lacerations were the most common alcohol-related injury (45 per cent), followed by burns (32 per cent) (caused by drinkers rolling into or stepping on camp fires). Women sustained a high proportion of head injuries. Illness consultations included cases of pancreatitis, pneumonia and cirrhosis. Alcohol-related deaths constituted 30 per cent of all deaths in the community over a 10-year period (from violence, neglect, burns, motor vehicle accidents and illness).

The direct and indirect effects of alcohol use upon Aboriginal women are now coming to prominence. Harris et al. (1987) compared consumption figures with those of Kamien recorded 14 years previously, and concluded that the proportion of abstinent men had increased from 10 per cent to 31 per cent, while fewer women had become abstinent (from 71 per cent in 1971 to 55 per cent in 1985). While fewer Aboriginal women than men consume alcohol overall (Watson, C., et al. 1988; Kamien 1975; Brady and Palmer 1984), it is disturbing to note that hospital separations associated with homicide and injury have increased among Aboriginal women in the Northern Territory (Devanesen et al. 1986, p. 222), and at least one community-specific study found that more women than men had died as a result of alcohol-related violence (Brady and Palmer 1984). The extent of alcohol-related violence against Aboriginal women by their spouses and others is becoming increasingly apparent as Aboriginal people themselves voice their concerns. Bell and Ditton (1980), interviewing Aboriginal women for the customary law brief of the Australian Law Reform Commission, documented their concerns about violence against women and their criticisms of legal aid services, which were seen to protect men charged with such crimes (Bell and Ditton 1980, p. 17). McCorquodale's digest of major criminal cases involving Aborigines provides some interesting examples of legal argument surrounding customary law, the role of alcohol, and violence against women (McCorquodale 1987). The extent of alcohol-related injury to women is also documented by Barber et al. (1988) for Palm Island, Queensland, and evidenced by the expressed need for, and establishment of, Aboriginal women's refuges (for example, in Tennant Creek, Northern Territory).

Petrol sniffing and other substances

The use of petrol as an inhalant is having an increasing impact on the mortality and morbidity of young Aborigines. Health reports from Aboriginal health services reveal a high rate of hospitalisation among petrol sniffers for symptoms such as convulsions, lead toxicity, burns and trauma (Freeman 1985; NHC 1989). Although there is controversy among medical professionals about the extent and nature of permanent neurological damage as a result of tetraethyl lead—the heavy metal that is a component of leaded petrol—local health services note permanent impairment in at least some chronic petrol sniffers. Organo-lead compounds are readily absorbed through the respiratory and gastrointestinal tract and through the skin, with the brain being the organ most sensitive to lead toxicity. Kaelen et al. (1986) and Rischbieth et al. (1987) report on cases of encephalopathy in Aboriginal petrol sniffers. Recovery from lead toxicity is, however, reported in the literature (Seshia et al. 1978; Brown 1983). Petrol contains many other toxic components—the aromatic hydrocarbons—which are associated with polyneuropathy and with 'sudden sniffing death' in which spontaneous cardiac arrhythmia can occur (Bass 1970; Coulehan et al. 1983).

Until recently, mortality as a result of chronic petrol sniffing has been extremely difficult to assess. With the establishment of a nationwide system of reporting deaths due to volatile substance abuse (coordinated by the National Drug Abuse Information Centre), coroners' records are now perused annually by state and territory-based drug and alcohol authorities. The official number of deaths associated with petrol sniffing between 1980 and 1988 is 20 (from information provided by the National Drug Abuse Information Centre 1989). However, more detailed documentation

(Brady 1989*a*) brings the number of Aboriginal deaths associated with petrol to 35 (34 males and 1 female) in the same period, the mean age of those who died being 19.22 years. It is probably safe to assume that other petrol-related deaths occur that do not find their way into the data collection system. Significant factors that may influence mortality associated with petrol sniffing are the health and nutritional status of users (Grandjean, 1984; Mahaffey 1985). There is considerable evidence to show that nutritional status (particularly the inadequate intake of certain vitamins and minerals) as well as erratic food intake, affect an individual's susceptibility to lead toxicity. These research findings are reviewed by Brady (1989*b*).

Petrol sniffers are treated by some hospital physicians with chelating agents (see Morice et al. 1981 for details), which are chemical compounds that bind heavy metals including lead. The treatment, if administered intravenously or intramuscularly, requires intensive care in hospital. One chelating agent, penicillamine, can be administered orally and is used to treat outpatients. There is some controversy among health professionals about the efficacy of chelating agents in the treatment of organic lead poisoning, and their use varies from state to state. Petrol sniffers in Canada and elsewhere, primarily Indian and Inuit (Eskimo) patients, were, until recently, treated by chelation (Boeckx et al. 1977).

To date only one pilot study has been undertaken to assess the health implications of kava use, by Mathews et al. (1988), mentioned earlier. Their findings are suggestive of minor health problems such as scaly skin and low weight, as well as the possibility of toxicity to liver cells. Health workers report informally that kava users can develop scaly skin, and puffiness of the face.

Prevention and intervention strategies

Many existing drug and alcohol treatment programs run for and by Aboriginal people use the Alcoholics Anonymous approach, employ ex-alcoholics who are Aboriginal, and rarely require formal training in treatment or clinical rehabilitation on the part of staff. For these and other administrative reasons, their success rate appears to be poor, as indeed are the national success rates for rehabilitation (Wilson n.d.). It appears that the lack of trained staff is compounded by a lack of professional support and advice from federal and state governments. There has also been a history of state–federal bickering over who should fund services for Aboriginal people.

Nevertheless some programs have had positive outcomes, particularly Benelongs Haven in New South Wales (Bryant and Carroll 1978; Miller 1982). Val Bryant, who developed Benelongs Haven, stresses that Aborigines become alcoholics in groups, whereas white people become alcoholics one by one. 'The Aboriginal can get out of his [sic] alcoholic problems', she writes, 'but he must realise that he cannot go into alcoholism the Aboriginal way (IN A GROUP) and out the white man's way (ONE BY ONE)' (Bryant and Carroll 1978). In this way the group approach has achieved success, and new programs started as a result.

Associated with the disease model of substance abuse (or chemical dependency, as it is known), the Holyoake model of 'co-dependency' is increasingly in use with Aboriginal drug and alcohol users. This model makes use of concepts developed from Alcoholics Anonymous, and Al-Anon and the Hazleden Institute in the USA, and asserts that 'chemical dependency is a progressive disease...which is characterised by highly developed patterns of denial and delusion in both the dependant and those close to him or her' (CAAPS unpub.). The model, enacted by family workers based in Aboriginal communities (particularly in the Northern Territory), has at its core the notion of 'tough love', and diverts attention away from the user, and towards the family members and others who inadvertently support the user. Residential programs are also offered, and Aboriginal people attend centres in Darwin and Perth from outlying communities. In the north, co-dependency counselling is directed at the use of alcohol, petrol and kava among Aborigines. While it is undoubtedly true that family members may support the drug/alcohol use of another (in the manner described by Merv Gibson, quoted earlier), the notion of tough love is decidedly difficult for Aboriginal people to enact; there have been suggestions that it is culturally inappropriate for Aboriginal people.

Another form of direct intervention has occurred in central Australia, with particular emphasis on petrol sniffing. The Healthy Aboriginal Life Team (HALT) has developed a family-based counselling and intervention program in which the team

Figure 5.4 *One of the posters commissioned for the federal government's Drug Offensive campaign uses 'x-ray' figures to show the effects of alcohol and smoking on pregnant women in a Top End coastal setting. (M. McMahon/Redback Graphix)*

attempts to mobilise Aboriginal family members who are not fulfilling their obligations to supervise and care for young petrol users. Franks, a member of the team, has published an article describing the work of HALT (Franks 1989). As well as direct one-to-one counselling, the team has branched into prevention strategies, using Aboriginal art depicting the spread of alcohol and petrol use and of AIDS. These have been reproduced and distributed as colourful posters to Aboriginal communities.

The use of such media aimed specifically at Aboriginal people around Australia has gained currency in recent years. The Drug Offensive funded workshops involving Aboriginal health workers and a graphic artist, which produced health messages in the form of illustrations (and minimal written content) for Aboriginal audiences. These posters cover the use of petrol, kava and alcohol, drinking and smoking in pregnancy, and AIDS. They are distributed by the Commonwealth Department of Community Services and Health (Frape et al. 1988; Spark and Mills 1988). Posters, T-shirts, videos and TV advertisements (on Aboriginal-run networks) with messages about drug and alcohol use are now an established part of prevention efforts aimed at Aboriginal people. Whether or not these media-based approaches will bring about change is an issue still under discussion; so far, few evaluation attempts have been made.

In contrast with North American indigenous peoples, who have integrated traditional healing practices into alcohol rehabilitation programs, there seem to be few, if any, traditional mechanisms available for Aboriginal Australians in this context. North American peoples use sweat lodge ceremonies for purification, drumming, herbalists, shamans and medicine men, among other techniques, in the treatment of alcohol abuse, although as Wiebel-Orlando points out, neither program directors nor researchers studying the programs know what works systematically or consistently fails within these treatment programs. 'We still do not know if any sort of alcoholism intervention, conventional or indigenous, works at all or for long periods of time', she observes (Wiebel-Orlando 1989, p. 152). In two critical articles, Wiebel-Orlando addresses ethnic diversity in treatment settings, the efficacy or otherwise of 'native healers' and highlights the sometimes uncritical stance taken by anthropologists in their assessment of indigenous healing methods (Wiebel-Orlando 1987, 1989).

Conclusion: community motivation

Despite some lapses, there has been a welcome diversification of the approaches taken to Aboriginal drug and alcohol use over the last 30 years. Social scientists have come to focus on these issues as specific studies, rather than as addenda to other issues, and this has provided a deepening of our understanding of the lived reality of drug and alcohol use for Aboriginal people. Aborigines themselves are becoming more assertive and critical in their approach to these issues, moving away from a position that denies personal responsibility and the potential for change. The social and physical costs of substance abuse are still high, and the intensification of some drug uses (petrol sniffing, for example, and perhaps illegal drugs) are cause for concern. Community-based programs, supported by Aboriginal organisations, the churches and government, continue to evolve, and this process has been aided by the surge of interest in locally produced audiovisual media for use in prevention and awareness campaigns. Community involvement in and support for alcohol and drug intervention is undoubtedly crucial: several of the successes and failures may be traced to the strength or weakness of local commitment.

While health service delivery has a role to play in both prevention and treatment of drug and alcohol problems, health professionals may have only limited influence on behaviour change. In a provocative discussion of community-based health programs, Rifkin distinguishes between the 'top down' and 'bottom up' approaches to their development. She observes that both the medical approach and the health services approach are examples of 'top down' approaches to community participation. 'The third approach believes that people's perceptions of health and their motivation to change health care are the critical factors' (Rifkin 1986, p. 243). She suggests that community participation cannot be viewed as an 'intervention' to improve health care, because its inputs and outcomes are not easily defined. She stresses that motivation, not resource allocation, is the major ingredient, and that community participation grows out of specific situations (1986, p. 245).

These, then, are the dynamic factors now at work within Aboriginal populations. While some groups are still tolerating the social stresses and medical emergencies generated by the drug and alcohol use of their members, others are increasingly motivated to act, to lobby governments, to initiate local awareness campaigns, or to support legal restrictions on availability. For their part, researchers are becoming acutely aware of the conflicting pressures that accompany the need to 'tell it like it is' and not to deflate the problems associated with drug and alcohol use, while conforming to ethical and research guidelines established by Aboriginal organisations who control access to those under scrutiny. By contracting their own researchers, both medical and social scientists, Aboriginal organisations have shown that they value the contribution that can be made by research, be it ethnographic, epidemiological or clinical in orientation.

References

Alama, K., and Whitney, S. (1990), 'Ka wai kau o Maleka. "Water from America": the intoxication of the Hawai'ian people', *Contemporary Drug Problems* 17(**2**), pp. 161–94.

Albrecht, P. G. E. (1974), 'The social and psychological reasons for the alcohol problem among Aborigines', in B. Hetzel (ed.), *Better health for Aborigines*, University of Queensland Press, St Lucia, pp. 36–41.

Alexander, K. (1985), 'What is kava?' in K. P. Larkins, D. McDonald and C. Watson (eds), *2nd National Drug Institute proceedings; alcohol and drug use in a changing society*, Alcohol and Drug Foundation, Canberra, pp. 117–130.

Alexander, K., Watson, C., and Fleming, J. (1987), *Kava in the north: a research report on current patterns of kava use in Arnhem Land Aboriginal communities*, Australian National University, North Australia Research Unit, Darwin.

American Psychiatric Association (1987), *Diagnostic and statistical manual of mental disorders (DSM-III-R)*, 3rd edn, revised, American Psychiatric Association, Washington, DC.

Angas, G. F (1847), *Savage life and scenes in Australia and New Zealand*, Smith Elder, London.

Australia, Senate Select Committee (various dates), Hansard reports of evidence to the Senate Select Committee on Volatile Substance Fumes.

Backhouse, J. (1843), *A narrative of a visit to the Australian colonies*, Hamilton, Adams, London.

Bain, M. S. (1974), 'Alcohol use and traditional social control in Aboriginal Society', in B. S. Hetzel (ed.), *Better health for Aborigines?* University of Queensland Press, St Lucia.

Barber, J. G., Punt, J., and Albers, J. (1988), 'Alcohol and power on Palm Island', *Australian Journal of Social Issues* **23** (2), pp. 87–101.

Barnes, G. (1985), 'Gasoline sniffing', *Revue Canadienne d'Economie Familiale* **35** (3), pp. 144–58.

Basedow, H. (1929), *The Australian Aboriginal*, F. W. Preece & Sons, Adelaide.

Bass, M. (1970), 'Sudden sniffing death', *Journal of the American Medical Association* **212** (12), pp. 2075–9.

Beauvais, F., and Boeff, S. (1985), 'Drug and alcohol abuse: intervention in American Indian communities', *International Journal of the Addictions* **20** (1), pp. 139–71.

Beck, E. J. (1985), *The enigma of Aboriginal health: interaction between biological, social and economic factors in Alice Springs town camps*, Australian Institute of Aboriginal Studies, Canberra.

Beckett, J. (1965), 'Aborigines, alcohol and assimilation', in M. Reay (ed.), *Aborigines now*, Angus and Robertson, Sydney, pp. 32–47.

Beckett, J. (1984), 'Comments on Robin Room's "Alcohol and ethnography: a case of problem deflation" ', *Current Anthropology* **25** (2), pp. 169–91.

Bell, D., and Ditton, P. (1980), *Law: the old and the new. Aboriginal women in Central Australia speak out*, Aboriginal History, Canberra.

Boeckx, R., Postl, B., and Coodin, F. (1977), 'Gasoline sniffing and tetraethyl lead poisoning in children', *Pediatrics* **60** (2), pp. 140–5.

Bonnheim, M., and Korman, M. (1985), 'Family interaction and acculturation in Mexican-American inhalant users', *Journal of Psychoactive Drugs* **17** (1), pp. 25–33.

Bott, E. (1987), 'The kava ceremonial as a dream structure', in M. Douglas (ed.), *Constructive drinking: perspectives on drink from anthropology*, Cambridge University Press, Cambridge, pp. 182–204.

Brady, M. (1985*a*), 'Aboriginal youth and the juvenile justice system', in A. Borowsky and J. M. Murray (eds), *Juvenile delinquency in Australia*, Methuen, Sydney, pp. 112–25.

Brady, M. (1985*b*), *Children without ears: petrol sniffing in Australia*, Drug and Alcohol Services Council, Adelaide.

Brady, M. (1988), *Where the beer truck stopped: drinking in a northern Australian town*, Australian National University North Australia Research Unit, Darwin.

Brady, M. (1989*a*), *Heavy metal: the social meaning of petrol sniffing in Australia*, Report to Research Into Drug Abuse Advisory Committee, Department of Community Services and Health, Australian Institute of Aboriginal Studies, Canberra.

Brady, M. (1989*b*), 'Lead toxicity and nutritional factors: some implications for petrol sniffers', *Aboriginal Health Bulletin* **12**, pp. 15–18.

Brady, M. (1989*c*), 'Number One for Action', *Australian Aboriginal Studies* 1989/1, pp. 61–62.

Brady, M. (1990), 'Indigenous and government attempts to control alcohol use among Australian Aborigines', *Contemporary Drug Problems* **17** (2), pp. 195–220.

Brady, M., and Palmer, K. (1984), *Alcohol in the outback*, Australian National University North Australia Research Unit, Darwin.

Brown, A. (1983), 'Petrol sniffing lead encephalopathy', *New Zealand Medical Journal* **96** (733), pp. 421–2.

Brown, V. A., Manderson, D., O'Callaghan, M., and Thompson, R. (1986), *Our daily fix: drugs in Australia*, Australian National University Press, Canberra.

Bryant, V. (1987), 'Female alcoholism', *Aboriginal Health Worker* **11** (2), pp. 20–1.

Bryant, V., and Carroll, J. (1978), 'Aboriginal alcoholism—where are we going? White man's way or black man's way?' *Aboriginal Health Worker* **2** (4), pp. xix–xxi.

Calley, M. J. C. (1957), 'Race relations on the north coast of New South Wales' *Oceania* **27**, pp. 190–209.

Carr, D. J., and Carr, S. G. M. (eds) (1981), *People and plants in Australia*, Academic Press, Sydney.

Cawte, J. (1974), *Medicine is the law: studies in the psychological anthropology of Australian tribal societies*, Hawaii University Press, Honolulu.

Cawte, J. (1985), 'Psychoactive substances of the south seas: betel, kava and pituri', *Australia and New Zealand Journal of Psychiatry* **19**, pp. 83–7.

Cawte, J. (1988), 'Macabre effects of a 'cult' for kava', *Medical Journal of Australia* **148**, June 6, pp. 545–546.

CEIDA (Centre for Education and Information on Drugs and Alcohol) (1986), *An Australian guide to drug issues*, AGPS, Canberra.

Chief Protector of Aborigines (1911), *Annual Report for the year 1910*, Brisbane.

Clark, A. J. (1984), *Petrol sniffing: report of a survey conducted in the Pitjantjatjara area*, Uniting Church Northern Synod, AADS, Darwin.

Clarke, P. A. (1988), 'Aboriginal use of subterranean plant parts in southern South Australia', *Records of South Australian Museum* **22** (1), pp. 73–86.

Cleland, J. B. (1957), 'Our natives and the vegetation of southern Australia', *Mankind* **5** (4), pp. 149–162.

Cole, K. (1980), *Dick Harris: missionary to the Aborigines*, Keith Cole Publications, Victoria.

Collmann, J. (1979), 'Social order and the exchange of liquor: a theory of drinking among Australian Aborigines', *Journal of Anthropological Research* **35** (2), pp. 208–24.

Collmann, J. (1988), *Fringe-dwellers and welfare: the Aboriginal response to bureaucracy*, University of Queensland Press, St Lucia.

Coulehan, J., Hirsch, W., Brillman, J., Sanandria, J., Welty, T. K., Colaiaco, P., Koros, A., and Lober, A. (1983), 'Gasoline sniffing and lead toxicity in Navaho adolescents', *Pediatrics* **71** (1), pp. 113–17.

Dalton-Morgan, D. (1978), 'Petrol sniffing: Papunya...a community solution', *Forum. Australian Crime Prevention Quarterly Journal* **1** (1), pp. 32–3.

Department of Health (Drugs of Dependence Branch) (1985), *Abuse of volatile substances. Information paper 5: Petrol inhalation*, AGPS, Canberra.

Devanesen, D., Furber, M., Hampton, D., Honari, M., Kinmonth, N., and Peach, H. G. (1986), *Health indicators in the Northern Territory*, Northern Territory Department of Health, Darwin.

Dingle, A. E. (1980), ' "The truly magnificent thirst": an historical survey of Australian drinking habits', *Historical Studies* **19** (75), pp. 227–49.

Douglas, W. (1988), letter, *Medical Journal of Australia* **149**, 19 September, pp. 341–2.

Downing, J. (1985), 'Petrol sniffing: treat the causes not the symptoms', *Aboriginal Health Worker* **9** (3), pp. 38–43.

Dozier, E. P. (1966), 'Problem drinking among American Indians: the role of sociocultural deprivation, *Quarterly Journal of Studies on Alcohol* **27**, pp. 72–87.

Duncan-Kemp, A. M. (1934), *Our sandhill country*, Angus and Robertson, Sydney.

Eastwell, H. D. (1978). 'Signs of Aboriginal stress: eating clay and sniffing petrol', *Aboriginal Health Worker* **2** (4), pp. 8–11.

Eastwell, H. D. (1979*a*), 'Boys and girls sniffing petrol', *Aboriginal Health Worker* **3** (3), pp. 32–3.

Eastwell, H. D. (1979*b*), 'Petrol inhalation in Aboriginal towns. Its remedy: the homelands movement', *Medical Journal of Australia* **8** September, pp. 221–4.

Eastwell, H. D. (1984), 'Petrol and lead', *Aboriginal Health Worker* **8** (2), pp. 20–2.

Eastwell, H. D. (1985), 'Elevated lead levels in petrol "sniffers" ', *Medical Journal of Australia* **143**, 28 October, pp. S63–S64 (special supplement).

Eastwell, H. D. (1988), 'Aspects of drug use and Aboriginal culture', *Drug Issues Affecting Aboriginal Australians*, Technical Information Bulletin no. 79, AGPS, Canberra, pp. 1–7.

Eastwell, H. D., Thomas, B. J., and Thomas, B. W. (1983), 'Skeletal lead burden in Aborigine petrol sniffers', *Lancet*, 27 August, pp. 524–5 (letter).

Eggleston, E. (1974), 'Legal controls on alcohol', in B. Hetzel (ed.), *Better health for Aborigines?* University of Queensland Press, St Lucia, pp. 53–65.

Eggleston, E. (1976), *Fear, favour or affection*, ANU Press, Canberra.

Elkin, A. P. (1958), *Aborigines and citizenship*, Association for the Protection of Native Races, Sydney.

Evans, R., Saunders, K., and Cronin, K. (1975), *Exclusion, exploitation and extermination: race relations in colonial Queensland*, ANZ Book Company, Sydney.

Everett, M. W., Waddell, J. O., and Heath, D. B. (eds) (1976), *Cross-cultural approaches to the study of alcohol: an interdisciplinary perspective*, Mouton, The Hague.

Folds, R. (1987), *Whitefella school*, Allen and Unwin, Sydney.

Franks, C. (1989), 'Preventing petrol sniffing in Aboriginal communities', *Community Health Studies* **13** (1), pp. 14–22.

Frape, G., Mills, P., Sago, P., and Smallwood, G. (1988), 'Community action: a cooperative approach to Aboriginal-Islander workshops to develop materials on drug and alcohol and AIDS information', *Aboriginal Health Worker* **12** (2), pp. 44–7.

Freeman, P. (1985), 'Petrol sniffing in Amata, South Australia', in Nganampa Health Council (ed.), *Health report*, Nganampa Health Council, pp. 88–97.

Gerrard, G. (1988), 'Use of kava in two Aboriginal settlements', in J. Prescott and G. McCall (eds), *Kava: use and abuse in Australia and the South Pacific*, National Drug and Alcohol Research Centre, Monograph no. 5., University of New South Wales, Sydney.

Gibson, M. (unpub.), 'Anthropology and tradition: a contemporary Aboriginal viewpoint', paper presented to ANZAAS conference, 'Peoples of the North', Townsville, Queensland, 1987.

Gordon, P., Torres, M., Parker, G., and Drury, C. (1987), 'The Kimberley delegation in the Northern Territory', *Aboriginal Health Worker* **11** (4), pp. 32–7.

Graham, D. (1989), *Dying Inside*, Allen and Unwin, Sydney.

Grandjean, P. (1984), 'Organolead exposures and intoxications', in P. Grandjean (ed.), *Biological effects of organolead compounds*, CRC Press, USA.

Graves, T. D. (1967), 'Acculturation, access and alcohol in a tri-ethnic community', *American Anthropologist* **69**, pp. 306–21.

Gray, A. (1985), 'Limits for demographic parameters of Aboriginal populations', *Australian Aboriginal Studies* 1985/1, pp. 22–7.

Gray, D., Isaacs, R., and Willaway, G. (1981), 'Social conditions and Aboriginal Alcohol use in Collie', WA Alcohol and Drug Authority, Perth.

Hamilton, M. (1985), 'Drinking and drinking related problems—a total community', in K. P. Larkins, D. McDonald and C. Watson (eds), *2nd National Drug Institute (proceedings): alcohol and drug use in a changing society*, Alcohol and Drug Foundation Australia, Canberra, pp. 75–95.

Harris, M., Sutherland, D., Cutter, G., and Ballangarry, L., (1987), 'Alcohol related hospital admissions in a country town', *Australian Drug & Alcohol Review* **6**,195–8.

Hayward, L., and Kickett, M. (1988), 'An analysis of morbidity and mortality in 1981–1986 and the prevalence of petrol sniffing in Aboriginal children in the Western Desert Region in 1987', Drug Data Collection Unit, WA Health Department, Perth.

Healy, B., Turpin, T., and Hamilton, M. (1985), 'Aboriginal drinking: a case study in inequality and disadvantage', *Australian Journal of Social Issues* **20** (3), pp. 191–208.

Heath, D. B. (1975), 'A critical review of ethnographic studies of alcohol use', in R. J. Gibbins et al. (eds), *Research advances in alcohol and drug problems*, vol. 2, John Wiley, New York, pp. 1–92.

Heath, D. B. (1987*a*), 'A decade of development in the anthropological study of alcohol use, 1970–1980', in M. Douglas (ed.), *Constructive drinking: perspectives on drink from anthropology*, Cambridge University Press, Cambridge, pp. 16–69.

Heath, D. B. (1987*b*), 'Anthropology and alcohol studies: current issues', *Annual Review of Anthropology* **16**, pp. 99–120.

Heath, D. B. (1989), 'American Indians and alcohol: epidemiological and sociocultural research', in D. L. Spiegler, D. A. Tate, S. S. Aitken and C. M. Christian (eds), *Alcohol use among US ethnic minorities*, NIAA Monograph no. 18, Maryland, DHHS publication no. (ADM)89-1435, pp. 207–22.

Hetzel, B. S. (1975), 'Religion and change in an age of rapid social change', in I. Pilowsky (ed.), *Cultures in collision*, Australian National Association for Mental Health, Adelaide, pp. 274–81.

Hope, D., (1987), 'Policing in South Australia: a transcultural problem', in K. M. Hazlehurst (ed.), *Ivory scales: black Australia and the law*, New South Wales University Press, Sydney, pp. 93–105.

HRA (Historical Records of Australia) (various dates), Governors' despatches to and from England, Library Committee of the Commonwealth Parliament, Sydney.

HRSCAA (House of Representatives Standing Committee on Aboriginal Affairs) (1977), *Alcohol problems of Aborigines: final report*, AGPS, Canberra.

Hunt, H. (1981), 'Alcoholism among Aboriginal people', *Medical Journal of Australia* **1** (2), 2 May, special supplement, pp. 1–3.

Hunter, E. M. (1989), 'Commissions and omissions: the wider context of Aboriginal suicides in custody', *Medical Journal of Australia* **151**, August 21, pp. 218–23.

Julienne, A., Smith, L., Thomson, N., and Gray, A. (1983), *A summary of Aboriginal mortality in NSW country regions 1980–81*, NSW Department of Health, Sydney.

Kaelen, C., Harper, C., and Vieira, B. (1986), 'Acute encephalopathy and death due to petrol sniffing: neuropathological findings', *Australian and New Zealand Journal of Medicine* **16** (6), pp. 804–7.

Kamien, M. (1975), 'Aborigines and alcohol: intake, effects and social implications in a rural community in western New South Wales', *Medical Journal of Australia* **1**, pp. 291–8.

Kamien, M. (1978), *The dark people of Bourke: a study of planned social change*, AIAS, Canberra.

'Kava: a challenge to alcohol' (1986), *Aboriginal Health Worker* **10** (1), pp. 12–24.

Kunitz, S. J., and Levy, J. E. (1974), 'Changing ideas of alcohol use among Navaho Indians', *Quarterly Journal of Studies on Alcohol* **35** (1), pp. 243–59.

Kunitz, S. J., Levy, J. E., Odoroff, C. L., and Bollinger, J. (1971), 'The epidemiology of alcoholic cirrhosis in two south-western Indian tribes', *Quarterly Journal of Studies on Alcohol* **32** (3), pp. 706–20.

Lake, P. (1989), 'Alcohol and cigarette use by urban Aboriginal people', *Aboriginal Health Bulletin* **11**, May, pp. 20–2.

Landry, M. (1987), 'Addiction diagnostic update: DSM-III-R psychoactive substance use disorders', *Journal of Psychoactive Drugs* **19** (4), pp. 379–81.

Langton, M. (1989), 'Seeing the grog for what it is', *Land Rights News* **2** (13), p. 29.

Larsen, K. S. (1980), 'Aboriginal group identification and problem drinking', *Australian Psychologist* **15** (3), pp. 385–92.

Lindstrom, L. (ed.) (1987), *Drugs in western Pacific societies. relations of substance*, Association for Social Anthropology in Oceania, Monograph no. 11, University Press of America, Lanham.

Liversidge, Professor (1880), 'The alkaloid from piturie', *Royal Society of New South Wales Journal of Proceedings* **14**, pp. 123–32.

Lyon, P. (1990), *What everybody knows about Alice: a report on the impact of alcohol use on Alice Springs*, Tangentyere Council, Alice Springs.

MacAndrew, C., and Edgerton, R. B. (1969), *Drunken comportment: a social explanation*, Aldine Publishing, Chicago.

McCarthy, F. D. (1957), *Australia's Aborigines: their life and culture*, Colorgravure Publication, Melbourne.

McClay, D., and Christie, M. (1980), 'Petrol sniffing: what the teacher ought to do', *Aboriginal Child at School* **8** (5), pp. 39–42.

McCorquodale, J. (1987), *Aborigines and the law: a digest*. Aboriginal Studies Press, Canberra.

Macknight, C. C. (1976), *The voyage to Marege*, Melbourne University Press, Melbourne.

McKnight, D. (1986), 'Fighting in an Australian Aboriginal supercamp', in D. Riches (ed.), *The anthropology of violence*, Basil Blackwell, Oxford, pp. 136–63.

Mahaffey, K. R. (1985), 'Factors modifying susceptibility to lead toxicity', in K. R. Mahaffey (ed.), *Dietary and environmental lead: human health effects*, Elsevier Science Publications, Amsterdam.

Manderson, D. (1987), *'Proscription and prescription: Commonwealth government opiate policy 1905–1937*, AGPS, Canberra.

Marinovitch, N., Larsson, O., and Barber, K. (1976), 'Comparative metabolism rates of ethanol in adults of Aboriginal and European descent', *Medical Journal of Australia* **1**, special supplement 6, pp. 44–6.

Marshall, M. (1979), *Weekend warriors: alcohol in a Micronesian culture*, Mayfield Publishing, Palo Alto.

Marshall, M. (ed.) (1982), *Through a glass darkly: beer and modernization in Papua New Guinea*, Institute of Applied Social and Economic Research, Monograph 18, Boroko, Papua New Guinea.

Marshall, M. (1987), 'An overview of drugs in Oceania', in L. Lindstrom (ed.), *Drugs in western Pacific societies: relations of substance*, University Press of America, Lanham, pp. 13–50.

Mathews, J. D., Riley, M. D., Fejo, L., Munoz, E., Milus, N. R., Gardner, I. D., Powers, J. R., Ganygulpa, E., and Gununuwawuy, B. J. (1988), 'Effects of the heavy usage of kava on physical health: summary of a pilot survey in an Aboriginal community', *Medical Journal of Australia* **148**, June 6, pp. 548–55.

May, P. A. (1977), 'Explanations of native American drinking: a literature review', *Plains Anthropologist* **22**, pp. 223–32.

May, P. A. (1982), 'Substance abuse and American Indians: prevalence and susceptibility', *International Journal of the Addictions* **17** (7),pp. 1185–209.

Millar, C. J., and Leung, J. M. S. (1974), 'Aboriginal alcohol consumption in South Australia', in R. M. Berndt (ed.), *A question of choice: an Australian Aboriginal dilemma*, University of Western Australia Press, Perth, pp. 91–5.

Miller, C. (1982), 'A haven for alcoholics', *Australian Medical Journal*, 11 December, pp. 602–4.

Miller, M.-E., and Ware, J. (1989), *Mass-media alcohol and drug campaigns: a consideration of relevant issues*, National Campaign Against Drug Abuse Monograph Series no. 9, AGPS, Canberra.

Mills, P. (1985), 'Aboriginal issues workshop', in K. P. Larkins, D. McDonald and C. Watson (eds), *2nd National Drug Institute (proceedings): alcohol and drug use in a changing society*, Alcohol and Drug Foundation Australia, Canberra, pp. 105–8.

Mitchell, J. (1984), 'Methanol from the school', *Aboriginal Health Worker* **8** (2), special issue: 'Substance abuse disorders', pp. 25–32.

Morice, R. D., Swift, H., and Brady, M. (1981), *Petrol sniffing among Aboriginal Australians: a resource manual*, Alcohol and Drug Foundation Australia, Canberra.

Muirhead,J. H. (1988), *The interim report on the Royal Commission into Aboriginal Deaths in Custody*, AGPS, Canberra.

Muirhead, J. H. (1989), *Report of the inquiry into the death of Kingsley Richard Dixon, Royal Commission into Aboriginal Deaths in Custody*, AGPS, Canberra.

Myers, F. D. (1986), *Pintupi country, Pintupi self: sentiment, place and politics among Western Desert Aborigines*, Smithsonian Institute and AIAS, Washington and Canberra.

NAHSWP (National Aboriginal Health Strategy Working Party) (1989), *A national Aboriginal health strategy*, National Aboriginal Health Strategy Working Party, Canberra.

Nathan, P., and Japanangka, D. L. (1983), *Health business*, Heinemann Education Australia, Victoria.

National Council of Maori Nurses (1988), *Te hunga wahine te Wapiro*, The Place of Alcohol in the Lives of New Zealand Women Project, report no. 14, Department of Anthropology, University of Auckland, Auckland.

Neich, S., and Park, J. (1988), *The place of alcohol in the lives of some Samoan women in Auckland*, The Place of Alcohol In The Lives of New Zealand Women Project, report no. 12, Department of Anthropology, University of Auckland, Auckland.

(NHC) Nganampa Health Council (1989), *Health report 1986–1987*, Nganampa Health Council, Alice Springs.

Nichols, T. (1985), 'Petrol sniffing: now on TV', *Aboriginal Health Worker* **9** (3), pp. 44–5.

NSWAECG (NSW Aboriginal Education Consultative Group) (1986), *1986 survey of drug and alcohol use by Aboriginal school students in New South Wales*, 84/38.1, NSWAECG, Sydney.

Nurcombe, B. (1974), 'Petrol inhalation in Arnhem Land', in B. S. Hetzel (ed.), *Better health for Aborigines?* University of Queensland Press, St Lucia.

Nurcombe, B., Bianchi, G. N., Money, J., and Cawte, J. (1970), 'A hunger for stimuli: the psychosocial background of petrol inhalation', *British Journal of Medical Psychology* **43**, pp. 367–74.

Nurcombe, B., Bianchi, G. N.,Money, J., aand Cawte, J. (1973), 'A hunger for stimuli', in G. E. Kearney (ed.), *The psychology of Aboriginal Australians*, John Wiley, Sydney.

O'Connor, R. (1984), Alcohol and contingent drunkenness in central Australia', *Australian Journal of Social Issues* **19** (3), pp. 173–83.

Palmer, K., and McKenna, C. (1978), *Somewhere between black and white: the story of an Aboriginal Australian*, Macmillan, Melbourne.

Peele, S. (1985), *The meaning of addiction: compulsive experience and its interpretation*, Lexington Books, Massachusetts.

Phillips, W. (1980), ' "Six o'clock swill": the introduction of early closing of hotel bars in Australia', *Historical Studies* **19** (75), pp. 250–66.

Plomley, N. J. B. (1966), *Friendly mission: the Tasmanian journals and papers of George Augustus Robinson, 1829–1934*, Tasmanian Historical Research Association, Hobart.

Powell, K. (1988), *Drinking and alcohol in colonial Australia 1788–1901 for the eastern colonies*, National Campaign Against Drug Abuse, Monograph 3, AGPS, Canberra.

Prescott, J., and McCall, G. (1988), *Kava: use and abuse in Australia and the South Pacific*, National Drug and Alcohol Research Centre, Monograph 5, University of New South Wales, Sydney.

Read, P., and Japaljarri, E. J. (1978), 'The price of tobacco: the journey of the Warlmala to Wave Hill,1928', *Aboriginal History* **2** (2), pp. 140–8.

Reser, J. (1989), 'Aboriginal deaths in custody and social construction: a response to the view that there is no such thing as Aboriginal suicide', *Australian Aboriginal Studies* 1989/2, 43–50.

Richards, J., Binns, C. W., Blaze-Temple, D., Dowling, C., and Logan, J. (1989), *Terms and definitions for use in drug-related research in Australia*, National Centre for Research into the Prevention of Drug Abuse, Curtin University of Technology, Perth.

Rifkin, S. B. (1986), 'Lessons from community participation in health programmes', *Health Policy and Planning* **1** (3), pp. 240–9.

Rischbieth, R. H., Thompson, G. N., Hamilton-Bruce, A., Purdie, G. H., and Peters, J. H. (1987), 'Acute encephalopathy following petrol sniffing in two Aboriginal patients', *Clinical and Experimental Neurology* **23**, pp. 191–4.

Rogers, G. (1980), 'Petrol sniffing: a barrier to learning', *Pivot (SA Education Department)* **6** (4), pp. 24–5.

Room, R. (1984), 'Alcohol and ethnography: a case of problem deflation'? *Current Anthropology* **25** (2), pp. 169–78.

Sackett, L. (1977), 'Liquor and the law', in R. M. Berndt (ed.), *Aborigines and Change*, AIAS, Canberra, pp. 90–9.

Sackett, L. (1988), 'Resisting arrests: drinking, development and discipline in a desert context', *Social Analysis* **24**, December, pp. 66–77.

Sansom, B. (1980), *The camp at Wallaby Cross: Aboriginal fringe-dwellers in Darwin*, AIAS, Canberra.

Sargent, G. (1977), 'Petrol sniffing in East Arnhem Land: a resume', report by Welfare Officer Nhulunbuy, Northern Territory Department of Health, Darwin.

Seshia, S., Rajani, K., Boeckx, R., and Chow, P. (1978), 'The neurological manifestations of the chronic inhalation of leaded gasoline', *Developmental Medicine and Child Neurology* **20**, pp. 323–34.

Shulgin, A. T. (1973), 'The narcotic pepper—the chemistry and pharmacology of *Piper methysticum* and related species', *Bulletin on Narcotics*, **25** (2), pp. 59–74.

Simmons, L. (1988), 'The grog story: information paper for Central Australian Aboriginal Congress', Central Australian Aboriginal Congress, Alice Springs.

Skowron, S., and Smith, D. I. (1986), 'Survey of homelessness, alcohol consumption and related problems among Aboriginals in the Hedland area', Alcohol and Drug Authority, Perth.

Smith, D. I., Singh, H., Singh, M. N., and Skowron, S. (n.d.) 'Alcohol consumption and crime in two Aboriginal communities', Alcohol and Drug Authority, Perth.

Spark, R., and Mills, P. (1988), 'Promoting Aboriginal health on television in the Northern Territory: a bi-cultural approach', *Drug Education Journal of Australia* **2** (3), pp. 191–8.

Spencer, D. J. (1988), 'Transitional alcoholism—the Australian Aboriginal model', *Drug Issues Affecting Aboriginal Australians*, Technical Information Bulletin no. 79, AGPS, Canberra, pp. 15–21.

SSCVSF (Senate Select Committee on Volatile Substance Fumes) (1985), *Volatile substance abuse in Australia*, AGPS, Canberra.

Stanner, W. E. H. (1979), *White man got no dreaming*, Australian National University Press, Canberra.

Stone, A. C. (1911), 'The Aborigines of Lake Boga, Victoria', *Proceedings of the Royal Society of Victoria* **23** (NS), part 2.

Symonds, G. J., Albrecht, P., and Long, J. P. M. (1963), 'Report of 1961 Missions/Administration Conference Sub Committee on alcohol problem', Northern Territory Administration, Darwin.

Thomson, D. F. (1939), 'Notes on the smoking pipes of North Queensland and the Northern Territory of Australia', *Man* **76**, pp. 81–91.

Thomson, D. F. (1961), 'A narcotic from *Nicotiana ingulba* used by the desert Bindibu', *Man* **1** (2), p. 509.

Thomson, N., and Smith, L. (1985), 'An analysis of Aboriginal mortality in NSW country areas 1980–1981', *Medical Journal of Australia* **143**, pp. S49–S54.

Tomlinson, J. (1975), 'Petrol sniffing in the Northern Territory', *Australian Journal of Alcohol and Drug Dependence* **2** (3), pp. 74–7.

Walker, R. B. (1980), 'Tobacco smoking in Australia, 1788–1914', *Historical Studies* **19** (75), pp. 267–85.

Walsh, D. C., and Hingson, R. W. (1987), 'Epidemiology and alcohol policy', in S. Levine and A. M. Lilienfeld (eds), *Epidemiology and health policy*, Tavistock, New York, pp. 265–91.

Warner, W. L. (1969), *A black civilization: a social study of an Aboriginal tribe*, Peter Smith, Gloucester, Mass.

Watson, C., Fleming, J., and Alexander, K. (1988), *A survey of drug use patterns in Northern Territory Aboriginal Communities 1986–1987*, Northern Territory Department of Health and Community Services, Darwin.

Watson, D. (1983), 'The rinso eaters of Groote Eylandt', *British Medical Journal* **286**, 5 March, pp. 755–6.

Watson, P. (1983), *This precious foliage: a study of the Aboriginal psycho-active drug pituri*, Oceania Monograph 26, University of Sydney, Sydney.

Watson, P. (1988), Letter, *Medical Journal of Australia* **149**, September 19, p. 342.

Welborn, S. (1987), *Swan: the history of a brewery*, University of Western Australia Press, Perth.

WHO (1977), *Manual of the international statistical classification of disease, injuries and causes of death*, 9th revision, vol. 1, World Health Organization, Geneva.

WHO (1981), 'Nomenclature and classification of drug- and alcohol-related problems: a WHO memorandum', *Bulletin of the World Health Organization* **59** (2), pp. 225–42.

Wiebel-Orlando, J. (1987), 'Culture-specific treatment modalities: assessing client-to-treatment fit in Indian alcoholism programs', in W. Miles Cox (ed.), *Treatment and prevention of alcohol problems*, Academic Press, New York, pp. 261–83.

Wiebel-Orlando, J. (1989), 'Hooked on healing: anthropologists, alcohol and intervention', *Human Organization* **48** (2), pp. 148–55.

Wiesner, T. S., Weibel-Orlando, J. C., and Long, J. (1984), ' "Serious drinking", "white man's drinking" and "teetotalling": drinking levels and styles in an urban American Indian population', *Journal of Studies on Alcohol* **45** (3), pp. 237–50.

Wilson, P. (1982), *Black death white hands*, Allen and Unwin, Sydney.

Worrall, J. (1982), 'European courts and tribal Aborigines: a statistical collection of dispositions from the north-west reserve of South Australia', *Australia and New Zealand Journal of Criminology* **15**, pp. 47–55.

Young, E. (1981), *Tribal communities in rural areas*, ANU, Canberra.

Zinberg, N. (1984), *Drug, set, and setting: the basis for controlled intoxicant use*, Yale University Press, New Haven.

Unpublished material

CAAPS (unpub.), Council for Aboriginal Alcohol Programme Services, Gordon Symons Hostel, Darwin.

Stead, J. (unpub.), Under the influence: a comparison of drinking in two Australian aboriginal societies, BA (Hons) thesis, Australian National University, Canberra, 1980.

Watson, P. (unpub.), Machines of the mind: an anthropology of drug use, PhD thesis, Department of Anthropology and Sociology, University of Queensland, Brisbane, 1987.

Wilson, W. T. (unpub.), An analysis of federal government action on the provision of effective preventive treatment and rehabilitative services for Aboriginal alcohol abusers, Department of Aboriginal Affairs, Canberra.

CHAPTER 6

Aboriginal mental health: conflicting cultural perspectives

Joseph P. Reser

Department of Psychology and Sociology, School of Behavioural Sciences, James Cook University of North Queensland, Townsville, Queensland

The issue of Aboriginal mental health is embedded in a larger set of questions relating to culture and cultural differences, historical events, social and cultural change and coping. How do societies define and foster quality of life, define social problems, and cope with change? How do societies determine, explain, and deal with mental illness? Is behaviour disorder essentially uniform across cultures, differing only in language and superficial form, or does each culture shape psychological disturbance in more profound and basic ways? What impact do social and cultural change have on individual and community mental health? These questions fall into a domain that has variously been called ethnopsychiatry, transcultural psychiatry, and cross-cultural psychopathology (see, for example, Draguns 1980*a*). Increasingly, 'cross-cultural mental health' is used to describe both mental health as well as behaviour disorder. In this chapter, these questions are asked in the context of Aboriginal society, that is with respect to an indigenous minority culture, and from a Western cultural perspective whose assumptions, definitions, and understandings of health and well-being are, in many ways, very different from Aboriginal world views.

This chapter examines the attempts of the majority culture to come to terms with indigenous mental health in Australia. The discussion is placed within the broader context of mental health across cultures, and incorporates contemporary Australian Aboriginal perspectives on mental health. The status of Aboriginal mental health, past and present, is considered, based largely on Western psychiatric perspectives and reported findings. A number of conceptual frameworks and issues are addressed in some detail. These include the notion of acculturative stress, the role and importance of culture in mental health and psychopathology, the nature and importance of emotional experience and self-construction in the Aboriginal cultural context, and the nature and experience of relatedness. The chapter also includes a brief discussion of families and psychopathology, alcohol and violence, and Aboriginal self-injury and suicide. The chapter does not attempt to provide an adequate historical perspective with respect to European contact and the devastating impact this contact has had on traditional Aboriginal society—and in many ways continues to have on contemporary Aboriginal communities. While this historical perspective is critical to understanding Aboriginal views on mental health and has been summarised in chapter 1, it ultimately relates to a collective Aboriginal experience that is best summarised by Aborigines themselves.

Recent and dramatic media coverage of a spectrum of 'social problems' in Aboriginal communities has led to increased interest and concern with the issue of Aboriginal mental health. These problems include physical well-being, substance abuse, delinquency, domestic violence, AIDS risk and Aboriginal deaths in custody. Underlying and neglected mental health issues and concerns include the nature and current status of indigenous health practices, the cultural context of Aboriginal emotional experience and expression, the nature of individual and community cultural coping stratagems, family and kinship dynamics and support systems, adolescent conflicts and adjustment problems, and interconnections between alcohol, violence and mental health.

Not surprisingly, different disciplines conceptualise and address mental health and mental health issues very differently. This has certainly been the case for Aboriginal mental health. For the psychiatrist who might visit a remote Aboriginal community once every several years for an afternoon clinic or one lasting only a few days, impressions are governed by the cases that have been mustered by the health personnel for examination and treatment, and by a pervasive 'medical model' frame of reference. The anthropologist who has lived and worked with a community for a number of years will tend to be aware of the social and cultural context underlying the behavioural 'problems' of a particular individual or community, and of the social control implications of being ill and being cured. The cross-cultural psychologist might be more concerned with individual experience of, and response to, perceived stressors, and the underlying values and belief systems through which people, individually and collectively, make sense of their world and their experience.

On the whole, assessments of the mental health status of Aboriginal individuals and communities have been framed in ethnocentric terms. This is true of recent as well as past assessments:

Of all the cultures that have suffered as a result of European intrusion, the plight of the Australian aborigine [sic] is one of the most unfortunate in the English-speaking world. The aborigines never developed an agricultural system and until colonization they lived as hunters and gatherers off the naturally occurring fauna. Because the land is sparse and arid, a tribe would wander in nomadic fashion during the course of the year, returning annually to the same territory. The only two weapons they have developed were the boomerang and the woomera, the latter being a form of sling enabling them to throw spears accurately for up to 150 yards [140 metres approx.]. There was no written language and archeological remains are rare, but an intricate art form developed which can be seen on caves or on rocks in remote sacred sites [emphasis added].

Spencer 1983, p. 208

Language such as this, serving as a general introduction to and summary explanation of Aboriginal culture, subtly conjures up a people of limited capacity and resilience. Such observations, of course, substantially prejudice the case, and are juxtaposed with what sound to be damning psychiatric morbidity rates:

Based on population figures the overall aboriginal [sic] admission rate is 60% higher than that of the general population. It is almost certain that these figures are an underestimation as previous studies have indicated that only a small proportion of mentally disturbed aborigines are ever appropriately recognized and referred for help.

Spencer 1983, p. 209

A paradox with such observations is that the objective is often to present a sensitive and sympathetic account of what are seen to be major 'social problems'. The reality is that a distorting and culturally biased assessment is often made and reified.

An individual who has substantially influenced the direction and nature of studies of Aboriginal mental health is Professor John Cawte. In many ways Cawte set the 'ethnopsychiatric agenda' in Australia, which was to study 'contemporary Aborigines as they struggle to evolve new social institutions to cope with catastrophic upsets caused by Western influence' (Cawte 1974, p. xiv).

Australian physicians and anthropologists have the opportunity to establish knowledge in ethnopsychiatry, a field described by Sir Aubrey Lewis (1963) as an 'obscure, potentially rich area of inquiry'. What are the 'traditional' mental illnesses of the Australian Aboriginal cultures? What are the 'transitional' illnesses occurring during the present epoch of re-enculturation? Such inquiries are important not only for academic reasons, but for Australia's mental health and, perhaps, racial harmony...An urgent question is: to what extent should Australian Aborigines be regarded as a 'sick society'?

Cawte 1974, p. 264

Cawte felt that ethnography in Australia was concerned with two groups of illnesses: those characteristic of traditional life, and those transition illnesses characteristic of assimilating communities (Cawte 1964). He also felt that, in practice, in most remote communities these illnesses overlap. Unfortunately, the language, framework, and general character and tenor of these 'ethnopsychiatric' reports, along with typically unsupported conclusions, have distanced other mental health workers in Australia. Perhaps the problem was that individuals were defining what they thought the discipline of transcultural psychiatry should be, rather than having been trained or steeped in a tradition that was inherently more cross-cultural and multidisciplinary.

Australian Aboriginal people have not figured prominently in cross-cultural studies of mental health. In the 1980 *Handbook of cross-cultural psychology* devoted to psychopathology (Triandis and Draguns 1980), for example, there is no reference to indigenous Australians. Within Australia, the first professional descriptions of Aboriginal mental health commenced in the 1960s and early 1970s, with the work, for example, of Cawte (1964), Cawte et al. (1968), Kidson and Jones (1968), Cawte (1972, 1974), Jones (1972), Nurcombe (1976), Eastwell (1977) and Kamien

(1978). With the exception of Kamien's study of Bourke, all of these publications related to remote Aboriginal communities. The earliest discussions of urban Aboriginal mental health are largely restricted to adolescents and are found in Gault (1968), Gault et al. (1970), and Lickiss (1970, 1971). There was little sustained interest in the mental health of urban and country-town Aboriginal communities during the 1970s and 1980s; rather attention focused on particular cases and events, including, for example, the Alwyn Peter murder trial (Wilson 1982, and featured in the film *State of shock*), and the community violence and alcohol abuse which was reported to be endemic in Aboriginal communities such as Weipa South and Palm Island, north Queensland.

This last decade has seen a renewed and rather different social science interest in cross-cultural mental health. This interest in the 'indigenous psychology' of other cultures derives from very different understandings of the person (Carrithers et al. 1985; Heelas and Lock 1981; Shweder and LeVine 1984; White and Kirkpatrick 1985), emotions (Scherer 1988; Lutz and White 1986), the nature and importance of social constructions and social meanings (Miller 1984; Shweder and LeVine 1984), and the nature and dynamics of adjustments to social and cultural change (Berry and Kim 1988). This altered focus also reflects basic paradigm shifts with respect to our understanding of individual and cultural coping strategies (Janes et al. 1986; Lazarus and Folkman 1984; Marsella and Dash-Scheuer 1988; Triandis and Draguns 1980), and a recent bridging of anthropology, psychology, and psychiatry in the study of these phenomena (Kleinman 1980, 1986; Marsella and White 1984). Sadly this renewed interest also reflects the dramatic salience of mental health issues and problems in indigenous minority communities in North America and the Pacific. In Australia these 'problems' loom large on the health agendas of state and federal government bodies—substance abuse, youth suicide, domestic violence—but understanding of these phenomena is impoverished, to some extent politically driven, and 'straitjacketed' by prior and totally inadequate frameworks for understanding the other-culture realities of Aboriginal mental health.

Cross-cultural perspective

It is inordinately difficult to specify the essence or critical components of positive mental health. Does this consist of the absence of distress and disturbance, or does it equate with culturally relative 'quality of life'? It has been equally challenging to isolate the nature and causes of mental illness—indeed we have met with only limited success within the context of Western cultures, and with the advantage of a medical and social science history of hundreds of years. An adequate understanding of psychopathology in other cultures does not exist, and it will be realised only when there is a more widespread and genuine understanding that there exist basic cultural differences with respect to how the world, the self, and distress are experienced and responded to (see, for example, Geertz 1975).

Notwithstanding a shared humanity, the nature of human cultures and experience is also enormously varied. While it is often possible to recognise severe distress and behavioural disorder, the causes, meanings and consequences of disturbed behaviour in another culture are not self-evident, nor do they necessarily conform to a western European diagnostic manual or Western psychiatric assumptions. Less obvious behaviour problems rarely come to the notice of the cross-cultural observer. For example, the anxiety and distress that can accompany residence in Western housing in 'planned' communities for traditionally oriented Aboriginal groups may not be obvious but can be debilitating, requiring extensive security precautions on the part of individuals who are not living on their own country (see Reser 1979).

Over the past 20 years understanding of the interrelationship of culture, medicine and psychiatry has changed enormously, as has understanding of *illness experience* as distinct from *disease entity* (Kleinman 1986). Today, we better understand that cultural understandings of health and illness, and beliefs about causes and cures, are directly related to actual as well as perceived effectiveness, and ultimate recovery (Taylor 1990; Young 1982). Medicine has become far more 'social' and cross-cultural. This more encompassing, interdisciplinary and less culturally parochial perspective has not yet appreciably influenced discussions of Aboriginal mental health in Australia. At best our understanding is indirect and patchy, informed by a number of sensitive ethnographic accounts, and the occasional lucid and eloquent statements and observations by Aboriginal individuals and culture brokers. These statements suggest that mental health in an indigenous context is better thought of as a qualitative index of the integrity and strength of an individual's relationships with his or her natural, spiritual and social world. These accounts also suggest that the meanings and explanations employed with respect to behaviour disturbance are often profoundly different in Aboriginal communities, as are individual and community responses.

One of the basic questions asked with respect to mental health is: to what extent do the nature and incidence of psychiatric disorders differ across cultures? Kleinman, a psychiatrist and anthropologist, has frequently addressed this question from a multidisciplinary and multicultural vantage point:

An anthropological reading of the literature in cross-cultural and international psychiatry reveals a strong bias of psychiatrists toward 'discovering' cross-cultural similarities and 'universals' in mental disorder. First this bias should not come as any surprise. Much of the cross-cultural psychiatric literature has been initiated from a wish to demonstrate that psychiatric disorder is like other disorders: it occurs in all societies, and it can be detected if standardised diagnostic techniques are applied. Clearly this was an interest of the WHO's International Pilot Study of Schizophrenia (1973), which expected that core symptoms of schizophrenia would cluster together in more or less the same way in Western and non-Western, industrialised and non-industrialised societies. It should come as no surprise that this is what the IPSS found, in a non-epidemiological, clinic-based comparison that applied a template of symptoms to psychotic patients in a range of societies to identify groups of patients who seemed similar. The problem with this study is that it leaves out those patients who fail to fit the template, the very patients of greatest interest from a cultural perspective, because they could be expected to reveal the greatest amount of cultural diversity...A more valid interpretation of the data base emerges when the two viewpoints, both biased and in opposite directions, are reviewed together. The findings for schizophrenia, major depressive disorder, anxiety disorders, and alcoholism disclose both important similarities and equally important differences. Hence the first anthropological question (How do psychiatric disorders differ across cultures?) is a necessary complement to the regnant psychiatric question (How are psychiatric disorders similar across cultures?).

Kleinman 1987, pp. 448–9

Ethnopsychiatry, cross-cultural psychology, and medical anthropology all involve cultural comparisons, on a number of levels (Berry 1980). In addition to the explicit or implicit comparison one makes with one's own culture in describing and trying to understand adjustment problems in another culture, explicit comparisons are often made with other reference cultures. While the latter exercise is critical to cross-cultural understanding, it has rarely happened with respect to indigenous Australians. One of the few studies that have attempted this is that of Kahn (1982, 1986). His comparisons are of particular interest, as he has looked at two Native American cultures (American Indian and Inuit peoples) and Australian Aborigines.

Some of the highest rates of emotional disorder and psychopathology are found among ethnic minority, aboriginal people who live in proximity to and under the general domain of western culture and values. The association between socioeconomic-minority status and high rates of psychopathology and inadequate treatment is particularly well demonstrated with these aboriginal people of North America and Australia...These groups suffered the loss of traditional lands and gross disruption of culture. The resulting social disorganization and stress has resulted in high rates of similar forms of psychopathology. Alcohol excess is the most visible form that is implicated in child neglect, domestic violence and family breakups. Suicide, accidental death and homicide rates are three or more times higher than national rates.

Kahn 1982, p. 553

The 'forms of psychopathology' that Kahn outlines and describes in his article, are alcohol excess, depression and suicide, homicide, crime, delinquency, accidental death, and family disruptions and instability. The unsatisfying aspect of such catalogues is that what is discussed is not the psychopathology of individuals or a balanced spectrum of mental health problems and issues, but a glossary of community or societal-level 'social indicators'.

A related issue in cross-cultural mental health concerns the existence of 'culture-bound reactive syndromes' such as the *pibloktoq* or arctic hysteria of the Inuit people of northern Canada or the *latah* of Indonesia (Yap 1974). These are viewed as culturally distinct forms of psychopathology, with distinctive aetiologies, symptoms, and courses. A number of such culture-bound syndromes have been reported and described in the context of traditionally oriented Aboriginal communities. Perhaps the best described of these is *malgri* (Cawte 1974), which is reported to be a 'prominent disorder' at Mornington Island, Queensland. *Malgri* is characterised as a spirit invasion syndrome which is linked to totemic affiliation to land and certain behavioural proscriptions. Careless violation of such proscriptions can result in a painful, constant colic-like condition. The validity of such psychiatric syndromes is open to question. This, of course, raises the whole question of the utility and validity of another culture's classification and diagnostic system when dealing with experienced distress (Kleinman 1987; Mirowsky and Ross 1989).

It is perhaps significant that non-psychiatric researchers are those most likely to conclude that African mental health and mental disorder is culture-bound and not capable of being comprehended within Western psychiatric categories. To be fair, it is also of significance that most of those who insist that mental disorder in Africa is comparable with that found in Europe and North America, and is susceptible to similar classification, are clinical psychiatrists (albeit now mostly African ones). Among psychiatrists who repudiate nosological and classificatory systems of Kraepelinian or DSM-III type are to be found large numbers whose interests are primarily in psychoanalysis, social psychiatry, or psychiatric anthropology. The viewpoint clearly influences the conclusions reached.

German 1987, p. 436

Mental health professionals are only now coming to appreciate that mental health is a 'social construction' (Berger and Luckman 1966; Millon 1988) and that the 'causes' and 'problems' associated with assessments of mental health and 'social pathology' are a part of this 'making-sense' and rationalising-intervention process. Accounts of social pathology and behaviour disorder are, understandably, often accepted by indigenous minority communities who may have been able to make little sense of often bewildering sets of problems. In the south-west United States:

Hopis of all ages believe that social pathology began its increase after contact with the whites. But, whereas the older generation believes that the present state of affairs is due to increased immorality and, thus, a fall from a superior moral state, many younger Hopis are coming to accept the dominant society's view of these behaviors as symptoms of personal and societal 'illness' and are beginning to think of themselves as a sick society. Accepting the explanation that social deviance is the direct consequence of social disintegration permits the community to view deviance as a response to new social conditions. And because these conditions have been imposed by the dominant Anglo society, no blame attaches to the values of the parental generation. Indeed, many Anglos have encouraged the Hopis to view the modern Anglo world as the cause of all their ills.

Levy and Kunitz 1987, pp. 937–8

The current social science consensus with respect to mental health investigations within and across cultures is that sociocultural factors substantially influence and determine virtually every aspect of psychiatric disorder: aetiology, expression, subjective experience, course, outcome and epidemiology (see Comas-Diaz and Griffith 1988; Draguns 1980*b*; Kleinman 1986; Marsella and White 1984; Marsella 1988). Marsella points out that even in the most severe neurological disorders, culture strongly influences the individual's interpretation and experience of the disorder, behavioural effects, and the response of the social environment. While controversy still exists, with some authors arguing that cultural variations are largely superficial and could be resolved with improved and standardised interviewing and assessment techniques (Dohrenwend 1983), most researchers argue that cultural variations are far more fundamental: for example, cultural differences in the somatisation rather than cognisation of distress and the implications this has for depression (Marsella 1980). Even reported similarities in symptoms across cultures would not in themselves mean that real differences in aetiology, meaning, psychosocial implications and diagnostic category membership did not exist. Such differences pose daunting problems for cross-cultural comparisons of psychopathology, and for a majority culture assessment of Aboriginal mental health.

'Culture-bound' syndromes

Examples of 'culture-bound' mental health syndromes identified by psychiatrists to be present in the Aboriginal cultural context include pathological fear states, fear-of-sorcery syndrome, hysterical trance-states, prolonged mutism, hypochondriacal states and *amok* (see Eastwell 1982*b*; Spencer 1983). Examples given by Spencer (1983, p. 212) include the following:

Hysterical trance-states are described as being fairly common, especially in young aboriginal [sic] women. These may be very dramatic illnesses characterized by acute schizophreniform disorder, catatonia, total unresponsiveness, immobility, mutisms, negativism and automatic obedience. There is often a low systolic blood pressure and urinary retention. These illnesses are sometimes called temporary death. The patients usually recover within the space of a few hours or days: occasionally they need to be escorted to sacred sites. The cause of these states is thought to be precipitated by interpersonal conflict or taboo-breaking.

Amok. This is a condition described as murderous frenzy. This was first described in Malays who will attack and kill unless apprehended and controlled. This is not common but well recognized in aboriginal [sic] communities, and in Western Australia and the Northern Territories. It is usually referred to as 'going wild'. Alcohol may or may not be involved.

Whether these 'syndromes' exist as clearly identifiable and adequately described diagnostic entities is a matter of some debate. It is also questionable whether these states equate with psychiatric disturbance from an Aboriginal perspective. It is possible, for example, that there are alternative explanations for the behaviour which substantially de-emphasise the 'mental disorder' understanding of the phenomena. All cultures have identifiable forms of psychopathology. Yet, while Western researchers have labelled many of these as 'culture-bound' or 'culture-specific', Western psychiatry has not been willing to consider that its own disorders may also be culture-specific (Marsella 1988).

A detailed discussion and critique of another reported Aboriginal culture-bound syndrome, *malgri*, is found in Cawte (1974, pp. 106–19).

J. Reser

Indigenous perspective

Much has been written about the status of Aboriginal health generally, from a Western medical perspective, but much less has been written about the nature of traditional health systems, or the cultural assumptions, beliefs and values that accompany such systems (Berndt 1964; Reid 1982, 1983). Surprisingly little is known, for example, about the 'indigenous psychology' of Australia.

Indigenous psychologies have not before been systematically delineated or examined. They are the cultural views, theories, conjectures, classifications, assumptions and metaphors—together with notions embedded in social institutions—that bear on psychological topics. These psychologies are statements about the nature of the person and his [sic] relations with the world. They contain advice or injunctions about the ways people should act, should feel and how they can find happiness and success in life. Considering their importance, academic understanding is slight.

Heelas 1981, p. 3

Causality

There are a number of important cultural differences with respect to Aboriginal world views that influence how mental health is understood. One such difference is in terms of causal 'attribution biases'. Many societies tend to understand the world of events and contingencies in terms of 'external' causes and forces, while other cultures are more 'internal' in their causal attributions, seeing individuals as having considerable control over life events (Lefcourt 1982). In a Western cultural context, there is a clear bias to see causality in terms of human agency, and to 'explain' events in terms of individual intentions, motives and competencies, that is, in terms of internal causes. In an Aboriginal cultural context, there is reason to believe that a more external attribution bias is operating, with the explanations and perceived 'causes' for many events residing outside of the actor (Biernoff 1982; Brady 1988; Martin unpub.). These external causes are typically explained in terms of forces, supernatural agents, or impaired relationships with respect to more encompassing human and natural ecosystems. For example, death in many Aboriginal communities is often 'explained' in terms of murder or sorcery attributions rather than in terms of a diseased organ or a biological system breakdown. Similarly, few events occur by chance; rather a plausible external cause will be posited. In the case of mental disorder, there is a tendency to view such a condition as the result of external powers and forces, and/or disturbed relationships with the world. Clearly, the 'disturbed relationship' view of mental disorder has much in common with modern social psychiatric perspectives, but in a traditionally oriented Aboriginal cultural context it is based on rather different assumptions about totemic affiliation to species and land, and a complex skein of ritual and behavioural responsibilities and obligations.

Abnormality

Another area of cultural difference relates to the concept of, and community response to abnormality. Berndt and Berndt (1951) argue that the concept of abnormality in an Arnhem Land Aboriginal context connotes 'different' and that this notion has particularly powerful emotional meanings in terms of social rejection. Individuals who are 'different' typically fall into three categories: those who possess supernatural powers, those who are *bengwar* (that is, 'silly', or 'deaf' to their social environment), and those who are victims of sorcery or malevolent magic. Mental illness, from a Western psychiatric perspective, would presumably straddle the second two categories, but such disturbed behaviour would probably have a non-psychiatric explanation for most Aboriginal observers.

The criteria which these people employ [with respect to 'abnormality'] have both a physiological and a psychological basis, but do not correspond to those which a trained psychologist or a psychoanalyst from our society would use in making an analysis of this subject. Observation of physical deformities and overt behaviour is accompanied by subjective interpretations of thoughts and emotions, and the whole 'explained' in the light of an external influence acting upon an initially 'normal' child or adult.

Berndt and Berndt 1951, p. 88

It is interesting that extreme violence is not, from an indigenous perspective, a feature of mental illness according to the Berndts.

Extreme violence, or desire to inflict injury, does not seem to be a feature of 'abnormality' in this region. This may perhaps be due to the fact that aggressive tendencies are acknowledged to be strong, and are in consequence conventionally channelized. Arguments resulting in fights are common, especially away from the Mission station, and show a definite pattern of permissible violence, often resulting in death and leading to intertribal or even interfamily feuds.

Berndt and Berndt 1951, p. 87

Some of the most basic and important cultural differences have to do with differences in cultural meaning systems, and culturally different notions of the person (Geertz 1975; Miller 1984; Shweder and Bourne 1982) An excellent discussion of how culturally different meaning systems influence everyday explanation is found in Brady (unpub.), who specifically discusses the Pitjantjatjara perception and explanation of mental disorder.

There are at Yalata, as elsewhere, individuals who are 'different', those who are mentally or physically atypical in one way or another, whose disability, actions or behaviour mark them out from their fellows. They may not as individuals be necessarily disruptive to the flow of everyday life, but are nonetheless potentially disturbing to the social order... Within the extremely negotiable set of notions of customary action recognised at Yalata, were understandings of such atypical or 'deviant' events and individuals. These understandings, although clearly discerning those who were thought to be unusual, did not attribute blame or negativity to the individual concerned. Just as Yalata people have actively evolved strategies whereby they adapt aspects of the Law and of social convention in order to achieve self or group interest of an external nature, so too have they developed strategies for explaining and accommodating circumstances which are subjectively disturbing, incomprehensible or even threatening. These strategies serve to order the potentially dis-ordering into an overall view of the world

Brady unpub., pp. 132–3

In the context of mental health, perspectives on causality determine not only whether a condition is viewed as a 'mental disorder' or a temporary state of dysfunction, but whether an intervention 'makes sense' or would be at all efficacious. The medications used by Western medical practitioners make considerable sense to many traditionally oriented Aboriginal people because of their own rich pharmacopoeia, and because many behavioural problems and disorders are 'framed' or understood in terms of 'external' and potent poisons and objects that invade the body and control the patient.

Notions of sorcery and healing

Another perspective that sheds light on an Aboriginal point of view with respect to mental health and mental illness is discussed in writings on Aboriginal notions of sorcery and healing (Berndt 1964, 1982; Elkin 1977; Thomson 1961; Reid 1983;

Warner 1958). These sources clearly communicate that a within-culture or 'emic' perspective (Berry 1980) on health and illness is embedded in a wider worldview in which the relationships and responsibilities between people and their encompassing natural and spiritual world are central. This material again makes clear that traditional healing and malevolent magic are both central features of traditional social control systems, with illness, whether physical or social, suggesting the imposition of sanctions in response to spiritual or social wrong.

The Aboriginal approach to both prophylaxis and curing is a holistic one. It recognizes the physical, personal and spiritual dimension of life and health. In many ways the Aboriginal perspective on health and illness is closer than that of Western medicine to the World Health Organization's definition of health—'a state of complete physical, mental and social well-being and not merely the absence of disease or infirmity'.

Reid 1982, p. 91

An analysis of language itself provides a valuable avenue for better understanding Aboriginal concepts and assumptions relating to mental health. The most focused discussions of an Aboriginal language in the context of mental health are those of Morice (1978, 1979). Morice worked among the Pintupi people of the Western Desert, who were among the last Aboriginal people to 'come in'.

When language and cultural barriers intervene, the expression and interpretation of symptoms can become exceedingly difficult, and mental state examination even more so. In this situation, common in the practice of transcultural psychiatry, symptoms tend to become subservient to behaviour in the diagnostic process. A result could be the infrequency, in many epidemiological surveys conducted in transcultural settings, of disorders of mood, especially as manifested by subjective states of anxiety and depression.

Morice 1978, p. 87

Morice provides evidence for a sophisticated Aboriginal vocabulary relating to emotional states (including anger, fear, anxiety, depression, and shame) and behaviour disturbance, which, he argues, 'calls for a radical reassessment of the current psychological, sociological and anthropological perspectives' (Morice 1978, p. 89) on Aboriginal culture. It is worth examining Morice's glossary of Pintupi terms relating to fear and anxiety, both to provide something of a within-culture perspective on this emotional domain, and in light of the published psychiatric consensus that anxiety and anxiety disorders are rare in Aboriginal communities (see table 6.1).

Contemporary Aboriginal involvement and concern

Over the past 10 years Aboriginal people have become increasingly concerned about being more fully involved in mental health services for Aboriginal communities. This has been part of a more general tendency to view the health arena as an area where there exists an opportunity for involvement, professional advancement, and a cultural stand vis-à-vis majority culture misunderstandings of Aboriginal realities. It is clear, from all perspectives, that there exists a substantial mental

Table 6.1   The Pintupi glossary of fear and anxiety

Kamarrarringu	Sudden feeling, premonition that makes person turn around; frightened feeling. May be caused by someone approaching from behind, or by father's spirit warning of the approach of a malevolent spirit.	Ngulunyngulungpa	Extreme fear, which implies watchfulness and some degree of immobilisation. Fear of being killed.
		Nyirrkinyirrkinpa	Always watchful and alert, for example, always looking out for snakes.
Kanarunytju	Insomnia. Person prevented from going to sleep through fear of being harmed or killed by spirits or revenge killers.	Patapatanu	Shaking of body, often caused by fear.
		Tiltirrpa	Shaking from cold or fear.
Kurrun ngulutjarra	Sensation of fear, usually at night, but can occur in response to natural phenomena like storms. Conception is that the 'soul' is shaking with fear.	Tjulurrtjingami	Sudden fright affecting the spirit or soul, usually during sleep, and causing person to jump up to seek the reason. Also to dream.
Kututu wala	Rapid beating of the heart, palpitations. Accompanies fear, and if it occurs at night, will prevent sleep.	Tjulurrwangkangu	As for tjulurrtjingami.
		Tjumanu	As for tjulurrtjinganu.
		Tjuni miiltjunu	Sensation in stomach caused by fear, or interpreted as warning that something bad will happen to the person, leading to fear.
Nginyiwarrarringu	A sudden feeling of fear causing the person to stand up to see what is causing it.		
Ngulu	Fear, usually due to expectation of harm from another person seeking revenge, distinguishing it from fear of real objects, such as snakes.	Warrmaltjunu	Disorder of the spirit or soul caused during sleep by someone shouting. Also fear related to expectation of death (from warrmala = revenge killers).

Source: Morice 1978, p. 91

health 'problem' in Aboriginal communities today, a multifaceted problem that is largely ignored, and that this relates to complex historical causes as well as contemporary stresses and strains within Aboriginal culture and communities. The first formal Aboriginal mental health group was formed in 1979, at an Aboriginal training school in Canberra. It was sponsored by the Australian Foundation on Alcoholism and Drug Dependence. The Steering Committee elected to the new National Aboriginal Mental Health Association (NAMHA) framed the following declaration:

We declare that mental health problems in Aboriginal society are at least as common and as serious as in any other society in Australia.

We declare that Aboriginal society does not enjoy the services for the relief and care of mental illness enjoyed by other groups.

We hold that psychiatric services planned to assist people of European descent are not suited to relieve the distress of Aboriginal people.

Therefore:

We express the need to develop, with all urgency Aboriginal services to meet the needs of Aboriginal people suffering mental distress.

We maintain that these services should be conducted for and by Aboriginal people, with proper links to other health services.

We recognize that services are provided for Aboriginal problems of the body, but that mental health problems go overlooked and ignored.

Therefore we pledge ourselves to the National Aboriginal Mental Health movement, designed to promote professional and vocational development in this field.

Wood 1980, p. 11

Later in 1979 the inaugural Aboriginal Mental Health Conference was held in Sydney. The testimony heard at the conference, often from Aboriginal health workers, indicated that adequate mental health services were desperately needed:

Data on some psychiatric patients, hospitalized far from their communities, and dealt with by professionals devoid of cross-cultural understanding, indicated to the Steering Committee that the need was indeed urgent, and that social prescriptions could neither restore those who had suicided, nor prevent similar tragedies.

Wood 1980, p. 12

The following year, in 1980, the second 'Aborigines and Mental Health' Conference, jointly sponsored by the Australian National Association for Mental Health (ANAMH) and the National Aboriginal Mental Health Association, was held in Brisbane. This conference proved to be very controversial, as very different perspectives on Aboriginal mental health and indeed psychiatry were aired. The opinions of the two medical practitioners invited to address the conference were viewed as antipsychiatric and uninformed by some other professionals. The psychiatrist Cawte later wrote:

The two medical practitioners invited to advise the Aboriginal Health Organizations contributed antipsychiatric views. Both were leading figures politically, one an ophthalmologist and the other a vitamin therapist. The first began by saying that he was not an expert on mental health, nor on Aborigines. He said he had heard a lot about how Aborigines are 'going off their heads' but that his experience of Aboriginal people had been highlighted by their mental and emotional strengths. He gave what proved to be a rousing antipsychiatric address. The vitamin therapist then had his turn. He delivered a dietetic view of psychiatry, asserting that he had cured senile dementia by vitamins and minerals. Nether of these advisers had any conception of the practice of psychiatry or of mental health, but each voice gave powerful messages of prejudice.

Cawte unpub., p. 11

The proceedings of both of these conferences were published (ANAMH 1981; NAMHA 1980) and serve to underscore the very different professional perspectives that exist with respect to mental health in general and indigenous mental health in particular. These reports appear to have had a substantial impact on community and professional perceptions of the nature, complexity and magnitude of Aboriginal mental health problems.

Ten years later, the picture from an Aboriginal perspective remains much the same:

Mental distress is a common and crippling problem for many Aboriginal people and appropriate services are a pressing need. Advances in the understanding and treatment for mental health problems have been impressive since World War II; this progress has yet to benefit Aboriginal people. Culturally appropriate services for Aboriginal people are virtually non-existent. Mental health services are designed and controlled by the dominant society for the dominant society. The health system does not recognise or adapt programs to Aboriginal beliefs and law, causing a huge gap between service provider and user. As a result, mental distress in the Aboriginal community goes unnoticed, undiagnosed and untreated.

NAHSWP 1989, pp. 171, 172

There is no question that the current Aboriginal 'position' vis-à-vis mental health is in part political. Given the history of Aboriginal mental health in Australia, and the increasing frustration and militancy of Aboriginal communities, this is hardly surprising. It is noteworthy that in the recent *Mental health discussion paper* (1989) of the Australian Health Ministers' Advisory Council, the topic of indigenous mental health falls under the heading of 'Specific Needs Groups', including, for example, AIDS sufferers, brain-damaged people with behaviour disorders, and offenders, and finds no reference under 'Multi-Cultural Issues'. It is hardly credible that the defining criterion and arguably the most salient and important aspect of Aboriginality, Aboriginal culture, is simply overlooked in the case of indigenous Australians. The exasperation of Aboriginal people with such 'overviews' is remarkably controlled.

The discussion paper does acknowledge a pressing need for mental health services in Aboriginal communities:

The poor health status of Aboriginal and Torres Strait Islander people is clearly documented in morbidity and mortality data. A high incidence of alcohol and substance abuse seems to be related to cultural and socio-economic factors and may result in high risk for organic mental deterioration, community isolation, institutional care and early death. Among Aboriginal children and adolescents, petrol inhalation has reached crisis proportions in some parts of Australia. Mental health problems are common problems for many Aboriginal and Torres Strait Islander people and they suffer the same major psychiatric disorders as the general community. The health system does not recognise Aboriginal beliefs and law and thus much mental illness may go unnoticed, undiagnosed and untreated. The mental health status of this population requires specific examination in a culturally sensitive manner with particular reference to:

- *the needs of adolescents,*
- *domestic violence,*
- *child abuse and neglect,*
- *substance abuse,*
- *grief associated with family and cultural loss,*

- *the specific mental health problems of Aboriginal women and,*
- *suicide.*

The socio-cultural elements of mental health problems are particularly evident in Aboriginal communities and the promotion of mental health requires a broader approach than simply treating individual mental disorders.

Mental Health Discussion Paper 1989, pp. 29–30

This excerpt constitutes all that was said about Aboriginal mental health in a 50-page document. The emphasis in the statement on alcohol and substance abuse, and 'socio-cultural elements' is important and is discussed in greater detail in the section 'Alcohol, violence and mental health'.

Not surprisingly, there are many Aboriginal perspectives on mental health. The views expressed by Aboriginal authors in publications such as the *Aboriginal Health Worker* are often markedly different from the views of individuals living in traditionally oriented communities. It is essential to bear in mind the many cultures and very different life circumstances of Aboriginal communities in Australia.

The status of Aboriginal mental health

It is important to consider just what evidence exists on which to base an 'objective' assessment of Aboriginal mental health. It would appear that it has been largely public statements rather than systematic assessments that have influenced conventional wisdom. The following are typical and widely cited.

That psychiatric illness is absent from a primitive community undisturbed by outside influence is not accepted as true. However, there is little doubt that the disruption of a way of life and the added strains imposed by unfamiliar pressures increase the incidence of psychiatric conditions. While a psychiatric illness is difficult to define nevertheless, accepting the term in a broad sense, there is a higher incidence in the Aboriginal population than in the non-Aboriginal community.

Department of Health 1972, p. 322

A recent submission from the Australian Department of Health stated that there was a higher incidence of mental illness in the Aboriginal population than in the white and that this mental illness was likely to increase as contact with non-Aborigines at such places as mining sites became more common. 'There is little doubt that the disruption of a way of life and the added strains imposed by unfamiliar pressures is increasing the incidence of psychiatric conditions' (Submission to the House of Representatives Standing Committee on Aboriginal Affairs). Furthermore the amount of mental ill-health is likely to be higher than would appear, since Aborigines are poor and live in remote areas where mental health services often do not reach them; and Aborigines are culturally different and shun white men's institutions.

Lippmann 1974, p. 11

A sifting of evidence from many sources, however, provides a less clear picture of higher incidence:

Evidence was received that the levels of major psychiatric morbidity in Australian communities are about as high as those of non-Aboriginal communities. Some studies have shown minor psychiatric morbidity quantifiably different to that of non-Aborigines. It was not entirely clear whether Western diagnostic categories are appropriate for Aboriginal patients or whether attempts are being made in many areas to study and learn Aboriginal concepts of emotional illness or to utilise Aboriginal expertise.

HRSCAA 1979, pp. 25–6

An accurate quantification of the extent of mental health problems amongst Aborigines is virtually impossible as general data in this area are even more deficient than data on physical ill-health. A general assessment is made even more complex by the difficulties in cross-cultural interpretation of 'aberrant' behaviour.

Thomson 1984, p. 711

Slattery (1987), in a discussion of transcultural therapy with Aboriginal families, argues that there is a clear crisis in Aboriginal health, but that a comparable prevalence of serious mental disasters in Aboriginal and white Australian communities belies a 'much deeper psychological malaise' in Aboriginal communities evidenced by substance abuse, anxiety, depression, and hypochondriasis. Eastwell (1985) similarly argues that the extent of psychiatric disorders in urban Aboriginal populations is hidden because of underuse of mental health services and underdiagnosis. In many urban communities and country towns, however, Aboriginal mental health services simply do not exist.

There are many intertwined problems with cross-cultural assessments of mental health. These include the cross-cultural experience and sensitivity of the medical practitioner who may or may not refer a client, the familiarity and understanding of the psychiatrist or clinical psychologist who ultimately sees the referred individual with the indigenous cultural context and community of the client, the sensitivity and cultural appropriateness of assessment techniques developed and standardised in Western cultural contexts, and the appropriateness of the taxonomy of mental health problems and syndromes used by practitioners to classify the presenting problem of the client. It is also common for many Aboriginal mental health problems to be 'located' in a family or larger community context, with the presenting symptom of the client being an indicator of unresolved conflicts within the extended family of the client or the community (Reser and Eastwell 1981).

There are few avenues or sources for examining the incidence of mental disorder in Aboriginal communities. Existing sources consist of hospital admission and outpatient treatment data, social welfare department data, state health department annual reports, and occasional 'psychiatric surveys' of particular Aboriginal communities. It is useful to consider some published figures in order to familiarise ourselves with the type of information available. A recent publication from the Northern Territory, for example (Devanesen et al. 1986), provides the information on mental disorders given in tables 6.2 and 6.3. These tables are not particularly informative in that they include only those individuals who were actually admitted to a hospital. They do not indicate whether an individual was resident in an Aboriginal or mixed community, in a rural or urban setting, or whether he or she was voluntarily or involuntarily admitted. If one accepts these figures as a reasonable picture

Table 6.2 Most common mental disorders, Northern Territory, 1977–82: standardised hospital separation rates

	Aboriginal males %	Non-Aboriginal males %	Aboriginal females %	Non-Aboriginal females %
1. Alcohol-related problems (ICD-9 291, 205.0, 303)	53	53	32	17
2. Schizophrenia	19	11	14	11
3. Neurotic disorders	5	11	23	29
4. Personality disorders	4	7	3	8

ICD   International Classification of Diseases

Table 6.3 Mental disorders, Northern Territory, 1977–82

Year	No. of separations		World standardised rate	
	Aboriginal	Non-Aboriginal	Aboriginal	Non-Aboriginal
Males				
1977	60	406	485	930
1978	82	387	668	877
1979	95	363	676	736
1980	107	456	744	893
1982	88	522	658	852
Females				
1977	50	226	356	664
1978	51	214	366	594
1979	66	248	427	653
1980	79	239	589	542
1982	51	259	342	537

Source: Devanesen et al. 1986, p. 109

of psychiatric morbidity, it would appear that there is not an appreciable difference between Aborigines and non-Aborigines with respect to types of presenting disorders, nor is there any difference between Aboriginal and non-Aboriginal males with respect to alcohol-related problems. The separation data in the tables refer to events (admissions and discharges from hospitals), not individuals. The data may not reflect the prevalence of mental disorder because hospital admission depends on many social, cultural and situational factors, and the reliability of clinical information for Aboriginal clients may be very different from that for non-Aborigines. Keeping in mind these rather serious qualifications, it can be said that the hospital separation rates suggest that prevalence of mental disorder was appreciably less in the Aboriginal population as a whole, but that the separation rate for Aboriginal males was steadily increasing over this five year period. The same Northern Territory report considers 'alcoholism' separately and presents information relating to

Table 6.4 Alcoholic psychoses, Northern Territory, 1977–82

Year	No. of separations		World standardised rate	
	Aboriginal	Non-Aboriginal	Aboriginal	Non-Aboriginal
Males				
1977	5	25	38	62
1978	8	24	76	60
1979	22	45	165	97
1980	20	53	162	108
1982	31	57	254	109
Females				
1977	2	7	16	32
1978	–	7	–	25
1979	–	10	–	28
1980	8	11	70	23
1982	10	10	72	28

Source: Devanesen et al. 1986, p. 253

alcohol-related diseases, hospital separations and alcoholic psychoses. The data on alcoholic psychoses is presented in table 6.4. Alcoholic psychoses were the most common cause of alcohol-related hospital separations among Aborigines and non-Aborigines, with such cases accounting for 25 per cent of Aboriginal males. This was twice the proportion of separations accounted for by alcoholic psychoses among Aboriginal females and non-Aborigines. It is also clear from table 6.4 that the hospital separation rate among Aboriginal males has been steadily increasing from year to year.

In the *Annual report* of the Northern Territory Department of Health and Community Services for 1987–88 (NTDHCS 1988), mental health status is reported by hospital admissions. Figure 6.1 gives the only data reported that compare Aboriginal with non-Aboriginal figures. (Mental health data in general take up only two pages in a 150-page report and consist of three figures and no text. Absolute numbers are of little value in such a presentation. If these data are considered relative to the respective Aboriginal and non-Aboriginal populations of the Northern Territory in 1977–78, the relative treated incidence figures become 0.36 per cent (Aboriginal) and 0.50 per cent (non-Aboriginal) clients. No information is provided in the report about diagnostic classification of patients, nor are age breakdowns available for Aboriginal versus non-Aboriginal clients. In the opinion of the Deputy Director of Mental Health Services for the Northern Territory, the data in the report did not reflect the incidence of mental illness in the Northern Territory and mental health services were in an 'enchoate state' (private correspondence).

Some states now maintain a central data base which can examine by ethnic origin the relative numbers and diagnoses of inpatients and outpatients at state-run mental health institutions. Such information, for example, is kept by the Queensland Department of Health. This information is interesting in that it covers

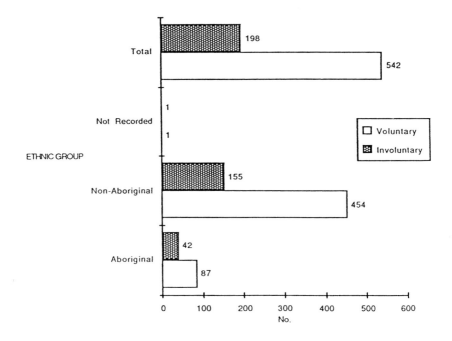

Figure 6.1 *Mental health: admissions by status and ethnicity. (NTDHCS 1988, p. 134)*

both urban and remote community referrals, and is based on state figures for the state with the largest Aboriginal population in Australia.

In 1988, for example, 43 per cent of Aboriginal outpatients and 47 per cent of Aboriginal inpatients were diagnosed as suffering from alcohol dependence or abuse, compared with figures of 18 per cent and 30 per cent for 'European' clients. Other noteworthy comparisons are with respect to neurotic depression and neurotic disorders generally, where comparison of 1988 figures for Aboriginal versus 'European' outpatients were 2.9 per cent versus 7.8 per cent and 3.2 per cent versus 5.0 per cent. A similar difference obtained for affective psychosis: 1.2 per cent of Aboriginal outpatients fell in this category, compared with 4.9 per cent of 'European' clients. Other categories showed very similar admission rates: for example, alcoholic psychosis, 1.2 per cent and 1.1 per cent, respectively; and schizophrenic psychosis, 14.7 per cent and 15.6 per cent, respectively. Overall, these 1988 data suggest that .86 per cent of Queensland's Aboriginal population, compared with .73 per cent of Queensland's non-Aboriginal population, were admitted for inpatient and outpatient treatment during 1988. These are not true prevalence figures, but are treated prevalence figures for state-run treatment services, including alcohol and drug dependence services.

Psychiatric surveys

The reporting of Aboriginal mental health in remote Australia has been characterised by 'psychiatric surveys', which attempt to 'survey' the prevalence of mental disorder in particular Aboriginal communities or regions for a given period of time. Published survey findings covering a number of regions and communities at different points in time include the following surveys:

1. Mornington Island, Queensland, population of 650 (Nurcombe and Cawte 1967; Cawte et al. 1968; Bianchi et al. 1970; Cawte 1972);
2. Warburton Range, Western Australia, and Yuendumu, Northern Territory, population of 300 (Kidson and Jones 1968);
3. Jigalong and Fitzroy Crossing (Western Australia), population of 300 (Jones 1972);
4. other Western Desert and Kimberley communities (Western Australia), population of 959 (Jones and Horne 1973);
5. the northern region of Northern Territory, population of 10 500 (Eastwell 1977).

An interesting overview and assessment of a number of these survey findings is found in Moodie (1973).

As the authors of these surveys themselves occasionally note, the comparability of epidemiological findings such as these is very limited, and depends as much upon case selection as on actual levels of morbidity. Additional problems include:

- these figures are often not broken down by sex or age categories;
- the actual population base figures are often very inaccurate;
- differing incidence frames are used (for example, over individual lifetimes versus last five years);
- it is not always clear whether the 'prevalence rate' (the number of cases active at a given time or for a given time period) include both treated and untreated cases;
- it is very difficult to find a regional psychiatric morbidity figure for comparison.

A number of successive psychiatric surveys were undertaken by Jones and colleagues in Western Desert and Kimberley Aboriginal communities in the late 1960s and early 1970s (Kidson and Jones 1968; Jones 1972; Jones and Horne 1973). These surveys were apparently based principally on elicitation of information from non-Aboriginal staff and 'native sources' rather than clinical interviews. Only frequencies by psychiatric disorder were reported, separately for adults and children and with no breakdown by sex. The findings of the second of these surveys are presented in table 6.5. The conclusions made by Jones and his associates on the basis of their several surveys were as follows:

1. Among Australian Western Desert Aborigines, dementia, depression, schizophrenia, hysterical conversion states and personality disorders exist, and in essential respects the features are similar to those states in European people, but the mode of presentation differs.
2. Among Western Desert Aborigines, overt anxiety, homosexuality and suicide are rare.
3. Possession states' are found and can sometimes be placed in the traditional nosological categories, but they are atypical.
4. The prevalence of psychiatric illness found in different communities varied between 2.7 and 9.2 per cent.

Table 6.5 Psychiatric disorders

	Jigalong	Fitzroy Crossing
Schizophrenia	3	1
Behavioural disorders of childhood	1	1
Organic disorders	2	2
Personality disorders	1	3
Possession	2	0
Hysterical fits	2	0
Anxiety	0	1
Subnormality	4	0
Hypochondriasis	0	3
Depression	0	0

Source: Jones 1972, p. 265

It should be noted that epidemiological studies of mental disorder in Western cultural contexts are fraught with their own problems. Dohrenwend (1983) notes that differences in the reported prevalence of various mental disorders can vary from rates of over 50 per cent to less than 1 per cent, depending on methods of research and beliefs about aetiology. According to Dohrenwend, the question of what information is required to make an informed clinical judgment and the question of what information is likely to bias such judgment constitute two horns of a dilemma that has received far less attention in epidemiological studies than it deserves.

Jones and Horne (1973) carefully qualify their findings with respect to physical inaccessibility, language barriers, cultural differences in the meaning and importance of particular behaviours and events, differences in the manifestations of some states, and small numbers. These factors, in addition to the limited information value of frequency-by-category data, do not allow very much to be concluded about the nature of Aboriginal mental health.

The most comprehensive psychiatric survey undertaken of remote Aboriginal communities is that of Eastwell (1977, 1982b) in the Northern Territory (see table 6.6 for the results of this survey). The problems with this, as with other surveys, include (Eastwell 1982b, pp. 231–2):

1. the lack of any specifics with respect to method or procedure:

a field team was sent to each of the small towns, along the lines used by Cawte (1972);

2. a reliance on the perceptions of white staff:

The field teams monitored psychiatric illness between trimonthly visits of the psychiatrist. They consisted of a white nurse at the town and one or two Aboriginal aids. In addition, non-medical white staff who knew many townspeople were also enlisted;

3. a reliance on another culture's classification and diagnostic scheme:

Table 6.6   Five-year survey of northern Aboriginal reserves (population 11 000): diagnoses using the International Classification of Diseases (ICD)

	Males	Females	Total
Reactive psychosis (a fear-of-sorcery syndrome)	53	4	57
Depressive neurosis (shame as dominant dynamic)	25	74	99
Hysterical neurosis-dissociation	11	43	54
Hysterical neurosis-conversion[a]	1	3	4
Hypochondriacal neurosis	14	33	47
Anxiety neurosis	7	3	10
Schizophrenia	10	17	27
Manic depressive psychosis and reactive depressive psychosis (often reactive to 'rolelessness')	13	14	27
Acute brain syndrome (all causes, usually alcohol)	15	–	15
Chronic brain syndrome (all causes,)	12	5	17
Moderate and severe mental retardation	10	4	14
Mild mental retardation (difficult to diagnose)	6	1	7
Major epilepsy ('idiopathic')	1	5	6
Transient situational disorder[b]	13	8	21
Personality disorders	12	8	20
Other diagnoses	3	2	5
Insufficient detail for diagnosis (in persons living remote from towns)	5	–	5
Total	211	224	435

[a] Many patients with minor conversion symptoms were included under their major diagnoses-depressive neurosis.
[b] Includes episodes of self-injury.
Source: Eastwell 1982 *b*

Only patients who corresponded to the World Health Organization definition of mental illness (1960) were included. This definition states that the symptoms of psychiatric illness should be severe enough to debar the patient from ordinary social life and work and that the illness should resemble some established psychiatric entity;

4.   a discounting of clear discrepancies between indigenous and Western labels and criteria:

Classification and diagnosis in any remote culture is always problematic and the field teams encountered practical difficulties. For example, extreme reactions of shame resembled reactive depressions but, because of the lack of indigenous labelling of such states of illnesses, many tended to be overlooked by Aboriginal field team members and none were recorded in some towns. As another example of difficulties, whites readily labeled repeatedly aggressive persons as personality disorders. But there was a surprising lack of agreement by Aboriginals [sic], who often refused to label them as ill;

5.   a cataloguing of culture-specific diagnostic categories: 'fear of sorcery syndrome', 'mimetic illness', 'shared depressive illness', which are then made

Contemporary anxieties, traditional fears, and diagnostic labels

Descriptions of Aboriginal people have tended to emphasise unreasonable and irrational fears and anxieties. Such descriptions, in a health context, have often taken on clinical and psychiatric connotations, with expressed fears being seen as evidence of disturbance and often psychosis. Discussion of the 'anxious' and 'fear-ridden' character of 'cases' is often linked to a psychoanalytic perspective on defence mechanisms.

Of the 11 male patients [identified as psychiatric cases], 5 had delusions of persecution by sorcery, while another performed sorcery rituals...Of the 25 cases encountered, 12 showed major use of projection, an ego defense mechanism whereby noxae such as sickness, injury, misfortune, or death were attributed to the malevolence of a rival clan. In addition 4 cases showed less pronounced use of this mechanism. This readiness to use projection has been previously noted among Aborigines. Roheim (1925) viewed it from a framework of orthodox psychoanalysis: 'the Australian rids himself of the contrition that follows the endopsychical acknowledgement of guilt—by projection to others' (207). More recently Cawte (1964) concluded, 'where the Western person feels guilt and blames himself, the [Aboriginal] person more characteristically feels afraid and blames others (471)...Projection was prominent in the following diagnoses and conferred a paranoid flavor on them [8 cases of transient delusional states, 4 cases of disassociative reactions, and 3 cases of severe depression]. (Eastwell 1977, pp. 43–6)

Eastwell (1987, p. 46) goes on to present these cases and explain how they are evidence of the defence mechanism of projection. All of the transient delusional cases, for example, 'were states of fear arising from putative sorcery...fear was always projected and took this delusional form; there were no cases of free-floating anxiety. Auditory hallucinations confirmed the fears in 4 cases'. This type of argument, based on the presentation of limited descriptive accounts, is difficult to evaluate and appears to be quite circular. The indigenous 'projection' explanation offered for the cases of dissociative reactions was 'that the patient's spirit had temporarily vacated the body, with the implication that unspecified sorcerers were responsible'. With respect to the cases of severe depression, Eastwell goes on to say that 'the clinical picture of hypochondriasis [following from depression] was seen rather more frequently after a death in the community that was ascribed to sorcery. Some of this behavior was thus motivated by the same fear, and hence projection was in operation'.

It is a tortured logic and a vague and encompassing notion of projection that ties these cases together. Such labelling of traditional explanatory frames and beliefs has tended to characterise the psychiatric perspective in Australia. It has also ensured that such beliefs were given a clinical interpretation. An argument that makes fewer cultural and psychiatric assumptions is that the contemporary anxiety and stress being experienced by many Aboriginal people living in crowded settlement communities is simply often given traditional labels. Attributions of sorcery and other forms of malevolent magic at least provide a familar and meaningful cultural explanation for many people, and suggest avenues of human intercession and control.

J. Reser

to 'fit' into conventional categories, in this case the International Classification of Diseases (ICD).

Such psychiatric surveys, though relatively few in absolute numbers, engendered numerous follow-up publications examining particular issues. It is arguable that these articles have not appreciably advanced cross-cultural understanding of Aboriginal mental health. Bianchi et al. (1970), for example, examined the relationship of cultural identity to incidence of psychiatric symptoms:

Our chief object in measuring cultural identity in the culture contact is to examine its relationship to the incidence of psychiatric symptoms...Acquisition of Western patterns—represented by reading, writing and speaking English, by travel and interest in radio and cinema—shows no relationship to the incidence of psychiatric symptomatology...Emulation of Western patterns—measured in our scale by preferences with regard to skin colour, place and type of housing, work and recreation—are not found to bear a relationship, either positively or negatively, to psychiatric symptomatology...The extent of retention of traditional beliefs [RB] — represented in the RB scale by belief in sorcery, the efficacy of native medicine and the existence of a Spirit Heaven in the East—is higher in the elderly, in the Kaiadilt subgroup and in the psychologically ill...The most striking finding in this study is that none of the parameters of cultural identity used by us are importantly associated with symptom levels.

Bianchi et al. 1970, pp. 315–18)

Quite apart from any reservations a critical reader might have about method, analysis and meaningfulness of results, such studies appear to have been undertaken within a problematic framework of majority culture and psychiatric assumptions. Observations made in reports such as these are telling.

With the Kaiadilt too, there is evidence that even before their sudden advent to a Westernised existence they were a miserable, paranoid group beset by bodily preoccupation.

Bianchi et al. 1970, p. 317

The Australian Aborigines were nomadic hunter-gatherers who built no permanent dwellings, made no pottery, and used spears rather than bows and arrows. They shared the honor of last place in the race toward cultural complexity with the Bushman of the Kalahari. This failure to advance technologically is explained by the unsuitability of the native animals for domestication and the native plants for growth as crops...There is a personal adherence to a philosophy of timelessness of life, entirely alien to Westerners, and an acceptance of magical explanations for events. Concepts of the individual's control over his own life and destiny are poorly developed...No Aboriginals [sic] have proceeded to tertiary education and only a handful have completed secondary school.

Eastwell 1982b, p. 229

These survey findings are difficult to interpret, given problems of language, frequent reliance on second-hand information from non-Aboriginal staff, and diagnostic classification. If the prevalence figures were to be taken at face value, overlooking additional problems of small numbers and comparability, and compared with figures found in other regions of the world, it would become clear that the prevalence of mental illness in these remote communities, at the time the surveys were undertaken, was not particularly high.

The estimation of the prevalence of mental illness in primitive societies is extremely difficult, and later studies which have met reasonable standards of precision and comprehensiveness did indeed find rates not too different from those encountered

Cultural relativity or cultural bias

In 1978, the *Journal of Psychological Anthropology* published what was to become a very controversial account of Aboriginal culture. The article, written by Arthur Hippler (1978), a North American psychiatrist and anthropologist, was entitled the 'Culture and personality perspective of the Yolngu of north-eastern Arnhem Land'.

The article attempted to describe broadly the cultural context of personality development among the clan groups of north-eastern Arnhem Land, with an emphasis on those child-rearing and socialisation practices deemed critical to the formation of personality and culture. This 'culture and personality' school of thought has its own critics (Draguns 1988; Jahoda 1982; Segall 1979), but Hippler's observations and conclusions, based on several weeks' field work and largely second-hand data, provoked a more specific and unprecedented repudiation on the part of anthropologists and psychologists working with Aboriginal communities in Australia.

Hippler's argument, based on very questionable 'evidence', was that Aboriginal child-rearing practices are characterised by a neglectful and hostile stance on the part of care-givers and a 'generalized impoverished socialization', which in turn creates serious developmental problems and adult emotional and intellectual 'deficits'. Specifically Hippler described the 'distance' of the father, the 'deep ambivalence', 'hostility' and 'inconsistent disinterest' of the mother, and the 'unceasing attacks' and 'teasing' of siblings and other children. Further supposed instances of 'harsh', 'brutal' and inconsistent child-rearing practices included frequent 'bogey threats',

amusement at the distress of young children, hostile and punitive 'toilet-training', and slapping and shaking. Such an upbringing, argued Hippler, leads to a complex of insecurities, anxieties and fears in the adult individual, evidenced in 'retardation of emotional maturity', 'massive projection', 'uncontrolled aggression as well as fear (by men) of women', 'unconsolidated egos', and 'defensive grandiosity'.

What particularly upset other researchers, apart from the dramatic discrepancy between Hippler's account of Aboriginal culture and their own extensive field experience, was that Hippler cavalierly ignored virtually all principles of cross-cultural research (Reser 1981, 1982) and based his synopsis/diagnosis of Aboriginal culture on totally inadequate evidence, extremely limited first-hand experience, and very distorting prejudices and value-judgments. The result was a caricature of Aboriginal culture, published in an international journal, which was quite damning in the eyes of readers with no independent knowledge of traditionally oriented Aboriginal society. Indeed the suggestion was that Aboriginal society is ridden with socialised, collective personality disorders and operates at a child-like level of emotional and intellectual functioning. The unprecedented condemnation of Hippler's views by anthropologists and cross-cultural psychologists in Australia (such as Hamilton 1979; Reser 1981, 1982), and Hippler's response (1981) encapsulate a spectrum of mental health issues with respect to indigenous Australians, and in particular the issue of the cultural relativity of other-culture diagnoses.

J. Reser

in industrialized societies. It seems that culture, as represented by different types of societal organization and development, is not related to total amount of behavior disorder but to the ways in which behavioral aberrations are manifested and in the distribution of specific diagnostic categories. This is strikingly illustrated by the ubiquitous 20-25% figure for the prevalence of emotional and/or behavior disorder found during the last 35 to 40 years in Midtown, Manhattan, Nova Scotia, New Haven, Iceland and two Ugandan villages.

Eron and Peterson 1982, pp. 241–2

As previously mentioned, Kahn (1982, 1986) is one of the few mental health professionals who has written about Aboriginal mental health from a cross-cultural perspective, and who has directly compared Native American mental health problems and issues with those of Aboriginal Australians. His observations are both more qualified and culturally sensitive than those of other researchers.

Diagnostic classification of psychological disorder is much influenced by culture. Abnormal behavior is largely a matter of deviation from a given culture's socially accepted norms of morality or actions. The norms vary from culture to culture. Cultural factors are also greatly involved in what appropriately stimulates emotion and how emotion is expressed. The DSM-III is a Western classification system developed for a particular culture and consequently may have limitations when applied to other cultural groups. Draguns (1980) and Marsella (1980) have discussed many of the complicated problems involved in classifying cross-cultural psychopathology. Most of the studies in Aboriginals have been done by Westerners using Western criteria and consequently must be viewed cautiously...There exists no adequate study of the forms of mental disorder among aboriginal people, although there have been a few notable attempts.

Kahn 1986, p. 47

Notwithstanding this more balanced perspective, there appears to be a tendency for psychiatric language itself to equate social problems loosely with 'disorder':

High rates for psychosocial disorders have been found among aboriginal people of the U.S. and Australia. The major disorders are similar for Native Americans (Indians and Eskimos) and for Australian Aborigines. Alcohol abuse is the most visible disorder, and is associated with other high prevalence disorders including depression, suicide, family instability, delinquency and accidental death. [Emphasis added.]

Kahn 1986, p. 45

Clearly 'disorder' loses useful clinical meaning when applied equally to such circumstances as depression, family instability, delinquency, and accidental death; its use also creates a psychiatric frame of reference that can be distorting. A major problem with the psychiatric view vis-à-vis indigenous Australians has been that, while giving explicit acknowledgment to some of the functions served by traditional 'medical' systems (for instance, Cawte's *Medicine is the Law*, 1974), there appears to have been little real understanding that symptoms of disorder were in many cases individual behavioural responses to social control sanctions, as noted by Biernoff (1982, pp. 139–40).

Though some of these studies recognize the role of social control mechanisms in mobilizing negative sanctions against the 'anti-social', none deals with the role of traditional structures and processes of social control that maintain and protect 'land' and 'law' in the subjective perception of physical and mental well-being. Thus although these studies provide useful data on personality and personality aberrations, they usually do not take into account the subjective reality of Aboriginal people. Nor do they explain individual situations and responses in ways that reflect Aboriginal understanding. The researchers' cultural and professional blinkers are understandable, but their reality does not coincide with the reality of many Aborigines in traditional settings. Aboriginal perceptions must be considered if valuable insights into the sociocultural dynamics and health of traditionally oriented communities are not to be missed.

The psychiatric frame of reference in the Australian context has also and more subtly ignored the emotional dimension of Aboriginal mental health, both because this was an area of cultural difference in presenting symptoms, and because of more basic majority culture assumptions about Aboriginal society. The dismissal of 'emotional problems' by Western practitioners working in indigenous cultural contexts has been a recurrent theme. German, for example writes:

Before the 1960s, the decade of African independence,…generalizations about Africans included the views that their brains were inferior, that they functioned in a childish manner, and that they lacked a sense of responsibility. Their emotional distress was the short-lived and charming emotionality of the child, but not the bravely-born pain of affective disorder. Responsibility was defined in terms of European priorities, while the responsible pursuit of African values was usually regarded as evidence of backwardness. Thus a series of cultural stereotypes was imposed on the African, and confirmation of these stereotypes came from epidemiological inquiries limited to patients in custodial mental hospitals—a highly select and unusual population.

German 1987, p. 435

While the state of knowledge, or more correctly, ignorance, concerning the prevalence of mental illness in Aboriginal communities may appear hardly credible, it is not an exceptional situation with respect to indigenous minorities. One could argue that the knowledge base for Native and Black American communities is just as problematic (LaFromboise 1988; Manson et al. 1987; Neighbors 1984). Indeed, there exist only three community-wide Native American epidemiological studies. The prevalence rates of psychological dysfunction range from a low of 1 per cent per 2000 to a high of 37 per cent per 1000 (LaFramboise 1988). Perhaps the saving grace with respect to Native American mental health surveys, however, is the fact that their findings are carefully qualified:

Gathering information of the type summarized in this report presents particular technical and methodological problems in Alaska. There is, for instance, no generally agreed upon and utilizable population base. Nor is there an inclusive statewide mental health reporting system…True figures for the incidence and prevalence of mental illness and alcohol abuse have not been established with any certainty for Alaska Natives or any other major United States population…It should be kept in mind, therefore, that the figures summarised here are incomplete, fragmentary, and deal with only one aspect of a complex problem. They are suggestive, not definitive; since they originate in a rudimentary reporting system with a considerable amount of under-reporting, they should be viewed as conservative.

Kraus and Buffler 1979, pp. 120–1

The quality of the epidemiological data in the Australian studies noted is very poor and non-comparable. Clearly there is a critical need for more systematic, comprehensive and valid data. A word of warning is in order, however. Conventional epidemiological data alone, whether in the context of physical or psychological morbidity, provides a weak basis for designing sound prevention strategies. Such description, without anthropological and psychological contextual data, simply misses crucial variables, interactions, and cultural meanings and processes (Janes et al. 1986). Research that promotes human well-being rather than frequency analyses over time and region will require genuine multidisciplinary involvement and cultural sensitivity. The value of the surveys is also questionable in any epidemiological sense; they tell us little about the incidence or true prevalence of mental health problems in Aboriginal communities. These studies are valuable, however, in underscoring the problems that the health professions have had worldwide in attempting to understand mental health cross-culturally and in forcing a reassessment of Western cultural assumptions and models.

Few studies of the mental health status of urban Aboriginal communities have been undertaken. Those that are reported (for example, Eastwell 1985; Kahn et al. 1978; Kamien 1978; Lickiss 1970, 1975) have either focused on a particular population (Lickiss 1970) or have been in the context of another objective, for example, in the context of an evaluation of a behavioural health program (Kahn et al. 1978). The consensus from such reports, and the opinion reflected in statements such as those of the National Aboriginal Mental Health Association, is that the mental health problems of urban Aboriginal communities are substantial and are not adequately met by existing health services.

One of the most recent investigations of urban mental health problems has been conducted by the Department of Primary Health Care and the Division of Sociology of Flinders University, along with the Aboriginal Education Foundation of South Australia, in Adelaide (Radford et al. 1990). The focus of the initial stage 1 report of this study, *Taking control*, was on stress and destructive behaviour among Aboriginal domestic care-givers. In particular, the study examined personal destructive behaviour with special reference to suicidal thoughts and attempts. The report is valuable because it constitutes a multidisciplinary attempt to consider mental health issues in historical, cultural, and situational contexts. The literature review of 'destructive behaviour' among Aboriginal people is one of the few existing balanced reviews of current psychiatric and anthropological perspectives on Aboriginal mental health. The findings of the study were that, out of a random sample of 88 Aboriginal heads of households (81 per cent female), 15 per cent had suffered sexual assault, 51 per cent had experienced physical violence, 24 per cent reported having deliberately 'hurt themselves', 31 per cent had thought seriously about taking their own lives, and 19 per cent had made at least one serious suicide attempt. The report includes a detailed discussion of the many factors implicated in the self-reported social and personal traumas that characterised the lives of many respondents.

Stress and coping

Acculturative stress

In many ways, the literature that has been seen to be most relevant to Aboriginal mental health is that dealing with stress and coping in the face of rapid social and cultural change, and associated individual and collective adjustment problems (see, for example, Berry et al. 1987; Berry and Kim 1988; Chance 1965; Hezel et al. 1985; Kraus and Buffler 1979; Murphy 1973; O'Neil 1986; Seltzer 1980). The mental health picture of indigenous Australians is almost invariably presented and discussed in terms of adjustment costs in the face of rapid sociocultural change, or in terms of cultural impediments to 'development' and acculturation. There are many assumptions and issues involved both in these larger arguments and with respect to their specific application to Aboriginal Australia. O'Neil (1986, p. 249) notes:

A large and multidisciplinary literature has generally argued that the health consequences of rapid sociocultural change are higher levels of morbidity and mortality along both physical and psychological dimensions. The prevailing view has been that rapid sociocultural change brings about social disorganization and cultural disruption which in turn is responsible for role confusion, cultural identity conflicts and feelings of alienation and anomie. This psychological 'stress' is then implicated etiologically in the development of a variety of health problems including alcohol abuse, suicide, schizophrenia, hypertension, diabetes and, increasingly other chronic illnesses including cancer.

Many authors have specifically applied such an 'acculturative stress' analysis to Aboriginal society, indeed most of the Aboriginal mental health literature is premised on such a conceptual framework (for example, Beckett 1965; Berry 1970; Cawte 1972, 1974; Kamien 1978; Kiloh 1975; Nurcombe et al. 1970). Kamien (1978, p. 44) writes of the people of Bourke, New South Wales:

The result of the contact of the two cultures was catastrophic for the Aborigines. They were dispossessed of their land by disease and by violence. The authority of their elders collapsed, together with the cultural practices that had sustained them for at least 30 000 years. The new settlers made few places available in their economy for 'Bourke Aborigines'. In order to survive they had to become dependent upon paternalistic charity from welfare or mission organizations. In their paternalism these welfare agencies further insulated the Aborigines from learning and developing new skills. The result was that in Bourke as in the rest of Australia, Aborigines had come to occupy the status of the lowest caste, excluded by behaviour as well as by colour from the mainstream of life in the town. They were generally despised, socially disparaged and their positive attributes were devalued. Their political and economic powerlessness gave few of them hope for the future. They exhibited the psychology of a persecuted and rootless people...In brief, most Bourke Aborigines were not beneficiaries of the basic freedoms from want, disease, ignorance, squalor, idleness or of the right to determine their own destiny. They exhibited all of the criteria of a socially disintegrated society.

The psychiatric literature on acculturative stress has typically not spelled out in any detail the nature of the relationship between the stress of culture contact and adaptation and mental illness. The suggestion is that there exists a reasonably simple and straightforward causal relationship between change itself and behaviour disorder. A further and typically confounded suggestion is that primitive and conservative elements of Aboriginal culture are impediments to 'development' and acculturation, and therefore mediate much of the culture-conflict which leads to psychopathology (Cawte 1972, 1974).

One of the very few studies in Australia to look systematically for evidence of the psychological effects of culture contact and change was that of Berry (1970). Berry's research was essentially an exploratory study carried out in a small coastal Aboriginal community in New South Wales in the late 1960s. In line with the predicted psychological effects of culture contact and change, he found evidence of psychological marginality, and particularly among the more traditionally oriented people:

The high level of acculturation of many of these highly marginal persons suggests that this more traditional orientation may be a reaffirmation rather than a retention of traditional values and that, psychologically, it is possible that these highly marginal, high-deviance, high stress persons have adopted this attitudinal position as a reaction to the dominant White society.

Berry 1970, pp. 250, 251

A subsequent study that examined the coping strategies of adolescents in a more traditional Northern Territory Aboriginal community undergoing substantial social change (Davidson et al. 1978) reported that substance abuse and aggressive behaviour were part of a characteristic response to pressures in conflict situations. However, research done in other indigenous cultures undergoing rapid Westernisation has not found any clear relationship between such change and mental health problems (Murphy 1973), nor do the research and theorists often cited in the context of acculturative stress theory (such as Chance 1965; Leighton 1959, 1968) in fact support the simple proposition that modernisation causes psychiatric disorder (although this research is often cited in support of such a proposition in an Australian context). Chance and Leighton's model not only is more complex in terms of indirect causation, but also underscores heightened vulnerability *in particular situations:*

The theoretical orientation of these investigations is that (a) throughout the entire course of an individual's life, events have the potential for precipitating psychiatric disorders; (b) sociocultural processes and situations experienced by adults are among the events that may influence disorder; (c) the conditions that most foster symptoms and disability are those that place the person at a disadvantage in terms of social support and opportunity for self-realization; (d) for social support to be present certain minimal integration of the socialcultural [sic] system is necessary; and (e) groups of people in the lower socioeconomic levels, in situations of cultural conflict, and in circumstances of rapid social change are in states of risk regarding sociocultural disintegration (Leighton, A. 1968). This orientation is different from the notion that modernization causes psychiatric disorder, which is sometimes referred to as acculturative stress hypothesis (De Vos and Miner, 1959). The idea here is that rapid change involving cultural conflict fosters vulnerability in the society and that the malfunctioning of the social system accounts for the distribution of the psychiatric disorders.

Murphy 1973, p. 240

The assessment of the psychiatric view with respect to acculturative stress by other social scientists has been very qualified (for example, Everett 1975: Levy and

Kunitz 1971, 1987; Segall 1979). What is really wrong with this perspective? Surely it is a reasonable proposition that transition stress and adaptation demands may exact a mental health cost. The real problems have to do with oversimplification of the process, a too-negative understanding of the stress of change, a misunderstanding of the nature and role of culture as change agent, the attempt to understand individual experience in exclusively structural and historical terms, and the consequences of such external attributions for the individuals and communities affected.

One of the oldest and most widely accepted generalizations about acculturation, among laypersons and specialists alike, is that individuals exposed to a rapidly changing culture find that exposure psychologically disruptive. Subjected often to conflicting values—for example, modern ones at school, traditional ones at home—they are thought to be living a schizophrenic-like existence in two conflicting cultures...Such pictures of acculturative stress are probably exaggerated and ethnocentric. They ignore the fact that, to many individuals experiencing culture change, elements of the contact culture are often not even perceived as foreign, because they have 'been there' throughout the lifetimes of those individuals...Still, the potential for some conflict and acculturative stress must exist in every culture-contact situation, particularly when the 'old' and 'new' cultural elements relate to contradictory values...But surely acculturative stress varies as a function of (1) the acculturative pressures brought to bear by a community, (2) certain traditional features of that community, and (3) certain characteristics of individuals.

Segall 1979, pp. 209, 210

Responses to stress

Contemporary social science perspectives on stress and coping constitute something of a revolution in traditional understandings of health and disease. Social and psychological factors are now viewed as critical mediating variables for understanding the aetiology, treatment and prevention of many disorders previously thought of in exclusively biological terms. Coping has emerged as a particularly apt notion for conceptualising the adjustment process that mediates between environmental stressors and human response. Rather than focusing on disease, distress and disability, coping considers health abilities, resources, and other positive aspects of human functioning. Coping models tend to emphasise individual appraisals of particular situations and their own coping capacity, and in particular *perceived* threats and *experienced* competence and felt control. This more psychological literature on coping (such as Dinges and Joos 1988; Folkman and Lazarus 1988; Lazarus and Folkman 1984; Rothbaum et al. 1982) is of particular relevance to the adjustment problems of indigenous minorities, as it is concerned with the individual and collective experience of change, conflict and stress in the face of continual and often contradictory adaptation demands. Culturally different modes of coping (Lee and Newton 1981; Levy 1973; Marsella and Dash-Scheuer 1988) are of particular interest to researchers and mental health professionals, because they suggest important differences in how problems and stressors are defined and experienced, and underscore the importance of strengthening culturally appropriate coping strategies in therapeutic interventions.

Many public statements relating to Aboriginal mental health make reference to underlying stress, the importance of felt control and implicit coping problems:

While symptomatic relief of the emotionally disturbed may be necessary in the short term, mental ill health is predominantly the result of extreme stress. Stress-related conditions, such as alcohol abuse, depression, hypertension, aggressive outbursts and other traumas result from chronic ill health, the breakdown of traditional and social authority structures, the loss of purpose and self-esteem, a perception that social and personal crises are beyond one's ability to change or control, suppressed fear and anger and discrimination...When people feel insecure and have no home which they see as permanent and inalienable, they crowd together in depressed, hopeless, dispirited groups having neither the confidence nor the motivation to create less crowded or more healthful living environments. The settlements on which they live take on the characteristics of institutions and the residents fall into a state of 'learned helplessness'. By contrast, when people have control over their physical environment they feel able to make and implement decisions for their own benefit, knowing that their decisions and actions are an assured investment in the future.
HRSCAA 1979, pp. 26, 58

The stress experienced by Aboriginal communities has been attributed to factors such as:

- the pressures and demands of transition,
- the experience and impact of discrimination and prejudice,
- the marginal social and economic status of most Aboriginal communities,
- the condition of the physical environment in which people live,
- poor health.

Few discussions have examined the coping process in an Aboriginal cultural context, although it is clear that stress is mediated through cultural assumptions and beliefs about what kinds of things are threatening and what can be done about them. It is also not often appreciated that some of the stresses that traditionally oriented Aborigines experience can be very different from the Western experience of and assumptions about stress. The importance of kinship proscriptions, for example, is shared with other indigenous groups, as Djikman and de Vries (1987, p. 551) note:

Rules of avoidance and their consequences...across cultures...often based on the fear and avoidance of sexual contact have been described in detail in the ethnographic literature (Malinowski, 1927; Wilson, 1951)...The strain involved in abiding by these rules may involve significant social stress, and the reality of breaching them may have profound psychological consequences that account for a certain percentage of mental health admissions in both Western and developing countries (Tseng and McDermott, 1981).

Features of Aboriginal culture that suggest important differences in coping strategies include:

- different cultural assumptions concerning causality and control,
- different ways of expressing and communicating emotional distress,

- different ways of thinking and feeling about self and others,
- very different objective life circumstances.

Research in other cultures suggests that coping can vary from more psychological responses in terms of emotional control, to somatically oriented coping, to social support, to direct environmental control attempts (Marsella and Dash-Scheuer 1988). Coping strategies are also often specific to particular types of stressors, and vary substantially across individuals within a culture.

Native American studies have been increasingly influenced by such 'stress and coping' formulations, and make use of an analytic framework that focuses less on historical discontinuities and structural change, and more on proximate mediators of stress, and how stress is experienced and dealt with. Dinges and Joos (1988, p. 12), for example, make the following observation:

Stress has been implicated as a causal, precipitating or perpetuating factor in virtually all of the disease categories described...Sources of morbidity and mortality which are prevalent among Indians and Natives, such as alcohol abuse and suicide, are clearly among these categories. Alcohol abuse may reflect maladaptive coping responses to a variety of environmental stressors and in turn contributes to mortality from accidents, suicide, homicide, liver diseases, and cirrhosis. Alcohol use has been related to hypertension among Navajos (DeStefano et al., 1979) and in non-Indian populations (McQueen and Celentano, 1982). Suicide has also been viewed as a result of failures in coping with respect to increasing environmental stressors. The concentration of suicides among young and middle-aged Indians and Natives may reflect this process at work.

The argument with respect to coping must be qualified in that it derives from a largely Western clinical literature and research program, and it is clear that the expression and communication of emotional distress and coping strategies are all culturally relative. In particular, Aboriginal coping strategies appear to rely more on the expression and communication of feelings, and a reliance on a collective coping response. Such a coping perspective also provides a particularly cogent explanation for a phenomenon such as the pattern of alcohol use in Aboriginal communities. Alcohol may constitute a particularly sympathetic coping strategy within an Aboriginal cultural context, as it directly connects with feelings and intensity of social interaction, and allows for heightened and oftentimes dramatic emotional expression, while at the same time providing a 'time out' in terms of sanctions and consequences. Hence tensions and anxieties are both biochemically and socially muted. Unfortunately, early dependence on alcohol as a coping mechanism can substantially interfere with the learning of more adaptive, long-term coping and problem-solving strategies.

A widely shared view of alcohol and other substance abuse is that such abuse is itself a coping strategy, with alcohol being a self-administered analgesic used to deaden anxiety or other emotional distress (see Abrams 1983; Barlow 1988; Shiffman and Wills 1985; Rodin 1985; Zinberg 1984). According to such formulations, uncontrollable stress leads to an experienced loss of control and associated anxiety and depression, which are 'treated' with doses of alcohol or other drugs. Substance abuse appears independently to minimise negative mood and maximise positive mood (Shiffman and Wills 1985). This view has in particular been applied to adolescents (Newcomb and Harlow 1986) and indigenous minorities (Pedigo 1983; Dinges and Joos 1988).

One obvious meaning alcohol and other drug usage has for the society is how it functions as a coping mechanism. A Task Force summary of information received from more than 50 tribes cited unemployment and poverty, related to loss of individual self-esteem, as a major cause for alcoholism. Loss of Native American culture that contributes to feelings of anxiety was also cited as a cause. Splits between old and young people and children going away to boarding schools was mentioned...Given the disintegration of social cohesion, and the positive social functions drug use may serve in that regard, the magnitude of Native American drug use does not seem inconceivable or even unreasonable. The additional role it serves as a coping mechanism enhances its desirability and justifies the Native American tendency to look the other way when faced with destructive use...In a study of high school students in a plains tribe, 84% of the boys and 76% of the girls claimed they drank regularly (Task Force 11, 1976). Such extensive chemical use has meaning as a coping mechanism that serves positive social purposes among Native American children.

Pedigo 1983, p. 275

Culture and emotional experience

A number of recent anthropological accounts of Aboriginal culture have suggested that the expression and communication of feelings is at the core of Aboriginal culture (Myers 1986; Morice 1978, 1979). Emotional well-being or distress is also perhaps our best barometer of mental health—indeed our psychiatric taxonomies are premised on the core importance of affective disturbance. The anthropology and cross-cultural psychology of emotions have become major areas of current research interest, with direct relevance to the understanding of anger, aggression and violence (Harre 1986; Izard et al. 1984; Levy 1973; Lutz 1988; Lutz and White 1986; Marcus and Fischer 1986; Scherer 1988; Shweder and LeVine 1984). The interrelationships between emotions, coping and substance abuse are also of central importance, with the research evidence suggesting that emotions and 'arousability' are significantly related to substance abuse (Adler 1990). Recent studies further suggest that youths scoring high in both negative feelings and arousability (a combination of reactivity and impulsivity) use drugs to try to handle negative feelings, with the problem perpetuated by a failure to learn alternative ways of dealing with negative emotions (Adler 1990). Recent research in north Queensland relating to the role of alcohol in Aboriginal self-injury and suicide suggests that culture-specific modes of emotional expression and coping are directly implicated in these phenomena (Reser 1989).

Ethnographic observations with respect to Aboriginal emotional expression and the role of emotions are few but noteworthy. The following are some examples:

Most Mardudjara adults are normally agreeable people of pleasant disposition. But both sexes have a capacity for rapid and passionate arousal of emotions to a violent pitch, seen most often in either anger or sorrow. At such times they may attempt to harm themselves; for example, when grieving over the sickness or death of a relative, or they may vent their anger on others in conflicts. Great anger can flare over seemingly trivial matters, resulting in quite intense confrontations between individuals.

Tonkinson 1978, p. 121

Each child at an early age is exposed to certain stereotypes which 'explain' problem behaviour. This is the system of role-types characterised by the predominance of a certain emotional and social response. The statement 'he is wild (anbaitjuda)' of a violent child does not merely describe his passing state but places him in a system of classificatory reference along with a number of other things...He is one of a class of 'wild' things, and membership in this class, attributed early in life, is likely to remain a reference point for his character as he grows older.

Hamilton 1981, p. 152

Among the Pintupi, the concept of walytja, meaning kinship or relatedness, is indeed critical to understanding social life, but their own emphasis is on the affective relationships among those who are relatives...The discourse of daily life is heavily nuanced with expressions and demonstrations of such emotions as 'compassion', 'melancholy,' 'grief,' 'happiness,' and 'shame'...Kin status is largely a matter of feeling, and if a person feels unkindly treated, he may complain that the other does not really 'like' him or her, and thus is not really walytja. The negotiation of such relationships is of critical concern to Pintupi...Thus, a full understanding of the Pintupi experience of life must grasp the cultural meaning of these emotions...Pintupi ethnopsychology seems to view an individual's internal states as extensively connected with a web of significant others.

Myers 1986, pp. 103–8

In this more 'psychological' and emotional Aboriginal world view, feelings are primary and at times must be expressed with conviction and force. Social intercourse takes place 'with feeling'. From childhood on, individuals are encouraged to give full expression to particular types of feelings, with other people and social context providing necessary checks and balances (see, for example, Hamilton 1981; Martin unpub.). In Western cultures, socialisation is in the direction of internal emotional control, or suppression of feelings. In an Aboriginal cultural context, communication, meaning, and support depend to a greater extent on expressing feelings, and structuring social reality through feelings and expressive behaviour. Feelings and connections with others orchestrate and define interactions and self in a more profound and consequential way than is the case for most Western cultures. The channels and cues employed are less directly verbal, and more physically expressive. Body language, non-verbal gestures, eye contact and movements, and touching are all more central to communication. Perhaps the most general observation that can be made about cultural differences in emotional expression is that in Aboriginal communities the *communication* of how a person is *feeling* is usually of paramount importance. Not to show 'proper feeling' in interactions with others is to question the relationship, and to violate not just an expectancy, but to threaten a severing of connectedness, which is critical to the sense of self and well-being. This can lead to an angry and aggressive response, as a person's very identity is genuinely threatened. As Martin (unpub., p. 7) explains:

The concepts of love, nurturance, respect, of obligation, have their approximate counterparts in Wik Mungkan linguistic terms, but it is in the sharing and exchange of material items—money, alcohol, food, consumer goods—that they are manifested. Like so much of social relations this too is encoded in the formal structures of kinship and its associated obligation correlates: these structures are realised in the interactions and the flows of goods and services between kin and at the same time are reproduced by them. Conversely, a refusal by someone to share with oneself, or a perceived inadequate share, is a denial of relatedness, of one's rights and interests in that relatedness, and a denial of a set of norms and values understood and represented as axiomatic.

A frequent and hurtful saying in north Queensland communities is 'I won't cry for you when you're dead', suggesting no connection, no feelings for the person thus spoken to. Such a comment will trigger a very strong emotional response and will often instigate a fight. Of strong emotions, Tonkinson (1982, pp. 236–7) also notes:

Powerful emotions are also seen to cause illness. Loss of appetite, weight loss, listlessness and pain are symptoms that are sometimes attributed to emotional causes. Yundiri (resentment, sulking) is by far the emotion most frequently linked to illness; in fact, a synonym for yundiri is wirla walygurini (the stomach becoming bad/sick). Some women expressed the view that men are more prone than women to become ill from yundiri. Gunda (shame, embarrassment) may also lead to sickness. With lesser frequency, worry, homesickness, grief and jealousy are said to be causes of illness.

Story about feeling

The emphasis on emotions and feelings in Aboriginal communities is more 'real' than non-Aboriginal people might think. Aboriginal people are in many ways more in touch with their own bodies and biology, and more attentive to non-verbal cues about how other people are feeling than people from Western cultures. This finds expression in how Aboriginal people describe their symptoms and problems, as well as in how they describe their connections with their world. This point is made by Bill Neidjie in the following poem from his appropriately titled book, *Story about feeling* (Taylor 1989, p. 4):

This story e can listen careful
and how you can feel on your feeling.
This story coming through your body
e go right down foot and head
fingernail and blood...through the heart
and e can feel it because because e'll come right through.

That tree, grass...that all like our father.
Dirt, earth, I sleep with this earth.
Grass...just like your brother.
In my blood in my arm this grass.
This dirt for us because we'll be dead,
we'll be going this earth.
This the story now.

J. Reser

There is frequent mention of 'emotions' and emotional distress in the psychiatric literature dealing with Aboriginal mental health concerns (see, for example, Kahn et al. 1976, 1978), but the meaning of such expressions as 'emotional problems' is very unclear and there is an obvious unfamiliarity with the within-culture context of emotions and emotional expression.

Depression

An emotional domain of particular interest to mental health generally and Aboriginal mental health in particular is that of depression, a domain singled out in the report to the House of Representatives Standing Committee on Aboriginal Affairs (HRSCAA 1979, p. 131):

Social disintegration leading to mental illness, in a vicious circle, is the central problem identified by Professor Cawte, whose studies over several years have pioneered this field. Depression resulting from problems which are essentially socio-economic in origin, rather than personality disorder based, looms as the largest single category of disorder in the Aboriginal community. Professor Cawte gave the Committee evidence which suggested that mental illnesses (especially those due to adaptational problems) were experienced in Aboriginal communities before contact with whites, but that these were essentially different from those presently predominant.

Depression would appear to be, from the Australian ethnopyschiatric literature and more general media coverage, a widespread and chronic condition in Aboriginal communities. Depression has also been implicated as a critical determinant of self-injury, substance abuse and suicide. There is, however, little consensus or clarity in the mental health literature. Cawte (1965, p.280) states that '[d]epression, from being a rarity in the traditional culture, is beginning to emerge more prominently in the transitional culture. With it comes suicide and attempted suicide, events uncharacteristic of tribal life'. Kahn et al.(1976, p 222), on the other hand, found that '[w]hile depression and suicide are problems frequently encountered among the Papagos, this does not appear to be parallelled among the Australian Aborigines': Two years later, in a follow-up study by Kahn et al. (1978), depression was reported to be one of the most frequent presenting problems at an Aboriginal health centre, second only to alcohol-related problems, and the rate had increased further at the time of a third follow-up report in 1982 (Kahn 1982, p. 556). Mental health observers suggest that depression is an ubiquitous phenomenon in Aboriginal communities, but it is not clear to what extent this refers to clinical depression. For example Eastwell (1982*a*, p. 232) notes:

In my five year survey (Eastwell 1982b) no aboriginal [sic] name was elicited for the commonest neurosis, apathetic depression, which was diagnosed in 100 of 435 patients and which is mediated by shame. Patients suffering from this neurosis typically lie on a blanket in a public place for weeks on end...These depressions are not regarded as illnesses but are seen as a normal reaction in the face of complications over bestowal and marriage.

Descriptions of the 'depression' found in Aboriginal communities do not provide for much construct validity; that is, it is not at all clear that what is being reported or 'measured' is depression:

A depressed tribal Aboriginal [sic] is more inclined to externalize his feelings by spear-throwing or other aggressive acts than to resort to self-destructive acts. The head-hitting seen with reactions to bereavement does not progress to suicide. During surveys of over 2000 tribal Aborigines in which details of individual patients are known fairly well over a ten year period, no case of suicide has been found. The depressed patient shows other signs of depression similar to Europeans, for example motor retardation, sleep disturbance and depression of affect. Ideas of unworthiness and guilt have been seen in a detribalized man, but not in tribal Aborigines. In tribal people it is difficult to obtain acknowledgement of guilt: they are much more likely to project these feelings on to others. They usually do not present complaining of depression of affect, but will come with somatic symptoms or a behavioural disorder.

Jones and Horne 1972, p. 346

Cawte (1986), indeed, outlines 11 'clinical' types of depression, ranging from *masked depression* ('a mild to moderate degree of depression evidenced by headaches, irritable bowels, poor sleep and not being able to go to work'), to *ill-health depression* (low spirits 'when ailing'), to *ill-use depression* (a depression mediated by self-hatred, manifested by self-injury and mutilation, and caused by abuse as a child), to *exhaustion depression* (giving and helping until 'all used up'). Such classifications do not correspond to any accepted taxonomy of affective disorder, nor are they particularly helpful or appropriate to cross-cultural diagnosis or counselling. As Marsella (1980, p. 243) points out:

One thing that becomes apparent in the various reports regarding the conceptions of depression is that the term is not well represented among the lexicons of non-Western people. This does not mean that depression, as it is defined in the West, is absent in cultures that do not have conceptually equivalent terms but, rather, that it is conceptualized differently and may be experienced differently. It is quite obvious that even though individuals from different cultural groups may have similar physiological changes, the recognition, interpretation, and behavioral representation of the problem may vary across cultures. Further, the social response to the behavioral representation may also differ. Thus, 'depression' would be embedded in an entirely different context and assume an entirely different meaning across cultures.

The issue and status of depression in Aboriginal communities has taken on added currency in that depression is frequently cited as the precipitating cause of many recent suicides and attempted suicides, as well as being seen more generally as a major factor in suicide (see Goldney and Burvill 1980; Goldney 1987). Depression is of particular interest because it has always been viewed as a core component of disturbed behaviour generally, and particularly in the case of affective disorders.

Additionally, depression is an important human emotion, and one in which cross-cultural differences in experience and expression might well be expected. Depression has, however, proven to be a singularly difficult phenomenon to specify or explain in a Western cultural context, with, for example, the distinction between depression and anxiety being very problematic (Kendal and Watson 1989), and depressive symptoms in children being held by some to be non-existent, while others simply regard it as different, and difficult to assess (Rubinstein and Perloff 1986; Quay et al. 1987). If alcohol and depression are interrelated, as most of the medical and psychiatric literature suggests, then assessment of client condition and cause of disorder becomes even more problematic (Edwards et al. 1981). As Marsella (1980) and other authors (such as Kleinman and Good 1985) have noted, the cross-cultural diagnostic perspective with respect to depression requires considerable qualification and cultural relativity. Perhaps the real problem with 'depression' is that it is a Western European *cultural category*, as distinct from a meaningful, cross-culturally valid diagnostic entity. Kleinman discusses the concept of 'category fallacy':

Shweder (1985), for example, suggests that among traditionally oriented rural populations, in many non-Western societies, the phenomenology of depressive disorder is better captured by local syndromes of 'soul loss' than by Western existential categories...Dysthymic Disorder in DSM-III (or neurotic depression in ICD-9) is a possible example. It may hold coherence in the more affluent West, but it represents the medicalisation of social problems in much of the rest of the world (and perhaps the West as well), where severe economic, political and health constraints create feelings of hopelessness and helplessness, where demoralisation and despair are responses to real conditions of chronic deprivation and persistent loss, where powerlessness is not a cognitive distortion but an accurate mapping of one's place in an oppressive system, and where moral, religious and political configurations of such problems have coherence for the local population, but psychiatric categories do not.

Kleinman 1987, p. 452

It is worrying that so much appears to have been written about depression in Aboriginal communities (see, for example, a special issue of the *Aboriginal Health Worker*, June 1986) with so little reference to the cultural context and meanings of depression-like behaviour. Indeed, there exists very little majority culture understanding of Aboriginal emotional experience generally, or how Aboriginally constructed 'emotions' mediate interpersonal behaviour, coping responses and mental health.

Relatedness and the cultural context of self

The *construction* of self is an important feature of an Aboriginal construction of reality which directly relates to the centrality of emotions and feelings. It is a commonplace that 'who' a person is in an Aboriginal cultural context is a nexus of relationships, a set of bounded expectations, obligations and human connections

(Coombs et al. 1983). This is an experienced reality for most traditionally oriented Aborigines, with parallels in many 'collectivist' cultures (see Sampson 1988; Westen 1985). It is evidenced not only in kinship terminology, self-reference, and address forms, but in the complex and rule-prescribed modes of interaction, in the way the world is divided, in the most fundamental cultural assumptions about relationships to the world, to others, to self. While there has been a Western predilection to try to understand these webs of relationships in abstract, classificatory terms, the 'emic', or within-culture, perspective appears to be far more oriented towards feeling and behaviour (Berndt 1971; Myers 1986). 'Self', in an Aboriginal context, incorporates in an almost literal way one's family and extended clan group, to such a degree that quality of interpersonal transactions can be intensely involving and consequential. While it would not be correct to characterise this sense of self as entirely 'collective' (Hui and Triandis 1986), it is clearly very different from a Western, more in-dividualistic orientation. Although a complex of relational bonds and reciprocal obligations ensure interdependence and 'collective' information processing, prob-lem solving and responsibility sharing, these exist in continual tension with a fiercely defended autonomy.

It is clear that there are substantive and profoundly important cross-cultural dif-ferences with respect to conceptions of self (Geertz 1975; Sampson 1988; Shweder and Bourne 1982) and that these differences in constructions of self can have impor-tant health care implications, with links to coping problems, individual and cultural identity crises, shame, self-concept, self-esteem, perceived rejection and so on (Marsella 1985; Weisz et al. 1984). Fabrega (1982, p. 39), notes:

I have assumed that an individual's theory of illness and self, which impact on one another and are complementary, strongly influence how an underlying psychiatric disease condition expresses itself psychosocially or in psychiatric illness generally. This means that (1) an individual's representation or attributions about illness, illness causes, mental functioning, symptoms, etc., together with (2) an individual's representation or attributions regarding personhood (e.g., volition, self control, boundaries of the self, social responsibility, etc.) play a critical role in how the underlying psychiatric disease process is expressed in behavior, how it unfolds, how it is handled, how long it lasts, and indeed how it is shunted about in the social system.

Geertz (1975) and others have argued cogently that an understanding of the nature and meaning of self in another culture is a natural and in many ways prerequisite starting point for understanding anything else about the culture. The meaning and mental health implications of Aboriginal understandings of self have never been adequately discussed or explored. It is possible, for example, that changes in the self construction of Aboriginal youth in many communities, associated with threatened identity and the attenuation of meaningful relationships, is placing them at particular risk with respect to self-injury and suicide.

A further aspect of Aboriginal culture that has never been fully explored or un-derstood is the issue of relatedness. While acknowledgment is made of culturally different and complex kinship networks (see Meggitt 1987), there has been little dis-cussion of what these networks *mean* in terms of emotional well-being, or of how they *function* in terms of social support, experienced connectedness and identity, and with respect to coping and adjustment. Notwithstanding the extensive writings which exist describing Aboriginal kinship systems, few authors have closely examined the emotional and psychological nature and quality of these relationships. Berndt is an exception in this regard, and places a particular emphasis on emotional bonds of varying intensity, referring to particular 'emotionally charged' relationships. The emotional closeness of these relationships can paradoxically create substantial stress and occasionally violent interactions:

One point must be made about kin-oriented Aboriginal societies. A different quality is involved in all forms of interaction from that in societies not organized predominantly along those lines. Living with people regarded as kin, even though many of them may only be classificatory kin, establishes a different sense of the intimate and personal. In such circumstances, within the structure of one's society or community there are virtually no strangers, no one towards whom one has no responsibilities and no obligations. The emotional connotations relevant to actual kin relationships are diffused as genealogical distance increases, declining in intensity but nevertheless retaining their essential substance.

Berndt 1971, p. 159

In all cultures relatedness is important (Pilisuk and Parks 1986), but few approach Australian Aboriginal culture in terms of the emotional and ontological intensity of particular relationships and interdependencies. Kraus and Buffler (1979, p. 119) describe relatedness among Native Alaskans:

The current difficulties of Alaska Natives can only be understood against the background of the traditional cultures...Each individual lived his life with a timeless, consistent, and supportive organization of human associations. The intimate traditional associations centered on family, kin, faith, and the land and the small, tightly woven networks of informal personal relationships which form the basis for social, religious, economic and political order were the organizing principles of life, a source of support that could always be relied on...For many Native Alaskans, and especially for the young, the breakdown of the organized, consistent, traditional relationships due to pressures from without has resulted in a reduced ability to find and hold a position of psychological integrity and centrality. Loneliness, anxiety, frustration, continuing stress, and at times despair characterize the lives of many Native Alaskans today. In the Western medical system these people come to be called mentally ill or alcoholic.

It is arguable that the extent of social breakdown, family fragmentation, and periodic absence (such as through relocation, imprisonment or schooling) in Aboriginal communities, along with intergenerational discontinuities, has led to an inevitable attenuation of social and extended kinship networks for many individuals. Those most affected are typically adolescents and young adults who, through structural marginality within their own communities or because of particular family histories or problems, have few meaningful or supportive connections with the community in which they reside. It is worth noting that virtually all studies of loneliness have documented that adolescents are particularly vulnerable, and highly dependent on social validation of self and social meaning (Breakwell 1986;

Figure 6.2 *The Rankin family of Bagot community, Darwin. For Aboriginal people, the family is of critical importance to health and well-being, providing social and emotional support as well as mediating adaptive coping. (From P. Taylor, ed., After 200 years, Aboriginal Studies Press, Canberra, 1988, p. 101; photo by Max Pam)*

Rook 1984; Weiss 1982). This state of non-relatedness is particularly salient and acute in a cultural context where one's place in such networks is self-defining, self-supporting and self-validating. A common Aboriginal, and particularly appropriate, descriptor for these individuals is that they are 'lost', typically without income, status, future, or meaningful connections to place or people. While such a circumstance might result in extreme loneliness in a Western cultural context, in an Aboriginal context it appears to engender a particularly stressful and painful relational vertigo, with dramatic and culturally different emotional concomitants and consequences.

It is clear that Western understanding of Aboriginal notions of self, relatedness, estrangement, and social support has been inadequate and has not recognised important cultural differences. It is only recently that there has been any real social science understanding of the critical importance of early bonding, social ties, and sense of community to human health and well-being. Indeed it is clear that meaningful interdependencies and relationships with others are prerequisite for the development of any sense of integrated self, life satisfaction, or semblance of mental health. The now vast literature on social support (for example, Cohen and Syme 1985) and the more recent perspective of 'network analysis' (Pilisuk and Parks 1986) have provided a far clearer understanding of the social, emotional and material linkages that confer connectedness, social order and coherence. A core and poignant dilemma in many Aboriginal communities today is the felt disconnectedness of youth.

The family and psychopathology

Most discussions of Aboriginal mental health have focused on culture conflict, the demands of change and adjustment costs. The levels of analysis typically involve historical and system level processes and problems. Just as little emphasis has been placed on the individual, the critical importance of the family to health and well-being has, until recently, been ignored. The family in many ways both provides social and emotional support and mediates adaptive coping. It serves some very basic psychological functions:

Caplan in particular has discussed the family as a principal support system, and under the term 'support' has subsumed the following functions: the collection and dissemination of information about the world; feedback and guidance about members' behaviour; the provision of a system of beliefs, values and codes of behaviour; guidance and mediation in problem-solving; the provision of practical service and concrete aid; the provision of a haven for rest and recuperation; the provision of reference and control group; a validation of a member's self-identity; and assistance in emotional mastery.

Orford 1986, p. 6

Unfortunately part of the reason why Aboriginal families have become a focus of recent attention is because many Aboriginal communities are suffering what appears to be a dramatic breakdown of the family structure. An additional factor is the salience and extent of domestic violence in Aboriginal communities.

Majority culture perceptions of the 'Aboriginal family' are reasonably confused and incorrect. Even in traditionally oriented communities the 'nuclear' family unit is very much a part of cultural and community life. Certainly Aboriginal cultural assumptions and ways of thinking about social reality in terms of extended kinship systems and relatedness make a difference, but people grow up in, relate to and identify as families. As in some European cultures, it is nonetheless common to spend extended periods of time with other relations, to 'invest' in extended family networks, and to identify strongly with larger clan groupings. As with many non-Western cultures, Aboriginal extended family connections are very important, and people tend to live in smaller human communities where the social fabric of relatedness is very powerful, in both positive and negative ways. (See also Gray et al., chapter 3 in this volume).

It is unfortunate that social science and mental health writings on the family have largely dealt with pathogenesis, that is, the role which families can play in 'causing' behaviour pathology (Hatfield and Lefley 1987). There has been much less attention paid to the therapeutic and supportive role of families. The cross-cultural literature has clearly underscored the supportive and therapeutic role of the family in non-industrialised societies. Many of the aetiological speculations and case reports of disturbed family dynamics are not supported by this cross-cultural evidence. Almost all research on families of the mentally ill, for example, has been conducted in Western populations. What complicates matters in the Aboriginal context is that many Aboriginal families have now been torn by several generations in which alcohol abuse has severely influenced one or more family members. The research done with children of alcoholics suggests that the cumulative impact of chronic alcohol problems and associated violence might severely impair the coping ability and resources of particular individuals and families. This is a rather different picture from that of the 'pathogenic family'. Having said this, it is clear that a very substantial proportion of the Aboriginal population does not drink (Reser et al. unpub.; Watson et al. 1988) and the strength of Aboriginal families in the face of dramatic stresses is testament to their resilience and health and stability-conferring role (see also Gray et al., chapter 3 in this volume).

It is nonetheless clear that a spectrum of mental health problems recur in particular families, and that the cumulative effect of problems of social marginality in a community, unemployment, alcohol problems, and long periods of incarceration of family members is devastating. In urban communities, in single parent families, these problems are exacerbated by an often total absence of support networks. The identification of such families is particularly important with respect to the provision of limited support and with respect to prevention. In the case of North American Indian research, such identifiable families are typically characterised by a particular structural marginality, which results in considerable stress while at the same time precluding the use of community support networks (Levy and Kunitz 1987, p. 935). A similar situation obtains in many Aboriginal communities, where particular families and groups, because of no legitimate ties to land, 'wrong-way' marriages, or the absence of a permanent male head of household or critical numbers in a community, may suffer the stress of exclusion in a small, tightly-knit community. Children growing up in such a family are particularly vulnerable. In other parts of Australia, and particularly in less traditionally oriented communities and settlements, the often routine forcible removal of children from their families and the occasional removal and dispersal of whole communities to distant settlements was devastating to the stability and integrity of Aboriginal families (see also Gray et al. on the stolen generations, in chapter 3 of this volume).

Alcohol and violence

The complex issue of the inter-relationship between substance abuse and mental health is beyond the scope of this paper. It is important to appreciate, however, that most discussions of indigenous mental health in Australia treat alcohol use and abuse as cause, symptom and mental health syndrome (see also the section on 'Conflicting models of drug and alcohol use' in Brady, chapter 5 in this volume). Kamien (1978, p. 137) characterises alcohol abuse in the following terms:

The most common psychiatric condition found was a form of personality disorder. I made this diagnosis in people who did not have a more recognizable underlying psychiatric disorder but whose social conduct persistently interfered with their family and community life. This condition was found exclusively in men and was manifest by drinking alcohol with subsequent behaviour which was unacceptable to the families of these men. Sixteen of these men and the three women were chronic alcoholics. The remaining men were periodic drinkers who indulged in more frequent drinking when they were particularly angry, anxious or depressed. Included in this category of personality disorder were three men who usually reacted to minimal provocation with excessive hostility and aggression and two men whose interpersonal relationships were characterised by overt suspiciousness and unreasoned jealousy of their wives.

Alcohol and violence are seen to be inextricably linked in the Aboriginal cultural context of Australia. Does this reflect an objective reality or is it part of the majority culture stereotype of Aborigines? Is this a general research finding in the case of other indigenous minority communities in similar circumstances to Australian Aborigines? If alcohol and violence are strongly linked in the contemporary Australian Aboriginal context, what is the nature of this interrelationship, and how might this relate to Aboriginal self-injury and suicide?

The specific role that alcohol plays in the violence found in Aboriginal communities is clearly a vexed and complex issue. There is nonetheless a clear consensus that the consumption of alcohol is an important mediator and facilitator of violence, as Callan, O'Connor and Wilson posit:

Alcohol abuse by Aborigines is often perceived to be of crisis proportions...Alcohol is related to higher rates of homicide, violence and riots in rural towns and Aboriginal reserves. Over half of all Aboriginal male adult deaths, and a fifth of female deaths, have alcohol listed as a cause on the death record (Goldstein, Hunt and Sharkey, 1981). In rural areas, alcohol was featured in 95% of all offenses committed by Aboriginal adults (Australian Law Reform Commission, 1980).

Callan 1985, p. 45

A common admission among drinkers is that inter-personal violence, socially disruptive behaviour and disintegration of families stem directly from the effects of alcohol...So we find people clinging tenaciously to drinking patterns that result in disease, injury, social disruption, marital and family breakdown, loss and destruction of personal property, removal of children, sanctions resulting from breaches of both Australian and traditional law and, ultimately, in death. Moreover the causal role of alcohol in these matters is acknowledged by many of the drinkers.

O'Connor 1984, pp. 174–5)

The most dramatic and worrying statistic, from the analysis of the cases of violence recorded, related to alcohol. It was found that in 95 per cent of homicides and serious assaults, alcohol in large quantities was directly involved. In more than 50 per cent of these cases, both offender and victim had been drinking...In only two of the 82 cases we analysed was there no record of alcohol consumption. [These] cases illustrate typical characteristics of the alcohol-triggered aggression that is almost a daily occurrence on many Aboriginal reserves.

Wilson 1988, pp. 48–50

There is a growing literature that addresses the institutionalised interrelationship between drinking and violence in an Aboriginal cultural context (for example: Brady 1988; Collman 1988; Martin unpub.; O'Connor 1984; Sansom 1980). These authors suggest that there exist social rules for drinking, that such drinking serves a number of functions that can relate to violence (such as 'time out' from other proscriptions, non-responsibility, bringing grievances to the fore), and that the behaviour that accompanies drinking—'drunken comportment' (MacAndrew and

Edgerton 1970) (including violence)—is largely a cultural and social product. These rules for drinking allow for the breaking or suspension of other rules of conduct, and are in many ways functional in a very role-prescribed culture undergoing rapid social and cultural change. Such 'time out' and non-accountability, however, can become untenable in terms of social order when they are chronic and widespread and are not confined to urban drinking sprees.

The comparative literature also clearly suggests that alcohol plays an important role in violence in indigenous communities (but this 'evidence' is largely impressionistic or inferential, for example Gibbs 1986).

There is considerable debate in the literature...about the role of alcohol abuse in the occurrence of violent behavior...Most authors feel that there is no direct relationship; the association of alcohol abuse with violent behavior requires some intervening sociocultural variables. Brod (1975) identifies deculturative and acculturative stresses as the intervening variables for most groups of Native Americans. According to a common theory, as the hunting and fishing lifestyle is discarded the usual methods of gaining respect and stature in the community are no longer available, so Native Alaskans resort to alcohol and violence to forget their perceived inadequacies and to prove their manliness (Brod, 1975; Seltzer, 1980). For Native Alaskans, alcohol abuse is both the result of psychosocial dysfunction and the cause of psychosocial dysfunction.

Phillips and Inui 1986, p. 143

There are few useful culture-specific research findings or analyses to draw upon in understanding the role of alcohol and violence in Aboriginal communities in Australia. Notwithstanding that alcohol and drug abuse is believed to be the most significant problem among American Indians, and that alcohol involvement has been a significant focus of the majority of studies conducted in Native American communities over the past several decades, very little is really known about it (Trimble 1984). This is particularly true in the case of young people (in Western as well as indigenous cultures), and with respect to the psychological, social and motivational factors that mediate substance abuse (Newcomb and Bentler 1989). This situation has not appreciably improved in the past five years, and is far worse in Australia, where there has been little substantive research other than quantitative surveys (for example, Shanahan unpub.; Eckersley 1988; Watson et al. 1988). The Australian indigenous cultural context is also significantly different from the North American situation, and what understanding has been gleaned from the substantial research investment in North America does not necessarily apply in Australia.

Nature of alcohol abuse

A further and important consideration concerns the nature and pattern of alcohol abuse, and how these contribute to aggression and violence. Much of the literature on alcohol abuse concerns alcoholism. Alcohol abuse in Aboriginal communities, in contrast to many North American Indian communities, does not conform to a picture of widespread and acute alcoholism. Rather what characterises many Aboriginal communities is recurrent binge drinking, accompanied by violent interpersonal and other

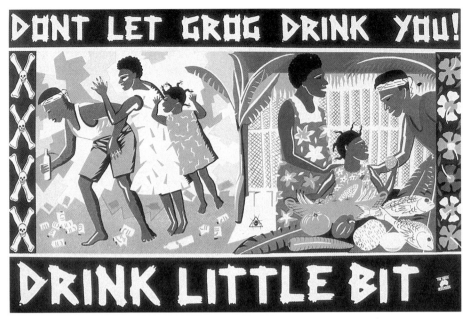

Figure 6.3 *A poster produced in 1987 for the National Campaign Against Drug Abuse. (M. McMahon/Redback Graphix)*

intercommunity episodes (Kamien 1986). There also appears to be a clear transition stage for many young males, similar in some ways to that described by Levy and Kunitz (1987) for Native American youth, but with a higher mortality in terms of those who continue as chronic binge drinkers. It is also clear that identifiable individuals and families in most Aboriginal communities account for a remarkably disproportionate amount of violent incidents, arrests, medical treatments and associated alcohol-related problems . Finally, to complicate matters further, a unique indigenous cultural context appears to underlie and maintain the relationship between alcohol and violence in Aboriginal communities—a particular contact history, and community and family-specific intergenerational histories that strongly influence more general alcohol-violence links. We are only now beginning to understand some of these longer term causal links in Western cultural contexts, for instance, the research on children of alcoholics.

Domestic violence

Much of the contemporary literature dealing with alcohol and violence concerns domestic violence. This in part reflects the fact that violence is an integral part of family life, as well a heightened awareness of the true prevalence of family violence and child sexual abuse. The high incidence of domestic violence appears to be generally true across cultures; roughly 30 per cent of married couples in North America, for example, reported that they had engaged in acts of violence against their spouse at some point in time during their marriage (Baron and Byrne 1987). There is a strange logic to this. Family members are more likely to see each other daily, to have close knowledge of one another, to share meals, to share material resources, to live under the same roof, to be dependent upon each other for emotional support (Orford 1986). The magnitude of the problem of violence within family contexts is evident in recent reports, submissions and articles dealing with Aboriginal violence (Kahn 1980; O'Connor 1984). The Queensland Domestic Violence Taskforce (QDVT 1988, p. 257) reported the following:

Indigenous people appear on the basis of available data, both qualitative and quantitative, to be suffering high rates of domestic violence. Aboriginal people to whom we spoke consistently estimated that domestic violence affects 90% of Aboriginal families living in Trust areas...Dr. Paul Wilson has analysed the homicide and serious assault statistics for this State over a three year period 1978–1981. He found that the homicide rate per year across 17 Aboriginal communities was 39.6 per 100 000 compared with an annual rate for the State of Queensland of 3.28 per 100 000...The rate for serious assault charges on reserves was 226.05 per 100 000 compared with a State figure of 43.85 per 100 000.

The links between alcohol and domestic violence in the general research literature are clear, but not entirely understood. Almost all studies report that most instances of domestic violence occur when the male partner is intoxicated (for example, Kantor and Straus 1989). Recent research also suggests that considerable domestic violence and substance abuse is embedded in a family context of psychopathology with characteristic stresses and vulnerability (see Goldstein 1988).

Notwithstanding the many current submissions that relate to domestic violence in Aboriginal communities, little systematic research has been undertaken. Questions concerning the role of cultural context with respect to this domestic violence have been neither adequately articulated nor answered. On the basis of information from Aboriginal paraprofessional behavioural health workers, Kahn (1980) suggests that battering has its origins in 'tribal traditions' and is supported by social sanctions. He also reports that the battering of Aboriginal women is related to alcohol ingestion and pervasive jealousy. The 'evidence' here, as with most such reports, is problematic, being based on selective and incomplete records, and the observations and anecdotal accounts of particular individuals.

The 'medicalisation' of alcohol abuse

A good example of the medicalisation of alcohol 'abuse' and a response from the Aboriginal community is found in the recent *Interim report of the Royal Commission into Aboriginal Deaths in Custody.* In this report, Commissioner Muirhead made the following recommendations (Muirhead 1988, recommendations 3, 4 and 7):

1. the decriminalisation of public drunkenness;
2. the provision of adequate funding for programs to care for and treat intoxicated persons;
3. the establishment of a national taskforce composed of all governments to examine the social and health problems created by alcohol for Aborigines, and then to assess needs and means of fulfilling needs, as well as appropriate facilities for short- and long-term care, education and training. The project

should have Aboriginal health and other medical representation and be essentially health-oriented.

The response of the National Aboriginal and Islander Legal Services Secretariat (NAILSS) to these recommendations was the following:

While these recommendations are no doubt intended to be humane, they do not provide an answer to the fundamental question of Aboriginal death. The substitution of one category of Aboriginal inadequacy with another is no solution. Now, instead of being 'criminal', Aboriginal people who are the victims of alcohol abuse will be treated as if they are 'sick'. While of course anyone affected by alcohol dependency may need medical care, that is not, from an Aboriginal perspective, what the problem is about.

Aboriginal people, if asked, will quite readily explain that alcohol has so many Aborigines in its grip because the pressures to choose between assimilation with white society, and the pain of trying to live an Aboriginal life without land and other strong cultural support is often too great to bear. Alcohol fills the gap. This is not alcoholism in the European sense at all. It is something completely different. The solution must come from Aboriginal culture.

By applying principles built up from the body of indigenous international law— that is the right to land, it is possible to reach a workable and highly practical recommendation to address the dilemma of Aboriginal cell deaths related to alcohol dependency...

By focussing on positive Aboriginal values like cultural recovery and skill development, the tendency to remain caught in the negative cycle of drunkenness and ill health could be broken.

NAILSS 1989, p. 15

Adolescents

The tendency of past writers to cast all behaviour problems in a psychiatric frame is particularly evident in the case of adolescents. There is little question but that the behaviour of adolescents in any community can often be disruptive and at odds with accepted convention. This is particularly true in many Aboriginal communities, where a permissive childhood and few formal social controls seem to lead to particular problems in contemporary settlement communities where traditional social control measures and intact families are the exception. The high incidence of petrol inhalation and alcohol abuse among young males in many of these communities further exacerbates problems of delinquency and conflict. These behavioural problems, however, cannot simply be equated with clinical '*disorders*' (Archer 1985; Edwards et al. 1981). The descriptions and terminology used by Nurcombe et al. (1970, p. 373) to describe the 'psychosocial background' of petrol inhalation in one community in northern Australia are interesting:

Petrol-inhalers appear to be much more disturbed psychologically; and this difference is manifest, particularly, in a pattern of tension-discharge...There is evidence that tension-discharge tendencies precede petrol-inhalation. In addition to this, there is clinical evidence that group petrol-inhalation releases and accentuates the same proclivities for tension-discharge...Petrol-inhalation in a group context is a complex phenomenon. An investigation of this disorder involves an appreciation of the interaction between individual developmental and environmental factors in a particular social setting... Difficulty in resolving these developmental problems leads to various forms of temporary or more chronic psychopathology. Among these the most common is tension-discharge, a pattern of behaviour by which internal conflicts are acted out. Tension-discharge involves the uninhibited expression of sexual, aggressive or acquisitive drives often in such a way as to bring the individual into conflict with external authority... Petrol-inhalation is one manifestation of the personal and social disorientation of the Aboriginal adolescent. Petrol is available. It affords instant gratification with an opportunity to regress to a state of pleasurable elation. Fantasy is stimulated and sexual, sadistic and acquisitive drives are disinhibited. Counterphobic behaviour is facilitated and the intergenerational conflict can be acted out.

There is continual reference in the discussion accompanying the above to 'tension-discharge disorder' and a suggestion that adolescents in particular are suffering from acute, generalised, acculturative stress.

Rapid transition, territorial uncertainty, the conviction of powerlessness in the face of incomprehensible forces, overcrowding, the near bankruptcy of tradition, the disruption of family relationships all contribute to a fragmentation of society, a tendency to split into mutually alienated groups. Adolescents reflect the conflicts of a people.

Nurcombe et al. 1970, p. 367

It is possible that there was and is a high incidence of behavioural problems of clinical severity among Aboriginal youth living at Elcho Island. It is more probable, however, that adolescent substance abuse in this and other such communities is functional and 'adaptive' in a number of ways, by reducing felt conflict, asserting identity and autonomy, and focusing and facilitating social support and a group identity among their age cohort.

It is important to note that the alcohol and violence equation with respect to adolescents and young people generally has its own character, with both behaviours linked psychologically, socially, and symbolically to critical developmental processes. This is particularly true for indigenous minority youth in Western cultural contexts, for whom a characteristic pattern of critical life events and a double identity crisis pose significant developmental problems (Berlin 1986; Harras 1987; Reser 1989a). In such contexts substance 'abuse' serves a variety of adaptive functions, often reflecting a 'stage' through which most young people pass as they accept adult responsibilities in their communities (Levy and Kunitz 1987). A recent general review of substance use and abuse among children and teenagers (Newcomb and Bentler 1989, p. 248) summarises our knowledge about the correlates and consequences of substance abuse:

Substance use and abuse are strongly associated with other problem behaviors such as delinquency, precocious sexual behavior, deviant attitudes, or school dropout.

Any focus on drug use or abuse to the exclusion of such correlates, whether ante-cedent, contemporaneous, or consequent, distorts the phenomenon by focusing on only one aspect or component of a general pattern or syndrome...Childhood and adolescence are critical periods for the development of both personal and interper-sonal competence, coping skills, and responsible decision making. Drug use is a manner of coping that can interfere with or preclude the necessary development of these other critical skills if it is engaged in regularly at a young age. For instance, if a young teenager learns to use alcohol as a way to reduce distress, he or she may never learn other coping skills to ameliorate distress. Thus teenage drug use may truncate, interfere with, or circumvent essential maturational processes and development that typically occur during adolescence. As one result, teenage drug users enter adult roles of marriage and work prematurely and without adequate socioemotional growth and often experience failure in these adult roles. Following the area of treatment, consequences of teenage drug use are the second least un-derstood and researched area of child and teenage substance abuse.

Clearly the 'gang' behaviour described by Nurcombe et al. in 1970 is now com-monplace in many northern Aboriginal communities and constitutes a substantial 'social problem' which communities must deal with. There is not, however, a strong case for describing the problem, for most petrol sniffers, in psychiatric terms. The whole question of where substance abuse becomes mental health syndrome and diagnostic category is of course an unresolved and vexed issue both within and across cultures (Edwards et al. 1981).

Aboriginal self-injury and suicide

A phenomenon that has seared its way into the Australian conscience and con-sciousness has been the issue of Aboriginal deaths in custody. This larger issue is in many ways beyond the scope of the present chapter. One aspect of particular relevance to mental health, however, is that of alleged Aboriginal suicides in cus-tody. It was the dramatic and apparent suicides of a number of young Aboriginal men in police custody that in many ways galvanised public concern and political response in the establishment of the Royal Commission into Aboriginal Deaths in Custody in August 1987 (Muirhead 1988). In that year, a nine-fold increase in the number of Aboriginal deaths by hanging while in custody took place. Considerable media and public speculation centred on the apparent 'copycat' character of these deaths, along with the countercharge that many of the reported 'suicide' deaths were in fact the product of either callous neglect or murder. Issues of obvious relevance were whether this pattern of deaths corresponded to a suicide 'cluster' (Reser 1989*a*), and whether or not there were other important and common mediat-ing factors, such as intoxication or mental health history. An additional question was to what extent this phenomenon was a reflection of a more widespread non-custody suicide phenomenon in Aboriginal communities. These questions forced a closer look at the whole issue of self-injury and suicide in the Aboriginal cultural context, as well as at the adequacy and availability of statistical information on

Aboriginal self-injury and suicide rates. At the same time that Aboriginal communities were seeing the deaths in custody issue as a powerful symbolic statement of oppression and injustice, David Bradbury's film *State of shock* was premiered, and later shown on national television. This film, documenting the celebrated murder trial and case of Alwyn Peter, communicated the bleakness, drunken violence, and ubiquitous self-injury that appeared to characterise Aboriginal communities such as that of Weipa South in north Queensland. The Royal Commission investigations themselves, psychiatric testimony, and prepared case histories of individuals who died in custody also raised further questions pertaining to individual psychiatric histories and psychiatric morbidity rates in the remote Aboriginal communities from which many of those who died in custody had originated.

An independent investigation was made in 1989 of all reported Aboriginal suicides in custody in Australia from 1980 to 1988 (Reser 1989*a*), giving consideration to geographic and temporal proximity, as well as to similarities in age, sex, method, involvement of alcohol, custodial authority, personal knowledge of other suicide victims, and other circumstantial and cultural factors. The data base used was that prepared by the Research Unit of the Royal Commission into Aboriginal Deaths in Custody. Particular attention was paid to nine reported Aboriginal suicides in custody in Queensland in 1986 and 1987. Findings strongly suggested support for a 'cluster' interpretation of at least eight of these Queensland deaths, which in themselves constituted 40 per cent of the total number of Aboriginal suicides in police custody in Australia between 1980 and the end of 1988. Such a cluster phenomenon (Coleman 1987; Phillips and Carstenson 1986) typically involves components of imitation and suggestion, wherein one suicide provides a 'model' for other at-risk individuals in a community. In these north Queensland cases, a number of distinct psychological, cultural, and community factors also appeared to be involved, including age, sex, alcohol and family-related self-injury and suicide attempts, circumstances (and prior history) of arrest, and interrelationships among the victims and communities involved. This is strikingly similar to circumstances of adolescent cluster suicide found in Native American communities (Bechtold 1988).

In 1987 a research investigation of self-injury and suicide in Aboriginal communities in Queensland was initiated at James Cook University of North Queensland, in response to a request by the Aboriginal Coordinating Council of Queensland that such a project be undertaken. An objective of this research was to examine the larger context in which the Queensland suicides in custody had taken place. The study examined the nature and incidence of suicide and attempted suicide in five selected Aboriginal communities between 1980 and 1988, through structured interviews with randomly selected individuals in each community between the ages of 15 and 65. Data was also collected in an urban centre for purposes of comparison. Fourteen people were identified who apparently died by suicide in the five Trust Area communities investigated over this period, including a number of alleged suicides in custody. At the time of preparing this chapter, the information relating to these deaths was incomplete. More complete information was available, however, on those who *attempted* suicide.

Suicide attempters were identified either through self-report during an interview, through the testimony of an immediate family member, or from at least two reliable sources (including medical records). The survey, using random samples and referred cases, identified 65 people from the five Trust Area communities who had attempted suicide, and structured interviews were conducted with 45 of these. Eight of those interviewed (4.6 per cent) appeared in the random samples of community residents, while an additional 37 were identified as attempters by others in the community and through health records. In the urban sample, 16 out of 110 Aboriginal and Islander respondents (14.5 per cent) reported that they had attempted suicide, compared with 9 out of 170 non-Aboriginal respondents (5.3 per cent). If only the 11 Aboriginal attempters in the urban sample are considered, the attempt figure for this Aboriginal community becomes 20.0 per cent. This is similar to the attempted suicide figure recently cited for Aboriginal heads of households in Adelaide of 17 per cent (Radford et al. 1990). It must be emphasised that these are not attempted suicide rates, which take into account a specified time period and the total population base. Rather these figures are the proportion of sampled individuals who reported having attempted suicide.

The 65 identified attempters from the north Queensland Aboriginal community included 44 males and 21 females. Eleven of these individuals had attempted suicide more than once. The age-at-time-of-attempt, where known, is presented in figure 6.4. It is noteworthy that 71 per cent of these attempts took place when the individuals were aged between 15 and 25.

Figure 6.5 presents the distribution of suicide attempts in the five communities over a period of 15 years. As in figure 6.4, this is a distribution of events, not individuals, hence some individuals are represented more than once. Respondents were asked to recall any suicides or attempted suicides they could remember over the previous 10 years, hence data before 1978–79 is fortuitous. Data for 1989 is incomplete, as data collection was initiated in mid-1988 and finalised in some communities midway

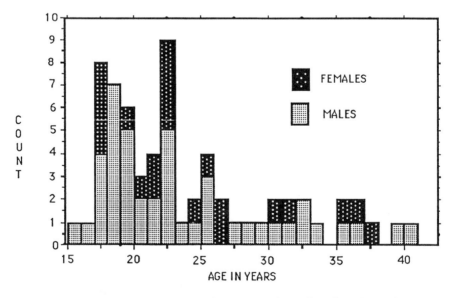

Figure 6.4 *Distribution of age-at-time-of-attempt and sex of confirmed suicide attempts in five Trust Area communities in north Queensland. Sample size, 65. Missing cases, 16.*

through 1989. These results must be further qualified with respect to inherent difficulties in determining suicide attempts over a 10-year period, in part because of denial and the likelihood of restructuring past and traumatic events. Reported figures are conservative. The cases presented in figure 6.6, for example, exclude 22 cases where reported attempts were not corroborated by at least two independent

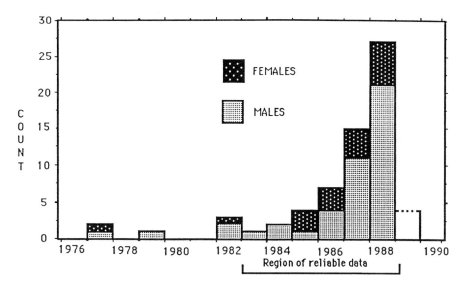

Figure 6.5 *Distribution of confirmed suicide attempts for five Queensland Trust Area communities by year and sex. Sample size, 72. Missing cases, 9.*

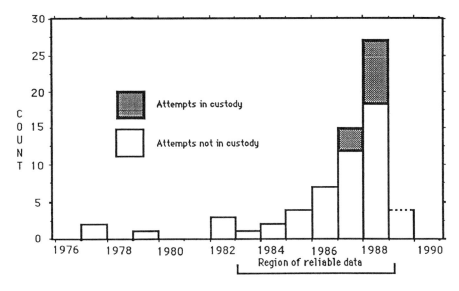

Figure 6.6 *Distribution of confirmed suicide attempts by year and custodial circumstances. Sample size, 72. Missing cases, 9.*

sources and it is clear that many genuine suicide attempts have been missed in the identified cases. Despite these qualifications, it is obvious that there are many suicide attempts taking place in the five communities concerned and that these events appear to have dramatically increased between 1986 and 1989. Seventy-two per cent of interviewed community attempters indicated that alcohol or drugs had been taken at the time of the attempt. Thirteen (19.4 per cent) of confirmed attempts took place in watchhouse custody circumstances (see figure 6.7), and alcohol was involved in 12 of these 13 cases. It would appear that suicide attempts in custody are a relatively recent phenomenon in the five communities concerned. They appear to have commenced following the suicides in custody in Yarrabah and other Trust Area communities.

Results relating to the role of alcohol in suicide attempts were unambiguous and dramatic. Virtually all male suicide attempts (97.7 per cent) were alcohol-related, while only one half (50.0 per cent) of female attempts involved alcohol. Over 25 per cent of interviewed suicide attempters indicated that in more than 10 instances during the past month they had been drunk enough to be sick, staggering, or to pass out, and another 30 per cent indicated that this was true for them three to nine times a month. Almost one-half of suicide attempters (46 per cent) indicated that drinking or drug use was causing personal problems, and 76 per cent reported that drinking gave rise to family fights. These findings must be placed in context. A recent and comprehensive survey of Aboriginal alcohol and drug use conducted in the Northern Territory (Watson et al. 1988) in 1986 and 1987, sampling 10 per cent of the target population (1764 individuals) reported that 60 per cent of Aboriginal people in the Northern Territory do not consume alcohol. The north Queensland research reported here found that 79.9 per cent of women in Aboriginal communities did not drink, compared with 64.7 per cent of men who did drink. It is clear that in the north Queensland data the pattern of alcohol use by a number of heavy regular and binge drinkers is placing them at a much higher risk of attempting suicide. Indeed this risk is over 18 times higher than that for those who drink only lightly, occasionally or not at all (Reser et al. unpub.).

Such research findings as these are difficult to evaluate without appropriate comparison figures, over time, and for both the non-Aboriginal population and other Aboriginal communities. Is the rate of suicide attempts in indigenous communities, for example, greater than that for similar age groups of non-Aborigines living in small rural communities in similar circumstances? Unfortunately there are few non-Aboriginal comparison communities that are really equivalent to Aboriginal communities. Also, attempted suicides are often not recorded as such nor are suicide attempt figures maintained. Separate Aboriginal and non-Aboriginal suicide figures are not available for Queensland or for Australia. It is nonetheless important to place the suicide and alcohol findings reported here in some kind of perspective. Many people are unaware that the suicide rate for young males aged 15 to 19 in Australia has more than doubled over the past 20 years (going from 6 per 100 000 to 13 per 100 000), and that this increase has been even greater for males aged 20 to 24 (going from 13 to 29 per 100 000) (Eckersley 1988). The suicide rate for young males in Queensland was higher in 1989 than the rate of deaths by motor vehicle accidents. It is possible that the apparently dramatic increase in suicides and suicide attempts by young Aboriginal males in part reflects this more general

A triggering case: distress or disturbance

The complex individual and family circumstances that can be involved in cases of self-injury and suicide are well-illustrated in the case of Perry Noble, whose suicide death in the Yarrabah watchhouse in December 1986 appeared to 'trigger' a suicide cluster in north Queensland communities.

At the time of his death, Perry was 21 years old, single, upset and intoxicated. His family situation was one in which his father frequently became violently drunk, often bashing Perry, his mother and his four younger brothers. Perry himself was a chronic heavy drinker by the age of 15, and had left school and had a criminal record at 14.

When drunk, Perry was violent and uncontrollable, and alcohol-related theft and violence were responsible for most of his confrontations with police and periods of incarceration. Perry's relationships with his parents and brothers were characterised by chronic and often violent conflict, with a number of arrests involving assaults on his father, including a stabbing to the face.

Perry's conflict with legal authorities commenced in 1981 with a charge of breaking and entering while armed, and continued through the next six years, culminating in four separate prison sentences between June 1984 and his death in 1986. He spent six months of 1985 in the Cairns watchhouse and Stuart Prison. Perry's repeated stints in the Yarrabah watchhouse for alcohol-related offences were perceived by him and others as sustained harassment and targeting by local police.

Perry's suicide was preceded by suicide threats, talk of suicide, a number of suicide attempts and numerous instances of self-injury. He made two attempts in 1982 and 1986, which involved shooting incidents while he was drunk, both resulting in serious injuries. Perry evidently witnessed a dramatic suicide of a relative during his youth. Two of his brothers also attempted suicide close to the time of his own fatal attempt. One brother, aged 18 at the time, shot himself two months after Perry's second shooting attempt and two months before Perry's death, and another brother, also 18 at the time, attempted suicide twice in the year following Perry's death, once by attempted hanging in the Yarrabah watchhouse, and once by shooting in non-custody circumstances.

Perry was placed in a watchhouse cell at Yarrabah police station at 11.00 a.m. on 4 December 1986. At about 12.50 p.m., another prisoner saw him hanging from the bars of the cell window from a bedsheet. At the time of his death Perry, had a blood alcohol concentration of 0.287 per cent.

In brief, the circumstances of Perry's life suggest a critical vulnerability, a deeply felt anguish at the absence of caring relationships with others, recurrent bouts of depression and low

J. Reser

phenomenon. Without accurate comparison figures, this possibility cannot be examined.

It could also be argued that a more appropriate basis of comparison would be other indigenous minority communities with similar problems and circumstances. Many common elements (as well as important cultural differences) exist in American Indian, Inuit and Australian Aboriginal communities: their status as an indigenous minority, residence in remote settlement communities, dramatically high unemployment, over-representation in custody, a welfare history of dependence and lack of self-determination, and very substantial problems relating to alcohol use and abuse. Youth suicide has also posed a very significant problem for Native American communities over the past two decades (Frederick 1973; Levy and Kunitz 1987; May 1987).

Recent Canadian suicide figures for the general population and Native people provide a useful comparison base. The suicide rate for men is much higher than for women. In 1986 there were 22.8 suicides for every 100 000 men compared with 6.4 for every 100 000 women. Overall, almost 80 per cent of all suicide victims in 1986 were men. Suicide rates are especially high among Native people. In 1986, there were 56.3 suicides for every 100 000 Native men, almost 2.5 times the rate for all men (22.8). At the same time, the rate for Native women (11.8) was almost double the rate for all women (6.4). The incidence of suicide is particularly high among young Native men. In 1986, there were more than 100 suicides for every 100 000 Native men aged 15–19 (Beneteau 1988). These findings underscore the more general extent and nature of indigenous suicide. There also exists a youth suicide phenomenon in some regions of the Pacific which shows basic similarities with the Australian Aboriginal situation (see Hezel et al. 1985; Hezel 1987). Suicide rates for males, aged 15 to 24, over the period from 1974 to 1983 have averaged, for example, from 200 per 100 000 (Truk) to 160 per 100 000 (Yap, Marshall Islands) (Rubinstein 1985).

An important diagnostic and prevention issue is the distinction between attempted suicide (parasuicide) and completed suicide. While this is a complex issue on which not everyone agrees, the consensus in the clinical suicide literature, deriving largely from Western cultural contexts, is that suicide and 'parasuicide' are distinct behaviours. It is difficult to make clear distinctions between self-injury, attempted suicide, and suicide in Aboriginal communities, but important differences in meaning, intention, and precipitating circumstance probably exist. It is clear that many attempts do not involve premeditation or planning, and constitute more of a reactive emotional response to a particular situation or set of events. It is also evident that many intentional self-injuries are not perceived by the individual involved as a suicide attempt (nor were they included in reported suicide attempts). It is possible that a number of the hangings in community watchhouses might well have been recorded as 'attempts' if the event had taken place outside of custody, in circumstances where other people would have intervened. The fact that individuals were typically drunk and upset when making the attempt, and using particularly violent methods, makes it probable that some attempts become actual suicides.

Actual suicide deaths are also typically under-reported and explained in other ways; death 'causes' and 'suicide' 'rates' indeed reflect Western cultural labels and biases (see Reser 1989b). It is understandable that the explanations given for such deaths in Aboriginal communities are culturally based, stressing external and system-level 'causes' that make sense to Aboriginal people. There is evidence that in communities such as Palm Island (Queensland), attempted suicide and associated alcohol abuse has a history of at least the past 20 years. On one psychiatric visit to the island in 1978, seven cases of recent suicide attempts were seen. In 1977, it was estimated that one half of the total weekly income of the island was spent at the canteen and on sly grog (Ruddock 1977). The high frequency of deaths by hanging in custody in northern Aboriginal communities is also noteworthy. Hanging is a particularly lethal method of attempting suicide, typically precluding change of mind and intervention, but is one of the few methods available when locked up alone in a watchhouse cell. For this reason, and because many individuals were locked up alone, it is possible that suicide attempts in police custody on Aboriginal communities, at least in the recent past, were more likely to end in death.

An alternative perspective on Aboriginal suicide deaths in custody has been offered by Ernest Hunter, a psychiatrist who has worked in Western Australia (Hunter
1988). The following is a description of findings from an interviewed sample of 100
Aboriginal individuals in the Broome lockup in 1987.

*In association with drinking 19 had experienced hallucinations (visual or
auditory), 27 paranoid ideation, and 28 panic or anxiety sufficient for them to
seek aid...A further 28 had had impulses to self harm by burning or otherwise
self-mutilating, with 17 having at some time acted on these impulses. Past suicidal
ideation was reported by 25, and a previous suicide attempt by 15.*

Hunter 1988, p. 277

Hunter essentially argues that part of the pattern that emerges for Aboriginal
suicides in custody is an often dramatic fear state when experiencing the dry horrors
(delirium tremens). He provides a statement by a respondent which captures this
recurrent experience of fear and suicide ideation:

*After heavy drinking you know, you get paralytic drunk and get the shakes, you
can hear voices, voices saying, 'I'll kill you'. I've been through that, hearing voices
and things. It makes you feel you want to commit suicide. Makes you think people
coming to get you, makes you think that before they get you you'll kill yourself,
commit suicide...When you're locked up and going through that thing you need
people around, you should have the lights on. In the light you're safe, but in the
darkness you think that person's going to come and kill you.*

Hunter 1988, p. 279

One might question the reasonableness of casting in psychiatric terms a fear state that
is brought about by heavy substance abuse and a traditional belief context. It would also
appear to be the case that most alleged suicides in custody have taken place within an
hour or two of incarceration, while the individual was still intoxicated. The importance
of traditionally oriented beliefs and their relationship to the meaning and consequences
of 'being drunk' cannot, however, be simply dismissed, nor can the history and pattern
of alcohol consumption for particular individuals and groups.

Finally, the issue of Aboriginal suicide has much in common with the acculturative stress debate discussed earlier in the chapter. A frequent argument is that these
suicides are an inevitable symptom of the more general social pathology that follows for indigenous peoples in the wake of rapid and enforced acculturation. This
psychiatric picture also suggests that those individuals who commit suicide are, by
definition, mentally disturbed. More qualified statements at least suggest that
psychiatric illness is often present in cases of suicide and parasuicide. Goldney and
Burvill (1980), for example, emphasise that in the majority of those who commit
suicide, and in no less than one-third of those who attempt suicide, psychiatric illness is present, most commonly depression. This mental illness argument is less
than convincing for many of the reported suicides in custody. Many of the
Aboriginal individuals were young, extremely intoxicated at the time of death, incarcerated in appalling facilities, in instances that were perceived as unjust, with histories of being targeted and harassed by community police, and at a time when prior
suicide deaths were salient and of particular symbolic poignancy.

Cawte, in an address to the Australian Academy of Forensic Science, takes the view 'that the majority of [Aboriginal] persons who take their lives in custody belong to the clinical category':

Some people do not enjoy life because of self-hatred. They slash their arms with razor blades, or thrust them through windows. In most cases these young people have been ill-used or abused when they were children. They have been neglected, beaten, treated harshly, or lived in homes where there was a lot of fighting or violence. They have hurting memories of being hurt. Sometimes the main contact with grown-ups which they had as children was being beaten. When they later become distressed or 'uptight' they revive this feeling of contact with grown-ups by repeating the beating. After their wrists are cut, they often feel calm and at peace for a while.

Cawte 1988, p. 232

The indigenous reality is more complex. It appears that Aboriginal suicides, both in and out of custody, reflect a number of contributing elements, some of these deriving from a traditional base, some from the exigencies of rapid change, institutionalised dependencies and social system collapse, and some from fortuitous historical and situational factors. The '*traditional* base' in the case of Aboriginal culture includes:

*   self-injurious behaviour;
*   coping mechanisms that involve overt and dramatic emotional expression and a participatory response on the part of significant others;
*   a culturally specific social meaning system involving self, relatedness, and reciprocity.

The more *classic* contributing elements include:

*   the particular vulnerability of structurally marginal families and individuals;
*   the identity and developmental conflicts of many indigenous youth;
*   the more general breakdown of social control and social support networks;
*   and the pervasive contributing role of substance abuse.

Historical factors include:

*   the institutional histories of many Aboriginal communities;
*   relocations and the alienation of rights to land for many groups and families;
*   the institutionalisation of attempted suicide as a mode of expressing and communicating anger and emotional distress;
*   the particular cultural elaboration and social construction of 'being drunk' in an Aboriginal cultural context;
*   the series of events leading up to the 'Deaths in Custody' issue in Australia and the associated symbolic salience of arrest and watchhouse incarceration.

Situational factors include those elements of suggestion, imitation, and modelling that can attend the suicide of a known individual or immediate family member, isolation while incarcerated, and common denominators of intoxication, arrest, perceived injustice and 'reactance' (Brehm and Brehm 1981). Finally, a number of these elements can interact, dramatically increasing their individual influence: for example, the interaction of Aboriginal emotional expression, coping style, and 'being drunk'.

Figure 6.7 *A cartoon that appeared in the* Sydney Morning Herald *in 1987.* *(M. Martin/John Fairfax Group)*

As part of the survey of suicide and self-injury in Queensland Aboriginal communities mentioned by Reser et al. (unpub.), an examination was made of the proportion of interviewed suicide attempters who had received some form of counselling as a psychiatric referral. This information was largely self-reported, but was validated against medical records where possible. Thirty-two per cent of interviewed attempters had made an appointment to see someone other than a friend or family member to discuss personal or psychological problems within two years of their suicide attempt. Fifty-two per cent of interviewed attempters indicated that they had personal or psychological problems for which they felt they needed special help during the preceding year, with 13 of these individuals actually seeking such help. Eighteen per cent had received psychiatric treatment of some form, and 32 per cent had at some point in time taken medication for 'emotional' or 'psychological' problems.

These findings and other interview responses indicate that this attempter group was experiencing considerable psychological distress and included a number of individuals who would have diagnosable behaviour disorders of clinical magnitude. The majority of this group, however, which was predominantly young and male, would not be considered 'mentally ill', and the uncritical use of the DSM III (the American Psychiatric Association's Diagnostic and Statistical Manual of Mental Disorders) categories of substance abuse and conduct disorder without regard to individual or community context would be problematic.

Aboriginal mental health in the 1990s

This chapter has considered majority culture attempts to come to terms with indigenous mental health in Australia. These attempts have, in the main, underscored the fact that majority culture psychiatric models and paradigms have been problematic, culturally insensitive, and in many respects inappropriate. Twenty-five years of ethnopsychiatric research has not resulted in an accurate or valid picture of the nature or incidence of Aboriginal mental health problems, or a genuine understanding of the constituent features of positive mental health. In hindsight, and from a multidisciplinary and cross-cultural perspective, it is not difficult to point out problems with the way this endeavour was conceptualised and carried out. Even today, there is little available knowledge of the indigenous psychology of Australia, that is, of indigenous accounts and explanations of behaviour or cultural meaning systems relating to mental health and well-being. It is also the case that the medical model has largely excluded 'social' from its causal explanations of mental health problems in physical or 'mental' terms, notwithstanding occasional reference to more general 'sociocultural' factors. 'Mental' thus became a residual and false category, with little explanatory power. The psychological and mental health picture of Aboriginal society was largely provided by the very few psychiatrists who were working with Aboriginal people and communities. The resulting 'clinical' and 'diagnostic' characterisation of indigenous personal and social functioning has typified many studies of other cultures (for example, Draguns 1980*a*).

It is only recently that these psychiatric accounts and observations have come under more general public and social science scrutiny, in part as a result of the growing awareness of contemporary Aboriginal mental health problems, in part because of a renewed social science interest in indigenous health, and even more recently because of the implicit mental health issues underlying the Black Deaths in Custody inquiry and as a result of concerns and protests by Aboriginal people themselves. Those few critiques that have been published (for example, Biernoff 1982; Dunham and Sendiony 1975; Langton 1981; Reid 1983) are salutary, suggesting that the starting assumptions, methodologies and conclusions of psychiatric surveys of Aboriginal communities are problematic, and provide a less than accurate picture of causes, cultural context and incidence of mental disorder. As Biernoff (1982, pp. 150–1) comments:

Finally, it is but a small step from explaining psychopathology in cultural terms, to describing culture in psychopathological terms...it is deceptively and dangerously easy to assert that, if sorcery, shared identity and socializing processes are factors that emerge as central in discussions with Aboriginal patients and their families, these factors themselves generate mental illness. This is clearly illogical, if not absurd. One does not, after all, conclude in Western society that if one person in a family becomes emotionally disturbed, all families are a mental health menace. And yet, it is this very position—the assumption that Aboriginal society is sick and maladjusted by reason of its culture—that emerges in many cross-cultural studies. This inference is not surprising in a profession whose concern is with psychopathology, but psychiatrists repeatedly paint a picture of Aboriginal communities as crumbling under the stress of the social environments in which they exist.

An objective and self-critical look at majority culture attempts to come to terms with Aboriginal mental health issues and problems is long overdue. This must be tempered, however, with a realisation that cross-cultural mental health is a relatively new field, and individuals who have had to deal with Aboriginal clients suffering from mental health problems have had little to fall back on except mental health insights and wisdom available within their own cultural context and experience. Assessments were often made under the most difficult circumstances, with fragmentary case information, often in the face of daunting communication difficulties, and in contexts where a client might be seen rarely and for very brief periods.

The situation at the beginning of the 1990s is very different: there exists a more helpful and available cross-cultural mental health literature; there are many social scientists as well as medical professionals working in the general area of indigenous mental health; and Aboriginal communities are both increasingly concerned about mental health issues and committed to finding solutions to community-defined health problems. This augurs well for what will hopefully be a spectrum of community-based mental health initiatives in many Aboriginal communities.

A crippling deficiency with respect to assessment and intervention, however, is the absence of systematic, comprehensive and reliable information on the nature and prevalence of stress and mental illness among Aboriginal people in Australia. Notwithstanding very substantial and challenging problems of access, and cross-cultural identification and diagnosis, such morbidity data is essential to an assessment of the magnitude and distribution of the problem. It is possible that prevalence will differ markedly across Australia, and between urban and remote communities. Whatever the naturally occurring incidence of mental health problems was in pre-colonial times or in the more recent past, contemporary Aboriginal communities are facing a number of problems which have no precedent and for which there exists no ready wisdom. Problems such as widespread binge drinking, youth gangs, child sexual abuse and suicide are relatively recent and bewildering problems for Aboriginal communities; dealing with them is beyond peoples' experience or the ability of faltering social control systems. There have been many formal and informal requests from communities for assistance, assistance which in some communities is desperately needed.

The contemporary picture is emphatically not one, however, of a destroyed Aboriginal culture, of a 'sick' society which somehow cannot take 'advantage' of acculturation and 'development' opportunities. Aboriginal culture is alive, dynamic, and pervasive throughout remote and urban Australia. In some areas of Australia, Aboriginal culture is in many respects non-traditional, but it is also very non-white-Australian. In many regions, traditionally oriented culture remains very strong, whatever superficial trappings of Western society it might judiciously select and use. This 'other-culture' reality must be acknowledged by mental health professionals. More than this, 'culture' must be seen and used as a critically important resource. Aboriginal culture is the change agent operating in Aboriginal communities, it informs and makes sense out of the present, it provides continuity to the past, it bonds people and communities, and, as a frame of reference and provider of identity, it is a powerful adaptive, therapeutic force.

There is not space in this chapter to address adequately issues of intervention, prevention, or indigenous community mental health programs. There now exists a substantial collective wisdom with respect to the implementation of community-based, culturally informed, indigenous mental health programs. An excellent forum that has critically discussed a variety of indigenous programs in the North American context is the *Journal of the National Center for American Indian and Alaska Native Mental Health Research* (see, for example, Guilmet and Whited 1989). The distilled social science wisdom of the past 30 years with respect to program development and implementation in indigenous communities is that viable programs must be community-initiated, community-based and community 'owned', as well as being culturally informed, consonant and, most important, meaningful. This does not mean that the knowledge and expertise of Western health systems is not highly valued and needed. It does recognise, however, that effective and appropriate change comes 'from within' communities and cultures, and that cultural experiences and understandings can be profoundly different from one another (Dasen et al. 1988).

Slattery (1987) argues for the importance of developing cultural sensitivity, competence and the role of cultural consultants in transcultural therapy with Aboriginal families. 'Cultural sensitivity' refers to the acquisition of knowledge of a particular culture's values, attitudes and beliefs as well as practices. 'Cultural competence' refers to the acquisition of the skill or ability to carry out cultural translation, that is, to work both within a specific culture or across cultural boundaries. A 'cultural consultant', knowledgeable about beliefs and practices, and with a high level of communication skills both within and across cultures can, Slattery argues, substantially facilitate communication and competence. Such individuals might be key indigenous people without qualifications, or indigenous or non-indigenous professionals or paraprofessionals, such as anthropologists, teachers, nurses or health workers. Such suggestions need to be seriously considered. There are now many examples in indigenous minority communities in other parts of the world of 'traditionally based solutions' where the indigenous culture itself has provided viable avenues for coping with contemporary mental health and social problems (see Manson 1982; Manson and Dinges 1988; Walker and LaDue 1986). While such strategies can be remarkably successful, they can also founder on widely shared misconceptions concerning cultural past and the complex and interdependent causes of contemporary problems. As Levy and Kunitz (1987, pp. 937–8) argue:

Community mental health meetings, held during the past few years, have devoted much energy to presenting traditional values and lifestyles as the antidote to contemporary mental health problems. From this premise it follows that, if alcoholism is defined as a disease introduced by the Anglos, it is their responsibility to provide cures and to undo the damage already done. But when a community perceives of itself as 'sick' and looks to the very source of its problems for a cure, it has abrogated responsibility for its own actions and done considerable damage to its self image. Moreover, to the extent a return to an idealized Golden Age is seen as a solution, innovative and adaptive strategies are precluded.

Alcohol perhaps presents the most intractable 'problem' and to date the most poorly understood challenge for many Aboriginal as well as Native American communities. A current Aboriginal perspective argues that Aboriginal society is 'caught in the strangle-hold of distorted and mythic traditions about alcohol' and that the social phenomenon of alcohol use among Aborigines is largely a distortion and exploitation, by Aborigines, of true culture and identity (Gibson unpub.; see also Gibson, 'A contemporary Aboriginal viewpoint', in Brady, chapter 5 in this volume). It could be argued that Western health professions have been no less caught in a 'strangle-hold' of distorted and mythic traditions about alcohol and mental illness among indigenous peoples.

Unfortunately there does not exist a coherent, culturally informed framework for understanding and communicating the nature and prerequisites of well-being in Aboriginal communities. Rather, the focus has been on pathology, viewed through some very distorting other-culture windows. If it is accepted that mental health is more than just the absence of illness, disease, or dysfunction and includes such components as effective functioning in daily life and the ability to deal with new situations (Berry and Kim 1988, p. 208), then what is necessary is a meaningful translation to an Aboriginal cultural context. An intriguing theoretical suggestion has been offered by Colby (1987), who attempts a synthesis of the perspectives of classical anthropologists, contemporary medical anthropology and the psychology of stress and coping in the context of physical health, satisfaction and happiness. Colby argues that a comprehensive cultural theory of well-being needs to encompass three broad worlds of human concern and behaviour:

1. the *ecological*: the material world of subsistence, technology, work, and economics;
2. the *social*: the world of interpersonal relationships, anchored in social structures and guided by ethics and social conventions;
3. the *interpretive*: the world of meta-thought, of symbolic systems and meta-level analysis.

Colby suggests that '[T]he cognitive systems representing these worlds in the mind of an individual combine in a "lifespace" that includes the many roles he [sic] assumes, the interrelationships he enters into and the assessments he makes of himself and of other people and situations' (1987, p. 890). Colby's emphasis on the immediate cultural surrounding and life-space of individuals is very sympathetic to the reality of needing to meet individual as well as community mental health needs and to appreciate and use local cultural values and understandings.

Aboriginal society has much to teach the rest of the world about sharing, caring and human connections—about human survival and well-being. It is ironic that these 60 000 years of collective wisdom with respect to mental health and human and ecosystem interdependencies are ignored at the same time that biomedical health sciences are just discovering the critical importance of supportive and caring connections between people. In the words of Pilisuk and Parks (1986, p. xi):

The case we present is that actual human interdependence is far greater than our contemporary values recognize. Understanding this interdependence is critical to our health, our sense of belonging, and even the survival of the human community. Where interdependency is nourished, it provides a healing web of remarkable powers for regeneration of the human potential. To survive—both individually and socially—we must reconnect with the ecology of our humanity, which is inseparable from the ecology of the world.

References

Abrams, D. B. (1983), 'Psychosocial assessment of alcohol and stress interactions', in L. A. Pohorecky and J. Brick (eds), *Stress and alcohol use*, Elsevier, New York.

Adler, T. (1990), 'Temperament tied to drug abuse risk', *American Psychological Association Monitor* **21** (2), p. 13.

ANAMH (Australian National Association for Mental Health) (1981), *Aboriginals and mental health: hitting our heads against a brick wall*, Australian National Association for Mental Health, Sydney.

Archer, D. (1985), 'Social deviance', in G. Linzey and A. Aronson (eds), *Handbook of social psychology*, 3rd edn, vol. 2, Addison-Wesley, Reading, Massachusetts.

Barlow, D. H. (1988), *Anxiety and its disorders, the nature and treatment of panic and anxiety*, The Guilford Press, New York.

Baron, R. A., and Byrne, D. (1987), *Social psychology*, 5th edn, Allyn and Bacon, Boston.

Bechtold, D. W. (1988), 'Cluster suicide in American Indian adolescents', *American Indian and Alaska Native Mental Health Research* **1** (3), pp. 26–35.

Beckett, J. (1965), 'Aborigines, alcohol and assimilation', in M. Reay (ed.), *Aborigines now*, Angus and Robertson, Sydney.

Beneteau, R. (1988), 'Trends in suicide', *Canadian Social Trends* **11**, pp. 22–24.

Berger, P., and Luckman, T. (1966), *The social construction of reality*, Pelican, Ringwood, Vic.

Berlin, J. N. (1986), 'Psychopathology and its antecedents among American Indian adolescents, in B. Lakey and A. Kaydin (eds), *Advances in child psychology*, vol. 9, Plenum Publishing, New York.

Berndt, C. H. (1964), 'The role of native doctors in Aboriginal Australia', in A. Kiev (ed.), *Magic, faith and healing*, Free Press, New York, pp. 264–82.

Berndt, C. H. (1982), 'Sickness and health in western Arnhem Land, a traditional perspective', in J. Reid (ed.), *Body, land and spirit: health and healing in Aboriginal society*, University of Queensland Press, St. Lucia, pp. 121–38.

Berndt, R. (ed.) (1970), *Australian Aboriginal anthropology*, University of Western Australia Press, Perth.

Berndt, R. (1971), 'Social relationships among two Australian Aboriginal societies of Arnhem Land, Gunwinggu and "Murngin", in F. L. K. Hsu (ed.), *Kinship and culture*, Aldine, Chicago, pp. 158–245.

Berndt, R. A., and Berndt, C. H. (1951), 'The concept of abnormality in an Australian society', in G. B. Wilbur and W. Muensterberger (eds), *Psychoanalysis and culture*, International Universities Press, New York, pp. 75–89.

Berry, J. W. (1970), 'Marginality, stress and ethnic identification in an acculturated Aboriginal community', *Journal of Cross-Cultural Psychology* **1** (3), pp. 239–52.

Berry, J. W. (1980), 'Introduction to methodology', in H. C. Triandis and J. W. Berry (eds), *Handbook of cross-cultural psychology: vol. 2, Methodology*, Allyn and Bacon, Boston, pp. 1–28.

Berry, J. W., and Kim, U. (1988), 'Acculturation and mental health', pp. 207–36, in P. R. Dasen, J. W. Berry and N. Sartorius (eds), *Health and cross-cultural psychology: toward applications*, Sage, Beverly Hills, California, pp. 207–36.

Berry, J. W., Kim, U., Minde, T., and Mok, D. (1987), 'Comparative studies of acculturative stress', *International Migration Review* **21**, pp. 491–511.

Bianchi, G. N., Cawte, J. E., and Kiloh, L. G. (1970), 'Cultural identity and mental health', *Social Science and Medicine* **3**, pp. 371–8.

Biernoff, D. (1982), 'Psychiatric and anthropological interpretations of 'aberrant' behaviour in an Aboriginal community', in J. Reid (ed.), *Body, land and spirit: health and healing in Aboriginal society*, University of Queensland Press, St. Lucia.

Brady, M. (1988), *Where the beer truck stopped: drinking in a northern Australian town*, North Australian Research Unit Monograph, Australian National University, Darwin.

Breakwell, G. (1986), *Coping with threatened identities*, Methuen, New York.

Brehm, S. S., and Brehm, J. W. (1981), *Psychological reactance: a theory of freedom and control*, Academic Press, New York.

Callan, V. J. (1985), *Australian minority groups*, Harcourt Brace Jovanovich, Sydney.

Carrithers, M., Collins, S., and Lukes, S. (1985), *The category of the person*, Cambridge University Press, Cambridge.

Cawte, J. E. (1964), 'Australian ethnopsychiatry in the field: a sampling in north Kimberley', *Medical Journal of Australia* **1**, pp. 467–72.

Cawte, J. E. (1965), 'Australian Aborigines in mental hospitals', *Oceania* **36** (4), pp. 264–82.

Cawte, J. E. (1972), *Cruel, poor and brutal nations*, University of Hawaii Press, Honolulu.

Cawte, J. E. (1974), *Medicine is the Law*, Rigby, Sydney.

Cawte, J. E. (1986), 'Aboriginal recovery from depression: eleven clinical types', *Aboriginal Health Worker* **10** (2), pp. 39–53.

Cawte, J. E. (1988), 'Aboriginal deaths in custody: the views of Aboriginal health workers', *Australian Journal of Forensic Sciences* **20** (2/3), pp. 224–33.

Cawte, J. E., Bianchi, G. N., and Kiloh, L. G. (1968), 'Personal discomfort in Australian Aborigines', *Australian and New Zealand Journal of Psychiatry* **2** (2), pp. 69–79.

Chance, N. A. (1965), 'Acculturation, self-identification and personality adjustment', *American Anthropologist* **67**, pp. 372–93.

Cohen, S., and Syme, S. L. (1985) (eds), *Social support and health*, Academic Press, Sydney.

Colby, B. N. (1987), 'Well-being: a theoretical program', *American Anthropologist* **89** (4), pp. 879–95.

Coleman, l. (1987), *Suicide clusters*, Faber and Faber, London.

Collman, J. (1988), *Fringe-dwellers and welfare*, University of Queensland Press, St. Lucia.

Comas-Diaz, L., and Griffith, E. E. H. (1988) (eds), *Clinical guidelines in cross-cultural mental health*, John Wiley, Brisbane.

Coombs, H. C., Brandl, M. M., and Snowdon, W. E. (1983), *A certain heritage*, Centre for Resource and Environmental Studies, Australian National University, Canberra.

Dasen, P. R., Berry, J. W., and Sartorius, N. (1988) (eds), *Health and cross-cultural psychology: toward applications*, Sage, Beverly Hills, California.

Davidson, G. R., Nurcombe, B., and Kearney, G. E. (1978), 'Culture conflict and coping in a group of Aboriginal adolescents', *Culture, Medicine and Psychiatry* **2** (4), pp. 259–96.

Devanesen, D., Furber, M., Hampton, D., Honari, M., Kinmonth, N., and Peach, H. G. (1986), *Health indicators in the Northern Territory*, Northern Territory Department of Health, Darwin.

Djikman, C. I. M., and de Vries, M. W. (1987), 'The social ecology of anxiety', *Journal of Nervous and Mental Disease* **175** (19), pp. 550–7.

Dinges, N. G., and Joos, S. K. (1988), 'Stress, coping, and health: models of interaction for Indian and Native populations', in S. M. Manson and N. G. Dinges (eds), *Behavioral health issues among American Indians and Alaska Natives: explorations on the frontiers of the biobehavioral sciences*, American Indian and Alaska Native Mental Health Research National Center, Denver, pp. 8–64.

Dohrenwend, B. P. (1983), 'The epidemiology of mental disorder', in D. Mechanic (ed.), *Handbook of health, health care, and the health professions*, The Free Press, New York, pp. 157–94.

Draguns, J. G. (1980*a*), 'Introduction to psychopathology', in H. C. Triandis and J. G. Draguns (eds), *Handbook of cross-cultural psychology: vol. 6, Psychopathology*, Allyn and Bacon, Boston, pp. 1–8.

Draguns, J. G. (1980*b*), 'Psychological disorders of clinical severity', in H. C. Triandis and J. G. Draguns (eds), *Handbook of cross-cultural psychology: vol. 6, Psychopathology*, Allyn and Bacon, Boston, pp. 99–174.

Draguns, J. G. (1988), 'Personality and culture: are they relevant for the enhancement of quality of mental life?', in P. R. Dasen, J. W. Berry and N. Sartorius (eds), *Health and cross-cultural psychology: toward applications*, Sage, Beverly Hills, California, pp. 141–61.

Dunham, H. W., and El Sendiony, M. F. (1975), 'Australian ethnopsychiatry: sociocultural factors and mental disorders', *International Mental Health Research Newsletter* **17** (4), pp. 1, 5–8.

Eastwell, H. D. (1977), 'Projective and identificatory illnesses among ex-hunter gatherers: a seven year survey of a remote Australian Aboriginal community', *Psychiatry* **40** (4), pp. 330–43.

Eastwell, H. D. (1982*a*), 'Overview: Australian Aborigines', *Transcultural Psychiatric Research Review* **19**, pp. 221–47.

Eastwell, H. D. (1982*b*), 'Psychiatric disorders among Australian Aborigines', in C. Friedmann and R. Faguet (eds), *Extraordinary symptoms in psychiatry: critical issues in psychiatry*, Plenum, New York, pp. 229–57.

Eastwell, H. D. (1985), 'Urban Aborigines: lifestyle and psychiatric disorders', *Patient Management*, January, pp. 63–8.

Eckersley, R. (1988), *Casualties of change: the predicament of youth in Australia*, Commission for the Future (AGPS), Canberra.

Edwards, G., Arif, A., and Hodgson, R. (1981), 'Nomenclature and classification of drug- and alcohol-related problems: a WHO memorandum', *Bulletin of the World Health Organization* **59** (2), pp. 225–42.

Elkin, A. P. (1977), *Aboriginal men of high degree*, 2nd edn, University of Queensland Press, St. Lucia.

Eron, L. D., and Peterson, R. A. (1982), 'Abnormal behavior: social approaches', *Annual Review of Psychology* **33**, pp. 231–64.

Everett, M. W. (1975), 'American Indian "social pathology": a re-examination', in T. R. Williams (ed.), *Psychological anthropology*, Mouton Publishers, The Hague, pp. 249–85.

Fabrega, H. (1982), 'Culture and psychiatric illness', in A. J. Marsella and G. White (eds), *Cultural conceptions of mental health and therapy*, D. Reidel, Boston, pp. 39–68.

Folkman, S., and Lazarus, R. S. (1988), 'Coping as a mediator of emotion', *Journal of Personality and Social Psychology* **54** (3), pp. 466–75.

Frederick, C. (1973), *Suicide, homicide and alcoholism among American Indians*, US Government Printing Office, Washington DC.

Gault, E. I. (1968), 'Psychiatric and behaviour disturbances in adolescent Aborigines in Victoria', *Australian and New Zealand Journal of Psychiatry* **2**, pp. 128–33.

Gault, E. I., Krupinski, J., and Stoller, A. (1970), 'Psychosocial problems of Aboriginal adolescents and their sociocultural environment', *Australian and New Zealand Journal of Psychiatry* **4**, pp. 174–82.

Geertz, L. (1975), 'On the nature of anthropological understanding', *American Scientist* **63**, pp. 47–53.

German, G. A. (1987), 'Mental health in Africa: 1. The extent of mental health problems in Africa today: an update of epidemiological knowledge', *British Journal of Psychiatry* **151**, pp. 435–9.

Gibbs, J. J. (1986), 'Alcohol consumption, cognition and context: examining tavern violence', in A. Campbell and J. J. Gibbs (eds), *Violent transactions: the limits of personality*, Basil Blackwell, Oxford, pp. 133–52.

Goldney, R. D. (1987), 'Suicide in young persons', *Medical Journal of Australia* **147**, pp. 161–2.

Goldney, R. D., and Burvill, P. W. (1980), 'Trends in suicidal behaviour and its management', *Australian and New Zealand Journal of Psychiatry* **14**, pp. 1–15.

Goldstein, M. J. (1988), 'The family and psychopathology', *Annual Review of Anthropology* **39**, pp. 283–99.

Guilmet, G. M., and Whited, D. L. (1989), 'The people who give more: health and mental health among the contemporary Puyallup Indian tribal community', *American Indian and Alaska Native Mental Health Research* **2** (2), pp. 1–140.

Hamilton, A. (1979), 'A comment on Arthur Hippler's paper, "Culture and personality perspective of the Yolngu of north-eastern Arnhem Land, part 1" ', *Mankind* **12** (2), pp. 164–9.

Hamilton, A. (1981), *Nature and nurture: Aboriginal child-rearing in Arnhem Land*, Australian Institute of Aboriginal Studies, Canberra.

Harras, A. (1987), *Issues in adolescent Indian health: suicide*, Indian Health Service, Tuscon, Arizona.

Harre, R. (1986) (ed.), *The social construction of emotions*, Basil Blackwell, Oxford.

Hatfield, A. B., and Lefley, H. P. (eds) (1987), *Families of the mentally ill: coping and adaptation*, Cassell Educational, London.

Heelas, P. (1981), 'Introduction: indigenous psychologies', in P. Heelas and A. Lock (eds), *Indigenous psychologies: the anthropology of the self*, Academic Press, London, pp. 3–18.

Heelas, P., and Lock, A. (eds) (1981), *Indigenous psychologies: the anthropology of the self*, Academic Press, London.

Hezel, F. X. (1987), 'Truk suicide epidemic and social change', *Human Organization* **46** (4), pp. 283–91.

Hezel, F. X., Rubinstein, D. H., and White, G. M. (eds) (1985), *Culture, youth and suicide in the Pacific*, University of Hawaii, Manoa.

Hippler, A. E. (1978), 'Culture and personality perspectives of the Yolngu of north-eastern Arnhem Land, *Journal of Psychological Anthropology* **1**, pp. 221–44.

Hippler, A. E. (1981), 'The Yolngu and cultural relativism: a response to Reser', *American Anthropologist* **83**, pp. 393–7.

HRSCAA (House of Representatives Standing Committee on Aboriginal Affairs) (1979), *Aboriginal health*, AGPS, Canberra.

Hui, C. H., and Triandis, H. C. (1986), 'Individualism-collectivism: a study of cross-cultural researchers', *Journal of Cross-Cultural Psychology* **17**, pp. 225–48.

Hunter, E. M. (1988), 'Aboriginal suicides in custody: a view from the Kimberley', *Australian and New Zealand Journal of Psychiatry* **22**, pp. 273–82.

Izard, C. E., Kagan, J., and Zajonc, R. B. (1984), *Emotions, cognition and behavior*, Cambridge University Press, Sydney.

Jahoda, G. (1982), *Psychology and anthropology: a psychological perspective*, Academic Press, New York.

Janes, C. R., Stall, R., and Gifford, S. M. (1986) (eds), *Anthropology and epidemiology: interdisciplinary approaches to the study of health and disease*, D. Reidel, Boston, Massachusetts.

Jones, I. H. (1972), 'Psychiatric disorders among Aborigines of the Australian Western Desert (II)', *Social Science and Medicine* **6**, pp. 263–7.

Jones, I. H., and Horne, D. J. de L. (1972), 'Diagnosis of psychiatric illness among tribal Aborigines', *Medical Journal of Australia* **1**, pp. 345–9.

Jones, I. H., and Horne, D. J. de L.(1973), 'Psychiatric disorders among Aborigines of the Australian Western Desert: further data and discussion', Social Science and Medicine 7, pp. 219–28.

Kahn, M. W. (1980), 'Wife beating and cultural context: prevalence in an Aboriginal and Islander community in northern Australia', *American Journal of Community Psychology* **8** (6), pp. 727–31.

Kahn, M. W. (1982), 'Cultural clash and psychopathology in three Aboriginal cultures', *Academic Psychology Bulletin* **4**, pp. 553–61.

Kahn, M. W. (1986), 'Psychosocial disorders of Aboriginal people of the United States and Australia', *Journal of Rural Psychology* **7** (1), pp. 45–59.

Kahn, M. W., Henry, J., and Cawte, J. (1976), 'Mental health services by and for Australian Aborigines', *Australian and New Zealand Journal of Psychiatry* **10**, pp. 221–8.

Kahn, M. W., Kennedy, E. V., and Cawte, J. (1978), 'Mental health services by and for Aborigines and Islanders: a follow-up report', *Australian and New Zealand Journal of Psychiatry* **12**, pp. 39–41.

Kamien, M. (1978), *The dark people of Bourke: a study of planned social change*, AIAS, Canberra.

Kamien, M. (1986), 'Alcohol and drug problems in minority groups', *Australian Drug and Alcohol Review* **5**, pp. 59–61

Kantor, G. K., and Straus, M. A. (1989), 'Substance abuse as a precipitant of wife abuse victimizations', *American Journal of Drug Abuse* **15** (2), pp. 178–89.

Kendall, P. C., and Watson, D. (1989), *Anxiety and depression: distinctive and overlapping features*, Academic Press, New York.

Kidson, M. A., and Jones, I. H. (1968), 'Psychiatric disorders among Aborigines of the Australian Western Desert', *Archives of General Psychiatry* **19**, p. 413.

Kiloh, L. G. (1975), 'Psychiatry amongst the Australian Aborigines', *British Journal of Psychiatry* **126**, pp. 1–10.

Kleinman, A. (1977), 'Culture, depression and the "new" cross-cultural psychiatry', *Social Science and Medicine* **11**, pp. 3–11.

Kleinman, A. (1980), *Patients and healers in the context of culture*, University of California Press, Berkeley, California.

Kleinman, A. (1986), *Social origins of distress and disease*, Yale University Press, New Haven.

Kleinman, A. (1987), 'Anthropology and psychiatry: the role of culture in cross-cultural research on illness', *British Journal of Psychiatry* **151**, pp. 447–54.

Kleinman, A., and Good, B. (eds) (1979), *Culture and depression*, University of California Press, Berkeley, California.

Kraus, R. F., and Buffler, P. A. (1985), 'Sociocultural stress and the American Native in Alaska: an analysis of changing patterns of psychiatric illness and alcohol abuse among Alaska Natives', *Culture, Medicine and Psychiatry* **3**, pp. 111–51.

LaFromboise, T. D. (1988), 'American Indian mental health policy', *American Psychologist* **43** (5), pp. 388–97.

Langton, M. (1981), 'Urbanizing Aborigines: the social scientists' great deception', *Social Alternatives* **2** (2), pp. 16–22.

Lazarus, R. S., and Folkman, S. (1984), *Stress, appraisal and coping*, Springer-Verlag, New York.

Lee, P., and Newton, N. (1981), 'Cultural aspects of coping', *International Journal of Psychiatry* **27**, pp. 13–22.

Lefcourt, H. M. (1982), *Locus of control: current trends in theory and research*, Lawrence Erlbaum, Hillsdale, New Jersey.

Leighton, A. H. (1959), *My name is Legion*, Basic Books, New York.

Leighton, A. H. (1968), 'Some propositions regarding the relationship of sociocultural integration and disintegration to mental health', in J. Zubin and F. Freyhan (eds), *Social psychiatry*, Grune and Stratton, New York.

Levy, J. E., and Kunitz, S. J. (1971), 'Indian reservations, anomie, and social pathologies', *Southwestern Journal of Anthropology* **27** (2), pp. 97–128.

Levy, J. E., and Kunitz, S. J. (1987), 'A suicide prevention program for Hopi youth', *Social Science and Medicine* **25** (8), pp. 931–40.

Levy, R. (1973), *Tahitians: mind and experience in the Society Islands*, University of Chicago Press, Chicago.

Lickiss, J. N. (1970), 'Health problems of Sydney Aboriginal children', *Medical Journal of Australia* **2**, pp. 995–1000.

Lickiss, J. N. (1971), 'Social deviance in Aboriginal boys', *Medical Journal of Australia* **2**, pp. 460–70.

Lickiss, J. N. (1975), 'Health problems of urban Aborigines: with special reference to the Aboriginal people of Sydney', *Social Science and Medicine* **9**, pp. 313–18.

Lippmann, L. (1974), 'Cultures in collision—Australia', in I. Pilowsky (ed.), *Cultures in collision*, Australian National Association for Mental Health, Sydney, pp. 11–14.

Lutz, C. A. (1988), *Unnatural emotions: everyday sentiments in a Micronesian atoll and their challenge to Western theory*, University of Chicago Press, Chicago.

Lutz, C. A., and White, G. M. (1986), 'The anthropology of emotions', *Annual Review of Anthropology* **15**, pp. 405–36.

MacAndrew, C., and Edgerton, R. B. (1970), *Drunken comportment: a social explanation*, Thomas Nelson, Melbourne.

Manson, S. M. (1982) (ed.), *New directions in prevention among American Indian and Alaska Native communities*, Oregon Health Sciences University, Portland, Oregon.

Manson, S. M., and Dinges, N. G. (1988) (eds), *Behavioral health issues among American Indians and Alaska Natives: explorations on the frontiers of the biobehavioral sciences*, American Indian and Alaska Native Mental Health Research National Center, Denver, Colorado.

Manson, S. M., Walker, R. D., and Kivlahan, D. R. (1987), 'Psychiatric assessment and treatment of American Indians and Alaska Natives', *Hospital and Community Psychiatry* **38**, pp. 165–73.

Marcus, G. E., and Fischer, M. J. (1986), *Anthropology as cultural critique*, University of Chicago Press, Chicago.

Marsella, A. J. (1980), 'Depressive experience and disorder across cultures', in H. C. Triandis and J. G. Draguns (eds), *Handbook of cross-cultural psychology: vol. 6, Psychopathology*, Allyn and Bacon, Boston, pp. 237–89.

Marsella, A. J. (1985), 'Culture, self and mental disorder', in A. J. Marsella, G. DeVos and F. Hsu (eds), *Culture and self: Asian and Western perspectives*, Tavistock Press, London.

Marsella, A. J. (1988), 'Cross-cultural research on severe mental disorders: issues and findings', *Acta Psychiatrica Scandinavica Supplementum* **78** (344), pp. 7–22.

Marsella, A. J., and Dash-Scheuer, A. (1988), 'Coping, culture, and healthy human development', in P. R. Dasen, J. W. Berry and N. Sartorius (eds), *Health and cross-cultural psychology: toward applications*, Sage, Beverly Hills, California, pp. 162–78.

Marsella, A. J., and White, G. M. (1984) (eds), *Cultural conceptions of mental health and therapy*, D. Reidel, Boston.

May, P. A. (1987), 'Suicide and self destruction among American Indian youths', *American Indian and Alaska Native Mental Health Research* **1**, pp. 52–69.

Meggitt, M. J. (1987), 'Understanding Australian Aboriginal society: kinship systems or cultural categories?', in W. H. Edwards (ed.), *Traditional Aboriginal society: a reader*, Macmillan, Melbourne, pp. 113–37.

Mental Health Discussion Paper (1989), a discussion paper presented to the Australian Health Ministers' Advisory Council in October 1989, AGPS, Canberra.

Miller, J. (1984), 'Culture and the development of everyday social explanation', *Journal of Personality and Social Psychology* **46** (5), pp. 961–78.

Millon, T. (1988), 'Psychiatric taxonomy: old wine, old bottles', *Contemporary Psychology* **33** (11), pp. 974–5.

Mirowsky, J., and Ross, C. E. (1989), 'Psychiatric diagnosis as reified measurement', *Journal of Health and Social Behavior* **30** (March), pp. 11–25.

Moodie, P. M. (1973), *Aboriginal health*, ANU Press, Canberra.

Morice, R. (1978), 'Psychiatric diagnosis in a transcultural setting: the importance of lexical categories', *British Journal of Psychiatry* **132**, pp. 87–95.

Morice, R. (1979), 'Psychiatric diagnosis in transcultural perspective', *Australian and New Zealand Journal of Psychiatry* **13**, pp. 293–300.

Muirhead, J. H. (1988), *Royal Commission into Aboriginal Deaths in Custody interim report*, AGPS, Canberra.

Murphy, J. M. (1973), 'Sociocultural change and psychiatric disorder among rural Yorubas in Nigeria', *Ethos* **1**, pp. 239–62.

Myers, F. R. (1986), *Pintupi country, Pintupi self: sentiment, place and politics among Western Desert Aborigines*, AIAS, Canberra.

NAILSS (National Aboriginal and Islander Legal Services Secretariat (1989), 'An interesting and informative chat is not what I had in mind', *Aboriginal Law Bulletin* **2** (36), pp. 12–15.

NAHSWP (National Aboriginal Health Strategy Working Party) (1989), *A national Aboriginal health strategy*, Department of Aboriginal Affairs, Canberra.

NAMHA (National Aboriginal Mental Health Association) (1980), 'Aborigines look at mental health', *Aboriginal Health Worker*, special issue 2, pp. 1–116.

Neighbors, H. W. (1984), 'The distribution of psychiatric morbidity in black Americans: a review and suggestions for research', *Community Mental Health Journal* **20** (3), pp. 169–81.

Newcomb, M. D., and Bentler, P. M. (1989), 'Substance use and abuse among children and teenagers', *American Psychologist*, February, pp. 242–8.

Newcomb, M. D., and Harlow, L. L. (1986), 'Life events and substance abuse among adolescents: mediating effects of perceived loss of control and meaninglessness in life', *Journal of Personality and Social Psychology* **51** (3), pp. 564–77.

NTDHCS (Northern Territory Department of Health and Community Services (1988), *Annual report: Mental Health Act 1987–1988*, Government Printer of the Northern Territory, Darwin.

Nurcombe, B. (1976), *Children of the dispossessed*, University Press of Hawaii, Honolulu.

Nurcombe, B., and Cawte, J. E. (1967), 'Patterns of behaviour disorder amongst the children of an Aboriginal population', *Australian and New Zealand Journal of Psychiatry* **1**, pp. 119–33.

Nurcombe, B., Bianchi, G. N., Money, J., and Cawte, J. E. (1970), 'A hunger for stimuli: petrol inhalation', *British Journal of Medical Psychology* **43**, pp. 367–74.

O'Connor, R. (1984), 'Alcohol and contingent drunkenness in Central Australia', *Australian Journal of Social Issues* **19** (3), pp. 173–83.

O'Neil, J. D. (1986), 'Colonial stress in the Canadian Arctic: an ethnography of young adults changing, in C. R. Jones, R. Stall and S. M. Gifford (eds), *Anthropology and epidemiology: interdisciplinary approaches to the study of health and disease*, D. Reidel, Dordrecht, pp. 249–74.

Orford, J. (1986), 'The domestic context', in P. Feldman and J. Orford (eds), *Psychological problems: the social context*, John Wiley, New York, pp. 3–38.

Pedigo, J. (1983), 'Finding the "meaning" of Native American substance abuse: implications for community prevention', *Personnel and Guidance Journal* **61** (5), pp. 273–7.

Phillips, D. P., and Carstenson, L. L. (1986), 'Clustering of teenage suicides after television news stories about suicide', *New England Journal of Medicine* **315** (11), pp. 685–9.

Phillips, M. R., and Inui, T. S. (1986), 'The interaction of mental illness, criminal behavior and culture: Native Alaskan mentally ill criminal offenders', *Culture, Medicine and Psychiatry* **10**, pp. 123–49.

Pilisuk, M., and Parks, S. H. (1986), *The healing web: social networks and human survival*, University Press of New England, Hanover.

Quay, H. C., Routh, D. K., and Shapiro, S. K. (1987), 'Psychopathology of childhood: from description to validation, *Annual Review of Psychology* **38**, pp. 491–532.

QDVT (Queensland Domestic Violence Taskforce) (1988), *Beyond these walls: report to the minister for family services and welfare housing*, Department of Family Services and Welfare Housing, Brisbane.

Radford, A. J., Harris, R. D., Brice, G. A., Van der Byl, M., Monten, H., Matters, D., Neeson, M., Bryan, L., and Hassan, R. (1990), *Taking control: stage 1, Aboriginal 'heads of household' study*, Department of Primary Health Care, The Finders University of South Australia, Adelaide.

Reid, J. (ed.) (1982), *Body, land and spirit: health and healing in Aboriginal society*, University of Queensland Press, St Lucia.

Reid, J. (1983), *Sorcerers and healing spirits: continuity and change in an Aboriginal medical system*, ANU Press, Canberra.

Reser, J. P. (1979), 'A matter of control: Aboriginal housing circumstances in remote communities and settlements', in M. Heppell (ed.), *A black reality: Aboriginal camps and housing in remote Australia*, AIAS, Canberra, pp. 65–96.

Reser, J. P. (1981), 'Australian Aboriginal man's inhumanity to man: a case of cultural distortion', *American Anthropologist* **83** (2), pp. 387–95.

Reser, J. P. (1982), 'Cultural relativity or cultural bias?', *American Anthropologist* **84**, pp. 399–404.

Reser, J. P. (1989*a*), 'Australian Aboriginal suicide deaths in custody: cultural context and cluster evidence', *Australian Psychologist* **24** (3), pp. 325–42.

Reser, J. P. (1989*b*), 'Aboriginal deaths in custody and social construction', *Australian Aboriginal Studies* **2**, pp. 43–50.

Reser, J. P., and Eastwell, H. D. (1981), 'Labeling and cultural expectations: the shaping of a sorcery syndrome in Aboriginal Australia', *Journal of Nervous and Mental Disease* **169** (5), pp. 303–10.

Rodin, J. (1985), 'The application of social psychology', in G. Lindzey and E. Aronson (eds), *Handbook of social psychology*, 3rd edn, vol. 2, Addison-Wesley, Reading, Massachusetts, pp. 805–81.

Rook, K. S. (1984), 'Promoting social bonding: strategies for helping the lonely and socially isolated', *American Psychologist* **39** (12), pp. 1389–407.

Rothbaum, F., Weisz, J. R., and Snyder, S. S. (1982), 'Changing the world and changing the self: a two-process model of perceived control', *Journal of Personality and Social Psychology* **42**, pp. 5–37.

Rubinstein, D. H. (1985), 'Suicide in Micronesia', in F. X. Hezel, D. H. Rubinstein and G. M. White (eds), *Culture, youth and suicide in the Pacific*, University of Hawaii, Honolulu, Hawaii.

Rubinstein, R. A., and Perloff, J. D. (1986), 'Identifying psychosocial disorders in children: on integrating epidemiological and anthropological understandings', in C. R. Janes, R. Stall and S. M. Gifford (eds), *Anthropology and epidemiology: interdisciplinary approaches to the study of health and disease*, D. Reidel, Boston, Massachusetts, pp. 303–32..

Ruddock, P. N. (1977), *Aboriginal health*, report from the House of Representatives Standing Committee on Aboriginal Affairs, AGPS, Canberra.

Sampson, E. E. (1988), 'The debate on individualism: indigenous psychologies of the individual and their role in personal and societal functioning', *American Psychologist* **43** (1), pp. 15–22.

Sansom, B. (1980), *The camp at Wallaby Cross*, AIAS, Canberra.

Scherer, K. R. (1988) (ed.), *Facets of emotion: recent research*, Lawrence Erlbaum, Hillsdale, New Jersey.

Segall, M. H. (1979), *Cross-cultural psychology: human behavior in global perspective*, Brooks/Cole, Monterey, California.

Seltzer, A. (1980), 'Acculturation and mental disorder in the Innuit', *Canadian Journal of Psychiatry* **25**, pp. 173–81.

Shiffman, S., and Wills, T. A. (1985) (eds), *Coping and substance abuse*, Academic Press, New York.

Shweder, R. A., and Bourne, E. J. (1982), 'Does the concept of the person vary cross-culturally?' in A. J. Marsella and G. M. White (eds), *Cultural conceptions of mental health and therapy*, D. Reidel, Dordrecht.

Shweder, R. A., and LeVine, R. A. (1984) (eds), *Culture theory: essays on mind, self and emotion*, Cambridge University Press, Cambridge.

Slattery, G. (1987), 'Transcultural therapy with Aboriginal families: working with the belief system', *Australian and New Zealand Journal of Family Therapy* **8** (2), pp. 61–70.

Spencer, D. J. (1983), 'Psychiatric dilemmas in Australian Aborigines', *International Journal of Social Psychiatry* **29** (3), pp. 208–214.

Taylor, K. (1989), *Story about feeling. Bill Neidjie*, Magabala Books, Broome, WA.

Taylor, S. E. (1990), 'Health psychology: the science and the field', *American Psychologist* **45** (1), pp. 40–50.

Thomson, D. (1961), 'Marrngit mirri and kalka: medicine man and sorcerer in Arnhem Land', *Man* **131**, pp. 97–102.

Thomson, N. (1984), 'Aboriginal health—current status', *Australian and New Zealand Journal of Medicine* **14**, pp. 705–15.

Tonkinson, M. (1982), 'The *mabarn* and the hospital: the selection of treatment in a remote Aboriginal community', in J. Reid (ed.), *Body, land and spirit; health and healing in Aboriginal Society*, University of Queensland Press, St Lucia, pp. 225–41.

Tonkinson, R. (1978), *The Mardujara: living the dream in Australia's desert*, Holt, Rinehart and Winston, New York.

Triandis, H. C., and Draguns, J. G. (eds)(1980), *Handbook of cross-cultural psychology: vol. 5, Psychopathology*, Allyn and Bacon, Boston.

Trimble, J. E. (1984), 'Drug abuse prevention research among Native American Indians and Alaska Natives', *White Cloud Journal* **3** (3), pp. 23–34.

Walker, R. D., and LaDue, R. (1986), 'An integrative approach to American Indian mental health', in C. S. Wilkinson (ed.), *Ethnic psychiatry*, Plenum Press, New York, pp. 143–94.

Warner, L. (1958), *A black civilization*, Harper, New York.

Watson, C., Fleming, J., and Alexander, K. (1988), *A survey of drug use patterns in Northern Territory Aboriginal communities, 1986–1987*, Northern Territory Department of Health and Community Services, Darwin.

Weiss, R. S. (1982), 'Issues in the study of loneliness', in L. A. Peplau and D. Perlman (eds), *Loneliness: a sourcebook of current theory, research and therapy*, John Wiley, New York, pp. 71–80.

Weisz, J. R., Rothbaum, F. M., and Blackburn, T. C. (1984), 'Standing out and standing in: the psychology of control in America and Japan', *American Psychologist* **39** (9), pp. 955–69.

Westen, D. (1985), *Self and society*, Cambridge University Press, Sydney.

White, G. M., and Kirkpatrick, J. (1985) (eds), *Person, self and experience: exploring Pacific ethnopsychologies*, University of California Press, Berkeley, California.

Wilson, P. (1988), *Black death, white hands*, George Allen and Unwin, Sydney.

Wood, C. M. (1980), 'National Aboriginal Mental Health Association: an outcome of studies in alcoholism', *Medical Journal of Australia*, Special Supplement 1, pp. 11–12.

Yap, P. M. (1974), *Comparative psychiatry: a theoretical framework*, University of Toronto Press, Toronto.

Young, A. (1982), 'The anthropologies of illness and sickness', *Annual Review of Anthropology* **11**, pp. 257–285.

Zinberg, N. E. (1984), *Drug, set, and setting: the basis for controlled intoxicant use*, Yale University Press, New Haven, Connecticut.

Unpublished material

Brady, M. (unpub.), Dealing with disorder, strategies of accommodation among the southern Pitjantjatjara, MA thesis, Australian National University, Canberra, 1987.

Cawte, J. E. (unpub.), The gap in Aboriginal health: a cry for a national Aboriginal school of healing, paper presented to the World Psychiatric Association Conference, May, Sydney, 1988.

Gibson, M. (unpub.), Anthropology and tradition: a contemporary Aboriginal viewpoint, paper presented at the 1987 ANZAAS Conference, Townsville, Queensland.

Martin, D. (unpub.), Nobody boss for me: a preliminary account of conflict and fighting at Aurukun, North Queensland, paper presented at the Bioscope Seminar, Anthropology Department, Australian National University, Canberra, 1987.

Reser, J. P., Reser, P., Smithson, M. J., and Taylor, J. C. (unpub.), Alcohol consumption patterns and consequences in North Queensland: a report of preliminary findings concerning the association between alcohol use and attempted suicide in Aboriginal communities in north Queensland, paper presented to the Remote Aboriginal and Torres Strait Islander Community Futures Conference, July, Townsville, Queensland, Australian Institute of Aboriginal and Torres Strait Islander Studies, 1990.

Shanahan, P. (unpub.), Communicating with the underage drinker, paper presented at the Drink Driving Education Conference, Maroochydore, Qld, 18–21 October, 1987.

Swan, P. (unpub), 200 years of unfinished business, paper presented to the 'Mental Health Status of the Nation' Conference of the Australian National Association for Mental Health, 1988.

CHAPTER 7

In sickness and health: the sociocultural context of Aboriginal well-being, illness, and healing

Robyn Mobbs

Palliative Care Unit, University of South Australia, Adelaide

This chapter focuses on the interrelationship between Aboriginal people and the dominant Anglo-Australian health-care system. It introduces Aboriginal health and illness beliefs, traditional healing systems, and the interactions between non-Aboriginal health practitioners and Aboriginal clients. The chapter is written in the recognition that it is an Anglo-Australian's representation of Aboriginal realities, but with the hope that non-Aboriginal readers (for whom it is primarily written) will become more aware of the cultural dimensions of well-being, illness, and healing.

Some of the data included here are based on extended anthropological fieldwork conducted at 'Mining City' with the Aboriginal people of two small reserves and the medical staff of the local 120-bed hospital. They allowed me to be a part of their lives between 1981 and 1983. Mining City is a pseudonym for a mining town in a remote area of Australia. The traditional owners of the area, the Gulgadunng, as well as other Aboriginal peoples, have camped on the fringes of Mining City since its inception. In the 1980s, there were two small reserves for Aborigines, referred to in this chapter as River Reserve and Camping Reserve. The reserve dwellers survived on welfare payments, mostly the age pension or supporting parent's benefit. Food was of primary importance in a community defined by poverty, and acquiring it was a daily concern. While people subsisted on essentials like tea, powdered milk, sugar and sometimes flour, they longed for, and sometimes obtained, bush meat like goanna, porcupine (echidna) and kangaroo. Health services in the area were limited. There was one elderly man who practised some traditional healing. Non-Aboriginal health services were also used, including the local hospital and the state government's Aboriginal Health Program. One elderly general practitioner was also consulted.

A sociocultural approach to the health of Aborigines

The health-care encounter between Aborigines and non-Aborigines is part of a web of interactions and processes that are shaped by history as well as by contemporary experiences of dealing with government agencies, health professionals and the health bureaucracy. An Aboriginal woman seeking help at a hospital, for instance, invariably brings with her all her previous contacts with the medical staff and all the expectations and perceptions arising from her previous contacts with Anglo-Australian society. Hers is an experience that is multifaceted and anchored in her personal and social history.

This notion that a health-care encounter is a total social experience highlights a number of points. First and foremost, it means that issues of health and illness cannot be separated from other processes that impinge upon Aboriginal society in the Australian setting. While it may be true that the blatantly racist attitudes of even a decade ago no longer typify the approaches of most health professionals (indeed there is greater understanding, and impressive goodwill and enthusiasm among many workers in the Aboriginal health area), certain outdated ideas and attitudes persist. Frequently, non-Aboriginal health professionals continue to operate, if only implicitly, with a benevolent or charitable attitude in their relationships with Aboriginal clients. Services largely continue to be provided with the assumptions that:

1. Aborigines are socially disaffected and grossly disadvantaged;
2. Aboriginal society is culturally simplistic;
3. the Western health and medical system is superior to Aboriginal traditions of healing and care.

The first of these assumptions—that Aborigines lack 'advantage' and education—can often lead practitioners who are new to Aboriginal health care into disillusionment and cynicism. Initially, feeling compassionate, they work hard to alleviate and cure with the ultimate intention of changing for the better the position of their 'disadvantaged' clients. When improvement, as they define it, is not forthcoming, some professionals try even harder to exact it, never questioning their own aspirations, nor reflecting upon the suitability of their methods. This kind of approach is ethnocentric and unproductive, and can lead to feelings of inadequacy and resentment. A sense of failure is then followed by disillusionment and cynicism, and frequently the health professional will withdraw emotionally and just 'do a job', or leave the area for good.

The other two assumptions—that Aboriginal society is culturally simplistic, and that the Western scientific health-care system is superior to any other for illness and disease management—both originate with the social theories of the last century. They can be traced to the underlying belief in the infallibility of biomedical science, which continues to be an intrinsic part of professionalised health education in the 1990s. Such beliefs derive in part from the nineteenth-century reworkings of Darwinism, which extrapolated ideas from the evolution of the animal kingdom and applied them to human societies. Thus, human groups were categorised as races and compared. Some were believed to be more evolved, and therefore more civilised, than others, which were thought to be more primitive. These ideas still inform the common Australian understandings of Aboriginal culture and society. One of the tenets central to these outdated philosophies is that known as the 'empty vessel' syndrome: the idea that Aborigines have no culture, or at least no civilised culture comparable to European culture with its technology and Christian humanism. Consistent with such theories, non-Aboriginal health-care professionals (mainly nurses and doctors), have held the view that Aborigines do not have a health-care system, or any body of indigenous knowledge that could be designated 'medical'. Although so-called 'medicine men' were known, they were considered to be purveyors of savage evil (that is, they were seen as witchdoctors). Their practice was dismissed in the same way as were the Aboriginal systems of land tenure and social organisation, and Aboriginal spiritual life and world views. Thus, throughout Australia's history, Aborigines have been presumed to be open to the filling of their emptiness with the 'superior' practices and beliefs of the dominant society.

With this kind of historical burden, it is perhaps not surprising that a patronising approach, often inflexible and self-justifying, still characterises much of the health care available to Aborigines today, regardless of where they live. Moreover, the problems with the present health-care system cannot be overcome simply by good-will and liberal idealism on the part of the individual non-Aboriginal health professional. To provide appropriate health care for Aborigines in all parts of Australia, it is necessary to unravel the sociocultural conditions in which Aborigines live and the historical and political contexts of their lives. This involves, among other things, gaining knowledge about Aboriginal culture and the way it is articulated or 'used' by Aboriginal people themselves in their daily dealings with the Australian health-care system.

Culture is that which members of a society share in the form of ideas, behaviours and artefacts. Culture in part arises from the propensity of humans to symbolise, that is to create and impose meanings on the objects around them and on the actions taken by them. Culture is the set of standards for perceiving, believing, valuing and acting that are imposed on, and make sense of the world, and that guide behaviours and relationships within a social group and with the environment. To give a classic anthropological illustration, humans are the only creatures that distinguish between water and Holy Water. Cultural knowledge is learned by living in a society where core traits and ideas tend to be transmitted from one generation to the next. This passing on through time gives continuity to a sociocultural community and its patterns of life. However, when social change takes place within a community, culture also tends to be transformed, with some traits and values being significantly altered while others are reinforced and strengthened in the new circumstances. Culture is never static nor dormant, never 'disappears', but changes continually through time.

Before the colonisation of Australia, more than 100 languages and many more dialects were spoken, and numerous groups of Aborigines could have been described as distinct cultural groups. Yet there were fundamental similarities in social organisation and cosmology, for example, which make it possible to describe the collective aspect of the cultural characteristics by which Aboriginality before colonisation could be defined. It is self-evident that Aboriginal lifestyles are not the same today as they were 200 or more years ago. Nevertheless, because all cultures are transformed through time, it is inaccurate to speak of 'deculturation', or loss of culture. Today, Aboriginal cultures remain distinctive, vital and changing, regardless of whether people reside on their own land in the Northern Territory, or in a rural township in Queensland, or in a cosmopolitan city in New South Wales (Keen 1988; Collman 1988).

For many Anglo-Australians, including health professionals, however, the idea of Aboriginality is controversial, and raises many of the myths and stereotypes with which Aboriginal people have had to struggle. The confident assertion by light-skinned individuals that they are Aboriginal often arouses indignation in many non-Aborigines who remonstrate that they are not 'dark enough', and that such people only call themselves Aboriginal to be eligible for the extra 'handouts' Aborigines supposedly receive. In a similar vein, many non-Aborigines will go to great lengths to explain how the 'full-blood' Aborigines are people of honourable character, while their 'half-caste' relatives are 'no good', the implication being that those who have retained their purity of 'blood' and pristine culture are somehow morally superior to those who no longer practise gathering and hunting as their basic economy.

The debate about Aboriginality highlights the dominance of British cultural ideology in Australia, because it is argued little in the Aboriginal community but at length by other Australians. Disputes about Aboriginality based on purity of 'blood' and culture are premised on the following beliefs:

1. that there is such a being as a racially pure, unmixed, undiluted human;
2. that a cultural group can be isolated absolutely from contact with any other culture;
3. that a group of people can be genetically and culturally contaminated and/or lost.

The scientific community has largely rejected the concept of race since research conducted after the Second World War showed that there is tremendous genetic diversity within any cultural group. Indeed in pre-1788 Australia, Aboriginal peoples varied greatly in height, hair colour and other physical characteristics. In north-west Queensland, Gulgadunng men were mostly over 6 feet (180 centimetres) tall, while the north Queensland rainforest people were short and small, akin to the African Pygmy groups. Thus, the physical appearance of different groups of Aborigines was of marked contrast, even within a relatively limited area. Moreover, the idea of racial purity could not have been applied to all Aborigines before 1788 even if it were a valid notion, because on the northern shores of the continent, long before the British invasion, children were born to Aboriginal women and Macassan seafarers who processed trepang on the coasts of Arnhem Land. As with the children of Aboriginal and non-Aboriginal unions since colonisation, they were assimilated by way of their maternal kin, and generally accepted as full members of their Aboriginal families.

The British, however, used the notion of racial purity and impurity (that is, caste) to separate children of dual descent from their Aboriginal mothers (see Gray et al., chapter 3 in this book). Theories such as these, now discredited, were used to justify practices such as the widespread sexual abuse of Aboriginal women by white men and many of the unlovely policies that controlled and undermined the indigenous population. The enforced removal of 'half-caste', 'quarter-caste' or 'quadroon', and even 'octoroon' children with 'white blood' running in their veins was supposedly to release them from hopelessness. By virtue of their superior inheritance, they were considered more able to live a civilised life than 'full-bloods'.

But this policy produced a dilemma and raised the question of when a less than 'full-blood' Aborigine ceases to be an Aborigine. That political predicament was put to rest only in the 1970s when the Australian government defined an Aboriginal person in other than racial terms: that is, an Aboriginal person is one who has Aboriginal ancestry, identifies as an Aborigine, and is identified by other Aborigines as Aboriginal. This social rather than genetic definition has clarified the identification of Aborigines for non-Aborigines, but it has not put an end to the 'Who is an Aborigine?' debate. Frequently, the accusation is now made that particular individuals or groups identifying as Aboriginal have 'lost' their culture; indeed, the idea that the majority of Aborigines in Australia (the urban dwellers) are deculturated is widespread. It is deeply offensive to Aborigines. It is like asserting that non-Aboriginal Australians have no culture because they have 'lost' their English identity. The observation that Aborigines are living changed lifestyles and have knowledge bases different from those of 200 years ago is no evidence of lack of Aboriginality, because Aboriginal culture has changed considerably since the arrival of Europeans. Furthermore, there is much that continues from the 'old', and much that has altered with the 'new', as is demonstrated in the discussion of the contemporary Aboriginal health-care system that follows.

The contemporary Aboriginal health-care system

All peoples have their own culturally determined and socially structured health-care systems, and some well-established premises underpin a cultural analysis of wellbeing, sickness and healing:

1.   that all groups at all times have experienced health and illness states;
2.   that all cultural groups have systematic ways of explaining illness and its causes;
3.   that all cultural groups practice healing.

In Aboriginal Australia, the indigenous health-care systems are part of a unique complex which includes descriptions of well-being, explanations of illness causation, healing practices, and prerequisite social behaviours for the person experiencing the illness and her or his kin. The 'traditional' remains relevant to today, as Landy (1983, p. 228) explains:

Through internal evolutionary processes and as a result of the forcible or peaceful influences of other cultures, each society and its culture—and its medical system—undergo continual change. When the term 'traditional' is used to describe an indigenous society, it should not necessarily imply that its culture is a replica of...its ancient medical heritage. In most systems there are clearly some lines, however tenuous, of continuity with the past.

Well-being

The meaning of health in any society is shaped by cultural traits, values and rules and is learned through participation in that society. Yet, it is difficult to draw a detailed picture of Aboriginal concepts of health and well-being, as there is little research and few early recordings. This scarcity of data is partly because anthropologists and other early writers did not include the subject in their descriptive analyses, although the physical attributes of adult Aborigines such as height and build were often considered by non-Aborigines to be indicators of health status. More recently, Aboriginal health beliefs and behaviours have become entangled with contemporary Aboriginal–white politics to such an extent that the former have been overshadowed by the latter. Thus, when Nathan (1983, p. 94) writes, 'To Aboriginal people, health includes food, water, electricity. It includes also the means to go into the bush and conduct ceremonial "business" ', the plea for better health is linked to a plea for land rights.

The politicisation of health has confused many non-Aborigines steeped in the medical paradigm, who assert that hygiene is what Aborigines need to attend to, not the regaining of land. It is certainly the case that Aboriginal health has, over the last decade or more, been a controversial topic for both state and federal governments. However, this health debate has taken place within a non-Aboriginal framework, focusing solely upon disease incidence, housing, and mortality and morbidity rates. By comparison, scant attention has been paid to the Aboriginal world view of well-being, which is socially, not biologically or pathologically, determined and which

Figure 7.1 *Aboriginal people protest in a street march at Alice Springs in 1975. Aboriginal concepts of health and well-being are closely linked with their relationship to their land.* (Herald and Weekly Times Ltd, *Melbourne*)

begins, and ends, with the land and its rightful indigenous inhabitants: the people, the animals, and the plants. As Rose (unpub., p. 15) clearly points out, health for Aborigines has many meanings but 'the most important is that of country, for it is in this context that *punyu* is given most forcible social expression.'

Rose is one of the few researchers to look at the Aboriginal meaning of well-being. She looks in some detail at the notion of health in Ngaringman culture in the north-west of the Northern Territory. From her understanding of Ngaringman ideas, she describes well-being or *punyu* as encompassing person and country. *Punyu*, according to Rose (unpub., p. 3), 'was variously translated as strong, healthy, happy, knowledgeable ("smart"), socially responsible (to "take a care"), beautiful, clean, and "safe", both in the sense of being within the Law and in the sense of being cared for'. Rose notes that there are at least three opposites to *punyu*:

1. *jangkayi* meaning sick, weak, sad, stupid, irresponsible, or in danger ('got a trouble', meaning at odds with Aboriginal law);
2. *wangkut* meaning 'buggered up', 'broken down' or 'no good';
3. 'rubbish', 'dirty', or 'no good'.

Both *punyu* and *jangkayi* are complete states of being. Working with the Groote Eylandters, Webber et al. (1975, p. 17) also found four categories of well-being, which broadly correspond with those described by Rose:

1. the strong (*wurringbuda*), which is similar to the European notion of well-being in which a person is functional and coping well both mentally and physically;
2. the weak (*wurrumurndagayuwaya*): temporary states of diminished strength induced by such conditions as diarrhoea, constipation, headache, rhinorrhoea, productive cough, toothache, abdominal pain (flatulence, nausea), or skin eruptions (boils, sores);
3. the wounded (*wurrugarburra*), which is not associated with weakness but requires appropriate care;
4. the sick (*angbilyuwa*), which is an extreme state of weakness induced by 'singing' or 'painting' (that is, by sorcery).

Certainly, Rose's *punyu* and Webber's *wurringbuda* appear to be similar states of well-being, both physically and psychosocially. Similarly, Soong (unpub., p. 21) writes:

Gunwinggu people do not have a word for health. The closest equivalents are strong, not sick, happy and good feelings. Those Aboriginals [sic] who were fluent in English said 'good health' means...'happy with my people' and 'feeling good during and after ceremonies'.

Rose (unpub., pp. 4, 5) elaborates on the concept of health, explaining that *punyu* is 'an achieved quality, developed through relationships of mutual care'. Furthermore,

In Ngaringman cosmology the known universe constitutes a living system the goal of which is to reproduce itself as a living system. Each part of the cosmos (country, Rainbow Snake, animals, people, etc.) is alive, conscious, and is basically either

punyu or not punyu. That which is punyu is not just alive but is also contributing to life.

At the level of the individual, the Ngaringman people see a human as what Rose (unpub., pp. 8–13) calls a single system, an extended system and an open system. The individual as a single system is an integration of three parts—the body and two spirits—which constitute well-being when they are in equilibrium. The extended system pertains to relationships of 'sameness', which derive from a common origin, that is from one Dreaming source, such as the kinship classification of subsection (or 'skin', as it is commonly known by Ngaringman), which 'places each person in a social category and defines types of relationships between people'. Similarly, totemic relationships between humans, and between humans and other species (such as the flying fox) are those of 'sameness'. The third system which defines humanness—the open system—is the interdependency of all species including humans, and the 'great many relationships which transfer life from one species to another...every link in the food chain is seen to have its own law, Dreaming, and place in the cosmos'. As Rose explains, 'The human life span, then, effects transfers of life from one species to another...When people and country are *punyu* the flow of energy keeps both strong, healthy, and fruitful'.

Given this detailed description of the traditional Ngaringman conceptual framework of well-being, what does 'health' mean for the urban-dwelling Aborigines who have been dispossessed of their land, who have therefore been isolated from the actualisation of their Dreamtime in the form of their Dreaming sites and places in their country, and who have been unable to uphold marriage rules and the complex social organisation that prevailed before their conquest and decimation? For the reserve dwellers in Mining City, 'being well' means having harmonious social relationships with kin, with others who are not kin, and even with strangers. Health constitutes, first, the absence of 'trouble' with other reserve residents and campers, and, second, active participation in the social exchanges that are never ending at River Reserve and Camping Reserve. Healthy people are not identified as being at the peak of physical fitness, exuding energy, and portraying beauty, but as individuals trying, however subtly, to draw attention to themselves, to retrieve, retain, or increase their social relatedness within the reserve community, and within their own family group.

Working with the Ritharrngu of Arnhem Land, Scarlett et al. (1982, p. 166) were told 'if you want to feel good (*djaalngamadhirri*), you should eat a mixed diet (*miilmarnabarn*), a diet of meat and vegetable food'. The Ritharrngu hold that weather as well as diet is ultimately related to health, demonstrating their acknowledgment of the 'relationship between physical cause and biological consequence'. While reserve dwellers at Mining City often say that a minor illness is caused by something eaten or by the weather, the converse does not prevail, even though 'bush tucker' is much prized and is thought to make one feel good.

For the Aboriginal people of Mining City's reserves, an individual's health status is largely a foregone conclusion, in that it is determined by that person's conception and birth. Consequently, the belief prevails that all individuals are what they were born as. This belief is not an acceptance of 'fate' as such, but rather an understanding that each individual is co-determined by many influences, some inevitable and some the direct results of particular incidents. During a discussion about alcohol abuse, one young reserve camper stated about the inevitable, that some members of a family would be drinkers, while the others siblings would 'go the other way', and be abstainers. This was suggested as something that individuals had no power to change, because people are born into this predetermined pattern. Likewise, while babies are expected to be born healthy, it is acknowledged that an infant could be born sickly (such a child is expected to die). This is reflected in the observation made by Toussaint (1989, p. 31) that Aborigines in the west Kimberley regard a healthy baby as 'one they "know" is healthy'. While such ability to 'know' for the west Kimberley people is based on the knowledge that health rituals have been performed for the baby, this is not the case for Mining City's reserve Aborigines. An unhealthy baby is one who contracts frequent major illnesses such as pneumonia, is hospitalised, and is consequently known to be born sickly. The case of Nina illustrates this acceptance of predetermined health status (see the case study: 'A tenuous hold on life').

For the people of the Mining City reserves, physique, beauty and personality are all subject to predetermination and this contributes to the acceptance of the uniqueness of each person (including positive and negative features) from birth. As a result, physical attributes are not the basis for ranking some individuals above others, even though an outstandingly beautiful young girl is expected to be courted

A tenuous hold on life

Nina* was 6 months old when she was admitted to hospital for the first time with a cough and severe bilateral conjunctivitis. She was ill again the following month, with a high temperature, diarrhoea and vomiting, but she was not dehydrated. The next month, when she was 8 months old, Nina was ill once more and was brought to hospital twice, being admitted on the second visit. On returning home she contracted measles and an upper respiratory tract infection, was well for the next three months, and then hospitalised for another upper respiratory tract infection. Two weeks later, she had pneumonia and was admitted to hospital. She returned within six weeks, and again five days after discharge.

Altogether, Nina was admitted nine times to hospital in 14 months, for a total of 81 days. Staff frequently noted that Nina's mother seldom visited her. After five admissions for pneumonia, medical staff referred the baby to a major hospital for investigation, where she was diagnosed as suffering from hypersecretory asthma. Her case was brought before the hospital committee for neglected children because of the frequency of her admissions and the supposed lack of interest shown by her mother.

*Pseudonym

Nina lived in a single-bedroom cottage at River Reserve with her mother, grandmother, young cousin, an older sister and her baby, as well as other transitory relations. Nina's grandmother headed a clean and neat household which boasted curtains and a working refrigerator and, while food was never abundant, there was usually something for the children to eat. Nina's mother was an outgoing woman whose other children were much older than the baby. She often travelled away from Mining City, usually taking Nina with her, but on occasion leaving her with a close relative. Nina's mother was always reluctant to talk about her baby's problems and when she did speak of her it was in a very defensive way, asserting that she took care of the child. There was always the feeling that Nina was not normal, which was reinforced by mild hirsutism. It was not until Nina was much older and less sickly that it became apparent to me that she had been expected to die. Given that expectation, and knowing she would be blamed for Nina's death, in particular by the hospital staff, her mother avoided the baby as much as she responsibly could while still caring for her.

R. Mobbs

by many young men, and a tall, good-looking man is frequently commented upon by the women. The lack of status attached to the body can be explained by the fact that marriage, for example, is arranged by kinship rules and social circumstances, rather than by the barter system of Anglo-Australian society (that is, the exchange of female beauty and male occupational status). The uniqueness of a reserve individual is also recognised by idiosyncratic markings on the body, which may be visible from birth (such as a birthmark, a scar from a fight, or a decorative incision in the skin of the arm). These marks come to be recognised as part of the bearer's identity and further establish his or her individuality. Reserve dwellers as a group do not therefore entertain the notion that health and well-being can be achieved through human endeavour. Instead they implicitly accept the normality of individuals and their health status according to age and sex.

In Victoria, Nathan (1980) found that urban Aborigines identify a healthy appearance by fitness, the brightness of eyes, the shininess of the hair, and the lack of a tired appearance. People with healthy attitudes and dispositions were described as follows:

Eats well, clean, tidy, regular meals.

A person who is cheerful, got a lot of get up and go and who can communicate with other people.

Someone who is active, looks after themselves. Drinks in moderation.

Regular exercise, regular meals, regular sleeping.

A person who has no worries and who is cheerful and energetic looking.

One who is vibrant, active, laughs a lot and has bright eyes.

A healthy person is one who doesn't indulge in too much alcohol. Looks after themselves. Exercises well.

Nathan 1980, p. 50

The Aborigines at Mining City's reserves would probably agree with these indicators, as they too suggest that shiny skin and lively eyes depict good health. More importantly, however, an individual's physical appearance at any given time is seen to be a direct result of life circumstances. Shiny skin, fat babies and well-rounded women denote well-being and happiness, while unattractive skinniness indicates unhappiness, as seen in drinkers of methylated spirits and women who are the victims of domestic violence.

The physical manifestation of life circumstances is monitored and assessed by community members. I was told about a woman who had become very skinny, when months beforehand she had been much heavier and, it was implied, much happier. I knew that the woman's husband had started drinking and had become very violent, yet her social circumstances were not discussed by the women talking about her, merely the manifestation of these circumstances in her appearance. In a similar vein, when I returned to Mining City after an absence of some months, the husband of one of my closest friends peered at me searchingly. He said that he had to inspect my appearance so that he would know what had happened to me while I had been away.

The meaning of well-being for Mining City's reserve Aborigines is acted out through the sociability of their group—their own family and community. In addition to their bodily manifestation, healthy relationships are revealed in the social well-being of the individual. Conversely, it is often said to be 'known' that a trouble-maker disturbing others will become seriously ill or perhaps become the victim of an accident such as a car crash. Nathan (1983) indicates that Aboriginal urban dwellers describe well-being not only in terms of their sociability but also of in-dividual health behaviours. However, this was not observed among the people of the Mining City reserves, for whom notions of well-being comprise a variation on the pattern of well-being among the Ngaringman people and the Groote Eylandters of the Northern Territory. This is the view described by Nathan (1983, p. 72) when referring to the people of central Australia:

Health and illness...were not viewed or treated as separate entities. Rather, they had a holistic, animistic and sacred character. The maintenance of health was inex-tricably tied to spiritual, religious and social welfare. People in their ceremonial activities, remained in touch with the intimate and fundamental life processes.

The old Gulgadunng men of Mining City often decried the despoiling of their country, and had to send their young men interstate to learn ceremonies. But they did not link the land directly to well-being, focusing instead upon their own cir-cumscribed social group.

As described above, Aboriginal concepts of well-being are very different from those of Anglo-Australians. Aboriginal ways of maintaining health therefore also dif-fer markedly from those of Anglo-Australians (table 7.1). The stark contrast between these differing notions of well-being and prevention of illness can have important practical consequences for health-care delivery, as outlined by Soong (unpub.).

Table 7.1   Anglo-Australian and Aboriginal notions of health maintenance

	Western societies	Aboriginal society
Concepts of health	Physical, mental and social well-being — biomedical theory of health	Good social relationships, taking part in rituals, sociomedical theory of health
Health maintenance	Good food, good housing and environment, hygiene, immunisation checks, avoidance of alcohol, cigarettes*	Observing kinship responsibilities, and taking part in health rituals
Ways of communicating about health	The home, school, health settings and public education	Participation in social and religious activities

*These health maintenance activities were taught in the health centre.
Source: Soong (unpub.), p. 22

Being ill

Aborigines have systematic explanations for their loss of well-being and for the causes of illness and death. These have been described by Reid and Dhamarrandji

(1978*b*), Reid (1982), Nathan (1983), Tynan (unpub. *a*, unpub. *b*), Taylor (1977), Tonkinson (1982), Hamilton (unpub.), and the Yolngu sociomedical theory has been analysed in detail by Reid (1983). The Aboriginal experience of illness, and particularly the social behaviours and meanings associated with the sick role, have been little researched, but some work has been conducted by Sansom (1982). This was also a topic of enquiry during the research at Mining City, and the data obtained are used here as the basis of the discussion about Aboriginal sick-role behaviour.

Explanations of illness causation

The Aboriginal experience of sickness is linked to the severity of the illness episode: minor illness and injury are explained in an entirely different way from major and chronic problems. Writing of the indigenous medical system of the Thaayorre and the Wik Ngantjera of Cape York Peninsula, Taylor (1977, p. 423) says:

there were general words for sickness and a range of adjectives to describe its level of severity. A more specific indication of the nature of the malady was supplied by a descriptive phrase that referred to the main symptom/s, e.g. vomiting, coughing, lumps or swellings, wounds or broken bones, diarrhoea...

While minor illness and injury are non-threatening aspects of everyday living, serious illness may well disrupt the life of an individual and her or his family, and may also involve the whole community. The social importance of severe illness for the Yolngu is explained by Reid (1983, p. 32):

Yolngu ideas about the cause of...serious sickness rest on one assumption; that humans have the capacity to mobilise and to control the power which exists in the universe and are themselves vulnerable to attacks by others using that power...[This] power is derived from the spirits, the invisible beings who live in and beyond the tangible world.

The belief that sickness is caused by the spiritual brings added dimensions to Aboriginal illness and disease aetiology. Supernatural hazards are associated with places and people, and with the taboos that apply to them, which can be violated by an individual, deliberately or inadvertently. Consequently, Aboriginal people must behave correctly in their relationships with kin, abiding by such rules as the taboo on communication between son-in-law and mother-in-law, and to avoid illness or accident they must perform the required ritual for approaching certain places.

Four categories of illness causation are recorded by Nathan and Japanangka (1983, pp. 73–9): the natural, the direct supernatural, the indirect supernatural and the environmental. A fifth category called 'introduced' may be added to these and is similar, but not identical to, those causes termed 'emergent' by Reid (1983, p. 147), that is, explanations related to non-Aboriginal diseases brought to the continent, or based on observations of contemporary phenomena, or adapted from European ideas about aetiology.

1. Natural

Nathan uses this term to describe death caused by old age and death of the very young, while Taylor (1977, p. 423) also includes minor illness episodes, such as swollen eyes caused by flies, and diarrhoea resulting from eating over-fat meat. Scarlett et al. (1982, p. 166) include:

'wet' sores (djeli'), said to be caused by excessive sweating (wulburr), especially when sleeping in a hot place without a breeze; sores (djidji'mapay), caused by wounds from grass etc. or burns; coughs and lung complaints, attributed to being 'slack inside' as a consequence of a diet deficient in meat; diarrhoea (birlbirlgu),...caused by...vegetable food that is 'too dry';...headaches (rathala) resulting from 'dry' food or excessive exposure to the sun.

At the reserves in Mining City, 'natural' symptoms of being unwell are said to be caused by:

a.   excessive activity (such as jumping around too much at a disco);
b.   something eaten (stomach upsets due to too much ice-cream or bananas, or butter causing 'jaundice').

Working with the Western Desert people at Jigalong, Tonkinson (1982, pp. 236, 237) was told that powerful emotions such as resentment, sulking, shame or embarrassment, and (less frequently) worry, homesickness, grief or jealousy could cause loss of appetite, weight loss, listlessness or pain. At Yirrkala in north-east Arnhem Land, there is a more complex natural causation category, which includes contagion, emotional state, excessive exposure to the elements, food, heredity, neglect by responsible others, old age, physical assault and injury, predation, pregnancy, neglect of self, suicide or attempted suicide, and 'no attributable cause'.

In general, natural conditions can be debilitating, but are a part of everyday living; they come and go, and are not life-threatening except, of course, when death can be explained by old age. Mostly, illnesses due to natural causes result in temporary states of weakness such as those described above as *wurrumurndagayuwaya* and, probably, *wangut.*

2. Introduced

Throughout Australia, Aboriginal people differentiate between 'whitefella' and 'blackfella' sicknesses. The former describes illnesses that have plagued Aborigines since the arrival of Europeans, be they infectious or lifestyle diseases. It is usually claimed that introduced illnesses can be treated only with 'whitefella' medicine. According to Scarlett et al. (1982, pp. 169,170), the local Aboriginal people in part of Arnhem Land believe that the many cases of fish poisoning in their area were caused by the toxic wastes flowing from the bauxite mine into the sea. When one woman was asked if she could use bush medicine to treat such poisoning, 'She gave a withering look and said that [it] was a sickness caused by Europeans and therefore needed European medicine'. The introduced illnesses include health problems caused by factors ranging from environmental damage to alcohol abuse. 'Grog sickness' is a common condition at the Mining City reserves, and is known to be the effect of excessive consumption. Indeed, any and all ailments suffered by a drinker, as well as hangovers and alcoholic fitting, are attributed to 'grog sickness'. Reserve dwellers believe that Anglo-Australian medical treatment is appropriate for this syndrome (see also Tynan unpub. *b*, p. 138) and alcohol abusers are regular clients at the hospital casualty section. Writing about the people of north-east Arnhem Land, Reid (1983, p. 147) includes in her emergent cause category such afflictions as the effects of alcohol, alleged assault or mistreatment by medical or nursing staff, illnesses defined in Western medical terms, motor vehicle accidents, sin, smoking, and unsanitary or unhealthy living conditions on the settlement.

3. Environmental

In this category, Nathan and Japanangka (1983, p. 78), writing about central Australia, include: illnesses caused by the north winds, which carry little black stones inducing pain, stomach-ache, or diarrhoea; the moon, which may precipitate epilepsy or fitting in children; and poisons available in the bush which might be added to alcoholic drinks: 'Poisons were considered "proper dangerous and no good to talk about".' Excessive heat and cold are thought by Mining City reserve dwellers and by the Western Desert people at Jigalong to cause aches and colds (Tonkinson 1982, p. 236).

4. Direct supernatural intervention

This category is referred to by Reid (1978*d*, p. 63) as 'direct causation' by 'supernatural agencies'. It includes illnesses caused by the following:

a. Powerful spirits often referred to in central Australia as 'devil' or 'evil spirit', which will punish transgressors of the Law. Illness can be engendered by trespassing on men's and women's sacred places and dangerous sites, which are found on the Aboriginal spiritual maps of the Australian environment. Such a breach is particularly dangerous should a woman trespass in a 'men's business' place or a man trespass in a 'woman's business' site, but can also have less than fatal results. This is illustrated by my experience when working on a land claim for the Gagadu people in the Northern Territory some years ago. An old man who was knowledgeable about the area took me to a site which had to be recorded, just as he had taken the senior anthropologist researching the claim. It was a hill that protruded from flat floodplains. Arriving there, the man related the story of the site. A long time ago, a band of Aborigines had made camp on top of the hill, and in the group were a lot of babies who were crying continuously. The old people became concerned at all the noise and urged the babies' parents to quieten their infants. Still the babies continued to cry, and as a result the entire camp vanished. Having finished recording the old man's story, I suggested we climb the hill, only to be met with a point blank refusal. He explained that anyone who ventures up the hill will become ill, and told how he had climbed the hill with the other anthropologist for the sake of the claim and against his better judgment. Some days later he fell ill, and so too did the anthropologist. Although it was late afternoon, we drove a considerable distance before we stopped to make our camp.

b. Spirits of the dead, which may inhabit the body of a living person, and if disturbed may cause that person to become weak, vomit a lot and lose interest in living.

c. Spirits of dead relatives that are not at rest because proper mourning rituals were not followed. Such rituals include (Nathan and Japanangka 1983, p. 75):

- failure to shift camp after the death of a group member;
- use of a dead person's name, or the name of a living person which is the same as that of a recently dead person;
- a woman breaking the silence rule which can apply after the death of a husband or brother.

Spirits of the dead can also be malevolent, as described by Tonkinson (1970, p. 283):

At times the blame for an influenza epidemic or for an individual's illness is laid...on spirits of the dead from a particular locality. These spirits can be either benign or malevolent, depending on such factors as the personalities of the humans they were formerly part of, and whether or not they approve of the activities of their Aboriginal descendants. One influenza outbreak...was finally attributed to a malevolent and powerful old ancestral man whose home is said to be next to a salt lake in the desert...The man who went badundjari (a dream spirit journey) to put a stop to the outbreak was an old native doctor whose father's spirit was believed to live in the lake with other spirits of the dead and its ancestral totem...[He] discovered that it was his father's spirit that released the influenza mist and spread it westward, in a fit of bad temper. The elder, in badundjari form, went into the lake and picked up his father's spirit...After extracting a promise of good behaviour and a guarantee that the influenza mist would be kept shut up inside the lake , the old man returned to the mission.

5. Indirect supernatural intervention

This category is referred to by Reid (1978d, p. 62) as 'indirect causation' (sorcery), while Nathan and Japanangka (1983, p. 76) use the more specific terms 'singing' and 'boning'. Sorcery is implicit in the Aboriginal world view, and has been examined in detail by Reid (1983), Elkin (1977), Cawte (1974), Pounder (1985), Reser and Eastwell (1981), and others. Sorcerers use their connections to the spiritual world to bring harm to their victims, who usually die as a result. At Yirrkala in north-east Arnhem Land, the reasons given to Reid (1983, p. 44) for the use of sorcery were concerned with 'conflicts between individuals and groups' and 'breaches of social and sacred laws', so that everyone in the community took great care not to transgress the Law.

Although sorcery is accepted as part of the normal world, Aboriginal people do not live in fear of it. Rather it is a recognised cause of serious illness, accident and death, and it is considered along with all other possible explanations. At Mining City, a sign of sorcery is premature death. For instance, an old man from Camping Reserve, who had been admitted to hospital for multiple complaints in previous months, took ill once again and was taken by ambulance to hospital. He died the same day, and rumours about his death abounded back at the reserve. It was said that he died in a hospital toilet, even though he did not seem to be seriously ill, and his son remonstrated that his father had died even before he had time to take his clothes to the hospital. The old man had been a man of authority in the area and was knowledgeable in traditional ways, and real unease existed in the camp about his unacceptable death. Kin packed into the church for his funeral service and waited quietly while his sons carried the old man's coffin up the steps and into the church. As they went through the doorway, a handle fell off the coffin, and a fearful chill was experienced by all. The incident gave powerful support to the rumours that the old man had been killed by sorcery.

Sorcery can also be inferred from serious injury. Take, for example, the following transcription from a consultation between an Aboriginal woman from River Reserve and a senior resident medical officer in the hospital casualty section.

Doctor: G'day.
Woman: Hello.
Doctor: What's the trouble?
Woman: Well, I got a swollen leg...
Doctor: Yeah, what's that from?
Woman: I was hit by that stick, same stick...
Doctor: Same stick hit your husband? Yeah?
Woman: Well, both sides, my arms and my rib...
Doctor: Where does it hurt?
Woman: This one is hurting. It's swollen, see?
Doctor: How big was this stick? Must have been a big stick!
Woman: Oh, it was a nulla nulla—it was a big one, yeah.
Doctor: Which side did it hit you?
Woman: Well, this side. I had nothing to protect myself, see. I tried to get a bamboo or something to protect myself but...
Doctor: What did they hit you for though?
Woman: I told this woman that came down, mind your own business. Those boys are always going on, you have no business in going to say things to anyone of them. Go back to your cottage...we will stop it. Mind your own business. Then she went down and got this nulla nulla. That's a stick that I never seen before. It's been poisoned. It's not an ordinary stick that woman had—it's been poisoned.
Doctor: Seems they've done some damage.
Woman: Yeah, she did, because it is a poison stick...

The woman's elderly husband was also involved in this fight, and as a result of being hit with the 'poison stick' received a fractured elbow, which required hospitalisation and surgery to insert a screw. It was recorded that the muscles were split down to the bone at the point of impact. He was in hospital for a week.

Aboriginal sociomedical theories incorporate a range of explanations for sickness and injury, whether a minor inconvenience for an individual or a critical illness that unsettles a whole community. These explanations are placed firmly within a traditional explanatory model, even though Aborigines have had prolonged experience of biomedicine. Aboriginal people are usually familiar with lay Anglo-Australian ideas about germs, accidents and other explanations of ill health. Even the urban dwellers of Mining City, however, never mentioned germs as an explanation, and the idea of an accident was controversial because the older people would imply that sorcery was indicated. Often it was pointed out that the person who had been severely injured or killed in a road crash had been making a lot of trouble in the camp, and it was expected that something like this would happen.

Reid (1983) divides the Yolngu explanatory framework into proximate (or immediate) and ultimate levels of explanation of serious or fatal illness. Thus, the proximate cause of serious illness and/or death (the 'how') is sorcery, and the ultimate cause of that episode (the 'why') is the disturbed social relationships surrounding it. Reid (1983, p. 55) adds that any framework that lacks both levels of explanation is, for the Yolngu, incomplete.

Illness behaviour and the Aboriginal sick role

The Thaayorre and the Wik Ngantjera of Cape York Peninsula (Taylor 1977, p. 423) accept that 'The illness of adults [is] self-diagnosed. Their own statement about their condition [is] enough to indicate to others that they [are] sick'. Reid (1983, p. 94) agrees that the person experiencing the sickness is the first to recognise the loss of her or his own well-being. According to Reid, minor ailments in north-east Arnhem Land such as headache, stomach-ache or a cold were chiefly the concern of the sick themselves (although female kin sometimes obtained medications—herbal or pharmaceutical—if the ailment persisted) and the cause of the sickness was largely considered irrelevant. The sufferer would retire for the short period of time required for the complaint to pass.

Similarly, minor ailments at Mining City are considered to be under the control of the sick themselves. One source of discomfort that motivates the sufferer to seek relief is a 'hot' feeling. One elderly woman who complained of feeling 'hot in the stomach' called for her relatives to give her cold water, and a young man who felt 'hot from the waist up' purchased iced water from a local garage in an effort to alleviate his discomfort. Neither of the two developed any further symptoms. The Mining City reserve dwellers live in terrible hardship—physically, environmentally, and medically—and individuals manage many of their own symptoms (often by denial). Mostly, no treatment is sought for boils, conjunctivitis, coughs, diarrhoea and 'going berserk'. Other conditions also left up to the individual—and as a result often left unattended—are lassitude in adults, concussion, and injuries such as skin lacerations and soreness, aching and generalised pain.

At Yirrkala in north-east Arnhem Land, management of illness changes if and when it advances from something temporary and non-life-threatening to a critical condition. The severity of the symptoms is a primary factor in the way that the sick and their family respond to them. Among the Yolngu, there are identifiable symptoms that galvanise family members into action (Reid 1983, p. 96). These include:

1. *signs of internal bleeding—blood in stool, blood in phlegm, blood in vomit, blood in urine;*
2. *one or a number of severe symptoms which persist for several days, such as uncontrollable vomiting, diarrhoea or high fever*
3. *the person stares blankly, or is unconscious;*
4. *the person refuses or is unable to speak;*
5. *the person refuses or is unable to eat or drink;*
6. *the person experiences severe internal pain;*
7. *the person says he/she is very ill and calls for the clan songs to be sung;*
8. *the person attempts to sing clan songs him/herself or to imitate the dances of the totemic animals;*

9. *the illness is severe and chronic;*
10. *the illness is perceived to be 'spoiling' the body, as in a severe attack of boils or infected sores, leprosy, or a severe urogenital condition.*

At the Mining City reserves, individuals with fractures and prolonged but slow bleeding are frequently left to obtain help themselves, but just as often a kin member will call the ambulance. Coughing blood will cause a family member to urge the afflicted person to go to the hospital. Immediate help-seeking by kin and group was initiated only by collapse and unconsciousness, acting 'strange' or 'mad', and convulsive fitting.

When illness symptoms cause family members to seek help, the sick person assumes a new social role, described by Sansom (1982) as the sick who do not speak. Writing of Darwin's Aboriginal fringe camps, he says that the sick role is a 'relegation to impotence'. Aboriginal illness behaviour is

based not on enunciated complaining, but grounded instead in the ability of unaffected third parties to read signs. Those who progress into sickness yield up behavioural items: 'Thatfella doin something really different. He bin long time makin toilet.' Or, 'That ol Jenny she bin sleepin too much.'...[Or] The rigours of a long strain with diarrhoea are first noted then there is the struggling and deliberate, foot in front of foot pacing of the diarrhoetic...The next sign is the groan the emptied sufferer emits despite himself as he relaxes onto his blanket. A camper approaches...He diagnoses fever. Announcement of fever brings a few of those people who are beginning to worry to the bed. The sufferer then speaks. This is dismissed as babbling. 'That not Long Billy talkin. Thatta sickness talkin.'...Someone touches the patient, turns back an eyelid and reads a further sign, 'Thisfella really sick, you lookim eye!' Members of the company about the bed all look into the eye, exchange glances with one another and then the most prominent person amongst this grouping of concern sallies forth to announce to all fellow campers: 'We got trouble. Really sick.' An announcement of this order is a call and campers rally to it.

Sansom 1982, p. 191

Many Aboriginal people feel that a very sick person is completely taken over by an illness so that sick people's utterances belong to the illness, and after recovery, recall of that illness belongs to the carers involved rather than to the person who has been sick. This is in dramatic contrast to Anglo-Australian sick role behaviour, whereby the person experiencing an illness retains ultimate responsibility for her or his own recovery, even though dependency on carers and health professionals is characteristic of the role. This sick role has important implications for communicating with Aboriginal people when they are sick, as it could be inappropriate for them to give a history of their own problems, and much more suitable for a close relative or someone knowledgeable about the episode to give the history of the illness to the non-Aboriginal health professional.

Aboriginal illness behaviour and the adoption of the sick role can be displayed by deliberate inaction, such as retiring from social intercourse, staying inside the house or the camp, or failing to gather food. But it is the meaning of the illness episode to the sufferer and his/her kin and community that will largely determine how it is managed by them. It is also the conceptualisation of the cause of the illness that will influence help-seeking choices and the effectiveness of any non-Aboriginal health care sought and delivered.

Illness management

Aborigines in Australia today can choose between their own treatment methods, Anglo-Australian medical care, or a combination of both. It is now documented (Reid 1978*d*; Tynan unpub. *a*, unpub. *b*; Tonkinson 1982) that even the most traditionally oriented of Aboriginal peoples have integrated Anglo-Australian medical services into their own health-care system, so that treatment choices range from bush medicines to paracetamol for headaches, from a traditional healer to a biomedical specialist, or both, to manage a life-threatening disease. How such choices are made depends on:

1. the actual services available to the sick, their families and communities, whether these services are traditional healing, health clinic or hospital;
2. the family's opinion about the cause of the illness;
3. all the other circumstances influencing any one illness episode.

It is not possible here to analyse the way people seek help and the conditions under which they may choose certain options (Reid 1978*a*; Mobbs 1987). Instead, short descriptions are given of Aboriginal methods of healing and their uses in the 1990s. These include bush pharmacopoeia, lay healing rituals and specialised healing methods.

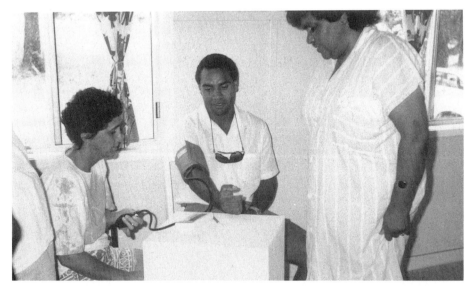

Figure 7.2 *Treatment choices for Aborigines today range from bush medicines and traditional healers to Aboriginal-Australian medical services such as those provided by the Aboriginal Health Program at Caroona community (New South Wales) pictured here. (Aboriginal Health Unit, NSW Department of Health, Sydney)*

Bush medicines

Non-Aboriginal documentation of Aboriginal knowledge of botanical pharmaceuticals ranges from incidental mentions of plants and their medicinal uses (such as Cleland and Tindale 1959), to longer inventories such as those given by Palmer (1883) and Webb (1969), extensive regional cataloguing (see Henshall and Devanesen 1982; Scarlett et al. 1982; Gott 1984), and recent works dedicated exclusively to Aboriginal bush medicines (such as Isaacs 1988). Most compilations use non-Aboriginal methods of categorising the plants, rather than Aboriginal taxonomies. However, referring to the Thaayorre and Wik Ngantjera of Cape York Peninsula, Taylor (1977, p. 425) comments that 'A native pharmacopoeia existed although the words *yuk-may* (Th.), *yuk-oparr* (W-Ng.) which denoted these bush medicines also denoted love potions, contraceptives, good luck charms, specifics against sorcery and poisons'.

An early examination of bush medicines was made by Webb (1969), who compared the numbers of plant species used for different medicinal purposes and found that 25 per cent were applications for skin lesions (sores, boils, wounds), 20.6 per cent for coughs and colds, 17.7 per cent for body pains (abdominal and muscular), 13.2 per cent for gastrointestinal disturbances, 5.9 per cent for sore eyes, 4.2 per cent for toothache, 2.9 per cent for postnatal conditions, and 1.5 per cent each for tonics, influenzas, skin irritations and rashes, leprosy, ear ache, headache, stomach ache, and contraceptives. Although there were recognised treatments for specific conditions such as sore eyes, colds and diarrhoea, most bush medicines were found to be broad-spectrum palliatives.

In the study of bush medicines, scant attention has been given to the sociocultural context of bush pharmaceutical usage, such as the social ownership of plants

Figure 7.3 Celtis philipinensis *is a bush plant used to relieve nasal congestion in the Northern Territory. (AIATSIS, Canberra)*

and authority to collect and prepare the treatments, and it remains unclear whether such proprietary rights apply or not. Henshall and Devanesen (1982, p. 10), for example, say that:

The collecting site is nearly always the country of a male Aboriginal present, and he alone will point out the plants and enumerate their uses. When women are collecting without men being present, the site, apparently, is of less importance. When questioned, a man will say that plants from his own country are stronger, and work more quickly. Often it is pointed out that plants belong to various skin groups or subsection systems.

Taylor (1977, p. 425) found that some bush medicines were the 'exclusive property of men and their agnates'. Scarlett et al. (1982, p. 163), however, note that there was 'No evidence of this...in north-eastern Arnhem Land, although certain plant preparations were said to be "women's business'. These included plants believed to control fertility and lactation'.

In the 1990s, bush medicines (if accessible) continue to be used by Aboriginal people interchangeably with Western medicinal palliatives. There is no loss of confidence in the bush pharmacopoeia, but it is usually easier to go to the local health clinic, hospital or chemist for medications for, say, pain relief. Reserve dwellers in Mining City always point out which grasses and plants are believed to have medicinal properties, but no effort is made to collect them for use in the camps.

Ritual healing

The healing and strengthening knowledge of older women and men may be used on occasion (Tynan unpub. *a*, unpub. *b*; Mobbs unpub., pp. 51–8), as in contraceptive songs sung by men for their wives, 'smoking' a woman after childbirth by female kin, and songs for strengthening a newborn. Some of these included the use of bush medicines. Songs can also be used for specific complaints: for example, Nathan and Japanangka record of the people of central Australia (1983, p. 83) that 'the eagle-hawk song is used by people with the sugar ant dreaming to remove the sputum associated with cold or flu'. Although such ritual care is still practised in many communities for weakness states and minor illnesses, it is at the time of serious illness and death that the traditional healing system can play a major role, because of the possibility of sorcery and the associated needs for specialist traditional healing and explanation of the ultimate cause of death.

Traditional healing

Non-Aboriginal health professionals are often believed to be unable to combat illnesses caused by breaches of taboos and sorcery; this is the preserve of the traditional healer. 'Medicine men' have intrigued non-Aboriginal observers for most of white Australia's history, and continue to do so (Reid 1983, 1978c; Elkin 1945; Cawte 1974; Soong 1983; Berndt 1964; Winterbotham 1951; Hamilton unpub.; Tynan unpub. *a*, unpub. *b*; Gray 1988; Thomson 1961). In earlier years, the interest in Aboriginal healing was tantamount to a fascination with witchcraft, illustrated by the words of Cook (1966, p. 560) when he wrote:

There was no knowledge of the aetiology of disease or of specific therapy. Decoctions of leaves or gum, hot sand or ashes might be used as local applications for the relief of pain;...For more intractable conditions, recourse was taken to magic—incantations supplemented by bleeding or incision and feigned removal of foreign bodies from the area of pain.

More recently, greater understanding of the sociomedical theories of the Aboriginal healing system illuminate better the role of the traditional healer.

In Aboriginal communities, healers are individuals who possess healing and divination powers which can be used for the benefit of the community. In most other respects, traditional healers are ordinary members of the community, sharing in social and family life. While they are held in high regard, they are not treated with awe nor do they necessarily possess any other special status. Based on his work at Carnarvon in Western Australia, Gray (1980, p. 173) explains that 'traditional medicine may be viewed as a specialised extension of religion; the native-doctors concerned have considerable prestige, but this does not result in any great status differentiation between them and other persons'. The healer can combat sickness caused by sorcery (the proximate cause) and divine the ultimate cause of the illness as well. Divination is particularly important in the case of a community member's death. As Reid (1983, p. 57) notes, 'It is the *marrnggitj* [traditional healer] to whom community members look for reassurance, healing, explanation and protection when serious illness and death threaten'. Healers are usually male, but women can also become reputable practitioners, and Reid's work at Yirrkala in north-east Arnhem Land has shown that children too can possess healing powers. In central Australia (Nathan and Japanangka 1983, p. 79), healers obtain their abilities in one of four ways:

1. inheritance (especially a son from his father);
2. predisposing qualities cultivated by community elders and existing *ngangkere*;
3. a psychic experience and serious illness;
4. powers latent in an individual that are 'opened up' by another *ngangkere*.

Among the Yolngu, at Yirrkala, as at Carnarvon, healing powers are not inherited but assigned, as an adult *marrnggitj* recounts in the case study 'The making of a healer'.

Traditional healers continue to be an important part of the contemporary Aboriginal health-care system and provide many Aboriginal peoples with comprehensive care. The suffering are able to use a range of biomedical and ethnomedical treatments, but which services an individual may choose is largely unpredictable. Sick people may visit the health clinic as well as consulting a traditional healer; they may accept treatment exclusively from a hospital or from a 'medicine man'; or they may treat themselves with 'bush medicines'. There can be a great deal of uncertainty about the actual cause of severe illness. The immediate or proximate cause may be an introduced illness, such as hepatitis, or a stroke, but the ultimate cause may be the sick person's troubled social situation that has provoked the practice of sorcery. In such cases, often both traditional healing and Anglo-Australian medical treatment will be sought by the family concurrently, to address both the underlying cause and its manifestation. And it is often because of this complexity that non-Aboriginal health-care workers find it difficult to comprehend the family's management of a relative's illness.

The making of a healer

'One night, as I was sleeping, I heard voices like wind rustling in the leaves. I thought it might be *galka* [sorcerer] and was very frightened. Then I felt something like an electric shock and some of this power that I have now, the little children [spirit familiars] or *manggata* entered me. I slept as though I was unconscious and in the morning woke up afraid that I had been attacked by *galka*. I thought I might die or be attacked by a crocodile as I was swimming across rivers on the way home...

'At sunset one day, as I was cooking a fish alone on a remote beach, I saw someone coming. I thought it was one of my brothers, but as the figure got closer it became huge and I could see it was carrying a *matjinydji* [special dillybag] across its chest and had fins running down its side and legs. "He's a *mokuy* [spirit]", I thought. "What's he going to do to me?" I was frightened and ran back and forth from the sea to the bush, but in each place he appeared next to me. I

decided to dig a hole and bury myself in the sand, but the *mokuy* just shrank to the size of a beetle and ran up and down my back. Suddenly I realised I was deaf, that my heart had stopped beating and that I was no longer afraid. "Why were you afraid?" it asked. "Don't you want my *gilapa* [magic things]? If you hadn't been afraid I'd have given you all of them. But now I've decided to give you half. I'll give you three *gilapa*." These are the stones I now use to heal people...[Later] I could hear a voice telling me not to reveal that I was a *marrnggitj* for at least three years...[Ten] years after this happened, my stepbrother died. I was so sad after the funeral that I decided to go and sleep by his grave. That night the ground shook like an earthquake and several *mokuy* rose from the grave. The boss *mokuy* said to me, "Why did you come to the cemetery?" "I was grieving for my brother", I replied. "What do you want?" he asked. "I want to become clever" ...He then gave me another *gilapa*.

From Reid 1983, pp. 59–61

Communication in the health-care setting

The considerable problems experienced by non-Aboriginal health professionals and Aboriginal people in both clinical and preventive encounters have been enumerated by Reid and Dhamarrandji (1978*b*), Nathan (1980), Nathan and Japanangka (1983) and Mobbs (1986). While there is evidence that many of the communication difficulties can be explained by the racist attitudes of some professionals (Harrison unpub.), it is also a fact that miscommunication is often the outcome of a complex mix of genuine goodwill and gross misunderstanding. The medical staff at Mining City's hospital listed the following reasons for disliking Aboriginal patients: communication difficulties, the lack of information with which to diagnose and treat, a perceived lack of self-help, absconding, and the frequency of presentation of alcohol-related problems, especially trauma. On the other hand, the two reasons most frequently given by reserve Aborigines for not seeking help at the hospital were fear of reproach ('they will growl at me'; 'they go mad') and lack of confidence ('they don't know what they're doing'). Indeed, the problems in this area are so great that mutual mistrust overwhelms most attempts to communicate in therapeutic settings. Often the health worker, motivated by professional obligation to treat, will simply do what is visibly required by the Aboriginal person and move onto the next, 'easier', non-Aboriginal client. Four issues underlie this discord:

1. the non-Aboriginal belief in the superiority of biomedicine and the institutionalised delivery of medical care;
2. contrasting concepts of care;
3. a lack of knowledge among non-Aboriginal health-care professionals of Aboriginal
   culture and social rules;
4. a lack of knowledge among non-Aboriginal health professionals of Aboriginal
   English language patterns.

1. Non-Aboriginal belief in the superiority of biomedicine

Medical institutions and health-care agencies in Australia have been, and continue
to be, powerful symbols of the colonial relationship between Aborigines and the
dominant society. In the recent past, doctors held positions as government officials
(such as 'Protectors') with enormous power over their Aboriginal wards. They also
controlled access to health care for people who were often sick and in pain. As a
result, many Aboriginal people have personally experienced feelings of intimi-
dation and humiliation in a health-care setting.

There is a much more fundamental problem here, however. The professionalised, scientifically based health-care system has been shaped by an intellectual framework now commonly referred to as the biomedical model. This is an
approach centred on a mechanistic view of the human body, such that a disease
appears as a failure in the physiological functioning of the biological system, with
minimal regard to its social meaning. It is a difficult leap for health professionals to
accept that this scientifically 'validated' ideology is also culturally shaped. Scientific principles are, however, founded upon key paradigms, and a paradigm is but
shared ideas about truth and reality agreed upon by men and women in the scientific community. Indeed, the 'laws' of science are influenced by personal, and therefore cultural, judgment and prejudice. Scientist, health professional and 'lay' person
alike can make sense of their observations only in terms of the world view with
which they have been socialised and enculturated. This does not mean that
biomedical pharmaceutical techniques and skills are not effective, but it does mean
that there are areas of human experience, suffering and meaning that they cannot
address.

Health professionals suffering from 'biomedical blinkerage' find it extremely
difficult to appreciate the complex health-care systems of other cultures, including
the Aboriginal system. And unfortunately, learning about different behaviours in the
health arena does not automatically mean that non-Aboriginal health professionals
will be more enlightened in practice. Take for example the health-care professional
who is ostensibly committed to the primary health-care ideal of awareness of cultural beliefs and wishes to engage the traditional health-care system in a way that
facilitates the delivery of Western health care to a community. Would that person
be willing to work alongside an Aboriginal person gifted in traditional healing,
respecting him or her as an esteemed colleague? Would that committed primary
health-care professional agree to the traditional healer as the first point of contact
for Aboriginal clients instead of herself or himself? And which practitioner will make
the final diagnostic decision in a controversial case?

All health-care systems are culturally described and defined, and this applies
not only to Aboriginal but to Anglo-Australian society. If it is understood that all

ideas are culturally influenced, including those in the health sphere, then it is also possible to understand that:

a. the Anglo-Australian health-care system is a product of the dominant, non-Aboriginal culture and social structure;
b. Aboriginal groups also have their own culturally determined and socially structured health-care systems;
c. for many Aboriginal people in the 1990s, non-Aboriginal health care is just one form of treatment available to them to use in conjunction with, or to alternate with, Aboriginal ways of managing illness.

2. Contrasting concepts of care

Caring in the clinical sense means practising 'good medicine', that is, showing dedication and thoroughness in the pursuit of an accurate diagnosis of a disease by means of systematic questioning, examination and testing. Clinical caring includes frequent examination to observe signs of disease, ordering numerous laboratory tests, and often combating critical illness when it seems futile. This kind of clinical care can be at odds with notions of caring in the Aboriginal community. Aboriginal people are familiar with an indigenous healing mode that is much more personal and involves family and community. A classical clinical approach can therefore conflict with Aboriginal clients' ideas of good treatment based on:

a. the health professional's manner and apparent interest in their problems;
b. whether the encounter has caused undue discomfort;
c. whether the prescribed treatment has met with expectations;
d. whether the health professional has inspired confidence.

Contrasting notions of care are further compounded by attitudinal differences towards human existence. These are illustrated in the case study, 'A time to die', in which an old man's preparation for death is contrasted with a medical practitioner's management of the final stage of the dying process.

The point at which to terminate resuscitation of a dying patient is a controversial issue among medically trained professionals. It is a particularly difficult ethical area for professionals who dedicate their skills to the prolongation of life, in large part responding to the Anglo-Australian social pressures to maintain life regardless of all costs. That ethos also underpins the care delivered by medical workers to old Aboriginal people, as indeed it must if there is to be equality of care for all. What is being questioned here, however, is the appropriateness of the prolongation of life in the case of an old man who had come to hospital to die. One can only ask if the dreadful suffering imposed on him during the multiple resuscitations was truly necessary. Would the medical officer in charge of Ralph's case have persisted for so long if she had been informed that this old man had decided that the end of his life was nigh?

3. Lack of knowledge about Aboriginal culture and social rules

One of the most disturbing experiences an Aboriginal person can have occurs with the frequency of the commonplace. It is the contravention of Aboriginal beliefs about gender. In Aboriginal society, women's business and men's business are

A time to die

An old man from an outlying community, Ralph,* was flown to hospital in a serious condition by the Royal Flying Doctor Service. Within a couple of days, the man was transferred to the intensive care unit, where he was in the charge of a senior resident medical officer. She monitored him constantly day and night, taking blood for blood gases and other laboratory tests, and expecting the hospital laboratory to examine these specimens before all others; prescribing drugs in response to every change in his condition; inserting a catheter to collect and measure urine; having him restrained when he needed oxygen but kept pulling off his mask; and propping him into a sitting position to improve lung drainage. On one occasion after the medical staff had left the room, the intensive care unit nursing sister asked rhetorically, 'Why do they keep on?' The doctor in charge did keep on. She gave her time, energy and knowledge to her patient's critical condition and, on the Sunday morning, Ralph sat up in bed, listened to his radio, and ate scrambled eggs for breakfast.

Later that day, I returned to the intensive care unit and to Ralph's bedside to find an emergency team fighting for his life. He had just suffered his fourth cardiac arrest. Assisted by a junior medical officer and nursing staff, the senior RMO commented to me that Ralph was near the end, but continued cardiac massage and again gave shock treatment. His fifth arrest signalled the end, his ribs were crushed, and the nurse's massage was no more than a gentle rubbing of his chest. The senior RMO spoke to Ralph

*Pseudonym

as though he were alive, even near the very end. She did not want him to die. She was silent when I accompanied her in the lift, away from the intensive care unit. Registering her feelings, I eventually said, 'That's a disappointment'. She replied that she had hopes for him that morning, but that they had done all they could.

Ralph's death scene left an enduring impression. The medical staff had made tremendous efforts to revive the old man, stopping only when it was clear that death could not be prevented. The medical determination to keep hold of life was paramount, yet Ralph had not fought death. It was only at the very end that there appeared to be agreement between the medical staff and Ralph about the inevitability of death.

When an opportunity arose, I visited the distant community that had been Ralph's home. I did so to seek out his family, and, if possible (given the social restrictions on speaking of the dead), obtain information about the circumstances under which he left with the Flying Doctor Service. I was able to do this, and a family member described Ralph's departure. He had been taken to hospital a number of times before his final admission, and each time there was an expectation that he would see his family again. Before his last departure, however, he had said 'Goodbye' to his grandchildren and family, and they had waved their last farewell at the airstrip. Ralph was going to hospital to die, and when news came of his death, it was only to confirm what the family already knew.

R. Mobbs

discrete and segregated modes of discourse and activity upheld by strict social rules, which can result in punishment if breached. When a health professional treats a member of the opposite sex, such as treatment of an initiated man by a young female doctor, or care of an Aboriginal woman by a male practitioner during pregnancy, it is an experience of great shame; so great in fact that it can cause the complete withdrawal of the Aboriginal person. Often, a young Aboriginal woman in labour will absolutely refuse to allow a male medical practitioner to examine her progress, and the midwife may also be refused while the attending male doctor is in the room. For those women who do consent to such an examination, the experience is one of shame: the dreadful humiliation caused by the breach of intimacy rules regulating female–male contact. 'Shame' is attached to all physical examinations involving the female reproductive system, so that a routine procedure such as the taking of a Pap smear will usually be avoided. I remember an elderly woman at River Reserve who had been subjected to just such a procedure during the morning session of the outpatients' clinic at Mining City hospital. During the afternoon the normally chatty woman was very withdrawn. After some hours, with only women present, she said, 'But they're different, those doctors, aren't they?' It emerged that a young male doctor had taken a Pap smear when she had presented with a problem she thought was unrelated to her pelvic region. It was not the supposed misdiagnosis that concerned her. Rather she was grappling with the idea that the male doctor was not 'just a man' with all of the associated overtones of male sexuality, but was a man trained into the professionalised role of medicine, and therefore 'different'.

Most Aboriginal groups have complex and multiple avoidance rules determined by kin relationships, such as mother-in-law/son-in-law avoidance. While a son-in-law has many obligations towards his wife's mother (providing food, giving money from wages), neither must ever speak to, touch, or make eye contact with the other. The far-reaching prohibition of any interaction between these two relatives often means that they will stay some distance from each other. To breach this rule is profoundly disturbing, as happened on one occasion at Mining City. With other members of my adoptive family, we had decided to go to the store to buy provisions to make the evening meal. Suddenly, my honorary sister's husband pushed his way drunkenly into the car. Arriving at the store, my 'mother', 'brother-in-law' and I waited in the car, while my 'sister' and her children shopped. Being very tall, my sister's husband tried to stretch one of his legs into the front of the car where his mother-in-law sat. In doing so, he touched her. Given his state of inebriation, he withdrew his leg very quickly, but he had breached the avoidance rule and not even drunkenness could excuse his scandalous behaviour.

Acceptable social behaviour as it is determined by avoidance rules can apply to many different kin relationships, but varies according to group. Consequently, health professionals must enquire about avoidance rules at their work place, preferably from an Aboriginal person of the same sex (and ideally, about the same age). It is also a common practice across Australia for Aboriginal people to avoid using the name of a dead person, even if it is also the name of a living person or persons. Instead, such people are addressed using a language term that indicates that their usual name cannot be used because of the death of the namesake, or otherwise they take another name. As death is so frequent in Aboriginal communities, familiarisation with the appropriate language term or name change will greatly enhance the social skills of the health professionals in an Aboriginal community.

Hospitalisation is, by definition, disruptive of a person's normal daily lifestyle. This is especially true for remote area Aborigines, for whom evacuation to a major hospital is very disorienting, involving removal to an environment dramatically different from their own. It is not only lifts and medical equipment that can be intimidating, but also the inexplicable behaviour of hospital staff. Why, for example, are inpatients expected to sit in wheelchairs to be taken to their beds when they are physically able to walk? Why are they expected to wear pyjamas for the length of their stay, even though they are capable of dressing each morning? For Anglo-Australians, these behaviours are an accepted part of the sick role, but for many

Aboriginal people, they merely reinforce the strangeness of the hospital environment.

Many Aborigines grow and live within a totally familiar social environment, where every other person is probably known to them and many are related. Evacuation to a distant hospital means removal from these familiar surroundings and contact with strangers. Temporary loss of family and community usually results in loneliness so intense that it can be defined as a state of bereavement induced by withdrawal from the high level of social activity to be found in the closely knit community of Aboriginal kin. Thus, when Aboriginal people speak of being 'lonely', they are expressing an intolerable emotional state which can motivate young and old alike to end it by, for example, absconding from hospital.

Being outside their own group is also very threatening to many Aborigines because it means contact with strangers. For instance Anglo-Australians insist upon prolonged, direct eye contact when speaking with another person, and conclude that Aborigines are shy because of their silence and averted gaze upon a first encounter. More to the point, however, is the fact that introductions to strangers, be they Aboriginal or not, present awkward situations. Von Sturmer (unpub., pp. 6–8) describes some ways of alleviating this discomfort.

1. Do not press the Aboriginal person to tell you her or his name immediately.
2. Should it be preferable to learn the person's name immediately, offer your own full name and then ask in 'deliberately polite English—"I hope you don't mind me asking this question but could you tell me your name?" '. It must be noted, however, that for Aborigines, 'names are subject to extreme variability and change dependent on such circumstances as deaths, ceremonies, and other social considerations'.
3. Once names have been exchanged, then either party may begin to establish which people they both know, be they Aboriginal or non-Aboriginal.

Terminating a conversation is also an uneasy time, as von Sturmer (unpub., pp. 27–9) relates:

1. Departures must not be arbitrary, and a reason for leaving or specific details of the destination should be given.
2. Often the Aboriginal person/s will make quite detailed arrangements about a future meeting, which may or may not eventuate and von Sturmer (unpub., p. 29) explains that 'it would be wrong to take arrangements at face value. They have a symbolic rather than a factual force'.
3. 'The likening of a departure to a death can be treated as a guiding principle.'

For Aboriginal people, their social relationships always take priority, overriding medical appointments and even illness itself. Thus, keeping prior arrangements for a subsequent visit to or from a health practitioner will always be secondary to the person's social circumstances at the actual time of the scheduled visit.

4. Lack of knowledge about Aboriginal English language patterns

Research conducted at Mining City's hospital showed that the resident medical officers there experienced many difficulties in communicating with Aboriginal people who attended the hospital for treatment (Mobbs 1986). So-called 'difficult' patients were said to fall into two categories: the unresponsive and the unreliable. The former refused to answer the questions the doctor asked in an attempt to establish their medical problems. The latter responded to questioning, but would not volunteer new information. This was construed as uncooperative behaviour by the doctors. It is in fact a clear example of what happens in a medical interview when the interviewer does not have the social knowledge or the linguistic skills necessary to communicate with Aboriginal clients who use Aboriginal English.

Eades (1982), working with an Aboriginal researcher and the Aboriginal people of south-East Queensland, has contributed considerably to the understanding of Aborigines' use of Aboriginal English, much of which can be extrapolated to the clinical encounter. Her work focuses on the sociocultural aspects of Aboriginal information-seeking, with particular regard to the role of questioning in the transmission of information. She makes three main points (Eades 1982, p. 99):

1. Aboriginal people have differing 'RIGHTS to knowledge, be it religious, special or everyday knowledge. All knowledge is considered an inalienable part of relationships between people and has no value of its own separate from these relationships'.
2. There is no obligation on an addressee to answer a question.
3. Constraints on the use of questions 'are bound up with permanent relationships and a sense of the right time to say and do things'.

Figure 7.4 *Mary Barker (right) checks Molly Warrawina's blood pressure at Dodge City, Brewarrina, in north-western New South Wales. In the clinical encounter, Aboriginal people find it easier to talk about their medical problems if the health professional first establishes a personal relationship with them. (From P. Taylor, ed.,* After 200 years, *Aboriginal Studies Press, Canberra, 1988, p. 72)*

Most doctors attempt to take medical histories using multiple questions. As Eades states, however, Aborigines do not normally feel an obligation to reply to a question. Thus the impression is often given to health professionals that Aboriginal clients are uncooperative—that is, unresponsive and unreliable providers of information. Furthermore, the transmission of information is by means of an exchange of knowledge or information within the context of social interaction, such as during story telling. Eades (1982, p. 107) explains that 'In Aboriginal society the passing of information doesn't result from a direct query. It is the result of normal two-way interaction between people'. Demonstrating a willingness to exchange information and personal experiences is obligatory in the context of social relatedness. For instance, an Aboriginal friend told me how a European man had told him about some of his life experiences at a place known to both of them. My friend commented, 'Well, what could I do? I had to tell him my story!' This point is of particular relevance to health professionals, as shown by the success of one resident medical officer at Mining City hospital in communicating with his Aboriginal clients (Mobbs 1986, p. S4).

[One doctor] attempted to approach an Aboriginal patient 'as another person' and without 'a stethoscope hanging out'. After greeting the patient with 'Good day', he would ask where the patient lived, whether they had relatives in hospital and probably relate some of his own experiences of the area. He also felt it was important to use colloquial terminology during a conversation.

This doctor preferred talking in a social manner within the hospital. In doing so, he unwittingly adopted a communication mode eminently suited to Aboriginal clients. He communicated as though he were in a non-medical context, establishing a communicative social relationship which enabled Aborigines to tell him about their medical problems.

The three main social constraints on Aboriginal transmission of knowledge (Eades 1982, pp. 100, 101) are:

1. the individual's right to know or his or her lack of right depending on the information and its surrounding circumstances;
2. the obligation to wait for the information to be given by the knowledgeable person;
3. the person requiring information must present some known, inferred or guessed information, in an appropriate mode.

Eades also presents more technical data about the linguistic strategies used for acquiring 'orientation information' and 'substantial information'. It is sufficient to say here, however, that if a health professional asks a direct question such as 'Are you sick?', an answer will probably not be forthcoming. If instead the health practitioner says 'You look a bit sick there. Can you tell me where you are sick?' or 'You have come here because you have problem. Can you tell me now what the problem is?' a response is more likely to be given.

To quote Eades (1982, p. 108), the art of information gathering in Aboriginal society is to:

consider information exchange as a part of your relationship with someone, and for specific issues start with known information and share it, then use triggering devices and wait until the knowledgeable person is prepared to give his information. Furthermore, accept that the person may exercise his right to withhold the information.

Given these complexities, a health professional can be greatly assisted by obtaining as much information as possible about an Aboriginal client from the client's family, and from health personnel familiar with that person. A good start to sharing information, however, is for the health professional to relate and share information about the health-care service or the surroundings, such as a guided tour of a hospital floor.

Understanding the client's view

This chapter has been devoted to describing Aboriginal views of health, illness and healing. It cannot give the reader more than a glimpse of the myriad ways in which Aboriginal people think about themselves, their maintenance of well-being, and how they manage illness.

It is true to say, however, that the culturally construed meanings attached to these human experiences will be very different for an Aboriginal person and a non-Aboriginal health professional. A useful construct for understanding the different world views held by a health professional and a lay person about a particular illness episode is that of 'explanatory models' (Kleinman et al. 1978; Katon and Kleinman 1980). It introduces the notion of a client aetiology of illness and validates this lay model for explaining personal 'dis-ease'. The idea of an explanatory model is particularly pertinent to the cross-cultural consultation between an Aboriginal client and non-Aboriginal practitioner, in which not only the cause of the illness but all aspects of the episode may have meanings for the Aboriginal person completely outside the professional and personal world view of the health professional.

A client's perception of her or his illness episode is referred to by Katon and Kleinman (1980, p. 259) as 'the patient's explanatory model'. They suggest that the health professional must 'have genuine interest in the meaning the sickness has for the patient, and make explicit to the patient his [sic] intent to draw on this essential information in constructing an appropriate treatment plan'. Kleinman et al. (1978) suggest that asking the following questions will help to elicit the patient's explanatory model. It is vitally important, however, that the health professional who wishes to utilise these questions as part of clinical practice should change both the structure and content of the questions to a format appropriate to the language patterns and colloquial expressions of the group to which the interviewee belongs. The questions are:

1. What do you think has caused your problem?
2. Why do you think it started when it did?
3. What do you think your sickness does to you?
4. How severe is your sickness? Will it have a short or a long course?
5. What kind of treatment do you think you should receive?
6. What are the most important results you hope to receive from this treatment?

7. What are the chief problems your sickness has caused for you?
8. What do you fear most about your sickness?

Whether the sick Aboriginal person is a 'town camper', stockrider, community elder or nurse, and whether the setting is a remote community clinic, a rural town hospital, or a specialised unit in a city hospital, understanding the Aboriginal person's conceptualisation of his or her condition can be of great assistance to communication and therapy. Seeking to understand the client's view of the illness and the meaning it has for him or her, however, does more than enhance the clinical encounter. It also helps to overcome the barriers of mistrust, misunderstanding and anxiety between client and professional, by signalling the desire of the latter to learn and to comprehend. In settings where the staff are Aboriginal, and the environment is conducive to Aboriginal use (such as Aboriginal medical services), these barriers are much less formidable. But while the majority of institutions and practitioners continue to be non-Aboriginal, the quality of care received by Aborigines will depend largely on the capacity of staff to respond sympathetically, and thoughtfully, to their Aboriginal clients.

References

Berndt, C. H. (1964), 'The role of native doctors in Aboriginal Australia' in A. Kiev (ed.), *Magic, faith and healing*, Free Press, London New York, pp. 264–82.

Cawte, J. (1974), *Medicine is the Law*, University of Hawaii Press, Honolulu.

Cleland, J. B., and Tindale, N. B. (1959), 'The native names and uses of plants at Haast Bluff, Central Australia', *Transactions of the Royal Society of South Australia* **82**, pp. 123–40.

Collman, J. (1988), *Fringe-dwellers and welfare: the Aboriginal response to bureaucracy*, University of Queensland Press, St Lucia.

Cook, C. E. (1966), 'Medicine and the Australian Aboriginal: a century of contact in the Northern Territory', *Medical Journal of Australia* **1** (14), pp. 559–65.

Eades, D. (1982), 'You gotta know how to talk...: information seeking in south-east Queensland Aboriginal society', *Australian Journal of Linguistics* **2**, pp. 61–82.

Elkin, A. P. (1945), *Aboriginal men of high degree*, Australasian Publishing Company, Sydney.

Gott, B. (1984), 'Victorian ethnobotanical records', *Australian Aboriginal Studies* **1**, p. 56.

Gray, D. (1980), 'Traditional medicine on the Carnavon Aboriginal Reserve', in R. M. and C. H. Berndt (eds), *Aborigines of the west: their past and their present*, University of Western Australia Press, Perth, pp. 169–83.

Henshall, T. S., and Devanesen, D. M. (1982), 'A study of plant medicines in Central Australia', *Aboriginal Health Project: Information Bulletin* **1**, April, pp. 10, 11.

Isaacs, J. (1988), *Bush food: Aboriginal food and herbal medicine*, Weldon, Sydney.

Katon, W., and Kleinman, A. (1980), 'Doctor–patient negotiation and other social science strategies in patient care', in L. Eisenberg and A. Kleinman (eds), *The relevance of social science for medicine*, D. Reidel, Boston, Massachusetts, pp. 253–79.

Keen, I. (ed.) (1988), *Being black: Aboriginal cultures in settled Australia*, Aboriginal Studies Press, Canberra.

Kleinman, A., Eisenberg, L., and Good, B. (1978), 'Culture, illness and care: clinical lessons from anthropologic and cross-cultural research', *Annals of Internal Medicine* **88** (2), pp. 251–8.

Landy, D. (1983), 'Medical anthropology: a critical appraisal', in L. J. Ruffini (ed.), *Advances in medical social science*, vol. 1, Gordon and Breach Science Publishers, New York, pp. 185–314.

Mobbs, R. (1986), 'But I do care! Communication difficulties affecting the quality of care delivered to Aborigines', *Medical Journal of Australia* **144**, special supplement, pp. S3–S5.

Mobbs, R. (1987), 'Suffering on the fringe: Aboriginal help seeking in an urban environment', *Psychiatric Medicine* **5** (1), pp. 57–61.

Nathan, P. (1980), *'A home away from home': a study of the Aboriginal Health Service in Fitzroy, Victoria*, PIT Press, Preston Institute of Technology, Bundoora, Vic.

Nathan, P., and Japanangka, D. L. (1983), *Health business*, Heinemann Educational Australia, Richmond, Victoria.

Palmer, E. (1883), 'On plants used by the natives in north Queensland, Flinders and Mitchell Rivers, for food, medicine, &c., &c.', *Royal Society of New South Wales: Journal and Proceedings* **17**, pp. 93–113.

Pounder, D. J. (1985), 'A new perspective on Kadaitja killings', *Oceania* **56** (1), pp. 77–82.

Reid, J. (1978*a*), 'The dangers of surgery: an Aboriginal view', *Medical Journal of Australia* **1**, pp. 90–2.

Reid, J., and Dhamarrandji, B. (1978*b*), 'Curing, not caring: why Aboriginal patients "abscond"', *New Doctor* **8**, April, pp. 27–32.

Reid, J. (1978*c*), 'The role of the Marrnggitj in contemporary health care', *Oceania* **49** (2), pp. 96–109.

Reid, J. (1978*d*), 'Change in the indigenous medical system of an Aboriginal community', *Australian Institute of Aboriginal Studies Newsletter* **9**, pp. 61–72.

Reid, J. (1982), *Body, land and spirit: health and healing in Aboriginal society*, University of Queensland Press, St Lucia.

Reid, J. (1983), *Sorcerers and healing spirits: continuity and change in an Aboriginal medical system*, Australian National University Press, Canberra.

Reser, J. P., and Eastwell, H. D. (1981), 'Labeling and cultural expectations: the shaping of a sorcery syndrome in Aboriginal Australia', *Journal of Nervous and Mental Disorder* **169** (5), pp. 303–10.

Sansom, B. (1982), 'The sick who do not speak', in D. Parkin (ed.), *Semantic anthropology*, ASA Monograph 22, Academic Press, London, pp. 183–95.

Scarlett, N., White, N., and Reid, J. (1982), ' "Bush medicines": the pharmacopoeia of the Yolngu of Arnhem Land', in J. Reid (ed.), *Body, land and spirit: health and healing in Aboriginal society*, University of Queensland Press, St Lucia, pp. 154–91.

Soong, F. S. (1983), 'Role of the *margidjbu* (traditional healer) in western Arnhem Land', *Medical Journal of Australia* **1**, pp. 474–7.

Taylor, J. C. (1977), 'A pre-contact Aboriginal medical system on Cape York Peninsula', *Journal of Human Evolution* **6**, pp. 419–32.

Thomson, D. (1961), 'Marrngit Mirri and Kalka—medicineman and sorcerer in Arnhem Land', *Man* **131**, July, pp. 97–102.

Tonkinson, R. (1970), 'Aboriginal dream-spirit beliefs in a contact situation: Jigalong, Western Australia', in R. M. Berndt (ed.), *Australian Aboriginal anthropology*, University of Western Australia Press, Nedlands. pp. 277–91.

Tonkinson, M. (1982), 'The *mabarn* and the hospital: the selection of treatment in a remote Aboriginal community', in J. Reid (ed.), *Body, land and spirit: health and healing in Aboriginal society*, University of Queensland Press, St Lucia, pp. 225–41.

Toussaint, S. (1989), 'Aboriginal and non-Aboriginal healing, health and knowledge: sociocultural and environmental issues in the west Kimberley', *Aboriginal Health Information Bulletin* **12**, November, pp. 30–5.

Webb, L. J. (1969), 'The use of plant medicines and poisons by Australian Aborigines', *Mankind* **7** (2), pp. 137–46.

Webber, D. L., Reid, L. E., and Lalara, N. (1975), 'Health and the Groote Eylandter', *Medical*

Journal of Australia, special supplement, December, pp. 20–7.

Winterbotham, L. P. (1951), 'Primitive medical art and primitive medicine-men of Australia', *Medical Journal of Australia* **1** (13), March, pp. 461–8.

Unpublished material

Hamilton, A. (unpub.), Socio-cultural factors in health among the Pitjantjatjara: a preliminary report, unpublished paper, Department of Anthropology, University of Sydney, 1971.

Harrison, L. (unpub.), Racial ideas and the health care of Aborigines: an analysis of articles on Aborigines in the *Medical Journal of Australia* 1914–1979, MA thesis, Australian National University, Canberra, 1979.

Mobbs, R. (unpub.), Fertility controls elemental to human populations, focusing on Aboriginal Australia: a study in medical anthropology, BA Honours thesis, University of Queensland, 1979.

Rose, D. B. (unpub.), Concepts of health among the Ngaringman, paper delivered to the Australian Anthropological Society Conference, Sydney, 1984.

Soong, F. S. (unpub.), Roles, social relationships and health care in an Aboriginal community in western Arnhem Land : a preliminary report, paper presented to the Australian Anthropological Society Conference, Brisbane, 1980.

Tynan, B. J. (unpub. *a*), Traditional and Western medicine at Warrabri, a central Australian Aboriginal community, paper delivered to the Australian Anthropology Society, Sydney, 1979.

Tynan, B. J.(unpub. *b*), Medical systems in conflict: a study in power, Diploma in Anthropology thesis, University of Sydney, 1979.

von Sturmer, J. (unpub.), Talking with Aborigines, Newsletter no. 15, Australian Institute of Aboriginal Studies, Canberra, 1981, pp. 13–30.

Acknowledgments

I wish to thank Professor Janice Reid for her editorial comments, Dr Souchow Yao for his discussions and contribution to formulating the paper, and Peter, Elizabeth, Archina and Grace for their support and tolerance. Research at 'Mining City' was funded by: the Commonwealth Department of Health, Canberra; the Department of Anthropology and Sociology, University of Queensland; and the Australian Institute of Aboriginal Studies, Canberra.

CHAPTER 8

Contemporary issues in Aboriginal public health

Paul Torzillo

Royal Prince Alfred Hospital, Sydney, and Nganampa Health Council, *Alice Springs

Charles Kerr

Department of Publilc Health, University of Sydney

Public health can be viewed as the practice of health care for populations rather than for individuals. It provides a framework both for assessing Aboriginal health and for planning strategies to improve Aboriginal health status. Currently, there is active debate about the change in emphasis of the 'new public health' compared to the more traditional aspects of public health, such as environmental hygiene and immunisation programs. Many Aboriginal people still live in conditions comparable to those experienced now in developing countries or a century ago in developed countries. Therefore, the provision of acceptable physical living conditions and basic health-care delivery systems are of fundamental importance for Aborigines, in contrast to other Australians, who essentially take these things for granted. However, what has been termed the 'sanitation phase of public health' (Kickbush 1989) was closely linked to action and change in social policy, and this is clearly also necessary for the improvement of Aboriginal health. The concepts of the 'new public health' also contain elements that are integral to Aboriginal health, the most important of which are that:

- health status is influenced by many factors in society;
- it cannot be improved unless communities actively participate in the process;
- good health can be a tool for social development.

As Hafdan Mahler, the former director-general of the World Health Organization (WHO), said:

With this change in emphasis, public health is reinstating itself as a collective effort, drawing together a wide range of actors, institutions and sectors within society towards a goal for a socially and economically productive life.

Mahler 1986, p. 1

---

* Senior medical adviser

This social goal, set by the WHO member states at the World Health Assembly in 1977, moves health from being the outcome measure of social development to one of its major resources.

Improvements in Aboriginal health status are clearly bound to the 'community development' strategies of the Aboriginal nation. While 'community development' cannot be precisely defined yet, the process of its definition is occurring in different regions across the country. It is obvious that it will take quite different forms in different locations. However, in all areas, major objectives will be to improve the 'well-being' and the lifestyle options of individuals and groups. Initiatives that enhance identity and cohesion, increase the community skills base, provide economic development and strengthen political power are at once prerequisites for health improvement and direct causes of health improvement.

Illness profile

One prerequisite for developing priorities for appropriate public health programs is an examination of the illness profile of the population. Disease has clearly been a major weapon in the colonisation of Aborigines, whether by accident or intent. Epidemics of infectious disease are well documented (Basedow 1932; Cleland 1928) and clearly had a greater effect in reducing the Aboriginal population than did murder by poisoning or shooting, although the latter were widespread and devastating (see Reynolds, 'Such extraordinary terrorism' in Franklin and White, chapter 1 in this volume). Butlin (1983, p. 175) suggests that 'the combined effects of disease and resource competition may have reduced black numbers in the course of about 60 years to about 10 per cent of the 1788 level'.

It should be emphasised that a major problem in addressing Aboriginal health issues is the tendency to generalise statements about the whole Aboriginal nation. There are major differences in the prevalence and severity of certain conditions between regions. In particular, the serious infectious diseases affecting children are far less common in cities and large country towns than in remote communities.

Childhood illness

Twenty years ago, the major public issue in Aboriginal health was the extremely high *infant mortality rates* (IMR) (see also Thomson, chapter 2 in this volume). From 1964 to 1971, Aborigines in central Australia had a crude death rate of 19.4 per 1000, which was higher than that of any country listed in the 1967 *World Health Statistics Annual* (Kirke 1974). The infant mortality rate was 172 per 1000 compared to the Northern Territory non-Aboriginal rate of 19.5 per 1000. The leading causes of those deaths were respiratory disease and gastroenteritis. Since that time IMRs have markedly decreased (DAA 1987), but the precise reasons for this are uncertain. There is now less discrepancy between IMRs in remote areas and those in more settled regions, although major differences exist in the incidence of infectious diseases. Some of the factors that may have contributed to the reduction in IMRs are: falling birth rates; increasing expenditure on housing, sewerage and water supply; a decrease in the prevalence of severe malnutrition; increased access to antibiotics with more nurses and health workers available in communities; and improvement in aerial evacuation services from remote communities to hospitals.

However, the reduction in mortality has been achieved at the cost of an enormous *hospitalisation rate* for young children (see Gracey, 'Kylie's first two years', in Thomson, chapter 2 in this volume). In a review of rural clinics and hospital attendances, Hall (unpub.) studied 194 children randomly selected from a cohort of survivors of the neonatal period born between 1978 and 1982 in the Alice Springs and Barkly regions of the Northern Territory. He reported 586 hospitalisations for the study period. In Western Australia, despite a marked decline in admissions between 1971 and 1980, admission rates remained extremely high. For gastroenteritis and lower respiratory tract infections the rates were, respectively, 11 and six times higher than those for non-Aboriginal people (McNeilly et al. 1983).

The harmful consequences of hospitalisation for young children are well recognised. However, it creates special problems for Aboriginal children and their families. In particular, the hospitalisation of a child means that the family is obliged to deal with the complexity of problems created by institutional racism in Australian hospitals (Torzillo and Williams unpub.). In remote Aboriginal communities, the social consequences of hospitalisation are particularly severe. In many cases, a mother will either accompany her child to hospital or follow by road transport, leaving the rest of her children dependent on others for care. Although Aboriginal communities are often well equipped to deal with this situation, it is not always without negative consequences. Hospitalisation is frequently prolonged and mothers require financial support from their community or must return home. Town life is often dangerous for people from bush communities: with constant exposure to violence, alcohol and police. Aboriginal parents are often intimidated and uncomfortable within the hospital environment. This often prevents them from visiting their children frequently, even when they are accommodated near the hospital. Invariably, as a result, medical staff conclude that parents are uninterested in their children's care and a cycle of resentment is established. In addition, recurrent hospitalisation separates children from their communities during an important time for learning language and social behaviour. This may well impinge on later cultural and community cohesion.

Although mortality from *respiratory disease* in Aboriginal children is low compared to that in developing countries, it is still significant. For example, in the Northern Territory, it remains the leading cause of death of Aboriginal children, apart from perinatal conditions (Devanesen et al. 1986). Chronic respiratory disease and bronchiectasis were reported in Aboriginal children in the late 1960s (Maxwell 1972; Maxwell et al. 1981). The prevalence of these conditions is not known, but signs of chronic respiratory disease, at least in rural children, seem to be common (Torzillo et al. 1983). Acute respiratory infection remains the major problem. In central Australia, Aboriginal admission rates for radiologically proven pneumonia are approximately 80 times those for non-Aboriginal children (Torzillo and Erlich 1984), while in Bourke, western New South Wales, 25 per cent of Aboriginal children born in a three-year period developed at least one such episode (Harris et al. 1984). A similar pattern of illness is seen in Western Australia (Harris et al. 1986).

Chronic nasal discharge and middle ear disease are both extremely common (Moran et al. 1979; Sunderman and Dyer 1984), although their prevalence is clearly less common now in areas where living conditions have improved over the last 20 years. Middle ear perforation and a discharging ear can occur even in the first few weeks of life and are generally present in the first year. After that time, the ear is chronically discharging and continues to discharge intermittently until late in childhood. Many of the perforations heal in older children. Hearing loss is usually greatest at the time of the chronic ear discharge, which obviously occurs at a critical time for learning and the development of language skills. In some regions of Australia, it is estimated that up to 80 per cent of Aboriginal children may be suffering hearing loss related to middle ear disease (Nienhuys 1989). There is little evidence that medical therapy will alter the outcome of chronic ear discharge in children. The priority public health issues are to: reduce the prevalence of the condition; develop improved hearing aid devices for use in schools; and introduce training for teachers of hearing impaired children in Aboriginal schools.

Chronic nasal discharge (Freeman et al. 1985) is a characteristic feature of many young Aboriginal children. Research in Papua New Guinea suggests that this accompanies early colonisation of the upper respiratory tract by bacteria (Gratten unpub.), and that this is a key event in the pathogenesis of pneumonia in these children (Riley 1985). Recent work, again from Papua New Guinea, demonstrates that known bacterial respiratory pathogens such as *Streptococcus pneumoniae* can be carried on the hands of mothers and children (Pickering and Rose 1988). Basic public health strategies, such as provision of facilities for washing children, may therefore reduce the incidence of acute respiratory infection (ARI).

Diarrhoeal disease is the second of the two most common serious conditions that affect Aboriginal children. It is a major cause of presentation to clinics in rural communities (Hall unpub.; Freeman et al. 1985) and admission rates to hospital are extremely high (McNeilly et al. 1983; Kass and Win Law 1985). There are considerable problems in demonstrating the specific benefits of improved water supply and sanitation (Blum and Feachem 1983), but the weight of evidence suggests that improvement of these amenities would bring a substantial benefit (Esrey et al. 1985).

Skin infection is common in Aboriginal children (Freeman et al. 1985; RACO 1980). This is important not just because of the immediate morbidity and chronic discomfort but also because of the potential development of post-streptococcal renal disease.

Ocular infection, particularly trachoma, and its sequelae have been well documented by the National Trachoma and Eye Health Program (RACO 1980). Subsequent studies in several parts of Australia suggest that in some coastal regions the prevalence has reduced, while it probably remains much the same in inland communities (Freeman et al. 1985; Meredith et al. 1989). Trachoma has long been recognised as a condition that reflects the state of environmental hygiene (Hollows 1989), as has gonococcal conjunctivitis, epidemics of which have been reported in central Australia (Brennan et al. 1989). Bacterial meningitis is far less common than ARI, but its mortality rate and sequelae are substantial. The attack rates for this condition are extremely high (Hanna unpub.). Serious infection due to *Haemophilus influenzae* has an incidence among central Australian Aboriginal children that is as high as any reported in the world (Hanna unpub.). Rheumatic fever is also more common among Aboriginal children although precise incidence data are not available (Brennan 1989; MacDonald and Walker 1989). There are anecdotal reports that renal disease amongst these children is also common. Haematuria in remote area Aboriginal children is frequent and the likely causes include post-infectious glomerulo-nephritis, urinary tract infection and urinary calculi (Jones and Henderson 1989).

Mild to moderate *malnutrition* continues to be common, particularly in remote areas (NTDH 1985; Gracey and Hitchcock 1983; see also Harrison, chapter 4 in this volume). Although growth velocity may even be increased in the first three months of life compared to international standards (Gracey and Sullivan 1988), growth fall-off starts to occur between 6 and 12 months of life and children continue to be light and short in the following two years of life. However, severe malnutrition is rare (Freeman et al. 1985; NTDH 1985).

Several studies have documented the incidence of *low birth weight* amongst Aboriginal infants (Gracey et al. 1985; Gogna et al. 1986; see also Harrison, chapter 4 in this volume). The precise implications for subsequent mortality or morbidity are unclear, but there is agreement that the low birth weight of these infants is likely to be due to prenatal factors, particularly maternal nutrition (Lancaster 1989).

Hepatitis B surface antigen was first recognised in the serum of Aborigines (Blumberg et al. 1965), and an increased incidence of infection has long been known in Aborigines (Barrett 1972). Whilst Sydney blood donors have a prevalence of hepatitis B surface antigen positivity of 0.07 per cent (Britton et al. 1985), rates of greater than 20 per cent have been reported in some Aboriginal communities (Thomson and Honari 1989). It is likely that most infections occur in the first few years of life (Campbell et al. 1989). It is difficult to be certain about the burden of disease caused by this infection. Acute hepatitis B infection seems not to be a substantial problem. However, there is evidence that mortality from liver cirrhosis and the incidence of hepatocellular carcinoma are significantly increased. Although the actual number of cases is small, available data suggest that hepatocellular carcinoma is six to seven times more common among Aborigines (Thomson and Honari 1989).

Substance abuse, particularly petrol sniffing and alcohol abuse are major child health problems in many communities (for details, see Brady, chapter 5 in this volume).

Adult illness

Undoubtedly a major public health issue for Aborigines is the extremely high *death rates* for young adults (see also Thomson, chapter 2 in this volume). In western New South Wales, the death rate for Aboriginal males is 2.5 times the age standardised rate for the total male population of the state and 3.0 times the rate for females (Gray and Hogg 1988). In some age groups, the relative risk is up to eight times that for non-Aboriginal groups. Data from central Australia demonstrate similar patterns. In fact, for the 30 to 34 year-old age group the relative risk of death has been estimated as 17.5 (Khalidi 1989).

The New South Wales study (Gray and Hogg 1988) identified 'diseases of the circulatory system' and 'accidents, poisonings and violence' as the two major classes of cause of death, with circulatory disease accounting for approximately 40 per cent of the excess risk endured by both Aboriginal men and women. In particular, the 'relative risk of ischaemic heart disease' for Aboriginal men and women was approximately 13 times higher than for the total New South Wales population. Although a further calculation was based on records of only 11 deaths, it was found that between the ages of 25 and 44 this relative risk was approximately 40 times greater than in the total population of the state. This is consistent with extensive anecdotal accounts by experienced workers in the field that coronary artery disease occurs frequently and at a young age. It is likely that cigarette smoking, dietary patterns and carbohydrate intolerance (discussed below) all contribute to the risk of coronary artery disease. While it is particularly significant that this pattern of high mortality among young adults is seen across the country, nevertheless there are inadequate data available to show whether the contributory factors are similar in different regions.

Alcohol is clearly a major social problem with enormous health implications for Aboriginal people. Death and injury from trauma and violence are often linked to alcohol abuse. The public health implications of this will be described later in this chapter.

In the last 20 years, considerable research has demonstrated the increased incidence of *diabetes mellitus* and impaired carbohydrate tolerance of different Aboriginal groups (Wise et al. 1970; Wise et al. 1976; Cameron et al. 1986). The pattern and nature of the disease, characteristically non-insulin dependent diabetes, is similar to that seen in several other populations when lifestyle has altered from a traditional pattern to one with features of urbanisation or 'westernisation'. O'Dea et al. (1982, 1988) have provided evidence to support the theory that a genetic factor may be involved in predisposition to carbohydrate intolerance given certain changes in diet and exercise patterns. In the early 1970s, many researchers in the field believed that complications of diabetes occurred less commonly in Aborigines. Subsequent field experience and particular research studies have shown this to be a false hope (Stanton et al. 1985). The high prevalence of obesity is an additional independent risk factor for the development of diabetes (O'Dea et al. 1988; see also Harrison, chapter 4 in this volume).

Chronic renal disease appears to be common and in South Australia has been estimated to occur 11 times more frequently in Aborigines than in the overall population (Pugsley et al. 1983). However little is known about true prevalence rates or aetiology. The prevalence of *hypertension* appears to be increased in some Aboriginal groups studied (Pugsley et al. 1983; Simons et al. 1981), but the increase is not of the same order of magnitude as for diabetes or coronary artery disease.

The ancient diseases of *leprosy* and *tuberculosis* continue to affect Aborigines, the former having been essentially eradicated from non-Aboriginal society in Australia. (See also Hargrave, 'Leprosy in the Northern Territory' in Thomson, chapter 2 in this volume.) Both conditions reflect poverty and poor living conditions.

As is the case for many indigenous minorities, *syphilis* and *gonorrhoea* are clearly more common among Aborigines, but there are few regions where data are available (Freeman et al. 1985; NTDH 1985). There are no substantial data currently available about the prevalence of *HIV infection*.

Specific women's health issues

The high mortality rate for young adults applies to both women and men. In addition, it appears that the incidence of gestational diabetes is very high (Patel

1989). In general, gynaecological services for Aboriginal women have been poorly developed, and this has also lead to a significant lack of data in this area. There is some preliminary evidence that cervical cancer mortality rates are high in Aboriginal women, which may reflect late diagnosis (Durling 1989). Maternal mortality continues to be substantially greater than the overall Australian rate (Thomson 1984; Thomson, chapter 2 in this volume). The poor nutritional status of young Aboriginal women (Gracey et al. 1984) may not only impair their own health but also that of their babies. Certainly perinatal risk factors have been shown to be increased in one study of Aboriginal mothers (Julienne 1983). Pelvic inflammatory disease is common, as it is in most communities with high rates of sexually transmitted disease. Violence directed against women is also a major social health issue for Aboriginal people.

Deaths in custody

Data from the current Royal Commission into Aboriginal Deaths in Custody (RCADC) demonstrate that, during the period 1980 to 1988, Aboriginal people died in custody at a rate more than 20 times the rate of non-Aboriginal people. (Biles et al. 1989). This mirrors the similarly increased imprisonment rate of Aborigines in Australian gaols. The notion that Aboriginal suicide does not occur is clearly a myth (Reser 1989). But whatever the immediate causes of death, and there are likely to be several, there are many implications for social policy that arise from the RCADC.

Clearly a primary concern is to reduce the rate of arrests and imprisonment of Aboriginal people. While this requires changes in social policy, it also requires legislative change to reduce the intrusion of police into Aboriginal lives. In much of Australia the police act as 'front line troops' for the interests of the white community (Tobin unpub.). Particularly in rural towns, Aborigines are unable to use areas outside town because they are invariably owned by white station owners. On the other hand, continual police surveillance limits their activities to small 'settlement' and 'mission' areas around the townships. They are at once 'land locked and landless' (Phil Ayre, Brewarrina, pers. comm.). In 1982, the New South Wales Antidiscrimination Board (NSWAB) reported a study of street offences by Aborigines. In regard to police surveillance they comment: 'The Aboriginal population in the study towns are subjected to continuous police surveillance which alone constitutes a harassment by ordinary standards' (NSWAB 1982, p. 113).

Management and planning

The importance of a public health perspective is that it provides the critical link between health service planning and community development and political action. Management is a key element of this process. While it is possible to draw some parallels between current management requirements and traditional management of their land by Aboriginal groups, many of the current issues present new problems that require the development of new structures and management principles by Aboriginal people. Some of these issues are outlined in the following pages.

1. Decision-making processes

It is common in many communities for all decision making to occur in 'community meetings'. These meetings are now faced with an enormous number of issues. Invariably the meetings are conducted in such a way that complex issues are put as a choice between two alternatives. Very often a funding agency or government department is offering 'something' and demanding 'Do you want this or that?'.

Many non-Aboriginal administration and government officials equate Aboriginal decision making with the ability to obtain a consensus, a definitive statement on every issue at a single meeting. To some extent, many Aborigines have suffered under the hegemony of these ideas. People rarely ask for more information or seek advice, or simply defer decisions in order to give the issue some careful thought. Of course, there are other very powerful factors influencing Aborigines to always 'make a decision', in particular, the threat that funds, or the offer of funds, will be withdrawn.

In fact the establishment and reinforcement of 'real Aboriginal control' requires that decision-making processes are defined. These processes might well be different for issues that are as diverse as deciding on a standard protocol for treatment of young children or how health service vehicles should be used. Decisions may be made either by health service administrators, the health committee, or the health worker staff. The advisory role of white professional staff and deciding for which issues they should be consulted are also important areas of management. A further reason for defining decision-making processes is that all communities have internal political agendas and differing perceptions of the desirable roles of Aborigines and non-Aboriginal people in service delivery (see the case study by Myers, 'A community-controlled health service: different agendas', in Franklin and White, chapter 1).

2. Aboriginalisation versus Aboriginal control

Aboriginal control of health service delivery remains a central tenet in planning. However, 'Aboriginalisation' of health services is neither a prerequisite for Aboriginal control nor a guarantee of its establishment. Even if the training of Aboriginal nurses and doctors is dramatically increased, there will be insufficient numbers to staff Aboriginal health services for many years (if ever). Although Aboriginal health workers are playing an increasing role in health service delivery and management, there will always be a need for doctors and sisters in most health services. In many communities, the relatively small number of people precludes the possibility that an Aboriginal person from that area will be able to fill all the required service positions in the community. Even in an ideal world of training opportunities with unlimited funding, it is unlikely that many communities will be able to provide all the necessary teachers, plumbers, carpenters, maintenance officers, office workers, store workers, as well as health service staff. Again this requires the development of decision-making principles that ensure informed Aboriginal control without necessarily requiring that all staff will be Aboriginal. In particular, guidelines for the selection, employment and sacking of non-Aboriginal staff must be developed. This process should include the evaluation of professional competence and mechanisms for seeking advice from outside the community.

Meetings, meetings, meetings

Boollara is a fictional community but the meeting described here is based on the experience of Aboriginal people and the problems faced in Aboriginal communities as they try to regain some control over daily life, on their own terms. Arthur Reilly, the chairman of Boollara Community Council, has called everybody together for an unexpected meeting with a senior public servant, Ron McAllister.

Arthur: Now, look, the main thing we got to talk about today is this money that the department down there in Canberra wants to give us. Now we've got Mr McAllister here from the Department of—sorry?—Oh right, the Division of Agricultural Grants, sorry. Anyway, he's gonna explain how it's all been reorganised and how they've split up the budget or somethin' and changed the name. So, they've got this new program now and they reckon we can get some money.

McAllister: Good afternoon, ladies and gentlemen. The Minister has asked me to sit down with you people to discuss the recently developed equity program for the redistribution of scarce resources. Now, we've developed this program in response to a growing awareness in the Division that disadvantaged communities, like yourselves, should start to take some responsibility and really take control of your own affairs. Now, I know you people, particularly you Arthur and of course you Wally, and we've all been discussing the future of Boollara for some years now. I'm sure that we'll be able to do something of local relevance which will fit into the guidelines. These guidelines have been developed in order to ensure that efficient and effective initiatives are planned, implemented and monitored appropriately. And of course, we are very mindful of the need for cultural appropriateness. Now, I don't need to say that the Minister is very keen to see Boollara go ahead. In fact he said to me only the other day, he'd like to be the Minister to solve the Aboriginal problem—well, after full and frank consultation with yourselves, of course.

Arthur: Now you mob, we've all got to have a say about this, and especially you Wally, and then we got to make a decison quick smart, or there won't be any money for another year. Right, Mr McAllister?.

McAllister: Well, not as such, Arthur, although we would like to be able to acquit the funds out of our budget this year and we are not yet in a position to assess the allocations for the following year. I should also like to indicate at this point in time that future funding is very much contingent on this project being successful. But we'll talk a little more about appropriate evaluation later. Arthur, maybe you should talk to your people about the changes we think need to be made to the original idea.

Arthur: All right, well, okay, Mr McAllister—now, you lot'll all remember that when the Minister came up last time, after them big rains and we found out the drains were all shonky in the new housing project—yeah Maureen, my kids were sick along with the rest of them. Well, we talked to him then about how we don't just need more hand-outs we need jobs, and training opportunities, especially the young blokes—and Wally had some ideas. Well, then we had the big round of meetings about six months ago. We had to postpone that trip up north for ceremonies and it upset the old fellas. Then the community adviser wrote up our ideas and we got a lot of other advice and we sent that to Mr McAllister. Yeah, that's right, we worked out a sort of mixed farm with a bit of a market garden, yeah and some chooks for the old people. Yeah, everyone could have a job, even the kids, but these new guidelines we've heard about means they've changed the ideas around a bit. Yeah, yeah, no, they'll still fund it but—instead of, you know, a farm and all that, and I know it sounds a bit funny, but they reckon, well, they think we can get three years' funding if we start up a pilot project for the first Aboriginal controlled Atlantic salmon run.

Now look, it's nearly the same amount of money. No, Wally, I never seen an Atlantic salmon either. No, I dunno what they taste like. Yeah, well we might be better off with sheep but we can't get the money for that 'cos it's gotta come out of this program on equity and they reckoned there were already a lot of sheep up here but no bloody fish. So it really fits into the new guidelines, eh, Mr McAllister?

McAllister: Well, not as such, Arthur, we've still got some outstanding matters to finalise. For example, we need process and outcome evaluation built in from the outset. Now, our officers down there in Canberra have just developed a very comprehensive set of performance indicators and we'll be using these to review the project after 12 months. Arthur, have I said something funny?

Arthur: Now, look just calm down, the lot of you, this is serious. No, they're not performing fish! Look, this is a bloody good opportunity, even if it isn't what we expected. If they want to give us the money, we might as well take it—and get them kids back in here, that washroom's all overflowed again and they're puddlin' around in it.

What's that Wally, where we gonna put a dam the size of the Atlantic Ocean? Well, we could start with the washroom, by the looks of it. Now look, you're just cranky cos' they changed your ideas around. Come on, shut them dogs up, you kids sit down in front and stop still, and you young blokes get back in here. We got to appoint office bearers for the Boollara Atlantic Salmon Cooperative or we won't be digging a hole big enough to shit in.

Two hours later.

Arthur: Now look, you can't all be busy. Shirley, you're a great doer, what about you be the secretary? What do you mean you've got too much to do already? Now that Billy and Marie have left home, that only leaves the six kids with you and Wally. Oh yeah, fair enough, you're already the secretary of the Child Health Group and director of the Young Peoples' Skills Program. And you're coordinating Oldtimers' Home Care, and working as a health worker at the Women's Clinic? And doing consultations for a proposal into open cut mining? Gee, when did that turn up?

What about you, Harold? Harold, you—you're the oldest one here, how about you be secretary of this fish project? Why not? Now don't go gettin' sad about it all. Those young blokes have got to run the community. They can't always go out on huntin' trips and be sittin' around listening to stories and singin' with old blokes like you. We gotta try and do things the new way as well as the old way. Come on Harold,

what are you doin' with your time? You must only be on the Oldtimers Committee. Oh, I forgot there's the bush tucker project with the anthropologist, and you've got them sacred sites consultations as well. Yeah, maybe you are too busy.

Oh jeez, I dunno, we gotta appoint the community management committee today or Mr McAllister won't be able to go back to Canberra and authorise the project. What's that Wally? You reckon we got so many meetings we need a government grant just to scratch ourselves! Well, you might have a point—how many we got so far? There's this one, and the Women's Council, the Schools Committee, there's health worker training, there's the clinic to run, and three Oldtimers programs and that new Public Health Committee. We've got four research projects, and the new housing consultation, and the young women and girls health education, yeah, the local government—gee, maybe you're right. But if we don't elect the office bearers for this project we won't get any funding—and without any money how we gonna manage things for ourselves? Look at the stuff ups that happen when we don't have the community involved.

Wally! I don't bloody care if you're allergic to fish, I reckon you should be the coordinator of this project. You're the one who convinced the Minister that blackfellas should take responsibility for their own communities and have a chance to make a living.

Yes, I know you meant the farm proposal. Yeah, mate, it was a lotta work, a great idea. Remember, Mr McAllister, we did about nine months of consultation with the community and got real expert advice. It was broken up into several stages, so that the community could take on the next one when they were ready. It was gonna use that, you know, 'appropriate technology', and it had a relocation plan so we could move away from being near the swamp and have better houses. Gee, Mum was happy about that, big trees all around and no more frogs in the kitchen. We even got an accountant in to give us the real cost of it all.

Listen, Mr McAllister, people get pretty fed up with this. Wally, I'm not stupid, I know we're a thousand miles from the nearest ocean and we don't know a thing about these bloody fish, but it's three years' funding and they're practically throwing it at us.

McAllister: Arthur, I'm sorry that's how you feel. We thought you people wanted to take more responsibility for yourselves. You have to show independence, flexibility, vision—I feel I must reiterate, on behalf of the Minister, that it's very important for you to take this opportunity now, so that in the future we can be confident that you people can undertake proper planning, consultation and program design. What's more you should stay away from these politically inspired do-gooder advisers. Work in with the Division and the Minister. After all, we're here to help.

Margaret Miller, Policy and Public Affairs, Australian Consumers Association, Sydney; formerly of Australian Community Health Association, Sydney

3. The development of aims and objectives

Planning is a central component of public health and community development. Several useful models for health planning have been published in the international health literature (Simmonds et al. 1983; Tugwell et al. 1985). Major components include describing health status, assessing community needs, establishing priorities and programs, implementation, monitoring, evaluation and modification. It is particularly important in Aboriginal health-care to develop mechanisms for ensuring sustainability of programs so that they do not collapse when staff change.

Health services must develop both short-term and long-term aims and objectives. These goals will provide direction to staff, ensure that community priorities are adhered to and provide the basis for evaluating whether the health service is effective. Increasingly, community-controlled health services are devoting time and effort to the development of aims, objectives and strategic plans. At the level of an individual service in a community, short-term (for example three-monthly) objectives are helpful in assisting health staff to plan work and realise their achievements and problems in a systematic fashion. On a wider scale, health services such as those in the Kimberleys (Western Australia) and the Nganampa Health Council area of the Pitjantjatjara homelands (South Australia) have had to address issues such as the role of umbrella organisations. These groups have had to plan for coordinating service delivery and health policy, sharing of health service staff and the optimal use of resources for large regions with several constituent communities.

4. Integration of public health and community development strategies

Activities in both these areas are intimately linked. This has been increasingly recognised by health services and there has been increasing development of innovative and diversified programs in response to the need for a multisectoral approach to public health. This is partly reflected by the active involvement and political leadership of many health services in political issues affecting Aboriginal people. At another level, it is reflected by particular programs such as the development of an aged persons' hostel by the Redfern Aboriginal Medical Service in Sydney; the emphasis on welfare services and health promotion by the Central Australian Aboriginal Congress (CAAC); the campaigns related to alcohol and women's health conducted by Anyinginyi Aboriginal Health Service at Tennant Creek (Northern

Territory). All these health services have been characterised by the development of strong Aboriginal management practices.

5. Alcohol and community development

Aboriginal people now clearly recognise the major impediment to community development which occurs as a consequence of widespread alcohol abuse. Peter Copin, an Aboriginal leader at Yandiyarra in the Pilbara (Western Australia) summarised this in 1979 when he said, 'If we gonna run this place we got to be thinkin' all the time, see. If you drink, you just can't be thinkin' all the time' (pers. comm.).

Environmental health

It is widely acknowledged that many Aborigines have a poor living environment and that this is a major factor in their level of ill-health. In 1979, the House of Representatives Standing Committee on Aboriginal Affairs (HRSCAA 1979) stated:

It is universally accepted that the attainment of a satisfactory standard of health in any community depends on the provision of certain basic amenities including water supply, sanitation and sewerage facilities, housing and electricity. The high incidence and recurrence of many infectious diseases amongst Aboriginals [sic]...result largely from their unsatisfactory environmental conditions.

The data on living conditions of urban Aborigines are scanty but for those in rural and remote areas there is good evidence that this situation has hardly altered in 10 years.

A housing needs survey conducted by the Aboriginal Development Commission (ADC 1988) in 1987 reported that one-third of Aborigines across Australia are either homeless or living in inadequate conditions. It was estimated that 16 179 additional dwellings and 157 hostels were required (see table 8.1).

Table 8.1 Additional dwellings needed for Aborigines (excluding hostel type accommodation), 1989

State	Number of dwellings	Percentage of national total	Cost ($ millions)	Percentage of national total
NSW	3 274	20.2	249.9	19.6
Vic.	651	4.0	50.5	4.0
Qld	4 715	29.2	356.0	27.9
WA	2 565	15.9	222.5	17.5
SA	1 403	8.7	117.5	9.2
Tas.	56	0.3	3.9	0.3
NT	3 515	21.7	273.7	21.5
Total	16 179	100.0	1 274.0	100.0

Source: ADC, p. 91

Figure 8.1 *A traditional Aboriginal shelter of branches and tarpaulins, with a steel tucker box in the foreground, at a Western desert outstation, South Australia. Many of Australia's Aborigines in remote areas are homeless or live in inadequate conditions. (M. Brady)*

In 1987 the House of Representatives Standing Committee on Aboriginal Affairs (HRSCAA 1987) reported on submissions describing living conditions and infrastructure in homeland communities. The Central Land Council reported on 24 homelands in the area around Yuendumu, Lajamanu and Haast's Bluff in central Australia. There was a lack of adequate water supply in 19, ablution facilities in all 24, and sewerage/water disposal facilities in 21. Twenty-two had an inadequate power supply and the same number required more shelter. It was estimated that nine further homelands were required in the region. A more comprehensive review of homelands in central Australia during 1984 reported that 80 per cent had substandard facilities. The Kimberley Land Council (KLC) surveyed its homelands and reported that 28 per cent had inadequate water supply, 68 per cent improvised housing and nearly half had impassable roads in the wet season. Community profile data from the Department of Aboriginal Affairs (DAA) in 1985 reported that 61 of 76 outstations in South Australia, Western Australia and Queensland had inadequate supplies of good quality water and 29 had inadequate supplies of any water. A DAA survey of 400 small communities with an estimated population of 12 060 reported that 292 had no sewerage disposal facilities.

Access to remote communities is invariably poor, with inadequate roads that are often impassable during flood periods. Availability of vehicles is extremely important in terms of access and provision of services. Air strip construction in remote areas is expensive and requires on-going maintenance. Most homelands do not have telephone communications. Radios are usually the only means of communication and funding for these is also a long-standing issue in homeland development.

There is considerable evidence that living conditions are even worse for many larger communities in remote Australia (NHC 1987*a*; Memmott 1988). In more settled rural areas such as western New South Wales, there are fringe communities and settlements in which living conditions are better but certainly far from adequate (Human Rights Australia 1988).

The preceding information clearly indicates that a major problem exists with the Aboriginal living environment. However, it does not define the details of the specific environmental problems that are important in the genesis of ill-health. As a consequence, it provides no basis for an improvement in the living environment based on benefits for health status. A further problem in this area has been a failure of multisectoral involvement in the provision of essential services for Aboriginal communities. In the Pitjantjatjara homelands in north-western South Australia, the Nganampa Health Council (NHC) has conducted an extensive public and environmental health review (NHC 1987*a*). This project, Uwankara Palyanyku Kanyintjaku (UPK) ('a strategy for well-being'), provides a model for developing an approach to environmental health in remote Aboriginal communities. Much of the following discussion is taken from the report of that review.

A model project

This area of land is held in title by an incorporated body, Anangu Pitjantjatjara (AP). The population consists of approximately 2500 people who live in communities ranging in size from approximately 400 members to small family groups on homelands. NHC, the Aboriginal body responsible for delivering health care to these communities, sought financial and infrastructure assistance from the South Australian Health Commission (SAHC) in 1986 in order to perform the review, which focused primarily on the relationship between the living environment and the health of the people.

The idea for the project was initially discussed at a meeting of the AP Council held on the Pitjantjatjara lands. A large number of people from all communities attend the meetings of the AP Council. One of the Aboriginal NHC field officers introduced the proposal and then informal discussions took place between health service staff and council members over the following two days. The concept of environmental health had been of significant concern to several members of the Nganampa Health Council Executive, particularly the council chairman, Yammi Lester. In a 1983 policy statement, Yammi Lester said:

When the health service starts we need to make some changes. We can make decisions to improve on health.

We want to find good water and put down bores. People can live well where there is good water. When there is plenty of water people can wash clothes and blankets and wash themselves and keep their camp clean, taking away the rubbish. When people keep their place clean they won't pick up infections.

A lot of germs are said to live in rubbish and places that are not clean. When there is plenty of water people can wash their food plates, pannikins and billycans. They can keep their cooking things away from the dogs too, because when they lick the billycans and things they leave germs on them.

People need to be able to eat and drink without picking up germs. Keeping things clean is an easy way for people to help themselves. These are good ways to start using Nganampa.

The work of the doctors and sisters comes after this preventative health work.

NHC 1987b

In these early discussions, the review team emphasised that the project should not simply result in submissions to government for funding. The need for Aboriginal communities to develop strategies and plans for managing their living environment was stressed at the outset. As a consequence of this focus, many of the recommendations of the review are actually directed at Aboriginal communities rather than governments.

Conducting the review

The main activities of the review consisted of:

1. an extensive and detailed survey of the living areas and facilities in all communities on the lands;
2. a nutrition survey examining the source of dietary intake as well as nutritional content of store food available to Anangu (Pitjantjatjara word for Aboriginal people);
3. extensive investigation of relevant data held by government and non-government agencies outside the AP lands.

The field team, which was primarily involved in the living area survey, undertook two other simultaneous tasks. First, its data collection was closely linked with an on-going, ground-level education process. This involved continually placing the question of environmental and public health on the agenda of Anangu on the lands. Second, the team identified urgent environmental problems and triggered remedial action by community councils and staff. The key personnel for the project were two Anangu research officers, an anthropologist and an architect-planner. This group conducted the data collection for the field survey. The research team medical officer focused on health issues and providing information about illness patterns and related matters.

On the basis of reviewing previous (and inadequate) surveys of other regions, as well as preliminary visits to all major communities on the lands, the following issues were resolved:

1. The focus of the survey work was not on housing but on living areas. Over half the items surveyed concerned the area around the house, as it was clear even at this stage that much living activity occurred outside buildings.
2. Numerous requests were made for information held by external agencies which related to the provision of infrastructure and essential services on the lands.
3. The focus of the living area survey was on:
   a. safety (in particular electrical and structural);
   b. services provided by the outside living areas;

    c.   services provided by the house, for example hot and cold water supply, waste removal, power, temperature control facilities.

    d.   population and demand placed on the services of the house and yard area.

From the survey sheets completed in the field, information was tabulated in the following areas:

1.   occupants of the house (number, age, family);
2.   plan of the house and yard area;
3.   condition of the building fabric (walls, roof, ceiling, floor, doors, windows);
4.   services of the house including:
    a.   electrical (mains connections, switchboard fuses, light points, power outlets);
    b.   water supply:
        i.   cold water (taps in all areas/internal and external);
       ii.   hot water (hot water system type, capacity, condition);
      iii.   taps (condition and types of failure).
    c.   waste removal (bathroom, toilet, kitchen and laundry areas, all waste pipe diameters and condition, obvious failures, blockages and if infiltration was affecting other rooms in the house);
    d.   heating and cooking (provision for heating or cooling houses: for example. trees, fans, stoves);
    e.   fittings (for example beds, cupboards, refrigerator);
5.   yard information:
    a.   beneficial effects of the building orientation on the yard or house;
    b.   verandahs (number and beneficial effects);
    c.   fencing (extent and height; existence of external water points in the yard);
    d.   trees (number of mature and immature trees/plants in the yard area);
    e.   fire areas and other indications of the occurrence of outside living (*wiltjas* [traditional Aboriginal shelters], camps, cooking utensils, fireplaces).

Since review team members were living in the communities at the time of the study, they were able to observe closely how house and yard facilities were used at night and during the sleeping period. This provided valuable data about the services and use of the living areas.

The review team specifically intended to provide detailed information on the living environment. There appear to be no previous surveys that have addressed this issue in detail and with a focus on implications for health status. This is particularly important, as the detailed information about structural problems provides clues both to improved design and to the aspects of Aboriginal social life and cultural practice that produce particular patterns of usage.

A major feature of the methodology was the time devoted to the survey process. Even though the review team consisted of Aboriginal people from the lands, together with an anthropologist with long experience and appropriate language skills, the detailed examination of living areas might still have generated hostility. The review team spent at least a week in each community discussing the review process and familiarising community members with the aims of the project. Only after this familiarisation period did they make appointments to inspect houses or camps and collect data. Aboriginal field workers played a central role in this data collection process. A prolonged period of time in each community was also essential for other reasons. In most communities, activities such as business, ceremonies or sporting activities take up community time. In addition, the review confirmed the impression that Aboriginal communities in remote areas are overloaded by meetings initiated by outside agencies. Both government and non-government organisations are continually presenting communities with issues to be decided in the areas of health, education, welfare, land policy, transport, police and many others. At one community in the AP Lands, 143 such meetings were held in a three-month period. In this environment, it is quite understandable that Aboriginal people will simply feel the need to have a rest from meetings, no matter how important the issue may seem to outsiders (see Miller, 'Meetings, meetings, meetings' in this chapter).

A further key aspect of methodology was the ability of the review process to provide immediate benefit to individual community members. When review members identified problems in either housing or community facilities, they were often able to initiate immediate repair or maintenance. A central source of dissatisfaction with surveys in general amongst Aboriginal people is that benefits to the community invariably seem only long-term, and are often intangible or non-existent. It is interesting that the methodology of one other national program held in high regard by many Aboriginal people—the National Trachoma and Eye Health Program—was based on a similar principle: it provided immediate access to glasses for improved vision and field availability of corrective surgery.

At the conclusion of data collection in each community, the field team ensured immediate feedback to the communities about findings through meetings with the community council, general community members and health staff.

Findings

Some of the survey findings from the larger communities are as follows:

Number of houses surveyed	90
'Housed' population	743
Population per house	8.3
Bedrooms per house	2.1
Cold water	60 per cent
Hot water	45 per cent
Waste disposal facilities	45 per cent
Electricity	65 per cent
Number of yards with recent fires	1.6 per house

Since half the population were not housed, the occupancy figures are likely substantially to underestimate crowding and the demand on services for each house and living area. Interestingly, the degree of crowding did not correlate at all with size of house and it is clear that building bigger houses alone is unlikely to reduce crowding. In terms of the service provided by the living area, there was often a negative interaction. For example, even if a house had an effective hot water outlet, contamination by sewerage may have prohibited the effective use of that hot water.

Recommendations

Having described the current environmental inadequacies on the lands, the review team developed a list of nine healthy living practices that were considered essential for well-being in remote areas and were influenced by environmental conditions. These were placed in order of their likely importance in improving health status, as follows:

1. Washing people
2. Washing clothes/bedding
3. Waste removal
4. Nutrition
5. Reduction in crowding
6. Separation of dogs and children
7. Dust control
8. Temperature control
9. Reduction in trauma

The majority of these proposals relate to washing and cleaning of the living unit, that is to the group of people, their clothes, bedding and immediate living environment. For each of the nine areas, the review team attempted to define the likely health benefits for Anangu. This was done by examining current medical and public health knowledge and documenting the specific disease processes that might be reduced or prevented by improving a particular aspect of the environment. For example, effective removal of waste from living areas was likely to reduce acute and chronic diarrhoeal disease, skin infection, hepatitis and polio-like infections. Subsequently, the team developed a range of detailed recommendations about the design, installation and maintenance of the 'health hardware' necessary to carry out these healthy living practices. (Health hardware is a term first popularised for Aboriginal health by Professor Fred Hollows of the Prince of Wales Hospital, Sydney, to refer to the infrastructure and equipment, either small or large, that is necessary for basic healthy living.) With regard to waste disposal, it was considered particularly important to build 'fail-safe' mechanisms into design structures to allow for inevitable service failures. The review team recognised that for each healthy living practice a threshold level of improvement must probably be reached before any health benefit can be achieved. For example, washing children twice a week may provide no health benefit at all; benefits may occur only when children are bathed daily.

The findings of the survey supported experience elsewhere in Aboriginal Australia where communal washing and ablution blocks have been a failure. On many Aboriginal settlements, these structures remain standing as a monument to poor planning and design in which little thought has been given to responsibility for supervision and maintenance or to predicted patterns of use. The survey recommended that if communal washing and ablution facilities are built, they should be linked physically and in terms of responsibility to existing community structures. For example, if a new craft room is to be built in a community, then a toilet and washing block could be included in the design structure and physically attached to the building. The craft room committee could then take responsibility for supervision, cleaning and maintenance. For the last three years, a communal facility with washing machines has successfully operated at Kaltjiti community in the

Pitjantjatjara lands. This facility is physically attached to the clinic, which is responsible for its maintenance and administration.

Improved nutrition obviously involves a large number of factors, which are discussed in detail by Lindsey Harrison in chapter 4 of this volume. There are, however, a number of hardware factors involved, including the structure, organisation and management of stores; the internal structure and storage facilities of houses; and the development of horticultural activities in the living area.

Reduction in crowding is likely to reduce any disease that is spread by infected body surface secretions. In particular, crowding has been shown elsewhere in the world to be a major determinant in the prevalence of respiratory infection. Design strategies to reduce crowding may well involve the yard area rather than the house itself, since most living occurs outside the houses.

Dogs carry and transmit large numbers of bacteria and parasites. Reducing contact between dogs and children may reduce skin infection, diarrhoeal disease and gut parasitic infections. Improved dust control may reduce incidence or severity of respiratory disease, ocular disease and skin infection.

The major health benefit of temperature control in the living area is likely to be during cold periods, when the crowding of sleeping facilities should be reduced and mothers should be encouraged to wash young children. Access to cool areas during hot periods is important to reduce dehydration in sick children.

Strategies for reducing environmental trauma cover a broad range of activities, including appropriate selection of building materials (for example, excluding glass windows), control of hard waste and rubbish collection, and dump management.

The importance of management

A major thrust of the findings of the UPK project is the importance of management in the maintenance of public health. Public health is highly dependent on the planning, design, funding, installation, maintenance and use of essential services and community utilities. All these functions are dependent on management, both at the local and government/external agency level. This principle is applicable to Aboriginal communities throughout Australia. Management structures at both local and government level should see as their primary function the maintenance of the well-being of their community. At the local level, this clearly necessitates Aboriginal people having a real say in the processes involved in establishing and providing essential services (a fundamental principle of the new public health). There are immediate and obvious consequences whenever local management fails in communities. Generators, water systems, waste disposal and other utilities all need to be designed, installed and maintained. Once these services break down they cause an immediate threat to public health in the community. Appropriate management processes at the local level will allow real (and informed) Aboriginal decision making to occur. This will involve both the setting of priorities and the development of aims and objectives for all programs.

Since many Aboriginal communities have only a relatively small number of members, the physical and human resources to manage essential services are often inadequate. In areas where there is natural affinity between communities, regional sharing of personnel and equipment is essential if adequate services are to be provided in those communities in the future.

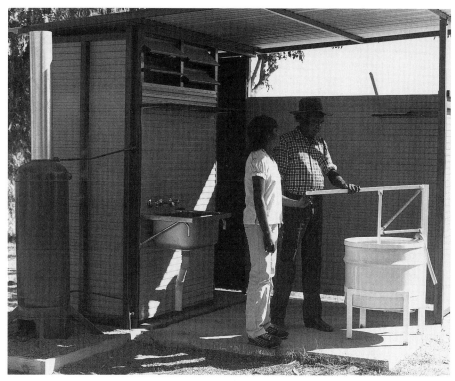

Figure 8.2 *This ablution facility was designed by the Centre for Appropriate Technology, Alice Springs, in response to the need for functional combined shower and laundry facilities in remote communities. Of simple design and sound construction, it is easily installed and maintained, and its uncomplicated drainage system allows blockages to be cleared easily. (Centre for Appropriate Technology, Alice Springs, Northern Territory)*

Health hardware

The focus of improving environmental health in rural communities should be the provision of health hardware rather than the provision of 'housing' per se. However any discussion of health hardware must involve housing program management. At the present time, housing programs are a priority of the Aboriginal and Torres Strait Islander Commission (ATSIC) and government at all levels. However, even conservative estimates of predicted housing costs constitute a major obstacle to planning for housing in Aboriginal communities. The UPK review estimated the cost of housing needed for Aboriginal people on AP lands over the period 1986–91. Despite a number of assumptions that were likely to cause costs to be underestimated, a figure of approximately $15 million over five years was deduced. The Aboriginal Development Commission (1988) estimates the current cost of backlog housing for Aborigines throughout Australia to be in the region of $1350 million dollars.

The pitfalls of inappropriate design

Access to effective washing facilities is essential for healthy living. As the following scenario indicates (see diagram A), bad design and faulty construction may lead to a chain of events that puts a washing and toilet area out of action and turns health hardware into a health hazard.

Diagram A

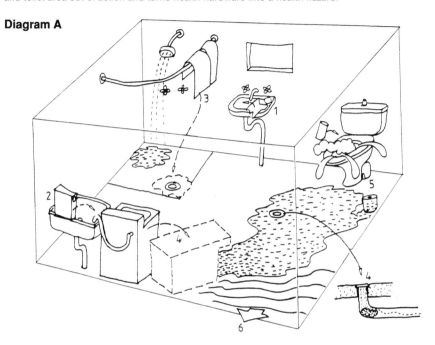

1. A new cake of soap is opened over the basin, the wrapper falls into the basin, gets wet and blocks the waste pipe trap.
2. A box of laundry powder is used for a load of washing. There is no high shelf, so the box is kept on a small ledge between the laundry tub and wall. The vibration from the machine knocks the box into the laundry tub. During the spin cycle, water softens the packet and soaks the soap powder. Pieces of wet cardboard and chunks of detergent disperse throughout the tub and enter the tub waste pipe. It is now difficult to wash a young child in the tub. Further loads of washing, with soap suds and lint, increase the blockage of the waste pipe.
3. In the shower, two nappies have been left to dry on a curtain rail near the small window. They fall to the ground and block the shower waste. The grading of the floor to the shower waste was set at the wrong angle and there is always a pool of water near the corner of the shower.
4. The washing machine pump motor fails. Dirty wash water can be released only by tipping the machine on its side. Water floods the floor but the floor waste cannot cope with the quantity of water. When the floor waste was installed, a small plug of concrete accidentally went down the open pipe. Even without additional blockage, the floor waste can release only a trickle of water.
5. A person coming to use the toilet finds that the roll of toilet paper has been soaked by washing machine water, uses an old piece of rag as toilet paper and flushes the toilet. Not long after, a young child flushes a soft drink can down the toilet. It seems to disappear. The next toilet user finds the toilet water-level backing up and flooding the room. Attempts to clean up the flooding are made difficult because of the faulty floor waste pipe.
6. Where does the water go if the blockages are not fixed?

There are a number of design improvements that can lessen the chances of breakdown in the use of the facilities described here. Checks during construction will ensure that installations will operate as intended. An obvious additional requirement is that maintenance of facilities must be rendered as easy as possible because of difficulties with obtaining the services of experienced tradespeople. Some points to be considered for minimising the foregoing chain of problems are given below (see diagram B).

Diagram B

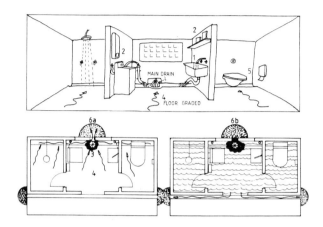

1. A deep laundry tub is used instead of a basin, not for the washing machine but for general purposes, including washing children. There is no connection between the tub and the in-slab drain, so any rubbish will clear the tub and go out to the main drain sieve.

2. Ideally, there should be a soap dispenser to avoid overuse of powder and clogging by waste detergent boxes. In any case, the washing machine should not have a waste tub, but rather a waste pipe that simply directs waste water to the main drain. Any lint or other debris will find its way to the main drain sieve. There should be a shelf above the washing machine, out of reach of children, but if the detergent box still falls onto the floor, it too will work itself towards the main drain sieve.

3. Assume that the two nappies fall in the shower area, but there is no shower waste as such to block. Two things may occur. First, the shower waste water flows around the nappies to the main drain sleeve or the nappies are washed down the main drain to the main drain sieve *outside* the shower area.

4. The floor, being graded steeply in one direction, can cope with this volume of water. The waste sieve can filter out any items likely to block the drain. The main floor waste should have a 100 millimetre pipe attached to it, which means that during construction you can physically check with your hand that no concrete has been dropped down the drain, thereby avoiding later obstruction of the water flow. The larger pipe diameter also makes it easier to unblock the drain.

5. By grading the floor down to the main drain in the toilet area and by separating the other wet areas from the toilet, there should be less water on the floor. It is preferable to install toilet tissue dispensers to reduce the volume of paper used in the toilet. Dry system toilets (pit toilets) provide an essential back up for failed flush toilets, as well as an important 'waste bin' method for dealing with disposable nappies and rags. The main problem area for blockages of toilets occurs between the toilet trap and entry to the septic tank. By using a 150 millimetre pipe to connect these (instead of the standard 100 millimetre pipe), there is a slightly better chance that blockages will be reduced. By positioning the main drain to the rear of the toilet area, it is possible to hose out the area for simple cleaning.

6. (a) If the main drain sieve becomes completely blocked, waste water flows through a hole in the main drain to a gravel sump. (b) A small dish drain leading to two more gravel sumps is a further precaution to prevent severe surface flooding.

Paul Pholeros, Consultant to Nganampa Health Council, Alice Springs, Northern Territory

However, inadequate funding is only one reason for the lack of housing for Aboriginal people. A number of other factors were identified in the UPK review:

1. Poor administration of funding to communities. This frequently involves inappropriate delays in the provision of funds, which leads inevitably to the loss of contractors and rising costs.
2. Inappropriate design structures. This involves both the lack of appropriate professional input as well as the essential consultation with and input by Aboriginal people in the communities to be serviced. Such consultation takes considerable time and expertise is acquired over years rather than days (Memmott 1988).
3. Inadequate and unprofessional documentation of design and building programs.
4. The selection of contractors on the basis of lowest tender price rather than background experience or reputation. In remote Australia, the building of a house may be far more dependent on whether a contractor has a truck that will not break down than on any more sophisticated factors.
5. Lack of appropriate contract structure and arrangements.
6. Lack of building supervision in remote areas
7. Lack of consideration of the standard and provision of mains services.
8. Inadequate funding and planning attention to the yard area and in particular inadequate horticultural input into the living space design.

Probably the most important factor in the long-term failure of housing programs is the lack of funding for or planning of maintenance. In fact, maintenance is a central issue in environmental health. There are numerous examples of the failure to plan adequately for housing programs. D'Abbs (1989 p. 253) provides an excellent example from the Northern Territory.

Myatt and Murringung are two town camps a few kilometres outside Timber Creek. In the past few months, six new houses have been built under a joint program involving the Commonwealth's Aboriginal Development Commission and the NT Department of Lands and Housing. Four of the houses are at Myatt, the other two at Murringung. When I visited the camps in February the builders had just completed their work, and the new houses were awaiting painters and electricians. Although none of the houses had been officially handed over, at least one family had already begun to move in, and I imagine since then the process has continued. Each house has its own private shower and flush toilet, connected to a septic tank and drain.

There is just one problem. Neither town camp has a mains water supply. Until now the 60 or so residents have hauled water up from a nearby creek. The PAWA has sunk bores to serve each camp, and stated its intention to equip them and reticulate water to the camps in the near future. In the meantime, six new houses are about to become occupied by families who will have received little or no training in the use and maintenance of the new toilet facilities; should they try to use the toilets, there is no water with which to flush them, and should they damage them, there is no budgetary provision for their repair and maintenance. The environmental health implications are, I think, fairly obvious.

A major obstacle to the provision of adequate health hardware is that no comprehensive plan for environmental health exists at the policy or budgetary allocation level in government departments. In most communities, there are multiple service agencies involved in essential services and housing. These include ATSIC and other Commonwealth government departments, various state agencies, and local and municipal councils. While there are sometimes specific contract arrangements for the maintenance of community facilities such as generators and power supply, no government agency accepts policy and funding responsibility for maintenance in and around Aboriginal houses. This situation leads to rapid breakdown of health hardware within houses. Most Aboriginal people in remote communities do not have the financial resources or access to tradespeople which would allow them proper maintenance services to their houses. Even minor maintenance is rarely possible, since the people invariably lack both the equipment and the skills to make such repairs. In addition, there are multiple cultural factors that mitigate against maintenance of houses by residents—for example, obligations to accommodate the extended family (Memmott 1988).

The current marginalised position of environmental health in government policy is recognised by many people in the field (D'Abbs 1989; NHC 1987*a*). Policy (and budgetary allocation) for maintenance of Aboriginal health hardware must be developed and must include commitment of 'on-going maintenance' funding in the initial budgetary allocation.

The impoverished state of remote Aborigines is well documented. Despite this, government organisations continue to argue that Aboriginal people should pay for maintenance of their homes. It is clearly impossible for rent from communities to provide adequate funding for maintenance of houses. In the UPK review, the team has recommended a division of maintenance work and expenditure according to its priorities for improving health, as follows (Paul Pholeros, NHC, pers. comm.):

1. Essential maintenance. This would include immediate hazards to safety and health, reduce future maintenance by systematic replacement policy and enable washing and waste removal. It is proposed that this component of maintenance be funded directly by government agencies.
2. Secondary maintenance. This would include reducing the risk of trauma, control of temperature and dust, and providing some separation of children and dogs. Funding for this maintenance would be provided by communities either through rent payments, Community Development and Employment Program funds or other community resources.

Remote communities need to have access to the appropriate tradespeople for the maintenance of health hardware, particularly plumbers and electricians. These positions need to be adequately funded on a long-term basis. Although there are considerable arguments in favour of training Aboriginal people for these jobs, it is inconceivable in the near future that there will be sufficient trained Aborigines to fill the need.

At the local level, Aboriginal people need to be able to identify health hardware problems in their houses and then notify the community council, which should be appropriately resourced to respond to their needs. In some Pitjantjatjara communities, a system with a 'house failure noticeboard' is being developed.

Household members simply put a cross in an appropriate square on a grid to indicate a particular system failure in the house and this serves as notification to the community council. An additional factor at the local level is the need for stores to stock appropriate house cleaning utensils and equipment.

Four prerequisites are necessary for people to be able to make the best use of their houses for healthy living (Stefan Rainow, NHC, pers. comm.):

1. Suitable design
2. Adequate maintenance system
3. Adequate access to supply of household hardware
4. Sufficient information and training to make the best use of the house

While the last of these four points is often emphasised and, in several places in remote Australia, homemakers projects have been implemented, these are of no value unless the first three components are in place.

Aboriginal Public Health Improvement Program

This program was initiated by the Commonwealth government in 1981 as a response to several reports about Aboriginal health status. Broadly the project aimed to fund capital works for water, sewerage disposal and associated power supply systems. A total of 50 million dollars was to be allocated over a five-year period, commencing in 1981. In the initial years, $8 million dollars was allocated to 100 projects in 58 communities.

In 1982, an appraisal of the effectiveness of the campaign was conducted by the Department of Aboriginal Affairs (DAA 1982). The review document highlights both the problems of the program and the fact that many major problem areas identified at that time still remain to be addressed by government policy. While the program was primarily aimed at improving public health, there was clearly insufficient examination of all the factors necessary to maintain health hardware in communities other than large capital works projects. The report states that the capital works projects were often not coordinated with housing programs or with other mains service projects. There are occasional references to maintenance in the document, but the issues of policy, funding and mechanisms for maintenance in Aboriginal houses is not addressed.

In regard to funding of maintenance, the report states that 'in the longer term communities should be required to contribute more directly to the cost of operation and maintenance of services' (DAA 1982, p. 9). This ignores the fact that remote Aboriginal communities are entrenched in poverty and there is no possible way that internal community funds could ever pay for adequate maintenance services.

The report also demonstrates another feature of government response to problems of environmental health: the attribution of most problems to a lack of education on the part of Aboriginal people. It is then assumed that implementing 'community health education' projects will somehow fix environmental health. In a masterful understatement, the report says: 'effective and sustained health education programs must also be mounted to ensure that toilet facilities are used, and kept clean, by all members of the community. Such a task is clearly made easier by adequate housing' (DAA 1982, p. 32).

Waste management in remote communities

Management of liquid and solid wastes in remote communities raises considerable problems. Inappropriate use or design of hardware associated with waste collection or disposal leads to difficulties that range from visual degradation of community space to a continuing source of microbial contamination. Some examples are considered below, each involving a different technology.

Two-hundred litre drums

In most remote communities, old 200-litre drums are used as the principal method of waste storage between the domestic living space and the waste removal system. Contrary to visual impressions, most living spaces are kept relatively free of organic wastes. Ground surfaces where people gather or sit are usually swept with branches or raked with leaf rakes. Resulting mounds of rubbish and topsoil or sand are transferred to the 200-litre drum or left positioned around the perimeter of the living space. Objectionable material is often removed before the raking process and placed in the drum, which generally does not have a lid and is easily ransacked by the camp dogs. The drum is difficult to lift or reposition in the living space. Occasionally, drums are burned out or used as incinerators. This leaves a fine ash deposit, which settles to the bottom of the drum and becomes quite heavy if mixed with rain water. The containers are also heavier than urban rubbish containers because of the large amount of soil raked up with the rubbish and placed in the drum. Trailers used by councils to collect rubbish are generally far too high to lift and tip 200-litre containers; consequently there is a large disincentive to collect rubbish.

It is obvious that large steel drums are far from ideal for waste storage as commonly used. Relatively light, cheap and robust metallic or plastic rubbish containers offer a more manageable alternative.

Trench and fill method

The most common method of treating solid waste in remote communities is the trench and fill method. In general, a series of trenches each 20 metres long, 3 metres deep, 3 metres wide and 20 metres apart are dug by a bulldozer. The bulldozer driver is usually a contractor who is not involved in the regular collection of rubbish. Rubbish trailers or trucks are reversed into the pit to dump their rubbish. Rubbish should be back-filled regularly, although most communities do not have a bulldozer or other appliance to do this. Another weakness of this option is that Aboriginal people often have an aversion to reversing vehicles. This is because many remote communities have plenty of open space and minimal use of reverse gears is required. Another reason may be that vehicles are often in poor mechanical condition, with poor brakes and no mirrors on tractors. Accordingly, it is easy to understand why the trenches are not used as designed. Under these conditions, it is not desirable to back into or up to a trench. In many cases, the distance between trenches precludes turning and backing up. There are a number of examples of rubbish trailers falling into the pits when reversing up to them. Unfortunately, the majority of available trailers and tip trucks have a rear-tipping action and are therefore not satisfactory in this application. Under such circumstances, and even when rubbish is collected in a town, it often does not find its way into the trench, or if it does, it can be at the expense of the trailer used to collect it.

A range of lightweight collection appliances and side-tip trailers may well provide a greater incentive to effect the lifestyle changes necessary to maintain new waste management strategies.

New techniques

New techniques for controlling waste in remote communities are the subject of research at the Centre for Appropriate Technology in Alice Springs. One promising development is contrary to the conventional dogma that it is essential to pick up all rubbish. This relates to light rubbish blown around settlements by the wind. Research indicates that this type of rubbish may be controlled by the selective placement of wire-mesh fences.

Fence lines in remote communities often show signs of dune formation. It is the build-up of wind-blown rubbish that is largely responsible for initiating this phenomenon, by trapping soil against the fence. After the initial deposition of soil/rubbish, a light rainfall will trigger the germination of wind-blown seeds. This growth stabilises the soil, which in turn enables more soil and rubbish to be trapped, thus increasing the rate of deposition. As the dune becomes higher, the topsoil is able to retain waste for longer periods of time, thus allowing the establishment of shrubs and bushes.

If fences are built to follow the contours of the land without spanning too great a distance, it is possible to establish numerous small water traps that enable larger trees to develop. The end result is an effective wind-break that needs absolutely no maintenance and continues to trap and slow surface run-off, wind-blown soil and rubbish.

If fences around living spaces are arranged to allow many access points for pedestrian traffic but to restrict vehicular access, the whole amenity of the living space is improved. The definition of the living space by a fence also establishes a clear demarcation of responsibilities for rubbish collection between individuals and council authorities.

Conclusion

Waste management poses as many problems for remote communities as it does for urban dwellers. A great deal of effort is needed to adapt technological methods to local needs and practices. Some procedures, such as the use of large steel drums for waste storage, create more problems than light weight cheap robust alternatives. Likewise, many communities find it difficult to effectively use the trench-and-fill method of waste disposal. Again, modifications to the rubbish transport system would assist in achieving better management. Appropriately sited wire mesh fences offer an imaginative solution to one aspect of rubbish pollution.

Successful adoption of more effective methods will only occur if the communities become convinced that better solutions are available. Accordingly, the promotion of alternatives remains an important task, requiring an understanding of established values and practices relating to waste management.

Bruce Walker, Centre for Appropriate Technology, Alice Springs, Northern Territory

Components of a health service delivery system

Many of the programs delivered by Aboriginal health services have particular public health significance. Before reviewing these activities, it is important to highlight differences between health service delivery in urban and remote areas. This is especially relevant when comparing the activities of different community-controlled Aboriginal health services as well as those of state-run services. Although there are similarities in the health needs of Aborigines in different parts of Australia, there are also marked differences in illness profiles, environmental resources and social setting. Urban Aboriginal children appear to have less frequent and less severe infective illness patterns. Even in many country towns, the incidence of pneumonia and severe gastroenteritis is less than that seen in remote Australia. However, alcoholism, increasing drug abuse, cardiovascular disease and other problems of urban living create different service requirements for Aboriginal health services in the city. The urban Aboriginal population is often more dispersed and those employed spend their time in a number of different locations. In these circumstances, community organisation is often more difficult than in remote areas. A number of primary clinical care services in cities may occasionally serve some of the Aboriginal population. In addition, Aboriginal people from country areas often visit cities for short periods. All these factors mean that traditional public health activities such as immunisation, screening programs, population registers and population-based activities in general are often more difficult to conduct for the urban health services. As a result such programs often need to be more flexible for urban groups. Despite these difficulties, urban health services are increasingly moving towards a program and public health approach to service delivery. The Aboriginal Medical Service (AMS) at Redfern in Sydney now has a full-time public health coordinator. The service conducts a variety of programs, covering such areas as infant care, methadone maintenance, child sexual assault and HIV infection (with two field workers). In addition, in response to a widely felt need in the community, the Redfern AMS has for some time managed a hostel for elderly Aboriginal people, which includes two respite care beds. The AMS also maintains a register of children aged less than five years, but not for other age groups.

The Central Australian Aboriginal Congress (CAAC) has a particularly complex population to serve. In addition to the Aboriginal people in the town of Alice Springs, a large number of Aborigines live in fringe camps and there is also a constant population of visitors from other communities. The CAAC runs a 'town camp' mobile health program and has had a welfare section operating for several years. In addition, this organisation has been prominent in public health activity on alcohol and AIDS in central Australia. The establishment of population registers and the identification of particular groups at risk are more difficult in such an area than they are in individual smaller remote communities.

Standard treatment regimens (STR)

Standard treatment protocols have been developed in several third world countries as important tools for the delivery of primary health care, initially as a response to the gross lack of doctors (Biddulph 1989). These countries typically have high mortality rates from a small number of infective illnesses which are readily treatable, usually with a single drug that can be administered by a task-trained health worker. Paediatric illness, in particular, follows a pattern that lends itself to the application of STRs. In remote Australia, there is an increasing trend to develop STRs, generally led by community-controlled health services that employ doctors and have been able to focus on improving primary clinical care services.

Some important issues regarding STRs are the following:

1. They need to be based on the best available data. This is often difficult, since it often involves a knowledge of medical and scientific literature relevant to the developing world as well as of studies done in developed countries. Because people working in Aboriginal health services often have little time and few resources, the development of STRs may be slow. In addition, STRs must be updated regularly as new information becomes available about Aboriginal health and from the wider medical literature.
2. Standard treatment protocols provide a key foundation for training both doctors, nurses and health workers, in regions where nursing staff and health workers provide some or all of the clinical care. For certain conditions, it is possible to construct a treatment regime that represents the optimal treatment, whether administered by doctors, nurses or health workers. The clinical prediction of pneumonia in areas without x-ray facilities provides an illustration of

this principle. There is now good evidence that the best predictor of pneumonia (and hence the need for antibiotic therapy) in young children is the presence of fast breathing, and that chest indrawing is the best predictor of severe pneumonia (Shann et al. 1984; Cherian et al. 1988). This means that listening to lung sounds through a stethoscope does not help diagnosis, whoever uses the instrument. Thus there is no reason to teach the use of a stethoscope to manage this disorder. In addition, the clinical examination will be the same, whoever is the clinical care giver. Obviously, not all conditions will fit such a stereotyped picture and there need to be limits to the clinical skills required of health workers and nurses, coupled with an appropriate upward referral strategy.

3. In areas of high staff turnover (as is the case in most remote areas), STRs provide a mechanism for continuity of care and practice, as well as a focus for orientation and education of new medical staff. Knowledge gained by previous staff is not lost and there is continuity of practice and policy for the health workers when new non-Aboriginal staff are employed in the service.

4. Effective treatment of infectious disease is particularly important for children. Malnutrition predisposes to infective illness, but it is also true that repeated infections exacerbate growth failure (Rowland et al. 1988). Therefore early and aggressive treatment is important in interrupting this cycle. In addition, such treatment is aimed at shortening the length and reducing the severity of illness, thereby avoiding hospitalisation. STRs therefore provide a significant public health strategy to reduce hospitalisation, particularly of young children.

Population register

The maintenance of a register of the local population is a traditional cornerstone of public health activities. As previously outlined, such registers are difficult to establish in some populations, but they have been developed and maintained in several areas, including an urban centre in Adelaide, the Nganampa Health Council region of the Pitjantjatjara homelands and in the Kimberleys. A population register is best organised as an age/sex register, which in smaller communities can easily be managed as a card file system; in some health services, computer data base programs are being developed. The register is particularly helpful for the identification of at risk groups in the population or of those who require special follow-up or regular monitoring: for example, patients with chronic renal disease, rheumatic heart disease or those requiring ocular or ear surgery. It also facilitates community screening programs.

Screening programs

Screening programs provide a number of functions for a health service, including the following:

1. A profile of illness patterns in the community for diseases that can be analysed appropriately by cross-sectional surveys. This will allow the health service not only to detect people who will benefit from treatment, but also to define the prevalence of conditions such as trachoma, poor vision, ear disease or diabetes. This information can assist the health service to determine program priorities

and plan the optimal use of resources, and also provide a tool for health education and health promotion activities in the community.

2. A mechanism whereby health workers can have a major role in a program rather than the limited role often provided in the clinic setting.

3. A method for detecting previously unrecognised and potentially correctable morbidity in the community: for example, conditions such as rheumatic valve disease, poor vision and deafness.

A screening program must include a mechanism for appropriately managing those individuals who are identified as having a problem that requires intervention.

Immunisation programs

Immunisation is a cornerstone of public health activities anywhere in the world. While the immunisation status of Aboriginal children has varied considerably between regions, a common problem has been poor documentation. A national immunisation status survey, conducted by the Department of Community Medicine at the University of Sydney, included information from 25 medical practitioners working in 15 Aboriginal medical services, predominantly in Queensland and South Australia (University of Sydney 1988). The study demonstrated that immunisation status overall was worse for Aboriginal than for non-Aboriginal children. In general, immunisation status is better in remote areas than urban centres.

Medical services in general are now applying more effort to the documentation and implementation of immunisation programs. A paediatric age/sex register facilitates opportunistic immunisation when children present to clinics for other reasons.

Improved systems for immunisation will be necessary with the inevitable availability of new vaccines for infectious diseases in children. *Haemophilus influenzae* vaccines that are immunogenic in young children have now been developed and tested overseas. There appear to be considerable differences in the immune response and vaccine efficacy in different populations (Ward et al. 1988; Dawn et al. 1988). There are no data examining these issues in Aboriginal children and clearly further research is needed. However, effective vaccines may provide a major tool to combat the high incidence of invasive *Haemophilus influenzae* disease (Hanna unpub.). It is likely that infection with *Streptococcus pneumoniae* is at least as common as *Haemophilus influenzae*. In developed countries, the indications for use of the current pneumococcal vaccine in adult populations remain uncertain. Only one randomised, controlled trial in young children demonstrates the vaccine's efficacy (Riley et al. 1986) in protecting against death. There are no published data, however, to indicate that the vaccine will lower morbidity or attack rates in children. Since the mortality rates from pneumonia in Aboriginal children are less than those from developing countries, it may be that if the vaccine only protects against death, it will be of limited value. Current research work on developing pneumococcal vaccines that are more immunogenic in young children will undoubtedly increase the attractiveness of such vaccines for use in Australian Aboriginal children. Rota virus vaccine studies are proceeding overseas and it is likely that these may be valuable in particular areas in Australia (Kapikian et al. 1989).

Hepatitis B infection

The availability of a safe and effective vaccine to prevent hepatitis B infection has required that a plan for its use in Aboriginal Australia be developed. In 1987, the Commonwealth government committed funds for the vaccination of all infants in high carriage rate ethnic groups. Specific funds have been targeted for programs in the Aboriginal community. Despite this the implementation of programs has been erratic and slow to develop. Among the reasons for these difficulties have been the following:

1. Although the prevalence of hepatitis B infection is high, the exact consequences of hepatitis B infection for Aborigines have not been defined. The number of individuals who develop primary liver cancer or severe chronic liver disease will always be relatively small. This has led to conflict among field staff about the importance of the vaccine.
2. Hepatitis B infection and AIDS have both been prominent issues in Aboriginal health care during the same time period. Because of some similarities in transmission, the diseases have often been dealt with by the same committee, either at government or local level. As a result, there appears to be some confusion about the relative seriousness of infection with hepatitis B virus compared to HIV, both among some field staff as well as among the Aboriginal community. (NSW Department of Health 1990).
3. In some states, there has been disagreement about how funds for hepatitis B programs should be spent. Some groups have argued for expenditure on education programs, the employment of field workers and the organisation of meetings and conferences. While such initiatives are clearly necessary to inform the Aboriginal population about the benefits of vaccination, the technical aspects of vaccine delivery have sometimes been neglected.
4. Current data suggest that most infection is acquired within the first few years of life (Campbell et al. 1989); however, there remains debate about which age group in the population should be vaccinated in a national program. In addition, the cost benefit ratio and logistic problems associated with pre-vaccination serological testing are uncertain. In considering the benefits to an individual, it may be important to know about hepatitis B antigen or antibody status before vaccination is given. Nevertheless, the public health priority is clearly to vaccinate those most at risk in the population and in particular neonates, so that in the longer term the disease will no longer pose a significant threat.

Sexually transmitted diseases (STD)

All Aboriginal health service delivery systems have seen STD as an important area of work. The traditional public health strategy of contact tracing is particularly difficult in Aboriginal communities. Despite this, several health services continue to explore ways to improve contact tracing, particularly given the major role played by Aboriginal health workers in STD management. Education programs have tended to focus on encouragement of early treatment for symptoms as well as promoting condom use. As has been experienced elsewhere, increased use of condoms because of AIDS education programs may well have a secondary benefit of reduction of other sexually transmitted diseases.

In remote communities, a number of health services continue to screen groups in the population for syphilis. Hart (1982) has studied the effect of repeated annual screening and follow-up treatment in four rural Aboriginal communities in Western Australia. Hart's study demonstrated that syphilis transmission could essentially be eliminated, provided that at least 90 per cent of the population was screened and treated annually for at least three years and that similar programs were conducted in adjacent communities. However, this required major resource and staff commitments. If the intensive level of activity was not maintained then syphilis transmission soon returned to its original level. Health services are now generally more selective in their screening strategies for syphilis. Nganampa Health Council (NHC) has had an active syphilis screening program for some time (NHC 1987b). At present NHC is concentrating on giving people an STD health education package whenever any procedures are performed.

HIV infection

There are no comprehensive data regarding the prevalence of HIV infection amongst Aboriginal people. However, evidence suggests that the absolute numbers of Aboriginal people currently affected are small (see Thomson, chapter 2 in this volume). Despite this, Aboriginal health organisations have been at the forefront of educational and preventative program activities. In some regions, the community interest generated by this issue has been unprecedented in comparison with other public health issues (Moodie 1989b).

Aborigines may be at particular risk from HIV infection for a number of reasons which include:

1. frequent and extensive travel of Aboriginal people between different communities;
2. the high incidence of sexually transmitted diseases and, in some regions, of ulcerative disease such as donovanosis;
3. the over-representation of Aboriginal people in prisons;
4. the high alcohol and substance abuse, which mitigate against safe sexual practices;
5. increasing problems with intravenous drug abuse amongst urban Aboriginal groups;
6. the possibility of virus transmission during ceremonial activities.

In New South Wales, staff of the Aboriginal Medical Service in Redfern cooperated with the AIDS Unit in the Department of Health to conduct a number of AIDS education workshops in 1987–88, as well as other health education activities. The same group has been conducting a workshop with other Aboriginal groups and this has allowed refinement and adaptation of the process in response to the earlier activities. The workshops have been attended by health workers and Aboriginal people involved in the administration of the Aboriginal health services. In addition the two HIV field workers of the AMS (Redfern) have been working especially with inner-city Aboriginal youth, as well as targeting intravenous drug users in the population. This is an extremely difficult and complex area of work, and for it to have any success, Aboriginal health workers must be involved at the front line.

Figure 8.3 *A booklet intended to inform Aboriginal people about AIDS and its prevention. (Aboriginal Health Unit, NSW Department of Health, Sydney)*

Health services in the Kimberley region of Western Australia have been extremely active in AIDS education activities. This has included HIV testing programs, education workshops, and the development of audiovisual tools such as videos and posters to promote condom use and safe sexual practices.

Central Australia has been the site of intensive activity in AIDS education and health promotion around the issue of HIV infection. Moodie et al. (unpub.) have highlighted the cooperation between government and community-controlled health services during this campaign. Strategies involved in the initial education programs included:

1. development of guidelines for a standard AIDS education talk;
2. education sessions for Aboriginal organisations;
3. in-service educational talks for key Aboriginal staff and community members in town camps;
4. condom distribution campaigns and the development of posters and stickers promoting the use of condoms;
5. radio sessions and advertisements related to AIDS issues.

A number of other activities have been conducted by various Aboriginal health services in central Australia together with the Healthy Aboriginal Life Team funded by the Department of Aboriginal Affairs. This team has developed the idea of presenting AIDS information using traditional desert painting symbolism, thus allowing Aboriginal people to adapt the skills they already possess to this new public health issue.

The evaluation of AIDS education and health promotion activities remains extremely difficult. It is impossible to evaluate factors such as a reduction in HIV prevalence. It may be possible to evaluate the reduction of non-AIDS STD prevalence using some indirect measures. However, since baseline prevalence data are so difficult to obtain, it is doubtful that this will provide a valuable evaluation tool in the future. Moodie et al. (unpub.) have highlighted the need to evaluate process as well as outcome. This has been attempted in the central Australian project in a preliminary fashion. In that area, an AIDS questionnaire was administered to 63 Aboriginal people between three and six months after the initial phase of the education campaign. Some important findings of that questionnaire were that:

1. AIDS and condom use were being widely discussed at the family and community levels;
2. most people knew about the use of condoms and where to obtain them;
3. condom use still remains infrequent and irregular;
4. serious gaps in knowledge about HIV transmission existed within the population;
5. there was significant confusion about how individuals or the community would react to the knowledge of an HIV-positive community member.

Despite the controversy generated in the white community about population screening for HIV infection, many Aboriginal communities have opted for community-wide screening, especially for monitoring disease. This process should provide reliable data about infection prevalence and groups at risk in the community. However, Stevens (1989) and others have raised the problem of obtaining informed consent among community groups. In some communities, it appears that where screening has been performed and no sero-positive individuals identified, communities have then felt that they are not significantly at risk of HIV infection and so there may be less impetus for behaviour change than before the screening.

An extremely difficult issue is the question of HIV infection being spread during ceremonial activities. In many parts of remote Australia, Aboriginal men have shown significant concern about possible spread of disease during ceremonies. These issues can only be addressed in an Aboriginal forum if appropriate information about HIV infection is given by health professionals.

Eye health

It is appropriate to discuss eye health by reviewing the National Trachoma and Eye Health Program (NTEHP) conducted in the late 1970s (RACO 1980). This project was a landmark in Aboriginal health care and yielded practical conclusions extending beyond eye health which are central to public health action. Trachoma has been endemic in Aboriginal society since at least the eighteenth century. In the 1940s, Father Frank Flynn examined large numbers of Aboriginal people and documented a high prevalence of the disease. In the 1950s, Professor Ida Mann conducted surveys in Western Australia demonstrating a high prevalence of both trachoma and blindness. These two studies provided valuable background information, but the NTEHP provided a comprehensive analysis of ocular disease among Aboriginal people on a national basis. The program examined more than 100 000 individuals, including more than 60 000 Aborigines throughout Australia.

The NTEHP aimed to describe the epidemiology of trachoma and ocular disease among Aboriginal people across the country, and also to define the prevalence of trachoma in all its stages, as well as of other ocular diseases and blindness. It defined the differences in prevalence between age groups, geographical zones and according to differences in environmental living conditions.

The screening programs contained a number of key elements that provide a model for future programs in Aboriginal Australia. From the outset, Aboriginal people were actively involved in the planning, administration and delivery of the program. Extensive consultation was undertaken throughout the program, with extensive use of Aboriginal liaison officers, local Aboriginal people and health workers. In fact, field staff for the program often included Aboriginal political activists with long-standing involvement in community affairs and politics. This greatly assisted the program to act as a focal point for community development activities, although it generated some hostility from non-Aboriginal politicians and bureaucrats, particularly in Queensland.

A high priority was given to technical and professional skill in screening. Considerable time was spent in ensuring that eye signs were recorded accurately and consistently by different team members. Critical aspects of ocular examination were defined and described by the program leader, Professor Fred Hollows, and where necessary these were taught to new doctors participating in the program. Attention was also given to the practical organisation of screening activity in any community.

There was a clear role delineation between different members of the team, and Aboriginal people played a prominent part in determining where and how the teams should work. In many communities in remote areas there are often complicated avoidance relationships between individuals that must be adhered to by Aboriginal people in communities. A lack of consideration for these relationships has been a criticism directed at many health service programs in the past. These problems were easily overcome by acknowledging that local Aboriginal community members would determine who would work with the team at any given time and where screening should be conducted. This is a good example of how Aboriginal decision making can very easily solve what has been thought to be a complicated problem.

Each community screened was given immediate feedback about the data collected and its implications for health-care delivery in the community. After a long day of screening, certain team members would work at night to prepare a summary of the screening data, which would be left in the community and discussed with appropriate community members the following day. There was no question that the program was collecting information without feedback or that this would be provided at some future or undefined time.

A central tenet of the program was that it involved not just screening for eye disease but the delivery of immediate eye care, including antibiotic treatment for infection, minor surgery and provision of spectacles. This brought immediate benefits to people within the community, who identified the program as being partisan and dependable. All teams included an optical dispenser who immediately assessed all those requiring glasses and organised for their prompt delivery.

The program had a political profile at both the national and community level. At the community level, program members saw participation as a responsibility to support local initiatives for improvement in community services or health-care delivery. In many locations, team members assisted communities to develop submissions for funding for essential services or community-controlled health services. The 'public health' approach of the program meant that activity in any area of community development was a legitimate function. On a national level, the program acted as a further focus for political activity to improve living conditions and health services for Aboriginal people. This was particularly assisted by the willingness of the program director to give unequivocal support to Aboriginal initiatives for public health improvement and to do this at a public level when requested. Once again this highlights principles of how health professionals should work with Aboriginal people: providing a high level of professional advice and technical skill, acting as advocates for Aboriginal people and following Aboriginal direction in political activity rather than initiating that activity.

The program made a number of recommendations, focusing on four issues:

1. It was the first national program to define requirements for healthy living. The recommendations included a list of minimum requirements necessary for healthy living in remote Australia. Although the details of these recommendations have been substantially modified and developed by other workers (NHC 1987*a*), the principle of defining these basic standards and linking ill-heath to living conditions was a key feature of the report.
2. The program recommended the expansion of health care services to Aboriginal people by the establishment of a large number of community-controlled Aboriginal medical services.
3. The program emphasised the need to develop the role and increase the training of Aboriginal health workers.
4. The program defined the requirements for ongoing eye health care in Aboriginal Australia.

Eye health care in some states remains inadequate and poorly organised. Invariably failure to adhere to the NTEHP recommendations can be identified as one of the primary reasons for the inadequacy of eye health care programs.

Improvement in eye health and adequate eye health care program management will require the following:

1. The provision of essential health hardware requirements necessary for healthy living for all Aboriginal Australians.
2. Accessible and appropriate primary clinical care services capable of rapid treatment of all acute ocular infections, screening for ocular disease and detection of visual impairment.

3. Access to corrective ocular surgery and a system for the rapid provision of glasses.
4. The increasing identification of diabetic complications will require that Aboriginal people have access to appropriate management of diabetic retinopathy.

Child health programs

In many remote areas, health services have adopted models of 'under fives' clinics which were first initiated in developing countries (Morley 1973). The benefits of these clinics in the underdeveloped world have been to allow large numbers of children to be seen and , ideally, health staff to concentrate on those children most at risk, as well as to attend to the major issues of child health. Since population numbers are much smaller in Aboriginal communities, these particular benefits are less important. Nevertheless, many health services have adopted similar models in order to focus on specific issues in child health. In some regions, a particular day each week will be set aside for a 'well baby clinic', whereas in others the contact is more opportunistic and depends on children presenting to the clinic for other reasons. These programs aim to monitor growth by regular weighing and recording on modified 'road to health charts' (Morley 1973). The clinics focus particularly on discussion with mothers about breast-feeding and subsequently on the need to introduce appropriate weaning foods in order to maintain growth and nutritional status. Immunisation status is checked and infective illness treated. Development of an age/sex register for this group allows clinic staff to identify those children in the population who are faltering in growth or who are being seen infrequently by the health service.

Women's health

Mortality data outlined earlier in this chapter demonstrate the increased risk of early death for Aboriginal women. They also highlight the importance of cardiovascular disease and trauma as causes of death. Similarly, diabetes mellitus and its complications are major health problems for adult Aboriginal women. In the context of such stark illness patterns, these problems, which affect both men and women, must be seen as a priority issue in women's health. However, there are also important issues that are specifically relevant for women. In particular, the provision of gynaecological health care for Aboriginal women has been inadequate in all parts of Australia. One manifestation of this inadequate service may well be the high mortality from cervical cancer, which may be related to late presentation (Durling 1989). The enthusiasm with which Aboriginal women take up appropriate gynaecological services when they are offered can be gauged by the success of the Congress Alukura Women's Health Services established in Alice Springs (Alukura Review Committee 1989). Although intended to focus primarily on birthing issues, because of limited funds the service has initially provided a broad health service to Aboriginal women in the region.

Domestic violence and violence against women in general has been the focus of a number of research projects conducted by both government and community-controlled health services in several states. Invariably, violence against women is linked to alcohol use and in some sense can be seen as a consequence of alcohol abuse (see Reser, chapter 6 in this volume).

There is evidence that Aboriginal women have more children at younger ages than do non-Aboriginal women and that this is associated with a higher incidence of child loss (Gray 1988). On the other hand, there is evidence that Aboriginal women are taking up contraceptive options and that this is at least part of the reason for the decline in fertility of Aboriginal women observed in the last 20 years (Gray 1987). The increased prevalence of antenatal risk factors and the poor nutritional status of Aboriginal women may in fact be tackled partly by increased contraceptive use and spacing of pregnancies.

Health worker training

Numerous health worker training programs have been developed throughout Australia by community-controlled Aboriginal health services, governments and some tertiary institutions. Regional differences between communities mean that health workers will have different training needs in different areas.

Before a training program is developed, the role of a health worker should be defined. Obviously the role will vary greatly according to the community in which that individual will work. In many places in remote Australia, it is essential that health workers are able to provide basic clinical care for the common illnesses that affect people in their community. In the health services of the Kimberleys (Western Australia), for instance, basic clinical skills are a major component of the training program. In urban centres, where doctors are more readily available, clinical skills are less important and will be infrequently used. In urban areas, therefore, skills such as counselling, health service management or program development may be far more important. In a number of programs, the role of health workers has been inadequately defined and this has led to problems for workers leaving those courses.

The education and literacy skills of health workers generally reflect the poor educational opportunities of Aboriginal people, but also vary greatly between regions. In some parts of remote Australia, particularly the Northern Territory, many health workers are functionally illiterate in English. Although this does not preclude them from developing many skills, it clearly creates significant obstacles to training, particularly training in the delivery of primary medical care. Various attempts have been made to overcome this problem. The Northern Territory Department of Health incorporated literacy training into the health workers' curriculum, but this strategy failed because infrastructure and trained staff were insufficient and teaching functional literacy on a part-time basis is very difficult (Willis 1984).

In urban centres, educational background is also an issue in the training of health workers. At the Aboriginal Medical Service in Redfern, Sydney, most trainee health workers have completed only two years of high school education (Dulcie Flower, AMS Redfern, pers. comm.). As with training health workers in remote areas, the incorporation of functional literacy teaching into curriculums poses significant problems.

How are health workers selected? In remote communities, it is usually assumed that health workers are 'selected by the community'. This assumption tends to suggest that Aborigines have some inherent knowledge of appropriate selection

Figure 8.4 *Aboriginal health workers with a medical student, Nganampa Health Council, South Australia*

criteria, which are always adhered to in the selection of health workers. This, of course, completely ignores the fact that communities have their own internal political agendas and that white staff are generally unaware of these agendas. The failure by white staff to appreciate the complexity of political decision making in Aboriginal communities has been well described (Gerritsen 1982; Myers 1986; see also Myers, 'Community-controlled health services: different agendas', in Franklin and White, chapter 1 in this volume.). The assumption that there is always a single community wish (predicated on what invariably turn out to be white values) is not a philosophy that supports Aboriginal decision making but a statement of paternalism. For example, selection by a community meeting may sometimes depend on which individual most requires an income. The long-standing controversy about older, more experienced individuals having more prestige than younger but more educated people continues as a dilemma in many remote areas. These problems should be addressed by thorough discussion about the role of the health worker in each community. It is then more likely that appropriate selection criteria can be developed.

In urban centres health worker trainees are often self-selected. They may be individuals who have been unemployed or who seek training in order to improve employment opportunities. Inadequately prepared students may fail in courses that are too educationally demanding. Lake (1989) has highlighted the demoralising effect of failure on individuals and has emphasised the need to screen potential trainees, not for the sake of exclusion but rather to determine who may need supplementary training.

Training courses are often conducted in centres far away from the homes of trainees. In particular, the full-time courses run in major capital cities provide significant social problems for trainees, who are often in a large city for the first time, isolated from community and family support, usually without great financial resources and often with inadequate accommodation. Their personal lives may be complicated by relationship difficulties, experimentation with alcohol and drugs as well as the significant demands of course work. In addition, the chronic ill-health of many Aboriginal people, as well as the need to attend to sick relatives and travel for funerals, often means that trainees miss a great deal of course time. Courses need to be flexible enough to allow for these difficulties. The Associate Diploma in Aboriginal Health and Community Development, for instance, at Cumberland College, Sydney, has adopted a 'block release' pattern. Mature-age and younger health workers come from Aboriginal medical services and government services throughout New South Wales for two weeks at a time several times a year. Between blocks, they continue their education as part of their work in the community.

Accreditation of health worker training remains a problem in most states. There are continuing problems with the formal recognition of courses and consequent difficulties in maintaining wage standards for health workers in employment. Health workers being trained in remote Aboriginal health services are invariably guaranteed at least some employment. However, in the urban centres, future employment is often doubtful. Many individuals complete courses and are unable to find employment as health workers. Because several health worker training courses provide broad educational skills with emphasis on personal development and improving management and counselling skills, trainees are often employed in Aboriginal organisations other than health services. In this way, the courses are contributing to the development of skills in the community and presumably helping to increase the general health knowledge of Aboriginal people. Hopefully, these courses will also provide individuals with the skills to continue their own educational development in fields of their choice.

Since many health worker training courses are inadequately funded, recruitment of teaching staff is always difficult. Particularly in remote area health services, teaching invariably is the responsibility of the clinic staff, who, although often possessing an appropriate knowledge of Aboriginal health issues, are rarely trained as teachers. Most courses available still lack staff who have appropriate knowledge and training both in health and teaching.

Health promotion

Many Aboriginal health projects have a significant health promotion component. State government Aboriginal health services have tended to label all their activities as being in health promotion and preventive health care. Particularly in Queensland

and New South Wales, government policy has proclaimed that adequate primary health care services are already available. However, many Aboriginal communities have clearly felt a need for primary care services that are more accessible and available. Aboriginal community-controlled services have invariably begun with the development of a clinical service. However, more recently all these services have placed emphasis on developing health promotion and preventive programs while maintaining the primary clinical care service.

Since most of these programs are difficult to evaluate, those developing them should provide Aboriginal people with evidence that the program will lead to an improvement in health. In particular, where significant behaviour change is hoped for, Aboriginal people must have some opportunity to decide whether they think the proposed behaviour change is worth the projected health benefits.

It is important to avoid dogmatism in the development of health promotion programs. This area in particular has been bedevilled by consultants with a strong belief that there is a single, magic solution to Aboriginal health problems: for example, God (in several denominations), participatory democracy, Aboriginal youth, vitamins, homelands, brown bread and growing vegetables, to name but a few favourites!

The Health Promotion Unit project

In 1986, a coordinator was appointed for this program of the Department of Health, New South Wales (Close 1987). Its aim was to fund a health promotion worker in each of 10 New South Wales Aboriginal communities that were thought to have particularly poor health status. The program was to focus on initiatives in environmental health, nutrition, maternal and child welfare, and immunisation.

In late 1986 the program coordinator travelled to communities involved in the project and held informal discussions as well as interviews for selection of field workers. Subsequently, orientation courses were organised with workshops on community development and health promotion strategies. Field workers were encouraged to develop programs using existing resources, having first identified community priorities. In addition, they were encouraged to devise mechanisms to provide information about health issues to community members.

A broad spectrum of activities have occurred as a consequence of the program, all with significant input by field staff. These have included: environmental landscape clean-up campaigns; applications by communities for funds to repair water, sewerage and other essential services; child-care centre funding; diabetes education workshops; AIDS education workshops; screening for hypertension and hypercholesterolaemia; immunisation education meetings; small group fitness campaigns; and general youth support work.

Evaluation of such campaigns is obviously extremely difficult. Very often significant activity has already occurred in the community and a field worker may simply assist by increasing interest in a particular issue. The Aboriginal Health Unit in the New South Wales Health Department has conducted a review of the program (Williams 1989). In descriptive terms, this relates to significant achievements in the number of activities being conducted in communities. There is a clear need for more infrastructure support to field workers as well as clarification of their role in individual communities.

Such programs are often extremely dependent on the skills of the field worker. Guidelines for the selection of field workers in this project do exist, but are mainly concerned with the requirement that the person live and work within the community. A more precise job description may well clarify the characteristics of individuals to be appointed to the field worker positions.

Alcohol and drug abuse prevention

A project to develop health education materials for alcohol and drug abuse prevention (Sago 1988) was initiated in 1987 with funding from the National Advisory Council on AIDS and the National Campaign against Drug Abuse. Workshops were held in a large number of Aboriginal communities by a team of people, which consisted of a doctor, nurse, health educator, communication consultant and graphic artist. In each workshop, information about alcohol and drug abuse was provided, followed by sessions on communication principles and the development of media resources. Subsequently, the workshop discussed the aims and objectives of individual campaigns and how these should be expressed. The participants then developed their own objectives and ideas, which were expanded by the graphic artist and communication consultant in the team. Various visual presentations of the major workshop themes were developed the following day and these were then shown to other community members, so that their responses could be evaluated.

In the third phase of the workshop, action plans for specific community projects were developed. This phase included discussions about plans, networking and evaluation of program activities. Participants were encouraged to devise ways of involving community groups and organisations in the overall health promotion strategy.

The team members considered four major principles to be essential to their methodology:

1. Extensive consultation with Aboriginal people before the workshop process began and then at all subsequent stages.
2. Use of existing networks of Aboriginal workers, rather than appointing new positions and creating a second infrastructure in competition with existing systems.
3. Training of workshop participants in the principles of program development and education. This was aimed at providing double benefits from the project: not only the development of a health promotion campaign but also the training of Aboriginal people so that they could develop future campaigns without outside assistance.
4. The production of health promotion material, posters, stickers and radio advertisements during the workshop process. This principle is identical to that adhered to by the NTEHP, which brought immediate benefits to the community while the project was being undertaken. The audiovisual resources remained in the community with health workers after the project teams had left.

Televised health promotion

The Northern Territory Department of Health and Community Services has developed a program of health promotion using television media (Spark and Mills

1988). The program was particularly designed to take advantage of the introduction of Imparja Television into central Australia in 1988. The network has a large Aboriginal audience in central Australia who may benefit from such a program. Spark and Mills (1988, p. 194) emphasise that most televised health promotion campaigns are designed to influence the 'climate of opinion surrounding the issues and achieving incremental shifts in community awareness and attitudes, which in turn can facilitate behavioural changes'.

The project began with research to determine current Aboriginal health-related behaviour and what behaviour change was necessary. This was followed by selective presentation of material to sample target audiences and evaluation following their response. In the final stage of the project, short, specific issue advertisements were developed in Aboriginal communities, usually by Aboriginal health workers. In most cases, the commercial messages were developed in workshop sessions in the community. These concerned alcohol, nutrition, ear health, petrol sniffing and kava use. As a general principle, the commercials relied minimally on language and used culturally relevant visual symbols and sound effects to convey the main messages.

Anyinginyi Congress public health campaigns

Anyinginyi Congress (AC), a community-controlled Aboriginal Health Service based in Tennant Creek, has conducted two innovative health promotion programs. The first of these was directed against 'sex shows' being used to promote alcohol sales in local hotels. These shows served to increase alcohol consumption, encourage domestic violence and undermine the promotion of responsible sexual practices (Boffa and George 1989). AC organised two public meetings and conducted a media campaign which generated significant political activity.

AC has also conducted a research project describing the physical consequences of assault against women. Injuries sustained by a number of Aboriginal women in the area over a one-year period were recorded. The project acted as a focus for community discussion about violence and also triggered considerable Aboriginal interest in the development of a women's refuge in the area. This particular project is an example of how health services can be involved in dealing with very difficult and controversial public health issues within their own communities.

Nutrition promotion

This is clearly a priority area for public health initiatives (for a detailed discussion of nutrition, see Harrison, chapter 4 in this volume). In Aboriginal adults attention has focused on altering the pattern of high fat, high sugar and low complex carbohydrate diets which, together with a decrease in physical activity, appear to be linked to the development of carbohydrate intolerance and diabetes mellitus. In children, the emphasis has been on the encouragement of breast-feeding and, particularly in remote areas, on the appropriate introduction of weaning foods in order to prevent growth failure in this period.

The development of an appropriate nutrition policy and strategy is affected by almost all other areas of community activity. Most obviously, it is related to income and the general level of poverty in the community. Other issues to be considered are those of store management and funding, access to bush foods, the impact of heavy alcohol consumption on the nutritional status of the community and maternal attitudes to child feeding and growth.

A community-based food and health program

Biomedical research on Aboriginal communities was frequently regarded with suspicion on the assumption that non-Aboriginal researchers were using the people to further their own professional careers. Now strict guidelines exist to ensure that all research in Aboriginal and Torres Strait Island communities is conducted ethically. It is generally accepted that community-based projects must be directed towards practical benefits for the communities and individuals involved. Moreover, the methods and process of investigation must be fully understood and accepted by those who are being studied.

One example of this type of research project is a study conducted with the people of a small northern coastal community in the Northern Territory, a project that has shown the way for other Aboriginal communities to help prevent so-called 'lifestyle' diseases.

The project was initiated by health workers in the community, who were concerned about the origins of illness and premature deaths among the people. They expressed particular concern about disease associated with lifestyle changes among Aborigines, notably coronary heart disease and diabetes. For this reason, they enlisted the help of scientific workers from Darwin to identify which factors were contributing to ill-health among adults and what could be done about it.

Apparent food and nutrient intake, together with anthropometric measurements (height, weight, hip and waist circumference), biochemical measurements (serum cholesterol and other lipids, glucose tolerance test, renal and liver function tests, vitamin status) and haematological measurements, were used as a rational basis for the planning, implementation and evaluation of the project within the community. For a 12-month period from June 1989, all parameters were monitored at three-month intervals. As a control, dietary intake was also monitored in a similar community.

Nearly all the adults residing in the community participated in the initial screening. The results indicated a high prevalence of diabetes (10.3 per cent) and impaired glucose tolerance (8.8 per cent), high cholesterol levels (67.6 per cent), high fasting serum triglyceride levels (38.9 per cent), relatively low folic acid status (80.9 per cent), low levels of serum vitamin B_6 (55.9 per cent of men and 51.5 per cent of women), low beta-carotene concentration (81.4 per cent), and low status of several other vitamins. Dietary studies revealed that the community had an unusually high intake of saturated fat (more than twice the proportional recommendation) and sugar (up to 38 teaspoons of white sugar per person per day), but that the diet was extremely low in dietary fibre (less than half the recommended intake), particularly from fresh fruit and vegetables.

With the assistance of an Aboriginal nutrition worker employed to work specifically on the project, the results were explained to the people in the community. The community members and the scientists worked together to design intervention strategies which addressed two major issues, namely increasing motivation of community members and provision of a greater range of healthy food in the store.

Over the 12-month intervention period, there were significant changes in some indicators of health and nutritional status in the community, including a 14 per cent reduction in serum cholesterol levels and a doubling of red blood cell folate concentration. Overweight people tended to lose weight, while underweight individuals tended to increase their weight. However, there was little change in diabetic status over the year.

Dietary data derived from the turnover of foods through the store indicated a move towards a healthier eating pattern. For example, there was a marked increase in the consumption of fresh fruit and vegetables (from 83 grams to 182 grams per person per day); intake of wholegrain and kibbled bread doubled; the apparent intake of sugars decreased by 20 per cent; and there was a marked increase in the nutritionally preferred type of carbonated beverages and cooking oils consumed. Store profits also increased during this period.

Various community development initiatives were also supported drring the project. As one extension of the project, a nutrition policy has been implemented in several other community stores managed by the Aboriginal-owned enterprise responsible for the store in the intervention community.

This research project illustrates the value of community participation. The researchers were involved in continual discussion with health workers, store staff, council and community groups and with the individual subjects of research who had the results of their health investigations promptly explained to them. Without such interaction, there is little chance of any useful benefit resulting from this type of research, because the people will neither understand the reasons for attempting to change unhealthy practices nor be motivated to do anything about it.

Amanda Lee, Menzies School of Health Research, Casuarina, Northern Territory, with Ann Bonson and Daisy Yarmirr

Alcohol abuse

The subject of alcohol abuse is dealt with in detail by Brady in chapter 5 of this volume.

Alcohol abuse is clearly a consequence of colonisation and oppression, and health planners must always base their analysis on this important fact. Nevertheless, the consequences of alcohol abuse are so serious that programs to reduce the burden of alcohol immediately in Aboriginal communities must be a major factor in any public health strategy. In many areas, alcohol abuse prevents any significant public health or community development programs from being established. Programs that involve behaviour change such as safe sex practices, early introduction of weaning foods for children, and increased exercise for adults, are all nullified if some people are continually drunk. Invariably, some members of the community spend all their time caring for drunks and managing the consequences of drunks' behaviour, instead of attending to their own health needs. A reasonable living environment and basic health hardware facilities are impossible to maintain if people are continually having to repair damage done by drunks. Tangentyere Council (Northern Territory) provides an insight into this in this description of current circumstances in town camps at Alice Springs:

[L]arge scale abuse of grog undermines the campers' struggle for adequate housing, improved living conditions on the camps, cultural revival, and a secure future for their children. Drunks smash up houses and drain the camp of food and finances (leaving no money for rent or power and water bills), disrupt community life (especially for workers and children), and generally make things intolerable for people who are struggling to adapt to rapidly changing circumstances.

Cited in Simmons 1988, p. 12

Since much Aboriginal decision making occurs in large community meetings, drunks can be powerful negative forces in terms of community development initiatives. In many communities, drunks disrupt meetings, provoke fights where otherwise debate would occur and generally prevent thoughtful decision making. On the other hand, people who have recently stopped drinking and are 'off the grog' usually feel so unwell that they are not able to contribute significantly to community debate. There is a clear and unequivocal relationship between violence and alcohol in Aboriginal communities and this alone is sufficient to make alcohol a major public health issue (see Reser, chapter 6 in this volume).

There has been a tendency over the last 20 years for Aboriginal drinking to be viewed as a manifestation of traditional cultural practices. This view, common in anthropological writing, has often made it difficult for health workers to develop strategies to stop people drinking. Some Aboriginal people are now criticising this analysis and thus sharpening the attack on drinking. Gibson (unpub.; see also Gibson, 'A contemporary Aboriginal viewpoint', in Brady, chapter 5 in this volume) discusses the effect of this 'myth' about drinking in his own community:

It is time to stop portraying gambling in Aboriginal society as some kind of traditional re-distribution of wealth. It is time to stop interpreting alcoholism as some kind of helpless result of cultural clash. Rather we should be seeing it for what it is. That is: the deliberate distortion of tradition for the sake of fulfilling an individual physical desire for alcohol. It is time to stop portraying the contemporary Hopevale alcoholic as a passive victim of colonisation. Rather we must consider how he has actively created his own problem.

Such cogent analysis provides leadership for the feeling, widely held by many Aboriginal people, that the devastating effects of alcohol on their communities must be stopped. These people recognise that colonisation and racism are the root causes of alcoholism, but the views of Gibson and others provide a framework for dealing with the consequences of alcoholism now.

A range of integrated programs must be developed and adequately funded, and, because of the interdependence of such programs, this must occur simultaneously. Simmons (1988) has emphasised the interdependency of programs and the likelihood that individual programs may fail without a comprehensive, long-term and adequately funded and planned process.

Evaluation of health care programs

Evaluation has been a controversial issue in Aboriginal health care. In the past, it was widely held to have been initiated by government in order to limit or reduce funding. This has led to predictable suspicion of evaluation by many, particularly in the non-government health services. However, it is increasingly recognised that evaluation is not only an essential component of any health-care plan but also a pre-requisite for real Aboriginal decision making in health-care delivery. Evaluation is necessary if Aborigines are to assess the effectiveness of their health services and then make the necessary changes to these systems. What is needed is the development of innovative and appropriate methodologies for evaluating these systems.

In the second half of the 1980s, a number of government- initiated review projects have provided illustrations of inappropriate evaluation methods. In 1986, the Department of Aboriginal Affairs (DAA) circulated a draft set of performance indicators for Aboriginal health services (DAA unpub.). These were developed in isolation, without consultation either with the services or with appropriate experts in evaluation. The indicators aimed to assess health service performance, collect workload statistics and provide data on Aboriginal health status. Unfortunately, the

Wantamulla

The scenario described here is a realistic one, but the place is fictional. The events portrayed are drawn from experience and information gained in the last decade in New South Wales.

Wide, burnt plains drop from memory as the traveller slows down at Waratah, a small town in the far west, beside the Wentworth River. Crossing an ancient wooden bridge, most drivers glance only momentarily at the rough track leading off to the left along the river; few see the collection of rusty corrugated iron roofs, shimmering in the sun.

Behind them, they leave the Aboriginal settlement of Wantamulla. Over the river and three kilometres from Waratah, this has been an Aboriginal camping place for 35 000 years.

These days, Wantamulla is a string of timber and iron houses straggling along the river bank. Technically owned by the elected Land Council, it's the same housing built by the Welfare Board in the 1950s and some even as early as the 1930s. Poky two- or three-room huts with only cold water, a fuel stove and a toilet out the back, they have never been adequate. Weathered by the years, the collection of huts remind visitors of old photographs taken of slum areas and the camps of the unemployed during the depression.

The last few years have been difficult for the Wantamulla people. Their plight came to the notice of the press and public authorities, but well-meant measures to improve matters became as difficult to cope with as the neglect of the previous years. They convinced the Department of Aboriginal Affairs that the dirt road caused a lot of problems in the community, especially in wet weather. The sticking silt of the flood plains would quickly turn to slime and swelling side creeks would cut the settlement off from Waratah. Wantamulla would then be not only out of sight and mind, but out of contact with much needed services in the town. It was often necessary to ferry food across during floods, but more than one sick child had died who might have been saved if the road had been passable.

Just 5 kilometres on the other side of Waratah is a small village of 100 people, with a sealed road, culverts and bridges, and the people of Wantamulla know why this is so. This is a white township. The people of Wantamulla, however, never vote in Shire elections, have never enrolled in the electoral system. They also know that the federal government grant to the local council to construct their road has been earning interest for 18 months, yet barely 100 metres of surface has been laid. All they get are assurances that the engineers are still working on the design, that matters are well in hand and the road will soon be completed.

In the meantime, shopping remains a problem, as does getting the kids to school, or going to the doctor, even in emergencies. A lot of kids have had glue ear and other problems, and have had to put up with name-calling and racist taunts at the local school. None have ever got past year 6, but no-one seems to expect anything else.

A nurse comes out one day a week to the clinic, but people do not always get around to getting there, or they cannot go on the day the nurse comes. Water is a problem too. You cannot use the river any more, since the cotton industry began. Fish are found floating belly up after rain. People remember when fish were a good, free feed, but they cannot trust it now.

Cotton farmers employ the Wantamulla people to chip out weeds in the summer, but sometimes they are sprayed by the planes and get sick. They need the work, however, and the farmers say the spray will not hurt them. They know that sometimes they get skin rashes and itch from the sprays, but what can they do? It is a job, when jobs are hard to find.

The government agreed to do something about the water problem and tenders were called to build a new fresh water system. But the system put in by a local contractor has a lot of problems. The pressure tank fills up too slowly so there is only water for about 3 hours a day, and river water carted by hand has to be used for clothes washing and toilet flushing.

The flush toilets are supposed to be better than the old pans, but without water, they are far worse. And the septic has leaked up and created green islands of growth verdant with the promise of gastroenteritis and hepatitis. It would take about $50 000 to fix and the community agreed to maintain the system when the grant was first approved. But almost everyone is on social security payments. Where will the $50 000 come from? They have thought about going back to the government but they know that there is a long list of other places needing services.

Wantamulla, despite the difficulties, has a growing population. However, 50 per cent of the inhabitants are younger than 20, and few are working. There are no jobs in Wantamulla itself, and those jobs still around in a time of rural decline go to the whites in Waratah. The children of Wantamulla have a chance at school to learn how to provide for themselves, but who will employ them. Many have turned to drink, and alcoholism and its accompanying health and social problems cause further traumas.

Another problem is diabetes. The old bush tucker days are long gone, apart from the fishing upstream and the occasional kangaroo or porcupine. In welfare days, people were doled out flour, sugar and tea, with whatever meat and vegetables they could get. Nowadays, there is not much physical work to do, and white bread, soft drinks and cheap cuts of meat are what people can afford and are used to.

In an attempt to improve people's health and to provide some work, the community argued to get funds to start a market garden a few years ago, but the project has been carried mainly by one person. It took a costly feasibility study, and a government grant bought equipment worth $15 000. There had been a manager/trainer and subsidy for six young people to learn the work. It went well for a while, but people could not force their relations to pay for food and the Waratah shops would not take any of their produce, supposedly because they had contracts with other market gardens. Eventually, people got sick of being the only ones doing the work, and a few got jobs elsewhere for a while. The one who had pushed for the project got sick of being the one who 'copped it' from all sides. No-one has touched it for a few months and the system is falling apart. The community had taken out a loan to help set it up and the repayments have to be met, but there is no way they will be.

Despite all that has happened, or not happened, the people who grow up in Wantamulla love it. It is free of the tensions and restrictions of the town. Here, they say, you can be yourself. You know everyone; everyone is related. Kids grow up as part of one big family, and if there are rows or problems at home, they can go and camp with Aunty next door. The kids have their own lives, roaming the country, fishing, playing and trapping. As they grow older, that sense of freedom grates with the tightness of the outside, especially with the restrictions of school. No-one in Wantamulla is going to call you a 'boong', or say you are dirty, or refuse to serve you, or push any of the other things that come at you in Waratah. As you grow up, you grow to know that Wantamulla is your home and you look forward to having your own kids there. But that doesn't bring jobs, and too many of the kids get sick; twice as many babies die as in the white community outside, and people know that change is long overdue.

Recently, funds for a part-time community health worker have been granted by the Department of Aboriginal Affairs, under a six-month 'pilot' scheme.

David Morrissey, Tranby College, Sydney

methodology failed to achieve any of these aims effectively. The indicators focused on clinic activities and reflected a lack of understanding of basic epidemiology. For example, one indicator was recommended documenting the number of clients who had blood pressure recorded in a period of one month, and how many of these had an elevated recording. This would clearly be a useless indicator of either health-service performance or prevalence of hypertension.

A similar lack of expertise was demonstrated in a letter to the Walgett Aboriginal Medical Service from the DAA in 1986 (cited in Moodie 1989*a*). The DAA required the service to achieve the following improvement in health status within two years:

1. Reduce the number of hospital admissions by 20 per cent.
2. Reduce the incidence of insulin-controlled diabetes by 10 per cent.
3. Reduce the incidence of abnormal blood pressure by 10 per cent.
4. Reduce the incidence of sexually transmitted diseases by 10 per cent.

5. All children to have received the regular battery of immunisation shots
6. Reduce the incidence of ear infection by 20 per cent.

The major problems here are a lack of knowledge about the natural history of these illnesses and the factors that determine their prevalence, as well as a blind faith in arbitrary targets as program objectives.

Naive romanticism is another theme that has pervaded evaluation processes. This is often reflected in a rigid view of Aboriginal culture as unchanging, inflexible and fragile, combined with a basic lack of knowledge about comprehensive health service planning. The 'Bonner Review' (DAA 1988) was commissioned in 1987 by the DAA to undertake a broad investigation of Pitjantjatjara and Yankunjatjara communities. Although the review team had no members with expertise in public health, they made a number of recommendations to alter health-care delivery in the region. The review commented on the 'predisposition of Aborigines to good health' and 'what is more significant than formal qualifications is the capacity of these people (health staff) to work with Anangu in promoting a healthy life'. This reflects an almost Luddite mysticism that thinking about being healthy will magically transform people's health status.

Since changes in health status occur slowly, particularly in populations without high mortality from infectious diseases, it will always be difficult to evaluate the impact on health services of short-term changes in health status. The principles of what constitutes a comprehensive health care system are fairly well established. These include an accessible and available primary clinical care service; immunisation programs; antenatal protocols; health worker education programs; health promotion activities; environmental health policy; community participation and the establishment of evaluation procedures themselves. The important objective, however, is to evaluate the extent to which a given process achieves a desired outcome. Towards this goal, health services need to develop both short- and long-term aims and objectives that can act as focal points for the evaluation process.

Conclusion

A public health perspective allows health-care workers to contribute not just to curing illness but to 'the well-being' of the people. This requires a professional approach to planning, implementation and delivery of health services, on the part of both government and Aboriginal health organisations. If Aboriginal decision making is to be productive and liberating, then it must be informed. The knowledge required to improve Aboriginal health status is not innate; it must be acquired. It is the responsibility of those employed by Aborigines to present current and comprehensive information to their employers in an accessible fashion and to encourage careful evaluation.

Non-Aboriginal health-care workers need to develop a long-term perspective on health improvement and community development. It is important that they do not see their own time in a health service as more important than any other time in the history of the organisation—this is rarely the case. Building on the work of others is important for sustaining programs and avoiding the problem of 're-inventing the wheel'. New staff must therefore consult with more experienced personnel.

Staff turnover is inevitable in most health services, particularly in remote areas. For this reason, mechanisms for retaining programs and information should be formalised. Written protocols for clinic practices as well as program management must be developed and adhered to.

The origins of Aboriginal ill-health are social and political; the solutions to health problems will therefore require social and political change. These solutions will reflect the political directions and community development models that Aboriginal people choose for their future.

References

ADC (Aboriginal Development Commission) (1988), *Aboriginal and Torres Strait Islander Housing and Accommodation Needs Survey*, Canberra.

Alukura Review Committee (1989), *Report on review of the Congress Alukura Pilot Health Programme*, Northern Territory Department of Health and Community Services, Darwin.

Barrett, E. J. (1972), 'Hepatitis-associated antigen in Aboriginal groups in Northern Australia', *Medical Journal of Australia* **2**, pp. 472–4.

Basedow, H. (1932), 'Diseases of the Australian Aborigines', *Journal of Tropical Medicine and Hygiene* **35**, p. 177.

Biddulph, J. (1989), 'Standard treatment regimes—a personal account of Papua New Guinea experience', *Tropical Doctor* **19**, pp. 126–30.

Biles, D., McDonald, D., and Fleming, J. (1989), *Australian deaths in custody 1980–1988: an analysis of Aboriginal and non-Aboriginal deaths in prisons and police custody*, Research Paper 7, Royal Commission into Aboriginal Deaths in Custody, Canberra.

Blum, D., and Feachem, R. G. (1983), 'Measuring the impact of water supply and sanitation investment on diarrhoeal disease: problems of methodology', *International Journal of Epidemiology* **12**, pp. 357–65.

Blumberg, B. S., Alter, H. J., and Visnich, S. (1965), 'A 'new' antigen in leukemia sera', *Journal of the American Medical Association* **191**, pp. 541–6.

Boffa, J., and George, C. (1989), 'Strip/grog debate', *Central Australian Rural Practitioners Association Newsletter* **9**, p. 16.

Brennan, R. (1989), 'Rheumatic fever and rheumatic heart disease in a central Australian rural Aboriginal community', *Central Australian Rural Practitioners Association Newsletter* **9**, pp. 12–14.

Brennan, R., Patel, M., and Hope, A. (1989), 'Gonococcal conjunctivitis in central Australia', *Medical Journal of Australia* **150**, pp. 48–49.

Britton, W. J., Cossart, Y., Parsons, C., Burnett, L., and Gallagher, N. D. (1985), 'Risk factors associated with hepatitis B infection in antenatal patients', *Australian and New Zealand Journal of Medicine* **15**, pp. 641–4.

Butlin, N. (1983), *Our original aggression: Aboriginal populations of south eastern Australia 1788–1850*, Allen and Unwin, Sydney.

Cameron, W. I., Moffit, P. S., and Williams, D. R. R. (1986), 'Diabetes mellitus in the Australian Aborigines of Bourke, New South Wales', *Diabetes Research and Clinical Practice* **2**, pp. 307–14.

Campbell, D. H., Sargent J. W., and Plant, A. J. (1989), 'The prevalence of markers of infection with hepatitis B virus in a mixed race Australian community', *Medical Journal of Australia* **1**, pp. 489–92.

Cherian, T., Simons, E., John, T. J., Steinhoff, M. C., Mercy, J. (1988), 'Evaluation of simple clinical signs for the diagnosis of acute lower respiratory tract infection', *Lancet* **2**, pp. 125–8.

Cleland, J. B. (1928), 'Disease among the Australian Aborigines', *Journal of Tropical Medicine and Hygiene* **31**, p. 53.

Close, G. (1987), *Health promotion: implementing continuing awareness programmes*, report for Aboriginal Health Unit, NSW Department of Health, Sydney.

D'Abbs, P. (1989), 'Health in the bush: a study of public health policy in the Katherine Region, Northern Territory', in P. Loveday and A. Webb (eds), *Small towns in northern Australia*, Monograph, Australian National University North Australian Research Unit, Darwin.

Dawn, R. S., Marcuse, E. K., Giebink, G. S., et al. (1988), '*Haemophilus influenzae* type b vaccines: lessons from the past', *Pediatrics* **81**, pp. 892–7.

DAA (Department of Aboriginal Affairs) (1982), *Appraisal of the effectiveness of the Aboriginal Public Health Improvement Programme*, DAA, Canberra.

DAA (1985), *Aboriginal social indicators*, DAA, Canberra.

DAA (1987), *Aboriginal statistics 1986*, AGPS, Canberra.

DAA (1988), *Always Anangu: a review of the Pitjantjatjara and Yankunytjatjara Aboriginal communities of central Australia*, Adelaide.

Devanesen, D., Furber, M., Hampton, D., Honari, M., Kinmarth, N., and Peach, H. G. (1986), *Health indicators in the Northern Territory*, NT Department of Health, Darwin.

Durling, G. (1989), 'What do we know about cancer in the Aboriginal population in the Northern Territory?', *Central Australian Rural Practitioners Association Newsletter* **9**, pp. 1–3.

Esrey, S. A., Feachem, R. G., and Hughes, J. M. (1985), 'Interventions for the control of diarrhoeal diseases among young children: improving water supplies and excreta disposal facilities', *Bulletin of the World Health Organization* **63** (4), pp. 757–72.

Freeman, P., Holmes, W., and Torzillo, P. (1985), *Nganampa Health Council—medical report 1984*, Nganampa Health Council, Alice Springs.

Gerritsen, R. (1982), 'Blackfellas and whitefellas', in P. Loveday, *Service delivery to remote communities*, Australian National University, North Australian Research Unit, Darwin, pp. 16–31.

Gogna, N. K., Smiley, M., Walker, A. C., and Fullerton, P. (1986), 'Low birthweight and mortality in Australian Aboriginal babies at the Royal Darwin Hospital: a 15-year study', *Australian Paediatric Journal* **22**, pp. 281–6.

Gracey, M., and Hitchcock, N. E. (1983), 'Nutritional state of Aboriginal infants and young children in Western Australia', *Aboriginal Health Project Information Bulletin* **4**, pp. 22–7.

Gracey, M., and Sullivan, H. (1988), 'Growth of Aboriginal infants in the first year of life in remote communities in north-west Australia', *Annals of Human Biology* **15** (5), pp. 375–82.

Gracey, M., Spargo, R. M., Bottrell, C., Hammond, K., Mulholland, K., and Valentine, J. (1984), 'Maternal and childhood nutrition among Aborigines of the Kimberley region', *Medical Journal of Australia* **141**, pp. 506–8.

Gracey, M., Anderson, C. M., and Brooks, B. (1985), 'Low birthweight and impaired growth to 5 years in Australian Aborigines', *Australian Paediatric Journal* **25**, pp. 279–83.

Gray, A. (1987), 'Family planning in Aboriginal communities', *Community Health Studies* **11** (3), pp. 165–75.

Gray, A. (1988), *Aboriginal child survival: an analysis of results from the 1986 Census of Population and Housing, Canberra*, Occasional Paper cat. no. 41260, ABS, Canberra.

Gray, A., and Hogg, R. (1988), *Mortality of Aboriginal Australians in western New South Wales 1984–1987*, NSW Department of Health, Sydney.

Harris, M. F., Nolan, B., and Davidson, A. (1984), 'Early childhood pneumonia in Aborigines of Bourke, New South Wales', *Medical Journal of Australia* **140**, pp. 705–7.

Harris, L., Knight, J., and Henderson, R. (1986), 'Morbidity patterns in a general paediatric unit in rural Western Australia', *Medical Journal of Australia* **145**, pp. 441–3.

Hart, G. (1982), 'Syphilis control in populations previously exposed to yaws', *International Journal of Epidemiology* **11**, pp. 181–7.

Hollows, F. C. (1989), 'Trachoma down the track', *Medical Journal of Australia* **151**, pp. 182–3.

HRSCAA (House of Representatives Standing Committee on Aboriginal Affairs) (1979), *Aboriginal health*, AGPS, Canberra.

HRSCAA (1987), *Return to country: the Aboriginal Homelands Movement in Australia*, AGPS, Canberra.

Human Rights Australia (1988), *Toomelah report: report on the problems and needs of Aborigines living on the New South Wales–Queensland border*, Human Rights Australia, Sydney.

Jones, T. W., and Henderson, T. R. (1989), 'Urinary calculi in children in Western Australia 1972–1986, *Australian Paediatric Journal* **25**, pp. 93–5.

Julienne, A. (1983), *A comparative study of perinatal outcome among Aboriginal and non-Aboriginal confinements in rural New South Wales, 1981*, Working Paper 4, Aboriginal Health Unit, NSW Department of Health, NSW Government Printer, Sydney.

Kapikian, A. Z., Flores, J., Hoshino, Y., et al. (1989), 'Prospects for development of a rotavirus vaccine against rotavirus diarrhoea in infants and young children', *Review of Infectious Diseases* **2**, supplement, May–June, pp. S539–46.

Kass, R. B., and Win Law, E. (1985), *Childhood diarrhoeal disease in central Australia: a hospital based report*, Department of Paediatrics, Alice Springs Hospital, Monograph of Northern Territory Department of Health, Alice Springs.

Khalidi, N. A. (1989), *Aboriginal mortality in central Australia, 1975–1977 to 1985–1986*, Working Paper, National Centre for Epidemiology and Population Health, ANU, Canberra.

Kickbush, I. (1989), 'Health in public policy: a context for the new community health', in M. A. Miller and R. Walker (eds), *Health promotion, the community health approach*, Australian Community Health Association, Sydney.

Kirke, K. D. (1974), 'The traditionally oriented community', in B. S. Hetzel, T. A. Dobbin, L. Lippmann and E. Eggleston (eds), *Better health for Aborigines: report of a national seminar at Monash University*, University of Queensland Press, St Lucia.

Lake, P. (1989), *Aboriginal health studies course re-accreditation 1989–90*, Discussion Paper, Aboriginal Health Organisation, Adelaide.

Lancaster, P. (1989), 'Birthweight percentile for Aborigines', *Medical Journal of Australia* **151**, pp. 489–91.

McDonald, B. (ed.) (1983), *The health worker book*, NT Department of Health, Alice Springs.

Macdonald, K. T., and Walker, A. C. (1989), 'Rheumatic heart disease in Aboriginal children in the Northern Territory', *Medical Journal of Australia* **150**, pp. 503–5.

McNeilly, J., Cicchini, C., Oliver, D., and Gracey, M. (1983), 'Infectious disease in Aboriginal infants and children in Western Australia', *Medical Journal of Australia* **2**, pp. 547–51.

Mahler, H. (1986), 'Towards a new public health', *Health Promotion* **1** (1), p. 1.

Maxwell, G. M. (1972), 'Chronic chest disease in Australian Aboriginal children', *Archives of Disease in Childhood* **47**, pp. 897–901.

Maxwell, G. M., Elliott, R. B., Langsford, W. A. (1981), 'Respiratory infection in Australian Aboriginal children: a clinical and radiological study', *Medical Journal of Australia* **1**, pp. 990–3.

Memmott, P. (1988), 'Aboriginal housing: the state of the art (or the nonstate of the art)', *Architecture Australia*, June 1988, pp. 34–47.

Meredith, S. J., Peach, H. G., Devanesen, D. (1989), 'Trachoma in the Northern Territory of Australia, 1940–1986', *Medical Journal of Australia* **151**, pp. 190–6.

Moodie, R. (1989*a*), 'The politics of evaluating Aboriginal health services', *Community Health Studies* **13** (4), pp. 503–9.

Moodie, R. (1989*b*), 'AIDS Education—seeing it a different way', *National AIDS Bulletin* **3** (3), April, pp. 17–18.

Moran, D. J., Waterford, J., Hollows, F. C., and Jones, D. L. (1979), 'Ear disease in rural Australia', *Medical Journal of Australia* **2**, pp. 210–2.

Morley, D. (1973), *Paediatric priorities in the developing world*, Butterworth, London.

Myers, F. R. (1986), *Pintupi self, Pintupi country: sentiment, place, and politics among Western Desert Aborigines*, Smithsonian Institute Press, Washington, DC.

NHC (Nganampa Health Council) (1987*a*), *Report of Uwankara Palyanyku Kanyintjaku: an environmental and public health review within the Anangu Pitjantjatjara Lands*, Alice Springs.

NHC (1987*b*), *Anangu Winki Nyaa: Ku Pikatjararinganyi Nya: A-Nguru, health report 1985–86*, Alice Springs.

Nienhuys, T. (1989), *Conductive hearing loss in the Aboriginal population*, Menzies School of Health Research, Annual Report 1989, Darwin.

NSWAB (New South Wales Anti-Discrimination Board) (1982), *Study of street offences*, Sydney.

NTDH (Northern Territory Department of Health) (1985), *Annual report 1984–1985*, Darwin.

O'Dea, K., Spargo, R. M., and Nestel, P. J. (1982), 'Impact of westernization on carbohydrate and lipid metabolism in Australian Aborigines', *Diabetologia* **22**, pp. 148–53.

O'Dea, K., Trainedes, K., Hopper, J. L., and Larkins, R. G. (1988), 'Impaired glucose tolerance, hyperinsulinaemia, and hypertriglyceridimia in Australian Aborigines from the desert', *Diabetes care* **1**, pp. 23–9.

Patel, M. (1989), 'Should all pregnant Aboriginal women be offered a test for diabetes?' *Aboriginal Health Bulletin* **12**, pp. 24–9.

Pickering, H., and Rose, G. (1988), 'Nasal and hand carriage of *Streptococcus pneumoniae* in children and mothers in the Tari basin of Papua New Guinea', *Transactions of the Royal Society of Tropical Medicine and Hygiene* **82**, pp. 911–13.

Pugsley , D. J., Grimes, B., and Esterman, A. (1983), *The Aboriginal renal disease survey: first report*, Aboriginal Health Organization, South Australia.

Reser, J. (1989), 'Aboriginal deaths in custody and social construction: a response to the view that there is no such thing as Aboriginal suicide', *Australian Aboriginal Studies* **2** (1), pp. 430–50.

Riley, I. (1985), 'The aetiology of acute respiratory infections in children in developing countries', in R. Douglas, and E. Kerby-Eatson (eds), *Acute respiratory infections in childhood: proceedings of an international workshop, Sydney 1984*, Department of Community Medicine, University of Adelaide, Adelaide.

Riley, I. D., Lehmann, D., Alpers, M., et al. (1986), 'Pneumococcal vaccine prevents death from acute lower respiratory tract infections in Papua New Guinea', *Lancet* **2**, pp. 877–81.

Rowland, M. G. M., Rowland, S. G. M., Cole, T. J. (1988), 'Impact of infection on the growth of children from 1 to 2 years in an urban West African community', *American Journal of Clinical Nutrition* **47**, pp. 134–8.

RACO (Royal Australian College of Ophthalmologists) (1980), *The National Trachoma and Eye Health Programme*, Sydney.

Sago, P. (1988), 'Training Aboriginal health workers in the process of developing health education materials for alcohol and drug abuse prevention campaigns', *Technical Information Bulletin on Drug Abuse* **79**, pp. 9–13.

Shann, F. A., Hart, K., and Thomas, D. (1984), 'Acute lower respiratory tract infections in children: possible criteria for selection of patients for antibiotic therapy and hospital admission', *Bulletin of the World Health Organization* **62**, pp. 749–53.

Simonds, S., Vaughan, P., and Gunn, W. S. (1983), *Refugee community health care*, Oxford Medical Publications, Oxford.

Simmons, L. (1988), *The grog story*, Information Paper, Central Australian Aboriginal Congress, Alice Springs.

Simmons, L., Wish, P., Marr, B., Jones, A., and Simon, T. (1981), 'Coronary risk factors in a rural community which includes Aborigines: Inverell Heart Disease Prevention Programme', *Australian and New Zealand Journal of Medicine* **11**, pp. 386–90.

Spark, R., and Mills, P. (1988), 'Promoting Aboriginal health on television in the Northern Territory: a bicultural approach', *Drug Education Journal of Australia* **2** (3), pp. 191–8.

Stanton, K. G., McCann, V., Constable, J., and Welborn, T. (1985), 'Diabetes in part Aborigines of Western Australia', *Diabetologia* **28**, pp. 16–21.

Stevens, M. (1989), 'A North Queensland perspective in Aborigines and AIDS', *National AIDS Bulletin* **3** (3), pp. 19–20.

Sunderman, J., and Dyer, H. (1984), 'Chronic ear disease in Australian Aborigines', *Medical Journal of Australia* **140**, pp. 708–11.

Thomson, N. (1984), 'Aboriginal health—current status', *Australian and New Zealand Journal of Medicine* **14**, pp. 705–18.

Thomson, N, and Honari, M. (1989), 'A review of hepatitis B infection amongst Aborigines', *Aboriginal Health Bulletin* **9**, pp. 24–6.

Torzillo, P. J., and Erlich, J. (1984), 'Pneumonia in Aboriginal children: problems in management', in R. M. Douglas, and E. Kerby Eaton (eds), *Acute respiratory infections in childhood: proceedings of an international workshop, Sydney*, Department of Community Medicine, University of Adelaide.

Torzillo, P. J., Waterford, J. E., Hollows, F. C., and Jones, D. L. (1983), 'Respiratory disease amongst Aborigines in the Pilbara', *International Journal of Epidemiology* **12**, pp. 105–6.

Tugwell, P., Bennett, K. J., Sackett, D. J., and Haynes, B. R. (1985), 'The measurement iterative loop : a framework for the critical appraisal of need, benefits and costs of health interventions', *Journal of Chronic Diseases* **38** (4), pp. 339–51.

University of Sydney (1988), *Childhood immunization and infectious diseases survey: the immunization status of children attending general practitioners in Australia*, Department of Community Medicine, University of Sydney.

Ward, J. I., Broome, C. V., Shinefield, N., and Black, S. (1988), '*Haemophilus influenzae* type b vaccines: lessons for the future, *Pediatrics* **81**, pp. 886–92.

Willis, E. (1984), 'Has the primary health worker programme been successfully exported to the Northern Territory', *Aboriginal Health Project Information Bulletin* **6**, pp. 13–18.

Wise, P. H., Edwards, F. M., Thomas, D. W. (1970), 'Hyperglycaemia in the urbanized Aboriginal: the Davenport Study', *Medical Journal of Australia* **2**, pp. 1001–6.

Wise, P. H., Edwards, F. M., Craig, R. J., Evans, B., Murchland, J. B., Sutherland, B., and Thomas, B. W. (1976), 'Diabetes and associated variables in the South Australian Aboriginal', *Australian and New Zealand Journal of Medicine* **6**, pp. 191–6.

Unpublished material

DAA (unpub.), Performance indicators—Aboriginal health services, unpublished letter, DAA, Canberra, 1986.

Gibson M. (unpub.), Anthropology and tradition: a contemporary Aboriginal viewpoint, paper presented to ANZAAS Conference, Townsville, Qld, 1987.

Gratten M. (unpub.), Carriage and invasion of respiratory bacterial pathogens in Melanesian children, MSc thesis, University of Papua New Guinea, Port Moresby, 1986.

Hall R. (unpub.), Mortality and morbidity of central Australian Aboriginal children under five years of age, 1978–1983, treatise submitted in partial requirement for the degree of Master of Public Health, School of Public Health and Tropical Medicine, University of Sydney, 1986.

Hanna J. (unpub.), The epidemiology of invasive *Haemophilus influenzae* infections in children under five years of age in the Northern Territory and central Australia 1985–1988, Master of Public Health thesis, University of Adelaide, 1988.

Moodie, R., Djana, F., and Bailey, S. A. (unpub.), AIDS education and awareness: a program by and for Aboriginal people of Alice Springs and central Australia, paper delivered to 'Healthy Public Policy', Second International Conference on Health Promotion, Adelaide, 1988.

Tobin, P. (unpub.), A meeting of nations: Aborigines and the police, manuscript, 1976.

Torzillo, P. J., and Williams, E. (unpub.), Review of casualty services for Aborigines in rural New South Wales, report prepared for NSW Department of Health Task Force, 1989.

Williams, L. (unpub.), The NSW Department of Health Aboriginal health program, discussion paper, NSW Department of Health, Sydney, 1989.

Acknowledgments

Valuable suggestions on the draft chapter were generously given by David Scrimgeour, Rob Moodie and Chris George. Much of the section on environmental health is taken directly from work by Paul Pholeros and Stefan Rainow for Nganampa Health Council. Lesley Simmons willingly typed several drafts of the chapter.

CHAPTER 9

Policy and practice in Aboriginal health

Sherry Saggers

Department of Aboriginal and Intercultural Studies, Edith Cowan University,
Mount Lawley, Western Australia

Dennis Gray

Department of General Practice, University of Western Australia,
Nedlands, Western Australia

Policy is not an unambiguous blueprint for practice. The policies enunciated by governments are as often statements of ideals, or statements to placate and/or silence particular interest groups in society, as they are the basis of action.

Palmer and Short (1989, p. 22) have defined health policy as:

courses of action that affect that set of institutions, organisations, services and funding arrangements that we have called the health care system. It includes actions or intended actions, by public, private and voluntary organisations that have an impact on health. ... policy may refer either to a set of actions and decisions, or to statements of intention. Government policy includes what governments say they will do, what they do, and what they do not do.

The purpose of this chapter is to review the health policies of various Australian state and federal governments, and the effects of those policies on the health of Aborigines. It is important to understand, however, that Aboriginal health policy and practice must be viewed in the context of broader policies towards Aborigines, and that the ill-health of Aborigines is as much a consequence of the general policies and practices of non-Aboriginal Australians as it is of specific attempts to alleviate that ill-health. It is in this wider context that Aboriginal health policies will be examined.

The poor state of health of Aborigines relative to other Australians has been well documented (Kamien 1980; Moodie 1981; Thomson 1984, 1986). They suffer higher rates of morbidity and mortality and their health profile combines third world disease patterns for the young with the so-called diseases of civilisation for adults (Thomson 1984; Russell and Schofield 1986; Beck 1985). Since Moodie (1973) and Hetzel et al. (1974) wrote their wide-ranging reviews of Aboriginal health, much literature has accumulated on the extent of poor Aboriginal health and the reasons contributing to this. In spite of differences in emphases, however, what is striking about much of this literature is the unanimity with respect to the fundamental causes of Aboriginal ill-health (Kamien 1980; Moodie 1981; Russell and Schofield 1986; Thomson 1984, 1986). In Thomson's words (1984, p. 939):

The health status of Australia's Aborigines is far inferior to that of non-Aboriginal Australians. The factors underlying this low standard of health are complex, but relate to the gross social inequality experienced by Aborigines, even today. The social inequality, characterised by extreme socioeconomic deprivation and relative powerlessness, is the end result of the European occupation of Australia, which caused Aboriginal depopulation and dispossession.

The fact that Aboriginal Australians are more likely to live in poverty, with inadequate water and electricity supplies, poor sanitation and sewerage facilities, and in over-crowded and inappropriate housing, needs to be included in any analysis of health care for Aborigines. In particular, the economic, social and political factors that in concert have contributed to the position of Aborigines in contemporary Australian society must be central. Consequently, policies directed primarily at the provision of health services can only marginally affect the health status of Aborigines.

The poor health status of Aborigines is the direct consequence of invasion by a militarily superior society, which was soon able to establish its dominance over the indigenous hunter-gatherers, expropriate their land and effectively, if not consciously, destroy their mode of production. The 200 years that have passed since the initial invasion have seen the cementing of the unequal power relations that existed at the outset.

From the very beginnings of the first colony in New South Wales, the provision of health care for Aborigines has been a political issue. In more recent times, this has included conflicts about the respective roles of the state and the Commonwealth, the power and status of professional and paramedical workers, and the control of services by Aborigines and non-Aborigines. These conflicts occur in a broader political context of debate about the proper role of government in the provision of health care.

Historical overview

Early colonial policy—'amity and kindness'

As Franklin and White point out in chapter 1 of this book, early explorers' reports (Basedow 1932; Dampier 1729) suggest that, at the time of British settlement, the health of Aborigines was generally better than that of a large proportion of the British population. The hunter-gatherer lifeway, based on a varied, largely vegetable diet, semi-nomadic movements, and intimate social groups, maintained a basically well-nourished population whose major threats to life and well-being consisted of infant mortality and physical trauma (Kamien 1980).

From the time of the establishment of the first colony at Sydney Cove, the British colonial government denied any prior ownership of Australia by the indigenous inhabitants (despite a later, ingenious attempt by John Batman to secure a treaty with Aborigines at Port Phillip in 1835). Thus there were few legal impediments to the appropriation of land for European purposes. However, imperial policy stated that Aborigines were to have the full status and legal rights of British subjects. Their physical well-being was to be protected, and Aborigines were gradually to become civilised, largely through the teachings and practice of Christianity (Long 1979, p. 357; Elkin 1951).

Despite such positive statements from the British Colonial Office, from the early colonial period there was an ambivalence between the ideology of equality expressed through various policies designed to protect Aborigines from the depredations of the Europeans, and very desultory practice which saw neglect and abandonment of the policies in response to the growing demands of the land-owning class. For instance, in 1837 the Western Australian Legislative Council pronounced that the amelioration and civilisation of the Aborigines was a less urgent task than the protection of the lives and property of British subjects (Long 1979).

There were colonial administrators who were more liberal-minded than others. For instance, Macquarie set aside agricultural lands around Sydney for the use of Aborigines who were 'inclined to become regular settlers'. But he was disappointed when Aborigines appeared not to be interested. Attacks by Aborigines on Europeans and their sheep led to the declaration a few years later of martial law for the part of New South Wales west of Mount York (Reece 1974, p. 110). In the circumstances the actions of benevolent individuals could do little to address the wider question of the status of Aborigines in the colonies.

The period of expansionism

Throughout the nineteenth century, the production of wool became increasingly important to the colony's economy, and the pastoralists required larger tracts of land over which to graze their sheep. Hence, in the second part of the century the dispossession of Aboriginal people continued westward and north into Queensland. As European expansion continued, clashes with the Aborigines increased and there was a hardening of attitudes about the practicality of the policy of 'amity and kindness'. Along the frontier, Europeans took the law into their own hands by 'pacifying' Aborigines who were proving troublesome because they wished to use their territories for traditional purposes at the same time as the land was being fenced and cultivated (Elkin 1951). In 1880, the *Bulletin* reported that:

In North Queensland, the blacks are never allowed within the township. The whites hold possession of the valley and when the hungry black descends from the range in quest of food, perchance to spear a horse or bullock, he is shot. And what is happening in Queensland now happened every day in NSW.

Cited in Pollard 1988, p. 24

From the initial period of colonial settlement, exposure to previously unknown infectious diseases was to decimate the Aboriginal population. Although estimates of the pre-colonial population vary (see in this volume Franklin and White, chapter 1, and Gray et al., chapter 3), it is estimated by some writers to have numbered around three quarters of a million people when the Europeans arrived (White and Mulvaney 1987). A smallpox epidemic in 1789 is estimated to have resulted in the deaths of some 50 per cent of Aborigines in the area surrounding Sydney (Kamien 1980). Subsequently, as the frontier expanded, this and other epidemic diseases such as measles and influenza took further heavy tolls. As well as epidemic disease, violence also had a dramatic impact on the Aboriginal population. Punitive expeditions by European settlers and the police resulted in many deaths, some of which have been recorded in brutal detail (Evans et al. 1975, pp. 33–46). It is not possible to place any reliable estimate on the total numbers of Aborigines killed by non-Aborigines, but Elder (1988) documents many of those massacres for which records are available (see case study: Reynolds 'Such extraordinary terrorism' in chapter 1).

While the official policy towards Aborigines was that they should be afforded the protection of the colonial government, in reality Aborigines were dispossessed, decimated, and reduced to remnant pockets of population on the outskirts of European settlement (Evans et al. 1975). Without the means to provide for themselves, these Aboriginal remnants suffered from malnutrition and a host of infectious diseases. At the same time, access to alcohol contributed to social conflict and ill-health. The sight of drunken Aborigines reinforced the prevailing European stereotyped belief that Aborigines were innately lazy and addicted to alcohol (Evans et al. 1975, p. 92). Many of the changes to the health profile of Aborigines during this period mirrored those of large sections of the European peasantry who in the eighteenth and nineteenth centuries had been transformed by capitalism into a surplus population enduring both malnutrition and stress-related diseases (Eyer 1984).

Recognition of the disastrous impact of European diseases and lifestyle on the Aborigines led to attempts by evangelicals in Britain to establish inquiries into the condition of Aborigines (and indigenous people in all the British colonies). The rapid depopulation of Aborigines in New South Wales and Tasmania added fuel to these requests. A report by Bruxton in 1837, based on the findings of a committee of the House of Commons, was influential in a change of policy, in which the overall emphasis was on segregation, for the purpose of protecting the Aborigines. The report recommended that responsibility for the condition of indigenous people should rest with Her Majesty's Executive, but the costs of administration should be met by colonial governments; and that Protectors of Aborigines should be appointed to become acquainted with the Aborigines and assist them to pursue lives they chose. These recommendations, initially implemented in New South Wales, formed the basis for policies of 'protection' throughout Australia into the next century (Reece 1974, pp. 133–4).

The period 1840–80 also saw the introduction of legislation to control clashes between Europeans and Aborigines. However, few Europeans were brought to account under such legislation and the colonial governments themselves continued to use the police in punitive expeditions against Aborigines. The new policy of protection was accorded lower priority than the economic interests of the European settlers.

While these new policies were being enunciated, elsewhere in Australia the health plight of the Aborigines received little attention. Referring to the situation in Queensland, Evans et al. (1975, p. 96) write:

The manner in which sicknesses that were not usually fatal to Europeans—like measles or influenza—cut a swathe through native groups with a seeming ease and inevitability encouraged an indifference among whites to the point of callousness on the question of Aboriginal illness.

Although official policy protected some Aborigines from the excesses of the Europeans, the effects of dispossession itself were not considered. Secure in their belief in the innate superiority of European capitalism, the colonialists expected the Aborigines to embrace agricultural pursuits, settled living and the 'benefits' of Christianity. There was no expectation that this accommodation would involve parity of life chances for Aborigines. Rather it was assumed that they would slot naturally into the 'lower orders' of European society. Policies developed in the nineteenth century for Aborigines reflected this view, as well as the notion that Aborigines were a dying race whose need for protection was probably short-term.

The creation of reserves where these remnant populations could spend their time sheltered from the violence of white settlements was very much a product of this view (Pollard 1988). Stemming from the earlier Bruxton report, the reserves were seen as 'a powerful means of domesticating, civilising and making them [Aborigines] comfortable' (Report of the Protector of Aborigines 1882, cited in Pollard 1988, p. 25). By the beginning of the 1890s, most of the Aboriginal population of New South Wales was resident on the many reserves (Pollard 1988, p. 25) and the other colonies rapidly followed suit.

One of the lasting effects of the reserves has been the dependence of Aboriginal people on the wider Australian society for the most basic of human needs. Diet, movement, employment, marriage, child-rearing arrangements, and the exercise of religious belief were all subject to the wishes of the mission or settlement custodians. In addition, the systematic removal of Aboriginal children believed to be of 'mixed descent', in order that they would be successfully assimilated into the 'lower orders' of Australian society, created generations of dislocated families, many of whom would never see their close relatives again (see the discussion of the 'stolen generations' in Gray et al., chapter 3 in this volume).

The institutionalisation of Aborigines in the period from about 1850 to the early 1930s had a number of consequences, not the least of which being the deleterious effect on their health. The change from small, semi-nomadic communities into large aggregations of people from many different areas led to a rapid increase of both communicable diseases and social tensions resulting in physical violence.

References to colonial policies and practices with respect to health care are scattered (Biskup 1973; Beck 1985; Nathan 1980; Reece 1974; Rowley 1970). What is clear from the literature is that particular policies pertaining to Aboriginal health were circumscribed, and were part and parcel of the wider policies to contain and control Aboriginal people. This was to remain the pattern of Aboriginal health policy throughout Australia until the 1970s.

In the latter half of the nineteenth century, Aborigines in Western Australia employed under contract were legally entitled to free medical treatment and prescribed rations, although this regulation was not enforced. From the 1860s, resident magistrates dispensed medicines to impoverished, sick Aborigines and, infrequently sent very ill people to the nearest hospital, where they were treated either on the verandah or in the yard. It should, however, be noted here that medical care for Europeans was rudimentary and treatment at home was the norm until well into the twentieth century (Biskup 1973, pp. 111–2). Despite this, it is clear that medical treatment for Aborigines in many parts of Australia was crude, or non-existent. In 1873, the Maryborough Hospital in Queensland refused to admit a seriously wounded Aboriginal woman who subsequently died, on the following grounds:

It has been a rule of the Maryborough Hospital ever since it has been in exist-ence...that aboriginals [sic] should not be admitted as patients—both from lack of separate accommodation for them and the absolute dislike—we might say almost refusal of the servants to attend upon them.

Evans et al. 1975, p. 97

The impetus for the development of specific 'health' policies relating to Aborigines came from the Europeans' desire to protect themselves from the con-tagious diseases that had had such a devastating effect on the Aboriginal population since the arrival of the first settlers. Venereal diseases were of particular concern after outbreaks among Aborigines were first noticed. In Queensland, syphilis spread so rapidly that reports in the 1890s refer to more than half the Aboriginal population suffering from the disease in some areas. The initial solution was to relo-cate the Aborigines away from European settlement (Evans et al. 1975, p. 100).

In Western Australia, pressure for Aboriginal hospitals which would primarily isolate, but also treat, sufferers of venereal disease grew in the early 1900s and in 1908 the Western Australian government established hospitals on Bernier and Dorre islands west of Carnarvon, on the north-west coast of Western Australia. These so-called 'lock' hospitals received many of their patients in chains, after they had been hunted down by police and forcibly removed to the islands (Jebb 1984). Effective medical treatment was not available until the First World War, and so many Aborigines died on the islands that in 1910 a bone crusher was ordered so that it was possible to 'utilize all available organic matter for the object of improving the nutritive value of the soil' (Biskup 1973, p. 113). Conflict over the administration of the hospitals contributed to a high staff turnover, as did the Spartan living conditions on the islands. These difficulties, and the abysmal record of successful treatment, led to the closure of the island hospitals in 1919 when an Aboriginal hospital at Port Hedland was established.

The model of enforced isolation and largely ineffective treatment was also fol-lowed for Aborigines diagnosed as having leprosy (Hansen's disease), a disease generally believed to have been introduced by indentured Asian labourers. A tem-porary leprosarium was established in Western Australia on Bezout Island near Cos-sack in 1911. From there, patients were then taken to Bernier and Dorre Islands. Medical surveys in Western Australia in 1922 and 1928 recorded more cases of leprosy, mostly in the Kimberley region, and in 1931 a decision was made to send all diagnosed lepers to Darwin, with a leprosy compound of the Derby Aboriginal Hospital acting as a staging point. Some patients waited for transport in the com-pound for periods up to a year. The Moseley Royal Commission of 1934 described the building as consisting of a 'galvanized iron shed, open on one side, and rather less pretentious than the average fowl-house' (*West Australian* 1934, cited in Bis-kup 1973, p. 115). Obviously the 'protection' of the Aboriginal population did not extend to protection from the health consequences of their contacts with Europeans.

Apart from the Aboriginal hospitals at Port Hedland and Derby, the only hospital to which Aborigines in Western Australia had access before about 1935 was the Australian Inland Mission nursing home in Hall's Creek—and that treatment was provided only because of an annual subsidy of 100 pounds from the Aborigines Department. The inadequacy of these services was apparent when epidemics broke out in the Kimberley region in 1920, when 132 people died (Biskup 1973, p. 116).

Attempts to make employers of Western Australian Aborigines more responsible for their health were met with stern opposition. For instance, in 1937, proposed regulations requiring employers to contribute 2 pounds ($4) annually to the Native's Medical Fund for every permanent employee were opposed by the Pastoralists Association, and the government eventually agreed to voluntary contributions by employees.

The Western Australian example is typical of other parts of Australia. Beck's (1985) history of European medical services in the Northern Territory notes that only in the 1930s, when it was apparent that the Aborigines were not dying out as predicted, were health services for Aborigines initiated in any systematic way. Prior to the assumption of responsibility for the Northern Territory by the Commonwealth government in 1911, most legislation pertaining to the Aborigines was designed to restrict contact between European and Chinese males and Aboriginal females, thus attempting to isolate Aboriginal disease from the wider population.

An attempt was made to establish a health service for Aborigines in 1911. However, this failed when the three 'medical protectors' appointed left their posts and were not replaced. Instead, medical kits were dispensed widely throughout the Northern Territory, and infrequent visits by medical personnel took place. The Inland Mission Hostel at Stuart, established in 1916, did not treat Aborigines (Beck 1985, pp. 11–12). The appointment of C. E. Cook as Chief Medical Officer and Chief Protector in 1927 saw the establishment of the Northern Territory Medical Service and the gradual upgrading of medical and hospital services for the European and Aboriginal populations. In the decade 1929–39, five hospitals and a leprosarium were established outside Darwin.

The assimilation period

By the 1920s, throughout Australia it was evident that Aborigines were not dying out and that their numbers were on the increase. It was therefore necessary for governments to move away from policies of protection. The direction taken was to attempt to incorporate them into the wider Australian society—the policy of assimilation.

The first major policy statement on the assimilation of Aborigines was made in 1939 by Minister for the Interior John McEwan, who was responsible for the Northern Territory. He stated that the policy should lead to:

the raising of their status so as to entitle them by right and by qualification to the ordinary rights of citizenship, and to enable them and help them to share with us the opportunities that are available in their native land.

Cited in Rowley 1970, pp. 328–9

That the assimilation policy was not accepted by a joint Commonwealth-State Ministerial Meeting until 1951 is a reflection of the attitudes of the wider society. Through this policy Aboriginal people, it was reasoned, could gradually become absorbed into the non-Aboriginal community. An important premise of this policy was that prejudice towards Aborigines was insoluble, and that only by breeding out Aboriginality could these people expect to be treated as equals (Rowley 1970, p. 343).

Under the assimilation policy, the extensive Aboriginal reserves were gradually revoked without compensation to Aboriginal people, and other overt vestiges of the segregation of the past were dismantled. However, the proclamation that Aborigines will live in a similar manner to other Australians did not take into account the fact that many of those other Australians were unwilling to admit Aborigines into their society. From the early days of assimilation in the 1950s to the 1970s, there were explicit examples of exclusion, and health services were not spared from this.

The period following the Second World War saw gradual improvements to health services for Aborigines in Australia, both in public hospitals and the growing number of mission hospitals. However, as late as 1947 the Mullewa Aboriginal hospital in Western Australia required all patients to do their own laundry, feed themselves and collect firewood. Probably, improved health services in that state can be linked to the takeover of the Aboriginal hospitals by the Department of Public Health in 1949. There is a clear difference between the positive public health measures undertaken by this department—with the successful treatment of leprosy and trachoma, in particular—and the resistance of local hospital authorities to take on the responsibility for treating Aboriginal patients. The matron of Perth's King Edward Memorial Hospital in 1949 echoed the sentiments of many others when she said:

It is all very well to talk about the rights of natives, but I do not think that people who talk in this way would like to be in the next bed to some of these women.
Cited in Biskup 1973, p. 247

Until the 1960s, it was not uncommon throughout Australia for Aborigines to be refused treatment, or to wait in segregated rooms to see a doctor. The question of whose financial responsibility it was to provide individual medical insurance was also much debated. In Western Australia, the Aborigines Department paid for Aborigines not covered either by their employers or the Natives' Medical Fund (Biskup 1973).

In the Northern Territory, it was not until the 1950s that organised health services for Aborigines were resumed by the Welfare Branch (Beck 1985). A similar pattern existed in other states, where special provision for Aboriginal health, prior to the 1960s, consisted largely of negative policies designed to protect white Australia from possible contagion from infectious diseases. Compulsory examination and, in some cases, forced isolation, remained in the legislation up until the 1960s (Rowley 1971).

The precedence of economic interests over humanitarian or health issues was clear. Attempts to win equal wages for Aborigines in the pastoral industry were vigorously opposed by employers, and in 1946 leaders of the Aboriginal pastoral workers' strike in the Pilbara region of Western Australia were gaoled (Bennett 1989, p. 6).

Although 1972 is conventionally regarded as the dawn of a new era in Aboriginal affairs, the seeds for the policies enunciated later were sown largely during the latter half of the 1960s. Internationally, the Vietnam War had raised people's awareness of issues such as colonisation, and bodies like the United Nations were increasingly used by the newly independent nations to bring worldwide pressure on those countries whose indigenous minorities were still not equal citizens. In Australia, while the most overtly discriminatory legislation pertaining to Aborigines was being dismantled, there were still many inequities. Lower wages, restrictions on movement, and limited access to social security payments existed in many states at this time. Even the identification of Aboriginality was denied to Aborigines; this was determined in most states by a local magistrate (Rowley 1973, p. 189).

The assimilation period was not without its 'successes'. Some of the Aboriginal children who had gone through the European education system were beginning to understand their position in Australian society and began to agitate to change it (Pollard 1988). It is ironical, but understandable, that the very people selected by Europeans to take their place in European society in Australia would be those most critical of past and present policies towards Aborigines. Aborigines in remote areas were also becoming more vocal in their opposition, with the Gurindji people walking off Wave Hill station in the Northern Territory in protest at the delay in the implementation of the Arbitration Commission's equal wages decision of 1965 (Bennett 1989, p. 12).

The combination of international and internal pressures led to the announcement of the policy of integration in 1965. This purported to allow for the participation of ethnic minorities in the wider Australian community, but with the retention of their traditional cultures, if this was desired. For many Aborigines and other Australians, this was a case of too little and too late. The difference between assimilation and integration seemed inconsequential but the policy provided a bridge to what would become a more liberal stance purporting to recognise the right of ethnic minorities to participate and direct their futures in this country.

The passing of the 1967 referendum, which deleted the discriminatory sections of the Constitution regarding the inability of the Commonwealth to make special laws for Aborigines and to count them in the census, was a necessary prerequisite for the development of progressive policies in Aboriginal affairs. However, in the years immediately following the referendum, there was little change in the status of Aborigines. The urgency of the situation from the Aboriginal perspective was highlighted by the establishment in 1972 of the Aboriginal 'tent embassy' on the lawns of Parliament House in Canberra, in protest against the conservative government's refusal to grant land rights. With the election of the Whitlam Labor government later that year, Aboriginal affairs became a prominent part of the political agenda, not just for this newly elected 'socialist' party, but for all parties (Bennett 1989, p. 14).

Health policy: 1972–90

The 1970s saw a dramatic change in Aboriginal affairs policy. Following the 1967 referendum, the Commonwealth Office of Aboriginal Affairs was established. With the election of the Whitlam Labor Government in 1972, this became the Department of Aboriginal Affairs (DAA) and was charged with implementing the government's policy of self-determination for Aborigines. During its period in office, the Whitlam government increased direct Commonwealth expenditure on Aboriginal assistance programs from $89.8 million in 1973–74 to $173.1 million in the 1975–76 financial year (DAA 1987, p. 69)

During the years of the Fraser government, there was a significant cut in Commonwealth spending on Aboriginal affairs. In its first year in office, spending was cut by 14 per cent (DAA 1987, p. 69). Despite the funding cuts, an emphasis on 'self-management' rather than self-determination, and an attempt to hand some responsibilities back to the states, Aboriginal affairs policy remained surprisingly bipartisan throughout the Fraser government's period in office. The Aboriginal affairs policies laid down by the Whitlam government, with some changes to program priorities, essentially remain the basis of the Hawke government's policies today.

The Whitlam government took a major initiative in the development of Aboriginal health policy. Under Whitlam, the Commonwealth Department of Health prepared the Ten Year Plan for Aboriginal Health. Approved by the minister for health in March 1973, the statement proposed that the Australian government, through the Department of Health, be responsible for a national campaign to raise the standard of Aboriginal health (see also Franklin and White, chapter 1 in this volume). In particular, Aboriginal health was to be improved to the same level as that of non-Aboriginal Australians in the following areas: infant and child mortality and morbidity, infant and child nutrition, growth retardation, and chronic diseases and infectious diseases such as leprosy, trachoma, tuberculosis, gastroenteritis, and respiratory and ear infections. These objectives were to be achieved in 10 years (Department of Health 1977). As Thomson (1985) has pointed out, however, the plan was more like a statement of intention to develop a plan.

The strategy to accomplish the objectives involved a review of Aboriginal health, including data collection; a survey of current and planned programs; specification of health care resources available within Australia to Aborigines; promotion of preventive medicine and community health; and the development of a national campaign in consultation with all relevant Commonwealth and state authorities (Department of Health 1977). To tackle the first part of this strategy, the House of Representatives Standing Committee on Aboriginal Affairs was charged with the responsibility of investigating the health problems of Aborigines. Specifically, it was to examine the prevalence of disease; the relationship between environmental, social and cultural factors and health; the efficacy of current health programs; and alternative health-care delivery systems that might be more culturally appropriate for Aborigines (HRSCAA 1979). Recommendations from the standing committee were headed by items pertaining to the physical environment, a very clear indication of the role that living standards play in poor Aboriginal health. It was also recommended that account be taken of Aboriginal cultural factors in health-care services, and to the further development of preventive health programs. Evaluation of all Aboriginal health care services was recommended, a point taken up later in this chapter. The committee stressed self-determination, community development and the much greater involvement of Aboriginal people at all levels of health-care service delivery. It also indicated the need for training of non-Aboriginal staff (HRSCAA 1979).

While the Commonwealth government was at the forefront of developing policies for Aborigines, health remained a state government responsibility. Thus, in order to influence state policy, the Whitlam government made available funds for Aboriginal health by way of tied grants under section 96 of the Constitution. This practice was to play a continuing part in Australian public policy making. The states were desperately in need of federal funding but wherever possible resisted Commonwealth attempts to provide direction.

During the 1980s, as a basis for the formulation of a national health policy, there have been several government enquiries into the health of Australians. These include the Better Health Commission (1986) and the Health Targets and Implementation (Health for All) Committee (1988). Although the health of Aborigines remains the worst of all identifiable groups in the country, the fact that it was not accorded higher priority in these reports highlights the low priority that Aboriginal issues generally have for government and the community at large.

The basis of the Hawke government's Aboriginal policies is the recognition that Aborigines 'experience fundamental disadvantages and obstacles in achieving their aspirations and needs'. The cornerstone of these policies are the notions of self-determination and self-management. The key section of the platform reads:

[Labor will adhere] to the principle of self-determination and self management whenever developing programmes or engaged in projects for the benefit of Aboriginal people. It will ensure the active participation and adequate resourcing of those Aboriginal groups, organisations and communities during the planning, development and implementation of these programmes and projects.

Australian Labor Party (WA Branch) 1989, p. 1

The Labor Party platform goes on to propose a number of specific policies to assist Aborigines in overcoming these disadvantages and obstacles. The main thrust of the government's health policy is to: support the development of Aboriginal Medical Services (AMSs) as the main agents of health-care delivery, and to transfer Commonwealth funds from state administrations to AMSs; to establish a national system for the collection of Aboriginal health statistics; to support the training of Aboriginal health personnel; and to provide essential services to Aboriginal communities.

The Commonwealth has sought to improve the health of Aborigines not only through specific health policies, but through broader community development programs. Of the programs administered by the Department of Aboriginal Affairs (DAA, now the Aboriginal and Torres Strait Islander Commission—ATSIC) and the Aboriginal Development Commission (ADC), the most important are the following:

1. The Accelerated Community Infrastructure Program (which replaced the Aboriginal Public Health Improvement Program), the Aboriginal Communities Development Program, the Priority Communities Development Strategy, the Town Campers Assistance Program, the Rental Accommodation (Housing Grants) Program, and the Home Loan Program, all of which are aimed at improving the environment in which Aborigines live.

2. The Community Development Employment Program, the Enterprise Development Scheme, Small Business Funding, and Enterprise Support Services, the aim of all of which is to create Aboriginal economic independence (DAA 1989; ADC 1989).

As well as these programs, others are administered by Commonwealth departments such as the Department of Employment, Education and Training, which provides the majority of education and training programs, and Australian Construction Services. Over recent years, between 42 and 44 per cent of all expenditure on Commonwealth Aboriginal programs has been administered by these various other departments (DAA 1989, p. 18). For example, in the 1986–87 financial year, direct Commonwealth expenditure on Aboriginal assistance programs was $542.1 million, of which departments other than DAA or the ADC provided 44 per cent. The proportion of direct expenditure in some of these key program areas for the years 1982–83 and 1986–87 is set out in table 9.1. In each of these years, the single largest program area was housing, followed by education. Significantly, the amount allocated to employment has been increased. However, the amount allocated for income-generating enterprise schemes remains minuscule. These priorities are understandable, given the urgent need that many Aborigines have for shelter, and the fact that providing housing is a less sensitive political issue for non-Aboriginal Australians than Aboriginal enterprises.

Several studies have made the point that Aboriginal self-determination will remain an illusion in the absence of economic independence (Howard 1978; Tonkinson and Howard 1990). Unfortunately, despite the changes initiated by Whitlam, the illusion remains. Largely as a result of the relative paucity of funds allocated to the problems faced by Aborigines, the various programs of the Commonwealth have not been implemented in a coordinated manner at the community level. That is, they have not been implemented in a way that would lead to broad community development. Thus, for example, in the absence of other programs, targeting housing in some communities has lead to a decline in health status. This has resulted from a reduction in disposable income as a consequence of increased rental and utility charges and a decrease in funds for foodstuffs, in turn leading to undernutrition and greater susceptibility to infection.

In table 9.1, the fall in the proportion of the Aboriginal programs budget allocated directly to health reflects increases in other areas rather than a fall in the Aboriginal health budget. As well as making funds available for general health services provided by community-controlled health services and the state departments of health (both of which are discussed below), ATSIC has also funded 'health initiatives' targeted at specific health problems. Among those underway in 1988–89

Table 9.1 Direct Commonwealth expenditure on Aboriginal advancement programs

Function	1982–1983[a]	1986–1987[b]
Housing	32.0	25.7
Employment	13.6	20.5
Education and training	20.8	22.6
Enterprises	0.3	2.5
Health	10.0	7.0

[a] From DAA 1984, p.55; total expenditure $242.1 million.
[b] Approximate, derived from DAA 1987, p. 68; total expenditure $542.5 million.

Aboriginal health and political economy in Australia

In the early 1960s, the generalisation 'Aboriginal health' did not exist in any national sense in the way in which we understand it today. At that time, the health of our people was in the hands of two powerful groups: the state governments and the Church. The state governments had responsibilities for all citizens who lived within their borders (and while most people of Aboriginal descent were not strictly citizens, they were nonetheless the responsibility of state governments). For over 100 years, the Church had seen itself as both the colonial—and after 1901—the Australian social conscience, providing Aborigines with moral correction. In the period from 1920 to 1960, two important factors shaped events. The first factor was the failure of state governments to provide adequate funding for Aboriginal welfare agencies such as Church missions. The second factor was the growing Aboriginal population, which placed great stress on Aboriginal mission costs.

In the post Second World War social and political climate, the states controlled all aspects of Aboriginal life, through repressive legislation, similar to the racial policies in South Africa at that time. With our growing population, Aboriginal people were denied access to the improved social and economic (including improved health) services of the post-war era, and had a declining share of the national wealth, at a time when inflation was rising. Also at this time, especially in the Northern Territory (NT), the increasing centralised controls under native welfare policies made the struggle more obvious. The reasons were twofold: first, the ALP opposition saw Aboriginal infant mortality as a problem to be addressed; second, rural political groups came face to face with the federal ALP as an alternative government. There was little understanding in the 1960s that the root causes of Aboriginal ill-health were related to the kinds of 'social relationships' between whites and Aborigines, such as overcrowded habitats, poor diet, poverty due to unemployment, and finally low political consciousness. The 1967 referendum heightened the prospect that a future ALP government would establish a national policy on Aboriginal matters.

In 1971, the ALP had an Aboriginal policy but it lacked two things: a national Aboriginal health strategy and a strategy to take account of the idea that 'protection' of reserve lands was increasingly under threat by mining interests. These two anomalies were corrected at the 1972 ALP Hobart conference, which resulted in the Whitlam Labor government policies of 1972. Nevertheless, throughout the 1970s and 1980s parties holding power failed to put into practice a national Aboriginal health strategy. One positive achievement of the period, however, was the emergence of 'free' primary health services located in Aboriginal communities. These medical services were managed by Aborigines and each provided a general practitioner, community-based health services model. The project soon attracted government support.

In the latter part of 1975, Dr Archie Kalokerinos made his now famous claim that blindness rates among Aborigines were the highest in the world, a claim that the Labor government could not disregard. The government approved funding for the National Trachoma and Eye Health Program (NTEHP) for rural peoples (RACO 1980). This was significant in that many Aborigines were, at that point, rural dwellers. The program's report forcefully placed Aboriginal health in the social, economic and political arena. The NTEHP findings supported the proliferation of community-based health services; greater access to material resources such as clean water; better diets; Aboriginal involvement in health policy making (and practices); and greater federal and state financial and political support.

The major ingredient of the NTEHP was its scientific approach to health surveillance. Whatever current strategies entail, they are often biased towards political and not scientific solutions. Another weakness is the lack of emphasis on review of Aboriginal-controlled health services to cover health service delivery standards. Moreover, there is nothing in contemporary federal or state government policies on Aboriginal health that can prevent the return of the neglect and apathy of the past.

Gordon Briscoe, History Department, Faculty of Arts, Australian National University, Canberra were programs addressing hepatitis B immunisation, lifestyle diseases, ear health, women's health, and eye health (DAA 1989, pp. 86–9). Of all the special health programs mounted in Australia, the National Trachoma and Eye Health Program (NTEHP; see RACO 1980) has had perhaps the highest profile, for a number of reasons. It incorporated a number of central issues in Aboriginal health-care provision: Commonwealth versus state responsibility, Aboriginal participation, and a very clear demonstration of the environmental basis of Aboriginal ill-health. Gordon Briscoe's case study, 'Aboriginal health and political economy in Australia', in this chapter provides the historical background to the program and places it firmly within a political economy framework.

Despite its short-term success in providing much needed treatment to those Aborigines suffering from trachoma and its complications, the NTEHP had little long-term impact on prevention of the disease. This highlights the fact that targeted medical interventions have limited success in the control of non-immunisable disease. However, the program was not without its successes. In particular, it became a focus for attempts by Aborigines to improve their health status. Of key importance was the insistence in the NTEHP report that Aborigines take control of their own health. The program report also indicates that among the essential requirements for long-term improvements in Aboriginal health are adequate housing, safe water, good food, appropriate storage, and well-maintained sewerage and garbage disposal (RACO 1980, p. 181).

Health and medical services for Aborigines

As stated previously, before the late 1960s there was little recognition that the health of Aborigines warranted special attention. However, acknowledgment of the magnitude of Aboriginal health problems, focused attention on the capacity of the existing health-care system to deliver adequate services to Aborigines. With the incentive of Commonwealth funding, this led to the development by the states of specific health programs for Aborigines. At the same time, the introduction of the Medibank and, later, Medicare universal health insurance schemes made primary medical care more affordable to all Australians—including segments of the Aboriginal population.

The basis of primary medical care in Australia is the fee-for-service provision of care by private practitioners. Currently, under Medicare, the Commonwealth's Health Insurance Commission (HIC) reimburses to the patient 85 per cent of the scheduled fee for each service provided by an approved practitioner. Alternatively, practitioners may elect to bulk-bill the HIC for services provided to patients and forgo the difference between the scheduled fee and the reimbursable amount. Aborigines have become increasingly urbanised in the last 20 years, and, although no figures are available, it is probable that a large proportion of those residing in larger urban centres receive primary care from general medical practitioners under these arrangements.

Exceptions to these arrangements have largely occurred in rural or remote areas in which the conduct of private practice has been uneconomical and/or which have been unattractive to medical practitioners or their families as areas in which to live. In these areas, the states have taken responsibility and primary medical care has been provided by salaried medical officers from the outpatients' departments of district hospitals. For Aborigines in remote areas, primary care is often provided by nursing post staff, community nurses or Aboriginal health workers.

As well as providing primary care services in remote areas, the states provide a variety of other services and programs, and these are outlined below. It should be noted that information about these services comes from each state's official submission to either the 1979 parliamentary inquiry into Aboriginal health, or the 1989 National Aboriginal Health Strategy Working Party. Those requiring more detailed information about these services are referred to the annual reports of the various state health departments or commissions. (Another important source of primary care and other health services for Aborigines is the Aboriginal-controlled health services, which will be discussed separately.)

Victoria

The Special Services Health Section of the Health Department of Victoria was established in 1974, with DAA funding, in response to criticism that very little recognition was being paid to the special health needs of Aborigines in the state. Advised to concentrate on preventive medicine and community health, staff consisted largely of nurses and Aboriginal health aides (Nathan 1980).

Significant changes to Aboriginal health services in Victoria resulted from the recommendations of the 1981 Working Party into Aboriginal Health (Coombs 1983). The Aboriginal Health Resources Consultative Group, with voting rights restricted to Aborigines, was created to advise the minister directly. In addition, Aboriginal-controlled community-based health services were established in areas of high Aboriginal population. Aboriginal hospital liaison officers mediate between these services and the state's hospital services. Coordination of this operation was vested in the Aboriginal Liaison Unit within the Public Health Division of the Health Commission (Thomson 1985).

Currently a Koorie Health Unit exists in Health Department Victoria. Its main objectives are to encourage the participation of Aborigines in the formulation of health policy and the design of programs, and to improve access to public health services for Aborigines. Specific programs target women's and children's health, diabetes, hospital liaison, and hepatitis B (NAHSWP 1989).

Northern Territory

In the Northern Territory between 1973 and 1978, responsibility for Aboriginal health was with the Northern Territory Division of the Commonwealth Department of Health (the Northern Territory Medical Service), but this now rests with the Northern Territory Department of Health and Community Services. This department provides three types of health-care services. In remote areas where Aborigines are living on ex-mission or government settlements, primary health care is delivered by resident nurses and Aboriginal health workers. Medical facilities range from the fairly basic to the quite sophisticated. The Aero-Medical Service provides emergency transport for treatment by regional medical officers, and also holds regular clinics in remote areas. Specialised hospital treatment is available in Alice Springs and Darwin.

Beck (1985) comments that the current health services are oriented to technology-intensive hospitals requiring highly trained (European) medical professionals. Although the overall expenditure on health per head of total population compares favourably with the national average ($443 to $438 in 1975–78), the proportion of health expenditure on community health services has fallen, while hospital expenditure has increased. Given the distribution of the Aboriginal population in the Northern Territory, and their largely primary health-care needs, Beck (1985) contends that it appears that the health services are directed mostly at the European population.

Queensland

In Queensland, the Aboriginal Health Program was established under the Department of Health in 1973. It was staffed largely by public health nurses, Aboriginal health nurses, health assistants and health workers. Health education programs were also mounted by the Department of Aboriginal and Islander Advancement (HRSCAA 1979). In 1982, the Aboriginal and Islander Health Advisory Council was created in order to provide direct communication between Aborigines and the minister. The Queensland government also has responsibility for health services in the Torres Strait and Northern Peninsula Area. Hospitals at Bamaga (on the peninsula) and on Thursday Island are run by the Department of Health, while medical aid posts in each Torres Strait island community, the Maternal and Child Welfare clinic at Bamaga and the pharmaceutical supplies to each aid post are controlled by the Department of Community Services and Ethnic Affairs (NAHSWP 1989).

Western Australia

The Community Health Services branch of the Western Australian Department of Public Health (now part of the Health Department of Western Australia) was established in 1972, and it became responsible for Aboriginal health. The state was divided into six regions, each with a full-time medical officer, public health field nurses and Aboriginal health workers. Recent initiatives in Western Australian Aboriginal health programs include the employment of Aboriginal liaison officers in the north of the state, a health inspection service incorporating the Environmental Health Worker Training Program in the Pilbara and Kimberley regions, and the training of Aboriginal health workers. The Health Department of Western Australia has recently filled positions in a newly created Aboriginal Health Policy Unit.

New South Wales

In New South Wales, the Aboriginal Health Section was created within the Bureau of Personal Health Services of the Health Commission in 1973. Emphasis was placed in each region on the employment of community health nurses and community health workers. The section also employed alcohol counsellors, mental health counsellors and hospital health workers (HRSCAA 1979). In 1982, a task force report (cited in Thomson 1985) recommended the redirection of Commonwealth funds from the New South Wales Department of Health to the Aboriginal community-controlled services, and this has been implemented. This redirection in funds is an important initiative and the first indication of a state government's willingness to cede some power and resources to Aboriginal-controlled health services. The report also recommended the establishment of an Aboriginal health resources committee to provide a coordinating function similar to that of the Victorian Consultative Group. This is now operating and it oversees the work of the Aboriginal medical services and the Aboriginal Health Unit within the Department of Health (Thomson 1985). In addition, the Department of Health funds enhancement programs with drug and alcohol workers, dental vans, public health workers and programs for targeted Aboriginal groups such as women and children, the elderly, and diabetics (NAHSWP 1989, p. 47).

South Australia

In 1973, South Australia's Health Commission created the Aboriginal Health Unit, which mostly employed Aboriginal health workers and nurses to provide clinical and preventive services in the remote reserves (HRSCAA 1979). The Aboriginal Health Organisation of South Australia commenced in 1981, under a 10-member board of management, eight of whom were Aboriginal. Current Aboriginal health programs funded by the Aboriginal Health Organisation include those on AIDS/STD, ante-natal care and family planning for women, and renal surveying and follow-up. The employment of Aboriginal hospital liaison, workers also provides mediation between mainstream health services and Aborigines. In 1988, a review of Aboriginal health in South Australia proposed the establishment of an Aboriginal health co-ordinating unit within the Health Commission, to be concerned with policy development, research and liaison with the wider community (NAHSWP 1989:54).

Tasmania

Health services for Aborigines in Tasmania are mainstreamed within the Department of Health Services, except for the provision of a Commonwealth-funded non-Aboriginal nursing sister and the operating costs of a medical clinic at Cape Barren Island (HRSCAA 1979; NAHSWP 1989).

Funding and strategies

The various state Aboriginal health programs have received considerable funds from the Commonwealth. In 1987–88, from a total budget of $12.9 million, Western Australia received $7.2 million, Queensland $4.9 million, South Australia $0.8 million and Tasmania $44 400. Current figures for the Northern Territory are not available, but in 1978–79 its allocation was estimated at $9.3 million. Of all the states, only New South Wales has gradually taken over the funding of its health program, releasing more than $2 million of Commonwealth funds to Aboriginal medical services in the state (Thomson and Honari 1988).

Thomson and Honari (1988) identified the criterion for allocation of funds as the major difficulty with the states grants scheme. Rather than distribution of funds on a *per capita* basis, or on the basis of relative needs, allocations were made on the basis of the existing programs when the scheme began. Hence, Western Australia was comparatively well resourced, even though that state's program is less well developed than those of Victoria, New South Wales and South Australia in terms of the employment of Aborigines and their participation in decision making. The Aboriginal and Torres Strait Islander Commission (ATSIC) has reviewed these arrangements, and in between the 1988–89 and 1990–91 budgets, allocations to the Health Department of Western Australia were phased out.

Palmer and Short (1989, p. 252) identify three strategies policy makers can adopt to rectify inequalities in health. The first involves mainstream or generic service providers, and attempts to make these services more accessible and acceptable to targeted groups. The second calls for the development of services that are designed specifically for the targeted group. The third strategy addresses the more fundamental question of the causes of health inequality, and specific strategies are therefore more likely to be addressed to the political and economic realms.

As illustrated in this section health and medical services provided by the state governments for Aborigines have, sometimes reluctantly, gradually taken on the first strategy. With the recent exception of New South Wales, the states have been more cautious in their approach to the second strategy. Their strong emphasis on service provision, and ideological opposition, has excluded any serious consideration of the third strategy.

Health and medical services by Aborigines

In the 1960s and 1970s, a commonly reported problem among Aborigines was late presentation of illness to providers of medical care. The result of such late presentation was increased severity of illness, development of complications that could have been prevented, and sometimes death. Recognition of this problem was partly behind the attempts to ensure delivery of primary health-care services to Aborigines in remote areas in the early 1970s. However, simple provision of services is not sufficient to ensure their use. This is reflected in the fact that, despite the emphasis on service provision to remote communities, underuse of health services was also common in the cities and large rural towns. In these larger population centres, the problem was exacerbated by the migration of Aborigines from rural areas, which had accelerated during this period.

The thrust of the World Health Organization's Alma Ata declaration is that, in order for primary health-care programs to be effective, they should be affordable, accessible, acceptable and appropriate, and that the involvement of the communities for whom they are provided is essential to their success (WHO-UNICEF 1978). In the late 1960s and early 1970s, prior to the introduction of Medibank (and later Medicare) most mainstream health services were not affordable to Aborigines. Generally, they could afford neither the fees charged by private medical practitioners nor private health insurance. The services that were affordable—those provided by hospital casualty departments—were often unacceptable, like those provided by private practitioners. Aborigines reported racist and unsympathetic treatment and that there was little attempt to understand their situation. Common are stories of hospital staff who berated Aboriginal mothers presenting with sick children for not taking care of the children, rather that encouraging the mothers for their attendance and helping them to understand how health problems might be prevented or minimised.

Aboriginal medical services (AMSs)

This situation led to one of the most important developments in the area of Aboriginal health—the emergence of Aboriginal-controlled medical services. The first of these was established in the Sydney suburb of Redfern in 1971. It is particularly important to note that this Aboriginal initiative pre-dates much of the government-initiated action in the area of Aboriginal health (see the case study by Patricia Fagan, 'Self-determination in action'). This reflects the growing political struggle among Aborigines throughout the country to improve their lot. Other manifestations of Aboriginal initiative include the walk-off from Wave Hill station in the Northern Territory in 1966 by the Gurindji over conditions of employment and land claims; the freedom rides through rural New South Wales in 1965 which aimed to break down discrimination in access to public facilities; and the establishment of the

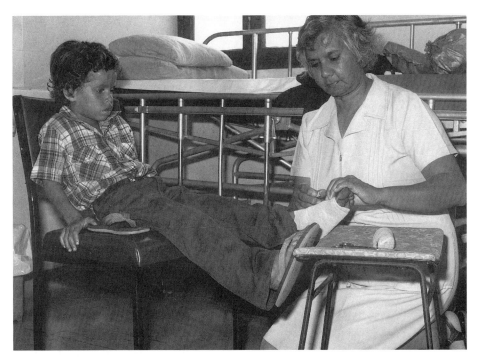

Figure 9.1 *A young patient receives care for an injured foot at Redfern Aboriginal Medical Service, Sydney, the first Aboriginal-controlled medical service in Australia. (R. Maccoll/Australian Foreign Affairs and Trade Department, Canberra)*

Self-determination in action

In 1970, Aboriginal people in Redfern, an inner suburb of Sydney, established the first Aboriginal legal service, a response to their overwhelming need for some redress and legal representation in the face of police harassment and frequent arrests in overcrowded and poverty ridden Redfern. This was the first ever community-controlled Aboriginal organisation, and the Aboriginal Medical Service followed in mid-1971. The significance of these events in Redfern is lost on many who look back in the 1990s. Few people understand that the establishment of the Aboriginal Legal and Medical Services involved a concerted struggle and was a historic political victory for all Aboriginal people in twentieth-century Australia.

In 1971, Aboriginal people knew that they faced severe health problems and had minimal access to mainstream medical care. The solution to these problems, to set up an independent community-controlled medical service, was an entirely Aboriginal concept. It was neither instigated nor supported by any section of government nor the health bureaucracy. In fact, non-Aboriginal Australia had always implied that Aboriginal people had neither the will nor the capacity to control their own affairs.

Initially, the Aboriginal Medical Service (AMS) was a shop front in Botany Road, Redfern. It was staffed by Aboriginal people and by volunteer non-Aboriginal health professionals. It was greeted with popular support from the community in Redfern. For the first time, they were offered a health service that was free, accessible and available on their own terms, and in a place they could call their own.

For the first 12 to 18 months the AMS functioned with next to no government assistance. But the government was eventually embarrassed into acknowledging that here was a much needed service that was accepted and used by the community—an achievement no non-Aboriginal health agency had ever been able to claim. Subsequently, some funding became available.

It should be realised that, from the very beginning, government tried to undermine the AMS's independence through the funding process. The justification for doing this was the use of 'public monies'. Aboriginal people consider that the relatively minute amounts of money that were made available at that time were neither 'public monies' nor handouts. They represented a tiny contribution to the massive compensation due for their dispossession.

The early years of AMS Redfern were characterised by this annual wrangle for funding—a process that required a great deal of time and energy spent rallying support. Aboriginal people resented this. They understood it as an attempt to control and trivialise their work and demoralise the workers. It seemed that, despite the by then official policy of self-determination, self-determined action by Aboriginal people was perceived as a threat and was to be thwarted in every possible way.

Aboriginal people describe the philosophy of the AMS as community control. In the 1970s, community control was a popular political sentiment of the left, worldwide. It was a term often loosely used but tending to refer to community action not initiated by government and not run by professional bureaucracies. In Aboriginal terms, community control also meant the revival of a mechanism for community decision-making that was already a part of traditional Aboriginal culture. Consensus is the goal; 'having your say' and 'talking it out' is the process.

Aboriginal community control over health services allows communities an opportunity to determine their own priorities in program development, and it ensures the continuing relevance and appropriateness of the services provided. Because community control requires an awareness of and an ability to respond flexibly to community concerns, it means that the health service necessarily sees health not only at the individual disease level but also at the community level, and so adopts a more holistic view, involving itself in the broader concerns of the community that have an impact on health.

An important consequence of community control in a medical service is that, unlike hospitals and most other health institutions, the AMS is client- and community-centred, not doctor-centred. The doctors and other health professionals are welcome and their skills are valued and respected, but their priorities are only one factor that contributes to the AMS's determination of its priorities.

The structure of the AMS reflects this philosophy of community control. Community input and participation is maximised through the AMS's governing body, the board of directors, all of whom are local Aboriginal people who are elected annually; and, at the clinic level, through the contribution of Aboriginal health workers, themselves members of the local community.

All this happened in 1971 in Redfern. It preceded the Alma Ata Declaration of 1978—the World Health Organization's declaration that recommended that community involvement and participation in primary health-care services was both essential and desirable.

So, far from being a government initiative, far from being founded at the instigation of non-Aboriginal people, far from being a consequence of a widespread development in primary health-care delivery in Australia, the establishment of the AMS in Redfern, with its philosophy of community control, was an exciting and innovative Aboriginal initiative and an expression of Aboriginal self-determination—of the conviction that ultimately Aboriginal people are the experts and that given time and opportunity they can find the solutions to their problems.

These were the true beginnings of the Aboriginal Medical Service in Redfern. They had a profoundly positive impact on Aboriginal Australia and they should not be forgotten.

Patricia Fagan, Aboriginal Medical Service, Redfern, New South Wales

Aboriginal 'tent embassy' outside Parliament House in Canberra in 1972 (Bennett 1989, pp. 6–12).

Briscoe (1974) and Foley (1975) have documented the establishment of the Redfern Aboriginal Medical Service and the difficulties, particularly with regard to funding, that were encountered. Subsequently, Aboriginal groups in other areas followed the lead set by the people of Redfern and established medical services of their own. Among these other services, published reports are available on those at Fitzroy in Melbourne (Nathan 1980) and at Perth (Reid, D. B., 1978).

Role of the AMSs

The Aboriginal medical services (AMSs) originally concerned themselves mainly with the provision of primary health care. The services are situated in locations where there are large numbers of Aboriginal people. Recognising that proximity is not the only factor involved in the accessibility of services, the AMSs often provide transportation for those who might otherwise be unable to attend, and they often conduct evening clinics for the benefit of those members of the community who might be working. As well as clinic-based services, the AMSs employ Aboriginal health workers to make home visits. The role of such health workers varies: in the major cities, there is an emphasis on educative, preventive and advocacy roles, while in rural and remote areas the health workers play a greater role in the provision of therapeutic services.

One of the most important features of the services provided by the AMSs is their *acceptability* to Aboriginal people. The majority of the staff are themselves Aboriginal and have an understanding of the consumers of the services, and the rules of etiquette appropriate in the community. Medical and nursing staff employed by the services, if not Aborigines, generally have an interest in Aboriginal health and an empathy with their patients. Also clinic facilities are small and non-threatening. According to Reid, AMSs most nearly meet the goals outlined by WHO for the delivery of primary health care (Reid 1982, p. xiv).

The provision of primary health care has been the major focus of the AMSs, and this continues to be so among some of the smaller of the 64 AMSs which were being

An Aboriginal nutrition program

Before white settlement in this country, Aborigines led a healthy life, collecting and hunting foods in season. Aborigines were not an obese race. This soon changed when the fertile hunting lands were taken over and our people became fringe dwellers around the early settlements and the welfare mentality began.

In a very short space of time nutritional problems began; this included mature onset diabetes, lactose intolerance and undernutrition in babies, overnutrition in others and circulatory problems. Apart from the abrupt change in lifestyles, children were taken from their parents and placed in missions which, in turn, did not introduce the ideal concept of European eating, and in many instances, the children were fed on large amounts of bread and dripping, with very little meat and vegetables. In some instances the young girls were taught to cook European-style, which included all the food suitable for colder conditions: rice pudding, steamed pudding, dumplings and stews, all made with large amounts of refined flour.

Food for health was not a part of the input for our people. It was a case of the motions and not the intricacies of culture being passed on. This can be seen on a broad plane in Australia today, with the inclusion of foods from different nationalities, particularly Chinese food. More specifically, in the early 1970s there was a general migration of Aboriginal people from the rural and remote areas when the country became mechanised and the national wage system was set in place. There was no place for the families to live in their homelands and work on the sheep and cattle stations. Until then, they had led a semi-tribal lifestyle, eating many of the foods off the land and catching kangaroos for meat.

This came to an abrupt end with the movement of Aborigines to the large towns and cities and the upsurge of eating high fat protein in mutton and beef and filling up with bread and cake. High fat and fast foods were on the tidal wave of success at that time, so this set the scene for the majority of our people who, without background knowledge of this lifestyle, and with little money and no education in basic needs for health and nutrition, had to struggle through a quagmire of ill-health due to poor eating habits.

It is very difficult for those of us working in the area of nutrition to present a program on healthy eating patterns in theory, for the following reasons:

1. Adults have an eating pattern in place.
2. Children have little say in buying household food.
3. When there is very little money, budget is a word that no-one recognises.
4. Carbohydrates, proteins and vitamins are foreign words, which people can't transpose into food, although fat is easily identified.

A program must be real and alive and be seen to work for it to be accepted. It was never very interesting for me, but in 1976 when I went to India to look at village health programs, I saw the Indian nurse with a group of women at the clinic squatting outside and cooking food on an open fire. When I asked what she was doing, she said: 'When the mothers come to the clinic, I teach them about nutrition by preparing food and cooking it as the people would in their homes'. I brought this innovative idea back, and when we started the health education program at the Aboriginal Medical Service in Perth, we endeavoured to Aboriginalise the program by looking at the type of food more likely to be eaten by Aborigines; this was particularly relevant for diabetic diets. We had long tasting sessions. The Nutritional and Dietary Department from Royal Perth Hospital cooperated with us and supplied a large variety of the foods that are offered to people with diabetes.

We always have a few diabetics among the students, so it was very interesting tasting the foods and comparing them with other foodstuffs of equal nutritional value. For example, one point for discussion was: 'Would an Aboriginal person sent home on a diet consisting of lentils, vegetables and fruit, stick to the diet? NO! Well what of the foods available? Could we make a palatable, acceptable diet for an Aboriginal diabetic?'.

It is very important to get an educator who is willing to listen and learn at a cultural level, because without this there is a tendency to override the cultural aspect in content and techniques. There is also a need for a person who is able to use a language that students can relate to, without losing the message. We went about communicating the message by:

1. finding out what people already know; getting them to talk about eating patterns; writing out a 24-hour intake of food;
2. discussing what a balanced diet is; forming groups of three to four and making posters on 'glow, go, grow' foods;
3. going to supermarkets and reading labels for content and amount; comparing prices of different brands;
4. preparing a balanced 'cold, take-away' lunch for the staff.

The setting has poster displays and students explain about health foods. This is done with in each group. Sandwiches, fruit and salads are sold. This allows for more shopping and preparation.

Another strategy is planning community meals. A theme is agreed on, such as:

What makes little kids grow?
Senior citizen's snacks
Alcohol and diet
Lactating mothers' meals
Diabetic delights

We make arrangements with a local hostel for the use of the kitchen and dining room, invite guests and set about buying and preparing the food. This always turns out to be a happy occasion and the students learn more than nutrition, as preparation, food storage and hygiene are all part of the experience.

The seminar on diet and nutrition is completed with each student preparing food at home and bringing it along for a picnic or barbecue on the last day.

A short exam is given the following week, with follow-up sessions later in the year to review diet and diseases. This program has been by far the most effective for retention and application of knowledge.

Joan Winch, Aboriginal Medical Service, East Perth

funded by DAA in November 1989. However, Aboriginal health workers employed by the AMSs have long conducted preventive health-care programs (see the case study, 'An Aboriginal nutrition program'). Over the years, some of the larger medical services have further broadened the range of services they provide. The AMS at Redfern has been a leader in this respect, and also provides specialist services such as diabetic clinics and physiotherapy, a drug and alcohol program, and a hostel for the aged, as well as conducting a health worker training program (NAHSWP 1989, appendix VI). In the north of Western Australia, the Kimberley Aboriginal Medical Services Council (KAMSC), an umbrella organisation, has contracted with the Health Department of Western Australia to provide to particular Aboriginal communities in the region services such as the immunisation program, health and care of the elderly, and alcohol programs (HDWA 1986, p. 12).

As well as focusing on the provision of health-care services, the AMSs have always had a concern with the wider social issues that are the underlying cause of so much of the excessive burden of morbidity and mortality in Aboriginal communities. These concerns have found varying degrees of expression in the different medical services. From its earliest days, the Redfern AMS has played an important role in bringing attention to the political and economic causes of Aboriginal ill-health.

Apart from their health-care and advocacy roles, many AMSs have also been important vehicles for community development. Given the social context of Aboriginal ill-health, this is perhaps their most important contribution. With the possible exception of land rights, health has been the issue that has most galvanised Aboriginal communities to action. The success of these community-based organisations has demonstrated to Aboriginal people that, although they are structurally disadvantaged, they are not completely powerless and that they can organise to improve the conditions under which they are forced to live.

Umbrella organisations

The importance of health as a political issue has led to the formation of various umbrella organisations among the AMSs. The most prominent of these is the National Aboriginal and Islander Health Organisation (NAIHO), which was established in 1974. This body has played an influential role in focusing attention on the social, economic and political aspects of Aboriginal health. NAIHO has also acted as a lobby group, pressuring the federal government to provide increasing levels of funding to Aboriginal-controlled medical services. It has also provided assistance to Aboriginal communities in establishing their own medical services. As well as the national body, there are state-level associations of AMSs. These meet at regular intervals to discuss issues of common concern and to formulate joint approaches to government. Regional umbrella AMS organisations, such as the Central Australian Aboriginal Congress (CAAC) based in Alice Springs and the Kimberley Aboriginal Medical Services Council are also important. Acting in concert, the individual AMSs are enabled to expand the range of services they provide.

Influence on state government departments

The relative success of the AMSs in providing the type of services demanded by Aborigines has also had some influence on the provision of health services by state government departments. As long as Aborigines contribute only marginally to state health policies, it is not possible for the states to provide completely acceptable health-care services. Nevertheless, community demands and the activities of the AMSs have led the states to provide services that have gone some way to recognising the needs of their Aboriginal clients. For example, they have increasingly incorporated Aboriginal staff into the lower echelons of service delivery.

Figure 9.2 *After completing a course at Queen Elizabeth Hospital, Adelaide, in 1987, Aboriginal enrolled nurse Lisa Mason stayed on to work at the hospital. (From DEET, Aboriginal opportunities in employment, education and training, AGPS, 1989, p. 27)*

Administration and funding

All of the AMSs have elected councils, through which communities have the opportunity to have a say in the formulation of policy and the running of the organisation. However, there is some variation in their funding and administrative arrangements. A small number are funded entirely from grants by the Commonwealth (usually through ATSIC) or state governments. This type of funding includes both capital costs and recurrent costs, such as the salaries of medical staff, health workers, and administrative personnel and overheads. A more common arrangement is the bulk billing of services to Medicare to provide a base income, with ATSIC picking up the funding for the additional budgetary components. Thirdly, the larger services receive additional funding from other Commonwealth agencies such as the Department of Education, Employment and Training, and the Department of Community Services and Health, as well as from various state government agencies. In part, this variation in funding arrangements is a reflection of differences in the range of services provided. Also, some of the AMSs that were established earlier were often able to strike more advantageous funding agreements than the more recently founded services. There has been little or no attempt to restructure the allocation of direct grants on the basis of need.

Criticisms

The AMSs have not been without their critics. One of the most frequent criticisms levelled is that they duplicate services already provided by mainstream health services. The problem with this criticism is that it looks only at the type of service provided, and not at the crucial issue of its acceptability. One of the most important lessons of the 1960s and early 1970s is that government can provide services but, if they are not acceptable, they will be underused. In this light, AMSs do not duplicate existing services—or do so to only a limited degree. Rather, they provide services to those who would otherwise be unwilling to use mainstream services. The issue of duplication is most vocally raised in towns where there is a large Aboriginal population, and which have private medical practitioners. Here the objection is largely from a self-interested professional group opposed to any funding or public underwriting of primary health-care services. At least in the public sector, the complaint of service duplication is most frequently heard in state government head and regional offices. Among those working in the field it is more common to hear the view that, given the enormous work load, little duplication takes place and that there is a need for provision of more services, not the exclusion of one organisation.

Another of the criticisms levelled against the AMSs is that some of them provide limited service coverage. This is viewed as presenting difficulties for health planners. However, we believe that this criticism is misplaced. In the wider community, apart from remote areas serviced by government health services, there are no organisations which provide blanket primary health care services. In this regard, AMSs should be treated in a manner similar to other providers, with the states shouldering their obligations to provide services where no others are provided. The AMSs should not be obstructed because they provide only the same services as other non-government primary health care providers.

The very successes of the AMSs might now be working against them. The NAHSWP identified a total of 91 centres as requiring either large or small AMS clinics (NAHSWP 1989, appendix V). Similarly, the DAA, which in November 1989 was funding some 64 AMSs, has numerous requests from communities to fund additional services. This increase in demand, with its consequent funding implications, appears to have led to a cooling in DAA's receptivity to such requests.

Aboriginal health workers

In an attempt to make mainstream health services more acceptable to Aboriginal people, Aboriginal health workers have been increasingly incorporated into health-care service delivery throughout Australia. Internationally, the push for the utilisation of indigenous primary health-care givers was led by the World Health Organization, after reports from developing countries such as China gave glowing accounts of this type of care.

In Australia, Aboriginal health workers have been employed since the early 1970s, both by Aboriginal medical services and state-controlled health services. The role of the health worker varies somewhat throughout Australia, and this has consequences for the type of training program provided. In some health services (for instance, in many of the state programs, and some urban Aboriginal medical services) health workers are seen in a largely educative and liaison role. The provision of primary care is the focus in other settings, particularly the Northern Territory state program, and many of the remote-area Aboriginal medical services. While some health workers are given a great deal of responsibility, especially in remote regions, others have a very dependent, subordinate role.

The selection of Aboriginal health workers should ideally be made by the community in which that worker is expected to be employed, and all health services stress the importance of community nomination and acceptance of the program (NAHSWP 1989). However, this ideal is sometimes balanced rather precariously with the priorities of the health professionals with whom the health worker must work closely. Young, literate Aborigines may be preferable from the point of view of a nurse undertaking their health training, but they may not be acceptable to their communities because of their perceived immaturity and/or lack of experience in Aboriginal matters. In health worker programs throughout Australia, there is much variation in the prerequisites for admission, from very few basic skills, to reasonable literacy levels.

The variation in the role of health workers has led to the development of training programs with different emphases. Delivery of training ranges from individual on-site instruction, as with the Health Department of Western Australia, to the full-time year-long courses undertaken by health workers in some Aboriginal medical services. There are also tertiary courses, such as the Associate Diploma in Aboriginal Health and Community Development at Cumberland College, Sydney University, which primarily trains the Aboriginal health workers employed by the NSW Department of Health and some AMSs. The Northern Territory program has influenced other services, particularly those in remote areas. That program directs

Figure 9.3 *Aboriginal health workers in training*

training to four broad areas; primary health care, personal health care, community health action and health services management (Soong 1979). A similar model was followed by the East Kimberley Aboriginal Medical Service and the Broome Region Aboriginal Medical Service in Western Australia (Armstrong et al. 1987) and in the program now conducted by the Kimberley Aboriginal Medical Services Council program which replaced them.

Training programs for health workers have been the focus of much debate in recent years, and a recurring issue has been the mode by which training should be delivered, given the wide variation in Aboriginal communities. It seems that it may be preferable to tolerate a range of modes, from full-time courses, to short-term modules offered within particular communities, and to supplement this with regular, systematic on-the-job training.

In 1989, the National Aboriginal Health Strategy Working Party recommended the development of uniform, accredited courses for Aboriginal health workers to 'assist mobility and to enable health workers to gain entry to the related health and professional education and training arenas' (NAHSWP 1989, p. 89). This is not an easy recommendation to implement, because the training needs of Aboriginal health workers are as diverse as the communities in which they work. While some health workers may aspire to the established health professions, many see their role as providing a wider range of services. That is, an Aboriginal person working as a doctor or a trained nurse may provide more acceptable care to the majority of Aborigines, but at present the formal training these professionals undergo pays scant regard to the issues fundamental to Aboriginal ill-health. Unless that training places more emphasis on the structural basis of Aboriginal health, and the social and cultural factors exacerbating health problems, incorporation of Aboriginal health professionals into health-care services is thinly disguised assimilation.

A review of health worker education in Western Australia (Armstrong et al. 1987) recommended against the tertiary accreditation of health worker programs, on the basis that this simply institutionalises the position of Aborigines at the bottom hierarchy of providers. Instead, the review committee encouraged the enrolment of qualified Aboriginal people into mainstream training courses in nursing and medicine; and they suggested that technical colleges and other pre-tertiary institutions were more appropriate places for the training of health workers. This issue will remain problematic, with some programs opting for tertiary affiliation, while others seek alternative accreditation routes.

One avenue to formal legal status and recognition has been through the Arbitration System. The Northern Territory *Health Practitioners and Allied Professionals Registration Act (1986)* provides for the registration of Aboriginal health workers and issues certificates to practice to those who have passed the Basic Skills Certificate in the state program (NAHSWP 1989). A similar scheme was recommended by the Western Australian review committee into health worker education (Armstrong et al. 1987).

The absence of a clearly defined career structure for Aboriginal health workers has been widely criticised (Reid 1982; Thomson 1984), and this has been exacerbated by the lack of formal education and training received by many health workers. In the Health Department of Western Australia, there is only one position above basic health worker, that of the regional Aboriginal health liaison officer (Armstrong et al. 1987). In 1987 there were only seven of these positions in the state, and they were largely token, with no real authority.

The ability of Aboriginal health workers to organise to improve their status is inhibited because of their isolation, both within the state health systems in which they work, and in geographical terms. However, recognition of these problems is now more widespread and suggestions to improve career paths based on length of service, supervisory responsibility, isolation, qualifications and administrative responsibilities have been made, if not implemented (Armstrong et al. 1987).

To date, few of the Aboriginal health worker programs have been formally evaluated. This is not surprising, given the difficulties in establishing valid criteria for evaluation. For instance, should the health profiles of communities improve with the employment of health workers (probably an unreasonable requirement, given the structural basis of most ill-health), or given the very basic skills which some health workers receive during their training, should employment outcomes be more relevant? However the matter of evaluation is decided, it is important that Aboriginal-controlled programs not be targeted to the neglect of the longer established state programs.

The future of Aboriginal health workers will depend on the direction taken by state and Aboriginal-controlled health services. It may be that their roles will continue to differ according to policies at the state and Commonwealth levels. Any health service, particularly those in which Aboriginal health workers are employed as low-level educators and liaison officers, will be increasingly asked to justify the status quo, given the official rhetoric about the importance of having Aborigines in decision-making positions in the health-care system (NAHSWP 1989).

The problem unsolved

At first glance, the range of policies that we have outlined appear admirable, but how effective have they been? Certainly, there have been some changes in the social indicators. Infant mortality, for example, has fallen quite dramatically, particularly in rural areas. Much of this fall has been the result of focused intervention. In Western Australia in the Kimberley region, this has been achieved by evacuating all pregnant Aboriginal women to the Derby Regional Hospital for their confinement. In the Northern Territory, a similar policy saw women from communities around the central region transported to Alice Springs to deliver their infants. However, the limits of this kind of intervention appear to have been reached, and infant mortality rates appear to have stabilised at between two and three times those in the non-Aboriginal population.

While not belittling this achievement, it must be recognised that such focused interventions have not solved the problems of ill-health in Aboriginal children. Rather, they have changed the nature of the problem. The children of impoverished Aboriginal parents no longer die in infancy. Instead, many survive, but 'fail to thrive' (see Gracey, 'Kylie's first two years', a case study in chapter 2 of this volume). Similarly, women evacuated alone to distant hospitals for their confinements suffer loneliness and anxiety.

In addition, available statistics indicate that in other areas the health status of Aborigines is actually declining. As Thomson documents in chapter 2, increases have been recorded in chronic diseases such as diabetes and heart disease (the conservatively misnamed 'lifestyle' diseases). Furthermore, Aboriginal life-expectancy at birth remains about 20 years less than that of the non-Aboriginal population (Thomson and Honari 1988).

In an attempt to deal with these seemingly intractable problems of Aboriginal ill-health, the National Aboriginal Health Strategy Working Party (NAHSWP) was established. In outlining its brief the NAHSWP states:

To date there has been no agreed national Aboriginal health strategy, nor have there been the coordinating mechanisms to ensure and measure the success of such a strategy.

With this in mind Commonwealth, State and Territory Ministers for Aboriginal Affairs and Health agreed to the establishment of the National Aboriginal Health Strategy Working Party at a meeting in December 1987.

NAHSWP 1989, p. ix

While the NAHSWP's 1989 report identifies many problem areas and makes many valuable recommendations, in an overall sense it is a disappointing document. In part constrained by its terms of reference, the report deals mainly with the delivery of health services, rather than addressing the fundamental causes of Aboriginal ill-health. Furthermore, the strategies proposed are general and do not focus on implementation. This leaves considerable room for interpretation, particularly by the more tardy state governments, and does not auger well for the implementation of these strategies (see the case study by Tony McMichael, 'A National Aboriginal Health Strategy' in this chapter).

A National Aboriginal Health Strategy

In March of this year [1989], the report of the National Aboriginal Health Strategy Working Party was released. Chapter 2 of this report begins thus:

Aboriginals have the worst health of any identifiable group in Australia, they carry a burden of health and mortality far in excess of that expected from the proportion they comprise of the total Australian population. This state of affairs has been documented on many occasions and there is considerable literature describing Aboriginal ill health.

Yes, we have heard this bad news, with the attendant appalling statistics, before. But, nevertheless, non-Aboriginal Australia mostly remains cosily oblivious to the continuing illnesses, diseases, and demoralisation of the Aboriginal population. We are much more likely to read, in the daily newspaper, of the loss of life in a malfunctioning DC 10 aircraft somewhere overseas, or of the road toll, or of the rising epidemic of AIDS in backstreet Sydney, or of some tenuous link of a food additive with cancer of the whatnot. The disgraceful story of Aboriginal suicides in custody has also aroused a discomforting fascination.

No wonder, then, that the [Foreword] to this report is angry and lurid in its analysis of the historical and sociopolitical dimensions—'The reality and not the myth'—of the tragedy of Aboriginal repression, slaughter, and social disintegration since 1788. Robert Hughes had it wrong, we are told, in his construal of 'The Fatal Shore'. The deportation of convicted murderers, rapists, thieves, and vagrants, along with the dregs of the army and police (who could not make it to up-market India and East Africa) resulted in inevitable degradation, destruction, disease and death for Aboriginal Australians. It was for the First Australians that the deportation of convicts proved 'fatal'.

While the Working Party went about the preparation of this report during 1988, the 'vulgar trumpetings and epically Philistine commercialism' of the Bicentennial further served to 'sanitise [white Australia's] convict past'.

Recent historical background

Ten years ago the House of Representatives Standing Committee on Aboriginal Affairs reported the state of Aboriginal health as being 'intolerable', and made 18 recommendations and 24 suggestions to improve the situation. The Committee gave highest priority to the provision of basic environmental health facilities, especially safe water supplies. Today, however, many Aboriginal communities still do not have a safe and reliable water supply.

The inadequacy of the piecemeal and episodic approach has been plain for many years. It was plain to the members of the Better Health Commission when they carried out their work, on behalf of the Commonwealth Minister for Health, during 1985–1986. Indeed, the terms of reference of the Better Health Commission, whose central task was to review Australia's major health problems and the means for their reduction, specified paying particular attention to the needs of disadvantaged and minority groups, including Aborigines. The inadequacy was also plain to the subsequent Health Targets and Implementation Committee (1987–1988), charged by the Australian Health Ministers Advisory Council (AHMAC) with developing specific health promotion targets and strategies for all Australians.

Thus, both those national committees of enquiry gave primary emphasis to the needs of the overall Australian population. On large canvases, the details and the needs of minority groups were overshadowed by broader brush strokes. The National Better Health Program that has recently been spawned by these two enquiries specifies four major health problem areas and one needy group—the elderly.

Origins of the Working Party

In late 1987, recognising Australia's continuing lack of a cohesive approach to Aboriginal health, and presumably influenced by the ideas, rhetoric, and social health strategies of the World Health Organization's 'Health For All By the Year 2000' campaign, a meeting of Commonwealth, State and Territory Ministers responsible for health and Aboriginal affairs established a National Aboriginal Health Strategy Working Party.

The Working Party comprised 19 persons: two Commonwealth appointees, eight State/Territory representatives, and nine Aboriginal community representatives. It is worth noting that this was the first time that Commonwealth, State and Territory governments, and Aboriginal and Torres Strait Islander community representatives have worked together on a national health policy.

The Working Party was to review governmental and community funding of Aboriginal health (both short-term and longer-term), for promoting intersectoralism, and evaluating progress. The Working Party carried out extensive community consultations, and met ten times, in the course of its work.

The report

The resultant report documents in detail the current health status of Aborigines and—to the extent that incomplete earlier health statistics allow—time trends in health indices. Age-adjusted rates of disease, adult death, and perinatal death are, variously, two to six times higher than in non-Aboriginal Australia. The socioeconomic indicators display the other side of this dismal coin.

Subsequent chapters deal with a logical sequence of major issues: Commonwealth/State health care responsibilities; the structure of the health care system (including the relatively recently emergent Aboriginal health services) and the profound cultural dissonances between Aboriginal and non-Aboriginal perceptions of health and health care; the education and training of Aboriginal health care workers; intersectoralism; the need for, and nature of, social health strategies; strategies for coping with special problem areas—such as alcohol abuse, women's health (including the culturally sensitive area of birthing), a range of infectious, chronic, and traumatic diseases and injuries, and various health problems caused by antisocial and violent behaviours attributable to social and cultural degradation. Finally, there is discussion of the need for better Aboriginal health research—conducted from within, and not 'imposed' from without—and for systematic monitoring and evaluation.

The report identifies the need for some structural changes in the machinery of government, if a national strategy is to be viable and effective.

Since 1984, the Department of Aboriginal Affairs [and later the Aboriginal and Torres Strait Islander Commission] has had sole responsibility

for funding and administering all Commonwealth programs relating to Aboriginal health. The Commonwealth Department of Community Services and Health retains a broad policy responsibility for Aboriginal health matters.

Neither the Department of Aboriginal Affairs nor the Department of Community Services and Health has a direct role in providing health care services for Aborigines. This responsibility lies with the general Australian health care system, including that administered by State and Territory governments, and with the community-controlled Aboriginal health services.

The report recommends the creation of an Office of Aboriginal Health, to coordinate, monitor and evaluate Aboriginal health programs, and to promote an intersectoral approach across portfolios of government. The Office would be a nonstatutory body within the Aboriginal Affairs portfolio (not explicitly within or without the Department of Aboriginal Affairs). It also recommends the creation of a National Aboriginal Health Council, to act, intersectorally, as a standing committee of both the Health Minsters Council and the Council of Aboriginal Affairs.

Interim response

Not surprisingly, the political/bureaucratic response to the report's recommendations has been to establish a 'Development Group' (comprising the Working Party chairperson and various senior Commonwealth and State/Territory officials). This body will review the detailed recommendations of the report, and will recommend to a joint Health/Aboriginal Affairs Ministerial meeting in November 1989 on Aboriginal health problem priorities and preventive strategies, and organisational and funding needs.

Immediately, however, the Commonwealth Departments of Aboriginal Affairs and of Community Services and Health have agreed to take action in relation to environmental health matters (eg safe water, hygienic food, sanitation), education and training programs for Aboriginal health workers, and the development of a uniform system of Aboriginal health statistics. This last is an obvious task for the Australian Institute of Health. Hopefully, too, the incipient National Better Health Program, under the auspices of the Department of Community Services and Health, will find ways of interfacing its five specific health promotion thrusts—in relation to hypertension control, nutrition improvement, injury prevention, early detection of cancers, and health care needs of the elderly—with the manifest needs of Aboriginal communities. The work of this Working Party provides our best chance yet of starting to get Aboriginal health right. The year 2000 is little more than a decade off.

Reprinted from Tony McMichael, 'A National Aboriginal Health Strategy', Aboriginal Health Information Bulletin **12**, November 1989, pp. 36–38

What then have been the major obstacles to the improvement of Aboriginal health? First and foremost is the lack of real commitment to the fundamental structural changes that are required to end the interrelated problems of Aboriginal poverty and dependence. No government has been prepared to change the status quo. For instance, in the Northern Territory the granting of land rights excluded the possibility of claiming land under pastoral lease. In Western Australia, opposition from the mining lobby led to the repudiation of land rights by the Burke Labor government. In 1990, the Hawke government was also back-pedalling on Aboriginal affairs, as it attempted to woo an increasingly conservative electorate. Despite continuing popular belief that the funding of Aboriginal affairs represents a bottomless pit, in 1986–87, total Commonwealth funding for Aboriginal affairs was $542.5 million (DAA 1987, p. 69). The Aboriginal population in 1986 was 227 645 (DAA 1989, p. 227). Hence—ignoring the fact that a large proportion of this funding does not go directly to Aborigines—the *per capita* spending amounts to $2383. This is hardly an amount likely to transform the status of the demonstrably most disadvantaged socioeconomic segment of the Australian population. The continuing dependence of Aboriginal people is assured until support is given that fundamentally changes the economic base of Aboriginal society (Rowley 1986, p. 152). This has proved too politically difficult for any government to achieve.

Fragmentation of service provision and coordination

Before 1972, most services for Aborigines were provided by umbrella departments such as the New South Wales Aborigines Welfare Department, and the Western Australian Native Welfare Department. In the eyes of the legislators who founded them, these departments were designed to protect Aborigines and cater for all their needs, including housing and general welfare.

Upon the establishment of the Department of Aboriginal Affairs in 1972, the Whitlam Labor government took responsibility for Aboriginal affairs. With the exception of Queensland, the other states either abolished their own departments that had been responsible for Aboriginal affairs or diminished their role. In these circumstances, the functions of the Aboriginal specific departments were reallocated to specialist, mainstream departments dealing with welfare, housing, and health.

Apart from the restrictive legislative framework they imposed on Aborigines, the old state Aboriginal affairs departments worked under a further handicap. They did not have the expertise to provide the specialised services for which they were nominally responsible. Under the new legislative arrangements, it was hoped that Aborigines would receive the same standard of general welfare services that were available to the wider community.

At this time, again with the notable exception of Queensland which retained its own essentially assimilationist policies, the states were generally willing to cede responsibility for Aboriginal affairs to the federal government. In this, the states were enticed by the Whitlam government's willingness to make grants to them to fulfil their responsibilities in areas such as health and housing. It could be asserted that some states actually abdicated their responsibility in these areas. They provided little in the way of funding for Aborigines from their own budgets, but instead largely relied on the funding provided by the Commonwealth.

The situation changed somewhat under the Fraser government's 'new federalism' policy. The states had been alarmed at what they regarded as the centralisation of power in Canberra under Whitlam. They therefore regarded with favour Fraser's claims that he was about to devolve recently abrogated responsibilities back to the states. However, while the states were more than willing to play a more decisive role, they were less willing to accept financial responsibilities. Thus, while asserting their right to conduct their own health programs, there was continuing demand for federal funds to support them. An example of this was the National Trachoma and Eye Health Program (RACO 1980), which was given initial approval under the Whitlam government and implemented in the early years of the Fraser government. However, for various reasons, states such as Western Australia and Queensland withdrew from the federally sponsored program and established programs of their own with federally allocated funds.

Consultation

When one speaks with senior public servants or government ministers, there is much talk of consultation. Indeed, we were told by one state government minister that the Commonwealth government spends so much time in consultation it does nothing. However, from an Aboriginal perspective the situation is entirely different. In their view *adequate* consultation generally does not take place. Common Aboriginal complaints centre on the determination of agendas by government officers, lack of adequate prior notification of meetings, and the inappropriate use of 'high English' as a medium of communication. These problems are compounded by an understandable reluctance on the part of some Aborigines to complain to departments upon which they are dependent for services (see also Miller, 'Meetings, meetings, meetings', in Torzillo and Kerr, chapter 8 in this volume).

These complaints reflect several factors. The first of these is that among many government officers, particularly outside specialist Aboriginal departments, there is a general lack of understanding of decision-making processes in Aboriginal communities. A consequence of this is the failure to recognise the inadequacy of the consultation that does take place. A second point is that consultation may be a lengthy and, for non-Aborigines, difficult process. Thus, attempts are often made to circumvent it. Finally, there are those instances where the process is cynically manipulated by bureaucrats in order to achieve their own desired outcomes.

One barrier to the implementation of policy that cannot be underestimated is the staff of the various Commonwealth and state bureaucracies. While departmental programs may be innovative and progressive, their successful delivery is sometimes

Figure 9.4 *Consultation is often an inadequate and lengthy process. (From* Health Issues **20**, *September 1989, p. 6; by S. Kneebone)*

dependent on staff who are philosophically opposed to self-determination for Aborigines.

Another problem exists with the implementation of the Aboriginal health policies that are determined by political parties. It is the role of the Commonwealth and state public services both to implement government policy and to advise on policy formation. The latter role is particularly problematic. Political parties, when in opposition, do not have the resources to develop detailed policies and plans for their implementation. Therefore, when in government, they must rely on advice from the public service. Senior public servants may be opposed on philosophical grounds to the policies of a particular government and the advice they offer may reflect their own political views dressed up in 'rational' arguments against a particular policy option. Furthermore, they might be unwilling to canvass all options and therefore they present a minister with a limited range of alternative courses of action. This reliance on public servants for policy advice is essentially an un-democratic process.

Recognising such conservative biases in the public service, the Whitlam government made extensive use of ministerial advisers and, to a lesser extent, made its own appointments to senior positions within the public service. This practice has since also been widely adopted by state governments. While it is possible to recognise the rationale behind political appointments, the practice has been widely criticised because of implications of 'cronyism'.

A further problem that can serve to frustrate the implementation of government policy is the range of interpretations that can be attached to many policy directives. For example, the requirement that there be consultation with Aborigines may be met with a two-hour community meeting. Unless policy is accompanied by strategies that set out in some detail how objectives can be met, misinterpretation will continue. Another specific example will illustrate the point. There are joint Commonwealth-state agreements to place more Aborigines in jobs, but at the local level this can be thwarted. For instance, one of the requirements for many jobs in Aboriginal affairs is an ability to communicate with Aborigines. We have come across an example where a regional-level public servant has interpreted such a provision to give equal standing to a non-Aboriginal person on the grounds that the person had lived in a country town and had met Aboriginal people through previous work. By no means all the difficulties of implementation are malicious in intent. As one public servant said, 'There is so much to do, it's easier for me to employ a non-Aboriginal person because he or she will require less support'.

Research and evaluation

Policy formulation and implementation is primarily a political process. It involves decisions about how to apply limited resources and in whose interests those resources should be applied, and concerns assessments of the political costs involved in particular decisions. This is not to say, however, that there is no place for 'rational' approaches to policy development. Rather, there is a need to recognise clearly the political and economic constraints that impose limitations on such approaches.

Rational models of policy development require an assessment of health problems and their causes, and the application of available resources in such a manner as to have the greatest benefit in the prevention and/or management of those problems. As Thomson discusses in chapter 2, a major impediment to this approach in Aboriginal health is the lack of basic Aboriginal health statistics and social indicators, on either a national or state level (Smith 1982; see also Thomson, 'The availability of Aboriginal health statistics', in chapter 2).

This state of affairs is a reflection of several factors. First, until recently states such as Queensland and Tasmania recorded little or nothing by way of separate statistics on Aborigines. In Queensland, this reflects the assimilationist policy of the National Party which governed the state for many years, until ousted in the 1989 elections. In Tasmania, it is a consequence of that state's reluctance, until quite recently, to give any recognition to people of Aboriginal descent. In other states, collection of Aboriginal health statistics has been of an essentially piecemeal nature. In their review of Aboriginal health for the Australian Institute of Health Thomson and Honari (1988, p. 108) write:

[I]n 1986 birth and infant mortality data were available only for 83 000 of Australia's 227 648 Aborigines (37%). Comprehensive data on Aboriginal deaths are not routinely available for any State or Territory, and hospitalisation data, while potentially available for Aborigines in all States and Territories except Tasmania are not routinely published and their accuracy has not been established.

In addition, in some states, a good deal of information is collected which is essentially of limited value in the assessment of Aboriginal health status. This includes data such as the number of client encounters by health service personnel. The problem with this kind of data is that it tells us little or nothing about morbidity and changes in it.

Some information, such as population figures, are available from census data gathered by the Australian Bureau of Statistics. In addition, the Aboriginal and Torres Strait Islander Commission (ATSIC; formerly the Department of Aboriginal Affairs) has attempted to maintain community profiles that document resources available in the communities. However, collection of this data has not been systematic, and it is extremely difficult to link the data and health statistics.

Paralleling the piecemeal approach to the collection of routine statistical data has been the research into Aboriginal health. There has been a lack of priorities and the research that has been undertaken reflects the interests of individual researchers as often as the pressing problems faced by Aborigines. Perusal of the annotated bibliographies on Aboriginal health prepared by Moodie and Pederson (1971) and Thomson and Merrifield (1988) show that a large component of research has been of the type that Jon Simon of the Harvard Institute for International Development has characterised as 'what is the bug' research (personal communication)—that is, a type of research that has been concerned with the proximal determinants of disease rather than with the underlying causes. Such an approach has led to increasing dissatisfaction among Aborigines. This is reflected in the Report of the National Workshop on Ethics of Research in Aboriginal Health (NWERAH), which states:

Research above all must be relevant to needs...In too many instances had researchers embarked on a research initiatives [sic] which had little or no relevance to the needs of Aboriginal communities. The Workshop considered that too often research had been used as a vehicle for aggrandisement rather than betterment of peoples.

NWERAH 1989, p. 15

There has been a change in this approach, with organisations such as the Australian Institute of Health and the Australian Institute of Aboriginal and Torres Strait Islander Studies taking a more active role in this area and the National Health and Medical Research Council earmarking special funds for Aboriginal health research.

In recent years, increasing emphasis has been placed on the evaluation of health services. Given the increasing Aboriginal health budget but continuing poor health status of Aborigines, this emphasis is not surprising. However, evaluation is not simply a methodological device. Whether an evaluation is conducted, the context of the evaluation, who conducts it and for whom it is conducted are questions with important political ramifications (Carr-Hill 1985, pp. 369–70).

The fact that health programs are singled out for evaluation usually says more about the power of the providers and consumers of those services than it does about possible problems with the programs themselves. Despite the fact that there are frequent critiques of many mainstream medical and surgical practices, rarely are there calls for their evaluation. Fear that evaluation may be used as a weapon against them, rather than to improve service delivery, has led some Aboriginal medical services to resist evaluation.

To date, few formal evaluations have been undertaken of either government or Aboriginal-controlled health services. A particular problem that has arisen is that of demonstrating unambiguously the causal relationship between provision of services and improvements in health status. For example, Copeman (1980) claims an association between the introduction of a community-based medical service and a fall in hospital admissions. However, as we have stressed throughout this chapter, health status is not primarily dependent upon health services, and it is likely that his findings are the result of confounding factors such as improvements in living conditions.

Equal chances: the way to improvement

The ill-health of Aborigines is a consequence of the past policies and actions of colonial and Australian governments and their non-Aboriginal citizens. The high levels of ill-health among Aborigines are directly attributable to their dispossession, their marginalisation, and the creation of their dependence on various government and welfare services. There is no doubting that there have been positive changes in the health of Aborigines over the past 20 years. However, there has been a slowing of such improvements and an increase in chronic diseases in the Aboriginal population. Despite the fact that both Commonwealth and state governments have developed policies directed at the improvement of Aboriginal health, the fact is that these policies are in conflict with more fundamental policy objectives of government. As Davis et al. write (1988, p. 10), from colonial times the Australian state has mobilised public resources for private gain. This has been the *raison d'etre* of all Australian governments, none of which have acted in a way that would significantly alter existing power relationships—the very relationships that need to be altered if Aborigines are to have equal life chances in Australian society.

References

ADC (Aboriginal Development Commission) (1989), *Annual report 1987–1988*, AGPS, Canberra.

Armstrong, C., Collard, D., Wronski, I., Gray, D., Williams, R. (1987), *Review of health worker education in Western Australia*, DAA, Perth.

Australian Labor Party (WA Branch) (1989), *State platform 1989*, Stephen Smith, State Secretary, Perth.

Basedow, H. (1932), Diseases of Australian Aborigines, *Journal of Tropical Medicine Hygiene* **35**, p. 177.

Beck, E. J. (1985), *The enigma of Aboriginal health: interaction between biological, social and economic factors in Alice Springs town-camps*, AIAS, Canberra.

Bennett, S. (1989), *Aborigines and political power*, Allen and Unwin, Sydney.

Better Health Commission (1986), *Looking forward to better health* (3 vols), AGPS, Canberra.

Biskup, P. (1973), *Not slaves not citizens: the Aboriginal problem in Western Australia 1898–1954*, University of Queensland Press, St Lucia.

Briscoe G. (1974), 'The Aboriginal Medical Service in Sydney', in B. S. Hetzel, M. Dobbin, L. Lippmann and E. Eggleston (eds), *Better health for Aborigines?*, University of Queensland Press, St Lucia, pp. 166–70.

Carr-Hill, R. A. (1985), 'The evaluation of health care', *Social Science and Medicine* **21**, pp. 367–75.

Coombs, K. (1983), 'Aboriginal health programs in Victoria', *Aboriginal Health Project Information Bulletin* **4**, pp. 8–11.

Copeman, R. (1980), 'The effect of an Aboriginal medical service on admissions of children to hospital in a NSW country town', *Medical Journal of Australia* **13**, special supplement on Aboriginal health, pp. 5–6.

DAA (Department of Aboriginal Affairs) (1987), *Aboriginal statistics 1986*, AGPS, Canberra.

DAA (1989), *Annual report: 1988–89*, AGPS, Canberra.

Dampier, W. (1729), *A collection of voyages*, vol. 1, Knapton, London.

Davis, G., Wanna, J., Warhurst, J., and Weller, P. (1988), *Public policy in Australia*, Allen and Unwin, Sydney.

Department of Health (1977), *The National Plan for Aboriginal Health*, submission to House of Representatives Standing Committee on Aboriginal Affairs, 1979, AGPS, Canberra.

Elder, B. (1988), *Blood on the wattle: massacres and maltreatment of Australian Aborigines since 1788*, Child, Frenchs Forest, NSW.

Elkin, A. P. (1951), 'Reaction and interaction: a food gathering people and European settlement in Australia', *American Anthropologist* **53**, pp. 164–86.

Evans, R., Saunders, K., and Cronin, K. (1975), *Exclusion, exploitation and extermination*, Australia and New Zealand Book Company, Sydney.

Eyer, J. (1984), 'Capitalism, health and illness', in J. B. McKinlay (ed.), *Issues in the political economy of health care*, Tavistock, New York.

Foley, G. F. (1975), 'The history of the Aboriginal Medical Service: a study in bureaucratic obstruction', *Identity* **2** (5), pp. 38–40.

HDWA (Health Department of Western Australia) (1986), *Review of Western Australian Aboriginal Health Programme: Phase One, Kimberley*, Health Department of Western Australia, Perth.

Health Targets and Implementation (Health for All) Committee (1988), *Health for all Australians*, AGPS, Canberra.

Hetzel, S., Dobbin, M., Lippmann, L., and Eggleston, E. (eds) (1974), *Better health for Aborigines*, University of Queensland Press, St Lucia.

HRSCAA (House of Representatives Standing Committee on Aboriginal Affairs) (1979), *Aboriginal health: report from the Standing Committee on Aboriginal Affairs*, AGPS, Canberra.

Howard, M. C. (ed.) (1978), ' "Whitefella business": Aborigines in Australian politics*, Institute for the Study of Human Issues, Philadelphia.

Jebb, M. (1984), 'The Lock Hospitals experiment: Europeans, Aborigines and venereal disease'. in R. Reece and T. Stannage (eds), *Studies in Western Australian history, European-Aboriginal relations in Western Australian History*, vol. 8, pp. 68–87.

Kamien, M. (1980), 'The Aboriginal Australian experience', in N. F. Stanley and R. A. Joske (eds), *Changing disease patterns and human behaviour*, Academic Press, London.

Killington, G. (1977), *Use of health services by Aborigines: Australian Government Inquiry into Poverty*, AGPS, Canberra.

Long, T. (1979), 'The development of government Aboriginal policy: the effect of administrative changes, 1829–1977', in R. M. Berndt and C. H. Berndt (eds), *Aborigines of the west: their past and their present*, University of Western Australian Press, Nedlands, pp. 357–66.

Moodie, P. M. (1973), *Aboriginal health*, ANU Press, Canberra.

Moodie, P. M. (1981), 'Australian Aborigines', in H. C. Trowell and D. P. Burkitt (eds), *Western diseases: their emergence and prevention*, Edward Arnold, London, pp. 154–67.

Moodie, P. M. and Pedersen, E. B. (1971), *The health of Australian Aborigines: an annotated bibliography*, Australian Government Printing Service, Canberra.

Nathan, P. (1980), *A home away from home: a study of the Aboriginal health service in Fitzroy, Victoria*, Pitt, Melbourne.

NAHSWP (National Aboriginal Health Strategy Working Party) (1989), *A national Aboriginal health strategy*, AGPS, Canberra.

National Workshop on Ethics of Research in Aboriginal Health (1987), 'Report', reprinted in NAHSWP, *A national Aboriginal health strategy*, AGPS, Canberra, 1989.

Palmer, G. R., and Short, S. D. (1989), *Health care and public policy*, Macmillan, Melbourne.

Pollard, D. (1988), *Give and take: the losing partnership in Aboriginal poverty*, Hale and Iremonger, Marrickville, NSW.

Reece, R. H. W. (1974), *Aborigines and colonists: Aborigines and colonial society in NSW in the 1830s and 1840s*, Sydney University Press, Sydney.

Reid, D. B. (1978), 'Aboriginal medical services, Perth, Western Australia', *Medical Journal of Australia* **1**, pp. 53–5.

Reid, J. (ed.) (1982), *Body, land and spirit: health and healing in Aboriginal society*, University of Queensland Press, St Lucia.

Rowley, C. D. (1970), *The destruction of Aboriginal society: Aboriginal policy and practice*, vol. 1, ANU Press, Canberra.

Rowley, C. D. (1971), *Outcasts in white Australia: Aboriginal policy and practice*, vol 2, ANU Press, Canberra.

Rowley, C. D. (1973), 'From humbug to politics: Aboriginal affairs and the Academy project', *Oceania* **42** (3), pp. 183–97.

Rowley, C. D. (1986), *Recovery: the politics of Aboriginal reform*, Penguin, Ringwood, Vic.

RACO (Royal Australian College of Ophthalmologists) (1980), *National Trachoma and Eye Health Program*, RACO, Sydney.

Russell, C., and Schofield, T. (1986), *Where it hurts, an introduction to sociology for health workers*, Allen and Unwin, Sydney.

Smith, L. (1982), 'Aboriginal health and Aboriginal health statistics', *Aboriginal Health Project Information Bulletin* **1**, p. 14.

Soong, F. S. (1979), 'Developing the role of primary health care workers (Aboriginal) in the Northern Territory: a challenge to the health professions', *New Doctor* **11**, pp. 29–31.

Thomson, N. (1984), 'Australian Aboriginal health and health-care', *Social Science and Medicine* **18**, pp. 939–48.

Thomson, N. (1985), *Aboriginal health, status, programs and prospects*, Department of the Parliamentary Library, Canberra.

Thomson, N. (1986), 'Current status and priorities in Aboriginal health', in Better Health Commission, *Looking forward to better health*, vol. 3, AGPS, Canberra, pp. 1–15.

Thomson, N., and Honari, M. (1988), 'Aboriginal health: a case study', in *Australia's health: the first biennial report of the Australian Institute of Health*, AGPS, Canberra, pp. 105–24.

Thomson, N., and Merrifield, P. (1988), *Aboriginal health: an annotated bibliography*, AIAS, Canberra.

Tonkinson, R., and Howard, M. C. (eds) (1990), *Going it alone: prospects*, AIAS, Canberra.

White, J. P., and Mulvaney, J. M. (1987), 'How many people?' in J. M. Mulvaney and J. P. White (eds), *Australians to 1788*, Fairfax, Syme and Weldon, Sydney, pp. 115–17.

WHO-UNICEF (1978), *Primary health care: International Conference on Primary Health Care*, Alma Ata, USSR, 6–12 September, WHO-UNICEF, Geneva.

Abbreviations

AADS	Aboriginal Advisory and Development Services
ABS	Australian Bureau of Statistics
ADC	Aboriginal Development Commission
AGPS	Australian Government Publishing Service
AHOSA	Aboriginal Health Organisation of South Australia
AIAS	Australian Institute of Aboriginal Studies
AIATSIS	Australian Institute of Aboriginal and Torres Strait Islander Studies
AIH	Australian Institute of Health
AMS	Aboriginal medical service
ANAMH	Australian National Association for Mental Health
ANU	Australian National University
ANZAAS	Australian and New Zealand Association for the Advancement of Science
ARI	acute respiratory infection
ATSIC	Aboriginal and Torres Strait Islander Commission, formerly Department of Aboriginal Affairs
BMI	body mass index
CAAC	Central Australian Aboriginal Congress
CAAPS	Council for Aboriginal Alcohol Programme Services
CARPA	Central Australian Rural Practitioners Association
CEIDA	Centre for Education and Information on Drugs and Alcohol
DAA	Department of Aboriginal Affairs
DCSH	Department of Community Services and Health
DEET	Department of Employment, Education and Training
DHHS	Department of Health and Human Services
HALT	Healthy Aboriginal Life Team
HDWA	Health Department of Western Australia
HRA	*Historical Records of Australia*
HRSCAA	House of Representatives Standing Committee on Aboriginal Affairs
ICD	International Classification of Diseases
ICIHI	Independent Commission on International Humanitarian Issues
IMR	infant mortality rate
KAMSC	Kimberley Aboriginal Medical Services Council
LBW	low birth weight
MJA	*Medical Journal of Australia*
NAHSWP	National Aboriginal Health Strategy Working Party
NAIHO	National Aboriginal and Islander Health Organisation
NAILSS	National Aboriginal and Islander Legal Services Secretariat
NAMHA	National Aboriginal Mental Health Association
NCHS	National Center for Health Statistics (USA)

NDG	National Diabetes Group
NHC	Nganampa Health Council
NH&MRC	National Health and Medical Research Council
NIAA	National Institute on Alcohol Abuse and Alcoholism
NIDDM	non-insulin dependent diabetes mellitus
NSWAB	NSW Anti-Discrimination Board
NSWAECG	NSW Aboriginal Education Consultative Group
NSWHC	New South Wales Health Commission
NTA	Northern Territory Administration
NTDH	Northern Territory Department of Health
NTDHCS	Northern Territory Department of Health and Community Services
NTEHP	National Trachoma and Eye Health Program
PHV	peak height velocity
QDVT	Queensland Domestic Violence Taskforce
RACO	Royal Australian College of Ophthalmologists
RCADC	Royal Commission into Aboriginal Deaths in Custody
RDA	recommended daily allowance
SAHC	South Australian Health Commission
SHFA	standard height for age
SSCVSF	Senate Select Committee on Volatile Substance Fumes
SWFA	standard weight for age
SWFH	standard weight for height
TO	take-off
VAHSC	Victorian Aboriginal Health Service Co-operative
WHO	World Health Organization
WHPRC	Women's Health Policy Review Committee

Index

Names of institutions, companies, government departments etc. are spelled out in full in this index, even when they are abbreviated in the text. Abbreviations used in the text are given in the list preceding the index. Page references to tables, graphs and illustrations are in *italics*.

ablution facilities: *see* washing facilities
abnormality, 226–227
Aboriginal and Torres Strait Islander
  Commission, 391, 411, 416
Aboriginal communities: *see* remote
  communities; urban communities
Aboriginal control: *see* community control; social
  control
Aboriginal Development Commission, 337, 345,
  391
Aboriginal English, 319–322
Aboriginal health and political economy in
  Australia (case study), 393
Aboriginal Health Service, Anyinginyi, 336, 368
Aboriginal health workers, xix, 363–365, 406–408
Aboriginal Health Unit, NSW Dept of Health, *109*
Aboriginality: *see* identification of Aboriginality
*Aboriginal Land Rights (Northern Territory) Act
  1976*, 27
Aboriginal Lands Trust, 108
Aboriginal languages: *see* language
Aboriginal Law: *see* Law, Aboriginal
Aboriginal Legal Service, Redfern, 103, 400
Aboriginal Medical Service, Redfern, 31, *71*, 353,
  363, *399*, 401, 403
  aged people's hostel, 336, 353, 403
Aboriginal medical services (AMSs), xix, xx, 106,
  117, *310*, 323, 361, 398–407
  nutrition programs, 158, 402–403
Aboriginal Mental Health Conference, 230
Aboriginal origins, 1–2
Aboriginal Public Health Improvement Program,
  350
Aboriginal versus white drinking in the Northern
  Territory (case study), 196
Aboriginal Women's Task Force, 102
Aborigines: *see* 'full blood'; mixed descent;
  Torres Strait Islanders
Aborigines Protection Board, 10, 93, 107
abortions, 85, 91
absconding from hospital, 319
absorption: *see* assimilation
abstainers: *see* alcohol abstainers
access roads, 338
accidents: *see* trauma
accommodation: *see* housing
accommodation (of European settlement),
  89–91, 385
acculturative stress, 245–248, 249, 266, 294: *see
  also* culture clash; deculturation; stress
  adolescents, 267
  alcohol, 187–188, 263, 371

petrol sniffing, 199
regional survey, 195
suicides, 275
Action revival movement, 199–200
adjustment problems: *see* acculturative stress
adolescents: *see also* children and infants
  coping strategies, 247, 268
  fertility and parenting, 40, 117
  gangs, 268, 279
  growth, 146–147
  loss of parents, 115
  relationships, 257–259
  substance abuse, 69, 247, 251, 263, 264,
    266–268
adoption, 97–98: *see also* stolen generations
adult health, 25, 110–116, 330–332
  nutrition, 152–157
Aero-Medical Service, 395–396
affective disturbance: *see* anxiety; depression
age-specific fertility: *see* fertility and sterility
age-specific mortality: *see* mortality
age/sex registers: *see* population registers
aged people
  hostel, Redfern, 336, 353, 403
  hunting and gathering groups, 137
  roles, 106, 118
aggression: *see also* violence
  adolescent coping strategies, 247
  personality disorder, 239
AIDS, 64–65, 331, 353, 356–359
  education programs, 356–359, 366
  media resources, *65*, 198, 208, *358*
Albrecht, Pastor P. G. E., 189
alcohol abstainers, 190, 193, 205, 261, 272
  predetermined, 299–300
alcohol and violence, 191, 204–205, 261–268, 273,
  363, 370–371: *see also* alcohol-related
  deaths
  adolescents, 267
  and kava, 201
  despair, 193
Alcoholics Anonymous, 184, 206
alcohol interventions and prevention, 180, 192,
  206–208, 367, 40?
  community involvement, 208–209
  media resources, 198, *207*, 208, *264*, 367, 368
alcoholism: *see* disease model of alcohol and
  substance abuse
alcohol-related deaths: *see also* alcohol and
  violence; Royal Commission
  homicide, 204–205, 262
  suicide, 67, 203–204, 269, 272–276

alcohol-related diseases, 203–205, *234*, 236, *239*, 304–305
  cirrhosis, 64, 195, 204
  psychoses, 235, 236
alcohol use, 68–69, 106, 173–197, 203, 205–209, 370–371: *see also* terms beginning with 'alcohol'; indigenous alcohol; legislation; media resources
  adolescents and children, 266, 330
  attitudes and responses, 190–192
  differences in metabolism, 189
  drinking styles, 190, 263–264, 272, 279
  early white settlement, 176–178
  effects on community, 337, 370
  effects on families, 193, 204–205, 260–261
  energy in diet, 135
  group activity, 190–192, 193
  mental health, 250, 256, 280
  rules for drinking, 191, 262–263
Alice Springs Hospital, 22–23, 60
American–Australian Expedition to Arnhem Land, (1948), 85, 131
American Indians: *see* Native Americans
amok, 225
amputations, diabetes, 154
analgesic use, 192, 195, 202
Anangu Pitjantjatjara, 339
Anbarra people (Arnhem Land), 84, 136–137
ancestral bones, 92
ancestral land: *see* land
Angoroko (NT), diet, 131
Angurugu, 85
anxiety, 228, 233, 237, *238, 239,* 240: *see also* depression
  alcohol use, 250
  housing communities, 222
  Pintupi language, *229*
Anyinginyi Aboriginal Health Service, 336, 368
apathetic depression, 254: *see also* depression
Areyonga, communal feeding, 133
Armed conflict in north-eastern Arnhem Land (case study), 4
army doctors, 24
army employment, 22
arrack, 176
Arrente people, alcohol use, 189
arrest: *see* custody; offences
arrowroot collection, *81*
asbestos miners, 25
aspirin: *see* analgesic use
assault: *see* violence
assimilation, xiii, 19–23, 93–100, 132–133, 387–389
  1961 definition, 26
  alcohol use, 192
  bush foods, 130
attempted suicide, *270, 271,* 269–275: *see also* self-injury, suicide
  alcohol and drugs, 272–275
attribution biases: *see* external attributions
audiovisual media: *see* media resources

Australian Construction Services, 392
Australian Drug Offensive, 185, *207,* 208
Australian Foundation on Alcoholism and Drug Dependence, 229
Australian Institute of Health, research, 411, 416
Australian Law Reform Commission, 205
Australian National Association for Mental Health, 230
autonomy, xv–xvi: *see also* self-determination
Availability of Aboriginal health statistics (case study), 38–39
avoidance rules, 249, 303, 318, 360

bacteremia, 60
bacterial meningitis, 329
Bagot population (NT), 132
Bamaga (Qld), health services, 396
Baryulgil (NSW), asbestos miners, 25
behavioural disorders of childhood, *238*
Benelong's Haven, alcohol intervention, 206
benzodiazepine use, 202
Better Health Commission, 391, 410
binge drinking, 178, 263–264, 272, 279; *see also* alcohol use
birth: *see* childbirth
birth weight: *see* low birth weight
Black Deaths in Custody: *see* Royal Commission into Black Deaths in Custody
blindness: *see* eye health; trachoma
blood pressure: *see* hypertension
body fat distribution, 153–154
body mass index, 153–154
Bomaderry Children's Home, 96
Bones of our ancestors (case study), 92
Bonner Review, 374
booklets: *see* media resources
botanical pharmaceuticals: *see* bush medicines
bottle feeding: *see* supplementation
Bourke (NSW)
  alcohol use, 69, 191–192, 195, 204
  food fortification, 158–159
  mental health, 221, 246
  pneumonia, 328
Bradbury, David, 204, 221, 269
bread fortification, 128, 158–159
breast-feeding, 55, 83, 85, 143, 151–152, 362
bush medicine, 312
  diet, 17, 140–141
  kava, 202
Broome Region Aboriginal Medical Service, 407
burns, 204, 205
bush foods, xvi, *81,* 130, 137, *138, 141,* 139–142, 299: *see also* diet; food; hunting and gathering
  animals, 130–131, 135–137, *138,* 139–140, 292
  diet studies, 126
  insulin levels, 156
  outstations, 135–136, 137
  plant, *81,* 136, 137, 142
  poster, *161*
  Tiwi, 130–131

bush medicine, 227, 311–312: *see also* traditional
    healers
  mine wastes, 304

Canadian Indians: *see* Native Americans
cancer, 46, *47,* 72
  cervical, 72, 332, 362
  liver, 64, 72, 330, 356
  lung, 72
carbohydrate, 142
carbohydrate intolerance, 331: *see also* glucose
    intolerance
cardiovascular disease: *see* circulatory system
    diseases
caring, 316
Caroona community, medical service, *310*
cars: *see* motor vehicles
cattle stations: *see* stations
causality, 226–227, 249: *see also* external
    attributions
cause of ill-health: *see under* illness
causes of death: *see* mortality
causes of drug abuse: *see under* substance abuse
Central Australian Aboriginal Congress, 192, 353,
    404
Central Land Council, facilities, 338
Centre for Appropriate Technology, *345,*
    351–352
ceremonial activities, 19, 302, 359
cervical cancer, 72, 318, 332, 362
childbirth, 17, 52, 90, 117, 311–312, 362: *see also*
    pregnancy
child-care centre funding, 366
child-rearing, 83–84, 117–118, 242, 266
children and infants, 19, 90, 353, 363, 390: *see
    also* adolescents; infant mortality; nutrition;
    stolen generations
  as healers, 313
  health programs, 108, 362
  illnesses, 14, 56–57, *56,* 59–60, 66, 110, *238,*
    300, 327–330, 354
  sexual abuse, 279, 353
  substance abuse, 330
chlamydial diseases, 59, 64, 86, 88: *see also*
    trachoma
Christian revival movements, 199–200
cigarette smoking: *see* tobacco
circulatory system diseases, 46, *46, 47,* 55, 57,
    113–114, 330–331
  body fat distribution, 153–154
  bush foods, 142
  childhood circumstances, 123
  deaths in custody, 204
  diabetes, 155
  drug and alcohol use, 203
  tobacco, 202, 331
  women, 362
cirrhosis, 64, 195, 204, 330
citizenship, 387
  and alcohol, 179–182, 189
city-dwellers: *see* urban communities
classificatory kin: *see also* kinship

clinical depression: *see* depression
cocaine, 203
co-dependency model, 206–207
colds and coughs, 305, 308, 311–312
colonisation, 327, 370, 371
Commonwealth funding, 108, 390–391, 397–398,
    405, 413
Commonwealth Office of Aboriginal Affairs, 389
communal eating, 14–15, 91, 133
communal facilities, 343
Communal feeding: a Northern Territory
    example of assimilation (case study), 132–133
communicable diseases: *see* infectious diseases
communication
  emotions, 249–254
  health-care setting, 314–322
Community-based food and health program, A
    (case study), 369–370
community control, xx, 27, 31–33, 327, 361,
    391–392, 394, 397, 408: *see also*
    decision-making; self-determination
  mental health initiatives, 279–280
  vs Aboriginalisation, 333
Community-controlled health service: different
    agendas, A (case study), 32–33
Community Development and Employment
    Program, 349
condom use, 356, 358, 359
Congress Alukura Women's Health Services,
    362
conjunctivitis: *see* eye health, infections
consensus: *see* decision-making
consultation, 413–415, *414*
Contemporary Aboriginal viewpoint, A (case
    study), 187–188
Contemporary anxieties, traditional fears, and
    diagnostic labels (case study), 240
contraception, 311–312, 363: *see also* fertility and
    sterility
Cooper, William, 18
Cootamundra Aboriginal Girls' Home, 96
Cootamundra Girls' Training School, *21*
coping, 247–251, 258, 260–261, 268, 280
copycat suicides: *see under* suicide
Coranderrk settlement (Vic.), 93
coughs, 305, 308, 311–312
Council for Aboriginal Affairs, 15
crime: *see* custody; offences
cross-cultural factors: *see* sociocultural factors
crowding, 342–344, 382
Cultural relativity or cultural bias (case study),
    242
culture, 19, 98, 242, 248, 279–280, 294–296,
    307–308, 389: *see also* acculturative stress;
    Law, Aboriginal; sociocultural factors
  and substance abuse, 275, 371
  knowledge of health professionals, 316–319
  mental health, 226–228
Culture-bound syndromes (case study), 225
culture-specific diagnostic categories, 223–225,
    239
Cumberland College of Health Sciences (NSW)
    courses, 406–407

custody: *see also* offences; Royal Commission
  AIDS, 357
  deaths, 204, 268–269, 272, 274–276, *277,* 332
  rates, 102, *103*
  substance abuse, 197, 203
customary law: *see* Law, Aboriginal

dead person's name, 306
deafness: *see* ear health
deaths: *see* mortality
deaths in custody, 102, 204, 332: *see also* Royal
  Commission; suicide
decision-making, 333, 342, 344, 360, 364,
  370–371, 408, 413: *see also* community
  control; consultation; meetings
deculturation, 294, 296: *see also* acculturative
  stress
definition of Aboriginality: *see* identification of
  Aboriginality
delirium tremens, 275: *see also* alcohol use
dementia, 237
dental health, 70–72, *71*
  Aboriginal nurses, 27
Department of Aboriginal Affairs, 27, 391, 411,
  412
dependence, 412–413: *see also* economic
  independence
  from early policy, 91, 385
  nutrition interventions, 157, 163
depopulation: *see* population, decline
depression, 224, 228, 233, *238, 239,* 237,
  239–240, 250, 254–256: *see also* anxiety;
  suicide
developing countries: *see also* international
  standards
  health and disease, 1, 44, 57, 60, 149, 353, 355
  health workers, 406
  infant and child health, 109, 362
  nutritional interventions, 159–160
development: *see* acculturative stress
diabetes, 55, 74, 154–157, 331–332
  and heart disease, 114
  body fat distribution, 153–154
  bush foods, 142
  complications, 59, 154–155, 331, 362
  deaths in custody, 204
  education, 157, 366
  lifestyle changes, 155–156
  urinary abnormalities, 72–73
  women, 362
diarrhoea, 66, 308: *see also* gastroenteritis
  bush medicines, 311
  children, 329
  dogs, 344
  essential services, 149, 343
  explanations, 304–305
  nutritional effects, 148
diary method: *see* diet, studies
diet, xvi, 3, 124, 299: *see also* bush foods; food;
  nutrition; rations
  and illnesses, 114, 156, 304, 331
  studies, 125–126, 128–130, 340, 343, 369

Dietary survey in a remote community (case
  study), 127
digestive system disorders, *46, 47,* 53
diphtheria epidemics, 88
Directorate for Aboriginal Welfare, 107
discipline, 83–84
discrimination: *see* racism
disease: *see* illness
disease model of alcohol and substance abuse,
  183–185, 206–207
disorders of mood: *see* anxiety, depression
Dispersal, alienation and re-possession: the
  southern Pitjantjatjara (case study), 28–29
dispossession, xii, xiii–xv, xviii, 89, 383–385
distribution of food: *see under* food
diversity of Aboriginal communities, xiii
divination powers, 313
Docker River, bush foods, 137
doctors, Aboriginal, 27
dogs and hygiene, *66,* 339, 343–344
  children, 344, 349
domestic service, *97,* 116
domestic violence, 362–363, 368: *see also* alcohol
  and violence
  and alcohol, 264–265
  tribal traditions, 265
donovanosis, AIDS, 357
Dreaming, 140, 299
drinking: *see* alcohol use
Drug Offensive, 185, *207,* 208
drug use: *see* substance abuse
drunkenness: *see* alcohol use
dry horrors, 275: *see also* alcohol use
Duboisia hopwoodii (pituri), 174–175
Dungalear Station, Walgett, 129
duplicating fluid as a drug, 202
dust control, 343–344, 349
dying race: *see* protectionism
dysentry: *see* intestinal infectious diseases

ear health, 58, 110, 354, 368, 390, 394
  bush medicines, 311
  children, 328–329
  hearing loss, 58, 329, 355
economic independence, 93, 391–392, *392,* 412:
  see also dependence
economic roles
  parental death, 114
  pre-colonial, 81–83, 86–87, 89
education, 118, 389, 392, *392: see also* health
  education
  by Aborigines, *99*
  hearing-impaired children, 58, 329
  literacy skills, 363
Eight—two—and a quarter (case study), 129
Elcho Island, 145, 267
elderly: *see* aged
electricity supply, 338, 342, 350, 382: *see also*
  essential services
emotions
  communication of, 228, 251–254
  mental health, 244, 274, 276

employers, medical insurance, 387–388
employment, 89–90, 100, 392, *392*
endemic diseases: *see* trachoma; yaws
endocrine and nutritional disorders, *47*
enterprises: *see* economic independence
environmental explanations of illness, 305
environmental health, 151, 249, 337–352, 391,
　　394: *see also* essential services; health
　　hardware; living conditions; National
　　Trachoma
　diseases, 148–150, 361
　facilities, 410, 411
　projects, 339–345, 348, 366
epilepsy, 68, 204, *239,* 305
Ernabella, bush foods, 137
essential services, 105, 150, 339–345, 348–349,
　　366, 391: *see also* electricity supply;
　　environmental health; toilet facilities;
　　washing facilities; waste disposal; water
　　supply
ethnicity and social disadvantage, xviii
ethnocentric health care: *see* sociocultural factors
evaluation, 359, 366, 371, 373–374, 416–417
exclusion of Aborigines, 68, 388
exercise and diabetes, 331
expansionism period, 383–387
expectation of life at birth: *see* life expectancy
extended families: *see under* families
external attributions, 226, 248, 274
eye health, 25, 58–59, 227, 304, 359–362, 394: *see
　　also* National Trachoma; trachoma
　blindness, 58–59, 360
　diabetes, 154
　dust, 344
　infections, 308, 329, 361
　sore eyes, bush medicines, 311
　surgery, 354, 361–362
　vision screening, 355, 361

families, *83*, 84, *259: see also* kinship; stolen
　　generations
　decline and rise, 80–118
　exclusion, 261
　extended, 100, 117, 257, 260
　female-headed, 99–100, 108
　mental health, 260, 269
　nuclear, 81, 86–87, 260
　single-parent, 115, 261
　size, 3, 83
　social functions, 116, 80, 82–83
　substance use, 186, 207–208
farms, 91, 93, *99: see also* stations
fat: *see* obesity
fate, 299–300
fear, *229, 239,* 240, 275
feelings: *see* emotions
Ferguson, William, 18
fertility and sterility, 40, 83, 88–91, 363: *see also*
　　contraception
　medicinal plants, 312
fetal mortality, 85: *see also* perinatal mortality
fires, 342

fish, 130–131, 136, 140–141, 304
Fitzroy Crossing (WA), 237, *238*
foetal mortality, *see* fetal mortality
food, xvi, 11, 14, *138,* 123–164: *see also* bush
　　foods; diet; nutrition; rations
　distribution patterns, 126, 137, 160
　gathering, 81, *124*
Food quest at Oak Valley Outstation, SA (case
　　study), 139
fourth world peoples, xiii–xv, xviii
Fregon (SA), store survey, 134
fringe dwellers, 104–105, 339: *see also* town
　　camps
　alcohol, 179, 190
fruit and vegetables, 137, 142, 158–159
'full blood' Aborigines, 18–19, 93–95, 295: *see
　　also* remote communities
funding, 126, 333, *392*
　AMSs, 400, 401, 406

Gagadu people, trespass, 305
Galiwin'ku (NT), 43, 134
gangs, 268, 279
gastroenteritis, 66, 106, 390: *see also* diarrhoea;
　　intestinal infectious diseases
　bush medicines, 311
children, 327–328
gender beliefs, 316–318
genealogy: *see* kinship
genetic factors
　carbohydrate intolerance, 331
　diabetes, 155
　size at birth, 148
genitourinary system diseases (ICD), *47,* 53
　genital herpes, 64
germs, 307, 339–340
glasses, 361–362: *see also* eye health
glomerulonephritis, 67, 73, 329–330
glucose intolerance, 155–156: *see also* diabetes
glue sniffing, 197: *see also* petrol sniffing
gonococcal conjunctivitis, 329
gonorrhoea, 63, 88, 331
Good intentions: a community nutrition program
　　(case study), 160
Goulburn Island mission, 145
Government health policy: *see* health policy
granuloma inguinale, 64, 88
graphic artist, media workshop, 367
grogging communities: *see* alcohol use
group experiences, 84
　alcohol intervention, 206
　alcohol use, 190–192, 193
　petrol sniffing, 199, 267
　revival movements, 199
growth, 54, 110, 137, 145–147, 390
　faltering, 56–57, 145, *146,* 148, 151, 330, 362
　measurement, 143–145
Gulgadunng, 292, 295: *see also* Mining City
Gunabibi cult, initiation, 140
Gundy, David, xviii
Gunwinggu people, 136, 140, 298 *see also*
　　Maningrida

Gurindji people: *see* Wave Hill Station
gynaecological health care: *see* women's health

Haast's Bluff, facilities, 338
Haemophilus influenzae, 59–60, 329, 355
'half-caste': *see* mixed descent Aborigines
hanging, 274: *see also* suicide
Hansen's disease: *see* leprosy
harassment, xvii, xviii
Harris, William, 18
Hasluck, Paul, 22
headache, 304, 308, 310, 311
head injuries, 204
head lice, town camps, 106
healers, 313–314
health: *see* health status
health education, 401: *see also* education; health
    promotion; media resources
  AIDS and STDs, 356–359
  alcohol and drug abuse, 367
  environmental health, 350
  public health, 340, 350
health hardware, xvi, xvii, 343, 349–350, 361,
    370: *see also* environmental health; housing
health information: *see* health education; media
    resources
health insurance, 388, 394, 398, 405
health policy, 30, 93–98, 381–417
*Health Practitioners and Allied Professionals
    Registration Act*, 408
health professionals, 293–294, 316–322, *320: see
    also* health workers
  nurses, Aboriginal, 27, *404*
health promotion, *302,* 355, 358, 365–368: *see
    also* health education
health rituals, 300
health services, xix, 313–322, 352–365, 374, 393:
    see also evaluation
  by state, 394–397
health statistics, 30, 38–39, 111, 391, 411,
    415–416: *see also* hospital statistics
  mental health, 279
health status, 1, 37–74, 232, 297, *302: see also*
    mental health; illness; mortality
  and relationships, 298
  and stress, 249
  at time of settlement, 3, 382
  attitudes and dispositions, 301
  Commonwealth expenditure, *392*
  declining, 409
  predetermined, 299–300
Health Targets and Implementation Committee,
    391, 410
health workers, *149,* 353–354, *364,* 406–408
  AMSs, 403
  role, 333, 355, 361, 363, 368, 395
  training, 353, 361, 363–365, 406–408, *407*
Healthy Aboriginal Life Team, 207–208, 359
hearing loss: *see* ear health
heart disease: *see* circulatory system disease
height gain, poor, 54
hepatitis B, 64, *65,* 356, 394: *see also* liver cancer

children, 330
waste removal, 343
hepatocellular cancer: *see* liver cancer
heroin, 203
high blood pressure: *see* hypertension
history taking: *see also* information gathering
    from client's family, 309, 320–321, 323, 322
HIV infection: *see* AIDS
Hollows, Professor Fred: *see* National Trachoma
Holyoake model of co-dependency, 206–207
homeland movement: *see* outstations
homicide: *see under* alcohol-related deaths
homosexuality, 237
honey, wild, 137
  for indigenous alcohol, 174
hookworm infection, 24
Hopevale community, alcohol, 187–188
horticultural activities, 344, 348
hospitalisation, 50–54, 66, 73, 354
  infants and children, 328, 409
  petrol sniffers, 205
  pregnancy, 409
  remote Aborigines, 318–319
hospital liaison officers, 395, 397
hospitals, 15, 22–23, 385–388
  primary health care, 395, 399
  segregation, 388
hospital statistics, 25, 50, *51, 52,* 111: *see also*
    health statistics
  alcohol-related, 69, 203–204, 234–236
  homicide and injury, 204–205
  infants, 66
  mental health, 233–235, *234, 236*
  skin infections, 66
hot feeling, illness behaviour, 308
housing, xvi–xvii, 222, 337, 348–349, 392, *392*
  costs, 105, 345
  homeland shelter, 338, *338*
  maintenance, 348–350
  town camps, 106
Housing Commission, La Perouse, 107–108
Housing on the reserve (case study), 107–108
hunting and gathering, 81–82, 131, 136: *see also*
    bush food
  contemporary, 130–131
  diseases, 86, 382
hyperchondriasis, 233, *239,* 240
hypertension, 55, 57, 74, 123, 331
  screening, 366
hysteria, 225, 237, *238, 239*

identification of Aboriginality, 30–31, 38: *see also*
    health statistics
  by local magistrate, 389
  definition, 30, 37, 296
illicit drugs, 203
illness, 3, 308–313, 327–332: *see also* names of
    specific diseases
  causes, 302–308, 382, 417
illustrations: *see* media resources
immunisation, 7, 64, 355, 362, 366, 403
immunological impairment, malnutrition, 149

Imparja television, 368
impetigo, water supply, 149
imprisonment: *see* custody
income and cash, 100, 133–134, 136, 368: *see also* poverty; social security
   food and housing, 159, 392
   motor transport, 131
   wages, 15, 388–389
indigenous, *see also* traditional
indigenous drugs and alcohol, 174–175
indigenous health care, 239, 294, 296–310: *see also* bush medicine; traditional healers
indigenous peoples, xiii–xv, xx
indigenous psychology, 225, 278
individuality, 300–301
Indonesia: *see* Macassan seafarers
infant mortality, 3, 15, 23, 73, 88, 108–110, 147, 327–328, 409
   causes of death, 84–85, 327
   infanticide, 3, 83, 84, 85
   statistics, 22, 25, 47–48, *48*, 85, 108, 327
infectious diseases, 3, 14, *46*, *47*, 47, 56–57, 59–67, 74, 148–150; *see also* intestinal infectious diseases; names of specific diseases; respiratory diseases; sexually transmitted diseases; skin infections, lesions and rashes
   child health programs, 362
   early settlement, 3, 383–384
   explanations, 304–305
   hospitalisation, 52, 53
   in institutions, 14, 385
   on outstations, 137
   standard treatment regimens, 354
infants: *see* children and infants
influenza, 6–7, 46, 88, 384–385
   bush medicines, 311
   caused by spirits, 306
information gathering: *see* history taking
information processing, collective, 257, 260
informed consent, HIV screening, 359
initiation, food taboos, 140: *see also* ceremonies
injury and poisoning, 46, *47*, 73, 203–205
   and sorcery, 307
   hospitalisation, 52, 53, 204
institutionalisation: *see also* missions; settlements
   health, 385
   suicide, 276
insurance: *see* health insurance
integration policy, 389: *see also* assimilation
interdependency, 281, 299
international attention, 30, 23, 389
international standards: *see also* Native Americans; Pacific Islanders
   diabetes, 155–156
   growth, 143, 145
   H. influenzae, 60
   infant mortality, 49
   life tables, 113
interventions: *see* alcohol interventions; petrol sniffing, interventions

intestinal infectious diseases, 47, 66: *see also* diarrhoea; gastroenteritis
intestinal worms, 86
intoxication: *see* alcohol use
introduced diseases, 5, 7, 110, 303
   explanations of illness, 304–305
Inuits: *see* Native Americans
ischaemic heart disease: *see* circulatory system diseases
isolation, infectious disease, 386, 388

jealousy and domestic violence, 265
Jesuit mission on Daly River, death information, 85
Jigalong (WA), 237, *238,* 304

Kalano Community Association (NT), 106
Kalokerinos, Archie, 25
Kaltjiti community, facilities, 343–344
kava, 177, 194–195, 201–202, 206–207
   and alcohol, 201
   television advertisements, 368
Kempsey, food studies, 125, 130
kidneys: *see* renal disease
Kimberley Aboriginal Medical Services Council, 403–404, 407
Kimberley East Aboriginal Medical Service, 407
Kimberley Land Council, facilities, 338
Kinchela school, *94, 95,* 96
kinship, 81–84, 117–118, 256–259, 299, 302: *see also* avoidance rules; families
   and alcohol, 187–189
   and feeling, Pintupi, 252
   children, 98, 115
   classificatory, 82, 258
   sharing, 82, 189, 253
   support, 100
Kintore, bush foods, 137
Kylie's first two years (case study), 56–57

Labor Party platform, 391
Labrador keratopathy, 25
lactation: *see* breast-feeding
Lajamanu, facilities, 338
land, xiii, xiv, 7–18, 118, 135, 302, 382–383
Land Councils, 108
land rights, xx, 27, 266, 276, 297–298
   demonstrations, 30, *297,* 389
   mining interests, 11, 27, 30, 412
Land Rights Bill (NT), 27
language, xiii, 294
   Aboriginal English, 319–322
   emotional states, Pintupi, 228, *229*
   for nutrition education, 161
   name of a dead person, 318
   sickness, 303
   Warlpiri for decisions, 84
   health and well-being, 86, 298
language skills and hearing loss, 58, 329
La Perouse settlement, 107–108

Law, Aboriginal, 191
    alcohol-related violence, 205
    and health, 231, 298, 305
    sorcery, 306
legal aid services, 205
legislation
    drug and alcohol use, 173, 177, 178–182, 189,
        196–197, 201–202
    to restrict contact, 387
leprosy, 61, 331, 386, 388, 390
    bush medicines, 311
Leprosy in the Northern Territory (case study),
    62–63
Lester, Yammi, 339
lice, 86
life expectancy, 3, 37, 43–44, 45, 111: see also
    infant mortality; mortality
lifestyle diseases: see circulatory system diseases;
    diabetes; hypertension
light-skinned Aborigines: see mixed descent
    Aborigines
Limbunya, 17
liquor licences, objections, 192
literacy training for health workers, 363
liver cancer, 64, 72, 330, 356: see also hepatitis B
liver disease: see also cirrhosis; hepatitis B
    toxic effect of kava, 201, 206
living conditions, xvi–xvii, 110, 337: see also
    environmental health
    diseases, 58, 59, 60, 328–329, 331
    infant growth, 55–57
    nutrition, 148, 151, 157, 163
Lizard Flat (WA), 56–57
loneliness, 258–259
    in hospital, 319, 409
Long Bay Gaol, protest, 103
low birth weight, 42–43, 54, 110, 147–148,
    330
low weight: see underweight
lung cancer, 72
Luritja camps, bush foods, 137
lymphogranuloma venereum, 88

Macassan seafarers
    fathers of children, 295
    introduced diseases, 5, 87
    trading pipes and alcohol, 176
maintenance, 342, 348–350
marijuana, 203
Making of a healer, The (case study), 314
malaria, 86
malgri, 223
malnutrition: see nutrition
management, public health, 332–337, 344: see
    also community control; self-determination
    self-management, 390–391
manic depressive psychosis, 239
Maningrida (NT), 84–85, 136
Maoris, xiv, xv, xviii, xix
Maralinga (SA), 28, 29, 139
marriage, 82, 84, 86, 108, 118
massacres, 2, 5, 11, 89, 384

maternal age, 40
    intrauterine growth retardation, 148
    maternal health, 85
    funding, 108
    mortality, 49–50, 332
    nutrition, 153, 159
matrifocality, 99–100, 108
McClelland, Mr Justice J. R., 29
meals: see food
measles, 6–7, 85, 88, 384–385
meat consumption, 133, 135, 139, 159
    bush meat, 130–131, 135–137, 138, 139, 292
media resources, 109, 198, 208
    AIDS, 65, 198, 208, 358
    alcohol and drug abuse, 198, 207, 208, 264,
        367, 368
    nutrition education, 403
    petrol, 198, 208
    radio, 338, 358
Medibank: see health insurance
Medical attitudes and health care (case study),
    24
medical model, 315–316
    alcohol abuse, 265–266
    diabetes, 156–157
    mental health, 219, 278
Medicare: see health insurance
medications, 227: see also bush medicine
medicine men, 294, 312: see also traditional
    healing
meetings, 333, 342, 370, 413: see also
    consultation; decision–making
Meetings, meetings, meetings (case study),
    334–336
meningitis, 60
menstruating women, food taboos, 140
mental health, 46, 47, 67–68, 218–281, 238, 245:
    see also suicide
    before white settlement, 253–254
    cross-cultural comparisons, 222–223
    incidence, 233, 235, 236
    indigenous perspective, 225–232
    surveys, 236–245
    town camps, 106
mental health services, 228–232
mental retardation, 239
metabolism of alcohol, 189
methadone maintenance, Redfern AMS, 353
methylated spirits, 179, 191
middle ear disease: see ear health
migration to cities, 100, 398: see also urban
    communities
Milikapiti (NT), 125, 130, 134, 135: see also
    Tiwi
Milingimbi (NT), 131, 145
mining, 30, 304
    land rights, 11, 27, 30, 412
Mining City (pseudonym), 292, 299–309, 314,
    318–320
miscarriages, 85
missionaries, 11–12, 177, 179
missions, 10–16, 91, 93, 385, 388
    bush foods 131

mixed descent Aborigines, 99, 295: *see also*
   stolen generations
   alcohol laws, 178–179, 181–182, 196
   assimilation, 19, 22, 94, 95
models for health planning, 336
Momega outstation (NT), 136
mood: *see* anxiety; depression
morbidity: *see* illness; mental health
Mornington Island (Qld), 223, 237
mortality, 3, 37, 43–50, *44–47*, 73, 90, *112,*
   115–116: *see also* deaths in custody; infant
   mortality; maternal mortality; perinatal
   mortality
   alcohol, 68, 203–205, 262
   and sorcery, 306–307
   effects on families, 114–115
   explanations, 226, 304
   petrol sniffing, 205–206
   young adults, 330–331
Moseley Royal Commission, 386
motor vehicles, 131, 139
   accidents, 73, 204, 338
Mount Isa, alcohol, 195–196
mourning rituals, 305–306
movement restrictions, 389
mudamuda: *see* mixed descent Aborigines
Muirhead, Justice *see* Royal Commission
Mullewa Aboriginal hospital, 388
murder: *see under* alcohol-related deaths

name of a dead person, 318
narcotics, 3, 177, 179
nasal discharge, children, 329
National Aboriginal and Islander Health
   Organisation, 404
National Aboriginal Health Strategy, A (case
   study), 410–412
National Aboriginal Mental Health Association,
   229–230, 245
National Advisory Council on AIDS, 367
National Better Health Program, 410, 411
National Campaign against Drug Abuse, *264,*
   367
National Police Custody Survey, 102
National Trachoma and Eye Health Program,
   58–59, 67, 329, 359–361, 393, 394, 413
Native Americans, xiii, xvii, xviii
   alcohol, xv, 184, 188–189, 195, 208, 263–264
   diabetes, 154–155
   mental health, 221, 223–224, 243, 244, 250, 279,
      280
   mortality rates, xv, 113
   petrol sniffing, xv, 206
   relationships, xiv, 258, 261
   suicide, 269, 273–274
Natives (Citizenship Rights) Act 1944, The, 180
Natives' Medical Fund, 387–388
natural explanations of illness, 304
neglect
   alcohol-related, 204
   of children, 94
Neisseria meningitidis epidemic, 60

neonatal mortality, 147: *see also* low birth
   weight; perinatal mortality
neoplasms: *see* cancer
neurotic disorders, *234,* 236
new public health, xii, xx, 326, 344
New South Wales, services, 396–397
newborns, ritual healing, 312
Newcastle Awabakal Cooperative, 102
Ngala people, 7
Nganampa Health Council (SA), 69 : *see also*
   Pitjantjatjara
   planning, 336
   population registers, 354
   syphilis screening, 357
   Uwankara Palyanyku Kanyintjaku (UPK),
      339–345, 348
Ngaringman culture (NT), 298–299
Ngiyampaa people, 10
Nicotiana ingulba (indigenous tobacco), *175*
Noble, Perry, 273
Noonkanbah Station (WA), 30
Northern Territory Drug and Alcohol Bureau
   survey, 195
Northern Territory, services, 395–396
nuclear families: *see under* families
Number one for Action: an ex-sniffer's account
   (case study), 200
nurses, Aboriginal, 27, *404*
nursing mothers: *see* breast-feeding
nutrition, xvi, 123–164, 332, 354, 402–403: *see*
   also breast-feeding; bush foods; diet; food;
   rations; weaning foods
   bush food content, 141–142
   children, 132–133, 143–152, 154, 159–160, 330,
      390
   early settlement, 384
   education, 160, *161, 162*, 163, 368–370
   hardware factors, 344
   infectious diseases, 55–57
   interventions, 157–164
   malnutrition, 74, 137, 143, 145, 153
   maternal, 363
   petrol sniffing deaths, 206
   town camps, 106
nutritional disorders, *47*
Nymboida Mission, *12*

Oak Valley Outstation, xvii, *136*
Ottawa Charter on Health Promotion, xx
obesity, 3, 55, 72, 153–154
   bush foods, 142
   diabetes, 155, 331
occupational diseases, 25
ocular: *see* eye health
Oenpelli (NT), 85, 127
offences, 102–103: *see also* custody
   alcohol-related, 182, 205, 262
   compared with whites, 190
   juvenile, petrol sniffing, 199
   street, police surveillance, 332
Office of Aboriginal Affairs, 27, 31
older people: *see* aged

On problem deflation (case study), 194
Ooldea Soak, 28, 29
Oombulgurri (WA), store survey, 134
opium, 177, 179
   opiate-like substances, 175–176
orphanhood: *see* parental death
outstations, 98, 338: *see also* land rights
   diet, 135–139
overweight: *see* obesity

Pacific Islanders
   drug and kava use, 177, 194, 201
   mental health and suicide, 221, 274
pain, 305, 311, 313
painting, desert, for AIDS information, 359
painting (sorcery), 298: *see also* sorcery
Palm Island (Qld), 205, 221, 274
pancreatitis, 204
Pap smears, 318: *see also* cervical cancer
Papunya, 32–33, 132–133, 137
paracetamol: *see* analgesic use
parallel development, 118
parasitic diseases, 46, 47, 86
parasuicide: *see* attempted suicide
parental death, effect on families, *114,* 114–115
parenting
   and petrol sniffing, 199–200
   stolen generations, 98
   teenage mothers, 117
'part Aborigines': *see* mixed descent Aborigines
pastoralists, 89, 179, 383, 387–388, 412: *see also*
   stations
pastoral workers, 106, 108, 388
peer influences on substance abuse, 186, 197–198
pelvic inflammatory disease, 88, 332
performance indicators, 371, 373–374: *see also*
   evaluation
perinatal mortality, 46, 47, 48, 48, 49, 85, 110,
   332
periodontal disease, 71–72
peripheral neuropathy, 55
Perkins, Charles, 21–22
personality disorders, *234, 237, 238, 239,* 239
Peter, Alwyn, 204, 221, 269
petrol sniffing, 69–70, 195, 197–200
   causes, 186
   children and adolescents, 266–268, 330
   deaths, 205–206
   interventions, *198,* 199, 206–208, 368
   lead toxicity, 198, 205–206
pharmaceuticals: *see* medications; bush
   medicines
physical appearance, 295, 297, 300–301
physical environment: *see* environmental health
pick-up services, 192
Pilbara (WA), 18, 99, 388
Pintupi, 32–33, 137, *229,* 252
Pitfalls of inappropriate design, The (case study),
   346–347
Pitjantjatjara, 69, 227, 374: *see also* Kaltjiti
   community; Nganampa Health Council
pituri, 174, 175

Plan for Aboriginal Health, 30
pneumonia, 46, 60: *see also* respiratory
   diseases
   alcohol-related, 68, 204
   children, 88, 328, 329, 354
   chlamydial, 88
   standard treatment regimens, 353–354
   vaccine, 355
poisoning and injury, 46, 47, 52, 53
   environmental explanations, 305
Poisons Act, kava, 202
police activities: *see also* custody; offences
   intrusion, arrests, xviii, 332
   Redfern, xviii, 103, *104*
   settlement protectors, 91
   training, 204
policy: *see* health policy
politics of Aboriginal health, 1–33, 297, 360
   leadership by health services, 336
polygyny, 82
polyneuropathy, petrol sniffers, 205
population, 1–3, 39–40, 383–384, 416
   decline, 2–3, 5, 86–91, 93, 384
   growth, 116, 387
population registers, 353–354
   children, 353, 355, 362
positive mental health, 221, 277: *see also* mental
   health
possession (psychiatric), 237, *238*
post-streptococcal renal disease: *see*
   glomerulonephritis
posters: *see* media resources
poverty
   and illness, xv–xvii, 331, 382, 412
   maintenance, 349, 350
   nutrition policy, 368–369
   urban Aborigines, xvi, 100
powerlessness, 382, 417
   alcohol abuse, 69
power supply, 338, 342, 350, 382: *see also*
   essential services
predetermination, 299–300
pregnancy, 363: *see also* childbirth
   antenatal risk factors, 363
   complications, 52–53
   diet, 17
   drug use poster, *207*
   food taboos, 140–141
   male doctors, 317
prejudice: *see* racism
prematurity: *see* low birth weight
pressures: *see* stress
prevention of illness: *see* health promotion
primary liver cancer: *see* liver cancer
prison inmates: *see* custody
private practitioners, 394: *see also* health
   professionals
problem deflation, alcohol use, 193–194, 209
prohibition: *see* legislation
protectionism, 10, 91, 93, 384–385: *see also*
   missions; reserves
protest, Long Bay Gaol, *103*
psychiatric disorders: *see* mental health

public drinking, 182, *183*
  2 kilometre law, 196–197
public health issues, 326–375: *see also*
  environmental health
public servants and policy, 413–415
punyu, 298–299

Queensland, services, 396
questioning: *see* information gathering

race, concept of, 24, 94, 293, 295
racism, xviii, 182, 249
  health professionals, 293, 314
  hospitals, 328, 399
  Royal Commission, 104
  town camps, 106
radio, 338, 358
rations, 11–13, *13*, 16–17, 89, 129, 131, 133: *see*
  also food
  tobacco, 177
reactive depression: *see* depression
Redfern: *see also* Aboriginal Medical Service,
  Redfern
  Aboriginal Legal Service, Redfern, 103,
    400
  police activities, xviii, 103, *104*
referendum (1967), 26, 182, 389
reform, 18–23
registers: *see* population registers
related people: *see* kinship
relationships, 299, 302
  alcohol, 187
  and health and illness, 228, 298, 303, 308
  expressed through food, 162–163
  take priority, 319
remains: *see* bones
remote communities, xx, 98: *see also* names of
  specific places
  alcohol, 191, 193
  culture, 247, 279, 389
  food, xvi, 130–135
  health care, 227, 352–353, 394–395, 401
  health workers, 363–365, 406, 407
  hospitalisation, 318–319, 328
  housing, 222, 349
  infants and children, 49, 84–85, 145, 362
  mental illness, 220, 223, 226, 236–245, 269
  relationships and family, 257, 260
  segregation, 93–94
renal disease, 72–73, 331
  and diabetes, 154–155
  children, 329–330
  glomerulonephritis, 67, 73, 330, 329
rented housing: *see* housing
research, 369, 411, 416
  Aboriginal attitudes to, 157, 192, 269
  alcohol, 188, 192
reserves, 10–16, 18–19, 93
  revoked for assimilation, 388
respiratory diseases, 46, *47,* 58, 344, 390: *see also*
  pneumonia

children and infants, 327–329
  hospitalisation, 25, 52, 53
  natural explanations, 304
  tobacco, 202
retinopathy, 55, 155
rheumatic fever, 329
rheumatic heart disease, 55, 57, 354, 355
right to drink: *see* legislation
right to vote, and alcohol, 180
ringworm, town camps, 106
Ritharrngu (NT), 299
rituals
  for approaching places, 303
  healing, 312
  mental health, 226
  mourning, 305–306
roads, homelands, 338
rotavirus vaccines, 355
Royal Commission into Aboriginal Deaths in
  Custody, xviii, 67–68, 102, 104, 203–204, 265,
    268, 332
  alcohol and drugs, 197, 203
  Research Unit, 269
rubbish: *see* waste disposal
rules of avoidance, 249, 303, 318, 360

sacred sites, Noonkanbah, 30
safe sex, 357, 358, 368
scabies, 66, 67, 106, 149
scaly skin from kava, 201, 206
scarlet fever epidemics; 88
schizophrenia, 237, *238, 239, 234*
  cross-cultural comparisons, 222, 236
school-based feeding programs, 159
screening, 354–355
  eye disease, 360
  HIV infection, 359
sea foods, 126, 130: *see also* bush foods
segregation, 384, 388
seizures, 69, 204
selection: *see* staff selection
self-determination, 390–392, 400–401: *see also*
  community control; economic
  independence
Self-determination in action (case study),
  400–401
self-esteem and drug use, 186
self-injury, 68, 203, 245, 254, 257, 268–277: *see*
  also suicide
self-management: *see* management;
  self-determination
separation rates: *see* hospital statistics
settlements, 91, 93, 98–108, 339: *see also*
  missions; reserves
  and bush foods, 131
  as 'total institutions', 15–16, 33, 91
  communal facilities, 343
settlers: *see* pastoralists
sewerage facilities: *see* waste disposal
sexual abuse, 90, 116, 245, 295
  and gonorrhoea, 88
  of children, 279, 353

sexually transmitted diseases, 5–6, 63–65, 88, 356–357
  AIDS, 64–65, *65*, 198, 208, 331, 353, 356–359, *358*, 366
  chlamydial diseases, 59, 64, 86, 88
  gonorrhoea, 63, 88, 329, 331
  isolation, 386
  sterility, 91
  pelvic inflammatory disease, 88, 332
  syphilis, 63, 88, 89, 331, 357, 386
shame and depression, 239, 254
sharing of material items: *see under* kinship
shelter: *see* housing
sick-role behaviour, 303, 309
singing (sorcery), 298: *see also* sorcery
single-parent households: *see under* families
skin infections, lesions and rashes, 66–67, 308, 329, 343–344: *see also* scabies
  and glomerulonephritis, 67
  bush medicines, 311
  natural explanations, 304
smallpox, 2–3, 5–6, 86–87, 384
smoking: *see* tobacco
soap powder as a drug, 202
social change: *see* acculturative stress
social control, 243, 279
  alcohol use, 184
  child-rearing 266
  medicinal plants, 311–312
  suicide, 276
social disadvantage, xviii
social distance between races, 190, 196
social factors
  drug use, 186
  mental health, 67–68
social justice, xix–xx
social relationships: *see* relationships
social rules for gender, 316–318
social security, 100, 108, 131, 292: *see also* income and cash
  child endowment payments, 22
  limited access, 389
social support, 257, 259–261
  coping with stress, 247, 250
sociocultural factors in health, xix, 221–224, 292–323
  mental health, 218–281
socioeconomic factors in health, xvi, xviii, 148, 150, 219, 249, 293–294
  alcohol and drug use, 186, 188–189
  mental health, 223, 254
  nutrition, 163–164
solid foods for babies, 151–152, 362
Somewhere between black and white (case study), 181–182
sorcery, 3, 240
  abnormality, 226
  and healing, 227–228, 312–313
  and illness, 298, 306–308
  explanation of death, 226
  fear of, *239*
  mental health, 278
sores: *see* skin infections, lesions and rashes

South Australia, services, 397
spectacles, 361–362: *see also* eye health
spirit invasion syndrome, 223
spirits and health, 228, 299, 303, 305–306: *see also* totems
squatters: *see* pastoralists; stations
staff selection, 333, 363–365, 367, 406
staff turnover, 336, 354
standard treatment regimens, 353–354
starch digestion, Aboriginal foods, 142
state government services, 391, 394, 397–398, 404, 413
State of shock, 204, 221, 269
stations, 16–18, 89–91: *see also* farms
  opium and tobacco supply, 177
statistics: *see* health statistics
stereotypes, xii
sterility: *see* fertility and sterility
still births, 85
stolen generations, 21–22, 93–98, *95*, *97*, 116, 295–296, 385
  current effects, 95–98
  kinship custodians, 118
stomach-ache, 305, 308
  bush medicines, 311
stores 126, 133–135, *161*, 369: *see also* diet, studies
  cleaning equipment, 350
  management, 344
Story about feeling (case study), 253
Strehlow, T. G. H., 26
Strelley (WA), *99*
streptococcal skin infections and glomerulonephritis, 67
Streptococcus pneumoniae: *see* pneumonia
stress, 240: *see also* acculturative stress
  and alcohol, 189, 204
  coping, 248–251
  diabetes, 156
  kinship, 258
  petrol sniffing, 198, 266–267
  stolen generations, 97
substance abuse, 173–209, 233, 250, 267: *see also* alcohol use; analgesic use; kava; petrol sniffing
  Aboriginal perceptions/opinions, 173
  adolescents, 69, 247, 251, 263, 264, 266–268
  AIDS, 65, 203
  causes, 185–189
  children, 330
  mental health, 250, 254, 276
  stolen generations, 97
Such extraordinary terrorism (case study), 8–9
sugar consumption: *see* glucose intolerance; obesity
suicide, 67–68, 102, 237, 257, 268–277, *277*: *see also* Royal Commission
  alcohol, 67, 203, 269, 272–276
  clusters, 268, 269, 273
  in custody, 268, 269, 332
  depression, 254–255
  town camps, 106

suicide attempts, 245, 268
  counselling, 277
supernatural explanations of illness, 303,
    305–308: *see also* sorcery
supplementation, baby food, 151–152, 362
support networks: *see* social support
survival: *see* life expectancy; mortality
survival of infants: *see* infant mortality
syphilis, 63, 88, 89, 331
  isolation, 386
  screening, 357

taboos, 303: *see also* avoidance rules
Tangentyere Council (NT), alcohol, 192, 370
Task Force on Aboriginal Health Statistics, 30
Tasmanian Aborigines, 10
Tasmania, services, 397
teachers: *see* education
teenagers: *see* adolescents
telephones in remote communities, 338
televised health promotion, 208, 367–368
temperature control (housing), 343–344, 349
Tennant Creek (NT)
  alcohol, 195–196
  Anyinginyi Aboriginal Health Service, 336, 368
  women's refuges, 205
tensions: *see* stress
tent embassy at Parliament House, 30, 389, 401
Tenuous hold on life, A (case study), 300
Ten Year Plan for Aboriginal Health, 390
Thaayorre, 303, 308, 311
third world countries: *see* developing countries
Thursday Island hospital, 396
Tiwi, 141, *146*, 162: *see also* Milikapiti (NT)
tobacco, 177, 195, 202
  chewing, 195
  heart disease, 202, 331
  indigenous, 174, *175*
  pipes, 175, 202
  in pregnancy, poster, *207*
toilet facilities, 346–347: *see also* essential
    services
Torres Strait Islanders, 37
  diabetes, 155
  early kava use, 177, 201
  health services, 396
  population, *39*
  tobacco trade, 177
totems, 3: *see also* spirits
  dances for severe illness, 308
  mental health, 223, 226
  significance of bush foods, 140
town camps, 104–108: *see also* fringe dwellers
  Alice Springs, drunks damage, 370
  group drinking, 190–191
  growth retardation, 150
trachoma, 58–59, 359–361, 388, 390: *see also*
    National Trachoma
  children, 329
  endemic, 3, 360
traditional, *see also* indigenous
traditional healing, 243, 312–314: *see also* bush
    medicines

alcohol rehabilitation programs, 208
  in biomedical context, 315
  mental health, 280
traditionally oriented Aborigines: *see* remote
    communities
traditional mental illnesses, 220
traditional resources: see bush foods
training of Aboriginal personnel, 391: see also
    health workers, training
tranquillisers, 203
transcultural psychiatry: *see* sociocultural factors
transition mental illnesses, 220: *see also*
    acculturative stress
transport
  emergency transport, 395–396
  motor vehicles, 73, 131, 139, 204, 338
  to AMSs, 401
trauma, 69, 85, 204, 302, 307
  environmental, 343–344, 349
  petrol sniffers, 205
  women, 362
treatment: *see* alcohol interventions; petrol
    sniffing, interventions
treponemal diseases, 86: *see also* syphilis;
    yaws
tribal: *see* traditional
Triggering case: distress or disturbance, A (case
    study), 273
tuberculosis, 6, 47, 60–61, 331, 390
Two hundred years of unfinished business (case
    study), 96

ulcerative disease, AIDS, 357
umbrella organisations, 404, 412
undernutrition: *see* nutrition
underweight, 54, 137
  kava, 201, 206
unemployment, xviii
United Aborigines Mission, 28
urban communities, xvi, xviii, 98–104: *see also*
    fringe-dwellers; names of specific places;
    town camps
  breast-feeding, 151, 152
  culture, 279, 296
  health service delivery, 352–353, 394, 398
  health workers, 363–365, 406–408
  living conditions, 25–26
  mental health; 221, 245
  migration, 100, 398
  support networks, 261
  well-being, 299, 301–302
urinary tract disorders, 72–73, 330
Uwankara Palyanyku Kanyintjaku, 339–345, 348

vaccination: *see* immunisation
vehicles: *see* motor vehicles
venereal diseases: *see* sexually transmitted
    diseases
Vesteys, 16–17
Victoria, services, 395

violence, 245: *see also* alcohol and violence
  against Aborigines, 8–9
  against women, 332, 362–363, 368
  institutionalisation, 385
  kinship, 258
  mental illness, 227
  town camps, 108
visual impairment: *see* eye health
vitamin availability, 128, 129–130, 131, 134
  food fortification, 158–159
  vitamin C in bush foods, 142
volatile substance use: *see* glue sniffing; petrol
  sniffing

wages: *see* income and cash
Walgett (NSW), food studies, 125, 128, 129–130
Wantamulla (case study), 372–373
wards of the government, 180
Warlpiri people, 84, 137: see also Yuendumu
washing facilities, xvii, 339, *345*, 343–344,
    346–347: *see also* essential services
  maintenance, 349
  respiratory infection, 329
waste disposal, 338, 342–344
  capital works, 350
  cause of ill-health, xvi, 382
  maintenance, 349
Waste management in remote communities (case
  study), 351–352
waterlilies, food composition, 141–142
water supply, 133, 149, 338–339, 342, 344
  capital works, 350
  cause of ill-health, 86, 329, 382
Wattie Creek, 18, 30
Wave Hill Station (NT), 17–18, 27–30, 389, 399
weaning foods, 151–152, 362
weather and well-being, 299
weight: *see* low birth weight; obesity;
  underweight
Weipa South (Qld), 204, 221, 269
welfare: *see* reform

Welfare Ordinance, 1953, 180
welfare payments: *see* social security
well-being, 297–302: *see also* health
Western Australia, services, 396
whooping cough epidemics, 88
Wik Ngantjera, 303, 308, 311
wild honey, 137
for indigenous alcohol, 174
  witchdoctors: *see* medicine men
Women and families (case study), 101
women's health, 88, 331–332, 362–363, 394: *see
  also* analgesic use; contraception; cervical
  cancer; childbirth; domestic violence;
  pregnancy
women's refuges, 205, 368
words: *see* language
working definition: *see* identification of
  Aboriginality
world: *see* international standards
Wujalwujal (Qld), 131, 134

Yalata (SA), xvii, 7, 14, 28, 29, 69, 93, 227: *see
  also* Pitjantjatjara
yams, 131, 136–137, 142: *see also* bush food
Yandiyarra, 337
Yankunjatjara, Bonner Review, 374
Yarrabah watchhouse suicides, 273: *see also*
  Royal Commission; suicides
yaws, 3, 88
Yirrkala (NT), 30, 85: *see also* Yolngu
  illness, 304, 306, 308–309, 313–314
  kava from Fiji, 201
Yolngu people (NT), 242: *see also* Yirrkala
  bush foods, 136
  explanatory framework, 303–308
youth: *see* adolescents
Yuendumu (NT), 14–15, 84, 338: *see also* Warlpiri
  food, 132, 134, 137
  growth studies, 147
  psychiatric surveys, 237

1 2 3 4 5 6 7 8 9 0
A B C D E F G H I J